globalization

Other titles in this
series include:

Culture: A Reader for Writers
John Mauk
(ISBN: 9780199947225)

Language: A Reader for Writers
Gita DasBender
(ISBN: 9780199947485)

Sustainability: A Reader for Writers
Carl Herndl
(ISBN: 9780199947508)

Identity: A Reader for Writers
John Scenters-Zapico
(ISBN: 9780199947461)

globalization

A READER *for* WRITERS

Maria Jerskey
LaGuardia Community College

New York   Oxford
Oxford University Press

Oxford University Press publishes works that further Oxford University's
objective of excellence in research, scholarship, and education.

Oxford   New York
Auckland   Cape Town   Dar es Salaam   Hong Kong   Karachi
Kuala Lumpur   Madrid   Melbourne   Mexico City   Nairobi
New Delhi   Shanghai   Taipei   Toronto

With offices in
Argentina   Austria   Brazil   Chile   Czech Republic   France   Greece
Guatemala   Hungary   Italy   Japan   Poland   Portugal   Singapore
South Korea   Switzerland   Thailand   Turkey   Ukraine   Vietnam

Published by Oxford University Press.
198 Madison Avenue, New York, New York 10016
http://www.oup.com

Library of Congress Cataloging-in-Publication Data

Globalization : a reader for writers / [compiled and edited by] Maria Jerskey,
LaGuardia Community College.

    pages cm

Includes index.

ISBN 978-0-19-994752-2

1. Acculturation--Study and teaching. 2. Acculturation in literature.
3. Cosmopolitanism in literature. 4. Globalization--Social aspects. 5. Essay--
Authorship. I. Jerskey, Maria, compiler, editor.

HM841.G575   2014

303.48'2--dc23

                                                2013038815

brief table of contents

preface   xxvii

1   Being & Becoming Global   1

2   Identity & Place   29

3   Body, Mind, & Spirit   77

4   Languages in Contact   133

5   Communication & Technology   183

6   Earning & Spending   243

7   Gender Matters   281

8   Pop Culture   337

9   Change & Transformation   383

appendix: researching and writing about globalization   463

credits   501

index   502

contents

preface   xxvii

1   Being & Becoming Global   1

Tyler Olsen, **"In Zarafshan"** *The Morning News*   2

"... using photos available on Google Earth, I find that from the ground, and despite the city's hellish location and less-than-organic creation, Zarafshan doesn't really resemble a 24th-century postapocalyptic ghost town."

Marcelo Gleiser, **"Globalization: Two Visions of the Future of Humanity"** *National Public Radio*   7

"Unless we find ways to respect and celebrate our differences while jointly creating an atmosphere of open exchange and mutual understanding, I fear that the utopian world of the future will have a very dystopian bend to it."

Kwame Anthony Appiah, **"The Shattered Mirror"** Excerpt from *Cosmopolitanism*   10

"You can be genuinely engaged with the ways of other societies without approving, let alone adopting, them."

Jeffrey N. Wasserstrom, **"A Mickey Mouse Approach to Globalization"**
Yale Global Online   20

"These examples of American products taking on distinctly new cultural meanings when moved from the US to China are useful in undermining superficial assertions equating globalization with 'Americanization'. But it is important not to stop there."

Tanveer Ali, **"The Subway Falafel Sandwich and the Americanization of Ethnic Food"** Good   24

"As generations settle in, the food, like the ethnic group itself, becomes subsumed into American culture: Think chow mein takeout, or drive-through Taco Bell. As later generations stabilize, they tend to cultivate an appreciation of ethnic difference alongside Americanness."

2   Identity & Place   29

Pico Iyer, **"Lonely Places"** Excerpt from Falling Off the Map   31

"So it is that Lonely Places attract as many lonely people as they produce, and the loneliness we see in them is partly in ourselves."

Justin Nobel, **"The Last Inuit of Quebec"** The Smart Set   38

"He was an ace student in high school but dropped out of a Montreal college after just three semesters, homesick. 'It wasn't the problem of going to school,' he said, 'it was more the problem that I couldn't go hunting.'"

Humera Afridi, **"A Gentle Madness"** Granta   48

"When I was twelve, my parents decided to leave Pakistan and move our family to Abu Dhabi. My heart, I thought, would never recover. But I needn't have worried. The country came with me: it moved in, set up home, breathing inside me a stream of remembrances that, for twenty-eight years, have inflected the most minute details of my present life."

Julian Hill, **"In Search of Black Identity in Uganda"** Glimpse   53

"Thinking that I could come to Uganda and, just by being black, relate in any meaningful way would have been rather naïve. It's not that I expected this; I just still held out hope that it was possible."

Julia Whitty, **"All the Disappearing Islands"** Mother Jones   62

"Today, roughly 1 million people live on coral islands worldwide, and many more millions live on low-lying real estate vulnerable to the rising waves. At risk are not just people, but unique human cultures, born and bred in watery isolation."

3   Body, Mind, & Spirit   77

Anne Fadiman, **"Birth"** Excerpt from *The Spirit Catches You and You Fall Down: A Hmong Child, Her American Doctors, and the Collision of Two Cultures*   78

"When a Hmong dies, his or her soul must travel back from place to place, retracing the path of its life geography, until it reaches the burial place of its placental jacket, and puts it on."

Latif Nasser, **"Do Some Cultures Have Their Own Ways of Going Mad?"** *Boston Globe*   88

"Depending on whom you ask, the notion that some cultures have their own ways of going crazy is either the ultimate in cultural sensitivity or the ultimate in Western condescension."

Andrew Guest, **"Pursuing the Science of Happiness"** *Oregon Humanities*   94

"Yet, even if we could have it all, even if we recognize happiness as dependent upon seemingly valorous statistical correlates such as healthy relationships, purposeful work, and making meaningful contributions to a community, there is room for critique."

Peter Manseau, **"Plasticize Me"** *Guernica*   103

"Is posing a dead man with a tennis racket wrong? Is a failure to make specific provisions for the treatment of one's remains the same as giving one's body to science? Does the education offered by an anatomy exhibit offer the same kind of public good as organ donation? To put all this in the simplest and starkest terms: What are the dead for?"

Elizabeth Dwoskin, **"Why Americans Won't Do Dirty Jobs"** *Bloomberg Businessweek*   115

"At a moment when the country is relentlessly focused on unemployment, there are still jobs that often go unfilled. These are difficult, dirty, exhausting jobs that, for previous generations, were the first rickety step on the ladder to prosperity. They still are—just not for Americans."

Stefany Anne Golberg, **"You Can Take It with You"** *The Smart Set*   124

"The backpack of the 1960s was roughly the size of one's back. It had straps to attach to the back and maybe a few extra pockets. The backpack of today is the size of a small person. It is equipped with external and internal pockets, and the pockets are often custom-fitted for specific items: umbrellas, iPods, water bottles, cameras, computers."

4   Languages in Contact   133

Lera Boroditsky, **"How Does Our Language Shape the Way We Think?"** *Edge*   135

"Language is central to our experience of being human, and the languages we speak profoundly shape the way we think, the way we see the world, the way we live our lives."

Stephen Pax Leonard, **"Death by Monoculture"** *University of Cambridge: Research*   145

"After having spent a year in a remote Arctic community which speaks a vulnerable, minority language and whose cultural foundations are being rocked by climate change, it is clear to me that the link between environmental and cultural vulnerability is genuine and that the two are interwoven."

James Angelos, **"Passing the Test"** *World Policy Journal*   149

"By pursuing more restrictive immigration policies in the name of integration, European political leaders are not only being disingenuous in their aims, but risk the opposite outcome—estranging the very immigrant communities they say they wish to see better integrated."

Reshma Krishnamurthy Sharma, **"The New Language Landscape"** *The Hindu*   164

"Fifty years down the line, will we be surprised if English becomes the single spoken language and kids go to special schools to learn India's regional languages?"

Pallavi Polanki, **"Operation Mind Your Language"** *Open*   167

"Wherever you go in Afghanistan, you will face Americans. That is why English has gained a very high position there. Before the Americans, there were the Russians. At that time, many of our people learnt the Russian language. God-willing, when we return, we will teach the new generation English."

Julie Traves, **"The Church of Please and Thank You"**
This Magazine 172

"In addition to the 380 million people worldwide who use English as their first language, it's estimated there are 350 million to 500 million speakers of English as a foreign language (EFL)—and the number is growing. For people from affluent and developing nations alike, it is clear that the secret passwords to safety, wealth and freedom can be whispered only in English."

5 Communication & Technology 183

Ethan Zuckerman, **"A Small World After All?"** *Wilson Quarterly* 185

"The unexpected outbreak of the Arab Spring, a mystery that's still unfolding, suggests that we may not be getting this full picture, or the deep, unconventional thinking we need. Had you asked an expert on the Middle East what changes were likely to take place in 2011, almost none would have predicted the Arab Spring, and none would have chosen Tunisia as the flashpoint for the movement."

Frank Bures, **"Can You Hear Us Now?"** *World Ark* 192

"I've always admired the ingenious ways that people in the developing world jerry-rig solutions to their problems. I've seen wheelbarrows assembled from sticks and boards, frying pans made from old car parts, and irrigation channels constructed from the husks of banana trees. I've even read of people making cars and a helicopter from scratch."

Natana J. DeLong-Bas, **"The New Social Media and the Arab Spring"**
Oxford Islamic Studies Online 197

"In cyberspace, the social restrictions that exist in reality in some places—such as gender segregation—disappear, providing groups of people who might otherwise never meet and converse the opportunity to connect and recognize what they share in common."

Teju Cole, **"The White Savior Industrial Complex"** *The Atlantic* 210

"@Teju Cole 5-The White Savior Industrial Complex is not about justice. It's about having a big emotional experience that validates privilege."

Rudabeh Pakravan, **"Territory Jam"** *Places*   219

"Iran's violation of the basic human rights of assembly and information access have long been condemned by the international community, most recently by the United Nations International Telecommunications Union, which declared that 'jamming is a fundamental violation, not only of international regulations and norms, but of the right of people everywhere to receive and impart information.'"

Rob Horning, **"The Accidental Bricoleurs"** *n + 1*   229

"Social-media companies don't facilitate community any more than fast-fashion companies elevate style; they cater to the fantasy of being a celebrity, the impossible dream of a mass audience for everyone. With that we either beat a retreat into vicarious fantasy or end up squarely in the realm of the creative class and its fiefdom of cool."

6   Earning & Spending   243

The Economist **"The New Grand Tour"**   244

"Even before they leave China, the travellers are nagged to mind their manners and told to act as 'ambassadors' for their country. Several times in the past few years the Spiritual Civilisation Steering Committee of the country's Communist Party has issued chivvying circulars calling on Chinese tourists to avoid queue-jumping, loudness or haggling in shops with fixed prices."

Charles Kenny, **"Haiti Doesn't Need Your Old T-Shirt"**
Foreign Policy   252

"Here's the trouble with dumping stuff we don't want on people in need: What they need is rarely the stuff we don't want. And even when they do need that kind of stuff, there are much better ways for them to get it than for a Western NGO to gather donations at a suburban warehouse, ship everything off to Africa or South America, and then try to distribute it to remote areas."

Tate Watkins, **"How Oliberté, the Anti-TOMS, Makes Shoes and Jobs in Africa"** *Good*   256

"The Oliberté brand is still niche, but to Dehtiar, part of the venture's value is in cutting a path that larger manufacturers can follow. 'Our goal is to be the reason that 1 million people are employed in manufacturing in Africa,' he says. 'We want to show that these models work and we want to encourage others, like the Nikes and Levi's of the world, to do the same.'"

Avantika Bhuyan, **"The Enchanted Bylanes"** *Open* 260

"Safely sourced, the toys make their way to Vidyanand Market, where sundry distributors and small-time traders buy them in bulk. Within days, the toys will be on display at cornershops across the country. Right now, though, it's time for some active bargaining; bundles of money exchange hands, even as wagonloads of toys are ferried around."

Simon Akam, **"The Long and Winding Road"** *More Intelligent Life* 264

"Toyotas are the car for Africa. But I did not want a Toyota. As with women and sex, for men the purchase of a four-wheel drive is often clouded with emotional baggage. As a child I once pined for a Land Rover, and a part of me still did. In Sierra Leone a Land Rover seemed to make sense. They looked better, they were different. I did not want a Toyota."

Maureen Orth, **"The Luxury Frontier"** *Wall Street Journal* 269

"Nothing illustrates the topsy-turvy nature of Mongolia today more than the capital city's main Sukhbaatar Square, where a bronze statue of Lenin once presided. Now a gleaming Louis Vuitton store, opened in October 2009, offers clients champagne in a circular VIP room outfitted with a lavish ceremonial Mongolian saddle and antique caviar case."

7 Gender Matters 281

Christina Larsen, **"The Startling Plight of China's Leftover Ladies"**
    Foreign Policy 282

"This is a country where 118 boys were born for every 100 girls in 2010, and by 2020 the number of men unable to find partners is expected to reach 24 million. So how could any women possibly be left over?"

Doug Clark, **"Crimson Leopard-Print Headscarves: Wearing the
    Veil in Banda Aceh, Indonesia"** *Glimpse* 289

"When travelling in more liberal parts of Indonesia—in parts of Jakarta or Indonesia's Christian provinces *jilbabs* are the minority—Aisha has experimented with not wearing a headscarf. She liked how the wind blew in her hair, that her hair didn't smell of sweat after taking her veil off, but ultimately she decided to keep wearing a *jilbab*."

Leila Ahmed, **"Reinventing the Veil"** *Financial Times Magazine* 304

"Occasionally now, although less so than in the past, I find myself nostalgic for the Islam of my childhood and youth, an Islam without veils and far removed from politics. An Islam which people seemed to follow not in the prescribed, regimented ways of today but rather according to their own inner sense, and their own particular temperaments, inclinations and the shifting vicissitudes of their lives."

Oliver Broudy, **"Body-Building in Afghanistan"** *Men's Health*   309

"How is it that, even as the fanatics are detonating their bodies in the marketplace, in the gyms men of a new generation of Afghans are exercising and building their bodies? For the careful student, there's a lot to learn here about what it means to be strong."

Mark Levine, **"Killing Emos, and the Future, in Iraq"** *Al Jazeera*   321

"In a conservative society, few behaviours or identities are more threatening to the keepers of public morality than perceived homosexuality. Especially in a culture in which men and women spend so much time segregated by gender, the need to police the boundaries between homosocial and homosexual becomes a central focus of government and social action in order to preserve the social order."

Chloé Lewis, **"The Invisible Migrant Man: Questioning Gender Privileges"** *openDemocracy*   330

"Griffiths' work has uncovered at least two ways in which male refused asylum seekers and those placed in detention face particular vulnerabilities. The first is through their not having a full legal identity; and the second, 'counterintuitively' she notes, emerges from 'gendered assumptions regarding privileged patriarchy, including an expectation that men can cope with destitution, detention and the loss of family.'"

8   Pop Culture   337

Roozbeh Shirazi, **"Beyond Mullahs and Persian Party People: The Invisibility of Being Iranian on TV"** *Jadaliyya*   339

"By dispensing with the diverse realities of being Iranian in the United States—notably the multiple ways in which Iranians articulate, enact, and experience race, citizenship, and community—and by instead magnifying a shallow Persian party scene, the Shahs of Sunset appears guilty of replacing one cultural stereotype with another."

Blake Gopnik, **"Revolution in a Can"** *Foreign Policy* 345

"The most elaborate images from Egypt, Libya, and Haiti today look very much like the 1980s paint jobs on New York subway cars and warehouse facades, and yet their point is not to function as art but to work as carriers of content and opinion."

Sarah Lacy, **"You Think Hollywood Is Rough? Welcome to the Chaos, Excitement and Danger of Nollywood"** *TechCrunch* 349

"Unlike Hollywood where the producers reside in glamourous offices and pirates operate in the shadows and basements of the Internet, in Alaba the content creators and those destroying their hopes of revenues reside in the same place, selling the same product side-by-side."

Jackson Allers, **"Voice of the Streets: The Birth of a Hip-Hop Movement"** *World Hip Hop Market* 357

"There was Boikutt formerly of Ramallah Underground repping Palestine; two young lions Khotta Ba and Tareq Abu Kwaik aka El Far3i from Jordan; veterans Edd from the Lebanese live hip-hop group Fareeq al Atrash and Malikah also from Lebanon representing as the lone female MC of the event; and you had your bevy of the best Egyptian talent—Deeb and the Arabian Knightz (E-Money, Sphinx, Rush) and MC Amin from a dusty-city called Mansoura 120km north of Cairo."

Charukesi Ramadurai, **"Fading Lights in Mumbai"** *More Intelligent Life* 367

"Nestled in the city's noisy bustle, Mumbai's single-screen theatres are exotic anachronisms. Many of them have grand English names—Strand, Metro and, most famously, Opera House—which have long been used to identify the surrounding neighbourhoods."

Jeff Chang, **"So You Think They Can Break-Dance?"** *Salon* 370

"While some fans on the message boards for 'America's Best Dance Crew' still don't know what a 'b-boy' is, the word in South Korea has become synonymous with national pride."

9   Change & Transformation   383

Martin Walker, **"The World's New Numbers"** *The Wilson Quarterly*   385

"The lower the birthrate, the greater the likelihood that a given society is developing—investing in education, accumulating disposable income and savings, and starting to consume at levels comparable to those of the middle classes in developed societies."

Damon Tabor, **"If It's Tuesday, It Must Be the Taliban"** *Outside*   397

"Tactically, our vacation had begun to feel similar to a military raid—rush in and rush out—and it was both exhilarating and unsatisfying. You were trying to be a tourist in a place that didn't allow for it. You could strike up a conversation with a shopkeeper, but he might be a Taliban informant. You could wander down some beckoning side street, but you might not be seen again."

Petina Gappah, **"Zimbabwe"** *Guernica*   414

"What Zimbabwe did particularly well in the first twenty years of its life was to correct the racial injustice that had denied quality universal education to the majority of the country's black children: throughout the history of the colony, state education was bottlenecked to ensure that fewer and fewer blacks had access to education as they progressed up to tertiary education."

Paul Salopek, **"The Last Famine"** *Foreign Policy*   428

"Last August, I took a long walk with Daasanach nomads in northern Kenya, well inside the disaster zone, to see what it was like to move, as most famine victims do, on foot, through a landscape of chronic hunger."

Francis Kuria, **"It's Time for the Turkana to Leave Their Wastelands and Settle Down"** *Daily Nation*   443

"In 35 BC in Rome, Virgil, the much-celebrated poet, asked the rhetorical question why a country man would hearken to the city of Rome. The answer was, to obtain freedom from want and war, and to eat."

Abhijit Banerjee and Esther Duflo, **"More than 1 Billion People Are Hungry in the World"** *Foreign Policy*   447

"What if the poor aren't starving, but choosing to spend their money on other priorities? Development experts and policymakers would have to completely reimagine the way they think about hunger."

appendix: researching and writing about globalization   463

credits   501

index   502

rhetorical contents

academic

Marcelo Gleiser, **"Globalization: Two Visions of the Future of Humanity"** 7

Kwame Anthony Appiah, **"The Shattered Mirror"** 10

Jeffrey N. Wasserstrom, **"A Mickey Mouse Approach to Globalization"** 20

Andrew Guest, **"Pursuing the Science of Happiness"** 94

Peter Manseau, **"Plasticize Me"** 103

Lera Boroditsky, **"How Does Our Language Shape the Way We Think?"** 135

Stephen Pax Leonard, **"Death by Monoculture"** 145

Ethan Zuckerman, **"A Small World After All?"** 185

Natana J. DeLong-Bas, **"The New Social Media and the Arab Spring"** 197

Rudabeh Pakravan, **"Territory Jam"** 219

Leila Ahmed, **"Reinventing the Veil"** 304

Chloé Lewis, **"The Invisible Migrant Man: Questioning Gender Privileges"** 330

Roozbeh Shirazi, **"Beyond Mullahs and Persian Party People: The Invisibility of Being Iranian on TV"** 339

Martin Walker, **"The World's New Numbers"** 385

Abhijit Banerjee and Esther Duflo, **"More than 1 Billion People Are Hungry in the World"** 447

argument and persuasion

Marcelo Gleiser, **"Globalization: Two Visions of the Future of Humanity"** 7

Kwame Anthony Appiah, **"The Shattered Mirror"** 10

Jeffrey N. Wasserstrom, **"A Mickey Mouse Approach to Globalization"** 20

Julia Whitty, **"All the Disappearing Islands"** 63

Elizabeth Dwoskin, **"Why Americans Won't Do Dirty Jobs"** 115

Stefany Anne Golberg, **"You Can Take It with You"** 124

Stephen Pax Leonard, **"Death by Monoculture"** 145

James Angelos, **"Passing the Test"** 149

Ethan Zuckerman, **"A Small World After All?"** 185

Frank Bures, **"Can You Hear Us Now?"** 192

Natana J. DeLong-Bas, **"The New Social Media and the Arab Spring"** 197

Teju Cole, **"The White Savior Industrial Complex"** 210

Rudabeh Pakravan, **"Territory Jam"** 219

Rob Horning, **"The Accidental Bricoleurs"** 229

Tate Watkins, **"How Oliberté, the Anti-TOMS, Makes Shoes and Jobs in Africa"** 256

Chloé Lewis, **"The Invisible Migrant Man: Questioning Gender Privileges"** 330

Roozbeh Shirazi, **"Beyond Mullahs and Persian Party People: The Invisibility of Being Iranian on TV"** 339

Blake Gopnik, **"Revolution in a Can"** 345

Martin Walker, **"The World's New Numbers"** 385

Francis Kuria, **"It's Time for the Turkana to Leave Their Wastelands and Settle Down"** 443

Abhijit Banerjee and Esther Duflo, **"More than 1 Billion People Are Hungry in the World"** 447

cause and effect

Pico Iyer, **"Lonely Places"** 31

Humera Afridi, **"A Gentle Madness"** 48

Julia Whitty, **"All the Disappearing Islands"** 62

Latif Nasser, **"Do Some Cultures Have Their Own Ways of Going Mad?"** 88

Elizabeth Dwoskin, **"Why Americans Won't Do Dirty Jobs"** 115

Reshma Krishnamurthy Sharma, **"The New Language Landscape"** 164

Julie Traves, **"The Church of Please and Thank You"** 172

Teju Cole, **"The White Savior Industrial Complex"** 210

Rob Horning, **"The Accidental Bricoleurs"** 229

Charles Kenny, **"Haiti Doesn't Need Your Old T-Shirt"** 252

Maureen Orth, **"The Luxury Frontier"** 269

Christina Larsen, **"The Startling Plight of China's Leftover Ladies"** 282

Oliver Broudy, **"Body-Building in Afghanistan"** 309

Chloé Lewis, **"The Invisible Migrant Man: Questioning Gender Privileges"** 330

Martin Walker, **"The World's New Numbers"** 385

Paul Salopek, **"The Last Famine"** 428

Abhijit Banerjee and Esther Duflo, **"More than 1 Billion People Are Hungry in the World"** 447

comparison and contrast

Jeffrey N. Wasserstrom, **"A Mickey Mouse Approach to Globalization"** 20

Julian Hill, **"In Search of Black Identity in Uganda"** 53

Julia Whitty, **"All the Disappearing Islands"** 63

Anne Fadiman, **"Birth"** 78

Latif Nasser, **"Do Some Cultures Have Their Own Ways of Going Mad?"** 88

Andrew Guest, **"Pursuing the Science of Happiness"** 94

Peter Manseau, **"Plasticize Me"** 103

Stefany Anne Golberg, **"You Can Take It with You"** 124

Stephen Pax Leonard, **"Death by Monoculture"** 145

Ethan Zuckerman, **"A Small World After All?"** 185

Frank Bures, **"Can You Hear Us Now?"** 192

Charles Kenny, **"Haiti Doesn't Need Your Old T-Shirt"** 252

Tate Watkins, **"How Oliberté, the Anti-TOMS, Makes Shoes and Jobs in Africa"** 256

Avantika Bhuyan, **"The Enchanted Bylanes"** 260

Doug Clark, **"Crimson Leopard-Print Headscarves: Wearing the Veil in Banda Aceh, Indonesia"** 289

Leila Ahmed, **"Reinventing the Veil"** 304

Chloé Lewis, **"The Invisible Migrant Man: Questioning Gender Privileges"** 330

definition

Humera Afridi, **"A Gentle Madness"** 48

Julian Hill, **"In Search of Black Identity in Uganda"** 53

Julia Whitty, **"All the Disappearing Islands"** 62

Anne Fadiman, **"Birth"** 78

Andrew Guest, **"Pursuing the Science of Happiness"** 94

Lera Boroditsky, **"How Does Our Language Shape the Way We Think?"** 135

Ethan Zuckerman, **"A Small World After All?"** 185

Teju Cole, **"The White Savior Industrial Complex"** 210

Rudabeh Pakravan, **"Territory Jam"** 219

Abhijit Banerjee and Esther Duflo, **"More than 1 Billion People Are Hungry in the World"** 447

description

Pico Iyer, **"Lonely Places"** 31

Julian Hill, **"In Search of Black Identity in Uganda"** 53

Julia Whitty, **"All the Disappearing Islands"** 63

Anne Fadiman, **"Birth"** 78

Peter Manseau, **"Plasticize Me"** 103

Elizabeth Dwoskin, **"Why Americans Won't Do Dirty Jobs"** 115

Stefany Anne Golberg, **"You Can Take It with You"** 124

Lera Boroditsky, **"How Does Our Language Shape the Way We Think?"** 135

James Angelos, **"Passing the Test"** 149

Pallavi Polanki, **"Operation Mind Your Language"** 167

Frank Bures, **"Can You Hear Us Now?"** 192

Rudabeh Pakravan, **"Territory Jam"** 219

Rob Horning, **"The Accidental Bricoleurs"** 229

Avantika Bhuyan, **"The Enchanted Bylanes"** 260

Simon Akam, **"The Long and Winding Road"** 264

Maureen Orth, **"The Luxury Frontier"** 269

Doug Clark, **"Crimson Leopard-Print Headscarves: Wearing the Veil in Banda Aceh, Indonesia"** 289

Oliver Broudy, **"Body-Building in Afghanistan"** 309

Sarah Lacy, **"You Think Hollywood Is Rough? Welcome to the Chaos, Excitement and Danger of Nollywood"** 349

Jackson Allers, **"Voice of the Streets: The Birth of a Hip-Hop Movement"** 357

Charukesi Ramadurai, **"Fading Lights in Mumbai"** 367

Jeff Chang, **"So You Think They Can Break-Dance?"** 370

Damon Tabor, **"If It's Tuesday, It Must Be the Taliban"** 397

Petina Gappah, **"Zimbabwe"** 414

Paul Salopek, **"The Last Famine"** 428

division and classification

Marcelo Gleiser, **"Globalization: Two Visions of the Future of Humanity"** 7

Jeffrey N. Wasserstrom, **"A Mickey Mouse Approach to Globalization"** 20

Tanveer Ali, **"The Subway Falafel Sandwich and the Americanization of Ethnic Food"** 24

Pico Iyer, **"Lonely Places"** 31

Humera Afridi, **"A Gentle Madness"** 48

Julian Hill, **"In Search of Black Identity in Uganda"** 53

Anne Fadiman, **"Birth"** 78

Peter Manseau, **"Plasticize Me"** 103

Lera Boroditsky, **"How Does Our Language Shape the Way We Think?"** 135

Rob Horning, **"The Accidental Bricoleurs"** 229

The Economist, **"The New Grand Tour"** 244

Doug Clark, **"Crimson Leopard-Print Headscarves: Wearing the Veil in Banda Aceh, Indonesia"** 289

example and illustration

Jeffrey N. Wasserstrom, **"A Mickey Mouse Approach to Globalization"** 20

Pico Iyer, **"Lonely Places"** 31

Julian Hill, **"In Search of Black Identity in Uganda"** 53

Julia Whitty, **"All the Disappearing Islands"** 62

Anne Fadiman, **"Birth"** 78

Andrew Guest, **"Pursuing the Science of Happiness"** 94

Elizabeth Dwoskin, **"Why Americans Won't Do Dirty Jobs"** 115

Lera Boroditsky, **"How Does Our Language Shape the Way We Think?"** 135

Stephen Pax Leonard, **"Death by Monoculture"** 145

James Angelos, **"Passing the Test"** 149

Pallavi Polanki, **"Operation Mind Your Language"** 167

Julie Traves, **"The Church of Please and Thank You"** 172

Frank Bures, **"Can You Hear Us Now?"** 192

Natana J. DeLong-Bas, **"The New Social Media and the Arab Spring"** 197

Teju Cole, **"The White Savior Industrial Complex"** 210

Rudabeh Pakravan, **"Territory Jam"** 219

Rob Horning, **"The Accidental Bricoleurs"** 229

The Economist, **"The New Grand Tour"** 244

Charles Kenny, **"Haiti Doesn't Need Your Old T-Shirt"** 252

Chloé Lewis, **"The Invisible Migrant Man: Questioning Gender Privileges"** 330

Blake Gopnik, **"Revolution in a Can"** 345

Martin Walker, **"The World's New Numbers"** 385

Abhijit Banerjee and Esther Duflo, **"More than 1 Billion People Are Hungry in the World"** 447

explanatory

Julia Whitty, **"All the Disappearing Islands"** 62

Peter Manseau, **"Plasticize Me"** 103

Lera Boroditsky, **"How Does Our Language Shape the Way We Think?"** 135

Natana J. DeLong-Bas, **"The New Social Media and the Arab Spring"** 197

Teju Cole, **"The White Savior Industrial Complex"** 210

Rudabeh Pakravan, **"Territory Jam"** 219

Rob Horning, **"The Accidental Bricoleurs"** 229

The Economist, **"The New Grand Tour"** 244

Charles Kenny, **"Haiti Doesn't Need Your Old T-Shirt"** 252

Tate Watkins, **"How Oliberté, the Anti-TOMS, Makes Shoes and Jobs in Africa"** 256

Maureen Orth, **"The Luxury Frontier"** 269

Christina Larsen, **"The Startling Plight of China's Leftover Ladies"** 282

Martin Walker, **"The World's New Numbers"** 385

Abhijit Banerjee and Esther Duflo, **"More than 1 Billion People Are Hungry in the World"** 447

explorative

Kwame Anthony Appiah, **"The Shattered Mirror"** 10

Pico Iyer, **"Lonely Places"** 31

Humera Afridi, **"A Gentle Madness"** 48

Julian Hill, **"In Search of Black Identity in Uganda"** 53

Julia Whitty, **"All the Disappearing Islands"** 62

Andrew Guest, **"Pursuing the Science of Happiness"** 94

Peter Manseau, **"Plasticize Me"** 103

Stefany Anne Golberg, **"You Can Take It with You"** 124

Ethan Zuckerman, **"A Small World After All?"** 185

Natana J. DeLong-Bas, **"The New Social Media and the Arab Spring"** 197

Rob Horning, **"The Accidental Bricoleurs"** 229

Leila Ahmed, **"Reinventing the Veil"** 304

Mark Levine, **"Killing Emos, and the Future, in Iraq"** 321

Roozbeh Shirazi, **"Beyond Mullahs and Persian Party People: The Invisibility of Being Iranian on TV"** 339

informative

Anne Fadiman, **"Birth"** 78

Elizabeth Dwoskin, **"Why Americans Won't Do Dirty Jobs"** 115

James Angelos, **"Passing the Test"** 149

Reshma Krishnamurthy Sharma, **"The New Language Landscape"** 164

Pallavi Polanki, **"Operation Mind Your Language"** 167

Natana J. DeLong-Bas, **"The New Social Media and the Arab Spring"** 197

The Economist, **"The New Grand Tour"** 244

Avantika Bhuyan, **"The Enchanted Bylanes"** 260

Maureen Orth, **"The Luxury Frontier"** 269

Oliver Broudy, **"Body-Building in Afghanistan"** 309

Mark Levine, **"Killing Emos, and the Future, in Iraq"** 321

Sarah Lacy, **"You Think Hollywood Is Rough? Welcome to the Chaos, Excitement and Danger of Nollywood"** 349

Jackson Allers, **"Voice of the Streets: The Birth of a Hip-Hop Movement"** 357

Jeff Chang, **"So You Think They Can Break-Dance?"** 370

Martin Walker, **"The World's New Numbers"** 385

Abhijit Banerjee and Esther Duflo, **"More than 1 Billion People Are Hungry in the World"** 447

journalism

Tanveer Ali, **"The Subway Falafel Sandwich and the Americanization of Ethnic Food"** 24

Julia Whitty, **"All the Disappearing Islands"** 62

Latif Nasser, **"Do Some Cultures Have Their Own Ways of Going Mad?"** 88

Elizabeth Dwoskin, **"Why Americans Won't Do Dirty Jobs"** 115

James Angelos, **"Passing the Test"** 149

Reshma Krishnamurthy Sharma, **"The New Language Landscape"** 164

Pallavi Polanki, **"Operation Mind Your Language"** 167

Julie Traves, **"The Church of Please and Thank You"** 172

The Economist, **"The New Grand Tour"** 244

Charles Kenny, **"Haiti Doesn't Need Your Old T-Shirt"** 252

Tate Watkins, **"How Oliberté, the Anti-TOMS, Makes Shoes and Jobs in Africa"** 256

Avantika Bhuyan, **"The Enchanted Bylanes"** 260

Simon Akam, **"The Long and Winding Road"** 264

Maureen Orth, **"The Luxury Frontier"** 269

Doug Clark, **"Crimson Leopard-Print Headscarves: Wearing the Veil in Banda Aceh, Indonesia"** 289

Oliver Broudy, **"Body-Building in Afghanistan"** 309

Mark Levine, **"Killing Emos, and the Future, in Iraq"** 321

Sarah Lacy, **"You Think Hollywood Is Rough? Welcome to the Chaos, Excitement and Danger of Nollywood"** 349

Jackson Allers, **"Voice of the Streets: The Birth of a Hip-Hop Movement"** 357

Charukesi Ramadurai, **"Fading Lights in Mumbai"** 367

Jeff Chang, **"So You Think They Can Break-Dance?"** 370

Damon Tabor, **"If It's Tuesday, It Must Be the Taliban"** 397

Paul Salopek, **"The Last Famine"** 428

narrative

Tyler Olsen, **"In Zarafshan"** 2

Pico Iyer, **"Lonely Places"** 31

Justin Nobel, **"The Last Inuit of Quebec"** 38

Humera Afridi, **"A Gentle Madness"** 48

Julian Hill, **"In Search of Black Identity in Uganda"** 53

Julia Whitty, **"All the Disappearing Islands"** 62

Anne Fadiman, **"Birth"** 78

Andrew Guest, **"Pursuing the Science of Happiness"** 94

James Angelos, **"Passing the Test"** 149

Julie Traves, **"The Church of Please and Thank You"** 172

Teju Cole, **"The White Savior Industrial Complex"** 210

Simon Akam, **"The Long and Winding Road"** 264

Doug Clark, **"Crimson Leopard-Print Headscarves: Wearing the Veil in Banda Aceh, Indonesia"** 289

Oliver Broudy, **"Body-Building in Afghanistan"** 309

Damon Tabor, **"If It's Tuesday, It Must Be the Taliban"** 397

Petina Gappah, **"Zimbabwe"** 414

Paul Salopek, **"The Last Famine"** 428

preface

For students in today's classrooms, perhaps no topic or perspective is more urgent to the workplaces and communities for which they are preparing than "globalization." *Globalization: A Reader for Writers* generates for student writers a practice of continual inquiry not only into what globalization means to them personally, but also its implications for our collective future. Through the vibrant, challenging, and diverse selections in this reader, students learn to refine and sharpen the lens of globalization. The practice of writing in response to these selections encourages students to use that developing lens of globalization to unpack and make sense not only of what they read in this book but also of what they see, hear, and experience in the surrounding media and culture.

Importantly, *Globalization: A Reader for Writers* takes a more open-ended, less determined perspective than the "West and the Rest" agenda implied by popular and mainstream perspectives on globalization. This open-ended perspective allows for the consideration and interrogation of the multiple ways in which globalization has been defined: Does globalization represent the homogenization of culture and commerce? Is globalization a recognition of the ways in which heterogeneous localities have emerged and responded to dominant cultures and powers? As an age-old concept that has become a ubiquitous and key 21st-century term, globalization has many facets of meaning depending on disciplines and contexts. The writers, scholars, artists, journalists, and activists represented in this book transcend globalization as theme or content, challenging students to see globalization as an *esprit*, an *ethic*, and ultimately a term they need to define for themselves. Many of these readings are at once personal and local, even as they engage a broader, perhaps global audience. By seeking to understand the ways in which these authors negotiate language, context, prior knowledge, and other factors, student writers are encouraged to situate themselves in a larger conversation with the world—and become participants in an academic discourse critical to success in their college careers and beyond.

Globalization: A Reader for Writers presents a broad spectrum of writers who are researching, reflecting on, and arguing about the experience and impact of globalization. Each chapter takes on a particularly compelling aspect of today's conversations about globalization: being and becoming global; identity and place; body, mind, and spirit; languages in contact; communication and technology; earning and spending; gender matters; pop culture; and change and transformation. Within each of these subjects, selections embody a range of experiences, ideas, and approaches to writing— from scientific research to poetic reflection, from powerful argument to playful celebration. We have retained the rich language and conventions of the readings as they were originally published, including variant spellings indicative of World Englishes. The diverse readings in *Globalization: A Reader for Writers* demonstrate how codes and conventions are arbitrary. When students learn these codes and conventions—and how they vary— they can use them as agentive rhetorical *choices*, rather than as passive correct/incorrect rules. Students learn that codes and conventions have a history of power that can be actively challenged, so that when they choose to conform to or deviate from standards and conventions, they do so from an informed position and because they have thought about the needs and values of their target audience, their purpose in writing, and the constraints of their text's form.

Globalization: A Reader for Writers is part of a series of brief single-topic readers from Oxford University Press designed for today's college writing courses. Each reader in this series approaches a topic of contemporary conversation from multiple perspectives and is:

- **Timely:** Most selections were originally published in 2010 or later.
- **Global:** Sources and voices from around the world are included.
- **Diverse:** Selections come from a range of nontraditional and alternate print and online media, as well as representative mainstream sources.

In addition to the rich array of perspectives on topical (even urgent) issues addressed in each reader, each volume features an abundance of different genres and styles—from the academic research paper to the pithy Twitter argument. Useful but non-intrusive pedagogy includes:

- **Chapter introductions** that provide a brief overview of the chapter's theme and a sense of how the chapter's selections relate both to the overarching theme and to each other.
- **Headnotes** introduce each reading by providing concise information about its original publication, and pose an open-ended question that encourages students to explore their prior knowledge of (or opinions about) some aspect of the selection's content.
- **"Analyze" and "Explore" questions** after each reading scaffold and support student reading for comprehension, as well as rhetorical considerations, providing prompts for reflection, classroom discussion, and brief writing assignments.
- **"Forging Connections" and "Looking Further" prompts** after each chapter encourage critical thinking by asking students to compare perspectives and strategies among readings both within the chapter and with readings in other chapters, suggesting writing assignments (many of which are multimodal) that engage students with larger conversations in the academy, the community, and the media.
- **An appendix on "Researching and Writing about Globalization"** guides student inquiry and research in a digital environment. Coauthored by a research librarian and a writing program director, this appendix provides transferable, real-world strategies for locating, assessing, synthesizing, and citing sources in support of an argument. The appendix includes a student's research paper on a theme of globalization that models MLA citation style.

about the author

Maria Jerskey is an associate professor in the Department of Education and Language Acquisition at LaGuardia Community College/City University of New York (CUNY). She teaches writing and linguistics to undergraduate students and academic writing to graduate students at CUNY's Graduate Center. Her practice focuses on cultivating and advocating for learning environments and curricula that build on students' language and literacy resources. Her strands of scholarship have included the connection between multilingual students' writing self-efficacy and their participation on Web 2.0 platforms, as well as the writing and publication practices of multilingual scholars. She founded and coordinates the Literacy Brokers Program at LaGuardia, which fosters networks of support among multilingual scholars and promotes equitable writing and publication practices in English-medium contexts. She also co-leads LaGuardia's professional development seminar, Community 2.0, in which teachers design social pedagogies to connect students across courses and disciplines. She currently serves as co-chair of CUNY's ESL Discipline Council and as a member of the Conference on College Composition and Communication's Committee on Second Language Writing.

acknowledgments

This project began with piles of readings organized and reorganized on a picnic table while "on vacation" last July, then further piled and reorganized yet again on the dining room table in August. Chapters began to emerge, take shape, and finally settled into the table of contents now transformed into the book you hold. There is no way this could have happened without the conversations, support, and interest of several people whom I would like to thank.

My amazing students—some of whom are teachers themselves now—were first and foremost on my mind as I worked on this book and imagined their responses. I'd especially like to thank Kiersten Greene and Clyde Barretto for their suggestions and advice.

At Oxford, I work with a fantastic team that sets—and reaches—a high bar for quality textbooks. Executive editor Carrie Brandon has been steadfast in her support of this project, her confidence in its excellence, and her delight in the results. Mine was the great fortune to have Meg Botteon as development editor *extraordinaire*. Her intelligence, enthusiasm, and critical eye for detail helped bring out the best in the drafts and their revisions. On the production end, I owe much to the careful reading and editing of Diane Kohnen and Bonnie Kelsey.

Kim Helmer, Leigh Jones, and Cheryl Smith, my colleague-friends at CUNY, offered perceptive feedback and teacher perspectives during our writing group get-togethers. I'm also grateful to my colleagues at LaGuardia—Habiba Boumlik, Ruhma Choudhury, Monika Ekiert, Ann Feibel, Jack Gantzer, Rebekah Johnson, and Max Rodriguez—for invaluable discussions on integrating concepts of globalization into our teaching practices and curriculum.

Most of all I'd like to thank my sonny-boy Gene. His passion for learning about global issues combined with his sense of wonder and discovery breathed life into this book.

Finally, the generous and in-depth feedback, suggestions, and critique from a group of outstanding reviewers helped me make improvements to *Globalization: A Reader for Writers*. I thank Gwen S. Argersinger, Mesa Community College; Stacia Bensyl, Missouri Western State University; Kara Bollinger, New Economic School (Moscow, Russia); Barbara Eaton, College of DuPage; Sharon Harrow, Shippensburg University of Pennsylvania; Eric Hyman, Fayetteville State University; Joan D. S. Maynor, Savannah State University; Sandra Park, Ohlone College; Hem Sharma Paudel, University of Louisville; Cary D. Ser, Miami Dade College; and Tanja Stampfl, University of the Incarnate Word.

globalization

Being & Becoming Global

1

What does it mean to you to be part of a *globalized* world? To what extent is globalization something new: Is it a phenomenon of 21st-century living in which access to travel, migration, and digital media allow for connections and reconfigurations with more people, places, and ideas than imagined possible in previous centuries? To what extent is globalization something old, or even eternal: Is it a human impulse or imperative that has been actively embraced—and resisted—by individuals and communities for millennia? How do your responses to these questions—ones that you will surely revisit and revise as you read this chapter and others in this book—reflect your understanding of being and becoming global?

The authors of the collected readings in this chapter grapple with these questions in ways both obvious and oblique, offering a range of approaches against which you can measure your own written responses. In "In Zarafshan," we are privy to one man's armchair journey via the Internet to a place he's never heard of or been to before. How do the questions and musings posed and explored in this article by Canadian journalist Tyler Olsen (writing for an online cultural magazine) compare to the key question asked by theoretical physicist Marcelo Gleiser in "Globalization: Two Visions of the Future of Humanity" (writing for a major radio station's blog)? How might we reconcile our emerging concept of globalization with the concept of cosmopolitanism introduced by philosopher Kwame Anthony Appiah in "The Shattered Mirror," excerpted from his book *Cosmopolitanism: Ethics in a World of Strangers*? The historian Jeffrey N. Wasserstrom, writing "A Mickey Mouse Approach to Globalization" for a major academic online journal, complicates the notion of globalization, which he points out is often conflated with the notion of *Americanization*, even as writer Tanveer Ali reports on the Americanization of an ethnic food in "The Subway Falafel Sandwich and the Americanization of Ethnic Food" for the online platform *Good*.

Together, the readings persuade us that no matter how we define what it means to be part of a globalized world, it is difficult to dispute that we are all in a dynamic process of both being and becoming *global*. It is a process that we as writers can describe individually and together from our local desks (or screens), bearing in mind the global contexts within which we can't help but find ourselves.

Tyler Olsen
"In Zarafshan"

Tyler Olsen is a reporter for the *Chilliwack Times* in Chilliwack, British Columbia. He is a recipient of several community journalism awards for his series "Growing Concern," which reports on marijuana grow houses in Chilliwack. "In Zarafshan" was published in the October 27, 2011 edition of *The Morning News*, an online magazine of essays, art, humor, and culture. In this article,

Olsen writes of his virtual exploration through the little-known Uzbekistani city of Zarafshan. Why Zarafshan? Olsen reasons: With a mouse, Wikipedia, and Google maps, why *not*?

In what ways does the Internet allow you to become more global?

The orange sand slides away beneath me as I meander down a long boule- 1 vard, the harsh sun stabbing at me from behind the trees. The ground soon turns to pavement as I cross four lanes of deserted, unused roadway and find myself alone in the middle of a massive, barren public square. *Is this place abandoned or, markedly worse, inhabited by zombies?*, I think, as I walk to the fridge to grab another beer.

I came here, to Zarafshan, Uzbekistan, via Google Earth and the Internet connection in my very suburban, very Canadian apartment because I could and I was bored and I didn't know much about the vast expanse of Earth between Beijing and Moscow. And I also came here because Google Earth promised to make the visit free, solitary (no tourists, no beggars, no tips!) and, thanks to the six-pack of beer beside my desk, well lubricated. In the past, to get a sense of the scenery of the Eastern steppe or a Pacific Island or a jungle village without actually visiting those locales, you would have had to read a book. Fortunately, those days are long gone. Today, you can explore remote destinations from the La-Z-Boy comfort of your own home. Nauru, Bolivia, the Democratic Republic of the Congo, Oman: on my salary of not-very-much, I've been able to visit places that are too out of the way, too dangerous, too people-y, or other- wise too boring to visit in person.

> "Wikipedia must have lied, I thought, as Google swooped me down to ground level."

Wikipedia must have lied, I thought, as Google swooped me down to ground level. There was no way this city of squares could be home to "over 65,000 people" as I had been assured. Indeed, at first glance, Zarafshan didn't appear to consist of much more than a chicane in a highway and a collection of Soviet-era apartment blocks. A couple quick flicks of the ol' mouse turned up little else and I considered moving on. Lesotho is beauti- ful this time of year. But the hardy, resilient traveler that I am, I pressed on, figuring that surely there must be something worth seeing. If there wasn't, the sheer absence would be noteworthy. It turns out the latter is true.

Uzbekistan, in case your globe still includes Rhodesia, is one of those countries in the dead center of Asia that was formed when Russia went to shit. If a map of the old Soviet Union (very, very) vaguely resembled a (male) bear, with eastern Siberia as the head, then Uzbekistan would have been in the gonad area. But since 2000-era military adventures are the touchstone for most people's knowledge of Asian geography these days, it's probably best to just say that the country's southernmost tip touches Afghanistan.

5   In the west, the country abuts the slow-moving ecological disaster that is the rapidly shrinking Aral Sea. In the east, it bangs up against the Himalayas. And in the middle, amidst the Kyzyl Kum desert and miles and miles (and miles and miles) of sand and scrubland sits Zarafshan, a city that looks shitty and rundown in the Google satellite image and which, I am told by the Internet's only English-language travelogue on the city, isn't much better in real life.

"So, you want to travel to Zarafshan," wrote a volunteer named Jon, on the website network54.com in 2005. "There is no real reason to ask why you want to come to Zarafshan. There can be no logical reason to do this. Therefore, any attempt to ask 'why' will only be futile."

Jon writes that there is a seedy hotel in town and a restaurant that serves "low-end Tashkent food" and that "While the buildings represent the height of Soviet architectural design, the most striking thing to see in Zarafshan is actually outside of the city: nothing."

Jon doesn't seem like a fan and early indications aren't promising for me either, especially since I'm exploring a town through a computer monitor on which "nothing" does not exactly come across as interesting. My self-assigned mission seems kind of like multiplying "0" a thousand different ways and expecting a new result. It seems, in other words, like an idiotic waste of time. So as I bore into the strange town, I'm not confident that the 6,000 miles or so between my computer and the residents of Zarafshan will make me like the city any more. But I'll go there virtually, guzzle a beer, and after an hour or two, come back and drink another. Travel has never been so risk-free.

• ⋮ •

It's the geometry of the place—the square blocks and the rectangular buildings and the straight roads—that first confronts me. Like many Soviet cities, Zarafshan seems to have been planned by a communist who played a pre-computer version of SimCity. All residential building comes in the form of apartment blocks, which are crammed into a very-square square mile of land. At first, I think the roads are canals, but they just turn out to be roads colored teal by a crappy camera. I congratulate myself on catching the detail before declaring Zarafshan to be the Venice of Uzbekistan in my future best-selling travelogue. (See, virtual travel has adrenaline-inducing risks too.) Zarafshan, it turns out, is more like what happens when Butte, Mont., meets Mad Max.

I zoom out until the city's perimeter reaches the edges of my screen. 10 From the air, Zarafshan looks like a city whose purpose was to ravage the surrounding landscape—which it was. However, using photos available on Google Earth, I find that from the ground, and despite the city's hellish location and less-than-organic creation, Zarafshan doesn't really resemble a 24th-century postapocalyptic ghost town. Somehow, the sand and the gray streets and the cement buildings and the blazing blue sky all direct one's eyes to the trees, which exclaim, "Look at us! Something lives here!" The greenery and the car-less streets give a sense of calm to the place. But then, I am startled by the question, *So where are all the cars?*

Amidst the buildings meant to house most of the city's residents, there is little evidence that Zarafshan remains a populated city. I do spot a turtle on the city's outskirts. But I have less luck with warm-blooded creatures. Just south of the apartment block complex, I come across a new-ish shopping plaza featuring a cafe. There are Russian-types and Afghan-looking types and other stereotype types, but they're all spaced very, very far apart.

I scroll-stroll a little farther west, where there is a reservoir that you might be able to swim in. But what may or may not be a public beach is deserted. Further up the shore, a couple of houses have docks that step out onto the water, which is piped in from the Amu Darya River 200 miles away.

Number of people: five, maybe 10. One of the things I like about virtual tourism, whether I wish to admit it or not, is that one does not have to deal with people. So the absence of other sentient creatures shouldn't really disturb me. But it's still strange to look at photo after photo of a city and not see more than a dozen people in total.

Unfortunately, or not, there are no on-the-ground pictures of the industrial rectangle that can be seen in the satellite photo of the city. There seems to have been enough jobs in the area at one point. But there's no telling if the people here are underemployed, overemployed, unemployed, or properly employed, although they are likely one of those.

15   I almost overlook it entirely, but eventually I spot evidence of post-Gorbachev activity in the form of a large neighborhood west of the reservoir that seems to be either too recently built to allow for much visible-from-space shrubbery or too impoverished for its residents to invest in it. The buildings could be slum-like shacks erected by those desperate for work after the collapse of the Soviet Union. Or they could be multi-story family compounds. Again, it's hard to tell, and not just because I'm on my fourth beer. I feel fortunate to escape the dust that would surely have forced me to take a shower if I had been on the ground. The neighborhood is slap-dashed tacked onto the western edge of town and, like Zarafshan itself, remains a mystery.

Finally, an hour into my journey, my heroic determination and perseverance pays off as I meet Igelya (a.k.a. Lara) on YouTube. In a photo slideshow, Lara, who now lives in North Dakota, takes me from Zarafshan's beginning as a mining city that sprung from the desert in the 1960s to more recent times, when the city was considered the center of Uzbekistan's gold industry and the home base for the nearby Muruntau open pit mine. Lara lived for 20 years in the city and the photos show a family building snowmen, working in the mines and sharing meals. There are camels (!), more turtles (!!) and some smiling people (!!!). Back in the day, there were motorcycle races and swimming races and people selling food.

Some of the photos look like they were taken in the last five years. So, if you physically follow in my digital footsteps, it is possible you will find people there. Poor them. Poor you.

Analyze

1. Using visual images and words, create a snapshot of Tyler Olsen's room as he traveled to Zarafshan and beyond. Be sure to include details from the reading, but elaborate on these details by "showing" what you pictured in your mind's eye as you read. How does your "picture" compare to those of others in your class?

2. Who are Olsen's readers? What age, education, and other defining characteristics do you imagine they have? What words, phrases, and

images offer hints? Who might feel excluded from this audience? Do you feel part of his audience? Explain why or why not.

3. What are the benefits and drawbacks of visiting an exotic place, as Olsen does, without actually leaving home?

4. Create a hybrid-text travelogue of a trip to Zarafshan in which you add your own visual images or images from an image-sharing platform such as Flickr.

Explore

1. Choose a city or region you are unfamiliar with. Research and explore it the same way that Olsen researches and explores Zarafshan. Write a narrative essay in which you recount your journey and discovery.

2. Olsen uses the words "shit," "shitty," and "crappy" in his article, words we generally would not associate with academic writing. Revise those sentences to sound more academic. What is lost and/or gained in your revision?

3. Olsen jokes that he will have a "future best-selling travelogue," presumably of his virtual travel adventures. Write a summary for the back cover blurb that lets readers know what they would find in Olsen's book. What does a travelogue based on virtual travel enable you to do? What are its limitations?

4. What mystery does Olsen "solve" about Zarafshan? If this were an academic essay, how would it differ in its account of the rise and fall of Zarafshan?

Marcelo Gleiser
"Globalization: Two Visions of the Future of Humanity"

Marcelo Gleiser, a theoretical physicist, teaches physics and astronomy at Dartmouth College. He is the author of several articles and books, including *A Tear at the Edge of Creation* (Free Press, 2010), *The Dancing Universe* (Dartmouth, 2005), and *The Prophet and the Astronomer* (W. W. Norton, 2003). "Globalization: Two Visions of the Future of Humanity" is a post from the

National Public Radio-sponsored blog *13.7: Cosmos and Culture,* which Gleiser co-founded. In this post, Gleiser concedes that technological advances make the realization of a true global village possible; yet, he also questions whether it is sustainable, given the human tendency toward tribalism and group culture.

Do you think it's possible to live in a global village and still participate in one's tribe or group cultures?

1   **W**ill the steady pace of globalization make the world better or worse? On the one hand, the shrinking of our planet due to increased speeds of travel, trade and Internet exchange all contribute to create a true global village. On the other, due to deeply ingrained human traits, cultural differences and distrust for those outside our "tribe" remain entrenched.

Futurists have long predicted that the world will evolve to a techno-driven state of oneness. Take, for example, Mikio Kaku's *Physics of the Future* (Doubleday, 2011). A theoretical physicist by training, Kaku interviewed over 300 scientists to dream up a utopian world defined by science: By the year 2100, intelligent computers will work in tandem with humans; people will have access to the Internet through contact lenses and will move objects with the power of their thoughts; nanobots will cure cancer by intervening directly with the diseased cells; laser-propelled rockets will change the face of space exploration and Mars will be the next frontier of colonization. Furthermore, trade barriers will be practically nonexistent, and the same culture and foods will be shared by all. As people share the same values and goods, wars will be isolated events.

These technological marvels are, of course, extrapolations of what we already have. If someone had predicted, in 1920, that by the year 2000 we would have laptop computers capable of downloading gigabytes of information from across the world in seconds, no one would have believed it.

The unexpected is hard to predict.

5   But how realistic are visions of scientific utopia, of a world made better and peaceful through technological advances and, more importantly, through the percolation of the scientific modus operandi of sharing information in a democratic way into politics and culture?

Michael Shermer, in his *Skeptic* column for the August issue of *Scientific American*, brings up a new book by Pankaj Ghemawat, a professor of strategic management, and Anselmo Rubiralta, chair of Global Strategy at IESE Business School at the University of Navarra in Barcelona, where such visions are strongly criticized. Globalization, understood as representing the vanishing of cultural and value barriers, is unattainable due to our evolved tribal natures. The book puts numbers to this claim, showing that, indeed, most of societal relations and trading remains local: international mail constitutes 1% of the total; international phone calling, less than 2%; international Internet traffic, between 17 to 18%; exports as percentage of GDP, 26%; first-generation immigrants, 3% (I'm one of them).

One of the most obvious and terrifying responses to tendencies of cultural merging is the upsurge of fundamentalism. If values and traditions that have defined how you and many generations of your ancestors have lived become threatened by "outside" forces, you have two choices: You either open up and absorb them to a lesser or greater extent, or you entrench and fight back. Humans have evolved in tribes and are still tribal. Beyond our families and blood relations, many of our social and cultural relations are vested in allegiance to certain groups, from the Red Sox or the New York Yankees to being an American or Mexican to being White or Hispanic to being an Episcopalian or a Muslim. We pledge allegiance to this or that flag, and many are ready to die defending it.

There is enrichment in the exchange of ideas but impoverishment in their homogenizing.

Many of the technological extrapolations Kaku and others discuss are definitely coming our way (see, e.g., Freeman Dyson's wonderful *The Sun, The Genome and The Internet*). That's a good thing, as I believe that one of the central tasks of science and technology is (or should be) to alleviate human suffering. Questions of culture and trade are subtler. Again, no question that trade barriers will keep falling, and that goods will become ever more globalized and accessible to everyone. (Although you could also argue that even with the upsurge of new economies such as the BRIC countries, purchasing power is becoming more polarized and not less.)

The challenge is to reinvent our tribal make-up. Can we live without our flags? Unless we find ways to respect and celebrate our differences while jointly creating an atmosphere of open exchange and mutual understanding, I fear that the utopian world of the future will have a very dystopian bend to it.

Analyze

1. The reading opens with an either/or question: "Will the steady pace of globalization make the world better or worse?" How does the author answer this question?
2. How does Gleiser define globalization? Find a definition of globalization from a different source. How do the two definitions compare and contrast? Sharing the range of definitions within your class, why do you suppose there are so many definitions of one concept?
3. What are the "two visions of the future of humanity" in the reading's title? Are they plausible in your view? Why or why not?

Explore

1. Gleiser recounts how physicist Mikio Kaku asked scientists "to dream up a utopian world defined by science." Dream up your own utopian world of the future using frameworks other than or in addition to science to define it.
2. The author claims that we as humans have evolved in tribes and are still tribal. Using an online tool such as Mindomo or iThoughts HD (or using paper and colored pencils), create a mind map that lays out the hierarchy and relationship of the "tribe" (or "tribes") that you belong to.
3. Gleiser asks, "Can we live without our flags?" (a) Create the front page of a newspaper or a news website that reports on the day the world becomes "nationless." What would be the lead article and image? What other kinds of articles would "make" the front page? Consider who would write the articles and in what language(s). (b) Taking into account Gleiser's reasoning, what would you personally gain and/or lose if you were a citizen of the world rather than of a specific country?

Kwame Anthony Appiah
"The Shattered Mirror"

Born in London but raised in Ghana, Kwame Anthony Appiah holds both B.A. and Ph.D. degrees in philosophy from Clare College, Cambridge University in England. He joined the Princeton faculty in 2002, as Laurance S. Rockefeller

University Professor of Philosophy, and the University Center for Human Values. Appiah has published three novels, as well as several essays and books on race and identity theory, political theory, moral theory, and semantics. This selection, "The Shattered Mirror," is from his book *Cosmopolitanism: Ethics in a World of Strangers* (W.W. Norton, 2006). In the book, Appiah argues that there is a middle ground between globalization and separatism, what he identifies as "cosmopolitanism." He believes that if we engage in an open exchange about our seemingly disparate ideologies, ideas, and identities, then we will find the shared values that bind us.

Do you agree that despite the differences that separate humankind, there exists a common value system that unites us?

A Traveler's Tale

We shall be meeting many cosmopolitans and anti-cosmopolitans   1 in this book, but none, I think, who so starkly combines elements of both as the character who will be the first companion on our journey. Sir Richard Francis Burton was a Victorian adventurer whose life lent credence to that dubious adage about truth being stranger than fiction. Born in 1821, he traveled, as a child, with his family in Europe, and spent time getting to know the Romany people; his English contemporaries liked to say that he had acquired some of the Gypsy's wandering ways. He learned modern Greek in Marseilles and French and Italian, including the Neapolitan dialect, as his family moved between the British expatriate communities of France and Italy; and he arrived at Oxford knowing Béarnais—a language intermediate between French and Spanish—and (like every other student in those days) classical Greek and Latin as well.

Burton was not just an extraordinary linguist. He was one of the greatest European swordsmen of his day. Before being expelled from Oxford (for ignoring a college ban on going to the races), he challenged a fellow student to a duel because that young man had mocked his walrus mustache. When this fellow didn't grasp that he had been challenged, Burton concluded that he was not among gentlemen but among "grocers." It is just possible, of course, that his adversary was a gentleman who had heard of Burton's prowess with the saber.

At the age of twenty-one, Richard Burton went to work for the East India Company in Sindh, where he added Gujarati, Marathi, Afghan, and Persian to his knowledge of modern and classical European languages, while deepening his mastery of Arabic and Hindi, which he had begun to study in England. Despite being (at least nominally) a Christian, he managed, in 1853, to be admitted to Mecca and Medina as a pilgrim, posing as a Pathan from India's Northwest Frontier Province. He traveled widely in Africa, as well. In 1858, he and John Hanning Speke were the first Europeans to see Lake Tanganyika, and he visited, among other places, Somalia (where he passed as an Arab merchant) as well as Sierra Leone, Cape Coast and Accra (in what is now Ghana), and Lagos. He knew large swaths of Asia and of Latin America; and he translated the Kama Sutra from Sanskrit and the *Perfumed Garden* and the *Thousand and One Nights* from Arabic (the latter in sixteen volumes, with a notorious "terminal essay" that included one of the first cross-cultural surveys of homosexuality). Aptly enough, he also translated Luiz Vaz de Camões' Lusiads—a celebration of that earlier global explorer Vasco da Gama—from the Portuguese. His translations made him famous (notorious even, when it came to the Oriental erotica); he also wrote grammars of two Indian languages and a vast number of the most extraordinary travel accounts of a century in which there was a good deal of competition in that genre. And, in 1880 he published a long poem that was, he said, a translation of "the Kasidah of Haji Abdu El-Yezdi," a native of the desert city of Yazd, in central Persia (one of the few substantial centers of Zoroastrianism remaining in Iran).

A qasida (as we would now write it) is a pre-Islamic classical Arab poetic form, with strict metrical rules, that begins, by tradition, with an evocation of a desert encampment. Although the form was highly respected before the rise of Islam, it saw its heyday in Islam's early days, before the eighth century AD, when it was regarded by some as the highest form of poetic art. But qasida have been written over the centuries through much of the Islamic world, in Turkish and Urdu and Persian as well as in Arabic. Burton's Haji Abdu of Yazd was devoted to "an Eastern Version of Humanitarianism blended with the sceptical or, as we now say, the scientific habit of mind." He was also, as one might guess from reading the poem, a fiction. For though the Kasidah is infused with the spirit of Sufism— Islam's mystical tradition—it also alludes to Darwin's evolutionary theory and to other ideas from the Victorian West. Burton, the "translator," offered to explain this by writing, in his notes, that Haji Abdu added

> to a natural facility, a knack of language learning, . . . a store of
> desultory various reading; scraps of Chinese and old Egyptian; of
> Hebrew and Syriac; of Sanskrit and Prakrit; of Slav, especially
> Lithuanian; of Latin and Greek, including Romaic; of Berber, the
> Nubian dialect, and of Zend and Akkadian, besides Persian, his
> mother-tongue, and Arabic, the classic of the schools. Nor was he
> ignorant of "the—ologies" and the triumphs of modern scientific
> discovery.

If the linguistic gifts of this imaginary Sufi read a little too like Burton's   5
own, Burton's conceit was not designed to deceive. At the start of the note,
we're told that Abdu "preferred to style himself El-Hichmakâni . . . meaning 'Of No-hall, Nowhere.'" And though Burton's point is, in part, that
Haji Abdu is, like himself, a man with no strong sense of national or local
identity (dare I say it, a rootless cosmopolitan), it is also, surely, to give us
the broadest of hints that El-Yezdi is his own invention.

Certainly the author of the Kasidah expressed views that, for a traditional Muslim, are more than mildly heretical. In one stanza he announces,

> *There is no Heav'en, there is no Hell;*
> *these be the dreams of baby minds . . .*
> In another he says,
> *There is no Good, there is no Bad;*
> *these be the whims of mortal will . . .*

In short, he can sound—appropriately enough, perhaps, for a native of
Zoroastrian Yazd—less like a Persian Sufi and more like Nietzsche's
Zarathustra. One thing, though, about the author is not a fiction: since
Burton had, in fact, made his pilgrimage to Mecca, the Kasidah's author
certainly was a hajji—one who has made the hajj.

Of course, one characteristic of European cosmopolitanism, especially
since the Enlightenment, has been a receptiveness to art and literature from
other places, and a wider interest in lives elsewhere. This is a reflection of
what I called, in the introduction, the second strand of cosmopolitanism:
the recognition that human beings are different and that we can learn from

each other's differences. There is Goethe, in Germany, whose career as a poet runs by way of a collection of Roman Elegies, written at the end of the 1780s, to the West-Eastern Divan of 1819, his last great cycle of poems, inspired by the oeuvre of the fourteenth-century Persian poet Hafiz (author, as Sir Richard Burton would certainly have pointed out, of extremely popular qasida). There is David Hume, in eighteenth-century Edinburgh, scouring traveler's tales, to examine the ways of China, Persia, Turkey, and Egypt. A little earlier still, across the English Channel in Bordeaux, there is Montesquieu, whose monumental Spirit of the Laws, published anonymously in Geneva in 1748, is crammed with anecdotes from Indonesia to Lapland, from Brazil to India, from Egypt to Japan; and whose earlier witty satire of his own country, the Persian Letters, ventriloquizes a Muslim. Burton's poet, too, seems mostly to speak for Burton: himself an agnostic of a scientific bent, with a vast store of knowledge of the world's religions and an evenhanded assessment of them all.

> *All Faith is false, all Faith is true:*
> *Truth is the shattered mirror strown*
> *In myriad bits; while each believes*
> *His little bit the whole to own.*

Burton's voracious assimilation of religions, literatures, and customs from around the world marks him as someone who was fascinated by the range of human invention, the variety of our ways of life and thought. And though he never pretended to anything like dispassion, that knowledge brought him to a point where he could see the world from perspectives remote from the outlook in which he had been brought up. A cosmopolitan openness to the world is perfectly consistent with picking and choosing among the options you find in your search. Burton's English contemporaries sometimes thought he displayed more respect for Islam than for the Christianity in which he was raised: though his wife was convinced that he had converted to Catholicism, I think it would be truer to say that he was, as W. H. Wilkins wrote in The Romance of Isabel Lady Burton, "a Mohammedan among Mohammedans, a Mormon among Mormons, a Sufi among the Shazlis, and a Catholic among the Catholics."

In this, he follows a long line of itinerant seekers. Menelaus may be most famous as the man the kidnapping of whose wife, Helen, was the casus belli of the Trojan War; but Homer has him boast of having roamed over

Kypros, Phoinikia, Egypt, and still farther
among the sun-burnt races.
I saw the men of Sidon and Arabia
and Libya, too ...

where the fecundity of the sheep ensures that "no man, chief or shepherd, ever goes/hungry for want of mutton, cheese, or milk—/all year at milking time there are fresh ewes." Centuries after the Iliad, Herodotus writes of how Croesus greeted the wise Solon: "Well, my Athenian friend, I have heard a great deal about your wisdom, and how widely you have travelled in the pursuit of knowledge. I cannot resist my desire to ask you a question: who is the happiest man you have ever seen?" (No "country can produce everything it needs: whatever it has, it is bound to lack something," Solon explains in the course of his reply.) Herodotus himself traveled as far south as present-day Aswan and told us something of Meroë (whose own language has still not been deciphered), a city whose glory days were not to come for another two centuries.

Such exposure to the range of human customs and beliefs hardly left the traveler untethered from his own. Burton illustrates this clearly enough. He was the least Victorian of men, and the most. Certainly he had many of the standard racial prejudices of his society. Africans he ranked below Arabs and most Indians, both of whom were below civilized Europeans. In the third chapter of his *To the Gold Coast for Gold*—an account of a trip to West Africa that began in November 1881—he speaks casually of the "pollution" of Madeiran blood "by extensive miscegenation with the negro." Describing a trip to East Africa in *Blackwood's Edinburgh Magazine* in 1858, he makes similarly unflattering asides: "the negro race is ever loquacious"; "even a Sawahili sometimes speaks the truth"; "Wazira is our rogue, rich in all the peculiarities of African cunning." At one point he turns to a lengthy description of the "Wanika or desert people of the Mombas hills": "All with them is confusion. To the incapacity of childhood they unite the hard-headedness of age." In their religion, he found "the vain terrors of our childhood rudely systematised."

Nor was his capacity for contempt limited to the darker races. He was an   10
odd sort of mélange of cosmopolitan and misanthrope. In his travels across North America through the summer of 1860, recounted in *The City of the Saints, and across the Rocky Mountains to California*, he manages to express hostility to the Irish ("At 9 p.m., reaching 'Thirty-two-mile Creek,'

we were pleasantly surprised to find an utter absence of the Irishry"), condescension toward French-Canadians ("a queer lot . . . much addicted to loafing"), distrust of Pawnee Indians ("The Pawnees, African-like, will cut the throat of a sleeping guest"), and gentle mockery of the uniform of the American army ("The States have attempted in the dress of their army, as in their forms of government, a moral impossibility"). Yet he is also capable of composing an elegant defense of a despised people, as in the litany of answers to the "sentimental objections to Mormonism" that runs for many pages of *The City of the Saints*. Still, there is little in Burton's life to suggest that he took seriously what I called in the introduction the first strand of cosmopolitanism: the recognition of our responsibility for every human being. Over and over again in his writings, he passes by opportunities to intervene to reduce human suffering: he records it, sometimes with humor, rarely with outrage. When he needs workers to carry his luggage into the Dark Continent, he buys slaves without a scruple.

Burton is a standing refutation, then, to those who imagine that prejudice derives only from ignorance, that intimacy must breed amity. You can be genuinely engaged with the ways of other societies without approving, let alone adopting, them. And though his Kasidah endorsed the kind of spiritualism that was common among the educated upper classes in late Victorian England, its image of the shattered mirror—each shard of which reflects one part of a complex truth from its own particular angle—seems to express exactly the conclusion of Burton's long exposure to the philosophies and the customs of many people and places: you will find parts of the truth (along with much error) everywhere and the whole truth nowhere. The deepest mistake, he supposed, is to think that your little shard of mirror can reflect the whole.

Beyond the Mirror

Life would be easier if we could stop with that thought. We can grant that there's some insight everywhere else and some error chez nous. But that doesn't help us when we are trying to decide exactly where the truth lies this time. Real disagreements of this kind often arise in the context of religious practices. So let me begin by thinking about one of those practices: the one, in fact, that Richard Burton wrote about so famously.

Most Muslims think they should go to Mecca—making the hajj, if you have the resources, is one of the five pillars of Islam, along with faith in God, charity, fasting, and daily prayer. About one and a half million Muslims make the trip every year. If you're not a Muslim, on the other hand, you don't think that Muhammad was a prophet, and so you are unlikely to think that you yourself should make the hajj. In fact, since unbelievers aren't welcome, what we should probably do is stay away: a tollbooth on the road to Mecca is helpfully signed NO ENTRY FOR NON-MUSLIMS.

Now, this might look, at first glance, like one of those cases where our obligations depend on our positions. You should be faithful to your spouse, we can agree, but I don't need to be faithful to your spouse. (In fact, I'd better not be!) Someone might say, in the same spirit, "Muslims should go to Mecca, Catholics to Mass." If you're not a Muslim, though, you don't really think Muslims should go to Mecca, and if you are a Muslim, you don't think that anyone, not even a Catholic, has a duty to go to Mass. On the other hand, unless you're some kind of libertine—or a rare survivor of one of those experiments with free love that erupted in the 1960s—you probably think that married people ought to keep their pledges of fidelity to their spouses.

Obviously, Muslims believe that they ought to make the hajj and   15
Catholics that they ought to go to Mass. But if you don't have the beliefs that give those acts their meanings, you presumably think that the people who do think so are mistaken. Either Muhammad was the Prophet or he wasn't. Either the Koran is the definitive Holy Writ or it isn't. And if he wasn't and it isn't, then Muslims are mistaken. (The same goes, mutatis mutandis, for Mass.) Of course, you probably don't think there's much harm done if people do go to Mecca. They think it's right. We don't. We don't think it's wrong, either, though. Indeed, since we think that integrity matters—that living by your beliefs is important—and since, in this case, there's no harm done in doing what conscience dictates, perhaps it would be a good thing if they made an effort to go.

It's important to insist, however, that to say that Muslims should go to Mecca for this reason isn't to agree with Muslims. It is to give our reason for them to do something that they do for a different reason. One way of seeing why this matters is to remind ourselves that no self-respecting Muslim would think that you understood, let alone respected, the reason they make the hajj if you said, "Of course you have a reason to go: namely, that you think you should, and people should follow their consciences unless to do so will cause harm." Because that isn't what Muslims think. What they think is that they should go because God commanded it through the Holy Koran. And that claim is one that you don't accept at all.

This disagreement is, nevertheless, one that doesn't have to be resolved for us to get along. I can be (indeed, I am!) perfectly friendly with Catholics and Muslims while not always agreeing with them about theology. I have no more reason to resent those who go to Mecca on the hajj than I have to begrudge the choices of those who go to Scotland for golf or to Milan for opera. Not what I'd do, but, hey, suit yourself.

Still, this live-and-let-live attitude is not shared by everyone: some people think that the worship of anyone but the true God is idolatry, itself an offense against divine law, and there are some Christians who think that Allah is not the God of Abraham, Isaac, and Jacob, whom Christians worship. Some Muslims (along with the Unitarians) have worried about whether belief in the Trinity is consistent with Islam's command that we should worship one God. And that possibility draws our attention to a second kind of disagreement.

For there are the cases, of course, where religious practices strike us not as morally indifferent but as actually wrong. Readers of this book are unlikely to think that the proper response to adultery is to take offenders before a religious court and, if they are convicted, to organize a crowd to stone them to death. You and I are no doubt appalled (as are a lot of Muslims, it should be said) by the very thought of a person being stoned to death in this way. Yet many people in the world today think that this is what sharia, Muslim religious law, requires. Or take what we often call female circumcision, which Burton documented among Arabs and East Africans (according to whom, he claimed, sexual desire in women was much greater than in men), and which remains prevalent in many regions. We mostly don't agree with that either. Disagreements like these are perfectly common, even within societies. If you are contemplating an abortion, which you think is morally quite permissible, and I think that you'll be killing an innocent young human being, I can't just say, "Fine, go ahead," can I?

20   The temptation is to look for a rule book that could tell you how to arbitrate conflicts like that—but then you'd have to agree on the rule book. And even if you did, for reasons I'll be exploring later, there's no reason to think you'd be able to agree on its application. So there has long been a seductive alternative. Perhaps, even if we agree on all the facts, what's morally appropriate for me to do from my point of view is different from what's morally appropriate for you to do from your point of view. Burton, with his

mastery of thirty-nine languages, was something of a freak of nature in his ability to penetrate different cultures—to "go native," as we say, and do so time and time again. But most of us have that ability to some lesser degree: we can often experience the appeal of values that aren't, exactly, our own. So perhaps, when it comes to morality, there is no singular truth. In that case, there's no one shattered mirror; there are lots of mirrors, lots of moral truths, and we can at best agree to differ. Recall the words of Burton's Haji Abdu:

> *There is no Good, there is no Bad;*
> *these be the whims of mortal will.*

Was he right?

Analyze

1. A theme throughout this selection is man's (for Appiah only cites men) search for knowledge through travel. Why else do people travel? How have changes in travel since Burton's time affected what people search for? Create a "mind map" around the word "travel" that branches out into the many ways and reasons.

2. Based on Appiah's two strands of cosmopolitanism, do you think Sir Richard Burton was cosmopolitan? Why or why not? Support your reasons with specific examples from the reading.

3. At different points in this reading, the author uses words and expressions that might sound overly academic or exclusive to certain readers. Could he have chosen less formal expressions? Revise two sentences that use vocabulary or expressions that were unfamiliar to you. What is lost and what is gained by using "simpler" words instead of "harder" ones (e.g., amity, chez nous, mutatis mutandis)?

4. In paragraph 17, Appiah writes informally, "Not what I'd do, but, hey, suit yourself." What effect does this vernacular phrase have on you, the reader?

Explore

1. Appiah persuades us that there are fundamental beliefs we'll never agree on. Write an essay about fundamental disagreements you and your "tribe" (e.g., your family, your friends, your political party, or your

religion) have with others. Describe how these fundamental disagreements are resolved (or not).

2. Describe a trip you'd like to take to a country or region you've never visited. Where would it be? Why would you want to go there? What knowledge do you expect you'd gain from going there that you could not obtain by staying "local?"

3. Paraphrase in your own words the two strands of cosmopolitanism that Appiah refers to in this reading. Using examples from personal experience, reading, or experiences of people you know, illustrate how each strand might play out in real life. How necessary or possible is it to be fully cosmopolitan?

Jeffrey N. Wasserstrom
"A Mickey Mouse Approach to Globalization"

Jeffrey N. Wasserstrom, a professor of history at the University of California, Irvine, is a specialist in Chinese history. His particular interests are gender, protests, social movements, and globalization. Such diverse concerns have influenced his many publications, including *China in the 21st Century: What Everyone Needs to Know* (Oxford University Press, 2010) and *Global Shanghai, 1850–1990* (Routledge, 2009). "A Mickey Mouse Approach to Globalization," which originally appeared on *Yale Global Online*, appeared again on the *Global Policy Forum*, an independent policy watchdog that monitors the work of the United Nations and scrutinizes global policymaking. In this selection, Wasserman challenges the assertion that globalization is synonymous with "Americanization."

Do you think it's possible to embrace products from other countries or regions on your own terms, without adopting or assimilating their values or ideologies?

From Buenos Aires to Berlin, people around the world are looking more   1
and more and American. They're wearing Levis, watching CNN, buying coffee at interchangeable Starbucks outlets, and generally experiencing life in 'very American' ways. Looking only at the surface of this phenomenon, one might erroneously conclude that US cultural products are creating a homogenized global community of consumers. But the cultural aspects of the globalization story are far more complex than might be assumed from looking at just consumer behavior. Even when the same shirt, song, soda, or store is found on all five continents, it tends to mean different things depending on who is doing the wearing, singing, drinking, or shopping. The 'strange' fate of global products in China illustrates these points.

Consider, first of all, the Chinese meaning of Big Macs. In *The Lexus and the Olive Tree*, Thomas Friedman says he has eaten McDonald's burgers in more countries than he can count and is well qualified to state that they "really do all taste the same." What he actually means, though, is they all taste the same to him. Nearly identical Big Macs may be sold in Boston and Beijing, but as anthropologist Yan Yunxiang has convincingly argued, the experiences of eating them and even the meaning of going to McDonald's in these two locales was very different in the 1990s. In Beijing, but not in Boston, a Big Mac was classified as a snack, not a meal, and university students thought of McDonald's as a good place to go for a romantic night out. To bite into a Big Mac thinking that you are about to do something pleasantly familiar or shamefully plebeian—two common American experiences—is one thing. To bite into one imagining you are on the brink of discovering what modernity tastes like—a common Chinese experience—is another thing altogether.

Or take the curious arrival of Mickey Mouse in China, which I witnessed firsthand. While living in Shanghai in the mid-1980s, two things I remember seeing are sweatshirts for sale on the streets emblazoned with the face of Disney's most famous creation, and a wall poster showing a stake being driven through Mickey's heart. Were these signs that a big American corporation was extracting profits from a new market and that local people were angered by cultural imperialism? Hardly. Yes, Disney was trying to make money, offering Chinese state television free cartoons to show in the hope that viewers would rush out and buy authorized products. But the plan went astray: the sweatshirts I saw were all knock-offs. The only people making money from them were Chinese entrepreneurs. And the wall poster was, of all things, part of a Communist Party health campaign.

A call had just gone out for all citizens to work hard to rid their cities of rats, which are called "laoshu," the same term used for mice. It wasn't long before enterprising local residents put up posters showing various forms of violence being directed at "Mi Laoshu," as Mickey is known in Chinese, not because they hated America but simply because he was the most famous rodent in China.

Flash forward to the year 2000, when Starbucks first opened in both the American town I live in (Bloomington, Indiana) and the Chinese city I study (Shanghai), and we see further evidence of the divergent local meanings of globally familiar icons. In Bloomington, Starbucks triggered mixed reactions. Some locals welcomed its arrival. Others staged non-violent protests or smashed its windows, complaining that the chain's record on environmental and labor issues was abysmal and that Starbucks would drive local coffee shops out of business. In Shanghai, by contrast, there were no demonstrations. The chain's arrival was seen as contributing to, rather than putting a check upon, the proliferation of new independently run coffeehouses.

5   The local meanings of Shanghai Starbucks do not stop there. For example, when outlets open in Europe, they are typically seen, for understandable reasons, as symbols of creeping—or steam-rolling—Americanization. In Shanghai, though, guidebooks sometimes classify Starbucks as a "European-style" (as opposed to "Japanese-style") foreign coffee house. To further complicate things, the management company that operates the dozens of Shanghai Starbucks outlets is based not in Seattle but in Taiwan.

These examples of American products taking on distinctly new cultural meanings when moved from the US to China are useful in undermining superficial assertions equating globalization with Americanization. But it is important not to stop there. The same thing has happened—and continues to happen—with the global meanings of Asian icons in America. Here, again, a Chinese illustration seems apt; that of a Middle Kingdom figure, Chairman Mao, whose face nearly rivals Mickey Mouse's in terms of global recognition.

One indication of the fame and varied meanings of Mao's visage is that in 2002 news stories appeared that told of the simultaneous appearance of the Chairman's image in three totally different national contexts. Representations of Mao showed up in the huts of Nepalese guerrillas; on posters carried by protesting laid-off workers in Northeast China; and in a London art exhibit. In Nepal, Mao was invoked because he endorsed peasant revolt.

In Northeast China, his link to the days when Chinese workers had iron rice bowls for life was what mattered. And in London, it was his status as a favorite subject of a pop art pioneer that counted: the exhibit was a Warhol retrospective.

There is, in sum, more to keep in mind about globalization than Friedman's divide between the worlds of mass-produced Lexus cars and individuated olive trees. One reason is simply that a Lexus can mean myriad things, depending on where it is. Whether one first encounters it in the showroom or working the assembly line matters. And it makes a difference whether the people who watch it are seeing it whiz by as they walk the streets of Toledo or seeing it crawl as they sit on a Tokyo-bound Bullet Train. It is not just in physics, after all, but also in cultural analysis, that the complex workings of relativity need to be kept in mind.

Analyze

1. Wasserstrom's article suggests we cannot assume that universal icons have universal meanings. Describe a time when you or a friend discovered how differently someone from another region or culture perceived or experienced a universal icon compared to what you had assumed.

2. Wasserstrom discusses globally familiar icons from the US that have "divergent local meanings". What globally familiar icons or symbols can you find that come from outside the US? What might be their "divergent local meanings"?

3. In the reading, how do Thomas Friedman and Yan Yunxiang differ in their opinions about how people experience Big Macs?

Explore

1. Choose an image of a visual icon from the Internet (e.g., Wasserstrom cites Mickey Mouse, Chairman Mao, and Starbucks) and research its range of meanings. Create a hybrid document with both visuals and words that demonstrates the range of cultural contexts in which your icon has been displayed and interpreted.

2. How does the author try to persuade his readers that globalization is not synonymous with Americanization? Did he persuade you? Why or why not? In an essay that analyzes Wasserstrom's assertions and evidence, explain your response.

3. The author shows that Americanization can be perceived in both negative and positive lights around the world, depending on one's point of view. Could the same be said for globalization? Write an essay in which you answer this question by comparing and contrasting Americanization and globalization.

Tanveer Ali
"The Subway Falafel Sandwich and the Americanization of Ethnic Food"

Freelance reporter, photographer, and Web designer Tanveer Ali was raised in Michigan and earned his B.A. in history from Columbia University and his M.S. in journalism from Northwestern University. Ali has reported for traditional news outlets such as the *Hartford Courant* and the *Detroit News*, as well as non-traditional outlets like *Mashable*, an online news blog that focuses on digital innovation in journalism. He has also contributed to *Good*, an online community that encourages "idealists to creatively and collaboratively engage with each other, our communities, and our world." Ali's post on *Good*, "The Subway Falafel Sandwich and the Americanization of Ethnic Food," appeared on February 10, 2012. Ali observes the process of a falafel sandwich premiering in a Chicago-based Subway sandwich shop and considers the threat of its fast-food mass production, the cultivation of the appreciation of ethnic difference, and the eventual setting-in of "food nostalgia" when the desire for authentic ethnic cuisine takes root.

What are your thoughts on selling ethnic foods in popular American fast-food chains?

1   **A** few years ago, Khaled Zaibak began promoting fried chickpeas in his sleep. "I started to have some dreams about falafel," says Zaibak, president of Chicago-based falafel wholesaler Zaibak Bros. "As a strong believer in faith, I felt as though it was a message from God."

Zaibak set about spreading the word. He assembled a research and development team and pitched the traditional Middle Eastern sandwich to Subway. Soon, Zaibak had the blessing of the chain's co-founder and CEO, Fred DeLuca, to start selling a falafel patty based on Zaibak's Turkish grandmother's recipe. Select Chicago-area Subways began offering foot-long falafels in April of 2010. They've since expanded to restaurants throughout Illinois and Northwest Indiana.

Falafel's foray into Subway stores is a logical step in the food's journey into the American mainstream. After watching the rising popularity of hummus in grocery stores across the country, Zaibak says he saw an opportunity for another chickpea-based Middle-Eastern food to become an American staple. If the Subway falafel sandwich goes national, it could give the ethnic treat the most American treatment of all: fast-food mass production.

"The history of American food is really a history of immigration, and the nostalgia that comes with a cuisine's decline is an indicator of an ethnic group's confidence in its American identity," novelist Dana Horn wrote in a 2009 *Wall Street Journal* piece. "When a group first attains critical mass in America, its restaurants are mostly for its own members." As generations settle in, the food, like the ethnic group itself, becomes subsumed into American culture: Think chow mein takeout, or drive-through Taco Bell. As later generations stabilize, they tend to cultivate an appreciation of ethnic difference alongside Americanness. "Shortly thereafter, food nostalgia sets in, and the quest for the 'authentic' begins," Horn writes.

The history of the falafel in America, particularly in Chicago, makes it   5 seem like it will conform to the trend. Much of the city's falafel joints are concentrated in Middle Eastern immigrant neighborhoods, particularly the northwest side's Albany Park, which saw an influx of Arabs and Assyrians from Iran and Iraq beginning in the 1970s. In recent years, several new lunch spots cropped up outside these traditional neighborhoods offering falafel of varying quality.

Unsurprisingly, reception of the Subway menu item wasn't met with much fanfare in a city with so many quality falafel outlets. *Chicago Tribune* columnist Steve Johnson called out Subway for "failing to stay in their place." But critics aren't customers. Zaibak says the falafel sandwich has proven to be extremely popular. Taking a cue from the McDonald's McRib, Zaibak Bros. and Subway have attempted to drum up a cult following for the sandwich with social media profiles on Twitter and Facebook.

"The Subway falafel sandwich is surprisingly not bad," one diner recently tweeted.

While his company expected to sell just one case of falafels per Subway store per month, Zaibak says the average is closer to 4.5 cases per store per month. (He wouldn't say exactly how many falafel pieces are in each case.) Of course, some quality has been sacrificed to bring the food down to American fast-food standards. Instead of fresh parsley, a dehydrated version of the herb is used. Falafels arrive flash-frozen from the Zaibak Bros. plant and are heated in Subway toaster ovens. The "cucumber sauce," which Zaibak says is intentionally not referred to by its more ethnic name "tzatziki," is a little watery. The patties offer a slightly mushy, orange-tinged version of the traditional falafel. These quirks are by design. "We take the whole ethnic feel out of it and create a relationship that is familiar to everybody," Zaibak says of the Subway falafel.

Though falafel snobs may scoff at an "Eat Fresh" version of a dish that usually packs an aromatic crunch, owners of Middle Eastern restaurants say Subway's falafel provides a major service to all Americans by expanding their palate. "It's almost kind of flattering that they want to be offering falafel," said Shadi Ramli, co-owner of Chicago's Sultan's Market. Ramli says Subway's sandwich is hardly competition, but it is a marketing campaign that could end up helping restaurants like his when Subway eaters and falafel newcomers want to try a more authentic version. "It gets the word 'falafel' out there," he says.

A Subway corporate spokeswoman said the fate of the falafel is unknown at the chain, but Zaibak expects the product to expand well beyond Chicago to new markets like Boston, Northern California, New York, and Houston. All of those areas have sizable shares of either ethnic populations, health-conscious communities, or both. In other words, they're places where falafel isn't entirely foreign.

10   If the falafel goes national with Subway, it would reach places where the food and the cuisine is un-American by virtue of unfamiliarity. Zaibak views this as an educational opportunity as much as a financial one. He sees the spread of falafel as a way to spread Middle Eastern cuisine, and by extension Middle Eastern Americans, to wider American culture.

"For a while in this country, anything Middle Eastern and Mediterranean was not accepted. The falafel's growing popularity shows we have become open-minded as Americans," Zaibak says. Besides: "Mediterranean food is delicious." It's about time everyone knew it.

Analyze

1. What ethnic food names, other than taco, falafel, and sushi, have been absorbed into the English language? Make a list of at least five regionally different ethnic foods and their languages of origin.
2. At the end of this article, Zaibak seems to conflate Middle Eastern and Mediterranean foods. Do some research on these categories and see if you agree.
3. Brainstorm other ethnic foods that have become "mass-produced" or at least ubiquitous in the US or other regions or countries you're familiar with.

Explore

1. Choose an ethnic food that has become part of a fast-food chain's menu. Research the food's local origin and its transformation into a food that appeals to people across cultures. How have the food's ingredients and preparations changed during this transformation?
2. Create a "mainstream ethnic food." Decide what the food is made of, where it's from, and how it's prepared. Which fast-food restaurant will adopt it? How will the ingredients and process of preparation change? Create at least 10 tweets (no more than 140 characters) that review the fast-food restaurant's success (or lack thereof) in introducing it into the mainstream.
3. Zaibak says, "We take the whole ethnic feel out of it and create a relationship that is familiar to everybody." Why do you suppose he thinks this is important to do? What does it say about his implicit beliefs of what it means to be global? Write an essay in which you agree or disagree with Zaibak.

Forging Connections

1. Write an essay about being and becoming "global." Begin by defining what globalization means to you. Cite at least two of the readings from this chapter to illustrate and support your point of view. Be sure to consider in your essay how one might argue against your point of view, again using examples from the readings in this chapter.
2. Gleiser writes, "There is enrichment in the exchange of ideas but impoverishment in their homogenizing." How do the readings in this chapter support and/or refute this statement?

Looking Further

1. In this chapter, themes of coming from nowhere (Appiah), being nowhere (Olsen), and the idea of a nationless world (Gleiser) emerge, suggesting that one could be just as much a stranger in a familiar place as one could be familiar in a strange place. Consider the readings in chapter 2, "Identity and Place," and write an essay that explores the theme of what it means to be familiar *and* strange in a globalized world.

2. Appiah describes Sir Richard Burton's astounding ability to acquire languages (Appiah claims he could speak 39 fluently), yet he held onto prejudices and ill-founded assumptions. Write an essay on the importance (or not) of knowing multiple languages in order to be a global or cosmopolitan citizen. Use readings from chapter 4, "Languages in Contact," to support your claims.

2 Identity & Place

The idea that our deep and abiding connection to a place (or multiple places) during our lifetime shapes how we understand—how we identify— ourselves has long been a resonant topic among writers, artists, scholars, researchers, politicians, and activists. But places don't simply shape us. Heewon Chang, an educational anthropologist, points out that as we connect to places, we "adjust to them, and, at the same time, effect changes to their natural context" (85). Although it's not a novel idea that identity and place are inextricably entwined, looking at identity and place through a lens of globalization offers fresh insight and exciting directions. How has an increasingly globalized world affected this symbiotic relationship in which one's identity shapes and is shaped by one's place? How might a globalized perspective offer and encourage a more complex and nuanced understanding and respect for place and identity?

To begin answering these questions, consider the impact of increasing numbers of people traveling and relocating far from their birthplaces at rates only dreamt of even a generation ago. For some, the change is welcome and intentional; for others (like the Tuvaluans we meet in Julia Whitty's "All the Disappearing Islands"), the change may be irreversible, the loss unfathomable. If you have lived in the same place all your life, how has that shaped your life differently from your peers who have moved once, twice, or many times? If you were plucked from your birthplace at a young age, as the writer Humera Afridi describes in "A Gentle Madness," does your memory of it make you different than if you had stayed there your whole life? If you live in a place that you've chosen, a place that you love, how does that affect your identity differently than if you live in a place that feels inhospitable, or even alien as some of the "Lonely Places" in Pico Iyer's piece? What place in your imagination has called to you so much that you feel homesick even though you've never been? Will you go in search of it, as Julian Hill recounts in "In Search of Black Identity in Uganda"? Does the place where you live now reflect back to you something unsettled and difficult to pinpoint? Justin Nobel ("The Last Inuit of Quebec") uses his writing to capture such an experience of place and identity in flux.

The authors in this chapter are your guides to places that allow us to ponder age-old connections in a new, global context. Indeed, these connections between place and identity take on deeper resonance at a time when travel and mobility are increasingly accessible for more people around the world, and at a time when ideas, cultures, beliefs, knowledge—and "stuff"—pervade and invade both place and identity. As you read, consider how this easy access to places affects our identities— as individuals, families, ethnicities, and nations. How do our own identities, conflicting as they may be, affect our beloved places—and our place in the world?

Works Cited

Chang, Heewon Chang. *Autoethnography as Method.* Walnut Creek, CA: Left Coast Press, 2008.

Pico Iyer
"Lonely Places"

Essayist and novelist Pico Iyer was born in Oxford, England. His father was a philosopher, and his mother a religious scholar. Iyer's work regularly appears in *Time*, *Harper's*, and *The New York Times*. "Lonely Places" is an excerpt from *Falling Off the Map* (Vintage, 1994), a collection of essays that explores "misfit" countries—the culturally and politically isolated places that tend to be outside of the tourist's radar. Iyer calls these countries the "lonely places" of the world. In this excerpt, Iyer explains why he identifies Cuba as one of these lonely places.

Think of the different places you have visited in your life. Did any of them ever come across to you as lonely? In what ways?

On every trip I took to Havana, the ritual was the same: I would get into a car with two of my friends (into a '56 De Soto most likely), and we would judder off towards José Martí International Airport. We drove past huge pictures of Che (BE LIKE HIM), past billboards that said SOCIALISM OR DEATH, THE MOTHERLAND BEFORE EVERY-THING, IT IS ALWAYS THE 26TH (of July, 1953), past long lines of women waiting for a bus. We spoke only in indefinite pronouns, so as not to arouse the driver's suspicions, pretending that we thought that every-thing was well, pretending that we did not hope to meet again. When we arrived at the airport, we would get out and sit under a tree just outside the battered terminal. There my friends would tell me about everything they planned to do as soon as they arrived in America: how they would open a bookstore, or take pictures of the clubs on Forty-second Street, or send all the jeans they could find back to their families at home. Then, when it came time for me to leave, they would turn and, without looking back, walk across the street to another tree and wait for a bus back into town. They couldn't bear, they said, to see me getting on the plane that they had been dreaming of for twenty-five, or twenty-seven, or thirty-one years.

That is one of the things that make me think of Cuba as a Lonely Place. Just like the old men sitting on the terraces of the cheap hotels, showing you photos of long-lost fiancées ("Miss Dade County 1956"), or the trim government officials who ask, in perfect Eisenhower-era English, "Do they still play tetherball in the States?" Just like the statues of Don Quixote set on lonely hills across the countryside, and the pictures of Ava Gardner in the downtown restaurants; just like the tiny huddle of worshipers singing hymns on Easter Sunday, or the messages people give you to take to unheard-from mothers in the Bronx, distant cousins in Miami, an Indian—of course you can find him—by the name of Singh. Cuba is ninety miles from the United States, but it might as well be a universe away. Letters pass only infrequently between the two neighbors, and telephone calls are next to impossible (though it was once my mixed fortune to befriend, of all things, a telephone operator: every night in Havana, she would call me up, unbidden, and serenade me with Spanish love songs, and for months after I returned home, the phone would ring, at 2:00 a.m., 3:15 a.m., 4:36 a.m., and I would pick it up, to hear *"Oye, oye!"* and the opening strains of "Guantanamera"). Exiled from the Americas, deserted by its Communist friends, its only ally these days a xenophobic hermit state run by an octogenarian madman ("Querido compañero Kim II Sung," run the greetings in the Cuban official newspaper, *Granma*), Cuba is increasingly, quite literally, a Lonely Place.

Lonely Places are the places that don't fit in; the places that have no seat at our international dinner tables; the places that fall between the cracks of our tidy acronyms (EEC and OPEC, OAS and NATO). Cuba is the island that no one thinks of as West Indian; Iceland is the one that isn't really part of Europe. Australia is the odd place out that no one knows whether to call an island or a continent; North Korea is the one that gives the lie to every generality about East Asian vitality and growth. Lonely Places are the exceptions that prove every rule: they are ascetics, castaways, and secessionists; prisoners, anchorites, and solipsists. Some are famous for their monasteries (Bhutan and, in some respects, Iceland); some are famous for their criminals and cranks (North Korea and Paraguay). And though no one has ever formally grouped them together—save me—every Lonely Place conforms to the Paraguay described by its native writer Augusto Roa Bastos as "an island surrounded by land."

Yet loneliness cuts in both directions, and there are 101 kinds of solitude. There is the loneliness of the sociopath and the loneliness of the only child, the loneliness of the hermit and the loneliness of the widow. And as with people, so too with nations. Some are born to isolation, some have isolation thrust upon them. Each makes its own accommodation with wistfulness and eccentricity and simple, institutionalized standoffishness. Australia, a part of the Wild West set down in the middle of the East, hardly seems to notice, or to care, that it is a Lonely Place; Bhutan all but bases its identity upon its loneliness, and its refusal to be assimilated into India, or Tibet, or Nepal. Vietnam, at present, is a pretty girl with her face pressed up against the window of the dance hall, waiting to be invited in; Iceland is the mystic poet in the corner, with her mind on other things. Argentina longs to be part of the world it left and, in its absence, re-creates the place it feels should be its home; Paraguay simply slams the door and puts up a Do Not Disturb sign. Loneliness and solitude, remoteness and seclusion, are many worlds apart.

Yet all Lonely Places have something in common, if only the fact that all   5 are marching to the beat of a different satellite drummer. And many are so far from the music of the world that they do not realize how distant they are. Both South Korea and North are zany, lonely places in their way: the difference is that North Korea is so cut off from the world that it does not know how strange it is and cannot imagine anything except North Korea. This is how life is, I imagine North Koreans thinking: being woken up each morning with loudspeaker exhortations in the bedroom; being told exactly what clothes to wear and which route to take to work; being reminded each day that Kim Il Sung is revered around the world. In the half-unnatural state of solitary confinement, Lonely Places develop tics and manias and heresies. They pine, they brood, they molder. They gather dust and data, and keep their blinds drawn round the clock. In time, their loneliness makes them stranger, and their strangeness makes them lonelier. And before long, they have come to resemble the woman with a hundred cats in a house she's never cleaned, or the man who obsessively counts the names in the telephone book each night. They grow three-inch nails, and never wash, and talk with the artificial loudness of someone always talking to himself.

Burma, out of the blue, decides to call itself Myanmar and to name its most famous city, unintelligibly, Yangon. Iceland speaks a tongue that Grendel would have recognized. North Korea, which sees no tourists, is building the largest tourist hotel in the world, 105 stories high. And for many years now in Havana, across the street from the U.S. Interests Section, there has stood a huge billboard, with a caricature of a "Ggrrrr"-breathing Uncle Sam, next to the message SEÑOR IMPERIALISTS!

WE HAVE ABSOLUTELY NO FEAR OF YOU! There are more things on earth, Horatio, than are dreamt of in your philosophy.

When people think of Lonely Places, they tend to think of moody outcrops off the coast of Scotland, or washed-up atolls adrift in the Pacific. They may even think of the place where I am writing this, a silent hermitage above the sea along the unpeopled coast of northern California. But Lonely Places are not just isolated places, for loneliness is a state of mind. The hut where I am sitting now is utterly alone. For days on end, I do not hear a single voice; and from where I write, I cannot see a trace of human habitation. Yet in a deeper sense, the place is packed. I am companioned—by rabbits, stars, and wisps of cloud—in worlds far richer than any capital. The air is charged with presences, and every inch of hillside stirs. I watch for the skittering of a fox on my terrace, listen to the crickets chattering in the dusk, catch a blue jay's wings against the light. Birds sing throughout the day, and the ocean's colors shift. Everything is a jubilee of blue and gold, and at night, walking along the hills, I feel as if I am walking towards a starlit Temple of Apollo. A Lonely Place in principle, perhaps, but certainly not in spirit.

More than in space, then, it is in time that Lonely Places are often exiled, and it is their very remoteness from the present tense that gives them their air of haunted glamour. The door slams shut behind them, and they are alone with cobwebs and yellowed snapshots, scraps of old bread and framed photographs of themselves when young. The beauty (and pathos) of Burma today derives from the fact that it is stranded amidst decaying remnants of its former glory, and the poignancy of Cuba that in the midst of leafy university quadrangles, you will find bird-spotted tanks. You wind back the clock several decades when you visit a Lonely Place; and when you touch down, you half expect a cabin attendant to announce, "We have now landed in Lonely Place's Down-at-Heels Airport, where the local time is 1943 and the temperature is . . . frozen."

Yet Lonely Places are generally sure that their time is about to come. North Korea is just waiting for Stalinism to sweep the world and the Olympics to be held in the stadia it has built for them (the secret of his longevity, says Kim II Sung, the world's longest-running dictator, is his optimism); Argentina is just waiting for the day when it will be a world power again, the cynosure of every distant eye. Lonely Places have seen Bulgaria, China, even Albania admitted, or awakened, to the world; they have seen the Falklands, Grenada, even Kuwait enjoy their moments in the spotlight. They tell themselves that even Japan was once a "double-bolted land," as Melville put it, and China, and Korea too; they tell themselves that tomorrow will bring yesterday once more.

Lonely Places are often poor places, because poverty breeds wonkiness   10
and a greater ability to visualize than to realize dreams. Lonely Places are often small countries, because smallness gets forgotten: the tiny voices of Tibet, or Benin, or East Timor are seldom heard at international gatherings. But even huge countries can be Lonely Places, or have Lonely Places inside them, as anyone who has been to Siberia or Ladakh, Kashgar or Wyoming, can attest. Everywhere, in some lights, is a Lonely Place, just as everyone, at moments, is a solitary. Everyone sometimes dances madly when alone, or thumbs through secrets in a drawer. Everyone, at some times, is a continent of one.

> "So it is that Lonely Places attract as many lonely people as they produce."

Lonely Places are defined, in fact, by their relation to the things they miss. You would expect the western fjords of Iceland, or the depths of Tierra del Fuego, to be lonely; but there is a more unanswerable kind of loneliness, and restlessness, in Reykjavik and Buenos Aires, the loneliness of people just close enough to the world to see what they might be. Both American Samoa and Western Samoa are pretty little South Sea bubbles a world away from anywhere, and both are isolated hideaways lost in their own surf-soft universe. Both are graced by palm-fringed beaches, Technicolor cricket games, and huts echoing with cries of "Bingo" in the dark. But what makes American Samoa a Lonely Place is that it also has a zip code, a Radio Shack, and a Democratic caucus. It has American-style license plates, yellow school buses, and *Days of Our Lives*. It sends a congressman to Washington, but he is not allowed to vote.

Other Lonely Places are happy in their loneliness, or able, at least, to turn it to advantage. The Australians, it seems to me, thrive on their remoteness from the world and see it as a way of keeping up a code of "No worries, mate," while peddling their oddities to visitors: nonconformity is at once a fact of life for many, and a selling point. Others, like Tibetans, pine for a loneliness that is tantamount to peace. Still others have the bitterness of outcasts: if they cannot play the game, say the Libyans, why should you? "Ye Visions of the hills! And Souls of lonely places!" sang Wordsworth, who found all his solace and scripture in his loneliness, and saw in it purity and a return to buried-over divinity. Everyone is a Wordsworth in certain moods, and every traveler seeks out places that every traveler has missed. Everyone longs at times to get away from it all. Finding a sanctuary, a place apart from time, is not so different from finding a faith.

So it is that Lonely Places attract as many lonely people as they produce, and the loneliness we see in them is partly in ourselves. Romantic when first I visited Iceland, I found in it a province of romance; returning, four years later, in a darker mood, I saw in it only shades of winter dark. The Gobi Desert, for a couple in love, is as far from loneliness as Hong Kong, for a single traveler, may be close. Even a jam-packed football stadium may be lonely for the referee. It is common these days to hear that as the world shrinks, and as more and more places are pulled into the MTV and CNN circuit, loneliness itself may become extinct. Certainly, many Lonely Places—Vietnam and Cuba, for two—grow less remote with every joint-venture hotel, and cities like Toronto and Sydney, London and L.A., already seem part of some global Eurasamerican village, with a common language and video culture. Yet the very process of feverish cross-communication that is turning the world into a single polyglot multiculture is producing new kinds of Lonely Places as fast as it eliminates the old. The lingua franca of parts of American Samoa is Mandarin, and Farsi is the second language of Beverly Hills. Japanese Joãos are returning to their grandfathers' homes from São Paulo as fast as German Hanses are taking Michikos back to Buenos Aires. Reykjavik is loneliest of all, I suspect, for the Thai girls who sit in the Siam Restaurant (on Skolavördustigur), alone with their mail order husbands. And even as the world contracts and isolation fades, half the countries around the globe are still off the map in some sense, out of sight, out of mind, out of time. There will never be a shortage of Lonely Places, any more than there will ever be of lonely people.

Lonely Places, then, are the places that are not on international wavelengths, do not know how to carry themselves, are lost when it comes to visitors. They are shy, defensive, curious places; places that do not know how they are supposed to behave. Yemen, Brunei, and Mali are Lonely Places; Paradise, Purgatory, and Hell are too. Desolation Isle is a Lonely Place, and Suriname, and California as seen by the Hmong. So, too, is the room next door.

Analyze

1. Iyer observes that he and his Cuban friends speak only in indefinite pronouns. Create a dialogue between Iyer and his friends using only indefinite pronouns to demonstrate how this might underscore Iyer's claim that Cuba is a Lonely Place. When and for what effect might you employ indefinite pronouns in your own writing?

2. The author wrote this essay in the 1990s. Find the cultural and political references that date it. What has changed that might make some of the places he refers to less lonely? Based on Iyer's criteria, what places might now be considered Lonely Places?

3. How does Iyer distinguish isolation from loneliness? Do you agree with him? Based on this reading, what do you suppose is Iyer's own relationship to Lonely Places?

4. In paragraph 9, the author writes that Lonely Places "tell themselves that their time is about to come" and that "tomorrow will bring yesterday once more." Why would they tell themselves that? To help clarify Iyer's claim, describe someone you know or have read about who thinks like this.

Explore

1. Iyer argues that Lonely Places are lonely by virtue of not being part of an international community, and that this is caused by their social "uneasiness." In this time of globalization, however, do you think it's possible not to be part of the international community? Write an essay to explore your response. Begin with a working definition of how you understand globalization. Then choose a group, region, or nation that resists or is inhibited from being part of a global community.

2. Iyer writes about Lonely Places as if they were people who have agency and choice and have purposely decided to isolate themselves. In paragraph 5, for example, he compares Lonely Places to cat ladies and men with compulsive disorders. Are these fair analogies? Why or why not? Find other comparisons of lonely places to people in this essay to support your claim.

3. Write an essay that describes your own Lonely Place(s). Begin by defining what "lonely" means to you. Use examples of places you're familiar with either because you've been there physically, or because certain places have occupied your imagination.

Justin Nobel
"The Last Inuit of Quebec"

Freelance journalist Justin Nobel earned an advanced degree in journalism from Columbia University. His writing has appeared in *The Huffington Post* and *Time*. "The Last Inuit of Quebec" first appeared in the independent online magazine *The Smart Set,* which is published with the support of Drexel University. In a statement on *The Smart Set* website, the magazine's mission states that "what unites its readers is their intellectual curiosity, and this cuts across age, gender, income, and education level." In his essay, Nobel explores his adventures in the Inuit territory of Arctic Quebec, where he went off in search of a place and a people who still "believed in magic and not God."

In what ways do you think a place can inspire beliefs in magic or God?

Three summers ago, looking for adventure, I left New York City and drove to California for a newspaper job. One evening while jogging, I noticed a glowing rock high on a hill. A few weeks later, I pitched my tent beside it. After work, I'd trudge up my hill in the moonlight and sit for hours under the rock. On some nights, strange howls kept me awake. I wondered if there was a land where people still lived in skins, gathered around fire, and believed in magic and not God. Looking for that land, I quit the paper and traveled to Nunavik, an Inuit territory in Arctic Quebec.

On Canada Day, I landed in Kuujjuaq, a community of 2,000 on the tree line. An icy wind spat cold rain. On the shores of the Koksoak River, families picnicked beside their SUVs and Canadian flags flapped in the drizzle. "Things are changing so fast," said Allen Gordon, the head of the Nunavik Tourism Association. I later learned that his wife was the first one in town to ship north a Hummer. We celebrated the holiday at the Ikkariqvik Bar, a cavernous dive without windows. There were darts and a disco ball. "If you're a woman, you'll win a sewing machine. If you're a man, you win nets. If you don't want either, you'll get four beers," shouted a lady selling raffle tickets. A teen dressed in black showed me a tiny silver pistol and someone collapsed on the edge of the dance floor. "We are drunk because it's Canada Day," said a man at the bar. When the raffle lady stumbled back on stage she was too drunk to announce who had won what.

Kuujjuaq is regarded as a *city*, severed from Inuit traditions. To find magic, I needed to go further north, so I boarded a propeller plane for Ivujivik, a town of 300 on the stormy coastline where Hudson Bay meets Hudson Straight. Trees disappeared then reappeared and then disappeared for good. This was tundra—a sopping, pitted landscape that shone brilliantly in the sun. Confused ribbons of water connected an endless splatter of lakes, some green, some yellow, some with red edges and bright blue centers. Ancient channels were etched in the stone. We unloaded and picked up passengers in Inukjuak and Puvirnituq. Over Hudson Bay, a passenger spotted a pair of belugas.

A drunk woman named Saira showed up at the airport in a Bronco packed with relatives and wanted me to live with her. We had met in Kuujjuaq at the home of a woman who peddled black-market booze. Saira was drunk on Smirnoff at the time, but had somehow remembered my travel plans. I ignored her. A construction worker dropped me at a drab house on the edge of town occupied by a security guard named Chico who I had been told would have a free room. A man with a beat-up face came to the door. "Why are you here?" he asked. I explained. "I can't wait to get the hell out," he said. "I hate this place."

I was in e-mail contact with a nurse who supposedly had a room, but   5 that too evaporated—her boss was in town. Reluctantly, I sought out Saira. She opened the door with a grin. "I'm drunk," she said, "but it's OK." I joined her and a niece with whittled teeth at a table covered with empty Budweiser cans. The women looked at me and giggled harshly. They bantered in Inuktitut. Saira explained that she was getting evicted in a few days. "We will live in a tent in the back," she said, "and come in to take showers."

I stepped out to clear my head. A stiff wind whipped white caps from the cobalt straight. I headed for it, walking over dinosaur egg-like rocks littered with ammo boxes and potato chip bags. At the edge of a headland, long rolling swells beat the boulders and blasted spray skyward. Beyond, the sea swirled. I stood there for some time, thinking about good meals and the New York subway. The strong wind dragged tears across my cheeks. I later learned this was the site where hunters once came to woo belugas into the bay so others could harpoon them.

Ivujivik had one store, a cooperative, which serves as a bank, post office, hardware store, and grocer. There were no bars and no restaurants. There was a school, a health center, a municipal building and a power plant that burned diesel fuel imported by a ship that comes twice a year. Homes were red, orange, blue, green; identical warehouse-like structures subsidized by the Quebec government. Each had a water tank and a sewage tank and trucks circled daily, refilling and relieving. All roads ended a few miles outside town. I was there in late July, and for children, who represent nearly half the population, these were the dog days of summer.

Kids began the day in small groups that expanded as night neared. Afternoon activities included hide and seek, cavorting atop shipping containers, pouring buckets of water over slanted wooden planks and watching a bulldozer demolish a building. By nightfall, which lasts from 9 p.m. until well past midnight, children can be roaming the streets in groups of 10 to 20. Often, they get rowdy. The summer I was in Ivujivik, youths regularly broke into the youth center to steal video games. In an adjacent community, a posse comprised of kids as young as 12 pummeled a man with a hockey stick and golf clubs.

Teens had rosier options. Some worked at the co-op or for the municipality, driving the water and sewage trucks. Some wandered like the younger ones, but with more gadgets. Several tore around on dirt bikes and quite a few had iPods. Gangsta Rap was very popular in the north and there was even a local group—the North Coast Rappers, or NCR. One morning, I hung outside the co-op with a teen in black jeans named Lukasi who said he would introduce me to a member. Sure enough, a thuggish youth emerged to meet us. He wore a baggy T-shirt with a picture of Tupac, his head in a bandana and bowed. Plastic diamonds protruded from the shirt, whose owner was also named Lukasi. He coolly lit a cigarette provided by the other Lukasi and discussed NCR, a three-man group that rapped over beats made by a computer synthesizer program. When I asked what they rapped about Lukasi paused briefly, then said: "Bitches and hoes, mostly."

10   In August, I noticed a flier in the co-op about a bowhead whale hunt in the community of Kangiqsujuaq, several hundred miles down the coast. Bowheads can live for 150 years and weigh as much as five school buses. The Inuit of Nunavik had not landed one in more than a century although locals had been pushing for a hunt since the mid-1980s. At that time, the Hudson Straight bowhead was designated as "endangered" and hunting

was prohibited. The Inuit claimed that the whales were plentiful. In 2005, a study by Canada's Department of Fisheries and Oceans confirmed the Inuit's suspicions and in 2008, the Inuit of Nunavik were granted permission to hunt one bowhead. Kangiqsujuaq was chosen as the hunt site for its proximity to known bowhead grounds and the hunting prowess of its inhabitants. I e-mailed an editor at the *Nunatsiaq News*, a paper delivered across the Arctic by propeller plane. She said they'd pay for a story and photos. I hitched a ride on a canoe headed south.

Kangiqsujuaq, a town of 600, was bursting at the seams. The Inuit were delirious over the chance to eat bowhead maktak, or whale skin. On a blustery day I joined a group of Inuit at a sort of tailgate for the bowhead hunt. We picnicked on a barren knoll outside town that overlooked a rocky cove with several fishing boats and a dozen or more canoes. Tinned anchovies, sandwich pickles, Ritz crackers, Spam, and a jar of Miracle Whip were spread over an impromptu plank table. A man with a buzz cut approached our group from the water's edge, his eyes hid by tinted shades, and the women shrieked. In each hand he grasped a fat glistening Arctic char. Two ladies with buns of gray hair tucked beneath colorful bandanas laid the fish on a dismantled cardboard box. We squat in the dirt and went at them with pocketknives and curved blades called *ulus*, slurping flesh from the skin as if spooning grapefruit. The meat was bright orange and sticky. "Chew the bones," the fisherman, whose name was Tiivi Qumaaluk, said. "They're the best."

The Inuit reached what is now northern Quebec more than 2,000 years ago. In winter they dwelt in igloos along the coast, skewering seals and walruses at breathing holes in the ice with ivory-tipped harpoons. In summer they tracked caribou into the interior, ambushing them at river crossings or chasing the animals toward hidden archers. Whales were corralled in shallow bays with kayaks made from sealskin stretched over bone. Polar bears were immobilized by dogs and then knifed. Still, famine was common. Elderly that slowed the group were left behind to die. Clans that settled near Kangiqsujuaq fared better than most. The large tides created caverns under the frozen sea that could be reached at low tide by chipping through the ice above. In times of hunger hunters scavenged these caves for mussels and algae. "There are numerous indications that starvation and famines accompanied by infanticide and even cannibalism were not rare," writes Bernard Saladin D'Anglure, a 20th-century anthropologist who spent time in Kangiqsujuaq.

By the late 1800s the Hudson Bay Company had built several trading posts in Nunavik and in 1910 Révillon Frères, a French fur company, opened one in Kangiqsujuaq. Inuit hunters stopped traveling with game and began searching for fox, which they traded at posts for nets, guns, and metal needles. Inuit began camping around stores rather than by hunting spots. They developed tastes for foods they had never eaten—flour, biscuits, molasses, tea, coffee. From the posts also came disease and dependence. "About 15 families camped in the settlement," reads the 1928 log from a Hudson Bay store operator in the Central Arctic, "they have no inclination to hunt or exert themselves but are content to sit around in a state of destitution."

By the 1960s, the north had become such a black eye that the Canadian government took steps to recuperate the region. Teachers, healthcare workers, and police were sent north. Homes and hospitals were built. Dogs were corralled by the police and shot. Some Inuit youth were shipped to southern schools against their will. The government's aim was to quell poverty and spur development, which to them meant providing Inuit with Western educations and eliminating sick dogs. But to many Inuit, these actions appeared to be part of a much more sinister agenda, the annihilation of their culture.

15   In 1975, the Inuit and their native neighbors to the south, the Cree, protested the Quebec government's seizure of their land for a massive hydroelectric project and received a settlement of nearly a quarter of a billion dollars in what was called the James Bay and Northern Quebec Agreement. The Inuit's share went toward the creation of the Makivik Corporation, a development agency charged with promoting economic growth and fostering Inuit-run businesses. Makivik is presently invested in construction, shipping, fishing, tanning, and air travel. They recently started a cruise ship company.

Kangiqsujuaq was trying to get itself on the adventure travel map. Much of the town's funding comes from a nearby nickel mine. Recent tourist oriented projects have included an elder home, a community pool, a new hotel with a $400 suite, and a visitor center for a remote provincial park that protects a two-million-year-old meteor crater said to contain the purest water on Earth.

When I entered the office of Lukasi Pilurtuut, who manages the Nunaturlik Landholding Corporation that oversees development in Kangiqsujuaq, I found him alone at the end of a long table with his laptop, wearing a cap, jeans, and sneakers. Sunlight streamed through large windows and the hilltops surrounding the town gleamed with freshly fallen summer snow. He was an ace student in high school but dropped out of a Montreal college after just three semesters, homesick. "It wasn't the problem of going to school," he said, "it was more the problem that I couldn't go hunting."

Dependence has made some people lazy, said Pilurtuut. The Canadian and Quebec governments subsidize housing and health care and many Inuit also receive welfare checks. In 2007, high nickel prices helped the mine turn record profits and each Inuit resident of Kangiqsujuaq received a check for $4,700. Some families got checks for $30,000. They bought ATVs, SUVs, dirt bikes, snowmobiles, motorized canoes, computers, and flat screen TVs.

Tourism money will be different, Pilurtuut said. Rather than destroying tradition, it could bring it back. In fact, this was already happening. As we spoke the phone rang several times. "Yes!" he cried during one call, and then turned to me, "We have good news, four single kayaks coming in today." The Inuit invented the kayak but no one in Nunavik remembered how to operate one. Kangiqsujuaq had to order kayaks from southern Quebec and hire an outside guide to train locals.

On a crisp summer evening, I raced into the Straight to greet the bowhead hunters on a bright orange government speed boat. The sun sank through thin clouds and spilled across the horizon like paint. "This is so special for us," our navigator, a man named Tuumasi Pilurtuut, said to me, practically speechless with joy. "We're back with our ancestors."

The hunters fired flares to mark their position. A tremendous cheer went up as we arrived and strips of maktak were passed aboard. "Better than beluga," Pilurtuut said between chews. Lines of turquoise fire billowed in the night sky—the northern lights, in their first appearance of the season.

The Nanuq, the boat to which the whale was secured, motored through the night and reached the cove near town where I had tailgated the week before shortly after dawn. The bowhead was moored to three orange buoys on the edge of the bay, where it bobbed, with a long knife called a *tuuq* stuck in its top, until early afternoon, when the tide lowered. Canoes ferried hungry onlookers to the site and the slicing of *maktak* began. Naalak Nappaaluk, a revered elder and the only man alive who remembered stories about the bowhead hunts of yesteryear, sat on a rock with a pad of maktak nearby and tears in his eyes. Nappaaluk had a shot at a bowhead as a teen, but it escaped through a lead in the ice. "Today, I have seen people standing on the bowhead for the first time," he told me through a translator. "It's overwhelming." A bulldozer that had intended to flip the whale had trouble making it to the site, and the majority of the meat rotted. When I returned three days later the stench was so potent that men were vomiting uncontrollably.

One tradition that had survived intact was the caribou hunt. Nearly a million caribou dwell in Nunavik and when a herd nears towns, offices empty. By mid-August the chatter around Kangiqsujuaq was that the animals were close. One morning at the grocery store I ran into Tiivi, the man who had caught the char at the tailgate party. He invited me to go hunting with him the following day.

Tiivi killed his first caribou at age nine while looking for bird eggs with his five-year-old brother. Unable to cut the carcass themselves, the boys rushed back to tell their mother. "She was so excited," Tiivi said, "she was like shouting of joy." In his teens he worked as a garbage man and at 21 he took a job pulverizing rock at the nickel mine, earning a $2,500 paycheck twice a month.

25   Tiivi married a janitor from the mine and they moved in together, living in a town on the Hudson Straight called Salluit. The marriage was a nightmare. Fights were frequent; in one she bit him, leaving a knotty scar over his bicep. Another time she plunged a steak knife into his chest. He was medevaced to a hospital on the other side of Nunavik for a tetanus shot. "The next day I couldn't lift my arm because all the muscles were cut," he said. One night, while she was asleep, he snuck out with just the clothes on his back. While visiting cousins in Puvirnituk, he met a second cousin named Elisapie. "A lot of different girls tried to be with me but I refused them all because I saw Elisapie and I wanted only her," said Tiivi. "She was so fine looking." They recently married.

I met Tiivi at his home just after 9 a.m. He wore muck boots, grease-stained pants, and a hunting cap. He carried a rifle for caribou and a shotgun for geese. We were joined by his aunt, Qialak, and his brother, Jimmy, who trailed us on a second ATV. On a ridge patterned with jackknifed rocks Tiivi signaled a shiny outcrop where carvers come for soapstone. Cumulus clouds splotched the sky and sunbursts lit mats of lichen red and orange. "There might be some gold particles," Tiivi said, as we crossed a stream. "Our land is full of minerals."

With mud splattering from the tires, we descended a spongy slope then looped around a lake where the week before Jimmy and Qialak had strung nets. Tiivi and Qialak reeled them in, half a dozen flapping Arctic char. "So fresh the heart is still beating," Tiivi said. Qialak sliced open the bellies of the females and wailed—two had eggs. I held a sandwich baggy open while she scooped in the long slimy packets.

We sat at the water's edge and slurped the bright orange flesh from flaps of skin. The meat was sticky and chewy, like a fatty piece of steak. The fresh blood tasted sweet. We drank tea from a thermos and ate packaged biscuits. Tiivi smoked two cigarettes and then we left. A muddy track led above the lake to the next ridge. Arctic poppies bobbed in the breeze. Jimmy spotted snow geese.

"They're going to land because of the wind," said Tiivi. We abandoned the ATVs and crouched low. Jimmy and I followed Tiivi along a sliver of wet land behind a low rock ridge. We crawled close on our bellies. When the geese took flight the men bolted upright and fired. Two birds fell. One goose lay sprawled in the tundra with wings still beating. Its handsome white coat was ruined by a single red smear. Tiivi pinned its chest with his arms. The long neck slowly lifted and the head cocked sideways and gasped. "Now it's dying because I'm holding the lungs," he said.

With a soft thud the head dropped. "Hurray!" Tiivi said and peeled a Clementine. He tossed the squiggled rind aside and gave me half. Qialak looked at me beaming, "You're probably getting the experience of a lifetime." 30

On a ridge above a river, under a sunset the color of skinned knees, Qialak spotted a large buck. Tiivi slowly extended his arms above his head, bent his elbows out, and pointed his fingers skyward, imitating antlers. The buck stared at us intently then resumed foraging. A smaller buck beside him followed suit. We splashed across the river and sped, sheltered by the ridge, towards the buck. Its impressive rack was just visible above the hill's crest in the grainy light.

"Stay low," Tiivi said. He crept up the ridge, rested on a rock, and fired several shots. The buck rushed forward frantically then halted. It seemed to not know where to step next. Tiivi fired again and it swayed. Its massive head lowered to the ground, eyes still opened. The body slumped. Labored, spastic breaths rose from the ground. The younger buck remained for a moment then darted.

Everyone produced knives; Tiivi held one in each hand. The buck lay on its side, its chest heaving. Tiivi approached from behind and it kicked the air violently. He jabbed a knife into its neck, then jostled the blade back and forth. As darkness fell the three Inuit dismembered the carcass. Everything was taken but the head and intestines. Tiivi tied his parts in a bundle—heart, hindquarters, filet, stomach, ribs. Recrossing the river we washed our hands and drank cold river water from our palms. "I'm all clean," Tiivi said.

During my last week in Kangiqsujuaq, I met with Father Dion, a Catholic priest originally from Belgium who had been in Nunavik for nearly five decades. He was a tiny, puckered man whose congregation was dwindling, but he was a bull. He laughed loudly, spoke with a thick French accent, and commanded respect from everyone in town, young and old, Inuit and non. His church was a pint-sized building in the center of town and he lived inside. When I knocked one drizzly day he didn't hear me. I entered. He was on the couch, in leather sandals with socks and a sky-blue sweater, watching CNN.

35   He shook my hand with a strong grip and heated a cup of tea in an old microwave then served it to me with the last two of a package of biscuits. He handed me a pair of ivory binoculars wider than they were long and suggested I view the Hudson Straight, which he had a clear shot of. When he was 19, the Germans invaded Belgium. Father Dion was in the seminary and went to war. When it ended he was given the choice of working in a hospital in his home country or being sent as a missionary to the Congo. He chose Congo, a dreadful two years. "It was hot," he said. "A lot of animal, a lot of sickness." Afterward, he requested to be sent to the Arctic, where Belgium had some missionaries stationed. He arrived in Nunavik in 1964, and spent his first nine years in a community of 300 called Quaqtaq. He survived a famine and a fall through the ice on a snow mobile. "I have a very strong esteem for these people and how they survived in such harsh conditions," he said. "I appreciate them very, very much."

Father Dion addressed some misconceptions. The dogs were shot because they were starving and had been eating Inuit babies. The schooling the government imposed on the Inuit helped create a generation of bright leaders. A change he wasn't fond of concerned the church. Newer community members were now following the Pentecostal church, whose loud hectic services made some think the group was a revival of shamanism. Inuit once depended on shamans to bring good results in a hunt or lift them out of famine, but shamans could also bring death. "It was a kind of liberation when they disappeared," said Father Dion. Shamans were replaced by the Catholic Church.

I asked Father Dion if the Inuit would be better off as Nunavik modernized. He chewed his cheek and looked out the window at the gray town. The tide was going out, leaving black pools of water between the rocks. A septic truck passed. "When I arrived, this land was empty," he said. "Nothing. No houses, nothing. People were living in tents in the summer and igloos in the winter. Now, they have enough to eat, warm houses, transportation, communication. They don't fight for survival."

Just before I left, Tiivi began a job managing the new elder home. I stopped in to stay goodbye. A hefty woman in a pink nightgown was working on a puzzle of a snowy European forest. The place smelled of new furniture and cleaning agents. Tiivi led me into his office. The walls were bare and he had taped a black trash bag over the window to keep the sun out. On his desk was a flat-screen computer; the screensaver was a shot of his son taken during the bowhead whale hunt. "So," said Tiivi, indicating his office items. "I have a good job."

Summer ended and I returned to Kuujjuaq days before the first blizzard hit. In mid-September, I flew to Montreal and boarded a Greyhound bound for the border. My bus crossed into the U.S. at midnight and by dawn I was in New York City. The day was warm and breezy, the city still smelled of summer. I began an internship at *Audubon* magazine but without enough money to get an apartment I moved back in with my parents, in the suburbs. Unable to sleep in my teenage room, still lined with posters of conspiracy and aliens, I set up the tent in a wooded spot near where my childhood dog was buried.

I imagine that in a far-off land, harbored by the heartwood of a massive   40 forest, there are a people that still remember how to do the things their ancestors did and there are still shamans and nobody has ever heard of God. I don't know how long that place will last or even if it deserves to, but surely it will soon enough be gone.

The leaves turned crisp yellows and oranges and fell to make large colored mats on the forest floor. Holes formed in the tent and spiders moved in. It got cold and I moved out. I had saved enough money from the internship for a cheap spot in Brooklyn.

Analyze

1. What prompts Nobel to set off in search of "a land where people still lived in skins, gathered around fire, and believed in magic and not God?" Write about an analogous yearning you've had for a time or place different from your own.

2. Throughout the essay, the author describes events in which he participates, but makes little or no commentary or analysis. Why has he chosen to observe rather than analyze? How does this benefit you (or not) as the reader?

3. How do Nobel's own material needs—and the choices he makes during his journey because of those needs—parallel those of the Inuit he meets?

Explore

1. Write an essay that makes an explicit claim about Nobel's quest to find "a land where people still lived in skins, gathered around fire, and believed in magic and not God." Using evidence and examples from Nobel's essay, as well as your own experience and readings, show your readers what Nobel has discovered—and what he may have missed.

2. Nobel travels to many places in this reading. Using an online tool such as Google Maps or MapQuest, create a detailed itinerary of his travels. How does tracking a journey on a map differ from tracking it in an essay? How would the presence of a visual map in this essay have affected your reading experience?

3. Father Dion offers to clarify for Nobel some "misconceptions" about the Canadian government's involvement with the Inuit during the 1960s (see paragraph 36). Does he believe Father Dion? How do you know? Using reliable sources, research (on your own or with partners in your class) the relationship between the Canadian government and the Inuit during the 1960s. Write a brief report that summarizes your findings.

Humera Afridi
"A Gentle Madness"

Humera Afridi, a New York-based writer, left her native Pakistan at the age of 12 with her parents for the United Arab Emirates. She was the recipient of a *New York Times* Fellowship at New York University, where she earned her M.F.A. in creative writing. Afridi's work has appeared in *The New York Times* and several anthologies, including *And the World Changed* (Feminist Press, 2008), *110 Stories: New York Writes After September 11* (NYU Press, 2002), and *Leaving Home* (Oxford University Press, 2001). "A Gentle Madness" was published in the April 2012 edition of *Granta* magazine. Founded in 1889 by students at Cambridge University in England, *Granta* claims no "political or literary manifesto," but instead aims to emphasize "the power and urgency of the story . . . to describe, illuminate, and make real." In the following essay, Afridi explores how the shifting of languages, cultures, and borders has failed to erase the memories that both haunt and define her.

In what ways have the language, culture, and memories of a place influenced your sense of self and identity?

When I was twelve, my parents decided to leave Pakistan and move our family to Abu Dhabi. My heart, I thought, would never recover. But I needn't have worried. The country came with me: it moved in, set up home, breathing inside me a stream of remembrances that, for twenty-eight years, have inflected the most minute details of my present life. No matter where I've lived since—Dubai, Dallas, Minneapolis, Jeddah or New York—fragments from those years merge and dissolve into the now so that walking down a street, or waiting underground for the subway to screech to a halt, I often feel as if I've accidentally slipped inside a video installation layered with disjunctive sound and imagery. The sounds are family lore, stories I've heard so many times that I can't free my memory from their telling, nor can I simply live in a present that isn't sieved through their mythology.

Pakistan is a nation of memory keepers. We feed our memories as if they are guests at tea, pay homage to them. Past and present skim close, brushing arms like almost-lovers strolling in a desert park. There is one memory that shoots through the aperture, into the present, with particular ferocity.

1971: Mother, Father, Ayah and I are driving to the Kohat Military Hospital. I have an ear infection, am burning up with a fever. From high above, somewhere in the darkening sky, East Pakistan is about to bomb us—the country is at war with itself. We live in Lahore but have driven north across the plains, through arid tribal terrain, to my father's ancestral village, Babri Banda, in the Northwest Frontier. My great-aunt has died.

Because my grandfather is in London, where he is serving as High Commissioner, and my uncles and aunts are visiting him and my grandmother there, as the eldest son, and the only one present in Pakistan, it falls on my father to represent his family at the funeral. Despite the danger of air raids, ritual demands that we make the journey from Lahore. Over the few days we spend in Babri Banda, amidst the wailing, keening, chest-thumping sorrow of the village relatives, I provide delightful distraction to the mourners who pull me out of Mother's or Ayah's arms to pet, kiss and rock me. My mother, squeamish about germs, is convinced I've been infected by a villager who kissed me on the ear.

In the Frontier, it is customary to remain indoors after sunset—kidnappers and robbers are everywhere—as it is lawless country, outside the government's jurisprudence. But I am listless and dehydrated and when my fever spikes, we have no choice but to drive out of the high mud-walled family compound at dusk to the hospital. Fifteen minutes into our drive, a somber wailing dissects the stark landscape. Warning gunshots follow. My father pulls up along a dirt path, flings open the passenger doors and drags Mother and Ayah into the adjacent field. My mother is carrying me in her arms. She hesitates, looking this way and that way into the empty distance, before jumping into the dugout.

5   We crouch in the dark. There is sticky blood on my cheek, my ear is oozing. The inside of my mouth, my throat, are choked with sand. The dizzying wails of the siren hem us tighter into the trench. The sound is high and deep all at the same time. There are leaves in my mother's hair, twigs caught in her chador, the end of which she's balled and stuffed into her sobbing mouth. My father is distracted and stoic, chanting *shush, shush, shush* through the warning. I can hardly breathe. The alarm pierces the humming in my ear, drives the fever so that it soars, vulture-like and wild.

All I want is to look into my mother's eyes. At rest they are luminous-green, startling in their stillness. Sometimes, her eyes bloom with purple flowers or glaze to rock-gray flecked with molten specks of bronze, taking their cue from shadows and surrounding hues—from the colour of her sari, from the clanking metal gate at home, the foliage of the almond tree in our garden. I want to look into her changeable eyes and understand. But my face is pressed into her clavicle. There is only darkness. The siren's wailing is as inconsolable.

My father plucks me from my mother, fumbles me into Ayah's arms, folds my mother into his chest. I recall the sensation of heat, despite the fact that it was winter, possibly from nearby bushes that caught fire, or piles of burning refuse, or the fever—the source is unclear. There is a precise moment when heat and pain crescendo and even the familiar haven of Ayah's bosom is a menace. Lit by a flame, I melt out of my skin, and fly away in the dust-speckled sky, first along with the siren and then high above the wailing, circling and circling until it fades. It's the first time I discover a way out of my body and become conscious on two planes. Borne aloft on invisible wings, I slip out of the trench into the smoke-filled air and peer down at our crouching bodies. The sensation lingers until a tiny aperture opens into the silence. A flautist's notes trickle in. Like faint oxygen they float down into the mud-filled dark. With my whole body I absorb the melody until fear, bitter as loam, dissipates. The reed swarms the trench with sweetness, lures me back into my skin, tunnels us into light and air.

This memory plays constantly, a frangent layer of film that dissolves and disperses into daily life. Fuelled by a will of its own it streams internally. Anywhere. Everywhere. Times when everything has felt new and unfamiliar— the pain of birthing, a beloved's betrayal—my mind returns to that moment when the world stopped underground. In that trench, in 1971, my eardrum burst. Pakistan lost its eastern wing and new borders defined the nation. A new country—Bangladesh—came into being. It was an unwitting birth—an accidental, even if inevitable, creation—just as it is unclear whether 'divine intervention' played a role in rescuing me.

I suspect that incident, its retelling over the years, and my own subconscious recreation of it, have had something to do with making me who I am. I walk into rooms and my eyes dart to the corners where shadows pool. I seek out their concealed exits, a dark trapdoor or window, out of which to fling my head for mouthfuls of fresh air. A part of me is always rooted in that elsewhere below ground, simultaneously hovering above, looking down. Rare is the person or circumstance in whose presence stillness comes. Most times I skip between land/trench, here/there, past/present.

There's nothing singular about this restlessness, the sense of needing to 10 map out escape routes, real and metaphorical. It's a shared Pakistani phenomenon, so deeply ingrained that we are hardly cognizant of it. Only by living away from Pakistan for many years, while still remaining oriented towards it, have I become aware of it. We are a nation that has foiled, even if just barely, one calamity after another, contorting our way out of military dictatorships and bungled democracies, warding off tidal waves with prayers to a Sufi saint. We manage to uphold the dream of a nation state that seems increasingly fragile. At any given moment, this is what it feels to be Pakistani: split, always seeking, a missing thing; often trapped in the gesture of looking back; of brushing against a past whose paint hasn't quite dried on the canvas for the present is perpetually being recreated.

That moment in the trench when my father extricated me from my mother's arms is visceral. I was too young to remember it but in the retelling and mythologizing, the memory has become muscular. In the act of being plucked from my mother, I lost a language I hadn't learned yet and gained a sensibility that is Pakistani.

This singular memory is the core around which I've come to orient myself, circumambulating it still, despite the passage of time and regardless of place. It thrusts into my days, dappling and splicing them, in a macabre ceremony of remembrance, of a place that is always elsewhere, whose heart is that excruciating space below ground where the most exquisite music trickles in, informing virtually every moment of my present.

Analyze

1. As the essay unfolds, the author goes back and forth in time. In some parts, she explicitly reveals her age or the year; in other parts, we understand her age and the year implicitly. How is this effective in her essay? How old, for example, do you think she is during the incident she recounts? What details inform your answer?

2. How does Afridi's memory inform her relationships with the places she's lived since leaving Pakistan?

3. Afridi claims that she was too young to remember the incident in the trench. How do you account for her detailed, visceral description? How reliable is this essay if it is not written directly from something she remembers? What does this imply about memory and identity?

Explore

1. Write a narrative that explores a place from your childhood that has taken on a "mythic lore" with your family or friends. Based on the themes that emerge as you write, consider how it has shaped and continues to shape who you are today.

2. In paragraph 11, Afridi writes that she lost a language she hadn't learned, but "gained a sensibility that is Pakistani." What does this enigmatic statement mean to you? Using examples from this essay,

your own life, or the personal experiences of others you know, explore the relationship between language and national identity. Explain how you can identify with a place (or not) even if you are not fluent in its language.

3. What prompted the conflict that occurred in 1971 between Pakistan and "East Pakistan" (soon to become Bangladesh)? Using reliable sources, familiarize yourself with the history, economics, and politics of that time. Write an essay that sheds light on Afridi's assertion of what it feels like to be Pakistani. Do you think she speaks for all Pakistanis? Why or why not?

Julian Hill
"In Search of Black Identity in Uganda"

Originally from Kankakee, Illinois, Julian Hill graduated with a degree in philosophy from Northwestern University, where he was active in student and campus affairs. He is currently studying international law at Harvard Law School, with a concentration in Latin America and East Africa. "In Search of Black Identity in Uganda" originally appeared on *Glimpse*, an online forum that allows writers, filmmakers, and photographers—all of whom are travelers in some way—a space to "create empathy across vast cultural and physical distances." In this piece, Hill describes Africa as his second home, even before he ever travels there. Eventually, Hill makes his way to Uganda and discovers that making a place home is not as straightforward or easy as he had anticipated.

At the beginning of the essay, Hill feels strongly that history and race can tie him culturally to the people of Uganda. Do you feel the same way about your own history, race, or ancestral culture?

Africa was my second home. I had never been there, though.
Instead, I daydreamed about it from the Black Student Alliance office at Northwestern University. I sat in my black reclining chair that no

longer quite . . . reclined, peering out of the window at our campus-turned-snow kingdom. Gusts of February winds seeped through the walls of the unheated building to reaffirm that I was definitely not in Africa, but Illinois.

I had just finished an AIM conversation with one of my best friends, B Chubbs.

I told him about my goal of getting to Africa soon.

5   I told him that it would be an opportunity for me to connect with my extended family.

I told him about my excitement over finding an organization in D.C. that I had heard could trace my ancestry to a specific region of Africa.

B Chubbs replied:

bchubbs1: even if you found out your family was from . . . i don't know . . . ghana, what you finna do? go back and help out?

For him, the idea of finding an African ancestry didn't mean much—we already had roots in the states. My Bahamian friend, Kortez, felt the same way. How his ancestors got to the Bahamas, or where they were before they got there, wasn't important. What mattered was where he was and what he was doing in the now. Other black friends of mine thought that without some little Congolese cousins or Senegalese grandparents, my claims to a connection with Africa were sentimental at best, and disingenuous at worst.

10   During this time, some four years ago now, I had no idea what "going to Africa" really meant. What country would I go to? What would I do? When would I go? I couldn't answer any of these questions. Though many of my black friends belittled my rationale (or lack thereof), something inexplicable kept calling me to the Continent.

I gazed at the walls of the office. There was a photo of seven black students standing around former NAACP Chairman Julian Bond, a black and white flier for a talk by rapper Chuck D, a painting of Africa. Composed of green, red and black stripes, the continent looked like a flag. A bronze chain penetrated the canvas just off of the coasts of Ethiopia and Senegal. Red paint dripped from the southern coast.

Another painting, cooled by pale blues and grays, hung on the wall next to my desk. There were dozens of dark brown people. They were lying down horizontally in large cubbies, which were stacked on top of each other. One white guy in a collared shirt and dark blue slacks was standing in the middle with a whip raised in his right hand.

Those enslaved blacks, ripped from Africa, are my ancestors. Jamaicans, Brazilians, Ghanaians, Black Britons—all are part of my larger family. Most of us share the inextricable link of slavery. Though unsure what having this link entailed, I knew that, for me, there was one way to find out.

Though half-dazed from the brightness of the sun and half-exhausted by the fourteen-hour trip from Chicago, I managed to find Frank. He stood just outside the terminal doors, busy conversing with a plump taxi driver with shades instead of holding up the sign with my name scribbled on it.

It was like meeting a long-lost brother. Tall, dark and thin, he greeted 15 me with a smile and an embrace.

"Welcome to Africa, my brother," he declared. I was being welcomed back home . . . for the first time.

Soon after piling into the black taxi, we were winding towards Kampala along the coast of Lake Victoria. A bicyclist rested on a palm tree as a light breeze passed over the lake into my window. Tall buildings began to appear, and with them a street sign saying "Kampala 09" that, like many light posts, bus stops, and trees, was covered in posters with pictures of politicians and the word "LONDA" in bold letters. Yellow buildings with an MTN logo blended with dry sun-scorched land and served as a canvas for streaks of Ugandans walking to and fro. Western influences were everywhere: two young men walking rapidly in conservative black suits; a Crane Bank building that took up almost an entire block; a Shell gas station filled to capacity with vans, cars, and motorcycles.

Passing a roundabout with a large clock tower in the middle, the city infrastructure slowly began to shift to rural landscapes. In the jungle-turned-farmland that lined both sides of the road, clusters of banana trees were scattered around one-story brick homes. Occasionally a town would pop up with stands and storefronts that sold everything from chickens to dresses.

We finally pulled in front of a house that looked just large enough to contain two bedrooms. Frank's wife, Christine, and their two sons walked out of the house to welcome me.

I took it all in—the towering tree draped in green mangos, the sweet 20 smell of hair grease as Christine hugged me, the gentle wind that dried pockets of sweat on my forehead, the laughing of kids playing games outside the neighbor's home. I was finally here.

By the end of my first week, I had learned enough of the local language, Luganda, to make a few friends. I would make the quarter mile walk into town, greeting elderly women in bright, multi-colored traditional dresses, called *gomesi*, and groups of shy children walking home from school in their yellow short-sleeved button-ups and maroon ties.

One day, I was making such a trip with Frank; we stopped to chat with a woman headed to the village. Though I couldn't understand what she or Frank was saying, her stares and smiles suggested that she made at least one comment about me. After she said her goodbyes, she continued down the bumpy dirt road.

"What did she say?" I asked Frank.

"She asked if you were my brother," he replied, chuckling lightly. It would not be the first time I was mistaken for an African.

25   Apparently, my five-year old host brother, Zach, asked Frank a few times if Frank was certain that I was indeed American and not Ugandan. According to Frank, his other son, Timothy, warmed up to me much quicker than he typically does to non-black volunteers. These situations made me feel the bond that I had hoped for on the Continent back on that frigid February day at Northwestern.

But it did not take long for me to see the limitations of race as a means of building relationships with Ugandans. Thinking that I could come to Uganda and, just by being black, relate in any meaningful way would have been rather naïve. It's not that I expected this; I just still held out hope that it was possible.

"Muzungu! How are you?"

I turned to see a grinning, shirtless boy whose head reached my waist. Almost immediately, three more children ran up asking the same. It was the first time anyone had called me a muzungu. I had heard it used to refer to whites and even my Taiwanese friend, but never anyone black.

That these children called me muzungu initially upset me. How could these kids refer to me as a European? Wasn't I more like them than any

European they've ever seen? I took it as if they were trying to ... disown me. *You're not one of us, you're one of them.* What perplexed me more than these initial feelings was that I was uncertain as to if they were right or not.

Putting my feelings aside, I generically replied, "I'm fine. How are you?" 30

Half-listening to their responses, I saw a matatu speeding down the road, honking to get attention. The conductor was sticking his hand out the window up into the air—the Gayaza route. I flagged the van down and the conductor hopped out and asked me where I was going.

In Luganda I asked him how much he charged to go to Nakumatt.

"3,000 shillings." (About $1.25).

I gasped and murmured, "2,500."

The conductor paused for a moment, looking at the ground and scratching his head, before replying, "Okay, we go."

Feeling a little guilty for negotiating, I squeezed my way into the vehicle. 35 I sat among fifteen others, cramped with four in my row, and called my friend to tell him that I was on my way.

"Yo, what's good? I'm chillin'. I'm mad on my way. I'll see you in like four-five. Fa sho. Word. Yuh."

As I ended the call, I looked around. Great. Four sets of eyes were on me—each pair screaming "Muzungu!"

Once the hour-long trip ended, I anxiously scurried along Jinja road to Oasis Mall, which I've dubbed Moneyville, to meet up with my friends at an upscale cafe. A security guard, in a red and black SECURITAS uniform, checked my bag and patted me down before I could even get into the parking lot.

In Café Javas, Southeast Asian men in collared button-up shirts and dress pants were speaking a language I could not understand; three white women, wearing wraps and carrying Black babies on their backs, were greeting three seated friends; an African man in a conservative dark blue suit was chatting with a young African woman in a black dress with flower imprints. I could smell the cooking oil and ketchup from the French fries they were sharing.

I sat down and greeted my friends—Chad, tall and athletic African- 40 American in jeans and a powder blue polo shirt; Monica, a Ugandan of British upbringing with hair twists, glasses, a brown skirt, and a yellow V-neck shirt; Tanya, a brown-eyed Londoner who was Malaysian, Italian, and a mix of other things, in black tights and a long white blouse. We fit in well.

I ordered a meal that cost ten times what I would pay at the local restaurant near my farm. Each bite of my quesadilla, which was literally the size of my head, unveiled a growing discomfort. It clouded my ability to concentrate on the conversation with my friends.

Sure, seeing a handful of African couples or groups at the café gave me some solace. At least there are some locals enjoying these spaces. I wondered, though, how I could forge any sort of solidarity with the neglected and exploited Ugandans in my village when my economic privileges presupposed the difficulties of so many of them. As an American, I could not ignore that U.S. trade and political policies help make it easier for countless Ugandan farmers to feed others around the world than to feed their own families. Who knows how much a local farmer got for the beans in my quesadilla? In a way, everyone in the café indirectly supported the economic exploitation of Uganda's small farmers.

By the time I finished dinner, streaks of reddish-yellow, blue, and pink filled the sky. People walked out of the mall into the once-full parking lot, most carrying plastic bags. As if programmed, the café's lights came on. Workers dressed in peach-colored polo shirts stacked wine glasses, typed away on the screens of their registers, and shared jokes with guests who generally looked like they did something important. My group soon left for my friend's apartment.

I felt disconnected, and uncomfortably recalled my trip to Eastern Uganda only a week before.

45   "Why the fuck am I here?" I sat on a tourist truck in a drunken trance. I had just taken a boat cruise along the Nile River. Now, I was headed just north of Jinja to a campsite in Bujagali where I was spending the weekend.

I sat at the end of the fifth row, with a view of the people on the side of the road. Ugandans . . . black people . . . my people. There was a crowd around a small stand where a teen was selling chapatti in scrap newspaper. A woman, in a red and white wrap with a black V-neck shirt tight enough to show she wasn't wearing a bra, walked slowly with a basket of roasted bananas on her head.

In front of me sat a hammered blonde woman with a thick build. She and the other dozen people on the truck (minus my friend and I) were white. This particular girl's right hand hung lazily over the truck's railing after she downed more of whatever was left in her red plastic cup

"Let's take a picture!" her friend yelled. A flash illuminated the night.

"Hey," the photographer rambled to me. "How do you say 'we go' again? Tugenda?"

"Tugende," I responded.   50

"TUGENDE SSEBO. TUGENDE!," the photographer friend yelled as she and her four friends laughed.

For as different as she was from me, we had much in common. Like myself, she and the others were able to travel to Uganda and volunteer or work—some with the hopes of sincerely making a difference. Like myself, some were taking a break from the real world and enjoying Uganda as an escape.

Still, I felt a million times more comfortable on my farm, in my village, among Ugandans, than I felt on this truck. I wanted to live in two different worlds, but they were inherently in conflict. Though thankful for and benefiting from the advantages of my Americanness, I also felt the alienation and exoticism that sometimes came with being black.

After we returned to the campsite, music and a noisy mixed crowd of people welcomed us—most with drinks in their hands—at the site's bar. Instead of going to the bar, my friend and I walked outside to an empty table. Aside from a Canadian rafter who had too much to drink, no one bothered us, and I was content with that. This was my way, though contrived, of not feeling like a tourist. Throw in a few of my patented Lugandan phrases with a local, and I felt less like the alien that I really was among Ugandans. As much as I wanted to deny the imperialist psyche, the hypocrisy, and the racist tendencies associated with much of America, I recognized that I would have had a much tougher time getting to where I am today had I been born in most African countries. How could I take the good of being American and being black and meld them together? It just seemed like I couldn't have it both ways.

One evening Frank and I were eating dinner and watching the news   55 on the thirteen-inch TV he carries into the kitchen from his nephew's bedroom every night.

"What do you and people in the village think of African Americans?" I asked after swallowing a spoonful of rice and fresh fish bought in town.

"For us, we believe that you are our brothers. We read in school about your history, and we know that you come from Africa. So, for us, we know that . . . there is no difference—you just got there because of slavery."

We shared a geographic origin, but also a racial category—black—that is arguably unlike any other. Across various countries and continents, blacks were condemned legally or extra-legally for something they could neither control nor hide from—their skin color. As trivial as I find race as an invention of society, its consequences even today cannot be ignored. Black people are still often harassed, assumed to be inadequate, and refused services in many parts of the world.

As the TV streamed videos of riots in Kampala, I thought about Uganda's history. The country had been plagued with intra-racial conflict and division even before independence from Britain. Though the population is largely Black, divisions on the basis of tribe, culture, socioeconomic status, political views, and religious affiliation are entrenched. Ugandan Presidents, including current President Museveni, have exacerbated problems by recruiting security forces and members of key governmental bodies from their native regions of Uganda.

On the screen, one image passed after another: President Museveni at a press conference, wearing a tan polo shirt, his bald head shining, his customary sun hat sat on the table in front of him; women and men being taken in gurneys to the Mulago Hospital from beatings and tear gas used by Ugandan police earlier that day; three officers, in blue and gray camouflage uniforms, chasing down a protester and clubbing him on the ground.

I wondered how these soldiers could treat their fellow Ugandans in such a way. I would ask the same of West Africans who enslaved their brethren during the slave trade or Hutus who murdered thousands of Tutsis.

The Black Diaspora is a mixture of people with various backgrounds. To expect complete unity ignores the real tribal divisions that have existed on the Continent since well before European presence. Some scholars say the last time Ugandans rallied together was against their British invaders. They had a common interest.

No common interest seemed to exist one afternoon when Melvin, a friend of Frank's, asked me to come and see his farm. Melvin wanted my opinion about his two-acre plot just outside the village. It seemed like a typical scenario—ask the muzungu to help you with something simple so that you can then ask him to give you money.

After giving me a walk-through, he asked me for advice.

"I'm no consultant, but I like that you have certain sections for certain   65
crops. Plus, it's good that you have a nice amount of space between them—
it will make weeding a lot easier."

"Mmm. Thank you, Julian. I would like you to take some of my greens—
cabbage, collards—yes?"

Over the next half an hour, we walked through thick vegetation as
Melvin pulled some of his best veggies—for me. Soon he and I were on our
bikes riding back toward Melvin's home. On the way, we discussed Ugandan
politics, economics, religion, and our aspirations. When we arrived, we
took tea and ate eggs as we watched a Nigerian movie with his wife.

An hour later, I was in town, sitting on a wooden bench outside of one of
the dozen storefronts located along the main road. Outside one stood a group
of four men; their chattering and laughing filled the air. People gathered in
clusters talking and enjoying the gentle evening. The stocky store owner next
door sat outside in her chair, frying meat patties, while the five pieces of
chapatti I had just ordered sizzled on a hot plate at a stand a few feet away.

As I sat there sipping a Fanta, the awareness hit me that soon I would be
leaving this place. Soon, I would be leaving Frank's farm. Next month, he
will harvest corn cobs on the same plot where I helped him plant seeds just
weeks ago. I wondered if he would think fondly of our time together, or if
he would think of me as just another outsider who stuck around for a bit.
I wondered if these Ugandans in town would think of me differently, or
would see me only in passing. I knew both of these responses were possible.
And truthfully, the same probably went for how I might think about them.

I finished my Fanta, and quietly watched the sun go down.   70

Analyze

1. What is calling Hill to "the Continent," his "second home"? How does
   his daydream in Illinois compare to the reality he finds? Think of a
   place you've never visited but might consider a "second home," as Hill
   does. What draws you to it?

2. What does the author let us know about Frank? How, for example, has
   the author come to know him? Why does Frank address Hill as "my
   brother"?

3. Hill writes, "... it did not take long for me to see the limitations of race as a means of building relationships with Ugandans" (paragraph 26). Why do you think Hill didn't expect this, "but still held hope that it was possible"?

Explore

1. Hill soon realizes that native Ugandans perceive him as "muzungu." What does this mean, what gave him away, and how does he react? Write about a time when you wanted to be part of a place, culture, or specific group of people, only to realize that you could not easily assimilate. How did you react? Why? Thinking back on it now, do you understand the situation differently? How and why?

2. The author asks, "How could I take the good of being American and being black and meld them together?" How does he answer his question? How would you answer the question for him?

3. We often meet people with whom we identify—whether because of nationality, race, gender, sexual orientation, linguistic background, or age—only to realize the subtle gulf of nuance that floods what we had assumed was common ground. Using Hill's essay as a backdrop, write an essay about the fluidity and changeability of one's identity with a place. Include what you hope Hill learned from his trip to Uganda.

Julia Whitty
"All the Disappearing Islands"

Julia Whitty was born in Bogota, Colombia, and immigrated to the United States when she was a child. She holds both US and Australian citizenships. A regular environmental correspondent for *Mother Jones*, Whitty is also a filmmaker and has published several works of fiction and nonfiction. "All the Disappearing Islands" first appeared in the July/August 2003 issue of *Mother Jones* magazine, a nonprofit publication that specializes in investigative, political, and social justice reporting. In this article, Whitty investigates both the environmental and cultural impact of melting ice caps on the South Pacific island nation of Tuvalu.

In your opinion, what moral obligations do the world's highest greenhouse-gas emitters and polluters—like Australia and the US—have to revise their industry-dependent cultures in the face of global warming?

From the air the tiny islets of Funafuti atoll appear as a broken pearl necklace scattered on the blue throat of the tropical sea. No other land is in sight, only an ocean without end and its own billowy breath rising as cumulus clouds that seem far more substantive than the tiny landforms below. As the twin-engine turboprop banks for final approach, the atoll assumes the classic dimensions of a desert island—a sand outpost studded with coconut palms and surrounded by impossibly huge swells topped with wave crests longer than the island is wide. This leaves me to ponder, as Charles Darwin did, how "these low hollow coral islands bear no proportion to the vast ocean out of which they abruptly rise; and it seems wonderful that such weak invaders are not overwhelmed, by the all-powerful and never-tiring waves of that great sea."

Although Darwin eventually discovered the reef-building mechanisms of corals that keep atoll islands from succumbing to the waves, even his prescient mind never considered the dread possibilities of the 21st century: that global warming could cause the sea to expand and rise faster than the corals could fortify themselves against it, and that these fragile spits of sand might disappear beneath the waves that tossed them into being in the first place.

Today, roughly 1 million people live on coral islands worldwide, and many more millions live on low-lying real estate vulnerable to the rising waves. At risk are not just people, but unique human cultures, born and bred in watery isolation. Faced with inundation, some of these people are beginning to envision the wholesale abandonment of their nations. Others are buying higher land wherever they can. A few are preparing lawsuits that will challenge the right of the developed world to emit the greenhouse gases threatening to cause the flooding of their homelands. But whatever their actions or inactions, the citizens of tropical island nations are likely destined to become the world's first global-warming refugees—although they contribute only 0.6 percent of greenhouse-gas pollution.

At no point is the sandy island of Funafuti higher than 13 feet above sea level, as is the case throughout the nine coral atolls of this South Pacific nation of Tuvalu. Surrounded by the sea, the people here have been shaped by it as few others on earth. Every afternoon, rain or shine, Tuvaluan children romp in its unsupervised playground. Fishing at dusk for the night's dinner, the men cast nets weighted with coral into the surf. Those islanders without outhouses wade into the privacy of the waves, where—they laugh and tell me—they feed the same fish who will soon feed them. Inescapably, this is a nation of waterfront property; even the plywood and corrugated-tin houses standing "inland" a block or two enjoy the ambience of the ocean. No one here has ever lived a moment without hearing the thunder of surf.

5   "Tuvaluans are blessed," wrote former Prime Minister Faimalaga Luka. "We have the sea, and above all we have our land. [We] are closely knit through kinship, a small population, and a single binding culture. What this mixture stirs up is a sensation that runs deep, a supreme sense of place."

That place, now in danger of disappearing beneath the waves, is located halfway between Hawaii and Australia. Once part of the British empire, Tuvalu is among the smallest and most remote countries on earth, with a total land mass comprising only 10 square miles, less than half the size of Manhattan and scattered over 347,400 square miles of ocean, an area larger than California, Oregon, and Washington combined. Nine thousand people live on these nine atolls, 95 percent of whom are Polynesians, having arrived variously from Samoa, Tonga, and Uvea over the past 2,000 years.

Life on a *motu* (the low island atop a coral reef) is always precarious, and when the first Polynesians arrived in Tuvalu, they found it hard going. With only sand for soil, they became dependent on the sea, coconuts, their pigs, and a threadbare agriculture of *pulaka* (a tarolike root). When high winds and waves from tropical storms and cyclones overcame their low-lying islands, the Tuvaluans sometimes tied themselves to spindly coconut palms, hoping the wind might spare these tenuous anchors.

Yet now, ominously, the high tides and resultant floods that used to visit Tuvalu in February are occurring nearly half the year, from November to March. And whereas in the past big cyclones rampaged through these islands only once or twice a decade—the most violent in recent memory being Cyclone Bebe, which in 1972 inundated Funafuti, killing six people, razing most buildings, flattening nearly every coconut palm—the 1990s saw seven of them. When three cyclones ripped through Fiji and Tonga in 1997, a 124-acre motu in the Funafuti atoll washed away. On my visit across the lagoon to see what is left, I find only a dome of petrified coral cement— the basement, as it were, for the sandy beaches and palm trees that once comprised a favorite Funafutian picnic site.

And these islands could be rendered uninhabitable by other effects of climate change. Floods and rogue waves raise the saltwater table underlying the atolls, poisoning the Tuvaluans' staple crops. Already some farmers have been forced to grow their pulaka in tin containers, and already some of the smaller motus have lost their coconut palms to saltwater intrusion. Nor are storms a prerequisite for disaster. "Last August," Prime Minister Saufatu Sopoanga tells me, "on a clear, calm day, a sudden wave surge rolled in from the sea and washed across Funafuti into the lagoon, flooding houses."

There was no apparent reason for it, and during my stay on the atoll,   10
I find the sensation of threat to be ever present—the sea on both sides, the constant drumroll of surf, a thin strip of land between—like living on a liquid fault line.

The Tuvaluans face a difficult choice. If the seas rise and they stay in Tuvalu, they will die. But if they leave, some part of them will die. In the event of abandonment, says Sopoanga, "we'd like to stay as close to Tuvalu as possible, where we could still have the same water and the same air." Despite a prevalent Western belief that all the world would like to emigrate to its shores, the Tuvaluans feel differently. Not at all happily, they are preparing to become a nation of *fakaalofa*—their word for landless people, which literally means "deserving of pity."

Because there are no motor scooters or even push-bikes in working order for me to rent, I am hitchhiking on Funafuti, although thumbs are not required here, simply a suitably heat-stricken gait. It's a good way to meet the locals, albeit only men, who immediately inquire as to my marital status. Recently a Funafutian married a *palangi* (white) woman, and his reports on the novelty of my kind are apparently piquing some interest.

Most of these men turn out not to be native Funafutians, but transplants from the outer atolls of Tuvalu. They have come here in search of economic opportunity, swelling the population of the capital to around 5,000. When I ask if they have seen many changes on the atoll since they arrived, they avoid talk of rising seas, turning instead to more immediate concerns. Eight months ago, the only road in the country was paved along a 7.5-mile span in Funafuti, and everyone agrees the island has gotten much hotter since the black tarmac usurped so much white sand. One elderly passenger complains that the Funafutians won't walk anywhere anymore, and worse yet, they won't go barefoot, but insist on wearing flip-flops. He blames this preponderance of newfangled footwear on the road too, saying the pavement is too hot to walk on, even for coral-calloused feet.

There is little or no television here, only a few hours of radio a day, and most of these drivers have never been farther than their home islands, although some have traveled to Fiji or New Zealand. But most don't have much to compare their country to, and when I mention that Tuvalu is graced with universal literacy and almost no violent crime (the only jail is currently empty)—the Funafutians smile and nod politely. Because it would be unseemly to acknowledge that their world is that much better than mine.

15   But whereas I had expected to meet a nation of people eager for me to broadcast their plight to the world, instead I am finding citizens wary of the topic of sea levels. To a person, they seem quietly disappointed that I am not a tourist. Despite the country's international airport code of FUN, virtually no vacationers make it to these islands. Perhaps the Tuvaluans are afraid that talk of flooded islands will squash any hopes that tourism will ever establish itself on their 13-foot-high shores. Yet I also sense something of shame, as if they feel responsible for their impending status as fakaalofa.

Thirty-one years ago, when Cyclone Bebe inundated Funafuti, its waves tossed coral rubble onto the windward side of the atoll, creating a rampart that still stands as the highest point on the motu. This rampart is now colonized by coconut palms, pandanus, and breadfruit trees, and I like to sit here in the late afternoons and watch the sea rolling ashore. As each wave climbs and then withdraws, it rolls the coral rubble back and forth. The chattering sounds these stones make are like the noise of thousands of falling dominoes, sharply audible even above the pounding surf.

The precariousness of dominoes seems an apt metaphor for Tuvalu's fate, where changes to either sea levels or the coral cover will likely result in the entire nation succumbing to what Darwin described as the "irresistible power" of the "miscalled Pacific." Snorkeling in the lagoon each afternoon, I see evidence of the struggle already under way. Stands of *Acropora* (staghorn) corals, the densest I have seen in more than two decades of diving and film-ing reef life, rise in a tangle as chaotic as blackberry thickets. Yet, by my estimate, 80 percent of these reefs are dead, killed in the 1997 and 2002 El Niños, which uprooted corals in a rash of cyclones and raised sea tem-peratures enough to cause the most massive, fatal, worldwide episodes of coral bleaching ever recorded.

The live corals still found inside Funafuti's lagoon are all young colonies, decorating the pointy tips of the dead staghorns like gaudy blue and pink fingernails. Below them, the thicket of what obviously was once a spectacular coral world is now choked in velvety algae and aswarm with the herbivorous species of parrotfishes, surgeonfishes, rabbitfishes, blennies, damselfishes, mollusks, and sea urchins. Together, these browsers and grazers form a bioerosive army that will eventually convert the bones of this reef to sand.

In the event that these corals—the backbone of the atoll—never recover their health, the whole island will eventually be swept away as well. Yet even with robust reefs, a rising ocean will likewise overwhelm these low-lying islands, and the most likely cause of rising oceans is rising global temperatures. Most scientists (even those employed by oil companies) now agree that the dangerous rate by which global temperatures are escalating is largely due to human activity. Forecasts predict the earth will warm three to nine degrees Fahrenheit over the next century—far more rapid than any previous fluctuations—with a three-degree rise akin to moving the climate bands poleward 30 feet a day. "Squirrels might be able to move at those kinds of rates, but an oak tree can't," says climatologist Ken Caldeira of the Lawrence Livermore National Laboratory. Neither can islands. At their best, the reef-building corals grow only an inch per year.

Evidence of global climate change is already mounting from the most   20
distant reaches of the globe. The snows of Kilimanjaro are melting away. In 2002, the ice covering the Arctic and Greenland shrank by a record 650,000 square miles, while a study published in Science found that Alaskan glaciers were melting at more than twice the rate previously assumed, adding 12 cubic miles of freshwater to the world's oceans each year. Also in 2002, a piece of ice the size of Rhode Island broke from the Larsen B ice shelf in Antarctica, where it had been firmly cemented for 12,000 years. New research reveals that the rapidly melting glaciers are even changing the shape of the planet, making the earth more oblate than spherical. Yet another study in Science suggests that the warming oceans might trigger intense eruptions of methane now frozen beneath the seafloor, leading to global warming on a catastrophic scale.

More alarming still is the fact that this melting creates a feedback loop difficult to escape. Because compact sea ice reflects 80 percent of the sun's heat back into space, and water absorbs 80 percent, any reduction in the ratio of ice to water further increases the warming of the oceans and the thermal expansion that will eventually raise sea levels worldwide—if it is not doing so already. "Once the process is set in motion," warns Robert

Watson, chairman of the U.N. Intergovernmental Panel on Climate Change (IPCC), "it cannot be slowed down in anything less than a few millennia."

But the evidence is not without controversy. Tangled up with the science is the reality that nations prefer not to alter the fossil-fuel-consuming habits that make them globally powerful, even at the expense of a stable climate. Chief among these are the United States and Australia, both of which refused to sign the 1997 U.N. Kyoto Protocol—calling upon the developed world to reduce greenhouse-gas emissions by 5.2 percent of 1990 levels by 2012—even though Australia is the world's highest greenhouse-gas emitter per capita, followed closely by the United States, the largest overall polluter.

Perhaps in light of this stance, in 1999 Australia was quick to trumpet its own evidence that sea levels in the Pacific are not rising after all. The report came from Australia's National Tidal Facility, which monitors a network of tidal gauges across the Pacific, including one on Funafuti. Yet much less noted was the evidence from the University of Hawaii's tidal gauge in Tuvalu—which has been recording sea levels for nearly three times as long as the Australians', and which indicates a mean one-to-two-centimeter rise per decade. Mark Merrifield of the Hawaii study tells me that what's really worrying is that the maximum sea levels—the highest of the high tides— have been increasing at a much faster rate. "This might explain why the inhabitants of Tuvalu have seen more extreme flooding events than one might expect from just looking at the change in mean sea level."

Aware of the ambiguities in the science, Prime Minister Sopoanga reminds me, "Here in Tuvalu we don't need to refer to reports because we see the evidence with our own eyes every day."

25   Because I am on foot in Funafuti, moving slowly through the heat and the afternoon rainstorms, I have ample time to savor the ambiguities. In 2001, Tuvalu began actively lobbying Australia and New Zealand to accept its entire population as environmental refugees, a request that Australia, with its strict no-refugee policy, refused, citing its tidal-gauge data. New Zealand, on the other hand, agreed to accept the citizens of Tuvalu, although only 75 islanders a year—at which rate the country will not be emptied for 120 years. By that time, according to the 2001 IPCC report, the seas may well have risen more than 35 inches, rendering the atolls uninhabitable.

Yet, paradoxically, Funafuti appears to be building like a nation with a long-term future. A three-story government office building is under construction in the center of town. Destined to be the tallest structure in the nation, this veritable high-rise is a thank-you gift from Taiwan, which won this round in the Pacific cold war by convincing Tuvalu to formally recognize it as the real China. Nearby, a new hospital is also under construction, funded by Japan. At both sites, Tuvaluan workers lounge in the shade, while their Australian handlers march around in Blundstone boots and khaki shorts.

On much of the rest of the atoll I see new houses springing up—evidence of Tuvaluans moving to Funafuti from the outer atolls, and of the growing prosperity of the nation as a whole, as money flows in from Tuvaluans working overseas, from foreign-aid organizations, and from a host of innovative money-making plans implemented by the government. Presumably in acknowledgment of the rising waters, the new houses are all being built on 10-foot-tall stilts—notably different from traditional dwellings—and overall, this tiny nation appears to be caught in a tidal cycle of doubt, ebbing and flowing between plans to abandon the country and hopes of developing it.

Of course, the stilt houses might also be due to the rising tide of garbage. Until recently, the only refuse the Tuvaluans created was coconut husks and fish bones, and in keeping with past practices, they now throw everything from plastic bottles to beer cans and disposable diapers more or less out their front doors. Paul Scells, an Australian aid worker who's helping to establish a waste-management program here, jokes that sea levels might or might not be rising, but for sure the housewives of Tuvalu are sweeping the island away. I, too, have heard the pleasant soundtrack of their work in the cool hour after dawn, as they brush away the leaves and fronds that have fallen in the night, and dutifully weed the tenacious green shoots growing in their yards. Apparently, the people here prefer un-vegetated plots (garbage or no), and the ex-pat Aussies and Kiwis, who gather each afternoon for lunch on the terrace of the Vaiaku Lagi—Tuvalu's only hotel—shake their heads in shared cultural confusion. But this is what I like best about this place, and what I fear most when I imagine its eventual abandonment: a different point of view that could only survive out here. Transplanted to New Zealand, the Tuvaluans will doubtless learn to grow lawns.

Before I left home, a friend suggested that Tuvalu might have a bright future as a postapocalyptic tourist destination, and with this in mind, I find myself assessing future attractions. The lobby of the Vaiaku Lagi would make a pleasant dive site—open and airy (watery), with the guest rooms adding the thrill of exploration, all of which might be clothed in pretty corals if the sea temperatures permit. The windowless kitchen would provide an excellent daytime sleeping site for white-tipped reef sharks, while the small dining room could house a large humphead wrasse and his harem of females. Ordering a can of Victoria Bitter, I see ample room behind the bar for a moray eel, and plenty of whiskey bottles to provide homes for shy octopuses.

30   Because of the building boom and the accompanying population boom of Aussie and Kiwi construction workers, I've been unable to get a room at the Vaiaku Lagi, or at any of the guest houses in the village, or even at the houses of relatives of the sympathetic young woman at the front desk. Her aunties' houses are filled with family from the outer islands, who have come to Funafuti for a weekend wedding. And so I find myself three miles out of town at the Hide-Away guest house, home of Rolf Koepke, a German who came to the South Pacific 40 years ago, and his Tuvaluan wife, Emily.

When they built their home on Funafuti 20 years ago it was a novelty: a two-story palangi house, Emily says, "way out in the bush." Her Tuvaluan family was mystified as to why she would want to live so high up or so far away. Rolf insisted on moving in before the house was completed, then stepped off the unfinished second floor in the dark one night, breaking a leg so badly that he spent the next nine months in the hospital, fighting the doctor's urge to amputate.

Emily ascribes Rolf's troubles to the fact that he loves his beer too much, although he is also a good man, she says, a "working-hard man." My first night at the Hide-Away, Rolf's legs have taken another hit, as he fell off his bicycle earlier that day. Oblivious to his blood dripping onto the bed where I will soon be sleeping, he tells me that he doesn't believe a word of this rising sea-level business. The Tuvaluans are building everywhere, he says, and he has personally seen no signs of rising waters, although he concedes that the climate is "all buggered up," and that none of the seasons arrive when they should anymore.

The next morning, when he looks surprised to see me there, and anxious over what to do about it, he delivers me into the company of Father Camille Desrosiers, better known among his tiny congregation as Father Kamilo— a fit, 74-year-old French Canadian Catholic missionary who has been on Funafuti for 17 years, where he claims, only half jokingly, to have been forgotten by his superiors. Father Kamilo also disdains the disappearing-island theory, citing the contradiction of the building boom. But the news of even the nearby world could easily pass him by, I realize. Chatting with me at his desk in his tiny office, he tells me that letters from England arrive "pretty fast"—this as he opens a Christmas card on Valentine's Day.

Father Kamilo strives mostly in vain against the dominant Protestant Church of Tuvalu, which has been in the islands for more than a century, and whose pealing bells call its brethren to services seemingly more often than a muezzin. The church's followers—97 percent of the population—hold to a strong belief in the Genesis story, in which rainbows are proof of God's promise to Noah that he will not flood the earth again. Apparently, Tuvalu's daily rainbows reinforce this belief, and whenever I hear the sound of Tuvaluan voices raised in *a cappella* church song, their harmonies weaving sweetly and effortlessly through the sky where rainbows blossom and fade, I can understand the comfort such faith could provide.

Somewhere in Father Kamilo's mind must be the thought that he will likely die on Funafuti, having converted few, having never been posted back to the bigger world, and having never even seen the outer atolls of Tuvalu. Perhaps he will end up like all the other Tuvaluans: buried in the private cemeteries gracing everyone's front yards, the graves surrounded by hog fencing decorated with plastic flowers. The Hide-Away has just such a cemetery, including the grave of Emily's and Rolf's 11-year-old son, who died of leukemia in faraway New Zealand, where Rolf, in desperation, took him for treatment.

It occurs to me that after 2,000 years of human habitation, a fair amount of Tuvalu's tiny landmass must be composed of the bones of its people, and when I think of the future, this thought saddens me as well. What will become of these other Tuvaluans—the ones whom the people still consider important enough to erect roofs over their graves for shade? Surely the New Zealanders will not accept the dead Tuvaluans, too, or the soil they have become.

Many young Tuvaluans are already being sent away. Promising students go to universities in Fiji, New Zealand, or Australia. At any given time 750 Tuvaluans—about 1 in 4 of the adult males—are employed as merchant mariners. When these young people return, despite being richer or better educated or both, they still have no pigs, a condition considered pitiable by the older generation.

Pigs and land have traditionally been the measure of wealth in Tuvalu. Although Emily says they love their pigs and cry when they must kill them,

35

when two rogue pigs go rampaging through her garden, she doesn't hesitate to tell me that, by law, she has the right to kill them, which would "give us all a good excuse for a feast." Apparently, slaughtering your neighbor's pigs sidesteps the sadness issue.

Because Emily is the groom's aunt, I am invited to the weekend wedding that has drawn so many people from the outer atolls. The feast is overflowing with pork, delivered whole on spits from underground *umu* ovens. In two days' time the newly married couple will go back to their university studies in Fiji. Meantime, they tear into the pig carcasses with their bare hands. Like a growing number of their countrymen, they are Tuvaluans who do not live in Tuvalu. Recent population estimates indicate that in the last two years some 2,000 have fled the rising waters, or the limited opportunities, and are now scattered across the South Pacific—many in Auckland, the largest Polynesian city in the world, and a place decidedly pigless and landless, at least for refugees.

40   During its brief decades of independence, Tuvalu has behaved differently from its South Pacific neighbors, many of which are considered among the most corrupt nations on earth. But a democratic Tuvalu has managed its resources well: growing the national trust fund to around $30 million; licensing its Internet country code (.tv) for $12.5 million (thereby funding the country's first streetlights, the first paved road, and U.N. membership); selling commercial fishing licenses within its waters; and producing postage stamps for the international philatelic trade. Other schemes, though lucrative, were canceled—including the sale of Tuvaluan passports (after evidence that terrorists were purchasing them) and a phone-sex service tied to the nation's "688" area code that once earned 10 percent of the federal budget (after Tuvalu's churches objected).

But perhaps the country's biggest revenue earner lies in the future. Currently, the government is seeking partners among other island nations for a lawsuit against the United States and Australia to be brought before the International Court of Justice in The Hague, suing for damages from global warming. The reparations from such "ecological debt" could be huge, including the potential to cancel the monies owed on developmental loans to the big polluters. At the very least, such lawsuits will give the World Court the means to punish the rich nations for practices that essentially amount to killing their neighbors' pigs.

There is skepticism over this lawsuit. Some see it as a cynical ploy for more foreign money. These tend to be the same people who privately mutter that garbage-strewn Tuvalu would benefit from a seawater flushing, and who appear to begrudge the Tuvaluans their clever capitalizing on the few opportunities available to them. "We hope to speak for the low-lying atolls and coastal areas of the world," says Prime Minister Sopoanga, although he admits that the suit is facing an uphill battle due to other litigants' fears that the powerful donor nations they'd be suing would seek reprisals. Still, the lawsuit is considered a threat, and Australian legal experts, at least, have advised their government to take it seriously.

Along with Tuvalu, many other island and coastal cultures have just grievances. Kiribati, Tuvalu's neighbor, has already lost two islands to the rising waters. The seas around the Carteret atolls off Papua New Guinea have cut one island in half and left 1,500 people dependent on food aid. In the Marshall Islands, World War II gravesites are washing away. Trinidad reports losing land at the rate of two to four yards per year. In the Indian Ocean, a third of the Maldives' 200 inhabited atolls are disappearing. And in Alaska, some Eskimo are being forced to move, as the tundra melts and their villages slip into the sea. Unlike other refugees displaced by wars or famines, these people on the edge of the ocean face the prospect of never again having homelands to return to.

Some help has been promised, but it pales in comparison to Western practices. In 2001, rich nations pledged $0.4 billion a year to help developing countries adapt to climate change, while spending $80 billion annually on energy subsidies, mostly for fossil fuels. In the Pacific, the frustration is apparent: "Tuvalu's voice in the debate is small, rarely heard, and heeded not at all," wrote former Prime Minister Faimalaga Luka.

Eventually, the cost will be high for all nations. The momentum of 45 global warming is such that—regardless of any curbs on emissions—sea levels are predicted to rise for at least the next 500 years, rendering a completely new map of the world, as river valleys become seas, and continents fragment into islands, and 13 of the world's 20 most populous cities submerge. During my time in Tuvalu, I find myself wondering what Darwin would have thought of it all. In the course of his long travels through the Pacific, he gleaned much about evolution and its shadow partner, extinction: "We have every reason to believe that species and groups of species gradually disappear, one after another, first from one spot, then from another, and finally from the world." Would he think the same lay in store for human cultures, and perhaps human existence, today?

Within the coming decades, the atolls of Tuvalu and elsewhere will almost certainly revert to sandbars and then nothing. Although the people themselves will not go extinct, without their home islands to anchor them, their beliefs and identity probably will, scattered person by person across the rising waters, to places where they will learn to wear real shoes and eat frozen pork—until, like Atlantis, the name of Tuvalu fades into myth.

Analyze

1. The Tuvaluan prime minister claims, "Tuvaluans are blessed" (paragraph 5). Do you agree with him? What evidence in Whitty's essay supports his reasoning? What contradicts it?
2. What is the difficult choice that Tuvaluans have to make, according to Whitty? What does she think they should do?
3. Based on this reading, do you agree that Tuvaluans "are preparing to become a nation of *fakaalofa*"? Why or why not? Why does Whitty sense some shame in the Tuvaluans' "impending fakaalofa"?

Explore

1. Whitty wrote this essay more than ten years ago. What has changed since then? Research current facts on global warming, Tuvaluans' status as "global warming refugees," and Australia and the United States' current positions on global warming as they affect Tuvalu. What action has Tuvalu taken? Make an annotated bibliography of your sources, briefly summarizing the information you have gleaned. Write an introductory brief that contextualizes your annotated bibliography.
2. Whitty provides several competing points of view with regard to the effects of global warming on Tuvalu. Create a chart with the name, occupation, nationality, opinion, and rationale about global warming and any other distinguishing categories for each person she describes in her essay. What motivations and assumptions underscore each of these points of view? How does this clarify your initial reading?
3. Whitty takes a dark view of Tuvaluans who migrate to New Zealand, fearing that they will "doubtless learn to grow lawns" (paragraph 28). Do you agree that they will adapt a new culture's practices with the

land? Why or why not? How might New Zealanders be influenced by their new Tuvaluan neighbors' relationship to land?

Forging Connections

1. Afridi and the Tuvaluans in Whitty's article have different positions about identity and place. For Afridi, Pakistani identity can be a deep part of her even though she moved away when she was a child; the Tuvaluans, on the other hand, have a word in their language for land-less people that literally means "deserving of pity." What do you think? How does a place affect identity? How does identity—of a nation, group, or individual—affect a place?

2. The authors in this chapter write about place and identity in different ways. Compare, for example, the pieces by Afridi and Iyer with those by Nobel and Hill. Do you think the writing itself has a way of shaping the writers' experience of place and identity? Why or why not? Write an exploratory essay in which you look as carefully at the approaches and styles of writing in this chapter as you do to the themes and ideas they generate. What have you discovered about the writers themselves?

Looking Further

1. Throughout this book that focuses on globalization as a theme, authors write about places they've visited in different roles—as jour-nalists, scholars, tourists, activists, and explorers—and places they've known since birth. Choose four authors from the other chapters whose points of view conjure distinct sensibilities of identity and place. With others in your class, create a transcript, a series of blog posts, or a series of tweets that document a panel discussion featuring the four authors. Cast one of the authors from this chapter (e.g., Iyer, Nobel, Afridi, Hill, or Whitty) as the moderator. The panel discussion should be on the topic of identity and place, and each of the author's responses should reflect the style and point of view you've observed in his or her writing.

2. Iyer writes, "Yet the very process of feverish cross-communication that is turning the world into a single polyglot multiculture is producing

new kinds of Lonely Places." Would you agree that the process of globalization is turning the world into a "single polyglot multiculture"? Why or why not? What evidence can you draw from the essays by Boroditsky and Leonard in chapter 4, "Languages in Contact," to test the validity of Iyer's assertion? What evidence can you draw from your own experience as a language user?

3 Body, Mind, & Spirit

W hat do you think about when you see the words "body," "mind," and "spirit" together? For some, they are separate entities that are fed, exercised, and shaped differently for different purposes. For others, mind, body, and spirit are abstractions of a unified self that is greater than the sum of its parts. One might categorize these views as Western and Eastern respectively. In our globalized era, how are these traditional Western and Eastern views of mind, body, and spirit melding, evolving, and even clashing as access to and engagement with cultural attitudes and knowledges become more accessible and necessary?

The readings in this chapter are not meant to represent an integrated vision of body, mind, and spirit in a globalized era; nor are they meant to expand your consciousness of the different ways in which people on this planet experience their bodies, minds, and spirits and the relationship among them. Rather, I chose these readings because each sheds light on conversations and topics that concern our most quotidian physical, cerebral, and spiritual experiences, and how those experiences are increasingly interpreted through a globalized lens.

Ann Fadiman's "Birth" contrasts traditional Hmong births with American hospital births. The idea of birth invites readers to step back and consider the ways we as humans can come into this world and how those around us—parents, doctors, shamans, priests, and teachers—will influence us as they define what is healthy or normal and what is diseased or harmful. But what happens when doctors, parents, priests, and shamans have different belief systems from each other? What collisions, insights, and possibly new ways of being emerge?

The themes explored in this chapter's readings provide opportunities for you as a writer to cast fresh perspectives and measured interpretations on universal topics related to our physical and nonphysical experiences. These include concepts about mental illness (in Latif Nasser's report on updating the *Diagnostic and Statistical Manual of Mental Disorders*), death (in Peter Manseau's thoughtful meditation on ethical treatment of the dead), and happiness (in Andrew Guest's contemplation of what he's observed about the pursuit of happiness—in the US and in Angola—in light of recent studies in the science of happiness). Notice also how mind, body, and spirit are invoked and interpreted in discussions about the changing economic and political implications of who does what kinds of physical labor (Dwoskin's "Why Americans Won't Do Dirty Jobs") and changing attitudes toward the things we carry—physically and otherwise (Golberg's "You Can Take It with You").

Anne Fadiman
"Birth"

Anne Fadiman is Francis Writer-in-Residence at Yale University, where she also teaches nonfiction writing. Her primary areas of interest are literary journalism, essay, memoir, and autobiography. The following selection is an excerpt from her book *The Spirit Catches You and You Fall Down: A Hmong Child, Her American Doctors, and the Collision of Two Cultures* (first edition published in 1997; 15th anniversary edition published in 2012 by Farrar, Straus and Giroux, LLC), which won the National Book Critics' Circle Award, the *Los Angeles Times* Book Prize for Current Interest, and the Salon Book Award. Often taught as a model of literary journalism, as well as a casebook for cross-cultural sensitivity, particularly in medical practices, *The Spirit Catches You and You Fall Down* examines the cultural, linguistic, and medical struggles of a Hmong family living in America. In this excerpt, Fadiman describes the birth of Lia, the 14th child born to Foua and Nao Kao Lee, and the only Lee child born in the US. Lia died at the age of 30 in August 2012.

How was your own birth shaped or affected by your family's rituals, customs, or ceremonies and/or the medical establishment?

If Lia Lee had been born in the highlands of northwest Laos, where her parents and twelve of her brothers and sisters were born, her mother would have squatted on the floor of the house that her father had built from ax-hewn planks thatched with bamboo and grass. The floor was dirt, but it was clean. Her mother, Foua, sprinkled it regularly with water to keep the dust down and swept it every morning and evening with a broom she had made of grass and bark. She used a bamboo dustpan, which she had also made herself, to collect the feces of the children who were too young to defecate outside, and emptied its contents in the forest. Even if Foua had been a less fastidious housekeeper, her newborn babies wouldn't have gotten dirty, since she never let them actually touch the floor. She remains proud to this day that she delivered each of them into her own hands, reaching between her legs to ease out the head and then letting the rest of the body slip out onto her bent forearms. No birth attendant was present, though if her throat became dry during labor, her husband, Nao Kao, was permitted to bring her a cup of hot water, as long as he averted his eyes from her body. Because Foua believed that moaning or screaming would thwart the birth, she labored in silence, with the exception of an occasional prayer to her ancestors. She was so quiet that although most of her babies were born at night, her older children slept undisturbed on a communal bamboo pallet a few feet away, and woke only when they heard the cry of their new brother or sister. After each birth, Nao Kao cut the umbilical cord with heated scissors and tied it with string. Then Foua washed the baby with water she had carried from the stream, usually in the early phases of labor, in a wooden and bamboo pack-barrel strapped to her back.

Foua conceived, carried, and bore all her children with ease, but had there been any problems, she would have had recourse to a variety of remedies that were commonly used by the Hmong, the hilltribe to which her family belonged. If a Hmong couple failed to produce children, they could call in a *txiv neeb*, a shaman who was believed to have the ability to enter a trance, summon a posse of helpful familiars, ride a winged horse over the twelve mountains between the earth and the sky, cross an ocean inhabited by dragons, and (starting with bribes of food and money and, if necessary, working up to a necromantic sword) negotiate for his patients' health with the spirits who lived in the realm of the unseen. A *txiv neeb* might be able to cure infertility by asking the couple to sacrifice a dog, a cat, a chicken, or a sheep. After the animal's throat was cut, the *txiv neeb* would string a rope bridge from the doorpost to the marriage bed, over which the soul of the couple's future baby, which had been detained by a malevolent spirit called a *dab*, could now freely travel to earth. One could also take certain precautions to avoid becoming infertile in the first place. For example, no Hmong woman of childbearing age would ever think of setting foot inside a cave, because a particularly unpleasant kind of *dab* sometimes lived there who liked to eat flesh and drink blood and could make his victim sterile by having sexual intercourse with her.

> "She labored in silence, with the exception of an occasional prayer to her ancestors."

Once a Hmong woman became pregnant, she could ensure the health of her child by paying close attention to her food cravings. If she craved ginger and failed to eat it, her child would be born with an extra finger or toe. If she craved chicken flesh and did not eat it, her child would have a blemish near its ear. If she craved eggs and did not eat them, her child would have a lumpy head. When a Hmong woman felt the first pangs of labor, she would hurry home from the rice or opium fields, where she had continued to work throughout her pregnancy. It was important to reach her own house, or at least the house of one of her husband's cousins, because if she gave birth anywhere else a *dab* might injure her. A long or arduous labor could be eased by drinking the water in which a key had been boiled, in order to unlock the birth canal; by having her family array bowls of sacred water around the room and chant prayers over them; or, if the difficulty stemmed from having treated an elder member of the family with insufficient respect, by washing the offended relative's fingertips and apologizing like crazy until the relative finally said, "I forgive you."

Soon after the birth, while the mother and baby were still lying together next to the fire pit, the father dug a hole at least two feet deep in the dirt floor and buried the placenta. If it was a girl, her placenta was buried under her parents' bed; if it was a boy, his placenta was buried in a place of greater honor, near the base of the house's central wooden pillar, in which a male spirit, a domestic guardian who held up the roof of the house and watched over its residents, made his home. The placenta was always buried with the smooth side, the side that had faced the fetus inside the womb, turned upward, since if it was upside down, the baby might vomit after nursing. If the baby's face erupted in spots, that meant the placenta was being attacked by ants underground, and boiling water was poured into the burial hole as an insecticide. In the Hmong language, the word for placenta means "jacket." It is considered one's first and finest garment. When a Hmong dies, his or her soul must travel back from place to place, retracing the path of its life geography, until it reaches the burial place of its placental jacket, and puts it on. Only after the soul is properly dressed in the clothing in which it was born can it continue its dangerous journey, past murderous *dabs* and giant poisonous caterpillars, around man-eating rocks and impassable oceans, to the place beyond the sky where it is reunited with its ancestors and from which it will someday be sent to be reborn as the soul of a new baby. If the soul cannot find its jacket, it is condemned to an eternity of wandering, naked and alone.

Because the Lees are among the 150,000 Hmong who have fled Laos 5 since their country fell to communist forces in 1975, they do not know if their house is still standing, or if the five male and seven female placentas that Nao Kao buried under the dirt floor are still there. They believe that half of the placentas have already been put to their final use, since four of their sons and two of their daughters died of various causes before the Lees came to the United States. The Lees believe that someday the souls of most of the rest of their family will have a long way to travel, since they will have to retrace their steps from Merced, California, where the family has spent fifteen of its seventeen years in this country; to Portland, Oregon, where they lived before Merced; to Honolulu, Hawaii, where their airplane from Thailand first landed; to two Thai refugee camps; and finally back to their home village in Laos.

The Lees' thirteenth child, Mai, was born in a refugee camp in Thailand. Her placenta was buried under their hut. Their fourteenth child, Lia, was born in the Merced Community Medical Center, a modern public hospital that serves an agricultural county in California's Central Valley, where many Hmong refugees have resettled. Lia's placenta was incinerated. Some Hmong women have asked the doctors at MCMC, as the hospital is commonly called, if they could take their babies' placentas home. Several of the doctors have acquiesced, packing the placentas in plastic bags or take-out containers from the hospital cafeteria; most have refused, in some cases because they have assumed that the women planned to eat the placentas, and have found that idea disgusting, and in some cases because they have feared the possible spread of hepatitis B, which is carried by at least fifteen percent of the Hmong refugees in the United States. Foua never thought to ask, since she speaks no English, and when she delivered Lia, no one present spoke Hmong. In any case, the Lees' apartment had a wooden floor covered with wall-to-wall carpeting, so burying the placenta would have been a difficult proposition.

When Lia was born, at 7:09 p.m. on July 19, 1982, Foua was lying on her back on a steel table, her body covered with sterile drapes, her genital area painted with a brown Betadine solution, with a high-wattage lamp trained on her perineum. There were no family members in the room. Gary Thueson, a family practice resident who did the delivery, noted in the chart that in order to speed the labor, he had artificially ruptured Foua's amniotic sac by poking it with a foot-long plastic "amni-hook"; that no anesthesia was used; that no episiotomy, an incision to enlarge the vaginal opening, was necessary; and that after the birth, Foua received a standard intravenous dose of Pitocin to constrict her uterus. Dr. Thueson also noted that Lia was a "healthy infant" whose weight, 8 pounds 7 ounces, and condition were "appropriate for gestational age" (an estimate he based on observation alone, since Foua had received no prenatal care, was not certain how long she had been pregnant, and could not have told Dr. Thueson even if she had known). Foua thinks that Lia was her largest baby, although she isn't sure, since none of her thirteen elder children were weighed at birth. Lia's Apgar scores, an assessment of a newborn infant's heart rate, respiration, muscle tone, color, and reflexes, were good: one minute after her birth she scored 7 on a scale of 10, and four minutes later she scored 9. When she was six minutes old, her color was described as "pink" and her activity as "crying." Lia was shown briefly to her mother. Then she was placed in a steel and Plexiglas warmer, where a nurse fastened a plastic identification band around her wrist and recorded her footprints by inking the soles of her feet with a stamp pad and pressing them against a Newborn Identification form. After that, Lia was removed to the central nursery, where she received an injection of Vitamin K in one of her thighs to prevent hemorrhagic disease; was treated with two drops of silver nitrate solution in each eye, to prevent an infection from gonococcal bacteria; and was bathed with Safeguard soap.

Foua's own date of birth was recorded on Lia's Delivery Room Record as October 6, 1944. In fact, she has no idea when she was born, and on various other occasions during the next several years she would inform MCMC personnel, through English-speaking relatives such as the nephew's wife who had helped her check into the hospital for Lia's delivery, that her date of birth was October 6, 1942, or, more frequently, October 6, 1926. Not a single admitting clerk ever appears to have questioned the latter date, though it would imply that Foua gave birth to Lia at the age of 55. Foua is quite sure, however, that October is correct, since she was told by her parents that she was born during the season in which the opium fields are weeded for the second time and the harvested rice stalks are stacked. She invented the precise day of the month, like the year, in order to satisfy the many Americans who have evinced an abhorrence of unfilled blanks on the innumerable forms the Lees have encountered since their admission to the United States in 1980. Most Hmong refugees are familiar with this American trait and have accommodated it in the same way. Nao Kao Lee has a first cousin who told the immigration officials that all nine of his children were born on July 15, in nine consecutive years, and this information was duly recorded on their resident alien documents.

When Lia Lee was released from MCMC, at the age of three days, her mother was asked to sign a piece of paper that read:

> I certify that during the discharge procedure I received my baby, examined it and determined that it was mine. I checked the Ident-A-Band* parts sealed on the baby and on me and found that they were identically numbered 5043 and contained correct identifying information.

Since Foua cannot read and has never learned to recognize Arabic numerals, it is unlikely that she followed these instructions. However, she had been asked for her signature so often in the United States that she had mastered the capital forms of the seven different letters contained in her name,

Foua Yang. (The Yangs and the Lees are among the largest of the Hmong clans; the other major ones are the Chas, the Chengs, the Hangs, the Hers, the Kues, the Los, the Mouas, the Thaos, the Vues, the Xiongs, and the Vangs. In Laos, the clan name came first, but most Hmong refugees in the United States use it as a surname. Children belong to their father's clan; women traditionally retain their clan name after marriage. Marrying a member of one's own clan is strictly taboo.) Foua's signature is no less legible than the signatures of most of MCMC's resident physicians-in-training, which, particularly if they are written toward the end of a twenty-four-hour shift, tend to resemble EEGs. However, it has the unique distinction of looking different each time it appears on a hospital document. On this occasion, FOUAYANG was written as a single word. One A is canted to the left and one to the right, the Y looks like an X, and the legs of the N undulate gracefully, like a child's drawing of a wave.

10   It is a credit to Foua's general equanimity, as well as her characteristic desire not to think ill of anyone, that although she found Lia's birth a peculiar experience, she has few criticisms of the way the hospital handled it. Her doubts about MCMC in particular, and American medicine in general, would not begin to gather force until Lia had visited the hospital many times. On this occasion, she thought the doctor was gentle and kind, she was impressed that so many people were there to help her, and although she felt that the nurses who bathed Lia with Safeguard did not get her quite as clean as she had gotten her newborns with Laotian stream water, her only major complaint concerned the hospital food. She was surprised to be offered ice water after the birth, since many Hmong believe that cold foods during the postpartum period make the blood congeal in the womb instead of cleansing it by flowing freely, and that a woman who does not observe the taboo against them will develop itchy skin or diarrhea in her old age. Foua did accept several cups of what she remembers as hot black water. This was probably either tea or beef broth; Foua is sure it wasn't coffee, which she had seen before and would have recognized. The black water was the only MCMC-provided food that passed her lips during her stay in the maternity ward. Each day, Nao Kao cooked and brought her the diet that is strictly prescribed for Hmong women during the thirty days following childbirth: steamed rice, and chicken boiled in water with five special postpartum herbs (which the Lees had grown for this purpose on the edge of the parking lot behind their apartment building). This diet was familiar to the doctors on the Labor and Delivery floor at MCMC, whose assessments

of it were fairly accurate gauges of their general opinion of the Hmong. One obstetrician, Raquel Arias, recalled, "The Hmong men carried these nice little silver cans to the hospital that always had some kind of chicken soup in them and always smelled great." Another obstetrician, Robert Small, said, "They always brought some horrible stinking concoction that smelled like the chicken had been dead for a week." Foua never shared her meals with anyone, because there is a postpartum taboo against spilling grains of rice accidentally into the chicken pot. If that occurs, the newborn is likely to break out across the nose and cheeks with little white pimples whose name in the Hmong language is the same as the word for "rice."

Some Hmong parents in Merced have given their children American names. In addition to many standard ones, these have included Kennedy, Nixon, Pajama, Guitar, Main (after Merced's Main Street), and, until a nurse counseled otherwise, Baby Boy, which one mother, seeing it written on her son's hospital papers, assumed was the name the doctor had already chosen for him. The Lees chose to give their daughter a Hmong name, Lia. Her name was officially conferred in a ceremony called a *hu plig*, or soul-calling, which in Laos always took place on the third day after birth. Until this ceremony was performed, a baby was not considered to be fully a member of the human race, and if it died during its first three days it was not accorded the customary funerary rites. (This may have been a cultural adaptation to the fifty-percent infant mortality rate, a way of steeling Hmong mothers against the frequent loss of their babies during or shortly after childbirth by encouraging them to postpone their attachment.) In the United States, the naming is usually celebrated at a later time, since on its third day a baby may still be hospitalized, especially if the birth was complicated. It took the Lee family about a month to save enough money from their welfare checks, and from gifts from their relatives' welfare checks, to finance a soul-calling party for Lia.

Although the Hmong believe that illness can be caused by a variety of sources—including eating the wrong food, drinking contaminated water, being affected by a change in the weather, failing to ejaculate completely during sexual intercourse, neglecting to make offerings to one's ancestors, being punished for one's ancestors' transgressions, being cursed, being hit by a whirlwind, having a stone implanted in one's body by an evil spirit master, having one's blood sucked by a *dab*, bumping into a *dab* who lives in a tree or a stream, digging a well in a *dab*'s living place, catching sight of a dwarf female *dab* who eats earthworms, having a *dab* sit on one's chest

2. Research at least one other culture's birth rituals. In the contrast that Fadiman shows between a birth in Laos and a birth in the United States, what might those in developed countries learn from practices in developing countries like Laos?

3. Write an essay in which you reimagine Lia's birth at the hospital, including Foua and Nao Kao's experience. The essay can be in narrative form—telling the story of the birth—that demonstrates how the medical team made culturally sensitive decisions that took into consideration Hmong beliefs. Based on your narrative, include your interpretation of what Western medical doctors would learn from the Lees, and what the Lees might learn about Western beliefs.

Latif Nasser
"Do Some Cultures Have Their Own Ways of Going Mad?"

A native of Ontario, Canada, and a graduate of Dartmouth College, Latif Nasser is a Ph.D. student in the history of science at Harvard. He is a writer and a blogger for the public radio program *Radiolab*, where "the boundaries blur between science, philosophy, and human experience." "Do Some Cultures Have Their Own Ways of Going Mad?" appeared January 8, 2012, in the *Boston Globe,* a daily newspaper owned by the *New York Times* Company. In this article, Nasser examines the notion of "culture-bound illness" and the debate over whether diagnosis in Western psychiatry is truly "culture-free."

Do you think it's possible for different cultures to have their own "ways of going mad"?

Anyone who follows psychiatry has noticed that the field is now in the midst of a debate that galvanizes its members every 10 to 20 years. At the center of the hubbub is psychiatry's most sacred text: the Diagnostic and Statistical Manual of Mental Disorders.

The DSM, for short, is a compendium of over 350 ways our minds can fail us, from autism to kleptomania to voyeurism. What makes it onto the list matters: The DSM's definition of "mental illness" can dictate whether an insurance company covers a treatment, or even whether a murderer is fit to stand trial. With the American Psychiatric Association gearing up to revamp the manual for the first time since 1994, mental health specialists have begun jostling over some of the most divisive issues in the field: whether someone mourning the death of a loved one can be justifiably treated for depression, for instance, or whether overdiagnosis and a black market demand for Adderall have trumped up a false ADHD epidemic.

And then there's the back of the book.

If you turn to page 898 of the current edition—past the glossary and the alphabetical index of diagnoses—you'll find a list of 25 little-known illnesses. These are the "culture-bound syndromes": mental illnesses that psychiatrists officially acknowledge occur only within a particular society. Take, for instance, susto—a distinctly Latin American fear that one's soul has panicked and left one's body. Or pibloktoq, also known as "arctic hysteria," in which Greenlandic Inuit strip off all their clothes and run out into the subzero Arctic tundra.

Depending on whom you ask, the notion that some cultures have their own ways of going crazy is either the ultimate in cultural sensitivity or the ultimate in Western condescension. And although these syndromes haven't attracted nearly as much attention as Asperger's or binge eating disorder, they are starting to come under fire from critics who don't think that the appendix belongs in the book at all. Since the last edition of the DSM, in lectures and research journal articles around the world, a cluster of psychiatrists, anthropologists, and historians has attacked the validity of specific disorders on the list. To these critics, the very notion of a "culture-bound illness" is an outdated relic from the days of European empires.

"A group of us think that the time has come to abandon it," says Dr. Dinesh Bhugra, the Indian-British president-elect of the World Psychiatric Association, an umbrella organization representing more than 200,000 psychiatrists in 117 different countries.

Partly in response to the critics, the DSM's editorial task force has convened a special committee of 20 advisers to figure out what to do with the category. Helming the committee is Dr. Roberto Lewis-Fernández, a clinical psychiatry professor at Columbia University who helped write the appendix nearly 20 years ago.

What to do with the appendix, however, is proving a thorny problem to solve. It's not because no one is sure whether pibloktoq is a real thing, although that's an open question. It's because the whole debate turns on an issue that psychiatry itself has yet to agree on: how much mental illnesses are a manifestation of the cultures in which they arise. And whether, when it comes to how culture and human psychology intersect, it's time to start seeing the West as a culture too.

The notion of a culturally specific disorder dates back to 1950s Hong Kong, where a British-trained psychiatrist named Pow Meng Yap found himself growing frustrated: The complaints he was hearing from his local patients in Hong Kong didn't always match up with the descriptions in the standard psychiatric textbooks he had studied. In 1951, he published an article titled "Mental Diseases Peculiar to Certain Cultures," in which he attempted to document ailments from far-flung corners of the colonial world, disorders that most Western psychiatrists had never encountered.

10   Collecting illnesses for his list, Yap drew on florid accounts written by anthropologists and psychiatrists around the turn of the last century. For instance, he mentioned three illnesses from colonial Malaya (now Malaysia): amok, an amnesiac homicidal spree which gave us the phrase "to run amuck"; latah, in which a startled victim falls into a trance and mimics or obeys anybody around her; and koro, the fear that one's genital organs are retracting into one's body, and that this will eventually lead to death. Yap himself was the first to admit that existing literature on these illnesses was a jumble, part observation, part "common prejudice." But if psychiatry didn't start looking at non-Western cultures, he argued, the field could never fully understand the human mind.

The first edition of the DSM, published the year after Yap's paper, never mentioned culture. Nor did its 1968 second edition. The notion crept into the 1980 third edition by way of a bureaucratic disclaimer: "Culture-specific symptoms . . . may create difficulties in the use of the DSM-III-R [either] because the psychopathology is unique to that culture or because the DSM-III-R categories are not based on extensive research with non-Western populations."

Then came the 1980s. Paradoxically, at a time when the manual was increasingly being adopted overseas as the ultimate arbiter of psychological truth, it was coming under fire in America. Critics charged it was too much a product of its own time and place—for example, it had labeled homosexuality a mental illness in earlier editions, and included a version of the possibly faddish premenstrual syndrome in later ones. At the same time, from all over the world, a critical mass of new practitioners was emerging who combined psychiatric expertise with training in anthropology. Many of these doctors worked in cultures previously unrepresented in the field, and they lobbied the American Psychiatric Association to give more space to the cultural diversity of mental illness.

The result was a seven-page appendix to the current edition of the DSM, published in 1994. After an essay advising practitioners "how to deal with culture in a clinical setting," the appendix lists all manner of conditions specific to locales such as Iran, Haiti, Korea, and Mexico.

One illness on the list is dhat syndrome, particular to the Indian subcontinent. Indian men report a vast array of symptoms—among them headaches, forgetfulness, and constipation—that they attribute to a lack of vital fluid, namely, semen. Patients may blame the semen loss on excessive sexual activity, masturbation, nocturnal emissions, or even loss through urine.

West African university students are mentioned as susceptible to brain fag ("fag" being old slang for fatigue). As first described in 1958, a young Nigerian male tired from "too much study" could spontaneously lose the ability to read. In addition, sufferers have complained of a burning scalp, blurred vision, and even sexual dysfunction (one student inadvertently experienced an orgasm during an exam). The Canadian psychiatrist who coined the diagnosis speculated that the syndrome was "an unconscious rejection of the education system."

Mediterranean peoples are wary of mal de ojo, or "the evil eye," which can prompt crying without apparent cause. In Cape Verde, sangue dormido, or "sleeping blood," can be blamed for paralysis, blindness, and even miscarriage. A culturally distinctive phobia in Japan is taijin kyofusho, a fear that one's appearance, odor, or movements will displease, embarrass, and offend other people.

Looking at the list of illnesses today, just 18 years after it was published, one can barely recognize the original impulse behind it. What once seemed to be a triumph for the forces of inclusivity now looks like a ghetto—or, as critics have called it, a "museum of exotica."

What has also struck some critics, though, is that some of these supposedly exotic disorders appear strangely familiar, if you look hard enough. Bhugra, who is also former dean of the Royal College of Psychiatrists, points out that 19th-century Americans had their own version of dhat—a semen loss anxiety that led, in part, to the development of health foods like Kellogg's corn flakes and Graham's crackers, whose inventors created their products as panacea for ills caused by, among other things, masturbation.

Nigerian-British psychiatrist Oyedeji Ayonrinde has similarly found an American wave of brain fag—the phrase was such a household term between 1890 and 1920 that the Chicago Tribune called it "the disease of the century." Quack cures proliferated around the country: thermal baths, a "brain fag pillow," even an electric hairbrush invented at Stanford University.

20   So what's really going on here? Is brain fag a universal phenomenon draped in West African garb, or is it a unique condition that only appears when the right cultural circumstances align?

The question gets to the heart of a debate in psychiatry about what mental illness really is. In one camp are specialists who see underlying mental disorders, whether they're caused by experience or biology, as universal. In the shadow of Sigmund Freud, many psychiatrists in the 20th century argued that basic human experiences shaped our psychological states—say, a child's relationship with his father. The past few decades of psychiatry have seen a powerful shift toward looking for biological causes like mutated genes, faulty brain wiring, and chemical imbalances. But these, too, would theoretically appear in humans all over the world.

If underlying mental illness is universal, then what looks like a "culture-bound syndrome" is likely to be a common problem that happens to show up differently in different settings. In this way of thinking, susto, or "soul loss," could be seen as just a Hispanic way of describing what Americans know as plain old depression. "Actually, [culture-bound syndromes] aren't really different," says Ayonrinde, who also lectures at the University of London, and has spoken out against the idea that "brain fag" is a specifically African problem. "They're all variations of somatic disorders, depression, anxiety disorders, and not really anything new."

However, there's another way to see the relationship between culture and mental health. A different group of thinkers—including, most prominently, cultural psychiatrists—sees culture as doing more than just giving different names to universal mental disorders. Culture doesn't just shape what a mentally ill person calls his or her illness, they argue—it determines what counts as illness in the first place.

"Culture tells us what is normal, what is abnormal, what is deviant, what is not deviant, and where you seek help from," says Bhugra.

If this is true—if it's culture that decides what's "crazy" and what's rea- 25
sonable behavior—then there may be no such thing as an illness that isn't
culture-bound. It's not that a handful of disorders no longer belong in a
cultural appendix; it's that perhaps they all do.

Lewis-Fernández and his team are now drafting their recommendations
for how the DSM should handle "culture-bound syndromes" in the next
edition. They suggest that a shorter appendix remain, winnowed down to a
handful of well-documented problems. They'd also like a stronger statement about culture's role in mental illness in the introduction, and the
disorders mentioned in the DSM itself. (Whether or not the editors of the
DSM-5 ultimately include the panel's suggestions is yet to be seen.)

What is not on the table yet—and considering that the DSM is ultimately published by American psychiatrists, may never be—is a deeper
acknowledgment that far more mental illnesses might be cultural than
we currently think. After all, commonly cited Western syndromes like
multiple personality disorder or anorexia nervosa are rarer in non-Western
countries, and yet the 1994 manual includes no British or American syndromes in its "culture-bound" category.

To put them there now, Lewis-Fernández says, would be "politically
unfeasible." But for many in the global psychiatry community, that argument is already over: It's time for Westerners to realize that their mental
illnesses might be, one way or another, just as much a local product as
pibloktoq.

"Diagnosis, we think, is culture-free," Bhugra says. "But it's not."

Analyze

1. The DSM is written by the American Psychiatric Association. Why
   would an American association's determination of culture-bound
   mental illnesses be important in a globalized context?

2. What do you think Nasser means when he writes, "when it comes to
   how culture and human psychology intersect, it's time to start seeing
   the West as a culture too"? In what ways do you think it's possible to
   define the West as its own culture? In what ways do you think the
   West might have multiple cultures?

3. How might health insurance companies and legal systems be affected
   in a globalized world in which diverse beliefs and cultures are increasingly in contact with each other?

Explore

1. Nasser writes, "If this is true—if it's culture that decides what's 'crazy' and what's reasonable behavior—then there may be no such thing as an illness that isn't culture-bound." Write an essay in which you consider the implications for treating mental illnesses in increasingly globalized communities. Begin by identifying and describing a behavior or symptom that could be considered either culture-bound "crazy" or "reasonable" behavior.

2. Consider that "dhat" and "brain fag" were once "ailments" that prompted so-called cures in the West in the form of corn flakes and thermal baths respectively. What "cures" have been developed for more modern ailments having to do with, for example, attention problems or lack of sunlight? What might be the implications about how we as a global community understand our minds?

3. Choose a country with a large immigrant population and research its mental health diagnosis practices. How have those practices been challenged by (a) their immigrant population's belief systems and (b) their own assumptions about mental health? Show your findings in a PowerPoint presentation.

Andrew Guest
"Pursuing the Science of Happiness"

Andrew Guest is an assistant professor of social and behavioral sciences at the University of Portland. He spent two years as a Peace Corps volunteer in the Republic of Malawi and six years conducting field research in the Republic of Angola. Guest's primary interests are culture and childhood, specifically child development in diverse and marginalized communities. "Pursuing the Science of Happiness" was published in the Fall/Winter 2010 edition of *Oregon Humanities*, a triannual magazine published by an independent, nonprofit affiliate of the National Endowment for the Humanities that seeks to "provide a forum for individuals and communities to raise questions, challenge assumptions, listen to others, and think critically about the issues that directly affect their lives and those of the people around them."

In this article, Guest contemplates a timeless philosophical concern—what it means to be happy—and explores what makes the pursuit of happiness at once interesting and complex.

How do you define happiness?

"I just want to be happy."

It sounds like such a simple, noble goal. When I overhear it in discussions by the generally earnest and well-meaning college students I teach, my first reaction is to think that worries about rampant materialism among today's youth are vastly overstated. But my second, more considered reaction is to wonder what they mean. Being happy, I want to tell them, is much more complicated than it sounds.

That considered reaction, that hesitation about a most American ideal—the inalienable right to "the pursuit of happiness"—is born primarily from my work as an academic psychologist. But the reason I do that work in Oregon is born of my own pursuit of happiness: Portland seemed like a place I could be happy. It may be a little out of the way for academia, but it's got a good quality of life—the trees are green, the coffee is rich, the ethos is a certain type of friendly. After six years here I sometimes think that has worked out. Sometimes.

I have, of course, had many happy moments in Oregon. The clichés have proven true: I've enjoyed beautiful mountain vistas, engaged with good friends and loving family, savored a fine meal accompanied by a hearty microbrew, felt part of conversations that might somehow contribute to a better community. Portland has even been good for idiosyncratic things, such as my soccer addiction: when the Timbers slice another slab off the victory log, it makes me happy. But am I a happier person?

My answer to that question is inevitably biased by some of my research   5 experiences. About a decade ago I spent the end of my graduate school years searching for happiness in unlikely places, including Angolan refugee camps. Ostensibly I was doing a dissertation in developmental psychology and focusing on the distinct cultural roles of play, games, and sports for children in marginalized communities. But implicitly, in the guise of social science, I was trying to figure out what it means to be happy—I was fascinated by the relationships between human psychology and the circumstances of our lives.

At the time, Angola was a paragon of bad circumstances; it was rated by the United Nations Children's Fund as the "worst place in the world to be a child" thanks to a twenty-seven-year civil war, decimated health care and education systems, and massive income inequality. The camps were hard-scrabble patches of ruby red dirt and quasi-permanent mud-brick homes, teeming with families bereft of tangible opportunities. And yet, when I asked the refugee youths in formal surveys about their psychological well-being, more than three quarters reported being generally happy. This is not meant to romanticize poverty, because the people I worked with were de-cidedly unhappy with their objectively dismal material realities. They wanted real schools, decent shelter, and opportunities for their parents and their future. They deserved a life expectancy beyond fifty years and the power to choose what they would do with their lives. But they did not nec-essarily internalize those problems; on a day-to-day basis they played with their friends, laughed with their siblings, and lived their lives. They found ways to feel happy.

Ironically, at that point in my life I was not sure how I would rate my own happiness. I was a lonely graduate student pining over a distant, ill-fated relationship and wracked with anxiety about whether I had any future in academia. I'm usually not an early riser, but during my six months in Angola I regularly woke at 4:00 in a lukewarm sweat only to stare for hours at the gritty white mesh of my mosquito net, listening to the spas-modic traffic in Luanda's old town. I genuinely appreciated the experience, and I felt deeply engaged with the research and the community, but I couldn't wait to leave. I wanted to settle in a place like Oregon to teach classes full of earnest and well-meaning college students eager to discuss the psychology of happiness. And fortunately, for the sake of that discussion, no matter how hard it is to live the science, a large and growing body of research has offered me a few things to say.

The modern science of happiness often goes by the name "positive psy-chology" and presents itself as an evolution away from psychology's his-torical focus on dysfunction—a focus seeded by Freud and fed by a desire to help the mentally ill. As University of Pennsylvania psychology profes-sor Martin Seligman, the generally acknowledged founder of positive psy-chology, framed it in a 2004 conversation with the Edge Foundation, "In the same way I can claim unblushingly that psychology and psychiatry have decreased the tonnage of suffering in the world, my aim is that psychology and maybe psychiatry will increase the tonnage of happiness in the world."

The core belief of positive psychology as a field is that science will lead the way. In the last decade new peer-reviewed scientific journals of happiness studies and positive psychology have appeared, which mostly dispense with the anecdotes and intuitions of self-help gurus. Institutions such as the august University of Pennsylvania have started offering degrees in applied positive psychology, and organizations such as the Templeton Foundation have invested millions of dollars in grants, conferences, and awards.

Amidst this flurry of modern science, however, lies a classical challenge: 10
there is no widespread agreement about how to define happiness. In fact, some contemporary psychologists go back to ancient Greek philosophic debates about hedonia and eudaimonia. In the 2001 *Annual Review of Psychology*, for example, Richard Ryan and Edward Deci contrasted contemporary scholarship taking "the hedonic approach," which focuses more on measuring subjective feelings of pleasure, with "the eudaimonic approach," which emphasizes the satisfactions of a meaningful life and self-realization.

Each approach tells us something about the human experience of happiness, but each has its limitations. The hedonic approach, for example, risks seeming superficial, while the eudaimonic approach risks unfair value judgments. From a research perspective, how can I decide whether someone's life is meaningful? In most cases researchers get around the thorny problem of judging meaningful happiness by keeping their measures as general as possible. The most common measures of what scholars call "subjective well-being" or "subjective happiness" essentially just ask people to define it for themselves, responding on a scale of 1 to 7 to prompts such as, "In general, I consider myself not a very happy person" (1) to "In general, I consider myself a very happy person" (7). A researcher can then aggregate results and suggest variables that do and do not correlate with happiness.

What those results rarely report is that most people in most places subjectively perceive themselves to be reasonably happy. For example, in her book *The How of Happiness*, University of California psychology professor Sonja Lyubomirsky mentions in passing, amidst various prescriptions for becoming happier, that the average adult scores around 5.6 on her 7-point scale; college students score lower—only around 5 out of 7.

What's more, our subjective perceptions of happiness don't tend to change much over time—even when our lives change dramatically. In one oft-cited 1978 study, for example, researchers from Northwestern University interviewed people at two extremes: people who had won the lottery and people who had been paralyzed in accidents. The point of the study was that, when asked, people in those groups agreed that the initial events had made a great difference in their lives: winning the lottery was joyful, becoming paralyzed was agonizing. But after six months or a year, the events seemed to make little difference. The lottery winners had settled into new stresses and burdens; they took less pleasure in the mundane realities of daily life. The people who had been paralyzed gradually found new satisfactions, challenges, and opportunities. They were nostalgic about the past, but also optimistic about the future. People in both groups adapted.

Combining the results of that study with findings from more recent research, Harvard psychologist Daniel Gilbert, in a 2004 TED conference talk, went so far as to say, "If it happened over three months ago, with a few exceptions, it has no impact on our happiness." This phenomenon has been much discussed and is occasionally controversial among psychologists, even garnering its own scientific-sounding name "hedonic adaptation," or sometimes, the "hedonic treadmill." The idea is that the more steps we take in our pursuit of happiness, the more we stay in the same place. There is, for example, an old newspaper poll finding that when you ask people making less than $30,000 per year how much income it would take to fulfill their dreams, they say $50,000. But when you ask people making just over $100,000 the same question, they say it would take $250,000. The technical terms for these ever-adjusting dreams are "relative deprivation" or "reference anxiety." The more human term is "jealousy." The end result is the same: we adapt.

15   Is this good news or bad news? Probably a bit of both. Our psychological ability to adapt means we can often cope better than we might expect with many of life's inevitable challenges, but it also means that our successes are more temporal than we might hope. When my team loses, it is never as devastating as I worry it might be, but when they win the joy is almost always fleeting.

In my mind, however, the most profound implication is what hedonic adaptation means for the pursuit of happiness over a lifetime. If I want to know how happy the students in my classes will be in twenty or thirty years, I could try to collect a lot of data: What will they do for a living? Will they fall in love? Have kids? Live in a vibrant community? Suffer tragedy? Make a lot of money? Have a fulfilling spiritual life? Make an artistic contribution? Cheer for the winning team? Get soft, wet kisses from a puppy?

I could try to learn about all that, but I don't need to. If I'm trying to make a statistical prediction of their future happiness, all I need to know is how happy they are now.

Researchers studying happiness sometimes talk about this phenomenon as a genetic "set point" for happiness, or perhaps a deeply rooted psychological dynamic—an emotional predisposition around which we vary from time to time, but to which we usually return. The idea of living in Oregon may have once made me happy, but based on my own predispositions, I might as well be back in Illinois or (shiver) Ohio.

Fortunately, however, the story is not quite that simple: the set point is, if anything, a set range within which there is much room for negotiation. As such, positive psychologists such as Sonja Lyubomirsky assert that although something around half of our happiness is determined by hard-wired dispositions, another forty percent is shaped by voluntary activities. Of course, that means a mere ten percent is down to the circumstances of our lives. In fact, in my reading, the science of happiness has as much to say about what is not likely to make us happy as what is.

Take money, for example. The voluminous (and sometimes controversial) research on wealth suggests that having more money correlates with happiness only up to a point. Being very poor creates hardships that can affect well-being, and having enough money to satisfy basic needs is important. But beyond a certain point (which seems to vary according to relative standards in different communities and cultures), more money seems to have little to do with happiness. In fact, according to statistics reported by Nobel prize-winning economist Daniel Kahneman and his colleagues, more than 80 percent of Americans at all income levels report being either "pretty happy" or "very happy."

What about other circumstances idealized by the popular imagination as being keys to happiness: Youth? Beauty? Intelligence? No. Nope. Not really. There are certain social advantages to being young, beautiful, or smart, but happiness does not seem to be one of them. In fact, compelling evidence suggests that our psychological well-being is highest in old age because we've dropped the pretense of wanting to be more attractive or intelligent than we are. Older adults tend to be more accepting of themselves and, in some cases, that can override even the challenging physical health problems of aging.

One other provocative example of a life circumstance that seems to have little relationship to happiness is having children. In the popular

20

imagination, children are often the joy of their parents' lives, but the evidence suggests otherwise. In a phenomenon some scholars call the "parenting paradox," no matter how you measure it—looking at overall well-being, day-to-day emotional states, broader life satisfaction—people with children are no happier than people without children (unless, some research suggests, the childless people wanted to have children but couldn't). Children bring joys, but they also bring burdens and anxieties. The fact that we are convinced children will make us happy may just be another peculiar trick of human nature. As Daniel Gilbert explained to *Harvard Magazine,* "Imagine a species that figured out that children don't make you happy. . . . We have a word for that species: extinct. There is a conspiracy between genes and culture to keep us in the dark about the real sources of happiness."

Most of the modern science exploring the source of real happiness seems to come back to a formulation that Freud famously (and perhaps apocryphally) proposed a century ago: love and work. Love, in its broadest definition as healthy social relationships and meaningful interpersonal engagements, seems to matter. Social isolation is one of the best predictors of depression and other mental health problems. Being married and having friends, however, is one of the best predictors of well-being. There are many nuances to how love can play out in our lives, but at the most general level, being connected to people matters.

Work, in the sense of engaging with meaningful projects that offer reasonable degrees of challenge and a sense of purpose, also seems important. Work does not have to be a remunerative job—it can be family responsibilities, community volunteering, artistic projects, and the like. But at its best it allows us to cultivate our strengths and contribute to something larger than ourselves.

Other statistical correlates of happiness often seem to integrate a healthy balance of these broad categories. There is, for example, convincing evidence that religious people are happier than the nonreligious, but this may be because religion often involves interpersonal connections within a community and a larger sense of purpose for our lives. It may also be the case that religion does not so much make people happy as happy people tend to be attracted to religion—teasing out the causal nature of these relationships is always as much an art as it is a science.

The presence of fulfilling love and meaningful work may also be condu-   25
cive to the types of voluntary activities that positive psychologists like to
prescribe for those looking to increase their levels of happiness. Practices
such as showing gratitude to others, intentionally savoring small daily plea-
sures, and spending time in activities that use our personal strengths seem
to have a significant impact on how we subjectively feel about ourselves and
our lives.

So does this kind of descriptive science give us a road map to happiness?
Should I just tell my students to stay connected to the people they love,
worry a little less about money, find work that offers them a sense of purpose, think twice before having kids, go to church, and give thanks for their
blessings? Maybe I should—but I can't. It may just go back to that classical
challenge of defining happiness, but I don't think I sat in Angola pining to
settle down in a place like Oregon because I wanted to boost my "subjective
well-being." I moved here because I thought it would make for a good quality of life. And what constitutes good quality in our minds may not be the
same thing as happiness.

In fact, the positive psychology movement has begun to generate a vocal
cadre of detractors to accompany its many acolytes. Books such as *Against
Happiness* by English professor Eric Wilson offer different critiques,
but fundamentally agree that framing happiness as an ultimate goal seems
shallow. Here even my college students tend to agree. If I offer them a
hypothetical choice between a constant, slightly positive emotional state—
permanent moderate happiness—or the chance to experience a range of
emotions with higher highs and lower lows averaging out to less gross happiness, most (though not all) make what classic economics would consider
the irrational choice: they are willing to sacrifice some happiness for the
full range of human experience.

Yet, even if we could have it all, even if we recognize happiness as
dependent upon seemingly valorous statistical correlates such as healthy
relationships, purposeful work, and making meaningful contributions to
a community, there is room for critique. In fact, social critics including
Barbara Ehrenreich, in *Bright Sided: How Positive Thinking Is Undermining America*, and Chris Hedges, in *Empire of Illusion*, argue that positive
psychology and the modern pursuit of happiness are ultimately related to
some of the deepest problems of modern society. Do you think gaping economic inequalities, unjust wars, and ferocious un/underemployment are
problems? Don't worry, be happy.

I appreciate the critics' perspectives and worry that adopting the baser tenets of positive psychology can blind us individually to broader social problems, but I also can't help but think that criticizing the pursuit of happiness is an oversimplification. Indeed, I sometimes remind my students that the founding documents of our country pointedly do not suggest that happiness itself is an inalienable right—only its pursuit. So perhaps the pursuit is the thing. Perhaps in their vast wisdom the founders offered us the primary lesson of happiness: that it is a process rather than an outcome.

30   So when I overhear my students saying they "just want to be happy," I like to imagine that the new science of positive psychology can help them. As University of Virginia psychology professor Jonathan Haidt points out in *The Happiness Hypothesis*, the research on happiness ultimately distills into the wise words of Shakespeare: "There is nothing either good or bad, but thinking makes it so." And for me, I've come to realize, there are ways in which thinking itself makes me happy.

In perhaps a final irony of my research experience, I often reminisce happily about that angst-ridden experience in Angola. I recall long days of equatorial sun glistening off the distant Atlantic Ocean, crafting amateur Portuguese into conversations with Angolans who challenged me, with their strength amidst adversity, to separate psychological well-being from structural well-being. And I think about long days in Oregon classrooms with the Willamette River flowing in the distance, hoping for chances to convey those experiences to students in ways that might challenge them to reconsider what it means to "just be happy." Happiness, I want to tell them, is more complicated than it sounds—but it is also much more interesting.

Analyze

1. In a small group, discuss what you think Guest's students have in mind when he hears them saying that they "just want to be happy." What clues are in the text? What assumptions have you made? Why?

2. As you read this article, how did you picture the author? Create or find an image online that illustrates how you pictured Guest. As you and your classmates share images, compare and contrast his features. Do you think how you picture an author influences the way you read his or her writing?

3. In paragraph 7, the writer describes the surprising results of his formal survey of children in Angola in which he found that it's possible to be

happy with one's life despite "a paragon of bad circumstances." Describe how it has been possible for you or someone you've known (or someone you've read about) to be happy despite material or physical hardship.

Explore

1. Do you think that happiness might be culture-bound in ways that are similar to mental illness in Nasser's article? Or is it a universal across all cultures? In either case, how might a globalized world affect individual, national, and cultural ideas of the "pursuit of happiness"?

2. Look up and analyze the use of the phrase "the pursuit of happiness" in the US founding documents. What do you think were the founding fathers' intentions about the pursuit of happiness? Were they thinking of a "hedonic approach" or a "eudaimonic approach"? Based on your experience, how have their intentions been interpreted?

3. Guest notes that critics of "positive psychology" like Hedges and Ehrenreich consider it and the pursuit of happiness to be *causes of* rather than *solutions to* society's deepest problems. Research other perspectives on the study of happiness, and write an essay that considers the possibility of being *both* happy and aware of others' suffering.

Peter Manseau
"Plasticize Me"

Peter Manseau is a doctoral candidate in religion at Georgetown University and the Patrick Henry Writing Fellow at the C. V. Starr Center for the Study of the American Experience at Washington College in Chestertown, Maryland. His essay "Plasticize Me" appeared in the March 2, 2011 edition of *Guernica*, an award-winning magazine of journalism, art, poetry, and fiction whose contributors come from dozens of different countries and write in almost as many languages. In his essay, Manseau considers the ethical treatment of the dead in light of the popular touring exhibition "Bodies," which uses preserved human corpses dissected and displayed for supposedly educational and artistic purposes. The exhibit has raised ethical and human-rights concerns, especially as all the corpses come from China. Manseau considers those ethical issues as he examines the science of human tissue preservation and its impact on Eastern and Western views of religion, death, and burial.

What traditions, rites, or rituals does your own family or culture practice when someone dies?

Questions concerning the ethical treatment of the dead have been with us at least since Sophocles, for whom a single act of leaving a corpse unburied brought mayhem that threatened the stability of society. In *Antigone*, the punishment King Creon gives to the murdered Polynices is so severe that it extends beyond the limits of life. According to Polynices's sister Antigone, death is only the beginning of the torments a body can face: "As for the hapless corpse of Polynices, it has been published to the town that none shall entomb him or mourn, but leave him unwept, unsepulchred, a welcome store for the birds, as they espy him, to feast on at will."

For Sophocles, to leave the dead unburied is an insult not just to the deceased or his family, but to the gods. That proper treatment should be given to human remains, Antigone insists, is among "the unwritten and unfailing statutes of heaven." She defies the state and risks her life in the attempt to see these statutes carried out, and calls upon others to do the same, even asking her reluctant sister, "Will you aid this hand to lift the dead?"

It's difficult to imagine how Antigone's plight might play out today. For those with the savings or the life insurance settlement to pay for it, there are any number of ways of dealing with human remains that are considered acceptable, and in every case the state requires, rather than prevents, some form of timely and permanent removal. Burial, cremation, resomation, organ donation, "whole body gifts" to science; all have become legitimate options. Although it is common for the preferred means of disposing of an individual's remains to be stated before death, often the method is chosen by the family of the deceased. In either case, there are few ethical concerns. Though a corpse has no autonomy, the treatment it receives, if carried out in accordance with specified wishes, can be seen as the last act of the will.

In just the past few years, however, new concerns have begun to arise concerning what it means to treat the dead ethically, and whether or not it is even possible to do so. Advances in technologies of tissue preservation—from cryogenics to chemical reduction to the injection of silicone polymers at the cellular level—have introduced unprecedented possibilities for the uses of human cadavers just as global markets have opened apparently limitless sources of bodies, creating tissue processing industries that never before existed. Corpses have always been commodities—even Saint Augustine complained of entrepreneurial monks roaming the countryside "hawking the limbs of the martyrs"—but never before has both the supply and the demand been so great.

Nowhere is this more apparent than in a wildly popular anatomy exhibit   5 currently touring the world. "Bodies . . . The Exhibition" is a for-profit traveling display of human cadavers that have been treated with a process that plasticizes tissue, allowing them to be manipulated and viewed in various states of artful dismemberment. Ostensibly the exhibition is scientific and educational in character, but given that there are no longer many mysteries within human anatomy, the most pressing questions it raises are ethical: Is posing a dead man with a tennis racket wrong? Is a failure to make specific provisions for the treatment of one's remains the same as giving one's body to science? Does the education offered by an anatomy exhibit offer the same kind of public good as organ donation? To put all this in the simplest and starkest terms: What are the dead for?

The use of humans as material is rarely simple or stark, however. "Bodies . . . The Exhibition" is produced by a Georgia-based company primarily for American and European audiences, but the human remains featured have come exclusively from the People's Republic of China, a nation and a culture that has its own history of ethical and religious reflection on the body. With this in mind, it must be asked if the questions such displays raise—questions that seem to Western audiences to arise naturally—are the appropriate questions. There are any number of ways in which Chinese notions of death differ from those held by Europeans and Americans. So whose conception of the body matters more, that of the Western living or the Eastern dead?

In every one of its scores of appearances, "Bodies . . . The Exhibition" has begun with a disclaimer. The exhibit about to be seen, a small placard reads, is in no way related to its chief rival in the world of anatomical exhibitions, "Body Worlds," or to other works conceived and managed by "Body

Worlds" founder Dr. Gunther von Hagens. The genealogy of these two anatomical education franchises, and the resulting competition between them, is inseparable from the ethical questions raised by each.

Von Hagens, a German physician turned entrepreneur and showman, is not only the originator of this new form of anatomical education, he is also the inventor of the process that makes it possible. Both "Bodies . . . The Exhibition" and "Body Worlds" make use of a new technology von Hagens calls "Plastination," by which all water is removed from human tissues and replaced with soft silicone polymers. ("Bodies . . . The Exhibition," it should be noted, uses the term "polymer preservation" to describe an identical process. "Plastination" as such is patented and trademarked by von Hagens for specific use of "Body Worlds" and its affiliates.) A macabre detail included in the story von Hagens tells of the development of this process hints at the ethical questions that were to come: He first thought of creating perfectly preserved cross-sections of human bodies when he was at a sandwich shop one day watching a butcher run a ham through an electric slicer. It was a flash of inspiration that foreshadowed the dehumanization of the bodies that would follow, for after the Plastination process is complete, von Hagens no longer calls them dead bodies, or corpses, or cadavers, but rather "plasti-nates." ("Bodies . . . The Exhibition," again, uses an alternate term, prefer-ring the untrademarked but equally impersonal "specimen.")

Terminology aside, the exhibits are nearly indistinguishable. Filled with displays of human remains that clearly required as much artistry as techni-cal ability to construct, each presents an average of twenty full corpses and hundreds of other disembodied parts arranged in a manner suggestive of a life-sized, three-dimensional anatomy text book. In each exhibit, corpses are made to throw footballs, stand on balance beams, even dance with their own entrails. The source of this similarity is neither an accident nor a mys-tery: "Bodies . . . The Exhibition" was founded by a former employee of von Hagens.

10   The main difference between the exhibits, it turns out, is ethical. More precisely, it is a matter of differing levels of attention to the practice, and the rhetoric, of ethics as it applies to the treatment of the dead. "Body Worlds" goes to great lengths to explain that every one of its "plastinates" was the willed gift of an individual, mostly from Europe, who had pre-arranged to donate his or her body for the use of scientific study or education. "Bodies . . . The Exhibition," on the other hand, makes no such assertion. It acknowl-edges that its bodies come exclusively from China, and that they had

formerly been in the possession of the Chinese government because they had died in hospitals with no kin to take responsibility for their disposal. As chief medical adviser for "Bodies . . . The Exhibition" Dr. Roy Glover told National Public Radio, "They're unclaimed. We don't hide from it, we address it right up front."

Von Hagens, by contrast, is a tireless promoter of the ethical difference between his exhibits and the others. "All the copycat exhibitions are from China," he told the *New York Times*. "And they're all using unclaimed bodies."

His exhibition has been gaining attention by holding gatherings for those so taken by his process that they have been moved to sign up for Plastination themselves. After joining a donor list von Hagens claims includes seven thousand names, would-be plastinates must fill out a form that keeps the terms of their donation open-ended in some respects (one can cancel one's donation at any time), but frighteningly specific in others. The matters of agreement range from the practical ("I agree that laypeople be allowed to touch my plastinated body") to the aesthetic ("I agree that my body can be used for an anatomical work of art") to the ontological ("The body donor's own identity is altered during the anatomical preparation"). With each granting of consent, donors assert that autonomy extends beyond the end of life. They may not know precisely what pose they will find themselves in for eternity, but in choosing their methods of disposal, they do know they will never be unclaimed. In a sense, they have preemptively claimed themselves.

Claiming, it turns out, is a crucial element in understanding the ethics of the dead. It is perhaps equally important in both the culture in which the bodies are displayed and the culture from which they have come. However, there is a significant difference in each culture's ethical assumptions about who has the right to do the claiming.

To the extent that any single set of ethical precepts guides Western attitudes toward the treatment of the dead, it is undoubtedly Christian teaching. Roughly 75 percent of Americans are buried when they die (rather than disposed of by some other means), and though changes in religious opinions like the recent acceptance of cremation by the Roman Catholic Church are sure to alter that percentage slightly, it is unlikely that the cultural disposition toward burial will disappear any time soon. The main reason for this preference seems to be not that anyone relishes the idea of lowering a loved one into the ground, or of being so lowered oneself, but rather that there is widespread acceptance of the notion that, as summed up nicely by Baptist theologian Dr. Russell D. Moore, "For Christians, burial is not the disposal of a thing. It is caring for a person. . . . The body that remains still belongs to someone, someone we love, someone who will reclaim it one day."

15   In the Christian conception, the resurrection of the dead is not just a belief in a future event; it's a reality that has immediate implications. The fact that the body "belongs to someone" who will "reclaim it someday" removes the remains of the dead from the category of that which must be disposed of, and places them in a category closer to valuables that must be safeguarded for their owner's eventual return. In other words, the belief in the resurrection of the dead is a de facto declaration of enduring ownership of the body by the person who has died. Because the body does not lose its personhood, it remains its own possession.

However, as in *Antigone*, ownership is not the only factor to be considered. If scripture is viewed as the Christian's primary ethical guide, treatment of the dead is derived, at least in part, from divine command. The first biblical burial is depicted as an almost automatic act with the ground opening its mouth to receive the blood, and presumably the body, of the murdered Abel. Thereafter, it is always one human who buries another. First there is Sarah's burial mentioned above, then that of Abraham, whose sons laid him beside his wife. Later, Rachel dies and Jacob sets a pillar on her grave. When it comes time for Jacob to die, he makes it clear whose wishes are to be followed in the disposal of his body:

Bury me not, I pray thee, in Egypt. But I will lie with my fathers, and thou shalt carry me out of Egypt, and bury me in their burying place. (Gen. 47:29)

Throughout the Bible, bodies are buried in the proper way and place because God finds the alternative shameful, and also, often but not always, because to do so is the preference of those who have died. The underlying notion in all of this is that the body is a gift that has been given by God to a specific individual. Though in death God relieves the dead of the burdens of the body, God does not rescind ownership.

Obviously, Christian notions of appropriate treatment of the dead do not apply to all who die in a secular and diverse society, regardless of its particular religious history. However, it does seem that certain elements of the Christian approach to the dead have carried over into the secular realm—specifically, the belief that there is ownership and free will even in death.

So it stands to reason that any viewers who suppose that the final desti-   20
nation of their own bodies will be their choice, may also suppose that any
body they view under the bright lights of an exhibit hall has chosen to be
there as well. Consciously or not, we want that to be the case. The alternative would be that we are seeing a display of bodies that tells us that our
conception of being dead—that there is any kind of choice involved—is
self-delusion. It's difficult to imagine that a different assessment of being
dead might be made in the place where the "specimens" lived and breathed
and, after dying, were transformed into objects for our benefit.

The lack of oversight by either government or medical authorities in
China has allowed the body processing market to boom in recent years.
Even von Hagens, who protests that "his" bodies are of European origin,
processes all the human remains for his exhibitions in China. Cases have
been cited of bodies discovered on farms, kept on ice, and destined for Plastination factories in the coastal city of Dalian. Doctors and medical students from Chinese universities, which are in every way complicit, admit
that they have no idea from where the bodies on which they work have
come. If press reports are accurate, these medically-trained professionals
seem little troubled by their work.

It would be easy to blame globalization for this situation. After all, the
Western desire for Eastern bodies is nothing new, and a newly-opened
China has the most Eastern bodies of all. Precedents for this interpretation
are easy to find: As recently as two years ago, European museums ran into
their own dilemma involving the ethical treatment of the dead when it
came to light that a number of major institutions still held collections of
disembodied Maori heads sent home by French and British adventurers in
the nineteenth century. The elaborately-tattooed heads, known as *toi moko*
in the Maori language, had been removed from bodies and remarkably well
preserved by the Maori themselves. A further level of complication arose
when it was determined that a number of the heads were not in fact of
Maori origin. They were, it seemed, the heads of members of other indigenous peoples of the South Pacific who had been captured, tattooed, and
decapitated specifically because of the booming *toi moko* market on the
other side of the world. Certainly the Plastination of anonymous Chinese
for display in North America has echoes of this unfortunate history.

However, it may be the case that there is another factor at play here: an
ethical foundation to the Chinese body industry that has not been explored. As in the Western context, the key to understanding the particular

ethics of the dead involves examination of the rituals of burial. In a study of Chinese mortuary practices, Sacramento State University archaeologist Wendy Rouse notes that the spiritual underpinnings of dealing with the dead are not so easily unpacked as in Christian and formerly Christian lands: "The development of the three major religions of China, Confucianism, Daoism, and Buddhism, significantly influenced the evolution of Chinese death rituals and beliefs," she writes. "Over the years, these philosophies became so intertwined that it is now difficult to determine which religion influenced the death ritual."

Although the origins of many of its components are difficult to identify, the Chinese ritual, like Christian burial, is a practice hundreds of years in the making. Its variations are endless, but in every instance the ritual does rest on the highest of Confucian ideals: honoring the ancestors. Every act of the ritual seeks to increase the comfort of the dead and to ease his or her way into the world to come.

25   The division of the body and the soul is generally taken to be a Western dualism, but a similar concept can be found in Chinese belief. This is not a body/soul divide in the usual sense but rather a division of the soul itself into two principles known as the hun and the po. The first of these, the *hun*, refers to the spirit and the intellect of a person, whereas the *po* makes physical action possible. As Rouse explains, "At death, the hun separates from the body and ascends to the realm of immortal beings, while the po remains with the body."

It is to the *po*, then, that the rites of death are directed. These rites include such elements that would seem familiar in the Christian context like prayers and the cleaning and dressing of the body. In fact, the attention paid to the dead is far more elaborate than that required by the Catholic Church. One of the original purposes of *fengshui*, which in the West usually refers to nothing more important than the arrangement of furniture, was the arrangement of the dead. Even one thousand years ago, it was a common practice to hire experts to make certain that a grave was properly oriented for the maximization of positive energy. As Rouse sums up the practice in the following passage, the first use of "deceased" refers to po whereas the second refers to hun:

The living could help the suffering of the deceased through chanting of incantations and burning offerings of food, money, and clothing. Once the deities in the netherworld received these appeals, the deceased could be granted a reprieve.

On the face of it, this does not imply an ethics of the dead very different from that which is suggested by Christian rites. The body is not merely a shell; it is a spiritual component of a person. For that reason, it must be treated with respect. However, the ethics involved shift when we consider the additional reasons for the undertaking of the rites of the dead:

The descendants considered the comfort of the deceased ancestor of utmost importance. If the po soul remained comfortable in the grave, the living would reap the blessing of their contented ancestor. Failure to provide for the deceased could result in punishment in the form of bad health, poor harvests, or a variety of calamities.

In the Chinese religious and cultural context, burial is an act performed not only for the dead but for the living. The same may be true in the Western context, but here it is much more explicitly built into the ritual's performance—and for that matter, its nonperformance. Unlike in Christian rhetoric of dealing with the dead, in the Confucian framing of the subject it is not assumed that everyone has the same rites awaiting them. All humans are not equal in death.

"The men of the family, especially the heads of the household, received the most ceremony at their death," Rouse explains. "Unmarried adults and young children received little, if any, attention. A person without descendants was simply placed into a plain wooden coffin and buried anywhere a gravesite could be obtained. Graves of convicts were dug in rows with no attention to the positioning of the graves according to the principles of fengshui."

In death as in life in the Confucian context, humans are valued based on their kinship connections. To be the patriarch of a large clan is to know that in death one's body will be celebrated and treated well. A fengshui expert will be brought in to make certain there is the right balance of energy in his final resting place. Prayers and offerings will be made before and for weeks after the funeral so that his hun may depart to eternal life and his po will rest in peace. As one traditional funeral chant makes clear, the dead are being constantly apprised of the ritual actions taking place on their behalf:

> *We are now cleansing your face*
> *The more your eyes are rinsed*
> *The brighter they become*
> *We are now cleansing your body*
> *The more your eyes are rinsed*

The brighter they become
We are now cleansing your hands and feet
When cleansed, they will feel so very light

To perform acts of respect toward the po but not to let the hun know about it is to risk the ritual going unnoticed. Such a situation invites the lingering presence of the spirit of the dead. Though the dead are revered, their continued influence is something to be avoided at all costs.

35   Through all this ritual action, the deceased is naturally the focus and the most pressing concern. However, it must be remembered that the underlying reason for the ritual is that the comfort of the dead is necessary for the welfare of his descendants.

If burial is performed for the benefit of living relations, it only makes sense that those without descendants would receive far less attention in the disposal of their bodies. I have suggested that in the Western/Christian context the primary claim on the bodies of the dead somehow remains the claim made by the dead themselves. Ownership of the body is so important to the Western sense of the self that it extends into the grave—or to the choice for no grave. In the Chinese/Confucian context, however, the primary claim on the body is that of the kinship network, those who have the most to gain or lose by its treatment.

In the place where the "Bodies . . ." specimens come from, to be unclaimed is nearly unimaginable. It is to be removed entirely from the system that, through ritual, leads to the appropriate treatment of the dead. In a sense, to be unclaimed is to lose both the hun and the po, a state that renders the dead, to borrow a term favored by von Hagens, as "former persons." They were individuals, but they have become mere material. As such, the unclaimed men and women who populate the displays of "Bodies . . . The Exhibition" may have arrived there, in part, because they fell beyond the protection of the Confucian ethics of the dead.

Although this reading of the Confucian tradition does suggest that it is somehow predisposed to uses of unclaimed bodies that the Western ethical view finds unacceptable, it is a useful reminder that though a rhetoric of rights, equality, and dignity of the dead exists in the West, this rhetoric does not always reflect reality. In the Washington, DC, morgue, for example, there has been in recent years a persistent problem of the overcrowding of unclaimed dead. Until an inspection report announced the problem "significantly reduced" in 2007, the District of Columbia Office of the

Medical Examiner had a decade-old reputation of failing to dispose of its dead. At one point there were over one hundred unclaimed bodies crowding a cold storage unit. Bodies were stored on carts, racks, and even the floor in a room occasionally lacking refrigeration, creating a stench so toxic it was judged a health risk to morgue employees. To blame for this apocalyptic scene were the four horseman of paperwork, budget strain, human incompetence, and an inevitable ambivalence felt toward those who die without a living soul to claim them.

The bureaucratic fumbling of a local government may be a far cry from the actual selling of perhaps thousands of unclaimed bodies by Chinese authorities, but nonetheless the point stands that, regardless of ethical assumptions or religious rhetoric, bodies without kin do badly in every corner of the world and in all religious contexts.

It also bears asking if there is something in the Western conception of 40
death—that is, the assumption that there is an element of choice involved in whatever state a corpse should find itself—that makes us particularly disposed to viewing the bodies of others.

There is an arrogance in individualism, just as there is an arrogance in the transaction that brings Eastern bodies before Western eyes. In each there is a sense that the anonymous dead died for our emphatically unanonymous benefit. Although it would be unbearable to most to consider one's parent or one's child put on display in this way, the experience is softened by what might be called the "willful assumption of choice": If it is only acceptable to view a body that has chosen to be viewed, and if I am viewing that body, then it must have chosen to be here.

Although it most likely makes no difference to the dead themselves, the concern over how they get where they end up—regardless of whether their final destination is in a display case or a grave—is more properly understood as concern for the living. In this sense, the problem of displaying or not displaying bodies resembles the much older debate surrounding the ethics of organ donation. Because such questions have been asked at least since the first successful kidney transplant in 1954, the discussion there is much more developed. In recent years, a push has been made to establish a global consensus that organs move between humans only as gifts and not articles of trade or commerce. Although that discussion is far too involved to go into here, it is worth noting that even within that global consensus there is disagreement similar to the essential differences between the two types of ethics of the dead we have here called Christian and Confucian: Does an individual own the body, or does the community? Do some individuals have less say in this than others? If an organ is a gift, who can claim the right to make it?

As with organ donation, the ethical concerns surrounding the exhibition of human bodies are as much about how things are as how they might be. Might plasticized corpses become so popular that—like non-Maori sources of Maori heads—people could be killed for the sake of being plasticized, packaged, and shipped around the world?

This is a question that might seem drawn from science fiction. Yet the most pressing ethical question of all comes from a much older text. If the questions raised by this example of "unburied" bodies are as troubling as those faced by Antigone, why is our asking of them far less urgent?

Analyze

1. What does the author want you to think about Gunther von Hagens, the founder of "Body Worlds"? What details does he give that reveal his point of view? Do you think this is fair? Why or why not?
2. Who represent Eastern and Western attitudes toward the dead in Manseau's article, and what are their different attitudes? Can you provide examples of other death rituals and attitudes toward the dead that are not so easily categorized?
3. Explain the difference between the Christian conception of death and the body's resurrection, and the Chinese beliefs in *po* and *hun*.

Explore

1. Manseau asks, "What are the dead for?" Write an essay in which you explore your own response to this question in dialogue with the reading. Begin by summarizing how Manseau frames and answers his question, then develop and ground your response by connecting your evidence and examples with Manseau's.
2. How do you think an increasingly globalized world might affect attitudes toward the dead and the "death rituals" in which we engage? Choose two or three places with large immigrant populations, and research how they address multiple cultures' death rituals. Based on your research, make a prediction of how new generations of local societies will address the ethical treatment of the dead.

3. In his final paragraph, Manseau wonders whether the questions raised by the display of plasticized bodies are as troubling as those faced by the character Antigone in the ancient Greek play by Sophocles. What factors, aside from Eastern and Western attitudes toward the dead, might play a role in what Manseau sees as a contemporary lack of urgency in the matter?

Elizabeth Dwoskin
"Why Americans Won't Do Dirty Jobs"

Elizabeth Dwoskin is a Washington-based staff writer for the magazine *Bloomberg Businessweek*. She was also a staff writer for the New York City–based alternative weekly *The Village Voice* and *The New York Times*. "Why Americans Won't Do Dirty Jobs" appeared in *Bloomberg Businessweek* in November 2011. In this article, Dwoskin analyzes the effects of Alabama's immigration law on industries that rely on manual labor to survive. Much of the employment that these businesses offer requires long hours and uncomfortable or even dangerous conditions for little pay. Historically, only undocumented workers were willing to accept such conditions. Since the law's enactment, however, thousands of undocumented workers who used to do this work have fled, and employers are finding it very difficult to hire American workers to take their place.

Under what conditions would you accept a poorly paid and potentially dangerous job?

Skinning, gutting, and cutting up catfish is not easy or pleasant work. No one knows this better than Randy Rhodes, president of Harvest Select, which has a processing plant in impoverished Uniontown, Ala. For years, Rhodes has had trouble finding Americans willing to grab a knife and stand 10 or more hours a day in a cold, wet room for minimum wage and skimpy benefits.

Most of his employees are Guatemalan. Or they were, until Alabama enacted an immigration law in September that requires police to question people they suspect might be in the U.S. illegally and punish businesses that hire them. The law, known as HB56, is intended to scare off undocumented workers, and in that regard it's been a success. It's also driven away legal immigrants who feared being harassed.

Rhodes arrived at work on Sept. 29, the day the law went into effect, to discover many of his employees missing. Panicked, he drove an hour and a half north to Tuscaloosa, where many of the immigrants who worked for him lived. Rhodes, who doesn't speak Spanish, struggled to get across how much he needed them. He urged his workers to come back. Only a handful did. "We couldn't explain to them that some of the things they were scared of weren't going to happen," Rhodes says. "I wanted them to see that I was their friend, and that we were trying to do the right thing."

His ex-employees joined an exodus of thousands of immigrant field hands, hotel housekeepers, dishwashers, chicken plant employees, and construction workers who have fled Alabama for other states. Like Rhodes, many employers who lost workers followed federal requirements—some even used the E-Verify system—and only found out their workers were illegal when they disappeared.

5   In their wake are thousands of vacant positions and hundreds of angry business owners staring at unpicked tomatoes, uncleaned fish, and unmade beds. "Somebody has to figure this out. The immigrants aren't coming back to Alabama—they're gone," Rhodes says. "I have 158 jobs, and I need to give them to somebody."

There's no shortage of people he could give those jobs to. In Alabama, some 211,000 people are out of work. In rural Perry County, where Harvest Select is located, the unemployment rate is 18.2 percent, twice the national average. One of the big selling points of the immigration law was that it would free up jobs that Republican Governor Robert Bentley said immigrants had stolen from recession-battered Americans. Yet native Alabamians have not come running to fill these newly liberated positions. Many employers think the law is ludicrous and fought to stop it. Immigrants aren't stealing anything from anyone, they say. Businesses turned to foreign labor only because they couldn't find enough Americans to take the work they were offering.

At a moment when the country is relentlessly focused on unemployment, there are still jobs that often go unfilled. These are difficult, dirty, exhausting jobs that, for previous generations, were the first rickety step on the ladder to prosperity. They still are—just not for Americans.

For decades many of Alabama's industries have benefited from a compliant foreign workforce and a state government that largely looked the other way on wages, working conditions, and immigration status. With so many foreign workers now effectively banished from the work pool and jobs sitting empty, businesses must contend with American workers who have higher expectations for themselves and their employers—even in a terrible economy where work is hard to find. "I don't consider this a labor shortage," says Tom Surtees, Alabama's director of industrial relations, himself the possessor of a job few would want: calming business owners who have seen their employees vanish. "We're transitioning from a business model. Whether an employer in agriculture used migrant workers, or whether it's another industry that used illegal immigrants, they had a business model and that business model is going to have to change."

On a sunny October afternoon, Juan Castro leans over the back of a pickup truck parked in the middle of a field at Ellen Jenkins's farm in northern Alabama. He sorts tomatoes rapidly into buckets by color and ripeness. Behind him his crew—his father, his cousin, and some friends— move expertly through the rows of plants that stretch out for acres in all directions, barely looking up as they pull the last tomatoes of the season off the tangled vines and place them in baskets. Since heading into the fields at 7 a.m., they haven't stopped for more than the few seconds it takes to swig some water. They'll work until 6 p.m., earning $2 for each 25-pound basket they fill. The men figure they'll take home around $60 apiece.

Castro, 34, says he crossed the border on foot illegally 19 years ago and   10
has three American-born children. He describes the mood in the fields since the law passed as tense and fearful. Gesturing around him, Castro says that not long ago the fields were filled with Hispanic laborers. Now he and his crew are the only ones left. "Many of our friends left us or got deported," he says. "The only reason that we can stand it is for our children."

He wipes sweat from beneath his fluorescent orange baseball cap, given to him by a timber company in Mississippi, where he works part of the year cutting pine. Castro says picking tomatoes in the Alabama heat isn't easy, but he counts himself lucky. He has never passed out on the job, as many others have, though he does have a chronic pinched nerve in his neck from bending over for hours on end. The experiment taking place in Alabama makes no sense to him. Why try to make Americans do this work when they clearly don't want it? "They come one day, and don't show up the next," Castro says.

It's a common complaint in this part of Alabama. A few miles down the road, Chad Smith and a few other farmers sit on chairs outside J&J Farms, venting about their changed fortunes. Smith, 22, says his 85 acres of tomatoes are only partly picked because 30 of the 35 migrant workers who had been with him for years left when the law went into effect. The state's efforts to help him and other farmers attract Americans are a joke, as far as he is concerned. "Oh, I tried to hire them," Smith says. "I put a radio ad out—out of Birmingham. About 15 to 20 people showed up, and most of them quit. They couldn't work fast enough to make the money they thought they could make, so they just quit."

Joey Bearden, who owns a 30-acre farm nearby, waits for his turn to speak. "The governor stepped in and started this bill because he wants to put people back to work—they're not coming!" says Bearden. "I've been farming 25 years, and I can count on my hand the number of Americans that stuck."

It's a hard-to-resist syllogism: Dirty jobs are available; Americans won't fill them; thus, Americans are too soft for dirty jobs. Why else would so many unemployed people turn down the opportunity to work during a recession? Of course, there's an equally compelling obverse. Why should farmers and plant owners expect people to take a back-breaking seasonal job with low pay and no benefits just because they happen to be offering it? If no one wants an available job—especially in extreme times—maybe the fault doesn't rest entirely with the people turning it down. Maybe the market is inefficient.

15   Tom Surtees is tired of hearing employers grouse about their lazy countrymen. "Don't tell me an Alabamian can't work out in the field picking produce because it's hot and labor intensive," he says. "Go into a steel mill. Go into a foundry. Go into numerous other occupations and tell them Alabamians don't like this work because it's hot and it requires manual labor." The difference being, jobs in Alabama's foundries and steel mills pay better wages—with benefits. "If you're trying to justify paying someone below whatever an appropriate wage level is so you can bring your product, I don't think that's a valid argument," Surtees says.

In the weeks since the immigration law took hold, several hundred Americans have answered farmers' ads for tomato pickers. A field over from where Juan Castro and his friends muse about the sorry state of the U.S.

workforce, 34-year-old Jesse Durr stands among the vines. An aspiring rapper from inner-city Birmingham, he wears big jeans and a do-rag to shield his head from the sun. He had lost his job prepping food at Applebee's, and after spending a few months looking for work a friend told him about a Facebook posting for farm labor.

The money isn't good—$2 per basket, plus $600 to clear the three acres when the vines were picked clean—but he figures it's better than sitting around. Plus, the transportation is free, provided by Jerry Spencer, who runs a community-supported agriculture program in Birmingham. That helps, because the farm is an hour north of Birmingham and the gas money adds up.

Durr thinks of himself as fit—he's all chiseled muscle—but he is surprised at how hard the work is. "Not everyone is used to this. I ain't used to it," he says while taking a break in front of his truck. "But I'm getting used to it."

Yet after three weeks in the fields, he is frustrated. His crew of seven has dropped down to two. "A lot of people look at this as slave work. I say, you do what you have to do," Durr says. "My mission is to finish these acres. As long as I'm here, I'm striving for something." In a neighboring field, Cedric Rayford is working a row. The 28-year-old came up with two friends from Gadsden, Ala., after hearing on the radio that farmers were hiring. The work is halfway complete when one member of their crew decides to quit. Rayford and crewmate Marvin Turner try to persuade their friend to stay and finish the job. Otherwise, no one will get paid. Turner even offers $20 out of his own pocket as a sweetener to no effect. "When a man's mind is made up, there's about nothing you can do," he says.

The men lean against the car, smoking cigarettes and trying to figure out   20 how to finish the job before day's end. "They gotta come up with a better pay system," says Rayford. "This ain't no easy work. If you need somebody to do this type of work, you gotta be payin'. If they was paying by the hour, motherf—s would work overtime, so you'd know what you're working for." He starts to pace around the car. "I could just work at McDonald's," he says.

Turner, who usually works as a landscaper, agrees the pay is too low. At $75 in gas for the three days, he figures he won't even break even. The men finish their cigarettes. Turner glances up the hill at Castro's work crew. "Look," he says. "You got immigrants doing more than what blacks or whites will. Look at them, they just work and work all day. They don't look at it like it's a hard job. They don't take breaks!"

The notion of jobs in fields and food plants as "immigrant work" is relatively new. As late as the 1940s, most farm labor in Alabama and elsewhere was done by Americans. During World War II the U.S. signed an agreement with Mexico to import temporary workers to ease labor shortages. Four and a half million Mexican guest workers crossed the border. At first most went to farms and orchards in California; by the program's completion in 1964 they were working in almost every state. Many braceros—the term translates to "strong-arm," as in someone who works with his arms—were granted green cards, became permanent residents, and continued to work in agriculture. Native-born Americans never returned to the fields. "Agricultural labor is basically 100 percent an immigrant job category," says Princeton University sociologist Doug Massey, who studies population migration. "Once an occupational category becomes dominated by immigrants, it becomes very difficult to erase the stigma."

Massey says Americans didn't turn away from the work merely because it was hard or because of the pay but because they had come to think of it as beneath them. "It doesn't have anything to do with the job itself," he says. In other countries, citizens refuse to take jobs that Americans compete for. In Europe, Massey says, "auto manufacturing is an immigrant job category. Whereas in the States, it's a native category."

In Alabama, the transition to immigrant labor happened slowly. Although migrant workers have picked fruit and processed food in Alabama for four decades, in 1990 only 1.1 percent of the state's total population was foreign-born. That year the U.S. Census put the combined Latin American and North American foreign-born population at 8,072 people. By 2000 there were 75,830 Hispanics recorded on the Census; by 2010 that number had more than doubled, and Hispanics are now nearly 4 percent of the population.

25   That first rush of Hispanic immigrants was initiated by the state's $2.4 billion poultry and egg industry. Alabama's largest agricultural export commodity went through a major expansion in the mid-'90s, thanks in part to new markets in the former Soviet Union. Companies such as Tyson Foods found the state's climate, plentiful water supply, light regulation, and anti-union policies to be ideal. At the time, better-educated American workers in cities such as Decatur and Athens were either moving into the state's burgeoning aerospace and service industries or following the trend of leaving Alabama and heading north or west, where they found office jobs or work in manufacturing with set hours, higher pay, and safer conditions—things most Americans take for granted. In just over a decade,

school districts in once-white towns such as Albertville, in the north-eastern corner of the state, became 34 percent Hispanic. By the 2000s, Hispanic immigrants had moved across the state, following the construction boom in the cities, in the growing plant nurseries in the south, and on the catfish farms west of Montgomery. It wasn't until anti-immigration sentiment spread across the country, as the recession took hold and didn't let go, that the Republican legislators who run Alabama began to regard the immigrants they once courted as the enemy.

A large white banner hangs on the chain-link fence outside the Harvest Select plant: "Now Hiring: Filleters/Trimmers. Stop Here To Apply." Randy Rhodes unfurled it the day after the law took effect. "We're getting applications, but you have to weed through those three and four times," says Amy Hart, the company's human resources manager. A job fair she held attracted 50 people, and Hart offered positions to 13 of them. Two failed the drug test. One applicant asked her out on a date during the interview. "People reapply who have been terminated for stealing, for fighting, for drugs," she says. "Nope, not that desperate yet!"

Rhodes says he understands why Americans aren't jumping at the chance to slice up catfish for minimum wage. He just doesn't know what he can do about it. "I'm sorry, but I can't pay those kids $13 an hour," he says. Although the Uniontown plant, which processes about 850,000 pounds of fish a week, is the largest in Alabama and sells to big supermarket chains including Food Lion, Harris Teeter, and Sam's Club, Rhodes says overseas competitors, which pay employees even lower wages, are squeezing the industry.

When the immigration law passed in late September, John McMillan's phone lines were deluged. People wanted McMillan, the state's agriculture commissioner, to tell them whether they'd be in business next year. "Like, what are we going to do? Do we need to be ordering strawberry plants for next season? Do we need to be ordering fertilizer?" McMillan recalls. "And of course, we don't have the answers, either."

His buddy Tom Surtees, the industrial relations director, faces the same problem on a larger scale. Where McMillan only has to worry about agriculture, other industries, from construction to hospitality, are reporting worker shortages. His ultimate responsibility is to generate the results that Governor Bentley has claimed the legislation will produce—lots of jobs for Alabamians. That means he cannot allow for the possibility that the law will fail.

"If those Alabamians on unemployment continue to not apply for jobs   30
in construction and poultry, then [Republican politicians] are going to

have to help us continue to find immigrant workers," says Jay Reed, who heads the Alabama Associated Builders & Contractors. "And those immigrant workers are gone."

Business owners are furious not only that they have lost so many workers but that everyone in the state seemed to see it coming except Bentley, who failed to heed warnings from leaders in neighboring Georgia who said they had experienced a similar flight of immigrants after passing their own immigration law. Bentley declined to be interviewed for this story.

McMillan and Surtees spend their days playing matchmaker with anxious employers, urging them to post job openings on the state's employment website so they can hook up with unemployed Alabamians. McMillan is asking Baptist ministers to tell their flocks that jobs are available. He wants businesses to rethink the way they run their operations to make them more attractive. On a road trip through the state, he met an apple farmer who told him he had started paying workers by the hour instead of by how much they picked. The apples get bruised and damaged when people are picking for speed. "Our farmers are very innovative and are used to dealing with challenges," McMillan says. "You know, they can come up with all kinds of things. Something I've thought about is, maybe we should go to four-hour shifts instead of eight-hour shifts. Or maybe two six-hour shifts."

McMillan acknowledges that even if some of these efforts are successful, they are unlikely to fill the labor void left by the immigrants' disappearance. Some growers, he says, might have to go back to traditional mechanized row crops such as corn and soybeans. The smaller farmers might have to decrease volumes to the point where they are no longer commercially viable. "I don't know," says McMillan. "I just don't know, but we've got to try to think of everything we possibly can."

Since late September, McMillan's staff has been attending meetings with farmers throughout the state. They are supposed to be Q&A sessions about how to comply with the new law. Some have devolved into shouting matches about how much they hate the statute. A few weeks ago, Smith, the tomato farmer whose workers fled Alabama, confronted state Senator Scott Beason, the Republican who introduced the immigration law. Beason had come out to talk to farmers, and Smith shoved an empty tomato bucket into his chest. "You pick!" he told him. "He didn't even put his hands on the bucket," Smith recalls. "He didn't even try." Says Beason: "My picking tomatoes would not change or prove anything."

While the politicians and business owners argue, others see opportu- 35
nity. Michael Maldonado, 19, wakes up at 4:30 each morning in a trailer
in Tuscaloosa, about an hour from Harvest Select, where he works as a
fish processor. Maldonado, who grew up in an earthen-floor shack in
Guatemala, says he likes working at the plant. "One hundred dollars here
is 700 quetzals," he says. "The managers say I am a good worker." After
three years, though, the long hours and scant pay are starting to wear on
him. With the business in desperate need of every available hand, it's not a
bad time to test just how much the bosses value his labor. Next week he
plans to ask his supervisor for a raise. "I will say to them, 'If you pay me a
little more—just a little more—I will stay working here,'" he says. "Otherwise, I will leave. I will go to work in another state."

Analyze

1. Describe the kinds of physically challenging jobs you, your friends, or
   people in your family or community have taken on. Compare them
   with others in your class.
2. What are the physical discomforts of the work described in this article? In what ways can business owners make jobs more tolerable?
3. The author writes, "It's a hard-to-resist syllogism: Dirty jobs are available; Americans won't fill them; thus, Americans are too soft for dirty
   jobs" (paragraph 14). What are other reasons Dwoskin finds to explain
   why "so many unemployed people turn down the opportunity to work
   during a recession?"

Explore

1. Does something similar happen with manual labor jobs in other countries? Research which jobs in which countries or regions go to immigrants because resident nationals are unwilling to do "difficult, dirty,
   exhausting jobs" (paragraph 7). Along with your class or writing group,
   use a Web 2.0 platform such as PB Works or Google Sites to create a
   wiki that describes manual labor jobs around the globe.
2. Choose a geographical country or region in the world and generate a
   categorized list of the kinds of jobs that immigrants in those regions
   do (e.g., skilled/unskilled, dangerous/safe, traditional/new, well-paid/
   poorly paid, physical labor/knowledge labor). Write a report in which

you interpret this data by considering how these categories affect who is willing or able to do these jobs.

3. Should immigrant laws consider more carefully the economic necessity for immigrant workers to sustain certain industries? Should local industries die their natural deaths as overseas competitors take over? Do you see a different solution? Write an essay in which you tease out the pros and cons of immigrant populations doing work that long-term resident populations will not do.

Stefany Anne Golberg
"You Can Take It with You"

Artist, writer, musician, and self-described "professional dilettante" Stefany Anne Golberg lives in New York City, where she is a founding member of the arts collective Flux Factory. Her article "You Can Take It with You" appeared in May 2012 in *The Smart Set,* an independent online magazine published by the Pennoni Honors College at Drexel University. Golberg is a frequent contributor to the magazine, which "feels that what unites its readers is their intellectual curiosity, and this cuts across age, gender, income, and education level." In her essay, Golberg ruminates over the ethos and evolution of backpack traveling.

What do you consider "essentials" when packing for a trip? What do those essentials say about your approach to travel?

Everywhere you travel, there are backpackers. You can see them herding at train platforms in Italy, or wandering past dusty tea stalls in India. They always have that look: something between yearning and exhaustion.

It's been more than half a century now that backpacking, for many young Americans, has become a rite of passage, a Grand Tour for the masses. The backpack has long ceased to be a mere choice of travel bag. It is a declaration of one's travel identity. Whereas the travel stories of yesteryear starred a traveler and a ship, these days, it is the traveler and the backpack. There is a literature of the backpack and literature for the backpack. There are the bibles of backpacking, usually a *Lonely Planet* guide. There is fiction for and about backpacking, like Alex Garland's *The Beach*. The backpack has become so essential for young travelers that the very word "backpacker" has become synonymous with the phrase "young traveler." There are backpacking clubs and blogs and magazines that link backpackers all across the globe. The backpacker has become a new form of life, prevalent on every continent, floating around each of the seven seas, exploring even the most remote nooks and crannies of this planet.

The backpack, as we now know it, is not a new invention. Its modern incarnation was developed in the mid-19th century for explorers and hikers. But its popularity grew alongside the relatively recent development of travel as a leisure activity that is open to average people: students, tourists on a budget—people who, in the past, would have only been able to travel if they were working their way through, on a cargo ship perhaps. Backpacks became truly fashionable in the Europe and America of the 1960s, and are still associated with the youth of that generation, many of whom set out to shed the bourgeois mores of the stationary life by traveling to distant lands where everything felt unfamiliar and strange. These young backpackers wanted to project a versatile, energetic attitude toward travel. A backpack meant motion, freedom, independence. Thus, the ethos behind traveling with a backpack was to pack as little as possible. Packing, like travel, was an act of abandon. The backpack should be as light as the traveler herself.

Many backpackers of the 1960s traced the paths of the Silk Road, the ancient network of trade routes that crisscrossed the lands and waterways in and around Europe, Egypt, Somalia, the Arabian Peninsula, Iran, Afghanistan, Central Asia, Pakistan, India, Bangladesh, Java-Indonesia, Vietnam, and China. The Silk Road was like a global, moving marketplace, a labyrinth of textiles, spices, medicine, jewels, perfume, and slaves. Religions were traded, technologies and languages, too, and many who traveled the Silk Road did so perpetually. The road, as Jack Kerouac would say, was life. In the 1960s and '70s, these merchant paths became known as the "Hippie Trail," filled with teenagers and 20-somethings journeying from Europe eastward, to countries in Southeast Asia and the Middle East along the Mediterranean. To this day, the legacy of backpackers along the old Silk Road is palpable, for example in Kathmandu, where a road named Jochen Tole is now known as Freak Street.

5   Packing was an important part of the Silk Road experience even for the
ancients. They packed supplies for basic travel needs. But they primarily
packed things to sell. Archaeological expeditions along the Silk Road have
uncovered clothing, goods. But mostly what they've found is money, bronze
and silver calling cards for the diverse travelers that made the Silk Road
home. Consciously or not, Hippie Trailers tried to transform what was,
historically, a journey of commerce into a journey of discovery and self-
fulfillment. Their choice of luggage reflected this transformation.

Open a random 1960s backpack and you would likely have found the
book *Siddhartha* by Herman Hesse. This novel about one man's spiritual
quest in the time of the Buddha was hugely influential for the '60s backpacker generation and, in its way, is a book about packing. In the beginning,
the eponymous Siddhartha is young and arrogant. He rejects the identity
forged by his father and religion. So he leaves everything behind to join a
band of ascetics. For years Siddhartha wanders hungrily, aimlessly through
the woods, until he realizes the ascetic's life has brought him no closer to the
enlightenment he seeks. So Siddhartha decides to go back to the town.
There, he meets a prostitute and a businessman, and becomes experienced
and wealthy. But one day, after years of living in decadence, Siddhartha decides that he has grown sick of all his stuff—his stuff is literally making him
sick—decides he must leave everything behind and go. The pleasure gardens
and the feasting have come to rule him, they have crowded him out of himself. Siddhartha's life has become an endless cycle of accumulation. So one
day, Siddhartha walks out of his house and into the forest. He packs nothing. He has no money, no food, no companions. He leaves his decadent life
in the city with the three things he arrived with: the ability to fast, the ability to think, and the ability to wait. And, he has the clothes on his back, in-
congruous rich man's clothes that look pretty silly on a man who is emptying
his life of external determination. Eventually, he sheds the clothes, too. It's a
common ascetic's tale. Go into the forest, go with nothing, expect nothing,
see everything. With his journey, Siddhartha posed a profound question.
What are we able to leave behind without losing ourselves completely?

Thus the 1960s. That specific spiritual journey, and the backpacking
that went with it, is over. The motivation for backpacking, however, remains. There is the desire to push one's limits, to see something new. But
the question is no longer, "What are we able to leave behind?" It is "How
much can we take?" In response, the backpack itself has changed.

Backpacks today are huge. They are so stuffed they can hardly fit in luggage racks. They are filled to capacity with supplies from home. The backpack of the 1960s was roughly the size of one's back. It had straps to attach to the back and maybe a few extra pockets. The backpack of today is the size of a small person. It is equipped with external and internal pockets, and the pockets are often custom-fitted for specific items: umbrellas, iPods, water bottles, cameras, computers. It straps to your back and also your waist and your chest. It has straps to hold a tent, compartments for sleeping bags, and fobs for watches and keys. It is padded and waterproof and fireproof. It is an infinity of zippers.

A random investigation of backpacking websites list the following items as today's backpack essentials:

water purification tablets
deodorant
toothpaste
2-in-1 shampoo and conditioner
sunscreen
insect repellent
camera
notebook and pen
Mp3 player
pack of cards
extra memory chip and battery pack for camera
USB cable
earplugs
sleepsheet
LED flashlight
hand towel
compass
small garbage bag
padlocks
ATM card
sandals (for the beach and to protect against hotel shower fungus)
travel tissues
inflatable pillow
Wet Wipes

Other suggested items include: a sleeping mask; money belt; hand sanitizer; alarm clock; two photo copies of passport and plane ticket; blister patches; important phone contacts such as one's embassy, credit card companies, and family; condoms; sewing kit; Swiss army knife; matches; bottle opener; Band-Aids; a first-aid kit; a sink stopper plug for washing clothes in a sink; a string for drying clothes.

10   It is always recommended that one should be careful not to over-pack.

The backpack of today is like a mobile home. Backpackers move through foreign lands with the hunched-over gait of mad scientists' assistants. The backpack was once meant to suggest the romance of an itinerant's carpetbag, or the sack on a stick carried by a hobo hopping onto a freight train. But carpetbags and hobo sacks held everything a person owned. The backpacks of today hold everything a person can take.

On a recent trip to Sri Lanka's hill country, I came across a middle-aged Spanish couple who were taking a yearlong adventure around Asia. They had large backpacks for their overall travels, but inside these backpacks were smaller daypacks that, for a daytrip in Sri Lanka's hill country, contained floppy hats for light rain, umbrellas for heavier rain, windbreakers for potential wind or rain, a microfiber blanket that could double as damp ground and wind protection, several sandwiches ("Sri Lankan food is not for me," the Spanish woman told us the previous evening), water bottles, and several bananas. They were dressed in trekking gear—hiking pants and sturdy boots. This was all for the purpose of a three-hour walk.

Backpackers are not about to travel unprepared. It is this thorough preparation that makes backpackers look absurd—and unexpectedly hostile. For, when we pack too well, we are telling the world that it isn't good enough on its own, that it makes us uncomfortable and scared. We don't know if we can depend on anything or anyone, and we've decided it's better not to take the chance. We will take our own umbrellas, our own bananas.

This attitude is equally expressed in what contemporary travelers pack on their bodies. For thousands of years the question, "What is your country?" would have been easily answered by the traveler's mode of regional dress. I think of the travelers along the Silk Road—Kazakh men wearing deerskin *qiapans* meeting up with saffron-robed Buddhist monks and Chinese women in silk brocade. The contemporary travel outfit makes a traveler's nationality often impossible to know unless you ask. Could you tell a New Yorker from a Walloon if both were wearing hoodies and cargo pants?

Today, the approach to travel dress is to be comfortable, which is to say   15
anonymous. Shorts, baseball caps, rubbery shoes. A few months ago, I met a
young German woman in Batticaloa on the eastern part of Sri Lanka. She had
been traveling alone throughout the country and by the time I met her she was
feeling distressed. When she was a baby, the woman told me, she had been adopted from India by a German family. The German woman had never known
India, and considered herself a German person through and through. Yet everywhere she went, people mistook her for a Sri Lankan. They would speak to
her in Sinhala or Tamil, expecting her to understand. Some people thought
she was Indian, but that came with its own set of expectations. She wanted
everyone to know she was a German person through and through, and she
wanted to be treated as such. She had even tried to dress as much like a German
tourist as possible, she told me in her thick Werner Herzogian brogue, and
pointed to her baggy tie-dyed T-shirt, her casual shorts, her Birkenstock sandals, and the big camera she wore on her chest. It was to no avail. Perhaps my
German acquaintance didn't know how many Sri Lankan tourists look equally
casual when they travel. What would the experience of the German traveler in
Batticaloa be like, though, if she wore lederhosen? I suspect what this woman
craved wasn't to be identified as German but rather to be left alone. The sweet
solace of urban anonymity is the first thing that goes when we travel.

There is an unavoidable truth about traveling: To travel is to make oneself a figure of potential ridicule. Travel makes us vulnerable. Most experienced travelers know their basic needs can be met wherever they may be.
You just have to ask for what you want and accept what you get. This is not
as easy as it might sound. It takes confidence. It takes faith. It is usually
easier to bring your own stuff.

This is not the backpack's fault. Anyone who has experienced being
dropped in the middle of a Warsaw winter with nothing but a giant suitcase on wheels that must be dragged over bumpy old cobblestones as it
careens and falls over and over again into the snow knows the so-called
comfort of this kind of luggage to be a farce. Wheeled-luggage travelers are
like an army of Queequegs who strap their sea chests to their wheelbarrows
only to carry the whole bundle up the wharf. The very act of packing is a
confrontation with who we are at home and who we can be when we are
away. It's never easy to leave home and harder still to make oneself temporarily homeless. This is true if you are traveling with a carpetbag or a steamer
trunk. But no luggage more bluntly—or more honestly—expresses the
fears about packing than the contemporary backpack.

We can see our souls in the contents of our baggage. Pack too much and we risk being weighed down by the place we're trying to leave. Pack too little and we risk losing ourselves.

In the 1960s, backpackers left as much as they could behind in order to release themselves from the burden of self. Now backpackers take as much as they can take in order to be self-sufficient. In the '60s, the backpacker's quest was to remove everything—often one's self-understanding, one's identity—to access something pure. Today, backpackers want to assert their identity across national boundaries with the help of the things they own.

20   Maybe the two lives of Siddhartha are the two sides of backpackers. The 1960s generation, it seems, was replaying the first part of Siddhartha's tale. They followed the young Siddhartha at the beginning of his journey of self-discovery, leaving everything behind in order to find their true selves. Contemporary backpackers are like the Siddhartha who goes back to the city in order to acquire as much as possible to fill the emptiness left by his ascetic life. Interestingly, Siddhartha only finds what he's looking for after he has possessed everything he can, becomes completely self-contained, creates for himself a fortress of belongings, and then lets it all go.

Analyze

1. In paragraph 2, Golberg writes "The backpacker has become a new form of life, prevalent on every continent, floating around each of the seven seas, exploring even the most remote nooks and crannies of this planet." Is this an extreme statement—hyperbole? Or is Golberg correct in her assertion? Does her choice of characterizing backpackers like this win or lose you as a reader? How so?

2. With images from the Internet, magazines, or your own collection, create a photo essay in which you display the contents of different backpacks. Create a narrative about each of the backpackers: Where are they from; where are they going; how old are they? Be sure to integrate in your narrative an analysis of the backpacks' contents and what they told you about their owners.

3. Golberg asks in paragraph 6, "What are we able to leave behind without losing ourselves completely?" What do you absolutely need when you travel? What do you miss the most? What could you ultimately do without? What might happen to you without your absolute essentials?

Explore

1. Golberg claims that contemporary backpackers are less interested in leaving things behind (as their 1960s counterparts did) and more interested in taking things along with them on their travels. Do you agree with Golberg? If so, what do you suppose accounts for this shift? If not, why not? As you answer these questions, consider whether you have taken on a broader or more global perspective than Golberg has.

2. If one side effect or byproduct of globalization is that people are beginning to look the same, as backpackers now do according to Golberg, is this good, bad, or neutral? What is lost? What is gained? Explain your response.

3. Golberg claims that "[w]e can see our souls in the contents of our baggage" (paragraph 19). Do an analysis of what you carry in the backpack, book bag, or briefcase that you bring to school or work. What is in your pockets? What do you wear? How does what you "carry" define your own essential self? Shape your answers to these questions into a personal essay. Be sure to integrate the insights you have gained.

Forging Connections

1. In the introduction to this chapter, I wondered what you think about when you see the words "body," "mind," and "spirit" together. As you consider the readings in this chapter (and others in this book), how might a global perspective influence your understandings of the body, mind, and spirit? Write an essay in which you develop a thesis and test it by further researching the communities and cultures you've read about in this chapter, including their beliefs about body, mind, and spirit connections. Based on your research, in what ways might these cultures and communities meld with others because of the effects of globalization? How might they retain their autonomies?

2. In a globalized era, what is becoming of the traditionally separated Western and Eastern views of mind, body, and spirit? Explore this question by identifying the Western and Eastern views in Fadiman's chapter "Birth" and Manseau's article "Plasticize Me." Do further research to flesh out these views, and see if you can identify where, on a continuum of Western and Eastern views, you would situate your own ideas about body, mind, and spirit.

Looking Further

1. How might a lens of globalization influence the ways in which we relate body, mind, and spirit to gender? Taking into account what you've read and written about in this chapter, look at the readings in chapter 7, "Gender Matters." Trace in an essay your own categorizations of body, mind, and spirit as they relate to your gender. Have your attitudes and beliefs been enriched or altered by the readings? Without feeling that you have to come to any definitive conclusions, pose your own questions and explore their tentative answers.

2. In reading and responding to the selections in this chapter, we've seen the different and complex ways in which human experience has been categorized across cultures into body, mind, and spirit. In an essay that can include elements of narrative, exploratory, and explanatory modes, show how you characterize the body, mind, and spirit connection and how it compares with and contrasts to those of the authors and/or the people they write about. Consider, for example, the people we meet in "Operation Mind Your Language" (chapter 4), "All the Disappearing Islands" (chapter 2), "You Think Hollywood Is Rough? Welcome to the Chaos, Excitement and Danger of Nollywood" (chapter 8), or "If It's Tuesday, It Must Be the Taliban" (chapter 9).

4 Languages in Contact

Languages are always in contact and can't help but influence one another. They contain in their utterances cultural values and knowledge, and reveal in their range of structures the cognitive wonders of what it is to be human. Languages are often in conflict because they are also containers and representatives of political ideologies. Together the readings in this chapter stimulate questions and insights about the connection between languages and globalization: How might a growing knowledge of language inform how we continue to understand and refine a working definition of globalization? And how might we use our contemporary lens of globalization to understand and use language equitably?

We begin with a selection by Lera Boroditsky, a cognitive psychologist who has conducted research on speakers of languages (as far away from each other as Aboriginal Australia, China, Greece, Chile, Indonesia, and Russia). Boroditsky illuminates the marvelously diverse ways that languages and cultures shape the way we think.

In his article "Death by Monoculture," linguistic anthropologist Stephen Pax Leonard bemoans the loss of the Polar Eskimos' language and culture, tying it in part to global warming and, perhaps just as frustrating, a seeming lack of concern from the very populace whose culture is waning. The Polar Eskimos' connection to the larger world via other languages, as well as through the Internet, is understandable, and it mirrors the desires of many people worldwide who are eager to start lives in new places or bring new places into their own lives.

Not knowing the "right" language presents more than a metaphorical barrier as James Angelos's article "Passing the Test" demonstrates. Is a required proficiency in a country's official language a helpful step toward "integration," or is it a passive-aggressive deterrent to undesirable immigration?

With well over 1,000 languages spoken in India, multilingualism is the norm, yet Reshma Krishnamurthy Sharma's article "The New Language Landscape" reflects both an anxiety to be part of a global economy and a logistical difficulty of maintaining regional languages in the face of India's increasing inter-regional marriages. The answer: The new generation is learning English—the language of the former colonizers—exclusively. In "Operation Mind Your Language," Pallavi Polanki sheds light on the demand for English teachers in Afghanistan as a result of the American presence. Indeed, the expansion of English as a global lingua franca has become a worldwide activity—for both those who want to learn and those who want to teach; but not without the justifiable ambivalence that Julie Traves captures in "The Church of Please and Thank You."

As this book goes to print, there are 6,909 living languages in the world. This number, however, is in decline: On average, one language dies every two weeks. At this rate, according to an article in *National Geographic*, "more than half of the world's roughly 7,000 languages will vanish by the end of this century alone."

Access to languages—and the wonder of human cultures that shape and are shaped by them—is increasingly available, even as that access spells, for some languages, their imminent extinction. Global languages such as English, and also Chinese, Russian, Spanish, and Hindi, seem to hold greater promise than a speaker's heritage language—the mother tongue, at least in the present, when economic need can make cultural heritage seem like a luxury. Resolving this conundrum that pits long-term heritage

against economic exigency becomes an ethical and cultural dilemma that
we as a global community must work out together.

Works Cited

Basu, Paroma. "What Happens When a Language Dies?" *National
Geographic News*, Feb. 2009; web accessed Jan. 23, 2013.

Lewis, M. Paul, ed. *Ethnologue: Languages of the World*, 16th ed.
Dallas, TX: SIL International, 2009; web accessed Jan. 23, 2013.

Lera Boroditsky
"How Does Our Language Shape the Way We Think?"

Lera Borodistky, who was born in Minsk in the former Soviet Union, holds a
Ph.D. in cognitive psychology from Stanford University and currently teaches
at the University of California, San Diego. She also works in Jakarta, Indonesia,
collecting data for her award-winning research on how languages and cultures shape human thought, and is editor-in-chief of the scholarly journal
Frontiers in Cultural Psychology. "How Does Our Language Shape the Way
We Think?" appeared in June 2009 in the online "salon" *Edge*, where individuals "seek out the most complex and sophisticated minds . . . and ask each
other the questions they are asking themselves." In this essay, Boroditsky
emphasizes the uniquely human gift of language, asserting its centrality to
human experience. As such, the language we each speak informs how we live
our lives, see our worlds, and think about ourselves.

Based on your experience as a language user, what ways do you think individual languages might shape the way their speakers think about the world?

Humans communicate with one another using a dazzling array of
languages, each differing from the next in innumerable ways. Do the
languages we speak shape the way we see the world, the way we think, and

the way we live our lives? Do people who speak different languages think differently simply because they speak different languages? Does learning new languages change the way you think? Do polyglots think differently when speaking different languages?

These questions touch on nearly all of the major controversies in the study of mind. They have engaged scores of philosophers, anthropologists, linguists, and psychologists, and they have important implications for politics, law, and religion. Yet despite nearly constant attention and debate, very little empirical work was done on these questions until recently. For a long time, the idea that language might shape thought was considered at best untestable and more often simply wrong. Research in my labs at Stanford University and at MIT has helped reopen this question. We have collected data around the world: from China, Greece, Chile, Indonesia, Russia, and Aboriginal Australia. What we have learned is that people who speak different languages do indeed think differently and that even flukes of grammar can profoundly affect how we see the world. Language is a uniquely human gift, central to our experience of being human. Appreciating its role in constructing our mental lives brings us one step closer to understanding the very nature of humanity.

> "What would your life be like if you had never learned a language?"

I often start my undergraduate lectures by asking students the following question: which cognitive faculty would you most hate to lose? Most of them pick the sense of sight; a few pick hearing. Once in a while, a wise-cracking student might pick her sense of humor or her fashion sense. Almost never do any of them spontaneously say that the faculty they'd most hate to lose is language. Yet if you lose (or are born without) your sight or hearing, you can still have a wonderfully rich social existence. You can have friends, you can get an education, you can hold a job, you can start a family. But what would your life be like if you had never learned a language? Could you still have friends, get an education, hold a job, start a family? Language is so fundamental to our experience, so deeply a part of being human, that it's hard to imagine life without it. But are languages merely tools for expressing our thoughts, or do they actually shape our thoughts?

Most questions of whether and how language shapes thought start with the simple observation that languages differ from one another. And a lot!

Let's take a (very) hypothetical example. Suppose you want to say, "Bush read Chomsky's latest book." Let's focus on just the verb, "read." To say this sentence in English, we have to mark the verb for tense; in this case, we have to pronounce it like "red" and not like "reed." In Indonesian you need not (in fact, you can't) alter the verb to mark tense. In Russian you would have to alter the verb to indicate tense and gender. So if it was Laura Bush who did the reading, you'd use a different form of the verb than if it was George. In Russian you'd also have to include in the verb information about completion. If George read only part of the book, you'd use a different form of the verb than if he'd diligently plowed through the whole thing. In Turkish you'd have to include in the verb how you acquired this information: if you had witnessed this unlikely event with your own two eyes, you'd use one verb form, but if you had simply read or heard about it, or inferred it from something Bush said, you'd use a different verb form.

Clearly, languages require different things of their speakers. Does this   5 mean that the speakers think differently about the world? Do English, Indonesian, Russian, and Turkish speakers end up attending to, partitioning, and remembering their experiences differently just because they speak different languages? For some scholars, the answer to these questions has been an obvious yes. Just look at the way people talk, they might say. Certainly, speakers of different languages must attend to and encode strikingly different aspects of the world just so they can use their language properly.

Scholars on the other side of the debate don't find the differences in how people talk convincing. All our linguistic utterances are sparse, encoding only a small part of the information we have available. Just because English speakers don't include the same information in their verbs that Russian and Turkish speakers do doesn't mean that English speakers aren't paying attention to the same things; all it means is that they're not talking about them. It's possible that everyone thinks the same way, notices the same things, but just talks differently.

Believers in cross-linguistic differences counter that everyone does not pay attention to the same things: if everyone did, one might think it would be easy to learn to speak other languages. Unfortunately, learning a new language (especially one not closely related to those you know) is never easy; it seems to require paying attention to a new set of distinctions. Whether it's distinguishing modes of being in Spanish, evidentiality in Turkish, or aspect in Russian, learning to speak these languages requires something more than just learning vocabulary: it requires paying attention to the right things in the world so that you have the correct information to include in what you say.

Such a priori arguments about whether or not language shapes thought have gone in circles for centuries, with some arguing that it's impossible for language to shape thought and others arguing that it's impossible for language not to shape thought. Recently my group and others have figured out ways to empirically test some of the key questions in this ancient debate, with fascinating results. So instead of arguing about what must be true or what can't be true, let's find out what is true.

Follow me to Pormpuraaw, a small Aboriginal community on the western edge of Cape York, in northern Australia. I came here because of the way the locals, the Kuuk Thaayorre, talk about space. Instead of words like "right," "left," "forward," and "back," which, as commonly used in English, define space relative to an observer, the Kuuk Thaayorre, like many other Aboriginal groups, use cardinal-direction terms—north, south, east, and west—to define space.[1] This is done at all scales, which means you have to say things like "There's an ant on your southeast leg" or "Move the cup to the north northwest a little bit." One obvious consequence of speaking such a language is that you have to stay oriented at all times, or else you cannot speak properly. The normal greeting in Kuuk Thaayorre is "Where are you going?" and the answer should be something like "South southeast, in the middle distance." If you don't know which way you're facing, you can't even get past "Hello."

10   The result is a profound difference in navigational ability and spatial knowledge between speakers of languages that rely primarily on absolute reference frames (like Kuuk Thaayorre) and languages that rely on relative reference frames (like English).[2] Simply put, speakers of languages like Kuuk Thaayorre are much better than English speakers at staying oriented and keeping track of where they are, even in unfamiliar landscapes or inside unfamiliar buildings. What enables them—in fact, forces them—to do this is their language. Having their attention trained in this way equips them to perform navigational feats once thought beyond human capabilities. Because space is such a fundamental domain of thought, differences in how people think about space don't end there. People rely on their spatial knowledge to build other, more complex, more abstract representations. Representations of such things as time, number, musical pitch, kinship relations, morality, and emotions have been shown to depend on how we think about space. So if the Kuuk Thaayorre think differently about space,

do they also think differently about other things, like time? This is what my collaborator Alice Gaby and I came to Pormpuraaw to find out.

To test this idea, we gave people sets of pictures that showed some kind of temporal progression (e.g., pictures of a man aging, or a crocodile growing, or a banana being eaten). Their job was to arrange the shuffled photos on the ground to show the correct temporal order. We tested each person in two separate sittings, each time facing in a different cardinal direction. If you ask English speakers to do this, they'll arrange the cards so that time proceeds from left to right. Hebrew speakers will tend to lay out the cards from right to left, showing that writing direction in a language plays a role.[3] So what about folks like the Kuuk Thaayorre, who dont use words like "left" and "right"? What will they do?

The Kuuk Thaayorre did not arrange the cards more often from left to right than from right to left, nor more toward or away from the body. But their arrangements were not random: there was a pattern, just a different one from that of English speakers. Instead of arranging time from left to right, they arranged it from east to west. That is, when they were seated facing south, the cards went left to right. When they faced north, the cards went from right to left. When they faced east, the cards came toward the body and so on. This was true even though we never told any of our subjects which direction they faced. The Kuuk Thaayorre not only knew that already (usually much better than I did), but they also spontaneously used this spatial orientation to construct their representations of time.

People's ideas of time differ across languages in other ways. For example, English speakers tend to talk about time using horizontal spatial metaphors (e.g., "The best is ahead of us," "The worst is behind us"), whereas Mandarin speakers have a vertical metaphor for time (e.g., the next month is the "down month" and the last month is the "up month"). Mandarin speakers talk about time vertically more often than English speakers do, so do Mandarin speakers think about time vertically more often than English speakers do? Imagine this simple experiment. I stand next to you, point to a spot in space directly in front of you, and tell you, "This spot, here, is today. Where would you put yesterday? And where would you put tomorrow?" When English speakers are asked to do this, they nearly always point horizontally. But Mandarin speakers often point vertically, about seven or eight times more often than do English speakers.[4]

Even basic aspects of time perception can be affected by language. For example, English speakers prefer to talk about duration in terms of length (e.g., "That was a short talk," "The meeting didn't take long"), while Spanish and Greek speakers prefer to talk about time in terms of amount, relying more on words like "much," "big," and "little" rather than "short" and "long." Our research into such basic cognitive abilities as estimating duration shows that speakers of different languages differ in ways predicted by the patterns of metaphors in their language. (For example, when asked to estimate duration, English speakers are more likely to be confused by distance information, estimating that a line of greater length remains on the test screen for a longer period of time, whereas Greek speakers are more likely to be confused by amount, estimating that a container that is fuller remains longer on the screen.)[5]

15   An important question at this point is: Are these differences caused by language per se or by some other aspect of culture? Of course, the lives of English, Mandarin, Greek, Spanish, and Kuuk Thaayorre speakers differ in a myriad of ways. How do we know that it is language itself that creates these differences in thought and not some other aspect of their respective cultures?

One way to answer this question is to teach people new ways of talking and see if that changes the way they think. In our lab, we've taught English speakers different ways of talking about time. In one such study, English speakers were taught to use size metaphors (as in Greek) to describe duration (e.g., a movie is larger than a sneeze), or vertical metaphors (as in Mandarin) to describe event order. Once the English speakers had learned to talk about time in these new ways, their cognitive performance began to resemble that of Greek or Mandarin speakers. This suggests that patterns in a language can indeed play a causal role in constructing how we think.[6] In practical terms, it means that when you're learning a new language, you're not simply learning a new way of talking, you are also inadvertently learning a new way of thinking. Beyond abstract or complex domains of thought like space and time, languages also meddle in basic aspects of visual perception—our ability to distinguish colors, for example. Different languages divide up the color continuum differently: some make many more distinctions between colors than others, and the boundaries often don't line up across languages.

To test whether differences in color language lead to differences in color perception, we compared Russian and English speakers' ability to discriminate shades of blue. In Russian there is no single word that covers all the colors that English speakers call "blue." Russian makes an obligatory distinction between light blue (goluboy) and dark blue (siniy). Does this distinction mean that siniy blues look more different from goluboy blues to Russian speakers? Indeed, the data say yes. Russian speakers are quicker to distinguish two shades of blue that are called by the different names in Russian (i.e., one being siniy and the other being goluboy) than if the two fall into the same category.

For English speakers, all these shades are still designated by the same word, "blue," and there are no comparable differences in reaction time.

Further, the Russian advantage disappears when subjects are asked to perform a verbal interference task (reciting a string of digits) while making color judgments but not when they're asked to perform an equally difficult spatial interference task (keeping a novel visual pattern in memory). The disappearance of the advantage when performing a verbal task shows that language is normally involved in even surprisingly basic perceptual judgments—and that it is language per se that creates this difference in perception between Russian and English speakers.

When Russian speakers are blocked from their normal access to lan-   20
guage by a verbal interference task, the differences between Russian and English speakers disappear.

Even what might be deemed frivolous aspects of language can have far-reaching subconscious effects on how we see the world. Take grammatical gender. In Spanish and other Romance languages, nouns are either masculine or feminine. In many other languages, nouns are divided into many more genders ("gender" in this context meaning class or kind). For example, some Australian Aboriginal languages have up to sixteen genders, including classes of hunting weapons, canines, things that are shiny, or, in the phrase made famous by cognitive linguist George Lakoff, "women, fire, and dangerous things."

What it means for a language to have grammatical gender is that words belonging to different genders get treated differently grammatically and words belonging to the same grammatical gender get treated the same grammatically. Languages can require speakers to change pronouns, adjective and verb endings, possessives, numerals, and so on, depending on the noun's gender. For example, to say something like "my chair was old" in Russian (moy stul bil' stariy), you'd need to make every word in the sentence agree in gender with "chair" (stul), which is masculine in Russian. So you'd use the masculine form of "my," "was," and "old." These are the same forms you'd use in speaking of a biological male, as in "my grandfather was old." If, instead of speaking of a chair, you were speaking of a bed (krovat'), which is feminine in Russian, or about your grandmother, you would use the feminine form of "my," "was," and "old."

Does treating chairs as masculine and beds as feminine in the grammar make Russian speakers think of chairs as being more like men and beds as more like women in some way? It turns out that it does. In one study, we asked German and Spanish speakers to describe objects having opposite gender assignment in those two languages. The descriptions they gave differed in a way predicted by grammatical gender. For example, when asked to describe a "key"—a word that is masculine in German and feminine in Spanish—the German speakers were more likely to use words like "hard," "heavy," "jagged," "metal," "serrated," and "useful," whereas Spanish speakers were more likely to say "golden," "intricate," "little," "lovely," "shiny," and "tiny." To describe a "bridge," which is feminine in German and masculine in Spanish, the German speakers said "beautiful," "elegant," "fragile," "peaceful," "pretty," and "slender," and the Spanish speakers said "big," "dangerous," "long," "strong," "sturdy," and "towering." This was true even though all testing was done in English, a language without grammatical gender. The same pattern of results also emerged in entirely nonlinguistic tasks (e.g., rating similarity between pictures). And we can also show that it is aspects of language per se that shape how people think: teaching English speakers new grammatical gender systems influences mental representations of objects in the same way it does with German and Spanish speakers. Apparently even small flukes of grammar, like the seemingly arbitrary assignment of gender to a noun, can have an effect on people's ideas of concrete objects in the world.[7]

In fact, you don't even need to go into the lab to see these effects of language; you can see them with your own eyes in an art gallery. Look at some famous examples of personification in art—the ways in which abstract entities such as death, sin, victory, or time are given human form. How does an artist decide whether death, say, or time should be painted as a man or a woman? It turns out that in 85 percent of such personifications, whether a male or female figure is chosen is predicted by the grammatical gender of the word in the artist's native language. So, for example, German painters are more likely to paint death as a man, whereas Russian painters are more likely to paint death as a woman.

25   The fact that even quirks of grammar, such as grammatical gender, can affect our thinking is profound. Such quirks are pervasive in language;

gender, for example, applies to all nouns, which means that it is affecting how people think about anything that can be designated by a noun. That's a lot of stuff!

I have described how languages shape the way we think about space, time, colors, and objects. Other studies have found effects of language on how people construe events, reason about causality, keep track of number, understand material substance, perceive and experience emotion, reason about other people's minds, choose to take risks, and even in the way they choose professions and spouses.[8] Taken together, these results show that linguistic processes are pervasive in most fundamental domains of thought, unconsciously shaping us from the nuts and bolts of cognition and perception to our loftiest abstract notions and major life decisions. Language is central to our experience of being human, and the languages we speak profoundly shape the way we think, the way we see the world, the way we live our lives.

NOTES

1   S. C. Levinson and D. P. Wilkins, eds., *Grammars of Space: Explorations in Cognitive Diversity* (New York: Cambridge University Press, 2006).

2   Levinson, *Space in Language and Cognition: Explorations in Cognitive Diversity* (New York: Cambridge University Press, 2003).

3   B. Tversky *et al.*, " Cross-Cultural and Developmental Trends in Graphic Productions," *Cognitive Psychology* 23(1991): 515–7; O. Fuhrman and L. Boroditsky, "Mental Time-Lines Follow Writing Direction: Comparing English and Hebrew Speakers." Proceedings of the 29th Annual Conference of the Cognitive Science Society (2007): 1007–10.

4   L. Boroditsky, "Do English and Mandarin Speakers Think Differently About Time?" Proceedings of the 48th Annual Meeting of the Psychonomic Society (2007): 34.

5   D. Casasanto *et al.*, "How Deep Are Effects of Language on Thought? Time Estimation in Speakers of English, Indonesian, Greek, and Spanish," Proceedings of the 26th Annual Conference of the Cognitive Science Society (2004): 575–80.

6   Ibid., "How Deep Are Effects of Language on Thought? Time Estimation in Speakers of English and Greek" (in review); L. Boroditsky, "Does Language Shape Thought? English and Mandarin Speakers' Conceptions of Time." *Cognitive Psychology* 43, no. 1(2001): 1–22.

7   L. Boroditsky *et al.* "Sex, Syntax, and Semantics," in D. Gentner and S. Goldin-Meadow, eds., *Language in Mind: Advances in the Study of Language and Cognition* (Cambridge, MA: MIT Press, 2003), 61–79.

8   L. Boroditsky, "Linguistic Relativity," in L. Nadel ed., *Encyclopedia of Cognitive Science* (London: MacMillan, 2003), 917–21; B. W. Pelham *et al.*, "Why Susie Sells Seashells by the Seashore: Implicit Egotism and Major Life Decisions." *Journal of Personality and Social Psychology* 82, no. 4(2002): 469–86; A. Tversky & D. Kahneman, "The Framing of Decisions and the Psychology of Choice." *Science* 211(1981): 453–58; P. Pica *et al.*, "Exact and Approximate Arithmetic in an Amazonian Indigene Group." *Science* 306(2004): 499–503; J. G. de Villiers and P. A. de Villiers, "Linguistic Determinism and False Belief," in P. Mitchell and K. Riggs, eds., *Children's Reasoning and the Mind* (Hove, UK: Psychology Press, in press); J. A. Lucy and S. Gaskins, "Interaction of Language Type and Referent Type in the Development of Nonverbal Classification Preferences," in Gentner and Goldin-Meadow, 465–92; L. F. Barrett *et al.*, "Language as a Context for Emotion Perception," *Trends in Cognitive Sciences* 11(2007): 327–32.

Analyze

1. In response to the question of whether language shapes the way we think about the world, what are the different reasons given by those who believe it does and those who believe it does not?
2. In empirically studying "whether or not language shapes thought" (paragraph 8), what has Boroditsky's group discovered?
3. What is grammatical gender, and how does it influence speakers of languages differently according to the author's research?

Explore

1. In a small group, create a visual chart or mind map that organizes the different language speakers that Boroditsky's group studied. What do those languages reveal about how their speakers think? How were the researchers able to test those speakers? How does your chart differ from others in your class?
2. In the last paragraph, Boroditsky claims that "[l]anguage is central to our experience of being human, and the languages we speak profoundly shape the way we think, the way we see the world, the way we live our lives." How does this change the way you view yourself and your relationship to others who speak languages different from your own?
3. Given Boroditsky's research into how language shapes the way we think, how might knowing the various orientations that different

languages have (e.g., regarding space, gender, or color) affect the way we understand the roles of language and culture in an increasingly globalized world?

4. If our language does indeed shape the way we think, how might you imagine the potential of a globalized world in which people from geographically diverse regions think in multiple languages? Write a fictional narrative in which you depict this world using examples from the languages described in this article.

Stephen Pax Leonard
"Death by Monoculture"

Stephen Pax Leonard is a research associate at the Scott Polar Research Institute at the University of Cambridge, England. An anthropological linguist, Leonard has carried out fieldwork in Iceland, the Faroe Islands, and Greenland. "Death by Monoculture" was published in September 2011 in *Research*, an online forum of Cambridge University. In this article, Leonard discusses observations he gathered during his one-year stay with a remote community of Polar Eskimos in northwest Greenland. His fieldwork reveals the dangerous effects of "synthetic monoculture" not only on this specific group's language and traditions, but with implications for minority languages and cultures worldwide. Leonard laments our weakening ethnosphere in the face of globalization and consumerism, and sees digital media and the Internet as ways to preserve it.

What various cultures permeate your day-to-day life and interests?

The 21st century is the make-or-break century for cultural and linguistic diversity, and for the future of human civilisation *per se*. An unprecedented and unchecked growth in the world's population, combined with the insistence on exploiting finite resources, will lead to environmental and humanitarian catastrophes as mass urbanisation meets fundamental problems such as the lack of drinking water. The actions that we collectively take over the next fifty years will determine how and if we can overcome such global challenges, and what the shape of the 'ethnosphere' or 'sum of the world's cultures' is to look like in years to come.

After having spent a year in a remote Arctic community which speaks a vulnerable, minority language and whose cultural foundations are being rocked by climate change, it is clear to me that the link between environmental and cultural vulnerability is genuine and that the two are interwoven. Cultural practices of the Polar Eskimos are based on a history of survival strategies in one of the world's most hostile environments. Their language and 'way of speaking' is a representation of that. When the sea ice disappears, their stories will eventually go with it.

We, human beings, rent the world for a period of approximately 80 years. It is our duty to future tenants to leave the house as we found it. The conservation issue goes beyond everything else and should therefore be at the heart of every policy decision. To do otherwise, would be to live in the 20th century. At present, linguists predict that over 50 per cent of the world's languages will no longer be spoken by the turn of the century. Instead of leaving the house in order, we are on the road to the fastest rate of linguistic and cultural destruction in history. Languages die for many reasons, but the current trend is driven by the juggernaut of the homogenising forces of globalisation and consumerism which seems unstoppable and whose language tends to be the new universal tongue, English.

I am a romantic and romantics are nowadays always disillusioned because the world is no longer how they had hoped it to be. I had gone to the top of the world and had wished to find elderly folk sitting around telling stories. Instead, I found adults and children glued to television screens with a bowl of seal soup on their lap, playing exceedingly violent and expletive crammed Hollywoodian video war games. Time and time again, I discovered this awkward juxtaposition of modernity meets tradition. Out in the Arctic wilderness, hunters dressed head to toe in skins would answer satellite phones and check their GPS coordinates.

5   Consumerism has now made it to every corner of the world. Some Polar Eskimos may live in tiny, wind-beaten wooden cabins with no running water, but Amazon delivers. Most 8-year-olds who live in Qaanaaq and the remote settlements have the latest smartphones. Media entertainment will, however, never be produced for a language of 770 speakers because it is loss-making. Technology, be it mobile phones, DVDs or video games may

support the top 50 languages maximum, but never more than that. Some languages are not suited to these technologies: Greenlandic words are too long to subtitle and to use in text messaging. Polar Eskimos tend to send text messages in Danish or English because it is easier.

As the world embraces the synthetic monoculture of populism and consumerism, linguistic and cultural diversity risk being erased right across the world. For consumerism to operate efficiently, it requires as few operating languages as possible. That way, the message is consistent and the producer's cost is minimised. This globalised consumerism is the product of a system which is based on an addiction to economic growth. Growth for the sake of growth is the ideology of the cancer cell, and yet it is difficult to hear US presidential candidates or EU officials talk about anything else. Some politicians speak oxymoronically of 'sustainable growth' but the combination of a rocketing world population and finite resources is the recipe of 'unsustainability' *par excellence*. Growth has become an abstract imperative that is driving humanity to destroy the ecosystem upon which life depends. If we can shake off the growth habit and focus on the 'local' and sustainability for its own sake, minority languages will have a chance to prosper providing they engage with new digital media technologies. The Internet represents surely the best opportunity to help support small or endangered languages and yet 95 per cent of Internet content appears in just 12 languages. The Internet offers also a chance to move away from television which is largely responsible for the spread of a phony, idiotic form of entertainment culture where production costs are too high to support minority languages.

I have never met anybody who is indifferent to the elimination of biodiversity or the protection of endangered animal species, but linguists and anthropologists are still being asked to defend linguistic and cultural diversity. In doing so, it should be remembered that a language is so much more than a syntactic code or a list of grammar rules. To treat language as such is to reduce it to its least interesting features. When languages die, we do not just lose words, but we lose different ways of conceptually framing things. For the Polar Eskimos, there is no one concept of 'ice', but over twenty different ways of referring to various forms of ice. Through different distinctions in meaning, languages provide insights into how groups of speakers 'know the world'.

A language is a collection of statements about the world delivered in a multitude of voices set to a background of music. There is a difference between being able to speak a language fluently and to speak a language like a native. The latter requires first and foremost a mastery of the language's paralinguistic features—in the case of Polar Eskimo, a rich and never random repertoire of sighs and groans and a specific mix of intonation patterns and gestures accompanying particular words and phrases. To be able to speak a handful of languages as a native, you have to be able to act and act well, reproducing exactly certain collocations of words to the rhythm, gestures, flow and timbre of its speakers. This is always more important than just having a large vocabulary or putting the verb in the right place. Each language of the world requires a different voice. When we lose a language, we lose an orchestra of voices that permeate the mind. As well as knowledge and perceptions of the world which are built into local language varieties, we lose the music and poetry of words and speech which elicit so much pleasure. There should be no need to defend linguistic diversity. It and the power of language are something to be celebrated. Without it, the world would be utterly dull. After all, who wants to listen to just Beethoven, when you can enjoy Rachmaninov and Shostakovich too? Not that there is any chance of the Polar Eskimos listening to Beethoven, they are too busy indulging in virtual reality Playstation war games whose only poetic content is 'fucking pacify him'.

Analyze

1. How does Leonard implicitly define "globalization"? Why does he blame it and consumerism for the decline of minority languages? How does he suppose digital media and the Internet would aid in their preservation? Do you agree with him? Why or why not?
2. What were Leonard's expectations when he arrived in the Arctic wilderness to live with the Polar Eskimos? What colored these expectations? Why was he disappointed?
3. According to Leonard, what is the difference between speaking a language fluently and speaking a language like a native? Can you think of examples from your own linguistic knowledge that support or disprove his assertion?

Explore

1. In your own words, how would you define "ethnosphere" after reading Leonard's article? What evidence does the author provide to persuade you that the planet's "ethnosphere" is endangered?

2. Create a dialogue between Leonard and Boroditsky ("How Does Our Language Shape the Way We Think?") in which Boroditsky helps to expand Leonard's statement, "Through different distinctions in meaning, languages provide insights into how groups of speakers 'know the world'" (paragraph 7).
3. At the end of his article, Leonard uses the metaphor of an "orchestra of voices" to illustrate the richness of any one language. What other metaphors could be used? Write a description of how you understand language using a metaphor of your choice.

James Angelos
"Passing the Test"

A graduate of Columbia University's Graduate School of Journalism, James Angelos is a freelance journalist based in Berlin, Germany. He has written for *The Atlantic, The New York Times, Foreign Affairs,* and *The New Republic.* The following article appeared in the "Speaking in Tongues Issue" (Spring 2012) of the *World Policy Journal,* published by the World Policy Institute, a think tank dedicated to identifying "critical emerging global issues in an interdependent world." In this article, Angelos examines the impact of Europe's increasingly common (and controversial) pre-entry language requirements on individuals looking to rejoin spouses already settled there. The supposed benefit of the language requirement is to promote among immigrant communities better communication with and participation in their new country's cultural mainstream. However, Angelos notes that such language restrictions do not so much integrate as further separate these very communities.

Who do you suppose would benefit most from pre-entry language requirements? Who would benefit least?

Hasibe Koyun has her first German class in Istanbul on a crisp January morning. She's so nervous that her hand, where she wears her large diamond engagement ring, quivers. When she introduces herself to the class, she twirls the ring around her finger and glances at the whiteboard, where the teacher has written the German words for "I'm called," *Ich heiße.* Koyun's cheeks turn red. "Ich hei-zze Hasibe," she stammers with a thick beginner's accent. For 23-year-old Koyun, these first words of German, spoken at the Goethe Institute in Istanbul, mark the beginning of an odyssey that will, she hopes, take her from her hometown of Ören—a tranquil village of 1,500 in Turkey's western Anatolia—to Germany, where she plans to join her new husband, Ilhan, in the Rhineland city of Düsseldorf.

Koyun has a lot to be nervous about. She has just moved from her village to Istanbul for the three-month language course. Moreover, people in the metropolis—like the two young women in class who sit near the windows with long, dyed hair, skintight jeans, and knee-high leather boots—often dress differently than people in Ören. Koyun is the only girl in class to wear a headscarf. It conceals her hair and matches the long gray skirt that stretches down to her shoes. But matters of wardrobe are not Koyun's primary concern this morning. All she has in mind is doing well on the German test. The exam is still a few months away, but if she does not pass, she can't get a German visa. If she does not get the visa, she can't join her husband. A marriage celebration has already been planned. It's to take place in the center of Ören that summer, with the villagers and her family dancing to the beat of the *Davul*, a deep-throated, goat-skin drum, and the nasal drone of the woodwind *Zurna*. If Koyun doesn't pass, it would be a disaster.

The entire class of 12 students has the same worry this morning. Almost all are engaged or recently married to someone of Turkish origin living in Germany. They plan to join their spouses there, on the condition, of course, they pass the exam.

Language Law

In 2007, the Bundestag passed a law requiring foreign spouses from most nations outside the European Union to possess basic German-language skills before entering the country to join their husbands or wives. Spouses with university degrees or those deemed highly skilled workers are exempt from the requirement, as are those from several developed countries—including the United States, Japan, Australia, and Israel. The measure also requires immigrating spouses be at least 18. The German Interior Ministry says the rules are intended to prevent forced or fake marriages and promote integration, or to ensure that the spouses "will be able to communicate in everyday situations using basic German and thus be able to take part in the society from the time that they arrive."

Pre-entry language requirements for foreign spouses are increasingly   5 common in an immigration-weary Europe. France, Holland, Austria, and Denmark have each enacted such rules, and near the end of 2010, shortly after David Cameron took office, so did the United Kingdom. While not all the language requirements are identical—France's, for example, is generally more flexible and accommodating towards spouses than the others—in their current form, the efficacy of pre-entry language requirements in promoting language learning or the integration of immigrants is questionable. Their real purpose of the rules appears to be to reduce the number of uneducated or low-skilled immigrants coming to European countries. By pursuing more restrictive immigration policies in the name of integration, European political leaders are not only being disingenuous in their aims, but risk the opposite outcome—estranging the very immigrant communities they say they wish to see better integrated.

"The tests are less about promoting integration than restricting immigration," says Thomas Huddleston, an analyst for the Migration Policy Group, a Brussels-based think tank that has studied the effectiveness of the language requirements. According to the group's research, pre-entry tests may have resulted in a reduction of immigration but have not proven effective in promoting language learning. Those who pass the tests, says Huddleston, often forget what they've learned by the time they immigrate, and there is no evidence to suggest that passing a pre-entry test helps spouses learn the language once they arrive.

Like their European counterparts, British government officials have said the measure will encourage integration and "assist in removing cultural barriers." But government officials have also said that the regulation is part of a larger effort to control immigration. "It is a privilege to come to the UK and that is why I am committed to raising the bar for migrants and ensuring that those who benefit from being in Britain contribute to our society," British Home Secretary Theresa May said before the language requirement was implemented. "This is only the first step. We are currently reviewing English language requirements across the visa system with a view to tightening the rules further in the future."

Though first conceived by the previous Labor government, the enactment of the language requirement, according to the *Economist*, is part of the Tories' effort to fulfill an election promise to reduce net migration. Much of the foreign spouses in question come from poor, rural communities on the Indian subcontinent, and as the magazine points out, "That might not be the sort of immigrant that governments prefer to attract, but it is the kind that a number of British citizens want to marry."

The pre-entry language requirements in Britain, as elsewhere, have proven controversial. Immigrant advocacy groups claim that requiring foreign spouses to learn basic English before they can immigrate violates a couple's right to a family life, guaranteed under the European Convention on Human Rights. The Joint Council for the Welfare of Immigrants in Britain has said the pre-entry requirement "is not about integration, social cohesion or any other laudable claim of the Home Office," but about "getting numbers of migrants down, pure and simple."

A Public Face

10   Recently, Rashida Chapti, a British citizen in her mid 50s, became the public face of the debate in Britain about whether the rule is justified. As one of a few spouses who recently challenged the rule in court, Chapti, pictured in British newspapers in a striped hijab, petitioned to have her husband of four decades, with whom she had several children, join her in Britain from India. He is too old to learn English, she contended, and finding a school for him to learn in rural Gujarat where he lives, would be difficult. In December, a British High Court judge upheld the language requirement, ruling that the government was acting within its right to promote integration and safeguard social services. Reacting to the ruling, the Joint Council for the Welfare of Immigrants said in a statement, "No one in their right mind would pretend that learning English is not a good thing for immigrants in the UK to do." But the ruling forcing them to learn English before they arrive, "will mean that many British citizens will continue to experience enforced and indefinite separation from loved ones, partners, and in some cases, their children," the statement added. "In countries experiencing conflict, poverty, natural disasters, and political instability," it can be "extremely difficult to acquire linguistic skills prior to arrival in the UK."

Many others in Britain, however, see matters quite differently. "This case goes to the heart of the debate over what a nation is and what it is that holds us together," reads one column in the Daily Mail. "And central to that debate is a shared language. It's got nothing to do with human rights, or the subjugation of minority cultures." The article continues: "The great multicultural experiment failed precisely because it encouraged incomers not to sign up to our common culture," resulting in "ghettos and isolation."

The notion that many immigrants have failed to become part of Britain's "common culture" was proclaimed by David Cameron last February in a speech at the Munich Security Conference. The prime minister blamed the "doctrine of state multiculturalism," which he described as a "hands off tolerance" for this state of affairs. One result, he said, was a growing security threat caused by the radicalization of Muslim youth in Britain. "Frankly," he added, "we need a lot less of the passive tolerance of recent years and a much more active, muscular liberalism." Presumably, the pre-entry language requirement is one aspect of the prime minister's brawny liberalism.

The concern that subsequent immigration of families, so called "family reunification," can exacerbate isolation of ethnic communities and hinder integration is widespread in Europe. As the *Economist* put it, "In countries founded through immigration, such as the United States, families have been seen as the key to integration; in Britain, like much of Europe, many fear that importing families reinforces inward-looking communities."

In Holland, anti-immigration sentiment has led to the rise of Geert Wilders, a right-wing populist who controls the nation's third largest parliamentary party and has called for a cessation of immigration from Muslim countries.

Since 2006, an overseas integration exam, testing basic knowledge of 15 Dutch language and society, has been required of foreign spouses. As part of the preparation for the Dutch test, spouses abroad are compelled to watch a video on Dutch society, part of a "study pack" that can be ordered for €110, though an English language version can be seen on YouTube. "I got quite a shock, of course," says one immigrant woman in the video. "I thought, my goodness, they really are white!" Though the video shows some contented immigrants, its goal appears, in large part, to shatter any illusions of Holland as an ideal place to live, focusing on problems related to immigration, poverty, and social housing. At times, it strikes an overtly discouraging tone. At one point in the video, the viewer visits the squalid flat where a Turkish family of six lives. The children, says the narrator, can't play outside, though we are not told exactly why. Introducing the mustachioed man of the house, the narrator says, "Life is different from how Akin imagined it would be." Then Akin, who is filmed pointing, apparently, at the leaky bathroom ceiling, says, "If someone from abroad was planning to come here, I would tell them, 'Think hard about what you're doing, what you're letting yourself in for. If I were 30 or 25, I wouldn't leave my country and come here. I'd stay in my own country, really."

Human Rights Watch has criticized that Dutch overseas test—as well as the exam fee of €350 ($450) and other financial barriers related to family immigration—as discriminatory. It targets spouses from Morocco and Turkey, the group charges, traditionally large sources of immigration to the Netherlands. The Dutch test, says the rights group, has served as a model for other European nations and resulted in a 20 percent decline in the number of applications for family reunification and formation in Holland the year it was implemented. While the Dutch government has a legitimate interest in advancing the integration of its migrant population, according to a Human Rights Watch report, the overseas test does not advance this aim. The requirement risks "alienating migrant communities in the Netherlands because it creates an impression that their family members (and hence they) are not welcome in the country," the report says. Such criticism has not dissuaded the Dutch government. In 2011, the level of Dutch required to pass the overseas exam was raised.

But the matter remains far from settled. Last Spring, Bibi Mohammad Imran, an Afghan woman who wished to join her husband and eight children in Holland, but who was refused entry because she had not passed the integration exam, brought her case to a court in the Netherlands. The Dutch court then requested a preliminary ruling from the European Court of Justice, the highest court concerning matters of EU law. At question was whether the EU's Family Reunification Directive—which compels member states to "respect family life," but also allows them to "require third country nationals to comply with integration measures"—permits a state to refuse a family member entry for not passing an exam abroad. At the time, the European Commission weighed in on the case, writing that EU states should not use these integration measures as a means of limiting family reunification. A member state, the European Commission said, cannot refuse entry to a family member solely on the grounds that this person has not passed an integration test abroad. Such integration measures, the observation said, should encourage successful integration and family life and must not be exclusionary. Before the Court of Justice could render an

opinion that could have threatened the legality of the pre-entry requirement, the Dutch embassy in Islamabad, Pakistan, gave Imran a provisional
residence permit, mooting the legal proceedings.

A few months later, another Dutch court ruled that imposing the
overseas test on Turkish citizens violates the EU Association Agreement
with Turkey, forcing the Dutch government to stop requiring Turkish
nationals to take the test. This April, a group calling itself The Foundation
for Victims of Integration, representing a potential tens of thousands of Turks
that were forced to take the exam, is planning to sue the Dutch government
for damages and for the recovery of costs associated with taking the test.

Die Türken

In Germany, the language requirement is deeply unpopular among Turks,
who account for the nation's largest ethnic minority. Indeed, many see the
law as a spurious effort to hinder further Turkish immigration. Even in
Turkey, when the rule was passed, then-Foreign Minister Abdullah Gül
called it "against human rights." And when Germany's federal commissioner
for integration, Maria Böhmer, visited Ankara, the Turkish newspaper
Hürriyet dubbed her "the German minister who brings brides to tears."

Around the time the measure was passed in Germany, four German-
Turkish organizations boycotted an "integration summit" hosted by
German Chancellor Angela Merkel to express their discontent with the
rule. The head of one of those organizations, the Turkish Community in
Germany, Kenan Kolat, claimed the law was discriminatory and said, "If
Helga and Horst are allowed to get their partners here, why not Ahmed
and Aische too?"

Many German newspapers have not responded with particular sympathy to the protests of their Turkish compatriots. "The Turkish officials
defend the importation of juvenile and preferably voiceless brides from
Turkey as if it were a question of the human rights of Turkish men," reads
one commentary in the *Frankfurter Allgemeine Zeitung*. The Turkish boycott
of a 2007 integration summit helped show that "some foreigners" come "to
live with their own kind in ghettos and parallel societies," reads another
commentary in the same newspaper. The government must send a clear
signal, it went on, "Germany is not a country of immigration, but a country
of integration."

20

Despite a sense among many in Germany that their nation has been overrun by foreigners, Germany is arguably becoming less of an immigration destination. Since the reunification of East and West Germany in 1990, the number of migrants entering Germany has generally been in a steady decline, though last year the nation did experience a significant rise in immigration from crisis-ridden EU nations like Greece and Spain. Each year from 2006 to 2010, more people left Germany for Turkey than arrived, a reversal of the longtime trend and a tribute to the booming Turkish economy. Nevertheless, marriage migration remains a major source of lingering Turkish immigration to Germany. It also remains of great concern to those who believe that the tendency of Turkish Germans to import spouses perpetuates a perennial immigrant culture with Turkish, not German, language and traditions remaining paramount within families. The spouses coming from Turkey tend to be seen as undesirable immigrants— uneducated women (though many are men) who come from poor and backward regions, unwilling to adopt European mores. Since the tests began, Turkish immigration through family reunification has decreased significantly. In 2006, before the test was instituted, 10,208 Turkish spouses were granted residency visas that allowed them to join their partners in Germany. That number fell by about a third in the years following the rule's enactment.

At the Goethe Institute in Istanbul, although many of the newlyweds eventually speak positively of their classroom experience itself, nearly all say that the exam sends an off-putting, exclusionary message. Perhaps, as some students say, it's because Germans fear the Islam that Turks bring, or because Germans simply believe that Germany is for ethnic Germans. But whatever the reason, as Hasibe Koyun puts it, "Everybody knows that the Germans don't accept Turks."

After School

After the class ends, Koyun makes her way downstairs to the school's lounge to meet her father, a round, gray-haired man, who has come with his daughter from their small village to spend some days with her in Istanbul. He has waited for her the entire morning, sitting at a small table next to a snack machine. "It's good that they learn German," he says. "But I wonder what the real motives are." Perhaps, he reflects, it has something to do with German opposition to Turkey joining the European Union. Or maybe there's a financial incentive. After all, the course and exam fee cost the equivalent of €670 ($875).

Koyun sits next to him and looks upset. Her teacher has told her she'd   25 be moving to another class. Koyun wonders if this was because she had never made it past the fifth grade in her Turkish school. She wonders if she'll be able to pass the exam—still three months away—at all. "I'm very stressed," she says. Like most of her classmates, Koyun never imagined she'd move to Germany. When a marriage offer from Germany had come a few years earlier, she refused because she wanted to stay near her family and help take care of her aging father. But this time is different.

"I love him," she says, talking about her husband Ilhan one day after school while walking through Taksim Square on the way to catch her bus home. Koyun does not want to discuss intimate details of their courtship, other than to say, "It wasn't flirty, the way we met." Her father and his father are cousins, she says, and he has a big supportive family in Germany, which gives her comfort. "There is no secret to falling in love," she says.

Many students tell similar love stories. No one describes theirs as an arranged marriage. Often, however, they seemed to know surprisingly little about the objects of their affection. One young woman says she met her fiancé at a friend's "promise celebration," something of an engagement party, when he was visiting Istanbul from Mannheim, Germany. Still, she's not quite sure what he does for a living, nor does she know very much about Mannheim, but she is convinced she'd made the right decision. "I won't ever meet anybody like him again," she says firmly.

The question of what awaits such women in Germany and their impact on German society is open to considerable debate, but more rarely discussed is the fact that many of the would-be immigrant spouses are men. In 2010, 43 percent of the spouses coming from Turkey were men, about the same percentage as 2006, the year before the exam was implemented.

On his second day of class in Istanbul, Tufan Cetindas, a 26-year-old website designer with large brown eyes and a thin patch of hair under his lower lip, leaves class 45 minutes early, but with a good excuse. He is getting married in the afternoon to his fiancée Hatice, who has come from Berlin for the ceremony. The couple had met at a narghile café along an Istanbul shoreline while Hatice was on vacation in Istanbul. He never wanted to go to Germany, he says, but his mother-in-law had argued for the advantages— from kindergarten for his children to affordable health insurance. The marriage takes place in an Istanbul courthouse, where after a short cere-mony, the couple poses for pictures near a portrait of Mustafa Kemal Atatürk, the founder of the Turkish Republic. Then they go to the groom's small apartment overlooking a traffic-choked highway on the outskirts of Istanbul. Amid a small gathering, an imam in a business suit sitting on the living room couch next to a small aquarium presides over a short religious ceremony. "Women are like roses," the imam advises the groom. "Be gentle. You should look after her like a rose."

Confidence Building

30   During the first few weeks of class, Koyun's confidence as a student begins to grow. She is diligent, poring over her notes during breaks while many of her classmates smoke in front of the building. She's even starting to enjoy the lessons. "This course prepares me so I can go to Germany and be independent," she says one day after class, adding, "I'm proud when I can answer the teacher's questions." Such favorable attitudes about the course itself—at least among those with the time and money to enroll in the three-month-long program at a Goethe Institute—are not uncommon. In the school's lounge one day after class, a group of young women wearing headscarves and diamond rings sit doing their homework. In their workbooks, they write German sentences like, "Since when have you worked as a taxi driver?"

"The first time I heard I had to take this course, I wondered, 'Why do I have to do this? What do the Germans expect from us?'" asks one student, Vesile Bayram. "Then I came here, and I realized that it's for me to learn. The Germans want to make it easier for me." Bayram plans to move to Munich to join her husband. The more she learns about Germany, she says, the more excited she is to go. Germans are more cultured, more interested in environmental protection and social justice, she observes, adding, "In Germany, every human being is equal, and the country exists for the people. In Turkey, the country comes first and then the people." But still, she says, passing the exam is her greatest worry. "Sometimes I have nightmares."

In 2010, 11,044 Turkish newlyweds and fiancés took the German language exam. Only 10 percent of those who took a preparatory "pre-integration" course at one of the three Goethe Institutes in Turkey—in Istanbul, Ankara, and Izmir—failed. But among the 88 percent of those who prepared for the test elsewhere, 37 percent failed. Advocates of the language exam emphasize that it tests only for basic proficiency, enough to greet someone, or fill out a form in a government office. But some of those taking the test have had such minimal schooling of any variety before they arrive in class that they would have difficulty filling out a form in Turkish. For them, such a feat in German can seem a Herculean task.

One class in Istanbul caters to such students with very limited schooling. Its teacher uses methods suitable for kindergarten. Students gather in a circle and clap in rhythm as they take turns pronouncing German phrases like "I come from Turkey." Correct answers are awarded with a round of applause. This method usually pays off, says the teacher, but this particular group is especially challenging. One student is unable to read at all. Several do not know what a verb is. One man comes to class without his homework and tells the teacher, "It was raining, and my homework disappeared."

Predictably, those who have the most trouble passing the exam are the most opposed to it. One afternoon in the school's lounge, a young woman pleads to a visitor, "Please help us." She had taken the exam twice and failed. Her husband, she says, is growing impatient. "He always says, 'Pass the exam or I will leave you,'" she explains. She will soon be taking the exam for the third time.

In the school's lounge, a stout 56-year-old woman named Ayse discusses 35 her daughter-in-law, Fatime. "Is there anything you can do to help us?" Ayse asks. Ayse has lived in a small city in Germany's Ruhr district for 40 years, where she had worked in a pickle factory before retiring. She speaks some basic German, enough to say phrases like "small village" as she explains how she'd found a wife for her son during a visit to her birthplace, a small village in central Anatolia.

Ayse saw Fatime, a quiet 20-year-old, at a marriage celebration. "I liked her, so I bought her," she says, letting out a high-pitched laugh. The expression in Turkish suggests an offer of marriage and not a literal purchase. Ayse's son, a house painter, came to meet his prospective bride. "They met, they talked, they liked each other," she explains. The couple agreed to marry in Turkey. The bride was decorated with henna for the wedding. Fatime, however, had already taken the exam once and failed. She had not made it beyond the eighth grade in Turkey, says Ayse, who claims she came to Istanbul to be with Fatime because the young woman had "angst" being alone. But the costs were becoming increasingly hard to bear. Ayse, a widow, left her 17-year-old daughter at home alone back in Germany, and the family has spent some $4,500 on courses, room and board, and private tutoring for Fatime.

Despite these difficulties, Ayse professes her love for Germany. It's the land where she had made a living and raised her five children, proudly adding that one daughter was nearly finished with medical school. Her German neighbors are nice, and she often cooks for the old German widow next door. But Ayse is not convinced Germany enacted the language requirement to promote integration. Though Ayse never learned much German herself, Fatime, she says, would be better off learning German in Germany, where the family could help her learn the basics and take her out shopping. "We are a big family," she says. "We could help her."

The Test

The busiest test-taking site in Turkey is on the eighth floor of a bland office building in downtown Ankara. One Friday morning, 31 test takers—18 men and 13 women, each having paid their exam fee of 140 Turkish lira ($93)—file into a florescent-lit room with rows of small desks and German tourism advertisements hanging on the walls. One reads, "Germany. Simply Friendly."

One of the test-takers is a 33-year-old woman named Hanim. She arrived the night before from Gaziantep, a city 435 miles away in southeastern Anatolia near the Syrian border. The white Volkswagen van that brought her was filled with a dozen passengers, other test takers and accompanying family members. After reaching Ankara late at night, they slept in the van. During the exam that morning, the family members wait outside, including one older man wearing baggy, traditional pants, who for a short time, long ago, had lived in Germany. He still keeps a tattered German medical insurance card in his wallet "for the memories."

40   The multiple-choice section lasts about an hour. Then the test takers break into small groups for oral exams. The students are asked to introduce themselves. Hanim answers mechanically, like a soldier trained how to respond to enemy interrogators: "I'm 33. I come from Turkey. I live in Gaziantep. I am a housewife. My hobby is shopping." Then she is told to pose a series of questions on different topics. Hanim, however, repeatedly says nothing, as if she did not understand the task. Her chances of passing the test seem remote. She finally seems to catch on when the administrator

asks her simply to make any kind of request. "Can you give me a rose?" Hanim replies in German.

After the exam, Hanim slips into a black hijab and ankle-length black garment so that only her face is exposed. Outside, she meets the crowd of family members, including her brother. Almost everyone begins complaining about the exam. "It is punishment. Maybe they don't want us to come to Germany," she says. "I am just a housewife. Why do I need to learn how to use the Internet or write a letter?" German words can get so terribly long, she explains, and of course the fact that she had not gone beyond elementary school did not make it any easier. "All you need to know is how to introduce yourself. You can learn the rest in Germany."

Gulcan Bayazit, a broad 39-year-old, chimes in. "This is psychological pressure," she says in perfect German, with a trembling voice. Raised in Germany, she lives in Mönchengladbach, as do her four children from a first marriage. She has come to Ankara to help her second husband study for the exam. He failed the first time he took it, even though he had attended university. "Once someone is over the age of 30, it is hard for them to learn a new language." Another man wearing a pinstriped suit who is waiting for his daughter adds, "They might as well tell us not to come to Germany."

Up on Stage

One day after her class at Istanbul's Goethe Institute, Koyun and a group of her classmates attend an optional theater workshop that allows them to practice their fledgling German. For some of the students, it would be their first time on a stage. In the theater, the instructor calls pairs of students to the stage to perform short skits. In one scenario, Barack Obama meets David Beckham on the street. The two young men playing the roles kiss each other on both cheeks. "What's up?" David Beckham asks Barack Obama. The class erupts in giggles. "Stand straight," shouts Koyun from the audience to the student playing Barack Obama. "You are a politician."

Koyun and another woman, a friend of hers from class, then take the stage. They are playing Angela Merkel and Shakira, the Colombian pop star. The two are to meet in a bus station. Koyun plays Merkel. "Who is Angela Merkel?" Koyun asks the instructor. A few of the students from class shout, "The German President," though actually, Merkel is the

Chancellor. Koyun, also seemingly unaware of Shakira's identity, then asks, "Which one holds the higher status?" as if this would influence the way she plays her role. "You are," responds one student. "You are the President." After class, Koyun walks toward the bus stop with a companion. "I did not know until today," says the other woman, "that the leader of Germany is a woman."

45   In the spring, Koyun takes the exam and passes. It is a huge relief. She has overcome the dreaded obstacle between her and her future. The wedding celebration will take place in her village that summer as planned. Koyun moves back to her village and awaits the changes to come, though, as the months drag by, much of the German she learns vanishes. While the life that lies ahead in Germany remains largely an unknown, during her time in Istanbul, the possibilities had seemed bright. "I'm 23 years old, but I have not done any great things," she said one day after class. "Until now."

What would become of Koyun and the others in her class in Germany? She had a sense, however vague, that she was hovering on the cusp of accomplishing great things. Still, her hopeful outlook could clash with her future in a nation where Turkish immigration is often perceived as a problem.

Of course, there are real immigration-related social problems in Germany, so it's no great stretch to imagine why Germans are so hesitant about more, new, unencumbered arrivals. Germany's immigration history, stemming largely from the arrival of waves of guest workers in the 1960s and early 1970s, has been fraught, over time resulting in complex social problems. But erecting barriers to family unification does not address, in any meaningful sense, the real social problems in Germany that integration policy should seek to remedy—underemployment, lower than average educational achievement, and other ills that disproportionately beset some migrant groups. The pre-entry tests only intensify a sense of social inequity by seeming to target the family life of those groups.

As barriers have been erected to keep out uneducated migrants, German policy makers are increasingly realizing the importance of luring highly skilled migration for a needy German labor market, especially as the German population is shrinking. Germany can better lure such workers by providing greater incentives and creating a society more open to cultural differences. Placing barriers on family life in order to stem what is perceived as "the wrong kind" of immigration is not part of the answer.

Whereas Koyun's experience at the Goethe Institute was very positive, she was among a fortunate minority in Turkey with the resources to take the course. German authorities should rather focus on making sure new immigrants have the opportunity for a similar experience once they arrive in Germany. The benefits of learning about German language and society should not be contingent on the threat of losing the possibility of being with one's family.

Political leaders across Europe should beware of pursuing alienating and 50 arguably discriminatory policies that masquerade as integration, lest they undermine the beneficial integration policies that might truly help alleviate long-simmering problems. The focus of wise integration policy should be to create conditions in Europe where migrants and their children have equal opportunities to participate in society—to receive a good education, to become school-teachers, police officers, politicians, and business leaders. Ultimately, a wise integration policy should improve life at home, not create barriers abroad.

Analyze

1. What are the main concerns that have prompted the pre-entry language requirements in Germany, France, the United Kingdom, and Holland? In what ways have advocacy groups, journalists, and the author of this article questioned those concerns?

2. The author quotes a commentary from the newspaper *Frankfurter Allgemeine Zeitung*: "Germany is not a country of immigration, but a country of integration." What is the difference between a country of immigration and one of integration? Based on what you've read in the article, do you think this is true about Germany? Why or why not? What other information might be helpful?

3. The author ends his article with strong suggestions about what European leaders should do instead of a pre-entry language requirement. Do you think leaders will be persuaded? What counterarguments might they use in response? What further evidence would Angelos need to provide in response to their responses?

Explore

1. In his article, Angelos neglects to mention that some European countries have multiple official languages. How do they address issues of integration and immigration? In small groups, research the language

policy of a European country with multiple official languages (e.g., Switzerland, Belgium, Finland, etc.). What are the linguistic expectations for new immigrants in the country you chose? How equitable are these expectations? Write a "letter to the editor" to flesh out Angelos's article.

2. What else could countries do to help immigrants "integrate" besides having them demonstrate competence in the language? What else is necessary to know besides language? Why?

3. In an increasingly globalized world, how important is it to adopt cultural and linguistic norms in order to effectively integrate into a society? What might be alternative ways to integrate new immigrants while preserving linguistic diversity? Research a few countries' language policies to familiarize yourself with some criteria for developing your own language policy.

Reshma Krishnamurthy Sharma
"The New Language Landscape"

Reshma Krishnamurthy Sharma is a writer, radio jockey, and freelance public relations executive based in Bangalore, India. She contributes frequently to *The Hindu*, an English-language newspaper founded in Chennai, India, in 1878. In "The New Language Landscape," published in *The Hindu* on February 12, 2012, Sharma explores the reasons behind a growing trend among the children of India's young professionals to learn English rather than their parents' regional languages.

What is lost and what is gained when children grow up speaking a language different from their parents' languages?

"**R**uchika, do you want this book on Winnie-the-Pooh or the Doraemon series toys?" asks Sandhya Rao to her two-year-old at a bookstore. It may seem ordinary, but the toddler replies in a language that was never her grandma's or even her mother's own. An increasing number of children, especially in urban areas, are speaking more English than any other language. Has English become the new mother tongue in many homes? Given the environments in which Gen X children are growing up, the answer seems to be 'yes.'

One contributing factor could be that in recent times the country has seen a significant rise in inter-regional marriages. Perhaps parents feel it is better to communicate in one universal language than to speak to the kid in two regional languages.

Shiril Pinto, a HR professional, talks to her three-year-old in English. "I am in a mixed marriage where my mother tongue is Konkani and my husband's is Bengali. As we were unable to learn each other's languages, we have resorted to speaking to our kid in English. Also, as we have always communicated to each other prior to marriage in this language, it just continued as a natural progression of communication at home."

Chaitra Kiran has different reasons for choosing English. "I do speak in Kannada and am married into my own community. Yet, I feel parents like me have started stressing English because we see children are not able to understand anything if they are not fluent in this language and somehow it has become the common spoken language in activity centres, play areas, in upscale apartments and so on." Book stores, children's activity centres, playhomes, and even workplaces encourage the use of English more than any other language. The presence of international schools in cities and strict codes in even regular schools on the use of one common language has somehow pushed English into homes as well.

Moreover, parents often believe that speaking in flawless English from a   5
young age, children are better equipped to work in global environments, so they converse in this language predominantly so that their child is not left behind.

Smitha Roy, a communication professional, did not make a conscious decision to speak in English to her three-year-old daughter Aahana. She and her husband have always spoken in English as a matter of convenience. She adds: "Somehow, even my parents conversed with me and my sisters generally in English, perhaps because we went to a convent school. I ensure Aahana learns Kannada from her grandparents. I don't want her to feel she did not get the opportunity to learn any other language."

According to Nandini Ashok, an educator who runs a preschool, "I personally think parents these days find the interview process at the kindergarten level cumbersome. It is unfair that the child is spoken to in English, and there are lesser opportunities for Indian languages to be learnt and of course, this in a certain way pressurises parents to speak more in English."

Yet parents who speak to children only in English are content that it is a global language and that their children will learn other languages if they are interested in them. Fifty years down the line, will we be surprised if English becomes the single spoken language and kids go to special schools to learn India's regional languages?

Analyze

1. According to Sharma, what factors have contributed to the trend toward English-only in India's urban areas?
2. How might speaking a different "mother tongue" from your parents affect your relationship with them? What examples do you have from your own experiences, the experiences of someone you know, or a character in a story you've read or seen?
3. There are several different dialects of English worldwide—some scholars call them World Englishes. (Dialects have distinctive aspects of grammar, vocabulary, and pronunciation, yet are mutually understandable.) What aspects of an Indian dialect of English can you discern in Sharma's article, as distinct from the English standard you use in school?

Explore

1. After two hundred years of British colonization, India gained its independence in 1947. Why is the English language still dominant in this country? Research India's current "language landscape" and suggest reasons for English's dominance. Based on your research, do you think English will become India's lingua franca? Why or why not?
2. Sharma asks, "Fifty years down the line, will we be surprised if English becomes the single spoken language and kids go to special schools to learn India's regional languages?" What other multilingual countries have become dominated by one language? What has been done, if anything, to preserve regional and indigenous languages?
3. As the world becomes more globalized, will it be more practical for people to choose between one language or another, as Sharma observes

in her article? Or is it realistic to become proficient in both a mother tongue and a national language? Find a scholarly article that addresses issues around language policy, education, and globalization and summarize in either a PowerPoint or poster presentation how the article addresses or answers these questions.

Pallavi Polanki
"Operation Mind Your Language"

Pallavi Polanki is a special correspondent for *Firstpost.com*, an online news source that offers thoughtful analysis of news in India and around the world. Polanki was also a special correspondent and launch team member for *Open* magazine, a weekly online current affairs and features magazine that "addresses the progressive, globally minded Indian" reader. "Operation Mind Your Language" appeared in *Open* in May 2010. In his article, Polanki describes the enthusiasm and earnestness of young Afghanis who are training as English-language teachers at the National Council of Education Research and Training in New Delhi, India, a collaboration meant to address the need for more English teachers in the public schools of troubled regions of Afghanistan.

As you read, take note of the different languages referred to in the article. How many have you already heard of? Which ones are new to you?

A back-bencher wearing a bright purple T-shirt and an even brighter smile raises his hand. "God is busy, may I help you?" says the writing on his T-shirt. Twenty-one-year-old Ehsan, from Wardak, a Pashtun-dominated province in central east Afghanistan, volunteers to explain his government's decision to sponsor 43 students at the National Council of Education Research and Training (NCERT) in New Delhi. Another 39 are in Mysore, at NCERT's Regional Institute of Education (RIE) campus, undergoing a similar 20-month programme.

"I am a student of teacher training for English language here," says Ehsan, before he delivers his kick-ass punchline. "As you know, USA nowadays means United States of Afghanistan. English has become our native language," he quips, making his classmates laugh.

He continues.

"Wherever you go in Afghanistan, you will face Americans. That is why English has gained a very high position there. Before the Americans, there were the Russians. At that time, many of our people learnt the Russian language. God-willing, when we return, we will teach the new generation English."

5   And so, with the new invasion has come the demand for a new language. Seven years of being the headquarters of the 'global war on terror,' and the subsequent arrival of 31 different nationalities on their soil, has brought with it a huge linguistic challenge that governments and private organisations, both local and international, are scrambling to address.

Pashto and Dari, Afghanistan's two official languages, now share space with a third language. Go shopping in Kabul, and the labeling on packets will be in three languages. A passport issued today in Afghanistan has text printed in Pashto, Dari and English.

English speakers are highly sought after in the job market. According to the Afghan Ministry of Education's statistics, nearly 50 per cent of the 12,000 public schools are in need of over 20,000 qualified English teachers. The quality of English teaching in schools is regarded as poor, and the proficiency of English teachers, lacking.

"Shortage of qualified teachers in general, and English teachers in particular, is a major national challenge. This challenge is bigger in rural, remote and less secure parts of the country. Since 2005, English is taught as a foreign language from Grade Four (it used to begin from Grade Seven). This change has added more demand on English teachers," says Susan Wardak, director general of the Afghan Ministry of Education's Teacher Education Department, in an email interview.

And so the Afghan government is hard at work trying to strengthen English departments at teacher training colleges, and giving out scholarships to students to be trained as English teachers abroad. "Collaboration on teacher education between Afghanistan and India is part of a broad bilateral agreement between the two governments," adds Wardak.

10   And so the stage was set for Operation Mind Your Language. It is a responsibility the students (the majority of whom belong to Afghanistan's

conflict-ridden southern provinces) take very seriously. Shy at first, they take their time to open up. But once they do, their warmth and sincerity, not to mention sense of humour, win you over.

For NCERT, this is a first-of-its-kind collaboration. "This 20-month diploma course on English Language and Teaching of English Language has been specifically planned for Afghan students. Initially, the idea was that students would be given teacher training in various disciplines. But later on, considering the interest in English in Afghanistan and its international importance in creating a niche for its youth, the Afghan Ministry of Education decided to focus on the English language," says Poonam Agrawal, head of the International Relations division of NCERT.

Abdul Hadi Hamdard is from Helmand, a volatile southwestern province that has seen many military operations by Nato-led forces in the last seven years. Abdul, 21, was working at a local radio station when he got the scholarship to study in India. "In the name of Allah, we welcome you to our class. My English speaking power is not very good . . . but I am doing my best. When I was in Afghanistan, I could not speak any English. Now I have improved a lot. It is our responsibility to learn English and go back to our country and teach in our schools."

According to 22-year-old Mehrabuddin Wakman, a student at the Mysore campus who's also from the Helmand region, this is a pathbreaking scholarship for students from Afghanistan's southern provinces: "Majority of the 40-odd students here are from the three-four provinces that are most affected by insurgents. The level of education there, therefore, is very low." English, says Mehrabuddin, is their passport to a job, a good salary and even opportunities abroad.

The students, say faculty members, have made tremendous progress since they first arrived. "Initially, we were speaking to them only in English, and they weren't used to that. But we have somehow managed to bridge the gap, and it happened because they watch Hindi serials back home and so they've picked up a little Hindi. . . . Once that language barrier was broken, the classrooms became very lively and interactive. Some Pashto words are very close to Punjabi, and so I would use a typically Punjabi word and they would immediately understand what I meant," says Kirti Kapoor, a member of the faculty at NCERT, Delhi.

For teachers, it's encouraging enough that students have found the confidence to converse in English. "They now know that their broken English is acceptable. That is a very big achievement after six months. Their

15

confidence is rising as they interact with more and more people. They are a young and adventurous lot," says Basanti Banerjee, also part of the visiting NCERT faculty.

"They have a kind of innocence that you don't find in our students," observes Prema Raghavan, coordinator of the Mysore batch, "In that sense, they seem far more honest in their interactions with teachers. They pretty much say what they think. It feels more like teaching young children. It is very refreshing."

Little gestures by students outside the class have endeared their teachers to them even more. Professor Raghavan relates an incident that happened when she ran into a group of her students at an ice-cream parlour. She had gone with her family, but the students quietly paid her bill before she could. "When I protested, they said, 'Let us have the honour.' They have these little ways that are very touching."

Hakima Zainul Abedin is one of the three girls studying at RIE, Mysore. Hakima, 24, used to be a school teacher in Helmand province.

Like most other Afghan students, her ideas about India came from watching Hindi movies. Only, she took them a little too seriously. "Before I came here, I thought India was a very dangerous place. I had only seen Bollywood films. But now, I've changed my mind. People of India are quite relaxed and they don't interfere." (So much for Bollywood's soft power. . . .)

20   Hakima says teaching and studying in schools, especially for girls, is very risky in her province. "It is extremely difficult for girls to go to school because of the insurgents," she reports, "So many of our schools have been burnt down. But we are rebuilding our schools. I will go back and teach English there. English is our link to the world, and it is very important for Afghanistan to connect with other countries."

Teaching can be a high-risk job in Afghanistan, and many students have chilling personal stories to tell. Abdul Wahid Karimy says he was shot at by the Taliban when he was working as a teacher in a school. "Three people surrounded me and they wanted to kill me. After they shot me in the stomach a couple of times, I fell unconscious. After that, they went looking for my father and uncle," says Wahid, whose father is a school principal in Helmand, where the incident occurred. Wahid moved to Herat province, which borders Iran, one-and-a-half years ago. He says he wants to study law in India after he has finished his diploma. He has also enrolled for computer classes, which he attends in the evening after finishing his lessons at NCERT. "I won't get this opportunity again, once I go back to

Afghanistan. I want to make the most of it. I am already 26," says Wahid, who, unlike the majority of his classmates, belongs to the ethnic community of Hazaras, the third largest group after Pashtuns and Tajiks in Afghanistan.

Twenty-year-old Sayed Khaled Folad's father is a member of Afghanistan's parliament. He speaks about how the government too is now keen on hiring people with English language skills. "There are some jobs that employ Americans to work for the Afghan government. Also, if you are consultant for the government, speaking English is a necessity. Then there are NGOs like US-Aid that employ Americans. So working in the administration requires knowledge of English," says Khaled, who is planning to do a degree in India before he joins the government back home. "The government needs good workers, people who want to serve country. If I am getting a degree, it is not for me. It is for my country."

Though studies and homework seem to dominate the agenda after class and on weekends, students are also learning about a new culture and sharing their own with their hosts. Holi and Diwali were celebrated with much enthusiasm on campus. They say they have the photographs to prove it. For their *navroz* or New Year celebrations, students at the NCERT campus treated the teachers and staff to a music and dance performance. Khaled has been playing cricket with his Indian friends at the hostel. Bollywood movies, of course, continue to be a favourite. Not to forget sightseeing. A visit to the Taj Mahal was accomplished on day two of their arrival in Delhi.

So, Operation Mind Your Language seems to be going rather well. Clearly, there is going to be no dearth of challenges for these newly trained English teachers once they return to their rugged provinces. But there's also no doubt that these young Afghans are intent on doing their government proud.

Analyze

1. Why do you suppose Afghani students are sent to India to study English and become English teachers?
2. What cross-cultural interactions and occurrences are documented in the article? What assumptions did the Afghani students have about India that changed? What assumptions did you have about Afghanistan that changed? What more would you like to know?

3. The author observes that "teaching can be a high-risk job in Afghanistan" (paragraph 21). What happened to Abdul Wahid Karimy, and why do you think he would choose to continue being a teacher? What are his aspirations?

Explore

1. Polanki writes, "with the new invasion has come the demand for a new language" (paragraph 5). What invasion is he referring to, and why would it be important for Afghanis to acquire the language of their invaders? What might be different for Afghanis learning English now compared to the previous generation that learned Russian?
2. The program Operation Mind Your Language is 20 months long, during which time students learn English and how to teach it. Do you think this is enough time to learn a foreign language well enough to teach it? How important is it to have native speakers teach a foreign language? What is the best way to acquire a second language as an adult? In order to have informed answers to these questions, find reliable sources that address second language acquisition.
3. From the article, we can see why Afghanistan would want and need to include the English language in its school curriculum. If you had to choose one essential foreign language to include in the school curriculum where you grew up, what would it be and why? In a proposal to the curriculum committee, outline and support your rationale.

Julie Traves
"The Church of Please and Thank You"

Formerly a book promoter, Julie Traves is now deputy arts editor at *The Globe and Mail*, the largest national newspaper in Canada. She is also a freelance writer whose works on the arts, society, and ideas have appeared in *Canadian Business*, the *Toronto Star*, and the *National Post*. "The Church of Please and Thank You" appeared in the March–April 2005 issue of *This*

Magazine, one of Canada's longest published alternative journals on politics, pop culture, and the arts. In her article, Traves suggests similarities between EFL (English as a foreign language) instructors and earlier Christian missionaries. She wonders if EFL has gone beyond the linguistic and entered the realm of the cultural—in effect, what she describes as a "linguistic imperialism."

Do you agree with Traves's observation that "English has irrevocably changed and acculturated the world"?

Michelle Szabo smiles encouragingly as a young businessman talks about his hobbies in broken English. She is a Canadian teacher at Aeon's language school in Kawagoe, Japan. He is a prospective student she's charged to recruit as part of her job. The two meet in a drab five-storey office building outside the train station. The room is so small it fits only a table and two chairs. But making the sell to would-be learners has little to do with décor. What counts is Szabo's final handshake.

More than contact with an attractive young woman, her personal touch symbolizes a grasp on a better life. In the competitive marketplace of Japan, English test scores make or break job applications. Getting ahead means getting into classes with teachers like Szabo. "I would ask so many people, 'do you expect to use English in your life?' And most people would say 'No, no, no, I just need this test score,'" says Szabo. "I think it's sort of a given for all families—it's like food, shelter, English." Some sarariiman (salarymen) were so excited they trembled when they took her hand.

In addition to the 380 million people worldwide who use English as their first language, it's estimated there are 350 million to 500 million speakers of English as a foreign language (EFL)—and the number is growing. For people from affluent and developing nations alike, it is clear that the secret passwords to safety, wealth and freedom can be whispered only in English. Even 66 percent of French citizens, linguistic protectionists *par excellence*, agreed they needed to speak English in a 2001 Eurobarometer poll. While thinkers such as John Ralston Saul proclaim the death of globalization, locals from countries around the world are clamouring for English training.

Enter thousands of Westerners who spread the English gospel overseas each year. Like the Christian missionaries who came before them, many are young, have a blind faith in the beliefs they've grown up with and are eager to make their mark on the world. Unlike the 19- to 26-year-olds who proselytize for the Latter-day Saints, however, these new missionaries are also out for adventure, good times—and hard cash. Part of a $7.8-billion industry, instructors can earn $400 a month plus room and board in China and up to $4,000 a month in Japan. That's a lot more than a McJob back home.

5   But students expect more than lessons in syntax and style. EFL teachers are also hired to share Western customs and values. "'Let's have lunch sometime' doesn't mean stop by my office tomorrow and we'll go out and have lunch. It means something more general, like 'It's been nice talking to you and maybe at some point I'd like to continue the conversation,'" says Diane Pecorari, a senior lecturer at the University of Stockholm. "When you're teaching formulae like 'Please,' 'Thank you,' 'Can I split the cheque?' you also have to teach the context in which they come up. That means teaching culture."

But what is the effect of that culture on students' dialects, customs—their very identity? Ian Martin, an English professor at York University's Glendon College in Toronto, points to a troubling precedent for the current explosion of EFL. "One of the big moments in the spread of English took place in India in 1835. [British politician] Thomas Babington Macaulay proposed that English be used to create a class of Indian middlemen who would be sympathetic to British interests, without the necessity of large numbers of British citizens coming out and running the show." Instead of invading India at great economic and human cost, English allowed the British to transform the country from within. With English on the tip of their tongues, Indians could much more easily swear allegiance to England.

Today's linguistic imperialism has a similar goal. Where once English facilitated the staffing of colonial offices, now it helps fill the cubicles of multinational corporations. Teaching locals Western speech and when it's appropriate to use it no longer transforms them into perfect Englishmen, it makes them into perfect businessmen and women. The politics of English haven't changed—the language simply serves a new corporate master.

To be sure, even those who are fascinated by the countries where they teach sometimes can't help transforming "the natives" as part of their work abroad. Canadian Michael Schellenberg, who taught in Japan more than a decade ago, loved learning about Japanese customs but also sheepishly admits he urged students to express themselves—quite against the Japanese grain. "One of the sayings in Japan is that the nail that sticks up will get pounded down. They wanted people to conform," he says. "I remember classes where I'd be like, 'Just be yourself!' As someone in my early 20s, I had a pretty good sense of how I thought the world should be. I felt pretty confident being forthright about that."

Teaching materials subtly suggest the superiority of Western values. Produced primarily in the US and UK, textbooks propagate the advantages of materialism, individualism and sexual liberation. For example, Ian Martin recalls an Indian friend's reaction to one textbook that showed Jack and Jane meeting in lesson one and dancing alone together by lesson three. "Where are the parents?" his friend wondered.

Some newer textbooks are more culturally sensitive. But in many of   10 the books currently in circulation, says Martin, "there's nothing about environmentalism, nothing about spirituality, nothing about, say, respecting non-native [English] speakers. And there's very little realism in any of the language learning material that I've seen. It's this mythic world of dream fulfillment through consumerism and Westernization." The Aeon language franchise in Japan uses Cameron Diaz and Celine Dion as its poster girls.

Of course, not all teachers aggressively peddle a mythic world—some have their soapbox thrust upon them. In her book *The Hemingway Book Club of Kosovo*, California writer Paula Huntley chronicles her experience teaching English to the survivors of the area's brutal ethnic clashes. Huntley doesn't believe her language and culture are better than any other. She wants to learn from the Kosovars as much as they want to learn from her. It's her students who are convinced that the American way is the way forward, that English is the true language of progress.

Before leaving for Kosovo, Huntley crams for four weeks to complete an English as a second language instructors' certificate. But this is not what impresses the owner of the Cambridge School in Kosovo, a man named Ahmet whose house and library of 5,000 books were destroyed by the Serbs. Barely looking at her CV, he tells her she's hired. "You are an American," he says. "So you can teach our students more than English. You can teach them how to live together, with others, in peace. You can teach them how to work, how to build a democracy, how to keep trying no matter what the odds."

Then there is the conflicted experience of Kathy Lee. She teaches at Guangdong Industry Technical College in China. In a suburb called Nanhai, the school is putting up satellite facilities eight times larger than the main campus. Teaching labs have banks of computers and a plasma screen TV. But like so much of the country, there is such impatience to forge ahead that Lee conducts her three classes a week amid construction because the school is expanding so fast.

Her pupils are equally anxious to take part in the country's massive business boom. Though most of them have been studying English since primary school, their fluency is strained. They tell her: "The world is growing and many people speak English. If I want to do business with them, I must speak English well too!" What students want is a foreign teacher to help them get up to speed. That's why the college has hired the 23-year-old Canadian at 4,000 RMB a month, two to three times the average salary for Chinese teachers.

15   The payoff is more than just monetary for Lee. Born in China but raised in Canada, she accepted the job so she could live in Hong Kong, within a short train ride from her sick grandmother. But now, her feelings have deepened. "When the schools were asking me why I wanted to teach in China, I BS'd and said it's because I wanted to learn about my 'other' culture," she says. "But the more I said it, the more I believed it. Now, I feel that I need to be here and learn what it means to be a Chinese person."

Yet the way of life Lee is trying to understand is challenged by her methodology in the classroom. By the end of term, her students will be well practised in communication modes that are entirely un-Chinese. Lee worries about this—and the general English fever sweeping the country that even includes television programs that aim to teach English.

"I know that if everyone spoke English in the world there would still be cultural differences, but the differences between cultures will become less and less," she says. "Why is China pushing English so hard? [My students] get the sense that their own language is not good enough. To prosper, they need English. What was wrong with the way it was before? Why do you have to be Western to be competitive in business?"

If it is tough for teachers to come to terms with these questions, it is even more complex for students. While some are in what Martin calls a "process of self-assimilation," others are much more ambivalent about the course they are on. These students may be struggling with the political implications of learning English in places where the language is associated with American or British hegemony. Or they may simply recognize that as English proliferates, the survival of their own customs and dialects is under threat.

Take 27-year-old Sanghun Cho of South Korea. He is a graduate student in Toronto and has a Canadian girlfriend. But when he thinks of English he also thinks of the US. "It's a kind of dilemma for Koreans," he says. "I don't like America in Korea because they want to control the Korean government, but to survive in this kind of competitive environment I have to speak English and I have to know what English culture is."

Another South Korean student puts it even more bluntly. Part of a mul-   20
tinational research project Martin has been conducting over the past five years to examine why students study English as a foreign language, the student was asked to draw a picture of his future with English, and describe the picture. He sketched Uncle Sam extending a fishing line from the US across the Pacific Ocean, a hook dangling above the student's open mouth. His description: "English is the bait that Americans are using to catch Koreans in their net."

Marta Andersson is a part of the last generation of Poles forced to learn Russian in school. When she was able to study English after the fall of communism, she was thrilled. On the one hand, it paid off: she got a good job in Poland, is now studying abroad and speaks English at home with her husband. On another level, though, Andersson is aware that using English is eroding part of what her people fought for. "I have just started to lose the sense of my native language and just wait when it will become moribund," she says, "Yet I cannot imagine my future without the presence of English."

Swede Hélène Elg is also concerned about the fate of her language as English words invade it the way they do in "Chinglish" and "Franglais." "I think it's important to separate the languages in order to 'protect' our own," she says. "I realize that languages evolve, allowing new words to come into use, but we should be aware of that development and be cautious about it. The reason I feel this is because languages are so much more than just words. Words have cultural connotations. As with languages, cultures evolve, but that development should not be about adopting another culture."

Can students fight back? It's arguable that withdrawing from English would exact too high a cost for those who want to be a part of a global economy. Instead, what's changing is how people from around the world use English. Rather than simply conforming to an English steeped in Western values, many students are co-opting the language for themselves.

On an internet discussion board for EFL teachers, one teacher writes: "I feel the need of reminding our students and young colleagues that the purpose of learning English is not for us to 'speak and act' like an English person . . . but to 'speak English' as an educated Indonesian." Similarly, one Cuban who participated in Martin's project drew a picture of a rocket being launched into the sky with the description: "English is the rocket which will allow Cuba to tell its own stories to the world."

25   A new "global" English is emerging that is a bridge language between cultures, not simply a language that supplants other cultures. As Salman Rushdie is quoted as saying in the best-selling history *The Story of English*, "English, no longer an English language, now grows from many roots; and those whom it once colonized are carving out large territories within the language for themselves. The Empire is striking back."

Along with students, many teachers are joining the fight to create a more egalitarian English. They do not want to be cultural colonialists. As David Hill, a teacher in Istanbul, writes in *The Guardian Weekly*: "English is global for highly dubious reasons: colonial, military and economic hegemony, first of the British, now of the US. . . . If we are not to be imperialists then we must help our students to express themselves, not our agenda."

To do that, new programs are emerging, like the Certificate in the Discipline of Teaching English as an International Language, which Martin coordinates at Glendon College. It pays close attention to issues of cultural sensitivity and autonomy when training teachers. As Martin says, "We're trying to come to grips with the effect of globalization on language teaching. Do we want a globalization that is going to be assimilationist to Western models of communication only? Or, do we want to help people gain a voice in English?"

Michelle Szabo is one teacher who has tried to give her students a voice. After her stint in Japan, she took a job at Chonbuk National University in South Korea from 2003 to 2004. On one November morning, she recalls encouraging discussion about the power of English. Her hope was to give pause to students who'd never considered the impact of studying English on their lives—as well as a place for those who had thought about it—a rare place to vent.

And there was plenty of venting as students heatedly debated face-to-face from desks arranged in a conversation-friendly horseshoe configuration.

"One side was feeling very pressured and resentful," says Szabo, "and one side was saying, 'No, [English is] opening doors for us.'" Szabo tried to "equalize" the class by sitting among the students. She also said little. She wanted a forum that conveyed the message, "I'm not here to change you, to acculturize you, to force my beliefs on you," she says.

But even Szabo's new self-consciousness about what it is she is selling to   30
her students along with English grammar has limits. English has irrevocably changed and acculturated the world already. Even if locals don't want to participate in the global capitalist machine, they need English to truly challenge it. As one of Szabo's students couldn't help but point out during the debate, "Isn't it ironic we're discussing the effect of English—in English?"

Analyze

1. Traves compares EFL teachers to Christian missionaries. In what ways does she demonstrate that EFL "converts" those who study it?
2. What does Traves mean by the term "cultural colonialists" (paragraph 26)? According to Salman Rushdie, how is the "Empire striking back"?
3. Of the various EFL teachers Traves quotes in the article, with whom do you most identify and why?

Explore

1. In paragraph 9, Traves claims that "[t]eaching materials subtly suggest the superiority of Western values." Is this true? With one or two classmates, analyze an EFL textbook (from your college library or bookstore) for images, exercises, and dialogues. Does it portray, promote, or critique Western values? How?
2. One EFL teacher quoted in paragraph 24 writes, "I feel the need of reminding our students and young colleagues that the purpose of learning English is not for us to 'speak and act' like an English person . . . but to 'speak English' as an educated Indonesian." How do you interpret his or her meaning? Write an essay in which you compare and contrast these two different approaches to teaching and learning English.
3. How apt is Traves's comparison of EFL teachers to Christian missionaries? Is learning a new language the same as converting to a new religion? Is linguistic tolerance the same as religious tolerance? Can

religions, like languages, be influenced by other religions and change over time? Use these questions as points of departure to respond in an exploratory essay to Traves's article.

Forging Connections

1. In paragraph 22 of "The Church of Please and Thank You," Hélène Elg says, "I think it's important to separate the languages in order to 'protect' our own." What does Elg want to protect? Do you think separating languages will effect this protection? Using the readings from this chapter and the research you may have conducted in response to them, write a cause-and-effect essay about languages in contact.

2. The introduction to this chapter asks: How might a growing knowledge of language inform how we continue to understand and refine a working definition of globalization? How might we use our contemporary lens of globalization to understand and use language equitably? Develop an essay in response to these questions, detailing how the readings in this chapter have helped to enrich your understanding of the esprit and ethics of globalization, particularly in reference to language.

Looking Further

1. Throughout the readings in this book, several non-English terms are used, even though the selections were written with an English-reading audience in mind. (For example, if you have not already, you will come across the words: *sheng nu, shia, shuzzuz, burka, hijabs,* and *qiezi.*) Why do you suppose foreign words enter languages instead of simply being translated? Do you think as the world becomes increasingly globalized, expressions from different languages will be adapted across languages? What recent "borrowings" or terms from other languages have you come across? Create a glossary of the non-English words that are part of your day-to-day life. List the word and its definition or translation. Include an example sentence to show its usage and anything significant you'd like to add. As you continue reading this book, add new terms you come across whose meanings you think you will need to remember. Alternatively, see if your class can together create and update a wiki of globalized terms.

2. In the following chapter, "Communication and Technology," we see how social media has been used to promote social change, challenge the ways in which free speech is suppressed, and create global witnesses to significant events. But how are global messages on social media (e.g., Facebook, Twitter, and blogs) able to transcend language differences? Write a research paper in which you identify an event (such as the Arab Spring, a political election, etc.) or a global concern (such as global warming, famine, or health), and investigate how language carries the message to others. Is English, as a global lingua franca, primarily used? If so, who translates? Are images used instead of language? Do people rely on translating platforms such as Google Translate or Bing? As you present what you have learned, consider the reliability of the information we have access to via social media. Take a step back and think: How can you verify and evaluate information from social media that is communicated in languages in which you are not proficient?

5 Communication & Technology

To what extent has the technology-enhanced communication of the 21st century aided and abetted our perceptions of a globalized world and our roles in shaping it? Access to instant information and constant connection even when we are physically worlds away continues to provoke awe and amazement, but also, as we shall see in this chapter, thoughtful commentary and creative criticism.

The first reading, Ethan Zuckerman's "A Small World After All?" begins with a consideration of 1979 Iran: Governmental intelligence worldwide is thrown off-guard by the Islamic Revolution and the undetected "small media" that stimulated it. Fast forward to the 2011 Arab Spring, stimulated by new social media, and you have Zuckerman claiming that the "challenge for anyone who wants to decipher the mysteries of a connected age is to understand how the Internet does, and does not, connect us." How do social media inform, inspire, and motivate us to understand and participate in issues beyond local networks?

Playing off a wireless company's famous slogan for the title of his piece "Can You Hear Us Now?" Frank Bures contrasts cell phone connections from Tanzania to the US 10 years ago (crackly with auditory lag) with now (crystal clear). Increasing access to innovative technologies has transformed the developing world in ways that, Bures points out, are "helping people of limited means gain a degree of control over their situations." Bures wonders, though, if notions of technology designed by charity will give way to more effective for-profit social entrepreneurship and, in turn, promote the self-determination that has eluded so many communities in developing nations.

Natana J. DeLong-Bas steps back to carefully analyze the wave of political revolutions that in 2011 rocked North Africa and the Middle East in "The New Social Media and the Arab Spring." Although the ability of the "Internet Generation" to topple intransigent leaders of totalitarian governments inspired the world, DeLong-Bas points out that it's too early to evaluate long-term results of the revolutions and reforms. To be sure, the creativity demonstrated by youth (and witnessed globally) in forging a virtual community has only just begun. But have our inclinations for succinct sound bites eroded our taste and attention for sustained communication? The reaction to novelist Teju Cole's seven-part response on Twitter to the now famous/infamous Kony2012 video posted on YouTube promoted fierce argument—and perhaps an airing of sentiment that has been too politically incorrect to convey otherwise. Standing his ground, Cole wrote "The White Savior Industrial Complex," our next reading in this chapter.

Iranian architect Rudabeh Pakravan examines the role of technologies in challenging repressive regimes through a discussion of satellite dishes in Tehran. Television programming, as with much of social life in contemporary Iran, is strictly monitored. Pakravan's account of the persistent presence of illegal satellites provides a window on how a hunger for cultural sustenance defies oppressive forces, fosters black market economies, and creates ambiguous public spaces. Rob Horning's ominous essay "The Accidental Bricoleurs" connects fashion to Facebook by positing that through fast fashion and social media, we are the coerced creators of our own self-branding. Will you agree with him?

The readings in this chapter provide both mirrors and windows into how we see ourselves and one another. They also offer models of how sustained and considered thinking through the act of writing allows us to provide our own readings and interpretations of one of the most dynamic aspects of contemporary life.

Ethan Zuckerman
"A Small World After All?"

Ethan Zuckerman is an American media scholar, Internet activist, and director of the Center for Civic Media at MIT. "A Small World After All?" appeared in the Spring 2012 issue of *Wilson Quarterly*, a magazine published by the Wilson Center, an independent think tank that seeks to "build a bridge between the worlds of academia and public policy, to inform and develop solutions to the nation's problems and challenges." In this article, Zuckerman urges readers to consider the true nature of our connectedness: Has the Internet genuinely broadened our worldview—or has our world become smaller?

Why do you think Zuckerman titled his essay "A Small World After All?" What does it reference, and why is it posed as a question?

When the Cold War ended, the work of America's intelligence analysts suddenly became vastly more difficult. In the past, they had known who the nation's main adversaries were and what bits of information they needed to acquire about them: the number of SS-9 missiles Moscow could deploy, for example, or the number of warheads each missile could carry. The U.S. intelligence community had been in search of secrets—facts that exist but are hidden by one government from another. After the Soviet Union's collapse, as Bruce Berkowitz and Allan Goodman observe in *Best Truth: Intelligence in the Information Age* (2002), it found a new role thrust upon it: the untangling of mysteries.

Computer security expert Susan Landau identifies the 1979 Islamic Revolution in Iran as one of the first indicators that the intelligence community needed to shift its focus from secrets to mysteries. On its surface,

Iran was a strong, stable ally of the United States, an "island of stability" in the region, according to President Jimmy Carter. The rapid ouster of the shah and a referendum that turned a monarchy into a theocracy led by a formerly exiled religious scholar left governments around the world shocked and baffled.

The Islamic Revolution was a surprise because it had taken root in mosques and homes, not palaces or barracks. The calls to resist the shah weren't broadcast on state media but transmitted via handmade leaflets and audiocassettes of speeches by Ayatollah Khomeini. In their book analyzing the events of 1979, *Small Media, Big Revolution* (1994), Annabelle Sreberny and Ali Mohammad, who both participated in the Iranian revolution, emphasize the role of two types of technology: tools that let people obtain access to information from outside Iran, and tools that let people spread and share that information on a local scale. Connections to the outside world (direct-dial long-distance phone lines, cassettes of sermons sent through the mail, broadcasts on the BBC World Service) and tools that amplified those connections (home cassette recorders, photocopying machines) helped build a movement more potent than governments and armies had anticipated.

As we enter an age of increased global connection, we are also entering an age of increasing participation. The billions of people worldwide who access the Internet via computers and mobile phones have access to information far beyond their borders, and the opportunity to contribute their own insights and opinions. It should be no surprise that we are experiencing a concomitant rise in mystery that parallels the increases in connection.

5   The mysteries brought to the fore in a connected age extend well beyond the realm of political power. Bad subprime loans in the United States lead to the failure of an investment bank; this, in turn, depresses interbank lending, pushing Iceland's heavily leveraged economy into collapse and consequently leaving British consumers infuriated at the disappearance of their deposits from Icelandic banks that had offered high interest rates on savings accounts. An American businessman on a flight to Singapore takes ill, and epidemiologists find themselves tracing the SARS epidemic in cities from Toronto to Manila, eventually discovering a disease that originated with civet cats and was passed to humans because civets are sold as food in southern China. Not all mysteries are tragedies—the path of a musical style from Miami clubs through dance parties in the favelas of Rio to the hit singles of British-Sri Lankan singer M.I.A. is at least as unexpected and convoluted.

Uncovering secrets might require counting missile silos in satellite images or debriefing double agents. To understand our connected world, we need different skills. Landau suggests that "solving mysteries requires deep, often unconventional thinking, and a full picture of the world around the mystery."

The unexpected outbreak of the Arab Spring, a mystery that's still unfolding, suggests that we may not be getting this full picture, or the deep, unconventional thinking we need. Had you asked an expert on the Middle East what changes were likely to take place in 2011, almost none would have predicted the Arab Spring, and none would have chosen Tunisia as the flashpoint for the movement. Zine el Abidine Ben Ali had ruled the North African nation virtually unchallenged since 1987, and had co-opted, jailed, or exiled anyone likely to challenge his authority. When vegetable seller Mohamed Bouazizi set himself on fire, there was no reason to expect his family's protests against government corruption to spread beyond the village of Sidi Bouzid. After all, the combination of military cordons, violence against protesters, a sycophantic domestic press, and a ban on international news media had, in the past, ensured that dissent remained local.

"To understand our connected world, we need different skills."

Not this time. Video of protests in Sidi Bouzid, shot on mobile phones and uploaded to Facebook, reached Tunisian dissidents in Europe. They indexed and translated the footage and packaged it for distribution on sympathetic networks such as al-Jazeera. Widely watched in Tunisia, al-Jazeera alerted citizens in Tunis and Sfax to protests taking place in another corner of their country, which in effect served as an invitation to participate. As Ben Ali's regime trembled and fell, images of the protests spread throughout the region, inspiring similar outpourings in more than a dozen countries and the overthrow of two additional regimes.

While the impact of Tunisia's revolution is now appreciated, the protests that led to Ben Ali's ouster were invisible in much of the world. *The New York Times* first mentioned Mohamed Bouazizi and Sidi Bouzid in print on January 15, 2011, the day after Ben Ali fled. The U.S. intelligence apparatus was no more prescient. Senator Dianne Feinstein (D.-Calif.), who chairs the Senate Intelligence Committee, wondered to reporters, "Was someone looking at what was going on the Internet?"

10   A central paradox of this connected age is that while it's easier than ever
to share information and perspectives from different parts of the world, we
may be encountering a narrower picture of the world than we did in less
connected days. During the Vietnam War, television reporting from the
frontlines involved transporting exposed film from Southeast Asia by air,
then developing and editing it in the United States before broadcasting it
days later. Now, an unfolding crisis such as the Japanese tsunami or Haitian
earthquake can be reported in real time via satellite. Despite these lowered
barriers, today's American television news features less than half as many
international stories as were broadcast in the 1970s.

The pace of print media reporting has accelerated sharply, with newspapers moving to a "digital first" strategy, publishing fresh information online
as news breaks. While papers publish many more stories than they did
40 years ago (online and offline), Britain's four major dailies publish on
average 45 percent fewer international stories than they did in 1979.

Why worry about what's covered in newspapers and television when it's
possible to read firsthand accounts from Syria or Sierra Leone? Research
suggests that we rarely read such accounts. My studies of online news consumption show that 95 percent of the news consumed by American Internet
users is published in the United States. By this metric, the United States is
less parochial than many other nations, which consume even less news published in other countries. This locality effect crosses into social media as
well. A recent study of Twitter, a tool used by 400 million people around
the world, showed that we're far more likely to follow people who are
physically close to us than to follow someone outside our home country's
borders, or even a few states or provinces away. Thirty-nine percent of the
relationships on Twitter involve someone following the tweets of a person
in the same metropolitan area. In the Twitter hotbed of São Paulo, Brazil,
more than 78 percent of the relationships are local. So much for the death
of distance.

As we start to understand how people actually use the Internet, the
cyberutopian hopes of a borderless, postnational planet can look as naive as
most past predictions that new technologies would transform societies. In
1912, radio pioneer Guglielmo Marconi declared, "The coming of the wireless
era will make war impossible, because it will make war ridiculous." Two years
later a ridiculous war began, ultimately killing nine million Europeans.

While it's easy to be dismissive of today's Marconis—the pundits, experts, and enthusiasts who saw a rise in Internet connection leading to a

rise in international understanding—that's too simple and too cynical a response. Increased digital connection does not automatically lead to increased understanding. At the same time, there's never been a tool as powerful as the Internet for building new ties (and maintaining existing ones) across distant borders.

The challenge for anyone who wants to decipher the mysteries of a connected age is to understand how the Internet does, and does not, connect us. Only then can we find ways to make online connection more common and more powerful.

There are at least three ways we discover new information online. Each of these methods has shortcomings in terms of giving us a broad, global picture of the world. Search engines, while incredibly powerful, are only as good as the queries we put to them. They are designed for information retrieval, not for discovery. If you had been able to ask Google in 1979 how many SS-9 missiles the Soviets possessed, you might have received a plausible answer, but you wouldn't have been told you should be asking about cassette recorders in Iran instead. Search engines tell us what we want to know, but they can't tell us what we might need to know.

Social media such as Facebook or Twitter might tell you to pay attention to cassette recordings in Iran, but only if your friends include Iranians. Social media are a powerful discovery engine, but what you're discovering is what your friends know. If you're lucky enough to have a diverse, knowledgeable set of friends online, they may lead you in unexpected directions. But birds of a feather flock together, both online and offline, and your friends are more likely to help you discover the unexpected in your hometown than in another land.

The most powerful discovery engines online may be curated publications such as *The New York Times* or *The Guardian*. Editors of these publications are driven by a mission to provide their audiences with the broad picture of the world they need in order to be effective citizens, consumers, and businesspeople. But professional curators have their inevitable biases and blind spots. Much as we know to search for the news we think will affect our lives, editors deploy reporting resources toward parts of the world with strategic and economic significance. When mysteries unfold in corners of the world we're used to ignoring, such as Tunisia, curators are often left struggling to catch up.

The limits of online information sources are a challenge both for us and for the people building the next generation of online tools. If we rigorously examine the media we're encountering online, looking for topics and places we hear little about, we may be able to change our behavior, adding different and dissenting views to our social networks, seeking out new sources of news. But this task would be vastly easier if the architects of Internet tools took up the cause of helping to broaden worldviews. Facebook already notices that you've failed to "friend" a high school classmate and tries to connect you. It could look for strangers in Africa or India who share your interests and broker an introduction. Google tracks every search you undertake so it can more effectively target ads to you. It could also use that information to help you discover compelling content about topics you've never explored, adding a serendipity engine to its formidable search function.

20   Why aren't engineers racing to build the new tools that will help unravel the mysteries of a connected world? They may be waiting for indicators that we want them and are ready to use them.

In 2004, journalist Rebecca MacKinnon and I founded Global Voices, an international news network designed to amplify and spread ideas and perspectives published online in the developing world. Our 800 correspondents translate and summarize content from the blogs of Russian activists protesting election fraud and Nigerian Facebook users discussing the latest hot Nollywood film. The project has won awards and recognition, but it's had only modest success building an audience. When a news story receives global attention, as Iran's Green Movement protests did in 2009, readership spikes. But our in-depth coverage of the protests in Sidi Bouzid went largely unnoticed until Ben Ali's government fell. We continue to report on coups in Madagascar and culture in Malaysia regardless of the audience these stories generate. But to convince Facebook to broker global connections or encourage *The Huffington Post* to cover global stories, people need to demand a broader view.

As Pankaj Ghemawat of Barcelona's IESE Business School reminds us in *World 3.0* (2011), we're not at the endpoint of globalization, but somewhere near the starting line. The age of connection is just beginning. Many people still view the world as dominated by secrets: How close is Iran to building a nuclear bomb? How can Western companies crack the Chinese market? Where are undiscovered reserves of oil? It's at least as possible that the questions that will dominate the next century are the ones we don't yet know to ask. Those who will thrive in a connected world are those who learn to see broadly and to solve the mysteries that emerge.

Analyze

1. Zuckerman wants to persuade his readers of the intelligence community's need "to shift its focus from secrets to mysteries." How does he define "secrets" and "mysteries" in the context of this article? Why is this an important distinction?

2. The author contends that despite the ease we have in sharing global information and perspectives, "we may be encountering a narrower picture of the world than we did in less connected days." What evidence does he give to support this view? What examples could you add from recent events in the world?

3. Why do you think people might not be interested in having what Zuckerman calls a "broader view"? What might be the dangers of unraveling "the mysteries of a connected world"?

Explore

1. Gugliemo Marconi, quoted in this reading, declared that radio would herald the end of war. Why do you think new technologies are so often greeted with predictions that society will be transformed by them? What have been the expectations of recent social media innovations? How have they fulfilled those expectations? How have they fallen short?

2. Zuckerman believes that curated publications have "inevitable biases and blind spots." To test this assertion, observe a variety of online news publications around the world over a 48-hour period, and document their top stories over that period. Even if you do not understand the language(s), you can document visual images, graphics, and/or use translation sites (such as Google Translate) to approximate meanings. What are commonalities? Differences? Compare your results with those of your classmates. What "picture" does this give you of the world?

3. Since Zuckerman published this article, what global "mysteries" have emerged? Visit Zuckerman's site, *Global Voices*, choose a recently published story, and explore how it's been "covered" by more conventional news sites. Provide a written analysis.

Frank Bures
"Can You Hear Us Now?"

Frank Bures, contributing editor at *Poets and Writers* magazine and the online travel magazine *World Hum,* has also published essays and articles in *Harper's* and *Esquire.* "Can You Hear Us Now?" originally appeared in the December 2010 issue of *World Ark,* a magazine published by the humanitarian organization Heifer International; the following version was published in the March–April 2011 issue of the *Utne Reader.* According to Bures, studies show that the boom in innovative technologies in the developing world has created new economic opportunities for people who live there. "Can You Hear Us Now?" documents several innovative technologies developed within and for developing countries and poses the uncomfortable possibility that for-profit social enterprises benefit the world's poor more than traditional charities and donations.

Do you believe that altruism and self-interest are fundamentally at odds with each other? How does Bures offer an alternative point of view?

B ack in the mid-1990s I was living in a semirural area on the slopes of Mount Meru, just outside Arusha, Tanzania. Now and then I had to make a phone call back home to America.

This was not then an easy thing to do. I would venture out to inquire about using one of the few phone lines at neighboring houses. Often, these lines would be broken, or working spottily, and it could take weeks to arrange a repair.

Usually, I would end up knocking on the door of a business in town (owned by friends of friends), trying to be unobtrusive as I listened to the crackly sound of the voice of the woman I would later marry. Our words seemed to run into each other, and we each had to wait a minute to be able to hear the other. In the lag, the distance seemed tangible.

These days, when I'm in Africa, I tell people this story and they laugh. They laugh as if I was telling them I used to hunt with rocks and start fires with sticks. Technology in the developing world has changed so much and so fast that it's almost hard to believe.

Last year I took a bus across West Africa. Somewhere in the middle of 5
Burkina Faso, as I sat looking out the window at the dusty trees, I took a
phone out of my pocket and called my wife. This time, the sound was clear.
There was no delay. It was almost as if she was sitting next to me.

I may have been the only passenger dialing America, but I was far from
the only one with a phone. There are now 415 million mobile subscribers in
Africa, and two-thirds of the world's 5 billion users are in the developing
world. India and China alone added 700 million new cell phone contracts
between 2000 and 2007, and the numbers continue to rise.

Among the many ramifications of this change, perhaps the biggest is
economic. Now, not only can people stay in touch with their friends and
family, they can also talk to business partners, get market reports, and
recruit clients. Mobile technology provides a significant boost to the incomes of those on the bottom rung of the ladder. In fact, a study from
the London Business School concluded that each 10 percent increase
in mobile phone use meant a 0.6 percent boost to GDP in developing
countries.

In Uganda, farmers can send text messages for commodity prices or
weather reports. In South Africa, a software service called Mobenzi allows
the unemployed to find and conduct work via cell phone. Jobs and revenue
are created as millions of people buy and sell phone cards. In Ghana, some
people even build towers for subscribers to climb (for a fee) so they can get
reception in hilly areas.

The rising popularity of cell phone technology in Africa is resulting in
startups with big business potential. A new service called PesaPal allows
people to shop by mobile phone. Founder Agosta Liko lived in the United
States for several years, working in banking and information technology,
before moving back to Kenya.

"There was no consumer payment system," Liko says. "People couldn't 10
open PayPal accounts, so I decided to build something. Now I can pay my
guys a good wage, which is the best way to alleviate poverty."

I've always admired the ingenious ways that people in the developing
world jerry-rig solutions to their problems. I've seen wheelbarrows assembled
from sticks and boards, frying pans made from old car parts, and irrigation
channels constructed from the husks of banana trees. I've even read of people
making cars and a helicopter from scratch.

There's also the case of William Kamkwamba, a Malawian boy who had
to drop out of school. In a library, he found an old science book, which he

used to build a windmill out of discarded parts. The homemade windmill powered lights in his parents' house and pumped water during a massive drought.

I first heard of Kamkwamba's story on AfriGadget, a website that showcases all kinds of technical ingenuity born of scarcity. The site is the brainchild of Erik Hersman, a web developer raised in Kenya and Sudan by American missionary parents.

Hersman is also the founder of Ushahidi.com. That site came together during Kenya's election violence in 2008, when Hersman and some friends developed a program that allowed people to report incidents of violence via text messages, which made possible the creation of a comprehensive crisis map. The platform is now called Ushahidi (Swahili for *testimony*) and is being used to monitor elections in India, to track violence in the war in Congo, and to monitor rainforest destruction in Madagascar.

15   Ushahidi is one more example of how technology is helping people of limited means gain a degree of control over their situations. Another is small-plot irrigation systems that are helping farmers in Ghana boost productivity through the dry season.

Even something like light can improve a poor family's situation. "Providing bright light impacts so many facets of people's lives," says Dorcas Cheng-Tozun of D.light Design, a company that has sold hundreds of thousands of low-cost solar lights to rural communities in more than 40 countries. "It allows them to work for longer hours and more productively. It lets children study longer. And people save a significant amount of money on kerosene."

The productivity boost associated with these technologies might seem small to us, but they're a great boon to the world's poor. One World Bank report found that advances in technology were key factors in reducing the number of people in developing countries living on less than a dollar a day from 29 percent in 1990 to 18 percent in 2004, with that number expected to drop to 10 percent by 2015.

One day when I was living in Tanzania, I was talking to a neighbor. He was from Germany and was not well liked in the area, for reasons that were becoming apparent. That day, he was complaining about an expensive solar water heater that had been donated from overseas but was already broken and in need of repairs. The problem, he told me, was that when you have a complicated machine, you need a white man to take care of it. A white man, he added, with his own car.

This statement left me speechless for several reasons. For starters, it was obviously untrue, a fact that has been clearly demonstrated in the years since.

"There are three myths about technology," says Harish Hande, cofounder 20 of SELCO-India, a "social enterprise" that has sold solar lighting systems to more than 115,000 households in India. "One is that poor people cannot afford sustainable technologies. Another is that poor people cannot maintain sustainable technologies. And a third is that social ventures cannot be run as commercial entities."

The trap the German fell into was what we might call the "solar-oven fallacy." The solar oven is a simple idea that has actually been around for a few hundred years. It is sometimes touted as a panacea for issues ranging from women's rights to global warming. The Peace Corps distributed them in the 1960s, and a cardboard version called the Kyoto Box recently won a prestigious $75,000 design prize. On the surface, the idea seems like a good one: Use the sun to cook food. Free heat. No chopping or carrying wood. And yet, ironically, the solar cooker has not set the developing world on fire.

"Solar ovens are not that complicated," says Paul Polak, author of *Out of Poverty: What Works When Traditional Approaches Fail* and founder of International Development Enterprises, which has sold half a million low-cost drip irrigation systems throughout the developing world. "What is complicated is learning the cultural patterns of people in Africa and how they might interact with that technology."

The drawbacks of solar ovens are many: They take several hours to cook food; they don't function in the rainy season; wind can knock them over; they simply won't work for people who are up before dawn or need to cook after dark. So while it may seem like a good idea to someone sitting in an office in Washington, D.C., the benefits might be less clear to a woman in a wattle house in Zambia.

"Poor people will enthusiastically embrace something if they can see it will improve their lives," says Polak. "But they're looking for practical solutions—things that work—for the problems they're facing."

In the end, the solar oven solves a problem very few people face: How to 25 cook lunch on a sunny day.

According to Hande, companies like SELCO-India are looking for practical solutions for real challenges in the developing world. "We look at what the need is, then tailor the product to the need," he says. "We are intervening with a product that either increases people's income or uplifts their quality of life, so it's a win-win situation."

SELCO sells not only low-cost solar lighting but also power inverters, biomass cooking stoves, and solar water heaters. And while it doesn't donate anything, its focus is neither simply making money nor providing charity, but embracing a new model, like that used by D.light Design.

"We feel strongly that market solutions and for-profit social enterprises will be a growing part of development," says Cheng-Tozun. "We see the customers we are trying to serve as just that: customers. We have to understand them and know what they want, because they ultimately have the choice: Do they like our product or not? They'll let us know by whether they choose to buy it."

This can be uncomfortable terrain for many of us who believe that altruism and self-interest are fundamentally at odds. But as ideas like these evolve, a more nuanced picture is emerging, and growth is not seen as a zero-sum game.

30   "The mobile-phone carriers are making money hand over fist and making a lot of great change happen," says Hersman, who also recently launched a technology innovation hub in Nairobi. "I think we're starting to see that businesses work here. Why not figure out a good business model, build it, and treat it like a real business instead of giving subsidies that provide a false floor and doom the project from the beginning?"

There is no false floor under 24-year-old Wilfred Mworia, a Kenyan software engineer who was sitting on his couch one day in his small apartment in Nairobi when an idea came to him: What if you could keep a journal on your phone—more specifically, on your iPhone—but instead of just writing, you could include pictures and audio? Mworia was able to scrape together funding to start a company to develop his "iScribe." Now that company, African Pixel, is doing its part to help the Kenyan economy grow.

At this pace, there's no telling what the lives of people in the developing world will look like in 10 years. For ambitious youths like Mworia, the path to the future is clear, and technology is helping them put it in their own hands.

Analyze

1. Make a list of the advances in technology Bures reports in this article and where in the world they were made. What kind of pattern do you notice about them?

2. When Bures writes in paragraph 17, "The productivity boost associated with technologies might seem small to us," who do you think he
means by the word "us"? Who is the audience for this article?
3. Think about the title to the article. Who might be asking the question
and to whom? What might they be saying?

Explore

1. There's an old adage that says "necessity is the mother of invention."
Choose a technology (from any historical period) that profoundly
changed the world. Trace its necessity, invention, proliferation, and
impact in an essay that demonstrates how technology has helped
people of "limited means gain a degree of control over their situations"
(paragraph 15).
2. Explore more deeply the inspiration behind one of the several powerful technological innovations Bures reports in his article. What has
happened to it and its inventor since this article was published? Has
the technology improved? Have there been downsides to it or disap-
pointments? What is its legacy?
3. Do further research on the efficacy of for-profit social enterprises in
developing countries that have created technology such as D.light
Design and SELCO. How can they provide better models for helping the world's poor than the charities and programs that provide
donations?

Natana J. DeLong-Bas
"The New Social Media
and the Arab Spring"

Natana J. Delong-Bas is a lecturer in theology at Boston College and deputy
editor of *Oxford Islamic Studies Online (OISO),* a resource for global Islamic
history, concepts, people, practices, politics, and culture. The selection that
follows appeared as one of the "Focus On" essays in *OISO,* a feature that

encourages in-depth exploration of select topics in Biblical studies. In her essay, Delong-Bas commends the use of modern technology and new social media by Tunisian and Egyptian youth who enacted peaceful political and social revolutions in 2011. She also notes that these triumphs were partly due to the governments' inability to control social media.

What are more recent examples of youth using social media such as Facebook and Twitter as vehicles for social and political protest?

Since January 2011, the eyes of the world have turned to the Arab Spring. Launched by the image of the self-immolation of the Tunisian vegetable vendor Mohamed Bouazizi as an outcry against the humiliation of citizens at the hands of authoritarian states and their security apparatuses, the Arab Spring has so far resulted in a mix of hope for reform and questions about the future of the Middle East and North Africa. Pivotal to the revolutions that peacefully overthrew regimes in Tunisia and Egypt and pressed for change and reform in other countries throughout the region has been the role of the new social media in translating ideas shared in cyberspace into real-life action on the ground.

Given the "youth bulge" in the Middle East—where between 55 and 70 percent of the population of any given country is under the age of thirty—the fact that social media and modern technology have been used to bring about political change should come as no surprise. Because of their experience with heavy-handed government control over the mainstream media, youth tend to be more likely to seek their news from and express themselves on the Internet, generally finding it to be more reliable and accurate and less filled with government propaganda than mainstream resources. Previously dubbed the 'Lost Generation,' and targeted as a potential source of recruits for jihadist and Islamist groups as they sought a collective identity, the youth are now being hailed as the "Facebook Generation," the "Internet Generation," and the "Miracle Generation" because they have accomplished in less than two months in some places what previous generations had not been able to achieve in over thirty years— and all of it without resorting to violence, terrorism, or appeals to jihad or even necessarily religion. Some of the most striking aspects of these uprisings have been their dedication to peaceful demands and nonviolent protests, their mix of male and female leadership and participation, and their refusal to engage in religious or political rhetoric reminiscent of past movements or more traditional social bases, such as the Muslim Brotherhood in Egypt. Most of the demands have focused on greater personal freedom of expression, expanded rights for political participation, resolution of economic challenges that have led to widespread unemployment and underemployment, and an end to corruption and authoritarianism. All of these are secular demands, rather than calls for an Islamic Revolution or a greater public role for religion.[1]

Although the outcome of such use of social media for political purposes appears to be relatively new, the seeds of activism have been consistently sown for the past two decades with rising access to the Internet, the end of government control over the mainstream media, and the growing availability of new levels of individual freedom of expression. Perhaps the greatest sense of empowerment has come through the ability to use cyberspace as a location for doing what could not otherwise be done in reality: assemble to discuss ideas, concerns, and complaints, and to share frustrations, while also providing the social networking opportunity to unite, strategize, and plan for change. In cyberspace, the social restrictions that exist in reality in some places—such as gender segregation—disappear, providing groups of people who might otherwise never meet and converse the opportunity to connect and recognize what they share in common.

For the past two decades, it has seemed that the jihadis have had somewhat of a monopoly on the use of social media—not only for political purposes, but also to evade detection of their activities, disseminate their ideas, plan terrorist attacks, and both recruit new members and make themselves accessible to self-recruiters. The shift to cyberspace was a deliberate strategic move. During the 1970s, 1980s, and even into the 1990s, radical Islamic preachers made use of cassette tapes to spread their message, often clandestinely due to their politically subversive messages and the strong presence of police intelligence throughout society. Such cassette tapes existed in the "underground" territory of individual reproduction and distribution by word of mouth, rather than being made publicly available. During the 1990s and more clearly after 2000, more popular preachers transitioned to satellite television broadcasts and websites to spread their message, given that these new territories were no longer as strictly controlled by government entities following the introduction of Al-Jazeera in 1996, and given the challenges of placing entirely effective filters on Internet access. Shifting to such a global format amplified voices that were previously restricted by geography and limited technology to a worldwide audience.

5   The Internet in particular opened a new communications territory, both in terms of accessing other peoples' ideas and in terms of individual expression. Websites quickly came to be used to generate awareness campaigns of many types, by individuals, organizations, movements, and even governments. In the Gulf, for example, e-government has started to streamline otherwise heavily bureaucratic procedures, such as applying for identification cards and permits, and providing information about how various services operate. In Saudi Arabia, websites like www.saudidivorce .org provide information about divorce laws and women's rights in order to ensure that women are aware of their rights both in Islam and under the law. The hope of website campaigns is that raising public awareness of these rights will result in greater justice.

Organizations further use websites both to proclaim their goals and to compile databases of like-minded individuals. Both organizations and individuals have used websites to post petitions requesting changes ranging from expansion of women's rights—particularly with respect to family law and access to the public sphere—to cleaning up the environment. Some of the most prominent Web petitions with respect to women's rights include the One Million Signature campaigns in Morocco and Iran, which seek to garner support for proposed reforms to be presented to the government. These efforts, among many others, demonstrate attempts to use the principles of democracy in new ways and to harness the new social media for social reform.

Perhaps nowhere have the attempts to use social media to promote the principles of democracy in new ways been more visible than in Tunisia and Egypt, where Facebook and Twitter have been used to quickly disseminate information and instructions that the government has not been able to control. Some believe that the new social media have created a new process for revolution. The process begins when someone establishes a page on Facebook, which is seen by various users, who then comment on it and begin interacting with each other. Once the group is solidified, users begin posting pictures, video footage, and links to YouTube. As this happens, news and comments also begin appearing on Twitter, ever expanding the network of people who are linked in to debates about these events and images. Since the network is not limited geographically, the scope can quickly become global. While this process can be promising in terms of reaching large numbers of people very quickly and creating instantaneous reactions, it also carries the inherent danger of being used to perpetuate sectarianism, tribalism, regionalism, racism, sexism, and discrimination through the proliferation of extremist or exclusionary content. It must be recalled that Facebook is not the private domain of "enlightened" values or democratic ideals. The reality of an open source is that it is open to everyone and anyone who cares to access and comment on it, whether constructively or destructively. Thus, there is the potential for both democratic change and retrograde reactionism that can have serious political and economic repercussions, and for both building and fracturing social cohesion.

Egypt provides a particularly instructive example of this new model for revolution. The popular protests that ultimately resulted in the 11 February 2011 overthrow of President Hosni Mubarak attribute their origins to a blog written by an Egyptian university student named Kamel. Kamel began writing his blog following an incident in which he fell off a train onto a platform. When policemen approached him, Kamel expected them to offer assistance. Instead, they beat him. Kamel started the blog to protest his public humiliation at the hands of representatives of the authoritarian government. He quickly gained a sympathetic audience, many of whom then turned to Facebook to discuss similarly degrading and brutal experiences, resulting in the creation of an online Facebook community.

The turning point came with the case of a young Egyptian businessman from Alexandria, Khaled Said, who was reportedly beaten to death by two police officers in 2010. Popular outrage against police brutality resulted in the Facebook community responding with a Facebook page titled, "We Are All Khaled Said," which quickly turned into a series of e-mail conversations and, ultimately, a network of wannabe activists. Although he was anonymous at the time, the Facebook administrator was the Google executive Wael Ghonim, who later became the face of the Egyptian revolution. Kamel and Ghonim worked together with others to plan Egypt's first day of protest on 25 January, bringing together activists in Cairo, Alexandria, and Damanhur to end the abuses of the Mubarak regime.

Said's case became a rallying point for the opposition because it shocked the moral conscience of observers—the incident demonstrated the degree to which the state had become abusive. The hope of the activists was to shock, in turn, the moral consciences of both the state and outside observers by juxtaposing the violence and oppression of the regime with the demonstrators'

10

own commitment to nonviolent methods, many of which were met with state violence and repression.

As more and more people joined the Facebook page, dissemination of information about planned gatherings, locations, and goals began. Through Facebook and Twitter, demonstrators were able to garner up-to-the-minute information about events, participants and leaders. In one case, ninety thousand people responded via Facebook and Twitter that they planned to attend particular demonstrations, giving organizers a vision of the intended scope of the event and also clearly showing the power of numbers. When so many respond to a social networking site that they intend to physically participate in an event, others are inspired to join, knowing that they will not be alone. By contrast, in cases where only a few respond to the calls for demonstrations—such as occurred for Saudi Arabia's not very impressive "Day of Rage," in March 2011—those debating whether to attend may have been at least partially discouraged from doing so because of the lack of numbers in the face of an intimidating police presence.

Although use of social media has not been credited with causing the uprisings, it clearly played a role in accelerating the events because of the speed at which communications were transmitted. Social media sites have proven difficult for governments to control, despite Mubarak's efforts to do so early in the protests by shutting the Internet down completely. Rather than having the desired effect of calming the situation, the attempt to regain control appears to have resulted in driving more people onto the streets. Had Mubarak chosen to monitor the social media rather than control it or shut it down, he might have at least come to understand the genuine depth and scope of popular frustration so as to respond to it more productively, or at least by meeting some of the demands of the protesters; instead, his decision to react with shows of strength served only to further inflame the situation.

In the case of Tunisia, another aspect of new social media played an important role in the Jasmine Revolution that brought down President Zine el Abidine Ben Ali on 14 January 2011: music disseminated via the Internet. In the early days of the revolution, the protesters found their battle hymn in "Rais Lebled," performed by one of Tunisia's most popular Internet rap artists, Hamada Ben Amor, a.k.a. El General. Rather than classical music or Qur'an verses, which might have left an older or more traditional stamp on the uprising, the deliberate use of a musical form popular with youth to rally the protesters against poverty and oppression made it clear that this revolution was being demanded by young people through methods and symbols of their own choice. The fact that rap had been banned from the airwaves by Ben Ali's regime made it an even more appropriate symbol for youth opposition, as did the fact that the song was unknown to the regime because it was circulated only via Facebook, and had not been made public before the uprising.

The song's lyrics directly targeted Ben Ali: "Mr. President, your people are dying / People are eating rubbish / Look at what is happening / Miseries everywhere, Mr. President / I talk with no fear / Although I know I will get only trouble / I see injustice everywhere," and, "We live in suffering / Like dogs / Half the population is oppressed and living in misery / President of the Country / Your people are dead." Because of its powerful imagery and popular format, the song was also adopted by demonstrators in Egypt and Bahrain, who were also protesting poverty and oppression. After Ben Ali's downfall, the song was broadcast on Tunisian television. Some protested the broadcasting of such music because of the swear words in it. Others believed the time had come for people to be vocal and public in their criticism of the government without fear of reprisal.

Since the downfall of Ben Ali, El General has composed a new rap   15
entitled "Vive Tunisie!" to honor Tunisian protesters and those killed during the uprisings there, as well as in Egypt, Algeria, Morocco, and Libya. In addition, rap artists gathered in late January 2011 to give a concert at the ten-thousand-seat La Coupole Stadium, followed by a political rally "in honour of the blood of our martyrs and our great popular revolution."[2] The concert also featured Tunisia's number one Internet rapper, Mohammed Jandoubi, a.k.a. Psyco-M, who declared his intent to shoot a video outside the long-feared Interior Ministry as one attempt to take back the government and the country by refusing to continue to be afraid of the state's power.

Inspired by varying levels of success, other Arab countries are beginning to engage in their own Facebook campaigns to address their particular problems. Overthrowing an existing regime is not always the goal. In the Palestinian territories, for example, a Facebook campaign led by Fadi Quran has set as the initial target goal the reconciliation and unification of Hamas and Fatah, so as to pursue the longer-term goal of ending the Israeli occupation. The hope is that the Palestinian youth, like their counterparts elsewhere, will be able to rise above the failed politics and rhetoric of preceding generations to find a new vision for achieving their goals and to do so united in their long-term vision, rather than the common hatred of a single leader that has fueled revolutions elsewhere. Although the Facebook activists themselves are divided as to how to best go about reconciling Hamas and Fatah, they all agree that the status quo cannot continue and that the Palestinian people need to be able to work and speak freely.

In Iraq, Facebook is being used to call for peaceful demonstrations demanding improved political and economic conditions, higher levels of security, and better government services, particularly regular access to electricity and clean water. Bloggers have been particularly active in both calling for protests and reporting what happened at them—especially in cases where peaceful protesters have been met with live fire—resulting in the creation of a new type of martyr, different from those associated with suicide attacks. Indeed, public sympathy toward martyrs of regime violence seems to be much higher and more likely to result in popular action than has been the case for those who engage in acts of so-called self-martyrdom that often result in the deaths of innocent Muslim civilians.

In the Sudan, activists have used Facebook to organize protests, but have also raised concerns that the police are using the site to compile lists of people to arrest. The openness of social networking sites has led some to be concerned about personal security because openness means that anyone, including the government, can access the information posted there and see who is talking to whom.

In places where the revolution has been achieved, such as Egypt, Facebook campaigns are not finished, but are changing focus. For example, the Tahrir Square veteran Ahmed Khalil is working to channel the revolution's momentum toward civic awareness of the need to take responsibility at an individual level for the construction of a new Egyptian society. His Facebook group is calling on Egyptians to protect their victory by building a better Egypt. He has combined his use of social media with older and more direct methods of reaching people, such as the distribution of leaflets throughout Cairo with practical recommendations for action, including, "Don't litter; don't blow your car horn for no reason; don't pay bribes; don't allow a police officer to humiliate someone in front of you; don't harass girls on the street; know your rights; stay positive; respect other opinions."[3] Khalil's work is premised on the reality that changing the leadership is just the first step in changing society. The longer-term and often harder work of constructing civil society remains to be done.

There are many lessons to be discerned from the successful use of social   20
media in garnering political and social change. The first is that information
technology today is used by such a wide variety of people that no one has a
monopoly over how it is used or for what purpose. This is expected to have
a powerful impact on how countries are perceived in the global arena. In
the past, governments were able to maintain relative levels of control over
the image of their countries, often focusing on levels of development and
artistic and scientific achievement. Today's reality of a variety of voices
shaping that image—most of which lie outside of the government—carries
the potential for a less cohesive or positive picture. One of the major
goals of the youth participating in these uprisings was to send what they
felt was a more accurate image of their countries to the rest of the world
by showing, through sheer force of numbers, what the majorities of these
countries believe is important, what their goals and aspirations are, and
how they intend to achieve them. Indeed, perhaps the most lasting and
powerful images from these uprisings are the vast numbers of people gathered in peaceful demonstrations. The participants have taken great care to
emphasize the nonviolent nature of their protests in an effort to take the
image of their country and culture back from extremists prone to violence,
whether pro- or antigovernment.

Another striking aspect of these youth revolutions is that they have been
careful to maintain that they are internal movements that have no need for
outside help or inspiration, other than, perhaps, other Arab youth. Part of
this insistence is due to the need to project an image of authenticity and
legitimacy, but the other part is due to the need to distinguish themselves
from the prior regimes that have been heavily dependent on the United
States, in particular, for their political and military strength. Many youth
activists see the United States no longer as the beacon of democracy envis-
aged by their parents, but as an active and deliberate supporter of regimes
guilty of horrific human rights violations and injustices and as concerned
only for its own self-interest, rather than the interests of the people. Thus, the
youth have been careful to avoid any hint of open association with the United
States in favor of focusing on their own capacity to solve the problems of their
societies, evidence of which lies most powerfully in having gotten rid of dictators in Tunisia and Egypt and successfully garnering reforms in other countries, such as Oman and Saudi Arabia, without U.S. support.

For the moment, the focus of the revolutions and protests has been
domestic. However, in the long run, whether this newly found relative

independence from the United States can be maintained remains to be seen. Some analysts and commentators are already suggesting that a dose of realpolitik and addressing of foreign policy will soon be needed if the revolutions are to have staying power, particularly because the youth, however enthusiastic and filled with good will, are lacking in the political and administrative experience necessary to run a state at both the domestic and international levels, particularly with respect to the economy. Simply changing the government or the leader does not change the surrounding context of tribal, provincial, regional, or sectarian loyalties or automatically result in the establishment of a fully developed and functioning democracy or even reform.

Finally, the strong participation of women as both leaders and demonstrators has challenged old stereotypes of Arab or Muslim women as passive, voiceless victims. Some of the most powerful and lasting images of the revolutions are of women marching; protesting; braving tear gas, tanks, and armed security forces; and shouting slogans. The Egyptian activist Asmaa Mahfouz became known as "The Leader of the Revolution" following the posting of her online video telling youth to get out into the streets and protest. When male youths challenged her right to protest, arguing that it wasn't safe for women to be out, she challenged them back by insisting that they come out to protect her. Another prominent Egyptian woman leader, Dalia Ziada, has engaged in both blogging and activism to train others in nonviolent means of effecting change. She has reported that the ideas of nonviolent uprisings, the struggle for civil rights, and the advancement of freedom through careful strategy and meticulous planning, all resonated with youth leaders in Egypt, who not only planned and coordinated demonstrations, but also made certain to keep their activities secret so that they could not be disrupted by the government security apparatus.[4] In Libya, women lawyers were among the earliest organizers of anti-Qaddafi protests in Benghazi. In Syria, women and children worked together to block a highway to protest the arrests of their husbands and fathers. In Yemen, the ongoing popular demonstrations against President Ali Ben Saleh have been led, since the beginning, by a woman, Tawaful Karman. Karman has been protesting every Tuesday since 2007 in front of Sanaa University, denouncing the expulsion of thirty families known as Ja'ashin from their village when their land was given to a tribal leader close to President Saleh. Karman insists that only the resignation of Saleh will allow Yemen to begin to address its problems. Thousands of Yemenis have joined her. In many cases, the protests have been broken up by either the police or armed supporters of the regime.

Women have also harnessed new social media to address social concerns. In Egypt, harassment of women is rampant, occurring openly and without much criminal recourse because parliament has failed to enact a law banning it. Women have found their own way to band together and fight back. In Cairo, a website called Harassmap provides a digital map of Cairo showing areas where it may be dangerous for women to go alone. Women can either send text messages or tweets to the site to report incidents of harassment that are updated in real time. The goal is to allow women to help other women create a climate of safety for each other since the police and the state have failed to assure such personal security.

Despite these hopeful beginnings, history cautions us not to expect that women's leadership and participation will be enough to guarantee them a solid place in the new order. In Iran, Algeria, and Kuwait, previous women's involvement in the liberation of their countries from the Shah, the French, and Iraqi occupation, respectively, did not translate into an expansion of women's rights or greater access to the public sphere. In fact, because women are the culture-bearers, typically in the aftermath of a revolution when emphasis is placed on the restoration of order, women are ordered back home so that the men can put the country together again. Women's rights are typically subordinated to the "greater" issues of democracy and domestic stability. Hints of such paternalism are already apparent in Tunisia, where women have expressed great concern about growing calls for the implementation of Shari'ah and the potential for the rise of political Islam, which women fear may threaten their rights and equality. Indeed, several postrevolution rallies organized by Tunisian women have been interrupted by men telling them to go back home to the kitchen. In Egypt, the "Wise Men's Council," which provides advice, and the Constitutional Committee, organized to handle the transition of government, do not include any women; the heady days of men and women working together side-by-side in Tahrir Square have devolved in some cases to a return of the culture of harassment of women. Women have noted the particularly disheartening situation in Egypt because women had played such a prominent role in the revolution.

In conclusion, it is simply too early to tell what the long-term results of these revolutionary and reformist endeavors throughout the Middle East and North Africa will be. The only thing that is known for certain is that

25

the use of modern technology and new social media has opened the door to new and creative thinking about how to assemble, organize, plan, and strategize activities ranging from political to social change that are immediately conveyed at a global level.

NOTES

1   Based on the results of the Gallup Poll of the Muslim world undertaken following 9/11, these realities are not surprising. The uprisings in the Middle East and North Africa have remarkably reflected the findings of this poll. For further information, see John L. Esposito and Dalia Mogahed, *Who Speaks for Islam? What a Billion Muslims Really Think*. New York: Gallup Press, 2007.

2   "Tunisia's Revolution Rap Hits the Big Stage," *Asharq Alawsat*, January 29, 2011.

3   Bobby Ghosh, "Rage, Rap and Revolution: Inside the Arab Youth Quake," *Time Magazine*, February 17, 2011.

4   Sheryl Gay Stolberg, "Shy U.S. Intellectual Created Playbook Used in a Revolution," *New York Times*, February 16, 2011.

Selected Bibliography

Alavi, Nasrin. *We Are Iran: The Persian Blogs* (Brooklyn, NY: Soft Skull Press, 2005). A thematic approach to a variety of Iranian blogs translated into English.

Bunt, Gary R. *Islam in the Digital Age: E-Jihad, Online Fatwas, and Cyber Islamic Environments* (London: Pluto Press, 2003). An analysis of the religious use of cyberspace by Muslim preachers and leaders.

Eickelman, Dale F., and Jon W. Anderson, eds. *New Media in the Muslim World: The Emerging Public Sphere*, second ed. (Bloomington: Indiana University Press, 2003). An edited collection of articles addressing the use of new media throughout the Muslim world.

Esposito, John L., and Dalia Mogahed. *Who Speaks for Islam? What a Billion Muslims Really Think* (New York: Gallup Press, 2007). An analysis of the findings of the Gallup Poll of the Muslim world.

Hammond, Andrew. *Popular Culture in the Arab World: Arts, Politics, and the Media* (Cairo: American University in Cairo Press, 2007). A discussion of various aspects of popular culture in the Arab world.

Inside Islam: What a Billion Muslims Really Think (Unity Productions, 2009). A documentary film discussing the construction
and findings of the Gallup Poll of the Muslim world.
One Million Signatures Campaign, Iran (http://www.we-change
.org/english/). Website for the English-language version of One
Million Signatures Campaign, Iran.

Analyze

1. What was your personal experience of the Arab Spring? Do you remember where you were or what you were doing as it unfolded? How
did the news of its events reach you? Since that time, what (if any) has
been your most reliable source of information about the continued
fallout of the Arab Spring?
2. The author writes that before social media, countries had better control of their images worldwide. How does she support this assertion?
What are recent examples of a country's image being exposed through
social media?
3. In what ways do you participate in social media? If a political movement or event were occurring where you live, how would you be
connected to it?

Explore

1. DeLong-Bas published her piece relatively soon after the Arab Spring in
2011. Does the article still hold up as you read it now? What has happened either with new social media or within the Arab world since the
article was published that might make the author consider updating it?
Research one of the countries in the Middle East or North Africa and
write a paper that considers a measured assessment of the strengths and
limitations of social media in effecting political change.
2. According to the author, what has social media done for women in the
Arab world? What have been its limitations in promoting the rights of
women?
3. In her conclusion, the author claims that "the use of modern technology
and new social media has opened the door to new and creative thinking
about how to assemble, organize, plan, and strategize activities ranging
from political to social change that are immediately conveyed at a global

level." What are some of the most powerful recent movements or events engendered by new social media? Working with a group in your class, choose an example of a recent movement or event and document its development using an online platform (such as Google Docs) that allows you to collaborate, insert media, and provide links. How did it begin, and on what social media platform(s)? In what ways has it been sustained? How were the issues it called for resolved? Compare your findings with those of other groups in your class.

Teju Cole
"The White Savior Industrial Complex"

Born in the United States and raised in Nigeria, Teju Cole now resides in Brooklyn. His debut novel *Open City* (Random House, 2012) was the winner of the 2012 PEN/Hemingway Award and a finalist for the National Book Critics Circle Award. "The White Savior Industrial Complex" was published on March 21, 2012, in *The Atlantic*, which was founded in Boston in 1857 as a literary and cultural commentary magazine. Now online, as well as in print, *The Atlantic* covers politics, business, entertainment, health, and international affairs. Cole's "article" reprints a series of tweets he originally posted to his Twitter account in response to Kony 2012, a video posted on YouTube that went viral, generating nearly as much outrage against the video-makers as it did against Joseph Kony.

How differently do people portray themselves on Twitter, Facebook, YouTube, or other new social media platforms compared to more conventional public forums like newspaper or magazine articles?

A week and a half ago, I watched the Kony 2012 video. Afterward, I wrote a brief seven-part response, which I posted in sequence on my Twitter account:

These tweets were retweeted, forwarded, and widely shared by readers. They migrated beyond Twitter to blogs, Tumblr, Facebook, and other sites;

Teju Cole
@tejucole

1- From Sachs to Kristof to Invisible Children to TED, the fastest growth industry in the US is the White Savior Industrial Complex.

8 Mar 12   Reply   Retweet   Favorite

Teju Cole
@tejucole

2- The white savior supports brutal policies in the morning, founds charities in the afternoon, and receives awards in the evening.

8 Mar 12   Reply   Retweet   Favorite

Teju Cole
@tejucole

3- The banality of evil transmutes into the banality of sentimentality. The world is nothing but a problem to be solved by enthusiasm.

8 Mar 12   Reply   Retweet   Favorite

Teju Cole
@tejucole

4- This world exists simply to satisfy the needs—including, importantly, the sentimental needs—of white people and Oprah.

8 Mar 12   Reply   Retweet   Favorite

Teju Cole
@tejucole

5- The White Savior Industrial Complex is not about justice. It is about having a big emotional experience that validates privilege.

8 Mar 12   Reply   Retweet   Favorite

Teju Cole
@tejucole

6- Feverish worry over that awful African warlord. But close to 1.5 million Iraqis died from an American war of choice. Worry about that.

8 Mar 12   Reply   Retweet   Favorite

Teju Cole ✓
@tejucole

7- I deeply respect American sentimentality, the way one respects a wounded hippo. You must keep an eye on it, for you know it is deadly.

12:39 PM - 8 Mar 2012

I'm told they generated fierce arguments. As the days went by, the tweets were reproduced in their entirety on the websites of the *Atlantic* and the *New York Times*, and they showed up on German, Spanish, and Portuguese sites. A friend emailed to tell me that the fourth tweet, which cheekily name-checks Oprah, was mentioned on Fox television.

These sentences of mine, written without much premeditation, had touched a nerve. I heard back from many people who were grateful to have read them. I heard back from many others who were disappointed or furious. Many people, too many to count, called me a racist. One person likened me to the Mau Mau. The *Atlantic* writer who'd reproduced them, while agreeing with my broader points, described the language in which they were expressed as "resentment."

5   This weekend, I listened to a radio interview given by the Pulitzer Prize-winning journalist Nicholas Kristof. Kristof is best known for his regular column in the *New York Times* in which he often gives accounts of his activism or that of other Westerners. When I saw the Kony 2012 video, I found it tonally similar to Kristof's approach, and that was why I mentioned him in the first of my seven tweets.

Those tweets, though unpremeditated, were intentional in their irony and seriousness. I did not write them to score cheap points, much less to hurt anyone's feelings. I believed that a certain kind of language is too infrequently seen in our public discourse. I am a novelist. I traffic in subtleties, and my goal in writing a novel is to leave the reader not knowing what to think. A good novel shouldn't have a point.

But there's a place in the political sphere for direct speech and, in the past few years in the U.S., there has been a chilling effect on a certain kind of direct speech pertaining to rights. The president is wary of being seen as the "angry black man." People of color, women, and gays—who now have greater access to the centers of influence than ever before—are under pressure to be well-behaved when talking about their struggles. There is an expectation that we can talk about sins but no one must be identified as a sinner: newspapers love to describe words or deeds as "racially charged" even in those cases when it would be more honest to say "racist"; we agree that there is rampant misogyny, but misogynists are nowhere to be found; homophobia is a problem but no one is homophobic. One cumulative effect of this policed language is that when someone dares to point out something as obvious as white privilege, it is seen as unduly provocative. Marginalized voices in America have fewer and fewer avenues to speak plainly about what

they suffer; the effect of this enforced civility is that those voices are falsi-
fied or blocked entirely from the discourse.

It's only in the context of this neutered language that my rather tame
tweets can be seen as extreme. The interviewer on the radio show I listened
to asked Kristof if he had heard of me. "Of course," he said. She asked him
what he made of my criticisms. His answer was considered and genial, but
what he said worried me more than an angry outburst would have:

> There has been a real discomfort and backlash among middle-class
> educated Africans, Ugandans in particular in this case, but people
> more broadly, about having Africa as they see it defined by a warlord
> who does particularly brutal things, and about the perception that
> Americans are going to ride in on a white horse and resolve it. To
> me though, it seems even more uncomfortable to think that we as
> white Americans should not intervene in a humanitarian disaster
> because the victims are of a different skin color.

Here are some of the "middle-class educated Africans" Kristof, whether
he is familiar with all of them and their work or not, chose to take issue
with: Ugandan journalist Rosebell Kagumire, who covered the Lord's
Resistance Army in 2005 and made an eloquent video response to Kony
2012; Ugandan scholar Mahmood Mamdani, one of the world's leading
specialists on Uganda and the author of a thorough riposte to the political wrong-headedness of Invisible Children; and Ethiopian-American
novelist Dinaw Mengestu, who sought out Joseph Kony, met his lieuten-
ants, and recently wrote a brilliant essay about how Kony 2012 gets the
issues wrong. They have a different take on what Kristof calls a "humanitarian
disaster," and this may be because they see the larger disasters behind it: militarization of poorer countries, short-sighted agricultural policies, resource
extraction, the propping up of corrupt governments, and the astonishing
complexity of long-running violent conflicts over a wide and varied terrain.

I want to tread carefully here: I do not accuse Kristof of racism nor do   10
I believe he is in any way racist. I have no doubt that he has a good heart.
Listening to him on the radio, I began to think we could iron the whole
thing out over a couple of beers. But that, precisely, is what worries me. That
is what made me compare American sentimentality to a "wounded hippo."
His good heart does not always allow him to think constellationally.

He does not connect the dots or see the patterns of power behind the isolated "disasters." All he sees are hungry mouths, and he, in his own advocacy-by-journalism way, is putting food in those mouths as fast as he can. All he sees is need, and he sees no need to reason out the need for the need.

But I disagree with the approach taken by Invisible Children in particular, and by the White Savior Industrial Complex in general, because there is much more to doing good work than "making a difference." There is the principle of first do no harm. There is the idea that those who are being helped ought to be consulted over the matters that concern them.

I write all this from multiple positions. I write as an African, a black man living in America. I am every day subject to the many microaggressions of American racism. I also write this as an American, enjoying the many privileges that the American passport affords and that residence in this country makes possible. I involve myself in this critique of privilege: my own privileges of class, gender, and sexuality are insufficiently examined. My cell phone was likely manufactured by poorly treated workers in a Chinese factory. The coltan in the phone can probably be traced to the conflict-riven Congo. I don't fool myself that I am not implicated in these transnational networks of oppressive practices.

And I also write all this as a novelist and story-writer: I am sensitive to the power of narratives. When Jason Russell, narrator of the Kony 2012 video, showed his cheerful blonde toddler a photo of Joseph Kony as the embodiment of evil (a glowering dark man), and of his friend Jacob as the representative of helplessness (a sweet-faced African), I wondered how Russell's little boy would develop a nuanced sense of the lives of others, particularly others of a different race from his own. How would that little boy come to understand that others have autonomy; that their right to life is not exclusive of a right to self-respect? In a different context, John Berger once wrote, "A singer may be innocent; never the song."

One song we hear too often is the one in which Africa serves as a backdrop for white fantasies of conquest and heroism. From the colonial project to *Out of Africa* to *The Constant Gardener* and Kony 2012, Africa has provided a space onto which white egos can conveniently be projected. It is a liberated space in which the usual rules do not apply: a nobody from America or Europe can go to Africa and become a godlike savior or, at the very least, have his or her emotional needs satisfied. Many have done it under the banner of "making a difference." To state this obvious and well-attested truth does not make me a racist or a Mau Mau. It does give me away as an "educated middle-class African," and I plead guilty as charged. (It is also worth noting that there are other educated middle-class Africans who see this matter differently from me. That is what people, educated and otherwise, do: they assess information and sometimes disagree with each other.)

In any case, Kristof and I are in profound agreement about one thing: 15 there is much happening in many parts of the African continent that is not as it ought to be. I have been fortunate in life, but that doesn't mean I haven't seen or experienced African poverty first-hand. I grew up in a land of military coups and economically devastating, IMF-imposed "structural adjustment" programs. The genuine hurt of Africa is no fiction.

And we also agree on something else: that there is an internal ethical urge that demands that each of us serve justice as much as he or she can. But beyond the immediate attention that he rightly pays hungry mouths, child soldiers, or raped civilians, there are more complex and more widespread problems. There are serious problems of governance, of infrastructure, of democracy, and of law and order. These problems are neither simple in themselves nor are they reducible to slogans. Such problems are both intricate and intensely local.

How, for example, could a well-meaning American "help" a place like Uganda today? It begins, I believe, with some humility with regards to the people in those places. It begins with some respect for the agency of the people of Uganda in their own lives. A great deal of work had been done, and continues to be done, by Ugandans to improve their own country, and ignorant comments (I've seen many) about how "we have to save them because they can't save themselves" can't change that fact.

Let me draw into this discussion an example from an African country I know very well. Earlier this year, hundreds of thousands of Nigerians took to their country's streets to protest the government's decision to remove a subsidy on petrol. This subsidy was widely seen as one of the few blessings of the country's otherwise catastrophic oil wealth. But what made these protests so heartening is that they were about more than the subsidy removal. Nigeria has one of the most corrupt governments in the world and protesters clearly demanded that something be done about this. The protests went on for days, at considerable personal risk to the protesters. Several young people were shot dead, and the movement was eventually doused when union leaders capitulated and the army deployed on the streets. The movement did not "succeed" in conventional terms. But something important had changed in the political consciousness of the Nigerian populace. For me and for a number of people I know, the protests gave us an opportunity to be proud of Nigeria, many of us for the first time in our lives.

This is not the sort of story that is easy to summarize in an article, much less make a viral video about. After all, there is no simple demand to be made and—since corruption is endemic—no single villain to topple. There is certainly no "bridge character," Kristof's euphemism for white saviors in Third World narratives who make the story more palatable to American viewers. And yet, the story of Nigeria's protest movement is one of the most important from sub-Saharan Africa so far this year. Men and women, of all classes and ages, stood up for what they felt was right; they marched peacefully; they defended each other, and gave each other food and drink; Christians stood guard while Muslims prayed and vice-versa; and they spoke without fear to their leaders about the kind of country they wanted to see. All of it happened with no cool American 20-something heroes in sight.

20   Joseph Kony is no longer in Uganda and he is no longer the threat he was, but he is a convenient villain for those who need a convenient villain. What Africa needs more pressingly than Kony's indictment is more equitable civil society, more robust democracy, and a fairer system of justice. This is the scaffolding from which infrastructure, security, healthcare, and education can be built. How do we encourage voices like those of the Nigerian masses who marched this January, or those who are engaged in the struggle to develop Ugandan democracy?

If Americans want to care about Africa, maybe they should consider evaluating American foreign policy, which they already play a direct role in through elections, before they impose themselves on Africa itself. The fact of the matter is that Nigeria is one of the top five oil suppliers to the U.S., and American policy is interested first and foremost in the flow of that oil. The American government did not see fit to support the Nigeria protests. (Though the State Department issued a supportive statement— "our view on that is that the Nigerian people have the right to peaceful protest, we want to see them protest peacefully, and we're also urging the Nigerian security services to respect the right of popular protest and conduct themselves professionally in dealing with the strikes"—it reeked of boilerplate rhetoric and, unsurprisingly, nothing tangible came of it.) This was as expected; under the banner of "American interests," the oil comes first. Under that same banner, the livelihood of corn farmers in Mexico has been destroyed by NAFTA. Haitian rice farmers have suffered appalling losses due to Haiti being flooded with subsidized American rice. A nightmare has been playing out in Honduras in the past three years: an American-backed coup and American militarization of that country have contributed to a conflict in which hundreds of activists and journalists have already been murdered. The Egyptian military, which is now suppressing the country's once-hopeful movement for democracy and killing dozens of activists in the process, subsists on $1.3 billion in annual U.S. aid. This is a litany that will be familiar to some. To others, it will be news. But, familiar or not, it has a bearing on our notions of innocence and our right to "help."

Let us begin our activism right here: with the money-driven villainy at the heart of American foreign policy. To do this would be to give up the illusion that the sentimental need to "make a difference" trumps all other considerations. What innocent heroes don't always understand is that they play a useful role for people who have much more cynical motives. The White Savior Industrial Complex is a valve for releasing the unbearable pressures that build in a system built on pillage. We can participate in the economic destruction of Haiti over long years, but when the earthquake strikes it feels good to send $10 each to the rescue fund. I have no opposition, in principle, to such donations (I frequently make them myself), but we must do such things only with awareness of what else is involved. If we are going to interfere in the lives of others, a little due diligence is a minimum requirement.

Success for Kony 2012 would mean increased militarization of the anti-democratic Yoweri Museveni government, which has been in power in Uganda since 1986 and has played a major role in the world's deadliest ongoing conflict, the war in the Congo. But those whom privilege allows to deny constellational thinking would enjoy ignoring this fact. There are other troubling connections, not least of them being that Museveni appears to be a U.S. proxy in its shadowy battles against militants in Sudan and, especially, in Somalia. Who sanctions these conflicts? Under whose authority and oversight are they conducted? Who is being killed and why?

All of this takes us rather far afield from fresh-faced young Americans using the power of YouTube, Facebook, and pure enthusiasm to change the world. A singer may be innocent; never the song.

Analyze

1. How does Cole support his statement, "Those tweets, though unpremeditated, were intentional in their irony and seriousness"? What kind of language is he referring to when he says in paragraph 6, "I believed that a certain kind of language is too infrequently seen in our public discourse"?
2. What does Cole mean by the expression "enforced civility"? Have you experienced "enforced civility"? Provide examples either from your own experience or from current events in which Web 2.0 platforms such as Twitter and Facebook have promoted and/or exposed "enforced civility."
3. What does Cole mean by the "White Savior Industrial Complex"? Why does he claim "there's much more to doing good work than 'making a difference'"?

Explore

1. Cole posted his seven tweets after viewing the Kony2012 YouTube video. How do his tweets compare to his article? Write a response to this article in seven tweets. Then write an essay that unpacks the tweets the way Cole has. Reading over your final draft, write a reflective piece on your process that responds to the question: What place is there for new social media in addressing global issues?
2. View (or view again) the Kony2012 YouTube video and read the responses by the African journalists and writers that Cole mentions in paragraph 9 of this article. How does this range of information complicate and/or clarify your understanding of what Cole calls "constellational thinking"?
3. Find a different example of an issue or problem that is being addressed by the White Savior Industrial Complex. Who are the saviors? Who are the victims? Provide examples of how this problem is explained and exposed through new social media platforms and compare them to examples of how it is explained and exposed through more conventional platforms of communication. Based on what you have discovered through your writing, how will you approach your own engagement with various communication and information technologies in the future?

Rudabeh Pakravan
"Territory Jam"

A member of the architecture faculty at the University of California, Berkeley, Rudabeh Pakravan is also principal of her own architecture and design studio. Her interests lie in how architecture operates on an urban scale, and how hidden networks affect urban space. She credits these hidden networks for the success of the Egyptian and Tunisian revolutions in her essay "Territory Jam," which appeared in *Places* on July 9, 2012. *Places*, an interdisciplinary journal of contemporary architecture, landscape, and urbanism, focuses on the public realm as both physical place and social ideal. In her article, Pakravan observes that part of what defines a democracy is the presence of legitimate public spaces. In the absence of such spaces, satellite dishes can provide legitimate *cyberspaces*, or "spaces of opportunity—for debate, leisure, discourse, spontaneous gathering and protest."

In what ways or under what conditions have you been limited in your ability to access information or entertainment—at home, at school, at work, or elsewhere? How did you respond?

Observers of Iranian politics can be forgiven for ignoring this recent headline: *Police clamp down on satellite TV users.*[1] The crackdowns on rogue television viewers have been reported periodically for the better part of two decades, though they're usually overshadowed by news of international economic sanctions, rigged parliamentary elections and the specter of war with Israel. Nevertheless, the satellite dish, or *mahvareh*, has been a fixture on Tehran's roofscape since the early 1990s, serving up American reality shows, Latin American *telenovelas*, domestic and international news, and dozens of other illegal alternatives to the ideological and religious conformity of the six state-controlled channels.

The Iranian Parliament banned satellite dishes in 1995, as part of an effort to limit the influence of "Western culture," but enforcement has proved difficult. Despite door-to-door sweeps and electronic signal jamming, satellite use in the capital is at an all-time high. (Although reliable statistics are hard to come by, a reported 40 to 65 percent of the capital's population has access to satellite television.²) Tehranis flout the ban, pay the fines, secretly reinstall receivers, engage in all manner of camouflage and subterfuge—anything to keep the TV on. Until a few years ago, apartment dwellers would hide satellite receivers behind air conditioning units or laundry drying on the line. These days, the typical Tehran roof is so crowded that residents simply place dishes in the open and resign themselves to periodically replacing those destroyed by police.³ Revolutionary guards who are denied entry to an apartment have been known to scale a building's walls with grappling hooks to dismantle receivers. It may seem like something out of a spy novel, but this cat-and-mouse game tells the deeper story of a complex exchange between the Islamic Republic and citizens of Tehran. In the absence of legitimate public space for discourse or demonstration, the satellite receiver opens a space for political dissent and cultural protest.

Delegitimizing Public Space

To understand how the satellite dish functions as a substitute for the spatial tactics of assembly and protest, we must first understand how Tehran's public spaces have been strategically delegitimized.⁴ The space itself is there. Unlike in Cairo, where Hosni Mubarak systematically dismantled public spaces, including Tahrir Square, Tehran's recent mayors have added nearly 3,000 acres of parks, plazas and green belts, and the city now has 1,800 parks serving a population of 9 million, a ratio roughly comparable to New York City.⁵ But Tehran's inhabitants are subject to strict behavioral laws, which mandate harsh penalties and imprisonment for socializing with a person of the opposite gender, deviating from the Islamic dress code, or participating in any but the most benign group activities. Women are publicly humiliated, fined and detained by police for showing hair beneath their headscarves, wearing makeup or even having a fake suntan. Meanwhile, young men are targeted for wearing Western-style clothing or long hairstyles, and both genders are prohibited from riding in the same car, speaking together in public or gathering in larger groups. The severity of the sentence varies with the political atmosphere but can include a fine, university expulsion, lashings and up to 60 days of imprisonment.⁶ These laws have become even more restrictive since the student uprisings in 2009.⁷

Today, activities in all parks, streets and other public spaces are tightly controlled and highly choreographed. Morality and vice squads—efficiently divided into the Makeup Unit, the Relationship Unit and the Hijab Unit—arrive unannounced in police minivans at parks, shopping districts and cafes popular with Tehran's youth. They round up offenders and take them to detention centers, often assaulting them verbally and physically. Shadowy officers on motorbikes accost groups of people talking or young couples walking alone on quiet streets. During crackdown periods, morality police appear weekly, sometimes daily, in the city's main public spaces, and it's not always clear which branch of Iran's complex law enforcement structure they represent. Some are agents of the Ministry of the Interior, charged with enforcing the Koranic principle of *amr-e be ma'ruf va nahy-e az monkar*, "commanding the just and forbidding the wrong."[8] Others are Islamic Revolutionary Guards, or special operations forces of the city police, or members of the even more extreme Basij, a volunteer national paramilitary unit notorious for violently suppressing demonstrations in 1999 and 2009.

In addition to punishing moral offenders, the Basij act as a neighbor- 5 hood task force, organizing religious ceremonies and parades in local parks.[9] Branches of the city government also participate in the choreography of public space. Tehran's Municipal Council has recently increased Basij street patrols under the guise of "public safety." The mayor's office sponsors cultural programs such as the "Imam of Piety," which celebrates the life of Ayatollah Khomeini with public exhibitions and events, and has ordered the construction of 400 mini-museums, scattered throughout the city, that recreate the homes of Islamic martyrs.[10] In 2010, the city's Religious Activities Department announced that all parks would be required to host congregational prayers every Friday at noon:

The tradition of Friday prayers and muezzins reading verses from the holy book in loud voices has helped keep Satan away from our cities and villages. We must now make sure that the same sound will be heard in all the capital's parks.[11]

The sounds of these mandated assemblies echo through the streets, bouncing off the hundreds of new minarets, mosques and prayer halls the government has built in public spaces across the city. Tehran's Municipal Council approved 30 new minarets in lower-income districts of South Tehran alone. In the greener, richer districts of the North Side, mosque projects are fewer but more noticeable, conspicuously placed across from secular venues like theaters and concert halls, reminding inhabitants of the regime's ubiquity.[12] Information about the funding and construction of these projects is murky. Officially, the Municipal Council works with planners and architects to approve plans, and construction companies hired by the city build the projects, but the Islamic Revolutionary Guards Corps and other high-level government agencies can bypass this process and advance their own initiatives. Various organizations, nominally "charitable foundations," actually fund much of the construction, bolstered by private donors who want to curry favor with the government.[13] Only 12 percent of city dwellers go to mosques by choice, and so these same groups work in parallel to fulfill attendance quotas by bussing in rural civil servants to join true believers for Friday prayers, passion plays and other state-sanctioned activities.[14]

Religious observances and events fill the parks several times a month; this January alone, there were four public holidays devoted to mourning religious figures. The rest of the time, they are used by groups that are usually left alone by the police: families picnicking with children, older men playing backgammon, citizens praying or engaging in city-sponsored activities. Sometimes there are periods of several months when even young people are left alone, creating an illusion that the spaces are becoming more democratic. But then the political climate shifts slightly, or summer arrives, and the morality squads once again dominate the public realm. During particularly tense days, police cars line the edges of the parks, watching over every move of the people. Predictably, this is jarring and creates a paranoid atmosphere even on calm days. As one student told me, "even when you are just walking in the street with your friends, you have to look over your shoulder. What was okay last week may not be okay this week."[15]

The Satellite Man

Spaces of opportunity—for debate, leisure, discourse, spontaneous gathering and protest—must therefore emerge behind walls, underground and, most commonly, in the home. Today the home is the true public realm in Tehran—the private place where residents can socialize comfortably and freely, unmonitored by the otherwise pervasive government. Some even invite strangers into their homes, hosting events for charities and non-governmental organizations and showing censored art in private "galleries."[16] Here residents piece together the news of their city, gathering information from illegal media, mounting daily challenges to the regime's monopoly on information.[17] Often the entire family gathers around a television in the center of the living room to catch up on Persian music videos filmed in Dubai or Los Angeles, watch dubbed soaps set in Mexico City or Miami, and catch up on news from London's BBC Persian Television or temporary channels set up by opposition movements. A particular favorite is *Parazit*, a satirical news program in the style of *The Daily Show*, broadcast by Voice of America in Washington, D.C.[18]

There is no more central character in this domestic narrative of cultural protest than the satellite man.   10

The satellite man is typically young, with an entrepreneur's zeal and a sense of adventure, often from the mercantile district of South Tehran. Trained by colleagues in the black-market niche of satellite TV installation, he begins by taking on overflow business, developing contacts with dealers smuggling dishes via boat and truck from Dubai or Central Asia; he then creates a loyal customer base through word of mouth.[19] He often works within groups of friends and families, driving around town to install the service for 150 dollars or so and returning for occasional maintenance. His predecessor, the video man, first joined the ranks of door-to-door vendors in the 1980s, carrying a black briefcase with videocassettes, alcohol, music and other black-market goods, developing relationships with people in homes all over the city. The satellite man carries on the tradition, but in a much more dangerous zone. The vendor hawking romantic comedies is breaking the law, but the real threat to the regime is the man on the doorstep providing access to a 24-hour television channel beaming news from the opposition movement.[20]

And the regime takes the threat very seriously. It deploys signal disruptions, known as "territorial jamming" or "downlink jamming," from "noise stations" set up in small circular buildings throughout Tehran that host radio equipment operated by the Revolutionary Guards, or from mobile stations that drive around the city emitting microwaves. These stations scramble satellite feeds within a localized area, and the signal emerges as black-and-white static on neighborhood screens. The government also deploys "vertical" or "uplink" jams, sending a signal up to the satellite itself, preventing it from receiving information from broadcasters. This tactic is used infrequently, as the entire satellite signal, which the government depends upon to broadcast its own programming worldwide, will then be inoperable. And although the government admits to jamming foreign channels that it deems "propaganda," permanently removing signal access is not an option, since regime supporters and government officials monitor the illegal channels.

When a signal is jammed, the broadcasting companies are then forced to rent frequencies from other satellites. This can happen quickly, but as household dishes are oriented toward the blocked satellite, the stations won't have the same coverage until everyone on the ground reorients their receivers.[21] Signal jams occur without warning and can last for days, especially during periods of extreme political tension. They interrupt all kinds of programs, but especially news and analysis of events in Iran.

It is during these disruptions that the satellite man makes his secret house calls, stopping in for a cup of tea and discussing the news or soap opera that was interrupted, then climbing up to the roof and repositioning the receiver to capture favorite channels from a new satellite. Although not overtly political, the satellite man, like many other young Iranians, is usually disillusioned with the economic and political climate, and so discussion comes easily.[22] Visiting up to eight homes a night, he becomes the purveyor not only of contraband television but also of a lengthening chain of local news that links one house to the next. His customer's own voices are thus folded into the narrative.[23] Penalties can be severe for installing and watching anything other than state television, so the satellite man and his customers are conspirators in a risky activity. Fines run from 500 dollars for individuals to over 50,000 dollars for dish importers; more worrisome is possible imprisonment and corporal punishment.[24] With repeat visits every few months to re-install or calibrate the dish, or just add a few channels, the satellite man brokers relationships between citizens who wouldn't necessarily have access to one another in public life.

15   In *Ambient Television: Visual Culture and Public Space*, Anna McCarthy argues that television reflects a media power structure that exerts control locally over its site, in the space of an airport or bar, for instance, or in the home.[25] In Tehran, the state television is site-specific, but its control is weak: viewers use the satellite man to find the spatial loophole that allows them to thwart signal jams. As households throughout the city tune into the same underground channels, and as entire neighborhoods are subject to the same signal disruptions at the same time, television transcends the boundaries of the local site and is embedded as a series of nodes in the

larger urban system, rendered visible by the network of satellite men moving from house to house, allowing communication to resume, temporarily unhindered.

Public Space, Temporarily

One reason that the revolutionary movements succeeded last year in places like Egypt and Tunisia was the element of surprise. Governments underestimated citizens' anger and frustration with years of oppression and were ill prepared to respond.[26] In contrast, the Islamic Republic (itself borne of violent revolution) anticipates exactly this type of group protest and reacts swiftly and violently. In June 2009, the immediate and brutal suppression of the Green Revolution crushed the nascent movement and sent the opposition further underground. In the years since, reformers' attempts to co-opt public space have been met with state violence, arrests and imprisonment. A group called the Mothers of Laleh Park, led by women who lost their children in the 2009 uprising, organized a demonstration in the spring of 2011 that led to detentions condemned by international human rights advocates. More recently, morality police have arrested young people who were using Facebook and other social media to organize flash mobs and seemingly apolitical gatherings, including "Bad Fashion Day," "The Meeting of the Curly Haired" and an 800-person water-gun fight.[27]

Iran's violation of the basic human rights of assembly and information access have long been condemned by the international community, most recently by the United Nations International Telecommunications Union, which declared that "jamming is a fundamental violation, not only of international regulations and norms, but of the right of people everywhere to receive and impart information."[28] Because legitimate public space is a critical element in any democracy, its absence can give rise to a more ambiguous set of spaces in which the people exercise their rights. Under these conditions, even a quotidian ritual like watching TV can be part of a broader spatial and political agenda.

Years ago the cultural critics Kristin Ross and Alice Kaplan observed that "the political . . . is hidden in the everyday, exactly where it is most obvious: in the contradictions of lived experience, in the most banal and repetitive gestures of everyday life. . . . It is in the midst of the utterly ordinary, in the space where the dominant relations of production are tirelessly and relentlessly reproduced, that we must look for utopian and political aspirations to crystallize."[29] Tehrani satellite-television culture doesn't guarantee a democratic future for Iran, nor does it substitute for public space, but it is a reminder of the various ways in which people find temporary places that allow them to remain connected, to gather spontaneously, and to create a sense of the public. We would do well to remember the debt that many democracies owe to such ambiguous spaces—places for people to gather their strength in preparation for change.

NOTES

1 "Iranian Police Clamp Down on Satellite TV Users Ahead of Election," Deutsche Presse-Agentur, February 18, 2012.

2 The official estimate is 40 percent, from "Roshd-e-Roozafnoon Hoozoor-e Mahvareh-Meeaan-e-Khanevadehayeh-Irani," Iranian Students' News Agency, November 2009, quoting Ali Darabi, Deputy Director of Islamic Republic of Iran Broadcasting. More recently, Golnaz Esfandiari of Radio Free Europe reported that the number is closer to 65 percent; see "Nothing Comes Between Iranians and Their Satellite Dishes: Not even the Police," March 13, 2012.

3 Paul Sonne and Farnaz Fassihi, "In Skies over Iran, a Battle for Control of Satellite TV," Wall Street Journal, December 27, 2011. See also Esfandiari, op cit.

4 As defined by Michel de Certeau — and recently discussed by Mimi Zeiger in The Interventionist's Toolkit: Project, Map, Occupy — strategy is "the calculus of force-relationships," in other words, the methodology used by those in power to maintain control, as opposed to the tactic, used by the powerless, which "can only insinuate itself into the other's place, fragmentarily, without taking it over in its entirety." By necessity, tactical spatial practices rely on improvisation, spontaneity and an aggregation of events that unfold over time. See Michel de Certeau, The Practice of Everyday Life (University of California Press, 1984) and Mimi Zeiger, "The Interventionist's Toolkit: Part IV," Places [at] Design Observer, March 27, 2012.

5 Data from Ali-Mohammad Mokhtari, Director, Tehran Parks and Green Space Organization.

6 See Damien McElroy and Admad Vahdat, "Suntanned Women to be Arrested Under Islamic Dress Code," The Telegraph, April 27, 2010, and "Crackdowns over dress codes begin again in Tehran," BBC Persian Service, April 27, 2012 (in Farsi).

7 Asef Bayat, "Tehran, Paradox City," New Left Review 66, November 2010.

8 Azam Khatam, "The Islamic Republic's Failed Quest for a Spotless City," Middle East Report 250, Spring 2009.

9 Farnaz Fassihi, "Inside the Iranian Crackdown," *Wall Street Journal,* July 2009.

10 Tehran Ministry for Cultural Affairs, official city website, en.tehran.ir.

11 "Tehran's Public Parks to be used for Friday Prayers," Shahrzad News Agency, April 17, 2010.

12 Bayat, "Tehran, Paradox City."

13 David Thaler, et al, *Mullahs, Guards, and Bonyads: An Exploration of Iranian Leadership Dynamics,* RAND Corporation, 2010, prepared for the Office of the Secretary of Defense, National Defense Research Institute. The Islamic Revolutionary Guards Corps, originally an ideological military body, has asserted itself in political and economic spheres since the election of President Mahmoud Ahmadinejad in 2005. Current and former members have run for office, donated money and gained control of real estate and agricultural entities, making them extremely powerful in many aspects of society.

14 Bayat, "Paradox City."

15 Author's discussion with students at Azad University, 2012.

16 Benjamin Genocchio, "Revolution's Long Shadow Over the Tehran Art Scene," *New York Times,* March 30, 2011.

17 Hossein Sadri, "A Human Rights Approach to the Politics of Space," presented at "Politics of Space and Place" conference, CAPPE Centre for Applied Philosophy, Politics and Ethics, University of Brighton, United Kingdom, September 2009.

18 "Al-Jazeera Takes on Parazit," Tehran Bureau, PBS Frontline, November 18, 2011.

19 Juliane von Mittelstaedt, "Smuggler's Paradise: Iran Sanctions Good for Business in Tiny Omani Port," *Der Spiegel,* January 20, 2012.

20 Meris Lutz, "Opposition launches new satellite TV channel," Babylon & Beyond, *Los Angeles Times* blog, September 3, 2010.

21 Sonne and Fassihi, "In Skies over Iran, a Battle for Control of Satellite TV."

22 Zahra Hosseinian and Hashem Kalantari, "Key Constituencies Disillusioned as Iran Votes," Reuters, 1 March 1, 2012.

23 Shahram Khosravi, Young and Defiant in Tehran (University of Pennsylvania Press, 2008).

24 Article 19, "Memorandum on Media Regulation in the Islamic Republic of Iran," May 2, 2006.

25 Anna McCarthy, Ambient Television: Visual Culture and Public Space (Raleigh: Duke University Press, 2001).

26 Chrystia Freeland, "How Anger Took Elites by Surprise," *New York Times,* December 26, 2011.

27 Parisa Saranj, "In Iran it's Fun to be a Rebel," NIAC Insight, National Iranian American Council blog, 1 September 2011.

28 Broadcasting Board of Governors, "New Pressure on Jammers of International Broadcasts," February 20, 2012.

29 Kristin Ross and Alice Kaplan, "Everyday Life," Yale French Studies, Fall 1987.

Analyze

1. How has the Iranian government's banning of satellite dishes backfired?

2. Explain what Pakravan means by her claim in paragraph 2 that "the satellite receiver opens a space for political dissent and cultural protest." How does satellite-television culture create "ambiguous spaces" according to Pakravan?

3. Why do you suppose Tehranis would go to such lengths to have satellite dishes installed on their roofs? What would it mean to you if you had limited or no access to television programs, and what might you do if that were the case?

Explore

1. The author observes that "Iran's violation of the basic human rights of assembly and information access have long been condemned by the international community." What has the international community done with respect to Iran, and what has been Iran's response?

2. One does not often consider the role of satellites in our everyday communications. How does the technology of satellites work to provide radio, television programming, and telecommunications globally? How are whole nations (like Iran) able to "jam" satellite information? What standards—regional, national, or global—are in place to ensure access to satellites and under what conditions? Who decides and who oversees? Choose from these questions and pose your own to develop an informative essay on the role of satellites in global communication.

3. Pakravan notes that the Iranian government only partially upholds its ban on satellites. Even though, as she claims, "the satellite receiver opens a space for political dissent and cultural protest," why might the government tolerate its citizens watching *telenovelas*, soap operas, and reality television programs? Write a research paper on the power of international television programs to promote and/or placate civil unrest.

Rob Horning
"The Accidental Bricoleurs"

Rob Horning is a blogger and editor of *The New Inquiry*, an online discussion space for the promotion and exploration of ideas. The following selection appeared in June 2011 in *n + 1* magazine, a triannual print publication for politics, literature, and culture founded in 2004. In the following article, Horning argues that social media companies, by encouraging their participants to repost a YouTube video found on a friend's Facebook wall or "like" a page they see pop up in a Facebook newsfeed, promote the perpetual recreation of new online identities based on the incorporation of others' identities. As Horning notes, ". . . we vacillate between anxious self-branding and the self-negating practice of seeking some higher authenticity."

How do you use your social media presence to "brand" yourself?

I've always thought that Forever 21 was a brilliant name for a fast-fashion retailer. These two words succinctly encapsulate consumerism's mission statement: to evoke the dream of perpetual youth through constant shopping. Yet it also conjures the suffocating shabbiness of that fantasy, the permanent desperation involved in trying to achieve fashion's impossible ideals. The *21* posits that age as a fulcrum, tenuously balancing the teenage idea of maturity grounded in the uninhibited freedom of self-presentation against the presumptive regrets of everyone older, who must continually be reminded of when it all began to go wrong for them, the day they turned 22.

Forever 21 began in 1984 as a single store called Fashion 21 in Los Angeles. After expanding locally, it spread to malls beginning in 1989, but it has only truly proliferated in the last decade. It now has 477 stores in fifteen countries, and projected revenue of more than $2.3 billion in 2010. The worldwide success of Forever 21 and the other even more prominent fast-fashion outlets, like H&M (2,200 stores in thirty-eight countries), Uniqlo (760 stores in six countries), and Zara (more than 4,900 stores in seventy-seven countries), epitomize how the protocols of new capitalism—flexibility, globalization, technology-enabled logistical micromanaging, consumer co-creation—have reshaped the retail world and with it the material culture of consumer societies.

Though retailers have long employed trend spotters to try to capitalize on bottom-up innovation, fast-fashion companies have organized their business models around the principle, relying on logistics and data capture to respond rapidly to consumer behavior. With small-batch production runs and a global labor market to exploit, fast fashion accelerates the half-life of trends and ruthlessly turns over inventory, pushing the pace of fashion to a forced march. Fast fashion's accelerated rate—and its unscrupulousness about copying branded designs—means that luxury houses and name designers, which once dictated fashion seasonally, now must increasingly adapt to the ramifications of fast fashion's trial-and-error approach.

Despite apparently democratizing style and empowering consumers, fast fashion in some ways constitutes a dream sector for those eager to condemn contemporary capitalism, as the companies almost systematically heighten some of its current contradictions: the exhaustion of innovative possibilities, the limits of the legal system in guaranteeing property rights, the increasing immiseration of the world workforce.[1] Their labor practices are in the long tradition of textile-worker exploitation, offering paltry piecemeal rates to subcontracted suppliers and overlooking how they treat employees. For instance, before the GATT Multifiber Agreement lapsed in 2005, allowing Forever 21 and other garment-makers to outsource much of their manufacturing to Asia, the company's domestic labor practices generated lawsuits filed on behalf of workers who alleged sweatshop conditions. In a press release, the Garment Worker Center, a California-based workers' rights group, noted some of the conditions that prompted the suits: withheld wages, long hours without legally mandated breaks, rat and cockroach infestations, and a lack of bathrooms and access to drinking water. The plaintiffs' lead lawyer claimed that companies like Forever 21 "create and demand these conditions. They squeeze their suppliers and make it necessary for them to get things done as quickly and cheaply as possible, no matter what the cost to the workers."

5   But why would the companies create these conditions? What logic drives the imperative to accelerate, regardless of the toll on workers? The all-purpose excuse for sweatshop practices once was the overriding need to offer bargain prices to Western consumers who have come to regard inexpensive clothes as an entitlement. Fast fashion has added the justification of

better responsiveness to consumers' fickleness. The companies overheat production schedules abroad so that they can constantly provide novelty and variety to customers who have come to expect it, who count on the stores not necessarily to meet their wardrobe needs but to relieve ennui. Shoppers come to witness and partake in the spectacle of pure novelty. On the chaotic retail floor and in the frantic dressing rooms of Forever 21's stores, amid the disheveled racks and the items abandoned by shoppers distracted by something else, creative destruction ends up being staged as semi-prurient guerrilla theater, in which an endless series of hurried consumer costume changes is the essence of the performance.

As the *fast* in fast fashion implies, the companies' comparative advantage lies in speed, not brand recognition, garment durability, or reputable design. They have changed fashion from a garment making to an information business, optimizing their supply chains to implement design tweaks on the fly. Zara "can design, produce, and deliver a new garment and put it on display in its stores worldwide in a mere 15 days,"[2] and this flow of information is by far the most significant thing the company produces, far more important than any piped pinafore, velveteen blazer or any of its other 40,000 yearly items. The company's system of constant information monitoring allows it to quickly spot and sate trends and at the same time largely avoid overproduction boondoggles and the need for heavy discounting.

Unlike earlier generations of mass-market retailers, like the Gap's family of brands (which includes, in ascending order of class cachet, Old Navy, Gap, and Banana Republic), companies like Zara and Forever 21 make no effort to stratify their offerings into class-signifying labels. They also don't adopt branding strategies to affiliate with particular luxe or ironic lifestyles, à la Urban Outfitters or Abercrombie & Fitch. Instead they flatter consumers in a different way, immersing them in potential trends on a near weekly basis and trusting them to assemble styles in their own images. Clothes reach stores with practically unspoiled semiotic potential, and consumers are invited to be expressive rather than imitative with the goods, to participate more directly in fashion. We become the meaning makers, enchanting ordinary cardigans and anoraks with a symbolic significance that has only a tenuous relationship to the material item. We work in lieu of advertisers to reconfigure trends and remix signifiers, generating new and valuable meanings for goods. The more new clothes come in, the more creative we can be.

Fast-fashion retailers reap the fruits of that creativity by capturing our preferences in successive generations of products and nearly synchronizing to our whims. Thanks to the rich data we generate as we select, reject, and recombine the items fast fashion offers, the companies need not develop their own brands so much as seize upon customers' ingenuity, distilling their choices into easily replicable trends and rushing the resulting products to market. If fashion functions like a language, then the fast-fashion firms are mainly interested controlling the underlying system and leave the meaning of the "words" to interchangeable designers and individual consumers. As long as customers are willing to speak fast fashion's language, the companies aren't particular about the specifics of the vocabulary. They are concerned only with the rate and volume of change.

In some ways, the fast-fashion companies are developing into post-brands—the apotheosis of the democratization of the designer label and the ready-to-wear revolution. Their lasting contribution to consumerism may be that they have excused themselves from the increasingly clamorous public sphere, already teeming with advertising, to make way for the budding personalities of their customers. Fast fashion itself is perhaps best understood as a kind of social medium, a communication channel that the companies attempt to administer in order to extract regular profits.

10   Facebook and other social-media companies have a similarly parasitic business model. They also appropriate the content and connections we generate as we recreate our identities within their proprietary systems, and then repurpose that data for marketers who hope to sell tokens of that identity back to us. Much as fast-fashion companies are routinely accused of pirating designs, Facebook continually oversteps once sacrosanct norms of privacy, opting users in to data-divulging mechanisms by default and back-pedaling only when confronted with public outcry. It offers a space akin to the fast-fashion retailer's changing room for the ritual staging of the self, inviting users to seize upon "stylistic elements" from wherever they can be grabbed. We become involuntary bricoleurs, scrambling to cobble together an ad hoc identity from whatever memes happen to be relevant at the time.

Like fast fashion, social media have brought with them a profusion of means and ways to reshape and display our identity. Constantly given new tools to share with, always prompted to say something new about ourselves ("What's on your mind?" Facebook asks thoughtfully), we are pressured to continually devise ingenious solutions to our identity, which suddenly appears to be a particular kind of recurring problem: one that can be solved by replenishing social media's various channels with fresh content. Just as fast fashion seeks to pressure shoppers with the urgency of now or never, social media hope to convince us that we always have something new and important to say—as long as we say it right away. And they are designed to make us feel anxious and left out if we don't say it, as their interfaces favor the users who update frequently and tend to make less engaged users disappear. One can easily fall out of fashion with the algorithms Facebook uses to select which content users see out of the plethora of material friends in their network contribute.

Social media teach us to seize potential signifiers of the self from any available source and spend our energy promoting them as attention-worthy. In this way, they actually abet and are abetted by the insidious creep of design ideology—the assumption that we can choose a desktop image to express our inner being or that housework will be less like drudgery with a tasteful dustpan and broom set. By coating consumer culture detritus with an aesthetic veneer, design ideology helps makes the idea of a self anchored in fonts and Uniqlo tolerable. Armed with the auric criteria of design, we can regard goods and ads and memes on websites as a rich source of inspiration ("Hey, these old Newport 'Alive with pleasure!' T-shirts are neat, think I'll riff on that logo for my Facebook profile picture!"), not as an inescapable blight.

In social media, where everyone can employ design ideology, the persistent messages of advertising—that magical self-transformation through purchases is possible, that one's inner truth can be expressed through the manipulation of well-worked surfaces—become practical rather than insulting. Not only do the methods and associative logic of advertising become more concretely useful, but its governing ideology no longer seems conformist but radically individualistic. Social media encourage us to appropriate whatever we want and claim it as our own without feeling derivative or slavishly imitative. On Facebook, if I link to, say, a YouTube video of Bob Dylan singing "I Threw It All Away" on the *Johnny Cash Show* in 1969, I am saying something particular about myself, not merely consuming the performance. I am declaring that video clip to be essentially equivalent to an update I may have written about a trip to Philadelphia or to pictures of me at a party that someone might have tagged. It is all bricolage for personal identity building.

With social media's sudden ubiquity, it's plausible that all other sorts of immersive knowledge by which we might invest our identity with meaning will become subordinate to the practice of clever sign manipulation, to adeptly choosing material and affixing it to one's persona online. Like fashion in its administered, industrialized form, social media seek a monopoly on the expression of individualism; they hope we will think of ourselves only in terms of the mechanisms they facilitate. Facebook wants to be the place where you feel most yourself, with the most control over how you are regarded. But in return, it wants you to think of yourself only in terms of what you can share on the site. It implements freedom of choice as a mode of control; our identities are "unfinished" but contained by the site, which ensures that more and more of our social energy is invested in self-presentation—selling ourselves like we are consumer goods.

15   The personal brand, in its concatenation of fame hunger and dismal self-exploitation, is the evolutionary end point of a tendency implicit in fashion since the rise of consumerism. As fashion strayed from its pre-capitalist role of expressing established hierarchies, it helped usher in a reflexive sense of self, set in terms of constantly shifting social meanings. It reconciled people to the idea of an identity not foisted upon us by birth and circumstances, but one for which we must hold ourselves personally responsible. Since then, fashion has been a form of institutionalized insecurity. It yokes us all to the zeitgeist, eradicating the orienting effects of tradition and leaving us all more vulnerable to existential doubt.

Once the nature of our identity can no longer simply be assumed as a function of our inherited place in the world, it becomes imperative to justify our conviction that we are somebody and prove it to the world. Sociologist Gilles Lipovetsky argued in his 1987 study *Empire of Fashion* that people rise to the challenge presented by the destabilization of the self by embracing fashion more thoroughly. Having "generalized the spirit of curiosity, democratized tastes and the passion for novelty at all levels of existence and in all social ranks," he argues, "the fashion economy has engendered a social agent in its own image: the fashion person who has no deep attachments, a mobile individual with a fluctuating personality and tastes."

Lipovetsky's "fashion person" sounds like an embryonic version of the sort of worker now required by neoliberalist capitalism, in which firms focus chiefly on the short-term, draw on a global workforce, and use technology to automate away manufacturing and clerical positions. Workers cannot expect a stable career with one employer. Instead, as the late-1990s business bestseller *Who Moved My Cheese?* sought to instruct, middle-class workers (likened unapologetically to mice in a maze) have to accept economic insecurity and respond by becoming even more cooperative with their masters. Neoliberalism demands that more and more of the working population tolerate a lack of job security, evince flexibility, and revise customary ways of doing things. Workers must be comfortable living off short-term projects secured through whatever means necessary—ceaseless networking and bootlicking, ruthless leveraging of friends and family contacts, spinning a series of half-truths on a résumé—and they must be more or less self-motivated to produce, to regard themselves as creative forces, to generate economic value in every aspect of how they live, instrumentalizing it all.

If one side of 1990s management discourse threatened the worker with the fate of becoming a helpless and confused laboratory animal, its optimistic flipside depicted precarity as a kind of liberation, with workers as "free agents" cut loose from burdensome corporate bureaucracy. The personal brand was part of that ideological offensive: in 1997, management guru Tom Peters wrote the definitive treatise on the concept for *Fast Company*: "The Brand Called You," which advises, "You're not a worker. . . . You are not defined by your job title and you're not confined by your job description. Starting today you are a brand."[3] Self-branding is "inescapable," Peters claims, so he encourages us to ask ourselves, "What have I accomplished that I can unabashedly brag about?" and "What do I do that I am most proud of?" and then promptly put these achievements up for sale, inviting capitalists to exploit them. He admonishes that we must be eternally vigilant about our personal brand strategy: "When you are promoting brand You, everything you do—and everything you choose not to do—communicates the value and character of the brand. Everything from the way you handle phone conversations to the email messages you send to the way you conduct business in a meeting is part of the larger message you're sending about your brand."

Assessing Peters's article in *One Market Under God* in 2000, Thomas Frank found it almost self-evident that personal branding was a form of coercive self-surveillance that corporations were anxious to induce. He heralded "The Brand Called You" as "a terrifying glimpse of the coming total-corporate state, a sort of Dress for Success rewritten by Chairman Mao." But with the advent of social media, which frankly invites us to "unabashedly brag" about ourselves and to take pride in even the most mundane of our accomplishments ("I just became mayor of Whole Foods on Foursquare!") and broadcast them, many of us now take that sort of self-branding behavior for granted and engage in it not with trepidation but with glee. By mobilizing all the qualities of the self as factors of meaning production, Facebook fuses Lipovetsky's "fashion person" and Peters's "personal brand," inextricably intertwining marketing with selfhood, so that having a self becomes an inherently commercial operation. Somehow, while we were optimizing our Facebook profiles and Twitter feeds, building up our LinkedIn contacts and building out Farmville empires, the total-corporate state may have arrived without our really having noticed it.

20   How did this happen? By seeming to mitigate the problems that neoliberalism creates by shifting economic risk onto workers, social media has been able to colonize the collective consciousness. Facebook, fast fashion, and the like provide new mechanisms of solace, quantifying our connections and influence (and thereby making them more economically useful to us) while enhancing the compensations of consumerism by making it seem more productive, more self-revelatory. Though we may be only one of a thousand friends in everyone else's networks, that never seems especially important when we're in the midst of posting new pictures.

In turning to social media for comfort, we've become happily dependent on digital devices, as we have come to rely on the accelerated rate of communication and exchange they facilitate. They offer us chances to articulate, evaluate, and augment who we are while archiving our identity-making gestures as a collection we can later fawn over and curate. The archiving makes the self seem richer and more substantial even as it makes it more tenuous. Our identity can never be so strong as to render any particular gesture negligible; it is cumulative at the same time that it is totally discontinuous. This has the effect of allowing everything we do to seem either significant or irrelevant, depending on which view suits our needs. The online repository has gradually become the privileged site of the self, the authorized version that redeems the frustration and desperation incipient with the provisionality of work life, that corrects the errors and discourtesies we commit in our confrontations with the physical world.

As this idealized online self becomes more articulated, recommendation engines and tracking databases begin to know better than we do what we want, what we should see, what we are going to do, and what sorts of choices we would like to have presented to us to give us a welcome sense of control over the actual surfeit of possibilities. The automated filters allow us to consume more, faster, which means we are producing more data, securing more opportunities for recognition within the social-media sphere.

They can direct us to those niches where we can feel important, where we can dominate the hierarchy. In that realm of quantification, the self can score points by innovating new ways to gain attention and by enhancing the value of various other branded goods (including one's friends, who in social media have become brands themselves). One is never far from a scoreboard for one's personality (number of Twitter followers, number of comments on a recent Facebook update, number of reblogs on a Tumblr post, et cetera) and because there are so many, we can cycle through them in search of micro-validation. Who needs ontological security when you can be repeatedly "liked" all day long?

With social media's rise, self-branding seems inescapable, as the stream of numerical data about our popularity makes it nearly irresistible to calculate our brand equity and devise ways of enhancing it. This becomes the price we pay for that delicious sense of autonomy that the consumerist emphasis on freedom of choice promises. But that doesn't necessarily mean we like it. When identity serves explicitly as a capital stock to be risked in ventures as opposed to something that exceeds or exists outside the dynamics of the market, we exist only insofar as we see ourselves profiting, we see our brand equity growing (or, alas, shrinking). We don't exist when we refuse to see how our brand plays in the market-driven world. This, of course, is a triumph for neoliberalism, as it suggests it has succeeded in imposing a fundamentally entrepreneurial subjectivity in its subjects to help rationalize its pitilessness.

Personal branding marks a striking departure from the prevailing norms of even a decade ago, when such bald self-promotion as one typically encounters on Twitter and Facebook would have been in questionable taste, and the idea of explicitly leveraging one's network of friends in order to maximize one's notoriety would have seemed preposterously alienating. Widespread ambivalence about the effects of commercial social media on intimacy suggests that the alienation is real, as a surfeit of weak ties suffocates stronger bonds yet stronger bonds seem available only through the online tools that have diminished them. The receptive, supportive community that recognizes you for who you are mingles uncomfortably alongside the host of advertisers that hope to persuade you to be something more, that are eager to hijack the self you share and make it a partner brand to help sell product. Such corporate identity expropriation can drive the quest for new, untainted ways to present oneself—the *real* me, not co-opted, not sold out, the one pushing trends rather than conforming—though these merely lead to fresh appropriations and perpetuate the cycle. Online, the reciprocity of friendship can start to seem indistinguishable from brand synergies; building trust can seem just another self-aggrandizing solo project in disguise.

25   We need a sympathetic community within which to realize our individuality. Social media tends to turn that effort to preserve that community into the pursuit of fame. And when we pursue fame, our behavior devolves into the familiar forms of self-commodification. We replace the pleasure of what we do with fantasies about the measurable notoriety we imagine we'll reap. Social-media companies don't facilitate community any more than fast-fashion companies elevate style; they cater to the fantasy of being a celebrity, the impossible dream of a mass audience for everyone. With that we either beat a retreat into vicarious fantasy or end up squarely in the realm of the creative class and its fiefdom of cool. To dissolve the creative class into universal creativity, the tyranny of "cool"—fashion as a mass-market business; trend spotting as an entrepreneurial vocation; friendship as a quantitative measure; influence as an end in itself—would have to be abolished, not universalized.

The pressure that sustains self-branding, it turns out, ultimately comes from ourselves, everyone on everyone else. We circulate the meanings, we empty out or alter their meaning, we grant the suddenly measurable attention that makes identity salient. We have more capability to share ourselves, our thoughts and interests and discoveries and memories, than ever before, yet sharing is in danger of becoming nothing more than an alibi that hides how voracious our appetite for novelty has become. It becomes harder for our friends and ourselves to figure out what really matters to us and what stems merely from the need to keep broadcasting the self.

And so we vacillate between anxious self-branding and the self-negating practice of seeking some higher authenticity: we have to watch ourselves become ourselves in order to be ourselves, over and over again. This futile process crystallizes in the irrepressible ideal of youth, the time when all that reflexivity seemed like second nature, was authenticity itself. When we were young, when our self-awareness was innocent and our curiosity was pure, our dreams were unsullied and our lives limitless—the memory of it remains vivid even as our self-scrutiny insensibly becomes anxious and narcissistic over the years, as calculating as youth was guileless. In social media, amid all the high school and college friends reconnecting, and the eager meme adoption and trend tracking, and the reawakening sense that the bands and books and clothes we like are of critical importance to the rest of the world, the great consumer promise of a return to the days of youth is perpetually reborn. Forever 21, indeed.

NOTES

1 Berfield, Susan. "Forever 21's Fast (and Loose) Fashion Empire." *Bloomberg BusinessWeek*, January 20, 2011.

2 Ferdows, Kasra, Michael A. Lewis, and Jose A.D. MacHuca, "Rapid-Fire Fulfillment." *Harvard Business Review*, November 1, 2004.

3 Peters, Tom. "The Brand Called You." *Fast Company*, August/September 1997.

Analyze

1. According to the author, what is the difference between "fast-fashion" retailers, like Forever 21 and Zara, and "mass-market" retailers, like the Gap and Banana Republic?

2. How does Horning compare fast-fashion retailers to Facebook and other social media companies? Do you agree with him?

3. What is Horning's purpose in writing this article? Who is his audience? Based on how he has presented and organized his argument, what do you think he hopes you will do after reading it?

Explore

1. How might you be a *bricoleur* of your own self-brand? Create a profile of yourself—your self-brand—as you would want to be perceived online. It can be in text, images, audio, and/or video. As you present your profile to your class (or to a group within your class), comment on the author's assertion that "we must be eternally vigilant about our personal brand strategy." How were the decisions you made as you created your profile reflective (or not) of this eternal vigilance?

2. In paragraph 11, Horning claims that "[j]ust as fast fashion seeks to pressure shoppers with the urgency of now or never, social media hope to convince us that we always have something new and important to say—as long as we say it right away." How does he support this claim, and are you convinced? Test his thesis by analyzing the Facebook pages or Twitter accounts of your friends, or, if you do not have a Facebook or Twitter account, ask those who do.

3. Ikea, the Swedish furniture store, is another international "brand." Analyze its website and describe in detail its global identity. How does its website accommodate customers from different countries? Building upon Horning's article, what insight about globalization does your analysis of the Ikea website provide?

Forging Connections

1. Zuckerman and DeLong-Bas seem to have conflicting ideas about the use of social media to promote social change. Zuckerman points out that its use is typically localized; DeLong-Bas has demonstrated that it has had enormous global effects. Using these articles as points of departure, write a research paper on the globalizing effects of social media to promote social change.

2. How does Cole's article align with the reading by Zuckerman in terms of helping those in need by bringing them into the support process? How might new social media provide bridges to allow that to happen? How might new social media exacerbate the problems of those in need?

3. Who are the emerging personas of global social media? Simulating a social media platform of your choice, create a discussion among the White Savior (Cole), Satellite Man (Pakravan), Fashion Person (Horning), and yourself. Make sure to explain the motivations of each of these "personalities" by citing specific parts of each article. As a presence in the discussion, you can ask questions, provide alternative perspectives and personas you've observed on social media, and/or tie the perspectives together into a whole.

Looking Further

1. This chapter has touched on how social media platforms, mobile telephones, and satellite dishes have transformed social issues, entertainment, and marketing at exponential rates. Although many of the readings in this book were first published online, many were published in hard-copy form, only to be disseminated later in digital and online media. How do the readings in this chapter (and others) make you more aware of the relationship between communication and technology in your own life? How competent and effective do you feel as a communicator using various technologies? Using the platform of

your choice (e.g., handwritten or word-processed copy, blog, Twitter, Facebook, Instagram, or Flickr, etc.), design a response to these questions. After you have completed your response, write a reflection that explains your process and what you've learned.

2. In what ways have communication and technology contributed to globalization? Further developing your working definition of globalization, consider now the impact of communication and technology. Use examples from a selection of readings in this book, or others you have researched, to illustrate your definition. Consider how issues of language, famine, conflict, economics, and environment in different parts of the world may complicate and add nuances to the relationship between communication and technology itself.

6 Earning & Spending

For many of us, the first thing that comes to mind when we hear the phrase "earning and spending" is *money*. And those who earn enough to provide food, clothing, and shelter for their families might have the luxury to think secondarily about earning and spending *time*. The readings in this chapter bring a global perspective to the seemingly inextricable relationship between earning and spending—especially, as we will see, in relationship to others' emerging economies and needs.

We begin with an article from the British weekly magazine *The Economist*, reporting on the habits and customs of tourists from China's emerging middle class. "The New Grand Tour" provides a fascinating window into what becomes a tourist spot and why. A deeper theme that begins to surface and takes us through the rest of the chapter is how earning and spending our time and money define (or are defined by) our circumstances. Are we active or passive? What is our role, and what choices do we have as participants in a global economy? Consider, for example, the provocatively titled "Haiti Doesn't Need Your Old T-Shirt," in which Charles Kenny analyzes how clothing and feeding the poor may do more harm than good for the economies of recipient countries. The next reading, "How Oliberté, the Anti-TOMS, Makes Shoes and Jobs in Africa," offers a compelling model of how buying products from developing countries promotes not only their economies but also their independence. The quality of environmentally conscious products made locally, the pride derived from selling them globally, and the creativity in their marketing provide a sharp contrast to the impulse purchases that line "The Enchanted Bylanes," in which Avantika Bhuyan reports on the Indo-Chinese toy market.

"The Long and Winding Road" traces Reuters reporter Simon Akam's desperate and humorous attempts to buy a car in post-conflict Sierra Leone, and provides at the same time an object lesson (if you needed yet another one) in how buying what's "cool" can blind us—with expensive repercussions—to what we really need. Reading his article reminds us that even in a globalized world, what people can earn and spend is affected first and foremost at a local level. The infrastructure in Sierra Leone has been so compromised by its volatile past, it remains to be seen how it will develop and with whose investment.

Our final reading in this chapter is an article from the *Wall Street Journal*, the US daily financial newspaper, on what may have been perceived until recently as an oxymoron: the presence of luxury items in, of all places, Mongolia, a country rich in resources, but poor in infrastructure. In becoming a global magnet for investment—and exploitation—will Mongolia's people and government resist immediate gain for long-term stability? How might it provide a model for other developing nations?

The Economist
"The New Grand Tour"

The following article appeared in the print edition of the weekly news and international affairs publication *The Economist* on December 16, 2010. Since its founding in 1843, *The Economist* has remained committed to the ideals of free trade, internationalism, and minimum interference by government, and also "considers itself the enemy of privilege, pomposity and predictability." "The New Grand Tour" examines a brand of tourism introduced to Europe by a new breed of Chinese tourist: the mobile middle class. These tourists are not following the historical and cultural itineraries of travelers past; rather, they are mapping out itineraries that best satisfy their penchant for spending. However, this fun and freedom does not come without condition; in exchange for foreign travel and consumer freedom, the Chinese government expects loyalty to one-party rule at home.

What do you make of this compact between the Chinese middle class and its government? Would you exchange political freedom for consumer freedom?

I n the grounds of King's College, Cambridge, grows perhaps the most famous willow tree in China. It was immortalised by Xu Zhimo, a 20th-century poet with all the attributes required for lasting celebrity: talent, a rackety love life and a dramatic early death (plane crash at 34). With each passing year, growing crowds of Chinese tourists visit the tree and a nearby marble boulder inscribed with lines from Xu's poem, "On leaving Cambridge."

Locals and tourists from elsewhere pass the tree without a second glance. But for educated Chinese, who learned Xu's poem in school, this tranquil spot, watched over by handsome white cows and an arched stone bridge, is a shrine to lost youth. Many are visibly moved, even as the cameras click and flash. Xu's verses help explain the great prestige Cambridge University enjoys in China, nudging it a notch or two ahead of Oxford. They also explain why many educated Chinese have heard of punting.

Xu's willow is just one stop on an emerging grand tour of Europe, the continent that routinely tops polls of dream Chinese destinations. China's newly mobile middle classes like to visit established spots like the Eiffel Tower, the Louvre and Venice's Grand Canal. But the visitors have also marked out a grand tour all of their own, shaped by China's fast-developing consumer culture and by distinctive quirks of culture, history and politics. The result is jaw-dropping fame, back in China, for a list of places that some Europeans would struggle to pinpoint on a map: places like Trier, Metzingen, Verona, Luxembourg, Lucerne and the Swiss Alp known as Mount Titlis.

For decades Asian economic might has gone hand in hand with government programmes to encourage newly affluent citizens to take holidays abroad. In Japan the Ministry of Tourism launched a "Ten Million Programme" to double outbound tourist departures from 5m to 10m between 1986 and 1991. Tourism from South Korea exploded a decade later. Officials in these countries hoped that despatching tourists around the globe would signal their new wealth. It also offered a tangible reward to citizens toiling in the pressure-cooker atmosphere of an economic boom. In China foreign travel is part of a slightly different compact between the state and the new middle classes: unprecedented freedom and fun in exchange for the maintenance of one-party rule at home.

In Search of Bordeaux and Hugo Boss

5   When the bamboo curtain lifted a generation ago, the first contact many Chinese had with the outside world was in the form of imported goods, whose foreign fame was viewed as intrinsic proof of quality. Even today, seen from a Chinese tour bus, the continent of Europe resembles not so much an ancient collection of cities and nations as a glittering emporium stocked with brands. Those brands are not always commercial products: the grand tour takes in the birthplaces of world-famous people, the seats of globally renowned institutions and—as in Cambridge—sites linked to well-known literary works.

A sketch map of the Chinese grand tour must begin in France, the country seen as offering all the essential European virtues: history, romance, luxury and quality. Paris shops such as Louis Vuitton are essential stops: witness their Mandarin-speaking staff. In 2009 Chinese tourists passed Russians as the highest-spending non-European visitors to France, according to a survey of duty-free shops. The south of the country is also popular, thanks in part to widely available translations of Peter Mayle's book *A Year in Provence* and in part to a slushy Chinese television miniseries, *Dreams Link*, which was filmed amid the lavender fields and walled citadels of the Midi.

China's freshly minted millionaires and billionaires are particularly obsessed with the wine country of Bordeaux, as red wine has taken over from expensive brandy as the business lubricant of choice. At the very pinnacle of desire is a visit to (or just a glimpse of) Château Lafite Rothschild, home of the claret which has become a favored show-off brand for Chinese plutocrats. Visits to Château Lafite itself are reserved for invited guests, but China's would-be tycoons are not put off. Jean-François Zhou of Ansel Travel, a Paris-based firm that brings 15,000 Chinese visitors to Europe each year, recently sent a group down to Bordeaux by bus. After an express tour, one of the coach party snapped up two cases of wine at €600 ($790) a bottle.

From France, Chinese groups typically travel south towards Italy via the casinos in Nice or Monaco (gambling is discouraged in China, but wildly popular). Venice and Rome are stops for every nation's tourists, but the Chinese grand tour also demands a visit to Verona. One site draws them: a 13th-century mansion linked, a bit spuriously, to "Romeo and Juliet." That play is doubly admired in China. It was one of the first of Shakespeare's works to be translated into Mandarin, and its storyline is hailed as matching that of a popular Chinese folk tale, the "Butterfly Lovers." Chinese tourists have their pictures taken below an ancient balcony said to be Juliet's, and next to a bronze statue of the tragic heroine. Then it is back on the bus, and northward.

In Germany cities such as Bonn and Trier are as important as more obvious sites like Cologne and Frankfurt (a hub for lots of China flights). Bonn means Beethoven: his birthplace there is a coveted stop for educated Chinese, who are avid fans of classical music. In Trier it is not the city or its Roman ruins that attracts the tourists. They come to see the Karl-Marx-Haus, birthplace of the revolutionary. The Marx museum estimates that 13,000 Chinese tramp around the house each year. Mandarin inscriptions fill the museum's guest books. In the early morning and evening, large crowds of Chinese have their pictures taken outside the house before heading to their next destination.

A stop in Metzingen involves a tribute to another German, the suit-maker Hugo Boss. A short drive from Frankfurt, Metzingen is home to several factory outlets, where Chinese shoppers vie with Russians and Indians as the biggest spenders. It is a standing joke among Chinese travellers that many products snapped up abroad bear "Made in China" labels. But there is some sense to this seeming madness. Thanks to hefty taxes and customs duties, European brands are routinely 40% more expensive back home. In China they are also quite likely to be fakes.

As France means wine and handbags, Brussels means chocolate. Chen Yongjie, a Suzhou native, works in the Pelicaen chocolate shop of Brussels, next to the Mannekin Pis (a small statue of a boy peeing that is unaccountably popular with tourists of all nationalities). Most Chinese think Belgian chocolate too sweet, Miss Chen reports. This does not stop them buying large quantities for friends and colleagues back home.

Many of the Chinese tourists in the Benelux countries are members of *daibiaotuan*, official or business delegations with a reputation as boon-doggles. As a result of this bureaucratic orientation, the grand tour's Belgian leg includes stops outside the Berlaymont, as the headquarters of the European Commission is known. Resplendent in the unofficial uniform of the *daibiaotuan*—dark trousers, dark polo shirt, dark blouson jacket and leather manbag—officials on tour queue up to have their pictures taken in front of the Berlaymont's nameplate, the nearest thing to a scenic spot in the glass and concrete canyons of the "European Quarter." The same delegations enjoy less success at NATO's headquarters which is off limits to tourists. The pluckiest *daibiaotuan* are not deterred. They can be seen parked on the roadside opposite NATO, taking pictures of its flagpoles across six lanes of traffic.

Taking pictures is a serious business for members of a *daibiaotuan*. Goofy poses are not encouraged. The Chinese word *"qiezi"*—pronounced chee-eh-dze and meaning "aubergine"—fulfils the same function as "cheese" in the English-speaking world, generating what is held to be a restrained yet photogenic smile. Childish pleasure can be derived from murmuring *"qiezi"* when walking past a delegation busy taking pictures: it reliably generates surprised cries of "did that foreigner just say aubergine?"

In Luxembourg the Chinese tourists pause just long enough to photo-graph the palace of its reigning grand duke. This pocket-sized country, with a population 3,000 times smaller than China's, is admired for its national wealth per person (the highest in the world by some measures). It also allows Chinese tour groups to knock off another country with minimal effort, allowing for extra boasting back home.

15   France, Germany, Belgium and Luxembourg all lie within the Schengen Area, a border-free zone that can be visited on a single visa. This appeals to Chinese tourists, who must submit reams of papers and face a long list of intrusive questions about their finances, employment and personal circumstances to obtain visas for Europe. In 2008 Switzerland joined the Schengen club and Chinese visitor numbers instantly soared.

In Switzerland the essential stop is the canton of Lucerne. With a lake, an historic city and mountains all in a compact area, it amounts to a "mini-Switzerland," saving time. The Lucerne brand includes Mount Titlis, easily reached by bus and cable car. The mountain is topped by a glacier, offering visitors the chance to visit an ice cave and mess about on sledges even in summer (high season for Chinese tourism). There are Chinese-speaking staff on the peak, and a Chinese restaurant. In perhaps Europe's oddest claim to Chinese fame, a Chengdu-born gymnast, Li Donghua, claims to have seen a vision of Buddha while visiting Mount Titlis. This he took as a sign that he would triumph at the 1996 Atlanta Olympics. He duly won a gold medal. His tale is recorded on a mountain-top plaque.

Surprisingly few tourists visit Britain. In August 2010 David Cameron, Britain's prime minister, noted with some bemusement that Germany is poised to enter the leading ten foreign destinations for Chinese tourists, while Britain languishes in 22nd place.

Mr Cameron called for promoting Britain's heritage—a departure from his Labour predecessors with their focus on modernity and "cool Britannia." Mr Zhou says his Chinese clients are fascinated that such a titchy island once ran such a large empire and dared start the Opium wars. In reality, as the leader of a Eurosceptic political party, Mr Cameron is unlikely to take the transformative step of joining the Schengen Area. If Britain followed Switzerland into the border-free zone, "half the Chinese tourists on the continent would head to London on the Eurostar," says Mr Zhou.

Enjoyment Isn't the Point

Chinese tourists know they are more coveted for their money than loved in Europe. In surveys of Chinese travel agents, the continent is most frequently described as "beautiful" and "historic"—but rarely as friendly. Europeans are described as both "civilised" and "cold." Even before they leave China, the travellers are nagged to mind their manners and told to act as "ambassadors" for their country. Several times in the past few years the Spiritual Civilisation Steering Committee of the country's Communist Party has issued chivvying circulars calling on Chinese tourists to avoid queue-jumping, loudness or haggling in shops with fixed prices.

The European travel industry uses the sniffy phrase "sleep cheap, shop expensive" to describe Chinese visitors. Chinese tour operators are Even before they leave China, the travellers are nagged to mind their manners. for bargaining down travel and hotel costs. A 2008 study by the European Travel Commission, an industry group, estimates that Chinese tourists reserve more than a third of their holiday budgets for shopping. It is "very difficult," the study laconically concludes, for established European tour operators to compete with rivals whose transport strategy may involve a

"Chinese-speaking waiter driving a minibus." Even Mr Zhou admits that Chinese travellers are "hard work," not like the "disciplined" Japanese.

Tourism is certainly not about discovering new food. A 2006 survey of Chinese coach travellers found that 46% had eaten "European" food only once, and 10% not at all, during holidays on the continent. Clients at Ansel Travel are typically offered foreign food once in each country: seafood in Paris, ham knuckle in Germany, pasta in Italy and so on. After that, "it's Chinese all the way." Many stay in suburban hotels and eat noodles.

This is because excitement and acquisition are prized over pleasant, relaxing experiences. The Chinese are keen on European luxury, says Andy Xie, a Shanghai-based economist—they just aren't so interested in luxurious hotels and lavish meals. Coming from a newly affluent, increasingly unequal society, they have a strong preference for the accumulation of material goods. After all, a Swiss watch lasts a lifetime, whereas "if you want a good bed, you can have that at home."

> "Even before they leave China, the travellers are nagged to mind their manners."

And Western goods may not be valued for the same reasons they are in the West. Château Lafite's astonishing fame in China is a story about the country's political economy, not about the enjoyment of wine, says Mr Xie. Too often at banquets in China he has watched first-growth claret being downed in joyless, glass-draining toasts, well into the small hours. "Château Lafite is for serving to high political officials in the hope of high returns. Government officials want to drink it because it is expensive. And people buy it because it is expensive. It becomes self-fulfilling."

A New Vision of Europe

Europeans may sneer at Chinese tourists who pursue Beethoven, Bordeaux and Hugo Boss with the same undiscriminating avidity. But Europeans used to tour their own continent in a similar way. The original Grand Tour was also a display of relative economic power, as the gilded youth of northern, industrialising Europe headed to France, Switzerland and Italy to pick up a veneer of continental "polish" and crateloads of antique souvenirs (many of them fake). Those tourists, too, had less fun than they let on: they grumbled about the food, their rapacious guides and the discomforts of travel.

The face of Chinese tourism is also rapidly changing. The heyday of the 25 *daibiaotuan* has passed. A decade ago, an official fancying a holiday more or less had to land a spot on one of these delegations, paid for from state or company funds or by joint-venture partners from the West. Today, such delegations are under much more scrutiny, and tourist visas are easier to obtain. Many travellers are now on their second or third visit to Europe: group tours are duly slowing down and stopping to savour local culture. Individual tourism is tipped as the next big thing. Yet individual visitors may create itineraries no more conventional than those dictated by tour groups.

In China, Xu Zhimo is loved not just as a romantic poet: his plain, passionate verse shook up a country grown exhausted and old. Xu is already a secular icon for Chinese students at Cambridge, whose diligence puts local undergraduates to shame. He would make a fine patron for the next waves of Chinese grand tourists—private travellers with the confidence to draw their own map of an old continent. Their list of important sights and experiences does not resemble the genteel image that Europeans have of their own homeland—it includes more duty-free shopping, for a start. But it is a fresh vision. With their economic power and hunger for new experiences, China's restless middle classes have conjured a new Europe into life.

Analyze

1. What is the origin of the notion of a "grand tour"? How does the new grand tour discussed in this article differ from that of the original?
2. How do you (or would you) prepare to visit a foreign place? How concerned are you with learning the customs and language of a particular culture? Would that be important to you—or not? Why?
3. What are the perceptions of Chinese tourists according to those quoted in the article? Do you think the author provides a fair depiction of Chinese tourists on the "new grand tour"?

Explore

1. Using creative online photo sites such as Tumblr, Fotopedia, or Pics4Learning, choose images that allow you to create a photo interpretation of the "new grand tour" as depicted in this article. How does the process of creating a visual essay compare to and contrast with a written essay?

2. Create an itinerary for a grand tour that you think a particular group would be interested in. It can be a group based on your nationality, regional or social background, or your peer group's cultural interests. Describe the group for whom the tour is designed, and describe the significance of each site or activity included on the tour. What is the purpose in visiting these sites; how will your group prepare; and what will your group bring back as souvenirs?

3. The article focuses on Chinese tourists in Europe because of their recent transition to a consumer society. Why are Chinese citizens encouraged to travel in ways they were not before? How does their motivation to travel shed light on what it means to be tourists in a consumer society? Finally, does this make you understand your own activities as a tourist differently? If so, how?

Charles Kenny
"Haiti Doesn't Need Your Old T-Shirt"

Charles Kenny is a senior fellow at the Center for Global Development, a nonpartisan and nonprofit think tank that researches the impact of wealthy nations on developing economies. He is also a contributing editor at *Foreign Policy*, a monthly magazine that covers international politics and global affairs. Kenny worked at the World Bank, with a particular focus on the Middle East and North Africa. In the following article, which appeared in *Foreign Policy* in November 2011, Kenny engaged the ongoing debate about some of the most popular—yet least effective—types of charitable giving.

What makes a donation truly "charitable"—the worth of the item, or the intent of the gesture? Is it "charity" to give away something you would have otherwise discarded?

The Green Bay Packers this year beat the Pittsburgh Steelers to win Super Bowl XLV in Arlington, Texas. In parts of the developing world, however, an alternate reality exists: "Pittsburgh Steelers: Super Bowl XLV

Champions" appears emblazoned on T-shirts from Nicaragua to Zambia. The shirt wearers, of course, are not an international cadre of Steelers die-hards, but recipients of the many thousands of excess shirts the National Football League produced to anticipate the post-game merchandising frenzy. Each year, the NFL donates the losing team's shirts to the charity World Vision, which then ships them off to developing countries to be handed out for free.

Everyone wins, right? The NFL offloads 100,000 shirts (and hats and sweatshirts) that can't be sold—and takes the donation as a tax break. World Vision gets clothes to distribute at no cost. And some Nicaraguans and Zambians get a free shirt. What's not to like?

Quite a lot, as it happens—so much so that there's even a Twitter hashtag, #SWEDOW, for "Stuff We Don't Want," to track such developed-world offloading, whether it's knit teddy bears for kids in refugee camps, handmade puppets for orphans, yoga mats for Haiti, or dresses made out of pillowcases for African children. The blog *Tales from the Hood*, run by an anonymous aid worker, even set up a SWEDOW prize, won by Knickers 4 Africa, a (thankfully now defunct) British NGO set up a couple of years ago to send panties south of the Sahara.

Here's the trouble with dumping stuff we don't want on people in need: What they need is rarely the stuff we don't want. And even when they do need that kind of stuff, there are much better ways for them to get it than for a Western NGO to gather donations at a suburban warehouse, ship everything off to Africa or South America, and then try to distribute it to remote areas. World Vision, for example, spends 58 cents per shirt on shipping, warehousing, and distributing them, according to data reported by the blog *Aid Watch*—well within the range of what a secondhand shirt costs in a developing country. Bringing in shirts from outside also hurts the local economy: Garth Frazer of the University of Toronto estimates that increased used-clothing imports accounted for about half of the decline in apparel industry employment in Africa between 1981 and 2000. Want to really help a Zambian? Give him a shirt made in Zambia.

The mother of all SWEDOW is the $2 billion-plus U.S. food aid   5 program, a boondoggle that lingers on only because of the lobbying muscle of agricultural conglomerates. (Perhaps the most embarrassing moment was when the United States airdropped 2.4 million Pop-Tarts on Afghanistan in January 2002.) Harvard University's Nathan Nunn and Yale University's Nancy Qian have shown that the scale of U.S. food aid isn't strongly tied to how much recipient countries actually require it—but it does rise after a bumper crop in the American heartland, suggesting that food aid is far more about dumping American leftovers than about sending help where help's needed. And just like secondhand clothing, castoff food exports can hurt local economies. Between the 1980s and today, subsidized rice exports from the United States to Haiti wiped out thousands of local farmers and helped reduce the proportion of locally produced rice consumed in the country from 47 to 15 percent. Former President Bill Clinton concluded that the food aid program "may have been good for some of my farmers in Arkansas, but it has not worked. . . . I had to live every day with the consequences of the lost capacity to produce a rice crop in Haiti to feed those people because of what I did."

Bottom line: Donations of cash are nearly always more effective. Even if there are good reasons to give stuff rather than money, in most cases the stuff can be bought locally. Economist Amartya Sen, for example, has conclusively shown that people rarely die of starvation or malnutrition because of a lack of food in the neighborhood or the country. Rather, it is because they can't afford to buy the food that's available. Yet, as Connie Veillette of the Center for Global Development reports, shipping U.S. food abroad in response to humanitarian disasters is so cumbersome it takes four to six months to get there after the crisis begins. Buying food locally, the U.S. Government Accountability Office has found, would be 25 percent cheaper and considerably faster, too.

In some cases, if there really is a local shortage and the goods really are needed urgently, the short-term good done by clothing or food aid may well outweigh any long-term costs in terms of local development. But if people donate SWEDOW, they may be less likely to give much-needed cash. A study by Aradhna Krishna of the University of Michigan, for example, suggests that charitable giving may be lower among consumers who buy cause-related products because they feel they've already done their part. Philanthrocapitalism may be chic: The company TOMS Shoes has met with considerable commercial success selling cheap footwear with the added hook that for each pair you buy, the company gives a pair to a kid in the developing world (it's sold more than a million pairs to date). But what if consumers are buying TOMS instead of donating to charity, as some surely are? Much better to stop giving them the stuff we don't want—and start giving them the money they do.

Analyze

1. What obligation do you believe one has to give charitably? Is there a process you go through to evaluate how your donations will be received and/or dispersed? How might you change your approach after reading Kenny's article?
2. According to the article, when might it be advantageous to donate "stuff" as opposed to money? What is the downside of donating "SWEDOW"?
3. How does the author build to his claim that it's "[m]uch better to stop giving them the stuff we don't want—and start giving them the money they do"? How can secondhand clothing and castoff food exports hurt local economies?

Explore

1. The author cites errors and "boondoggles" in providing SWEDOW to developing countries. What are the errors and boondoggles mentioned in the article? Explore more carefully the motivations behind the Pop-Tarts-for-Afghanistan incident or President Clinton's food aid program to Haiti. What was the chain of reaction? Who benefited, and who lost out?
2. Do some research on "philanthrocapitalism" (also called venture philanthropy) to see if it is effective. Is it as ineffective as Kenny states? Find other examples like TOMS Shoes. What have you been able to confirm or refute? What have you learned?
3. What is the most effective way to help those who are in need of food, clothing, shelter, and other basic needs? Conduct research on the efficacy of philanthropic organizations geared toward helping developing countries. How are they organized, and which ones seem to be most effective under which circumstances? Why? Compare, for example, a large, established international organization, such as the Red Cross or CARE, with smaller ones locally situated. Create a "What to Consider When You Want to Give" information sheet.

Tate Watkins
"How Oliberté, the Anti-TOMS, Makes Shoes and Jobs in Africa"

Tate Watkins is a freelance writer based in Port-au-Prince, Haiti. His writing on economic development, foreign aid, immigration, and technology has appeared in numerous print and online media, including the *Harvard National Security Journal, The Christian Science Monitor,* and *Wired.com.* The following article appeared in *Good,* an online global community "of, by, and for pragmatic idealists working toward individual and collective progress," on January 17, 2012. Watkins critically compares and contrasts the missions of two very different shoe manufacturers. Oliberté employs Africans to make premium footwear in Africa using African materials, thereby creating jobs for local economies; the business model for TOMS emphasizes giving shoes to poor children. Although critics accept that TOMS' mission is well-meaning, some have expressed concern that their "give-away-for-free" policy may do more harm than good.

Are consumer goods marketed with a charitable story any less genuine in their charitable intent? Can you "buy" altruism the same way you buy a pair of shoes, a T-shirt, or a handbag?

'**W**hy or how could anyone want to make shoes in a place full of so much poverty and corruption?'

That's the question many people asked Canadian Tal Dehtiar when he founded Oliberté Footwear, the first company to make premium shoes in Africa using African materials and explicitly linking shoes sold by Western retailers to job creation on the continent. Dehtiar started the Toronto-based company in 2009, and sales increased from a mere 200 pairs initially to 10,000 in 2011. He projects sales of between 20,000 and 25,000 this year.

"At Oliberté, we believe Africa can compete on a global scale," he says, "but it needs a chance. It doesn't need handouts or a hand up. It needs people to start shaking hands and companies to start making deals to work in these countries."

Oliberté shoes are stitched and assembled in Ethiopia with leather sourced from local free-range cows, sheep, and goats—the default in a country with many herders whose livelihoods depend upon ranging wherever grass may be. The livestock haven't been injected with hormones to speed their growth, a common practice in other parts of the world. The result is a light, limber, yet sturdy upper.

The shoes feature crepe rubber soles made from natural rubber processed   5
in Liberia and lined with soft, breathable goat leather. This spring, the company will expand its line to offer leather bags and accessories, some of which will be sourced in Kenya and made in Zambia. It produces woven labels and other branding materials in the African island nation Mauritius.

Oliberté—the name melds "liberty" with the "O" from the anthem of Dehtiar's home country—employs workers at factories selected because they pay relatively high wages, provide employee benefits like subsidized lunches, and employ women as about half of their workforces. The company plans to open its own factory in Addis Ababa in March while maintaining production at its existing third-party plants. It distributes across North America and Europe and sells online.

The best-known footwear brand with a humanitarian bent is TOMS Shoes, the Santa Monica, California-based company that gives a pair of shoes to a child in need for every pair it sells. From Nicaragua to New Orleans to Niger, TOMS has distributed shoes to more than a million children through "shoe drops," when staff and contest winners travel the globe to hand out shoes. In addition to helping prevent soil-borne diseases, the donations help recipients attend schools that in many places forbid bare feet.

"With TOMS," Dehtiar says, "the best thing is the awareness they've created." But he's skeptical of the company's one-for-one model because he believes the donations can pressure local shoemakers and vendors, in addition to reinforcing stereotypes about the developing world.

"TOMS Shoes is a good marketing tool, but it's not good aid," agrees Saundra Schimmelpfennig, an international aid expert who blogs at Good Intentions Are Not Enough, where she aims to educate nonprofit donors about effective charity. She's criticized TOMS for competing with local producers by handing out free goods and for being "quintessential Whites in Shining Armor." "The idea of creating jobs that pay a fair wage and provide necessary benefits," she says, "can have far more impact than aid."

According to its latest giving report, TOMS also uses factories in   10
Ethiopia, in addition to ones in China and Argentina. "I'm not saying ours

is a better way," Dehtiar says, "but people just continue to give away stuff to Africa, and there's no incentive for dependencies to end."

Dehtiar had experience in aid work abroad before starting Oliberté. After graduating from business school, he started MBAs Without Borders, a charity that consulted with small businesses in the developing world and helped them find venture capital. "It was basically Peace Corps for people who had done Peace Corps and now had a business degree," he says. The nonprofit worked in 25 countries, from Haiti to Pakistan to nations in West Africa. One impetus Dehtiar cites for founding Oliberté is that African friends kept telling him they were tired of charity—what the continent needed was jobs. "On a given day," says Dehtiar, "one to two hundred people are working on our shoes. Because we don't hire foreigners, we have local buy-in."

"For me, it is great," says Feraw Kebede, general manager of Oliberté Ethiopia, in a company video. "As an Ethiopian I'm very proud that we are exporting shoes to America."

Instead of striving to produce the cheapest shoes possible, the company focuses on quality. "When it comes to footwear," Dehtiar says, "we don't want people to think of Africa as the next China. We want them to think of it as the next Italy—think quality."

The strategy has begun to pay off with American retailers. "The first thing that prompted me was the style of the shoe," says Justin Davis, manager of Mint Footwear in San Diego. "They're attractive. The shoes demand attention." He noticed the materials and craftsmanship were better than "regular production stuff." Once he heard about how and where the shoes are produced, Davis says the line became even more attractive to him. "People crave products that have a little more purpose than just consumption," he says.

15   The Oliberté brand is still niche, but to Dehtiar, part of the venture's value is in cutting a path that larger manufacturers can follow. "Our goal is to be the reason that 1 million people are employed in manufacturing in Africa," he says. "We want to show that these models work and we want to encourage others, like the Nikes and Levi's of the world, to do the same."

Dehtiar says one of the top five footwear and apparel brands in the world recently inquired about acquiring the company, impressed that it built a high quality made-in-Africa brand rather than simply set up a cheap manufacturing center on the continent. But the company is not for sale, Dehtiar says, because he has yet to finish developing it.

"When we first started, I didn't want to do the Africa angle," he says, a seemingly strange statement about a company that markets the continent in its tagline. "Our first ad was very stereotypical Africa. It was a picture of an African face—a Maasai warrior. I hated it." He stopped using the ad the following year. "We've gone from portraying a very stereotypical image of Africa to now selling pride instead of pity. But it's a challenge, because some stores want the stereotypical Africa branding."

"The balance," says Dehtiar, "is how do I do the Africa angle without doing the part I hate: 'Buy because you feel bad about Africa.'"

Analyze

1. What stereotypes about the developing world are reinforced by companies like TOMS Shoes? How does Oliberté propose to provide an effective alternative?
2. Dehtiar says, "People crave products that have a little more purpose than just consumption." Do you think this is true? Do you crave products with purpose? Look at the way certain items are promoted. Who are they appealing to? Are their marketing devices successful?
3. Why is Dehtiar so hesitant to use the "Africa angle"? What might he lose in the short-term, but gain in the long-term, if he resists? What do you think a new "Africa angle" could be?

Explore

1. Since the publication of this article, how has Oliberté followed through with its intention of promoting equitable jobs in Africa and its promise for expansion?
2. "When it comes to footwear," Dehtiar says, "we don't want people to think of Africa as the next China. We want them to think of it as the next Italy—think quality." What do the references to China and Italy mean here? Has anything occurred in the past decade that might have changed either of their reputations? Based on your research, how do countries generate reputations about quality, and how do their reputations affect consumer interest?
3. What are important qualities to consider in the production of something you want to buy, like technology and clothes? How do those qualities affect your purchases? Make an annotated list of items you've

purchased in the past year (e.g., clothing, technology, etc.). Where were they made, and what were the conditions of the factories in which they were manufactured? Choose one of the items, and tell its story backward: from you owning it to how, where, and by whom it was made. If you go online to the manufacturer's website, be sure to verify their claims with reliable sources.

Avantika Bhuyan
"The Enchanted Bylanes"

Avantika Bhuyan has been the principal correspondent for *Open* magazine since 2008. She earned her B.A. in mass media and mass communication from Indraprastha College for Women, Delhi University, India. Although it is aimed primarily at the resident Indian reader, *Open's* webzine has attracted a more geographically sweeping readership. Bhuyan's article appeared in *Open* on April 9, 2011. In it she describes the heart of a successful business enterprise between Chenghai, China, and Old Delhi, India: the bulk manufacturing and wholesale purchase of toys. These toys are so popular, and the demand so great, that they are sold by everyone from street peddlers to shopkeepers—making toy-selling as lucrative an industry in India as toy-making is in China.

What kinds of immensely popular toys have you owned? Where in the world were they from?

Only the worthy can find their way to this enchanted land tucked away in the bylanes of Old Delhi. That is, if you can convince the cattle to move their conference from the middle of the road, navigate your way round the agitated horses at the *tonga* stand, and keep your feet from being flattened by one of the hundreds of speeding rickshaws. At every turn, you are given differing directions to the 'Indo-Chinese' toy market. But after jostling your way through it all, when you finally reach Vidyanand Market, Teliwara, in Delhi's Sadar Bazar, you will thank yourself for not giving up.

This happens to be one of India's largest wholesale markets for Chinese toys. Items from here make their way to Mumbai, Bangalore, Ahmedabad, Lucknow and many other cities—to be sold at traffic signals and toy stores. This is also where thousands of toys vie with each other to be declared the rage of the season. Dolls preen in their pretty dresses, superheroes flash their guns, and trick toys try their utmost to tickle you pink. But typically, only one toy gets to reign over the market every season. Earlier this year, that honour was won by a cute set of solar powered plants that shimmied their way into millions of Indian hearts.

Now, it is time again for a new toy to enter the spotlight as the year's in thing. It's an exercise in creativity that can be traced thousands of kilometres away to the bustling Shantou district of China. "It is also known as the toy district of China. Chenghai town, where most of the toy-making facilities are located, is very similar to Delhi's Okhla Industrial Area," says Vipul Gupta of Darling Toys, who regularly spends a third or fourth of his year in Shantou.

Importers like him work closely with Chinese toy makers to design toys specifically for the Indian market. This Holi saw many novel creations. Water cannons that not only soak you but do it musically too, *gulal* bombs that burst open with a pop like a Christmas cracker, dinosaur guns that glow and growl to the delight of kids, and *pichkaris* with Winnie the Pooh shields at the nozzle to save yourself a retaliatory drenching.

"I first went to Shantou in 1996 and started importing toys in 1998,"   5 says Vipul, who designs toys along with his father, Vijay. "Anyone can go to China, but you need to have an idea of the market. What items will be impulse purchases? What special features should be added to appeal to the Indian customer?" From idea to finished product, a toy takes three to four weeks. But importing it to India takes an additional three weeks.

What's lost to Indian bureaucracy is made up by Chinese enthusiasm. Such is the popularity of people like Gupta, that news of his arrival spreads like wildfire. "At least six people are always there to pick us up from the airport, hoping that they will get business from us. There is a lot of goodwill for us," says Vipul.

It's not easily done. Staunch vegetarians, particularly those who don't even eat garlic and onions, need to take their own food along (even teabags, in Vipul's case: "I've been told that they mix garlic even in their tea"), but that inconvenience pales in comparison with the business opportunity. Communication can be troublesome too, but toy marketers and toy makers have a way of understanding each other. This time round, Vipul is hoping to get hold of something novel like the petrol bike he got last year. "It was ideally meant for children who stayed in farm houses. The bike had a lot of power and was a big hit."

Safely sourced, the toys make their way to Vidyanand Market, where sundry distributors and small-time traders buy them in bulk. Within days, the toys will be on display at cornershops across the country. Right now, though, it's time for some active bargaining; bundles of money exchange hands, even as wagonloads of toys are ferried around. Enterprising one-man toysellers—the kind you see at traffic signals—are also jostling each other for the latest low-cost wares straight from China. They have little time to talk, and give clipped responses to your questions. Salim Khan, who sells these toys at a Seemapuri traffic signal in Delhi, has been coming here for the past one-and-a-half years. He has just bought 10 pieces of Ben Ten guns and 15 of Happy Girl mobile phones. "There are interesting toys such as ice cream cones that pop in your face, BlackBerry replicas that come for as little as Rs 11–15," he says, "The idea is to sell something compact and novel, something that would have the customer make up his mind in less than two minutes."

Ramesh Kumar, in contrast, is a veteran. He has been coming here for the past 11 years now. In the morning, he sells his wares at Teliwara, and in the afternoon moves on to one of the traffic signals in Old Delhi. "*Yeh poochcho ki kya nahin bikta* (ask what doesn't sell)," he says, adding that shopkeepers come from as far as Faizabad to pick up toys here.

10   Street vendors like Salim and Ramesh buy 30 to 50 pieces at a time, and sell out within two days, returning to recycle their cash for more inventory. "When we see a particular toy doing very well, like the solar-powered plant, then we start selling it more aggressively. Or if we notice other vendors buying more of some toy, we also start buying more pieces. And that's how a toy becomes a phenomenon," says Salim.

The wholesale market comes to life as early as seven in the morning. And fresh imports are not all that is hawked. You see people squatting along the pavement with old products as well. "People from in and around the neighbourhood come with toys that have been leftover from previous seasons. They sell them at very nominal rates. Earlier, that was a thriving market, but nowadays the cops have become very strict. They don't allow anyone to sit like this," says Mahesh Agarwal, who has been a toy vendor for the past 13 years. Once upon a time, he too was part of that lineup, squatting with old toys. Now he has his own shop, Single Toys. "By 11 am, some 500 people come to the market," he says.

On most days, shop owners such as Mahesh can sell up to Rs 26,000 worth of stuff, while on leaner days, sales slide to about Rs 10,000. Traffic-signal vendors like Salim and Ramesh, in contrast, manage sales of some Rs 500 every day. "All said and done, this is a fascinating job," says Mahesh, "Where else can you spend all your time being surrounded by toys of all shapes and sizes? It makes you feel like a kid again."

Analyze

1. One of the sellers in the article states, "The idea is to sell something compact and novel, something that would have the customer make up his mind in less than two minutes." How aware are you of this strategy when you shop? What kinds of items do you see displayed to purchase in "less than two minutes"? What makes you want to buy them—or not?
2. The author observes that there were several novel creations for the Holi (an Indian holiday). What "novel creations" are made for holidays that you celebrate? Do they change each holiday or remain the same?
3. Why do you think the author titled this article "The Enchanted Bylanes"? What does this image conjure up for you? What sense of enchantment, if any, do you glean from the reading?

Explore

1. Create a timeline on which you trace the cost of production of an item—a toy, a piece of clothing, or technology—in one part of the world to its purchase site in another part of the world. Comparing with others in your class, how do your timelines help you understand international commerce networks? What more information do you need?
2. How does the historical relationship between China and India affect their trade with each other now—particularly as they compete to position themselves in the global marketplace? Write a research paper in which you discuss the issues that promote and/or hinder the economic relationship between the two countries.
3. The article ends with a sunny depiction of a toy seller's delight as he observes, "Where else can you spend all your time being surrounded by

toys of all shapes and sizes? It makes you feel like a kid again." What might be an alternative view of India's largest wholesale markets for Chinese toys and those who make their living selling toys in its "enchanted bylanes"? Why do you suppose the author chose to end her article in this way?

Simon Akam
"The Long and Winding Road"

Simon Akam is a journalist and photographer based in Sierra Leone, West Africa. Born in Cambridge, England, Akam moved to Egypt after college to study Arabic, and then to New York City to attend the Columbia University Graduate School of Journalism. Upon graduation he joined *The New York Times* and eventually embarked on a career that has taken him to Istanbul and Berlin. A recipient of *The Guardian's* International Development Journalism Award, Akam's writing has appeared in *The Guardian, The Observer, The Economist*, and *The New Republic*. The following article was featured on *More Intelligent Life*, the online version of *Intelligent Life*, a bi-monthly lifestyle and culture magazine published by *The Economist*. In this article, Akam imparts an important lesson: Do not expect easy solutions to simple business transactions in countries emerging from devastating civil war.

What do you think Akam means when he states, "In a place like Sierra Leone, it is hubristic to believe even the most basic problem has an easy solution"?

M y Land Rover broke down twice on the first day. The first time—30-odd miles into the bush—the fan-belt snapped, the engine boiled over in a filthy froth, the brakes and steering seized up and the dashboard lit up like a Christmas tree. A young man vanished on a motorbike to a nearby village and came back with a replacement belt of the wrong size. As the tropical night came on fast and dark, a small mechanic from a nearby quarry upended himself in the engine cavity, only his legs visible. He built a bracket to stretch the oversized belt. We moved on.

An hour or so later, on a wretched road in clouds of dust, a front tire went down. The bolts on the spare were the wrong size for the wrench. More passers-by appeared, and by torchlight a local friend who had come to help chiselled notches in the bolts with a screwdriver till he could force them loose. I got home after midnight, filmed head to toe in laterite dust. It was fitting, somehow. Just another chapter in the saga of purchasing and owning a car in a post-conflict African state.

Last year I moved to Sierra Leone to work as a correspondent for Reuters. This desperately poor country is still recovering from the bloody civil war that took place in the 1990s. I was initially without private transport, and soon learned to cut about the muggy capital Freetown on the back of motorbike taxis called "Okadas." When "Upcountry"—the colonial-era phrase still used to describe all territory beyond the capital—I occasionally got around by UN helicopter, but more often by limping bush taxi or a hired geriatric jeep. Such vehicles can be relied on to consume the day's rationed drinking water in their gurgling radiators.

Last December I was in a government bus, returning from a tense by-election in the east of the country, when a tire blew at 50-odd miles per hour. The jalopy swung wildly across the road. The driver expertly held the skid and brought the bus to a standstill before we rolled into the scrub. Afterwards I noted that the maximum passenger capacity hand-painted on the side of the Mercedes was approximately twice what its German designers would have suggested. I decided I needed my own wheels.

This was plausible enough because I had just inherited a sum of money 5 from my grandfather, who died last year. He was someone I had long associated with an immaculately waxed car parked outside his genteel home in south-east England. To use this money to buy a car of my own seemed fitting.

But acquiring a vehicle in Sierra Leone would prove challenging. It is nearly impossible to conduct business transactions in an environment without trust. The task introduced me to areas of the beleaguered state that I had come to cover, a country that only recently lifted itself from last place on the UN human-development index. Gross National Income per capita in Sierra Leone stands at $340. One in eight women here will die in childbirth.

I knew I needed a four-wheel drive. For my work I regularly travel to the extremities of this diamond-shaped and diamond-rich little country. Beyond the regional capitals, linked to Freetown by ribbons of aid-project

asphalt, the roads are medieval. Even Freetown is a city of yawning pot-
holes, unfenced storm drains and alarming plank drawbridges.

In these conditions the thinking man's car is a Toyota. Despite its recent
embarrassments and recalls, the Japanese firm makes machines that can
withstand not only Africa's brutal roads but also the depredations of the
continent's mechanics. Bush-car doctors are men of extraordinary ingenuity
(I soon discovered). They get vehicles moving with wire, string, tape and a
mysteriously powerful compote of superglue and wood ash. But in the long
term, such tinkering is disastrous. These quick-fixes leave cars ravaged.

The United Nations in Sierra Leone uses Toyotas, along with other far-
eastern four-by-fours. The endemic NGO population drive Land Cruisers
too. Locals favour the 4Runner, a roofed Toyota pickup that was only
briefly on sale in Britain (perhaps because it looks like a scaled-up Tonka
Toy). Toyotas are the car for Africa. But I did not want a Toyota. As with
women and sex, for men the purchase of a four-wheel drive is often clouded
with emotional baggage. As a child I once pined for a Land Rover, and a
part of me still did. In Sierra Leone a Land Rover seemed to make sense.
They looked better, they were different. I did not want a Toyota.

10   "If you want to go into the jungle you drive a Land Rover," advised Nick
Fieldhouse at Kankku, an off-road driving school in the Lake District. "If
you want to come out again you drive a Toyota." I had contacted him for
advice. But then I closed my ears. The residual British army presence in
Sierra Leone—a leftover from Tony Blair's little war in 2000—reassuringly
drive Land Rovers. I went looking for one.

The mercantile Lebanese who dominate commerce in Sierra Leone keep
cars parked in rough compounds for sale. But their prices are spectacular.
Nine years after the end of hostilities, Freetown still has a war economy. This
makes one of the world's poorest nations a pricey place to live. After one
Lebanese-owned dealer quoted $27,000 for a ten-year-old vehicle, I knew
I had to venture into the murky world of private car sales in Freetown.

For help, I called David Komba James Kpakiwa, a tall and striking man
who hails from Kono in the east of Sierra Leone. He works as an intern at
the United Nations Development Programme, but his calling is elsewhere.
David is the man you find if you are an expat looking to buy a car in Freetown. I was given his number by another foreigner at a waterside bar. In
time, David became a friend as well as a fixer.

Car ownership is a funny thing in Sierra Leone. Local petrol is still
leaded and so destroys the catalytic converters of vehicles imported from

America or Europe. The country's resourceful mechanics deal with this problem by drilling through the clogged devices and replacing the system with a simple pipe. Such a solution does not filter the exhaust fumes in the way a catalytic converter should, but there are no environmental regulations to prevent such a thing here. Locals also have an elegant solution to the ominous flicker of warning lights on dashboards: they remove the bulb.

After much searching I found the right car, parked by the roadside with a beckoning 'For Sale' sign under the windscreen. It was a 1999 Land Rover Discovery just off the boat from America. The owner assured me that I had first right of refusal for the two weeks it would take to get the cash. Cars in Sierra Leone, like anything substantial, are priced in dollars. To buy one I needed wads of dollars in cash, but getting it was not easy.

A third of the country's educated population lives abroad, but trans-   15 ferring money back home is tough. Western Union and other transfer services charge a formidable commission. I decided to open a local dollar-denominated account, to which I would wire money from Britain. Expatriate friends recommended the Pan-African finance house Ecobank, so I signed on with them. With probate from my grandfather's will not yet complete, my father advanced me $10,000 and sent it south.

The money vanished. It was meant to take three days to arrive. After five had passed, Ecobank explained that tracking down the funds had to be done by the transmitting bank. The process took weeks. Meanwhile $10,000 had apparently gone into the ether, and cars I wanted to buy were leaving the lot. Finally I received a British document stating that the money had arrived in Sierra Leone days after I had sent it. This necessitated a harrowing confrontation with the bank manager. By then, the car I had intended to buy had been sold to someone else.

Buying a car in Sierra Leone requires a lot of haggling. Such negotiating is one thing when the object in question is a carved curio (though such craftsmanship has become rare here; a decade of war blunted such artisanal skills). But haggling over a car, where thousands of dollars are at stake, is something different. It turns out that the disparity in price between the first offer and the final sum is pretty much the same for cars as it is for carvings—about 40%.

Finally I bought a car David found, a 2003 Land Rover Discovery with a diesel engine (to avoid the dirty local petrol). It cost $10,000, which I carried in large-denomination greenbacks to its Nigerian owner in a leather bag, not unlike a participant in some ill-fated narcotics transaction.

With the car in my possession, I hoped to enter an age of smooth driving. The local Land Rover dealership had checked over the car before I bought it. I looked forward to an end to turning up at interviews filthy and matted with dust from journeys on the back of motorbikes.

20   But everything still broke. The fan belt was the first of a host of problems, minor but many and expensive: an oil leak, a belt tensioner. Like the viral haemorrhagic fevers that stalk west and central Africa, my car slewed oil and innards from every orifice. Maybe I should have bought a Toyota.

A trip to the local garage ultimately revealed that my Land Rover was a 1999 model dressed up to look newer. This unnerving revelation managed to place my car's problems in context. They were many, but they were relatively minor, and not unreasonable for a vehicle that was a dozen years old and with many miles on it. Still, when a Land Rover breaks in Africa, getting it going again is particularly difficult due to the scarcity of spare parts. I've grown accustomed to gleaning whatever advice I can from the odd sages who populate online Land Rover forums.

I've discovered that there are few things more humbling that the kind of rigmarole involved in getting something as simple as suspension springs for my car. Once that problem was solved, I enjoyed perhaps 45 minutes of trouble-free motoring before my key refused to turn in the ignition. As I write from a Lebanese restaurant in Freetown, a rare place with reliable electricity, my car is parked a mile or so away in yet another dirt road "garage." There two men are prodding its innards, after I realised this morning that the smell in the cabin was not a local simmering cabbage outside but rather the air conditioner compressor smoking in dissatisfaction.

And so it goes. But the lesson has been valuable. In a place like Sierra Leone, it is hubristic to believe even the most basic problem has an easy solution. The road is a long one, and it pays to not be in a hurry.

Analyze

1. What does the author mean when he writes, "It is nearly impossible to conduct business transactions in an environment without trust"? How is this statement backed up by his experiences in Sierra Leone?

2. What is the author's rationale for buying a car? How does it compare to your personal or family's need for transportation? How does his process in obtaining a car compare to the process you need to go through where you live?

3. The author notes that Sierra Leone is a "post-conflict African nation" and "only recently lifted itself from last place on the UN human-development index." What does he mean by "post-conflict," and how has this affected its placement on the UN human-development index?

Explore

1. Choose a film, book, or television program that depicts contemporary sub-Saharan Africa, and analyze how it portrays a region's economic situation. Examples of films include *Hotel Rwanda*, *Tsotsi*, *Disgrace*, and *Osuofia in London*.

2. In recounting his misadventures in purchasing a car, the author attested to the presence of other international corporations and institutions economically involved—directly or indirectly—in Sierra Leone. These include Reuters, Toyota, Western Union, the United Nations, as well as non-government organizations (NGOs). Write a research paper in which you examine the presence of one of them in a sub-Saharan country. How do they help and/or exploit the situation?

Maureen Orth
"The Luxury Frontier"

Maureen Orth is an award-winning journalist, author, and special correspondent for *Vanity Fair* magazine. Her career began in 1972, when she was hired to be one of the first female writers at *Newsweek*, where she wrote about pop music, entertainment, and lifestyles. In the following article, which appeared in *The Wall Street Journal* on June 24, 2011, Orth refers to Mongolia as "the luxury frontier." She cautions that as Mongolia's economy booms, policies and infrastructure need to be put in place lest the country risk losing everything it has gained.

How and where do you see signs of "luxury" marketing? Does that marketing emphasize—or ignore—social and economic divides?

There he stands alone on his horse, a fierce giant shimmering out of nowhere rising 131 feet against the vast Mongolian sky. Eight hundred years after he declared the Great Mongolian State in 1206, Genghis Khan rides again, all 250 stainless-steel tons of him. As I bump along on one of the few paved roads 20 miles outside the capital, Ulan Bator, this kitschy monument to the new mineral-rich and independent Mongolia seems more like a huge middle finger raised to its powerful neighbors, China and Russia. July marks the 21st anniversary of Mongolia's robust democracy after more than 200 years of despised Chinese rule followed by 70 years as a satellite of the Soviets, during which time the proud history of Genghis Khan, who spawned the largest contiguous empire in world history, was banned from public view and utterance. Today, owing to deposits of 80 different minerals, including immense reserves of coal, copper, gold and uranium, as well as ongoing exploration of oil, this sparsely populated country, twice the size of Texas, is undergoing a dizzying transition. No other nation today so squarely faces the choice that Mongolia does. Will it become Nigeria or Chile? Venezuela or Australia?

"Mongolia really is the land of opportunity," says Howard Lambert, head of corporate banking for ING in Mongolia. "Everything can be done here. The financial infrastructure doesn't exist, so you can be a part of building it. Instead of sitting in an office in London turning a wheel, you can build the machine. Every day I see new buildings, developments going up—people buying sports cars in a country that doesn't have roads. The social divide is getting wider."

Nothing illustrates the topsy-turvy nature of Mongolia today more than the capital city's main Sukhbaatar Square, where a bronze statue of Lenin once presided. Now a gleaming Louis Vuitton store, opened in October 2009, offers clients champagne in a circular VIP room outfitted with a lavish ceremonial Mongolian saddle and antique caviar case. Outside the store, however, several hundred yards away, a group of dissident poor have pitched their round felt and wood yurts (gers in Mongolian) to protest the government's cozying up to foreigners and not doing enough for them. "We want jobs. The poor need to have a better quality of life," 52-year-old I. Baganuur tells me. "The government is implementing policies for themselves, not for its citizens."

Sharing the same luxury mall with Vuitton are Burberry, Zegna, Emporio Armani and Hugo Boss. Burberry is planning a second store in a Shangri-La hotel currently under construction. Ferragamo and Dunhill are also looking for space. At the same time, the capital, which boasts the most vibrant democracy in Central Asia, does not have street addresses and has just begun to introduce zip codes. "The irony for Mongolia," says American ambassador to Mongolia Jonathan S. Addleton, "is the more successful they are, the more challenging it becomes."

How could it be that luxury retailers have come to Mongolia? The country has only 2.8 million people, almost half of them living in a capital built for 500,000, including 700,000 destitute former nomads whose gers crowd the surrounding hills and who burn coal and even plastic bottles in the harsh winters, choking the city with extreme pollution. I wanted to understand how a luxury brand could turn a profit in this antiquated land where the livestock outnumbers the people 16 to 1.

My first interview with a Mongolian official is the tieless, 38-year-old vice minister of finance, C. Ganhuyag, whose office sports a putting machine with a strip of artificial turf. "I decided to install casual Fridays," Ganhuyag proffers. (In Mongolia, last names go first, often indicated only by an initial, and people are routinely referred to by first names.) After recounting his latest stay at Davos and directing me to his website, which promotes the new Mongolian "Wolf Economy," because wolves can survive in Mongolia's minus-40-degree winters (Ulan Bator has the lowest average temperature of any world capital), Ganhuyag explains how Mongolia is trying to cope with its two largest mining treasures.

First, in October 2009, a $4 billion deal with Ivanhoe Mines of Canada and Australia's Rio Tinto for Oyu Tolgoi, the world's largest undeveloped copper-and-gold deposit, was finally signed by the government. Currently under construction, the mine is estimated to contain a staggering 40 million tons of copper and 46 million ounces of gold and should start operating in 2012. Next, six competing companies are waiting to hear which of them will win an even bigger deal to develop what will perhaps become the world's largest coal mine, Tavan Tolgoi. Both of these behemoths are situated in the southern part of the Gobi Desert not far from the northern border of the voracious, commodity-hungry China. The area today contains mostly nothing except a few nomads, rare animals and priceless scenery. To manage the coal mine, a city of 60,000 is being planned.

"Mongolia has always been here," Ganhuyag says. "With all our riches, with all our hearts, we were trying to reach out to the West. The West noticed us too late, fortunately for us. If we were Czechoslovakia, they would have grabbed us in the first five years and everything would have been snatched. We suffered through 200 years of Chinese rule, 70 years of Soviet rule and 20 years of being ignored by the West. In retrospect, we had time to educate ourselves. We learned all the tricks of privatization."

It took six years to hammer out the gold and copper deal of which the Mongolian government owns 34 percent and will get a healthy 59 percent of pretax profit without having to advance any money. Along the way there have been some bumps, however. At one point Mongolia instituted a 68 percent windfall profits tax on mining, since revoked, which scared all the banks away. During the last election, in 2008, politicians promised the populace cash handouts that amount to about $17 a month to everyone, rich or poor, taken from the down payments made to the government for the gold and copper deal. Today that cash is moving into the deficit zone and the handouts have been widely criticized for taking funds away from desperately needed infrastructure projects, as well as creating a welfare dependency.

10   Even so, Ganhuyag says Mongolia's current GDP of $7 billion a year is set to grow at least 20 percent a year for the next decade. "We are going to double our economy every three to five years—even the IMF agrees on that. That's why luxury retailers get a good smell from us. It all depends on the global markets. If China is trying to equip every man with a car, then the demand for copper, coal, iron, gold, gas, uranium, which we also have, will be endless."

Louis Vuitton, which first created its trunks for African explorers, is indeed pleased with its entry into the Mongolian market and the demand does not even have to be endless. Rather, LV CEO Yves Carcelle thought it was a special sign when he learned that "How are you?" in Mongolian is asked, "How did you travel?" I tell Carcelle that Burberry says their Mongolian customer base is little more than a thousand people and they are happy. He agrees. "One to two thousand people is all you need. You can't judge by average income—average doesn't mean anything. The question is, do you have a few thousand people who can afford luxury? What you need is a stable political environment and the necessary environment to put your store where you are the place."

What I observe in Louis Vuitton is a clientele of women ages 30 to 40 already sporting LV bags and men shopping for gifts. LV's interest, of course, was sparked after going into Russia and China. "In 20 years China has become our biggest client," Carcelle says. "Apart from that, our expansion is quite well spread around the world. Because of media today, luxury and fashion have become the universal language." Mongolia follows global trends too. "People look at fashion and TV online here. We get Russian Vogue, and Cosmo Mongolia just came out," B. Delgermaa, a fashionable Mongolian woman, tells me. "You have to subscribe to American Vogue and it's very expensive."

It is traditional for Mongolians to display their wealth on themselves. "Nomads move around the country four times a year," Ts. Ariunaa, executive director of the Mongolian Arts Council, says. "All your wealth goes to jewelry and costume, your horse and saddle." Adds Delgermaa, "Culturally, Mongolians like to show off. Mongolians are very proud of themselves—there is only one me. They think they deserve exclusivity."

A rich nomad today is known for having a satellite dish and a solar panel for his ger and a motorbike for himself. But his primary relationship has always been with nature. According to Ariunaa, "First you sing about the land, your horse, your mother, and then you sing about your loves and relationships. Mongolians are better at communing with nature than with each other. You live on the steppes in a ger. You don't need to know what your neighbor is thinking." Nomads are also used to "singing outside, so you need to listen in a big space."

Thanks to its years under Soviet rule, Mongolia has a literacy rate of 98 percent, as well as 151 universities where 70 percent of the students are female. A less fortunate hangover from Soviet rule is the rate of alcoholism, especially among Mongolian men, up to 25 percent of whom are classified as alcohol-dependent. I traveled to an orphanage in Mongolia's second-largest city, Darkhan, about a three-hour drive from Ulan Bator, where some of the 40 or so orphans had ended up because of the alcohol problems of their parents. "You can buy a bottle of vodka for 75 cents, less than a cup of coffee," says Meloney C. Lindberg, country representative for Mongolia of the U.S. NGO the Asia Foundation. I was told that if you collapsed on the street in the capital from a heart attack, no one would help you because they would probably think you were drunk. "We never before used hard drink like vodka," B. Baabar, one of Mongolia's leading intellectuals, tells me. "Our alcohol came from milk like sake [from rice]."

Baabar is one of the best-loved figures in Mongolia. He gave up his job as a biochemist to become a historian, writer, publisher and activist. He led the project to translate the Encyclopedia Britannica into Mongolian and was jailed by the Russians, whom he clearly does not like. He believes that the Mongolian government today is still too reflexively Socialist and the central-planning Russian model of state paternalism too often prevails. "The people here who are running the system still think like Communists or Socialists," he says. "Every five years the Soviet Union gave Mongolia $5 billion. This supplied Mongolian industry, agriculture and military. On the other side, it made Mongolia fully dependent."

He is angry that the Mongolian government started giving cash handouts that he calls "economic infantilism," a product of those educated under the Soviets. "Members of Parliament must go through elections and make many promises to the people. If the people are fed like children from this guy who acts like the father and promises cash money, free education and everything free because the state is getting richer and richer—that is the bad side of this sudden wealth."

The inner sanctum of the cash cow that everyone hopes the Oyu Tolgoi copper-and-gold project becomes is the Ulan Bator office of Cameron McRae, the redheaded, 52-year-old Australian CEO and president in charge of the site construction. The "first step" investment of Ivanhoe and Rio Tinto is $7 billion, he says, and they are currently spending $7 million a day to dig the mine.

His computer contains numerous animated models of the construction site, where a tiny Eiffel Tower is used for scale, towered over by the vast project. "We are building at a scale never tackled in this country," McRae says. "We are facing a shortage of artisans and technologists and people with large-scale construction experience." At its peak, the construction site will require 17,000 people and when completed, the mine is expected to produce 50 to 55 million tons of ore annually.

20   The government has already received about a half billion dollars in fees and taxes and has not had to put up a penny. Yet because of a lack of technically trained Mongolians, two of the mine's major contractors are Chinese—the mine is located only 28 miles from the Chinese border and up to 80 trucks a day from China carry in necessary building supplies. "We made a commitment to the Mongolian government to train up to 5,000 Mongolians," McRae says. Once the mine is built, "a minimum" of 90 percent of the workers will be Mongolian.

The mine's remote South Gobi location requires considerable amounts of power and water, not to mention an airport. "We'll help bring power to Gobi and upgrade roads. We'll build a powerline to China and tap into the Chinese grid," McRae says. But the amount of water required, especially in a desert, is unprecedented. "We're exploring for water. We found a very large ancient aquifer in a gravelly area not related to anything else." I ask McRae where he thinks they will be in five years. "We'll be the second-largest copper mine in the world with a very inexperienced workforce with a big training program."

Before World War II, Mongolia served as a buffer state between Japan and the Soviet Union, and after, between the USSR and China. Beijing is just 340 miles from the southern Mongolian border and the Great Wall was constructed mainly to keep out the Mongols; 70,000 Russian troops were once stationed in Mongolia. Those old enmities are hard to overcome. For example, the Trans-Mongolian Railway conforms to the gauge of the Russian railroad, not the Chinese one, so each train to China from Mongolia must go through a tedious re-fitting process. Under the guise of "national security concerns" there is now a major debate going on in Mongolian business and political circles over how to export the coal from Tavan Tolgoi—by rail to Russia or by truck to China? It would require hundreds of miles of new rail to be constructed to ship out through Russia, or the coal could simply be trucked 150 miles to the Chinese border.

"National security concerns is code for concern about the possible use of the railway for military intervention," says Graeme Hancock, who until recently was the senior mining specialist for the World Bank in Mongolia. "These Cold War concerns are still being played out all over Mongolia. They consider the Russians their Big Brothers, their friends, and for 70 years they've been told there's a big yellow evil to the south." He adds, "From our perspective, Mongolia places too much [emphasis] on national security interests and not enough on economic interests. Instead of basing decisions on what's good for the economy of Mongolia, decisions are based on geopolitical considerations." I actually came across the lingering reverence for Russia in, of all places, Mongolia's only five-star hotel resort, the lavishly appointed Terelj. I was startled to find the deposed statue of Lenin ousted from the main square of Ulan Bator in 1993 stuck behind the building in one of its gardens.

Changes in Mongolia are happening so fast that L. Sumati, the country's leading pollster, says it is impossible to group people into social classes—mobility is too rapid. At the same time the situation is made more complicated by the fact that almost all of the poor have accumulated in the ger areas of the capital city, many forced there after the horrendous winter of 2009–2010 caused nearly six million of their livestock to die. "An army of the poor is besieging UB. Any political party standing for election has a tough time negotiating with these people," Sumati says. "They are very volatile and just asking for survival. In some ways they are angry. They see a widening gap between the rich and the poor and they see no way out." I ask him why he can't classify who is wealthy. "We have a group of very rich people supported by their access to power," he says, referring to the crossover between business ownership and government. "The rich are not a class yet because there is still very high mobility both up and down." Although Mongolia has strict laws requiring top officials to publish their assets and a lively media that includes 22 daily papers in Ulan Bator plus 21 TV news channels, there is no freedom of information act and cross-ownership of media and business interests abound. I'm told editorial control is nearly always held by owners and there are ways to pay to get a story on the news.

25   Corruption here is endemic. The Asia Foundation pays Sumati to poll a thousand households quarterly to benchmark attitudes toward corruption and how many bribes they have paid in the previous three months—usually to doctors, teachers, administrators and police. The last poll showed that Mongolians consider corruption to be the government's third most serious problem after unemployment and poverty, and that while the number of bribes decreased from 16 percent of households in March 2010, to 13 percent in September 2010, the amounts of the bribes more than doubled. Of course, these surveys do not address the big guys and government officials who somehow may be secretly attached to these lucrative concessions, a lot of which are done on an all-cash basis, the preferred method of the Chinese. "The Chinese come in with a suitcase full of cash," says banker Lambert. "A Chinese guy buys a bottle of vodka and he will buy your mine for $7 million with no due diligence. Even though the Mongolians don't like the Chinese, they have a healthy respect for them."

The transition from Communism is still being felt. The alphabet is Cyrillic and there are many parts of the capital that look a lot like old Moscow. The era after the Soviet Union collapsed is still recalled painfully. Those who made out like bandits were similar to the apparatchik of Russia— people who had had contact with the West. One such person is national rich guy Kh. Battulga, one of the most controversial figures in political and business life today. He is a former national judo champion, a man who drives a Bentley and paid $10 million out of his own pocket to build the gargantuan statue of Genghis Khan on Mongolia's steppes. Battulga is a developer—he is turning the land around the statue into a resort—and also happens to be the minister of road, transportation, construction and urban development and a powerful leader of Parliament. He traveled the exterior as an athlete, started trading by selling electronic appliances from China, graduated to computers and now owns a large meat-processing plant that supplies the country. In 2004, "my own needs were met," he says, so he decided to run for Parliament.

Today, his grand vision is to build a $10 billion industrial complex the Mongolians call a "production city" named Sainshand, also in the middle of nowhere in the Gobi, 300 miles from the Russian border, 125 miles from China and about 200 miles northeast from the proposed Tavan Tolgoi coal mine. It would be connected by highway and rail to the capital and by rail only to Russia. Instead of selling unrefined ore and coal to the Chinese, who collect it in trucks, Sainshand would process the minerals and refine the oil. Mongolia could then sell its commodities at an increased profit of at least 30 percent, according to estimates, and create hundreds of thousands of new jobs. But first the city has to be created from scratch. Then the coal will have to travel 3,000 miles from the mine, including a connection to the Russian railroad, before reaching the port of Vladivostok. Battulga told me he got the Sainshand idea because a Buddhist thinker in the 19th century predicted that one day a great metropolis would grow there.

All over Ulan Bator I hear naysayers on Sainshand. The local gossip is that Battulga is in cahoots with the Russians. "The Russians quite naively believe if they monopolize the railroad around the minerals they'll have control of the mineral wealth," says J. Od, who with his brother is one of Mongolia's biggest businessmen and taxpayers, doing a lot of business with the Chinese. He dismisses it all as politics, declaring that's the way "the clowns" in government mix politics with business. "Sainshand," he continues, "is some so-called geopolitical policy of Russia. It cannot be implemented in Mongolia today—it's too late." Battulga counters: "For Mongolia it's not profitable to sell raw materials to China. It's not geo-political, it's business. We want minerals sold to the world market."

The fragile coalition government that is up for reelection next year is literally besieged on all sides. To hedge against inflation and to share the wealth, Parliament has passed a law creating a Sustainability Fund with money set aside from mining industry revenue including the Tavan Tolgoi coal profits; sometime in the future, all citizens will also be issued 10 percent of the shares of an IPO the government will offer on the Hong Kong and London stock exchanges. (The government has also established a more general Development Bank.) They know they cannot count on the fluctuating prices of commodities to sustain their long-term growth. When I spoke to Z. Gombojav, minister for foreign affairs and trade, he chose to spin the country's many immediate needs as "vast opportunities and room for investment in infrastructure, including roads and railways, energy, urban construction, light industry and food production."

30   The reality on the ground is more challenging. For example, Mongolia has the best cashmere in the world, but domestic producers who refine the wool say they are in danger of being put out of business because the government does not collect the 30 percent export tax from the Chinese, enabling them to buy vast amounts of raw wool from the herders at higher prices while domestic producers are fully taxed. According to D. Erdene-Ochir, head of sales for Goyo Cashmere, the government is sacrificing them to the herders. "It's terrible politics to treat herders badly. So there are no taxes and the Chinese manipulate the market. They are supposed to pay the government, but the government doesn't collect. Mongolian companies have to pay income and VAT taxes.... If I want to be elected, I cheat the producers not the nomads." He also accuses the Chinese of mixing the cashmere with wool, silk and cotton. "They mix it and call it anything they want. We will be extinct very soon."

There is no doubt that Mongolia is white-hot in multinational-investment circles. One night I attended GE's welcome reception celebrating Mongolia as the 130th country where it does business. GE will begin by selling MRI machines to the country's underequipped and overburdened hospitals. Caterpillar already has a $100 million business going there. "Mongolia is like baking a cake," says business consultant Jackson Cox. "All the ingredients are on the table. You've got everything you need in Mongolia to build a modern, prosperous economy. The only thing that's missing is the political leadership to make the tough decisions. You have to envision the Mongolia you want 25 years from now and then take on the decisions to plan the education, infrastructure and health care to get there."

Nevertheless, most of the Mongolian hands I dealt with seemed to believe things would somehow work out in the end, even though environmentalists rightly fear precious grasslands and watersheds could be destroyed in a country that so far has only been 25 percent geologically explored. As Graeme Hancock says, "There is a very, very active civil society. Companies don't get away with making a mess very long."

The looming question is what Mongolia will do once its finite treasures have run out. "Twenty years from now, if all this mineral wealth—which is not renewable—is not turned into renewable wealth, which is knowledge, then we will have missed the point," says newspaper columnist D. Jargalsaikhan. "This underground wealth needs to stay above ground to suit our will and aspirations."

"Money without policy does more harm than good," says J. Od, who believes "we are only at the tip of the iceberg" in knowing how rich Mongolia really is.

Analyze

1. The author claims that no other nation "so squarely faces the choice that Mongolia does" and wonders whether it will "become Nigeria or Chile? Venezuela or Australia?" What is the choice that Mongolia faces? What is the significance of citing each of these countries?

2. Orth published her article in *The Wall Street Journal*. What words, phrases, and concepts in the article distinguish *The Wall Street Journal* readers' interests from those of a more general readership? How do you compare to this group of readers?

3. What kind of political leadership does Mongolia need in order to transition from an emerging economy to a prosperous one? What is currently standing in the way?

Explore

1. The article briefly touches on the environmental risks of exploiting Mongolia's natural resources—coal, copper, gold, uranium, and oil. Research alternative points of view about the risks and gains that Mongolia faces in its move toward becoming an emerging global economy.

2. The CEO of Louis Vuitton opines, "Apart from that, our expansion is quite well spread around the world. Because of media today, luxury and fashion have become the universal language." Do you think this is true? How has the company positioned its products as global luxury items?

3. How will Mongolia's plan for development by mining its natural resources improve life for Mongolians? What do they stand to gain—and lose? Even if the demand is endless, what will happen when the resources run out?

Forging Connections

1. In a globalized world, what place do you see for luxury items like those mentioned in both "The New Grand Tour" and "The Luxury Frontier"? Do you think that the ability to buy luxury items is a good incentive for those who work? Do you think such items are important, or do you think they are obsolete? Using the readings from this chapter, write an essay on the relevance of luxury items in a globalized world.

2. This chapter focused on different countries and their peoples whose transformative political and economic changes have either sent them out into the world or attracted many in the world to them. How have these readings broadened your sense of globalization and its effects on earning and spending?

Looking Further

1. In his article on the shoe manufacturer Oliberté, Watkin quotes an international aid expert who criticized TOMS for competing with local producers by handing out free goods and for being "quintessential Whites in Shining Armor." How does this compare with Teju Cole's claims in his article in chapter 5, "The White Savior Industrial Complex"?

2. How does "philanthrocapitalism" relate to the discussion in chapter 5 about for-profit social entrepreneurs? Do further research on both of these concepts; summarize how they are defined and interpreted, based on your reading, and how they promote (or don't) a global esprit or ethic.

7 Gender Matters

Globalization, whether seen through the lens of economic opportunity, expanded communication, or multicultural awareness, has brought to the fore in many ways the range of attitudes and beliefs that underlie gender matters worldwide. The selections in this chapter offer contemporary snapshots of gender matters from a range of geographical locations that also hold mirrors to the ways in which gender matters to each of us personally. Christina Larsen's "The Startling Plight of China's Leftover Ladies" is startling not because young Chinese women are not sought by prospective husbands. Rather, China's gender gap has left millions of men single at a time when well-educated women prefer husbands who are as economically well off as they are. Perhaps the fact that they are called "leftover" is what is most startling.

From China, we move to Banda Aceh, Indonesia, one of the most conservative Islamic places in the world. Doug Clark continues the marriage theme detailing the preoccupations of 27-year-old Aisha as she prepares for her first date with Fajar: What message will her choice of hijab send to her prospective suitor about her own identity? His observations in "Crimson Leopard-Print Headscarves: Wearing the Veil in Banda Aceh, Indonesia" are given a more critical perspective in Leila Ahmed's "Reinventing the Veil." Ahmed, a feminist Egyptian academic living in Cambridge, US, finds herself at first surprised by contemporary young women choosing to wear a veil, and then even more surprised to find herself stumbling upon her own unchecked assumptions.

Is there a language that can be shaped and used to appeal to one gender over another? See if you notice a difference in Oliver Broudy's coverage of "Body-Building in Afghanistan." Does it seem geared toward a male audience with its graphic depictions of war-torn Kabul and the determination of the men he interviews to rebuild their country by rebuilding themselves first? The chapter takes an even darker turn in the next reading, "Killing Emos, and the Future, in Iraq." Have Iraqis who favor "emo-core" been attacked and murdered because they are effeminate? Or because the Shia society is homophobic? What is behind the impulse to control and contain sexual identity and traditional gender roles, and how are they challenged further by access to and identity with music? The final selection in this chapter makes what some might see as a surprising claim about the perception of male migrants and the privileges they are often denied because of their gender. As the world becomes increasingly globalized, and as we ourselves come to adapt a globalized perspective, how will gender matters emerge, be challenged, and be redefined?

Christina Larsen
"The Startling Plight of China's Leftover Ladies"

An award-winning magazine writer and editor, Christina Larsen has reported from across China and Southeast Asia. Her essays on China, the environment, climate change, and civil society have appeared in *The New York Times, The Atlantic,* and *Time.* She is a contributing editor to *Foreign Policy,* in which the following article appeared in the May/June 2012 issue. Larsen describes the modern Chinese woman, who benefits from extraordinary educational and financial opportunities while contending with an unusual demographic situation. In today's China, women who remain single beyond the ideal "marriageable" age (mid-20s) are known as China's *sheng nu,* or "leftover ladies."

In what ways does economic status—or economic anxiety—shape courtship rituals in your own community?

The Spicy Love Doctor was running late. A well-heeled crowd one recent Sunday afternoon had packed into the second-floor lounge of Beijing's Trends Building—home to the publishing offices of several glossy magazines, including the Chinese editions of *Cosmopolitan, Esquire,* and *Harper's Bazaar*—to hear Wu Di, a contributor to China's *Cosmopolitan* and author of an alluring new book, *I Know Why You're Left.* The poised, professional crowd, outfitted in black blazers, leather boots, and trendy thick-framed glasses, was composed mostly of women in their mid-20s to mid-30s—prime *Cosmo* readers and all there waiting patiently to hear Wu, who typically charges $160 an hour for "private romance counseling," explain their surprising plight: being single women in a country with a startling excess of men.

At last she sauntered to the front of the room, microphone in hand. Wu, a pert, married 43-year-old who resembles a brunette Suze Orman (and whose chief advertised credential, it turns out, is an M.B.A. from the University of Houston), surveyed her audience. Then she broke out into a practiced grin and, in the relentlessly chipper staccato common to Chinese public speakers, launched into her talk: a mix of sisterly homily, lovemaking tips, and economics lecture. It's unrealistic to expect that you will be madly in love with one person forever, she warned, or even that passion can be the right guide to marriage. Her authority? No less than the wandering eye of Bill Clinton, which, she told her solemnly attentive audience, "proves that there is no method to sustain feverish lust between long-married couples."

The majority of her talk was devoted not to such timeless aphorisms, but to describing a new conundrum in China: the plight of its *sheng nu,* or "leftover ladies." In popular parlance, sheng nu refers to women above a certain age—some say 27, others 30—who are unmarried and presumably "left over," too old to be desirable. Increasingly, sheng nu are a topic of alternating humor and alarm for Chinese newspaper columnists, TV sitcoms, reality dating shows, and studies by government bodies like the All-China Women's Federation; according to its 2010 survey, more than 90 percent of male respondents agreed that women should marry before age 27 or risk being forever undesired.

What's most startling about this national obsession with China's Bridget Joneses is that sheer numbers would seem to say it couldn't possibly be so. China has far too few women, not too many. This is a country where 118 boys were born for every 100 girls in 2010, and by 2020 the number of men unable to find partners is expected to reach 24 million. So how could any women possibly be left over?

> "By 2020 the number of men unable to find partners is expected to reach 24 million."

5   As science journalist Mara Hvistendahl, author of *Unnatural Selection*, and numerous scholars have documented, a confluence of factors has led to this deeply male-skewed national sex ratio. For centuries, Chinese families preferred male children because girls were obliged to leave home eventually and move into their husband's household rather than stay and take care of their parents; the advent of the one-child policy in 1980 only increased the stakes. Over the next decade and a half, the newly widespread availability of ultrasound scans led to a dramatic uptick in sex-selective abortions— banned since 1995 but still easy enough to arrange. The upshot is that by the 2020s, an estimated 15 to 20 percent of Chinese men of marriageable age will lack potential brides, according to Jiang Quanbao of Xi'an Jiaotong University. You might think this would create a sense of entitled ease among China's single ladies, but the reality is rather more complicated, as the attentive supplicants to the Spicy Love Doctor attest.

"Why do sheng nu happen now in China?" Wu asked. After a dramatic pause, she answered her own question: "It is a result of high GDP growth." At this point, several women in the audience fidgeted, wary of an economics sermon, but Wu continued. "In the past, there was no such word as sheng nu. But today women have more wealth and education—they have better jobs, and higher requirements for men." She reflected: "Now you want to find a man you have deep feelings for who also has a house and a car. You won't all find that."

She wasn't telling the women they should want less, exactly. What she was really pointing out was just how much better today's Chinese women have it. Thirty years ago, a marriage certificate was a passport into adulthood. "Until you married, there were no basic human rights. No right to have sex before marriage. No house allocated by your *danwei* [government work unit] before marriage." Today those barriers have crumbled, with rising sexual freedom and a booming private real estate market. Why marry unless you find someone just right? "The future is different," Wu predicted, waving her arms for emphasis. China's big cities will be filled with sheng nu. "Those who can bear the shortcomings and sufferings of men will get married," she concluded. "Those not, single."

All this grand theorizing was not remotely what Sabrina, a slender 26-year-old with sexy librarian glasses, wanted to hear. "I wish she had given more practical advice about how to enlarge my social circle," she whispered to me. Sabrina was there because she truly wanted to get married, and by her own anxious calculation, she feared she had about one year left. She had a graduate degree from a good university, held a respectable job in marketing, and was reasonably attractive. It had never occurred to her that finding an appropriate partner would be a struggle. Did I know any unmarried men? she asked. And if so, I should probably tell them she is just 24.

In 2006, China's *Cosmopolitan* ran the headline, "Welcome to the Age of the Leftover Ladies." One might expect the magazine to exaggerate women's angst to peddle copies, but the notion that marriage is fundamentally changing in China is borne out by the numbers: Women in urban China are marrying later, and the most educated marry latest—or, increasingly, not at all.

According to an old proverb, "The emperor's daughter need never fret   10
about finding a husband." But Wang Feng, a sociologist and director of the Brookings-Tsinghua Center for Public Policy, is eager to explain why the old legend just isn't true: "I've checked, and daughters of the imperial family actually had trouble getting married. They tended to wed much later," he told me.

It just so happens that with China's economic boom, more and more women are now sharing the dilemma of the emperor's daughters. In 1982, just 5 percent of urban Chinese women ages 25 to 29 were unmarried, according to Wang. By 1995, that percentage had doubled. By 2008, it had nearly tripled. Most of these women will eventually marry, yet the percentage of women in their 30s who are single, though relatively small, is also multiplying quickly: In 1995, just 2 percent of urban Chinese women ages 30 to 34 were unmarried. By 2008, 6 percent were.

Tellingly, the least likely to marry are the most educated. In 2005 fully 7 percent of 45-year-old Shanghai women with college degrees had never married, according to Wang's research. "That's a harbinger of what's going to happen in other places [in China] for more educated women," he told me. "It's a sharp departure from before, from near-universal female marriage." Indeed, there's a common joke that there are three genders in China: men, women, and women with Ph.D.s. Men marry women, and women with Ph.D.s don't marry.

But it's not just China. In many East Asian countries, women, especially the best-educated top-earners now thronging the cities, are increasingly rejecting the institution of marriage altogether. *The Economist* reported last year that roughly a third of Japanese women in their early 30s and more than 20 percent of Taiwanese women in their late 30s remained unmarried; not more than half those women will ever tie the knot. In Singapore, 27 percent of college-educated 40- to 44-year-old women were single. There's little reason to suspect that China, which is still 49 percent rural, won't evolve in a similar direction.

The geopolitical stakes are high for a region home to more than one-fifth of humanity and the factory floor of the global economy. Most East Asian countries, including China, have invested little in creating a social safety net; per tradition, children are expected to care for aging parents. But China's economic miracle has brought rising income levels and city skylines—as well as rising marriage ages and divorce rates, even as the one-child policy has driven down fertility. (In fact, childbearing across East Asia has plunged since the 1960s, from 5.3 children per woman to 1.6 children today.) So as the region modernizes and struggles to create First World health-care and retirement systems, fewer and fewer young workers will be there to pick up the tab to support the elderly. TVs, iPhones, and tennis shoes—all now made in China—could become much more expensive. And East Asia's humming factories could lose their competitive edge.

15   The Chinese government has undoubtedly seen this writing on the wall, as Leta Hong Fincher, a contributor to *Ms.* magazine and a Ph.D. candidate in sociology at Tsinghua University, told me. Why else, she asks, would the government-backed All-China Women's Federation take pains to conduct an exhaustive, 30,000-household survey asking about attitudes toward sheng nu? "This derogatory term has been aggressively disseminated by the

Chinese government," she points out. According to a state media report on the survey, "See What Category of 'Leftover' You Belong To," the All-China Women's Federation assigned young single women such hapless labels as "leftover fighters" (ages 25 to 27), "the ones who must triumph" (ages 28 to 30), and "master class of leftover women" (35 and over). The takeaway: Get worried, and get married. Or, as Fincher wrote for *Ms.*: "If you want to stand a snowball's chance in hell of ever getting married in this country, don't demand too much from your man."

Given China's unbalanced sex ratio, if more women opt for the single life, that simply leaves more unmarried men at the bottom of the social ladder. According to Wang's analysis of China's 2000 census, just 1 percent of college-educated men remained single at age 40, but among men in the lowest income and education bracket, fully 25 percent were single at 40. If some 24 million largely rural bachelors remain in remote villages to care for aging parents, who in turn will care for them? Moreover, a greater proportion of single men, in any society, is often linked with increasing rates of crime and violence. As one common Chinese slogan has it, a harmonious family is the cornerstone of a harmonious society. Clearly, Beijing is worried that the inverse is also true.

Certainly, a visceral anxiety about marriage and romance pulses through nearly every aspect of contemporary Chinese culture. Take the tremendous pressure on young men and their families to buy apartments and cars to make them more attractive in the marriage market. According to research by the Baihe matchmaking website, 68.3 percent of women in China's most developed cities say a man must own a home before they'll get married. Or take the popularity of the nerve-racking dating show *Fei Cheng Wu Rao* (*Don't Bother if You Aren't the One*), in which a bachelor faces an inquisition by 24 young women standing behind lighted podiums, presidential-debate style. Or the glib yet lovelorn features in women's magazines, from Chinese *Elle*'s recent slide show, "Love Guide: 8 Types of Men Whom Sheng Nu Love Most in 2012" (starring happy canoodling couples), to Chinese *Bazaar*'s advice article "From Senior Sheng Nu to Queen of the Wedding Veil."

Yet the editor in chief of China's *Cosmopolitan*, Xu Wei, told me that, after helping popularize the term sheng nu, she is now trying to downplay it: "We want instead to convey more positive images for modern women." Besides, she explained, "leftover ladies" is really a bit of a misnomer—it's women's own standards that are changing so quickly.

The singletons I interviewed in Beijing were anything but dowdy. At 5 feet, 9 inches, the slim woman who slipped into a seat at the table at trendy Opposite House cafe was, in fact, an utter knockout. Annie Xu has a strikingly angular face, large wide-set eyes, shoulder-length hair, and flawless skin. She is 30 years old and alternates between feeling panic and contentment. At one point, she told me, "Thirty is a very dangerous age," and at another, "I am 30 years old; I am not afraid of being alone. It's just like, when you pass the age, everything is just OK."

20   College-educated and financially independent, Xu is a whip-smart journalist for one of Beijing's most respected newsmagazines. She is, in short, a catch. She is also, somewhat to her own surprise, increasingly convinced that devoting her time and attention to work constitutes time better spent than dawdling on disappointing dates or "friends with benefits" (she's seen too many of both, she confided). She still hopes to get married one day, if she finds the right partner, but when I asked what would happen if she were still single at 50, she said, "I think it's OK. I am most afraid of marrying with the wrong man."

Before our meeting, I had asked her to read the recent *Atlantic* cover story about unmarried American women, "All the Single Ladies," to see whether it resonated. Yes, she told me, pointing especially to this passage: "When Gloria Steinem said, in the 1970s, 'We're becoming the men we wanted to marry,' I doubt even she realized the prescience of her words."

A generation ago, when Chinese society was simpler, there were fewer choices. But today, with colossal economic upheaval—and a yawning chasm between China's winners and losers—your spouse may be the largest single factor determining whether, in the words of one infamous female contestant on *Fei Cheng Wu Rao*, you ride home on the back of a bicycle or in a BMW. And that just crystallizes the problem: China's educated women increasingly know what they want out of life. But it's getting harder and harder to find Mr. Right.

Analyze

1. What is the source of the term *sheng nu* (leftover ladies)? Why is it considered a misnomer? Why is it being used to intimidate women to "get worried, and get married"?

2. What kinds of pressure are emerging in Chinese society for men who want to marry?

3. What expectations about marriage do you feel in your own community or culture? Have those expectations changed in comparison to those of your parents?

Explore

1. Read the article "All the Single Ladies" published in *The Atlantic* and referenced in this article. Write an essay about the changing state of traditional marriage. You can choose to focus on one specific culture other than your own or on multiple cultures around the world. Include predictions, based on these readings and your own experiences, about how this might affect gender roles in the future.

2. Larsen notes that the "Spicy Love Doctor," Wu Di, uses Bill Clinton as evidence that "there is no method to sustain feverish lust between long-married couples." Consider a selection of contemporary world leaders—female and male—and their marital statuses. How might they be representative—or not—of their nations' views on contemporary marriage?

3. Larsen makes no mention of a lesbian, gay, bisexual, and transgender (LGBT) community in China specifically or South Asia in general, where women "are increasingly rejecting the institution of marriage altogether." How might a consideration of gay rights and issues around same-sex marriage complicate the assumptions within the article?

Doug Clark
"Crimson Leopard-Print Headscarves: Wearing the Veil in Banda Aceh, Indonesia"

Doug Clark is a Fulbright Fellow in Banda Aceh, Indonesia, where he teaches English at a public high school and is completing a collection of short stories. He is a writer and correspondent for the online space *Glimpse,* which features the work of emerging writers, journalists, photographers, and filmmakers on the topic of travel. In his essay, which appeared on *Glimpse* on

January 27, 2012, Clark observes how young women negotiate the intersection of Western modernity with the deeply Islamic culture of Banda Aceh.

How do your clothes mark you as a member of a particular class, community, or group? Do you make deliberate choices about what you wear based on how you want to be perceived or understood?

A isha has a date tonight.

Aisha is twenty-seven. Most of her friends are married. She is still pretty, but worries she is losing her looks. Her figure, which she once described as "professional," has bagged down with plumpness, the result of a love of fried bananas.

And in Banda Aceh, Indonesia, where sharia (Islamic) law reigns, a single date signals a lot more than in the West. Meeting for coffee often means agreeing to be viewed as a couple in the eyes of Acehnese society. Certainly, after a second date, friends will start gossiping—jokingly and not—about a wedding.

Aisha isn't sure if other people are labeling her and Fajar a couple yet, but she hopes so. They work together at the bank: she's up front as a teller; he's in back as an accountant. They've never gotten beyond casual conversation when he drops papers off at her desk because the other tellers are eavesdropping. Most of Aisha's information about him comes from gossip and Facebook stalking, but she's liked what she's heard: quiet but friendly, a diligent employee, loyal to his widowed mother. She's also noted that he's older, expected to be promoted soon, dresses well, and drives an expensive Honda Tiger motorbike.

5   But in some ways he remains a mystery. Take, for example, the bruise—birthmark?—a little to the right of the center of his forehead. It's so faint she's not even sure it's there. Could it be a developing *zabiba*, the callus exceptionally devote Muslims earn through a great deal of prayer, bowing repeatedly until their heads bump the tiles? Everyone knows Fajar never misses any of the five daily devotions, but he dresses very modernly in jeans and knock-off Adidas. She has never seen him in a *peci*, the traditional hat religious men wear.

But Aisha can't waste too much time debating whether the spot is a *zabiba* or birthmark. It's 3:00 p.m. and her shift at the bank has just ended. The date is at 7:30 p.m. at Q&L Coffee. If the night is going to be a success she needs a new outfit, especially a *jilbab* (headscarf).

Aisha knows her best friend, Putri, is a terrible person to ask for fashion advice, but she can't imagine sorting through veils and weighing the messages they will send alone.

Aisha abandons caution and calls Putri.

Aceh, Indonesia, is a scarred land. It is still recovering from twenty-five years of separatist, Islamist rebellion and the devastating 2004 tsunami, which killed approximately 125,000 people in Aceh Province. In ten minutes Banda Aceh, the region's capital, lost about a fourth of its population: 60,000 souls.

The rebuilt Banda Aceh is a puzzle of crooked lanes. Motorbikes honk and swerve around stray cows and old men push *kaki limas*, wheeled food-carts, ringing bells. The buildings are drab and single story, shedding peeling paint. The domes of hundreds of mosques dominate the skyline, their calls to prayer filling the city with haunting music five times a day.

When the *azan*, the call to prayer, echoes through Banda Aceh, the frenetic city suddenly calms. Choked streets empty into eerie stillness; restaurants and shops lock their doors and draw their blinds; the population files towards mosques and prayer rooms.

Islam is central to Acehnese identity. Banda Aceh was the first place in South East Asia to convert to Islam, around 1200 C.E. It spread from there, eventually encompassing all of Malaysia, most of Indonesia, and portions of Thailand and the Philippines. The desire for sharia law has fueled separatist Islamic rebellions since the 1950s, as Indonesian's central government insisted the province remain subject to the country's secular constitution. In 2001, Aceh was allowed to implement sharia law for Muslims (though not for Aceh's minority Christian or Buddhist populations) in an attempt to appease the rebels. Special sharia courts and "morality" police were created. The rest of Indonesia, the world's largest Muslim country, continues to use a secular, constitutional legal system.

All Western forms of modernity in Aceh accommodate themselves to Islam: signs hang in internet cafes asking men and women not to share computers; the TVs in roadside coffee shops rarely show the provocative music videos common elsewhere in Indonesia, sticking instead to soccer; and though Acehnese women might wear jeans, they also cover their hair with headscarves. For a Muslim woman to show her hair on the streets is an offense punishable by law.

It is the responsibility of the sharia police to enforce prohibitions on infractions such as drinking, failure to attend Friday prayers, and all actions *mesum* (sexually inappropriate), from premarital sex to failing to wear a *jilbab*, a headscarf. Punishments can include: caning, fines, and public shaming, including having buckets of sewage dumped on offenders in front of a crowd. Although such cases are extremely rare, sharia courts can also sentence adulterers to be stoned to death. The most powerful enforcer of Islamic standards, however, is the censure and gossip of Acehnese society.

15   Correct dress and fashion for women are fraught issues in many Islamic communities. According to most Acehnese interpretations of the Koran, it is only appropriate for women to show their faces, hands, and feet. The neck and ears are a gray, verging into black, area.

But Banda Aceh is not Afghanistan or Pakistan. Burkas, the black "body tents" that conceal everything but a woman's eyes, are extremely rare.

Walking down the street reveals *jilbabs* of all colors and styles are combined in inventive ways with Western, Acehnese, and Islamic outfits. A daring student sports a sheer lime-green headscarf above a knee length dress and leggings; an old woman carries a basket of mangos on top of a tightly wound pashmina, her loose robe tangling around her; a housewife hurries down the street to buy sugar at a neighborhood convenience store, wearing only pajamas and a *jilbab songkok*, a pre-made headscarf favored for its ease of use; a rich woman keeps her chin high, careful not to disturb the elaborate, almost sculptural folds of her sequined veil....

The number of styles is almost endless, as are the signals they send, in a society that very much judges a woman on what she wears.

Aisha and Putri shop at Suzuya, Banda Aceh's biggest store, whose selection spans from durian fruit to knockoff Calvin Klein underwear. It has the feel of a scaled down Carrefour or Wal-Mart. They like it because they can try on clothes in the aisles and not bother folding them back up correctly, unlike in claustrophobic traditional market stalls where the owner always lurks, peeking over customers' shoulders.

20   Around 3:45 p.m., Putri stops Aisha at a table of discount tablecloths, picks one up, and tries to wraps it around her friend's head. "Here, this is it! And cheap too! Wouldn't you look beautiful?" Putri says, laughing.

Putri describes herself as a "firecracker," "a modern person who lives in *this* place [Banda Aceh]." Certainly, her style calls a lot more attention to itself than Aisha's. Putri wears a black and teal headscarf, the colors alternating in zebra stripes. The headscarf matches her outfit, a black pullover with a shimmering aquamarine dress below. Beneath that are tight black jeans and flip-flops pounded paper thin by long use.

It's often hard to notice Aisha next to the flamboyant Putri. Aisha's headscarf is black and without pattern or texture, wrapped in a simple style, and pinned with an unobtrusive rhinestone brooch. She wears a baggy maroon shirt with knockoff Louis Vuitton symbols stitched onto the sleeves. Her pants and flip-flops are the same mud brown. She thinks of herself as, "A good girl. Simple. Modest. I don't demand a lot." When someone talks to her, she has a habit of stepping back so that if the person reached out to touch her she would remain just beyond their fingertips. She lives at home with her mother who spends most of the day studying Arabic so that she can read the Koran without translation.

"Oh, so you're ready to serve?" Aisha says, slapping away Putri, who is still attempting to wrap the tablecloth around Aisha's head.

They continue through the aisles, heading towards the *jilbab* section. The women appreciate the air conditioning: headscarves and full body clothing are hot, especially in tropical climates. The loudspeakers play the Indonesian equivalent, in both sound and sappiness, of an American Christmas pop tune—"Insyallah," last Ramadan's big hit. When it is time for one of the five daily prayers, the market broadcasts the *azan* over the same loudspeakers.

They start sorting through the hundreds of *jilbabs* piled on the discount tables.   25

There can be almost infinite variation in what constitutes a headscarf. Throughout history, women in cultures across the world have implied modesty and piety by covering their hair, from Catholic Nuns who wear wimples, to the women of modern day Afghanistan who veil themselves with burkas.

The Islamic practice for veiling derives mainly from the following passage in the Koran, though there are other shorter elaborating verses and *hadith*. In them, Allah commands through Muhammad:

> O Prophet! Tell your wives and your daughters and the women of the believers to draw their *jalabib* [cloaks or veils] all over their

bodies. That will be better, that they should be known [as Muslim women], so as not to be bothered. And Allah is Ever Oft-Forgiving, Most Merciful.

What exactly women are being ordered to do has been heatedly debated ever since. Some Muslim religious authorities have interpreted the passage as a directive for women to cover everything except their eyes—or even a single eye, which is all that is necessary to see with. Others take a more relativist approach, recommending that women should be modest within the context of their society and time. Anthropologists have suggested that the full body burkas worn today are significantly more cumbersome than those worn in Muhammad's time.

Westerners often think of headscarves as designed to cover only a woman's hair, but they are also technically supposed to cover a woman's breasts as well. This directive is often obeyed cursorily, with women dangling a perfunctory corner of scarf down their fronts. A more orthodox woman, however, will wear a veil that covers her chest, or even extends to the waist.

30   The word *jilbab* in most Islamic countries denotes a long veil that fully covers a woman, often to the ankles, but in Indonesia it refers only to headscarves. Indonesian *jilbabs* come in a diversity of colors and materials. They can be arranged in an infinite variety of styles, left loosely flowing or arranged into artistic shapes with the help of pins. All sorts of accessories can be added, from glittering brooches to sun-visors. For every occasion, from playing volleyball to praying, there is a different kind of veil.

Today, in Indonesia, the first choice a potential *jilbab* buyer has to make is "pre-made" or "loose." Pre-made *jilbabs*, also known as *jilbab songkok*, are already formed, with a hood, facial opening, and drape sewn into place, so that a user only has to pull it on to be presentable. *Jilbab songkok* are considered unfashionable in Banda Aceh, partly because of their popularity in the province's many remote villages where women are more concerned with ease than style. These kinds of *jilbabs* are especially popular with children; many are made to look like popular cartoon characters or animals. A *jilbab songkok* with stuffed ears sewn onto the hood and tiger stripes was especially popular during the 2011 Ramadan season in Banda Aceh.

Aisha chooses a "loose" *jilbab*.

A "loose" or "free" *jilbab* starts as a square of cloth, usually measuring three feet long and two feet wide. They have to be arranged and pinned. Extra fabric allows for more elaborate designs, such as sculpted folds and whorls, while smaller cloths create tighter, sleeker fits. Scarves come in all colors and patterns, each with its own meaning. Dark solid colors convey conservatism or modesty; patterns of sequins or fancy stitching, often depicting flowers or religious themes, indicate wealth; western or non-traditional symbols, such as leopard skin or even the anarchist "A" show the wearer is "less fanatical," in Putri's words.

Paying attention to color is especially important when a woman is choosing a *jilbab* because Indonesia's standards of beauty favor pale skin. A woman with dusky skin can't wear a dark hue for fear of making her skin seem blacker, while those with middling skin tones tend towards neutral colors like pinks and creams to whiten their complexions by association. Only the luckiest, and fairest, can get away with bright hues; sometimes, Aisha gets jealous just seeing an orange *jilbab* float through a crowd. Her favorite color is orange and it has always seemed unfair that she cannot wear the color because of her muddy complexion.

"How about this?" Putri says, holding up an ocean blue scarf, with 35 a light blue and white pattern, like watercolor clouds, brushed on. By 4:15 p.m., the friends have thoroughly searched all the *jilbabs* in the store and winnowed them to four selections.

"I don't want Fajar to think I'm already married to the American president," Aisha answers. The headscarf Putri is waving is known as the "Obama headscarf" because of its popularity after the first lady of the USA wore it on a diplomatic visit to Indonesia in 2010.

So they're down to three *jilbabs*: the first is simple, black and unadorned except for a thin fringe of lace; the next is a leaf green scarf that still signals conservatism—the color reportedly was Muhammad's favorite—but which is a little more eye-grabbing than the black veil; the final choice is an almost-sheer magenta headscarf with tassels strung with ruby-colored plastic globes. But now the friends are stuck.

Part of the problem is that they can't figure out what, exactly, Fajar wants. Is he looking for a modern woman, someone with a little bit of flair and westernized views? Should they signal with the magenta *jilbab* that Aisha is bolder than the average woman?

Or does Fajar want someone more traditional? Will he be embarrassed by a showy *jilbab*, but impressed by Aisha's modesty and humility in wearing a simpler scarf? Or might the black or leaf-green *jilbab* strike him as dull and chilly and turn him off?

40   Aisha also has to consider her neighbors: what would they think if they saw her in the magenta, tasseled veil? They argue the choices over and over.

"You say he has the *zabiba*, that he's so religious. So chose something that would appeal to an *imam*," Putri says, exasperated. She had been pushing for something bolder even than the magenta *jilbab*, pointing out the tasseled scarf isn't *that* radical.

Eventually, they decide it is better to play it safe. No one will be offended by a conservative *jilbab*, but Fajar could discount Aisha immediately for wearing the magenta headscarf.

"Even if many guys say they don't want a traditional wife, they really do, deep down. Or want you to act like one, for most things," Aisha points out. That advice has been rattling in her head since reading an article in *Paras*, an Indonesian fashion magazine.

The magenta scarf is flung back onto the table.

45   Next, Aisha decides, "Green makes my skin look yellow," and picks up the black *jilbab*.

Aisha recognizes the black headscarf as the closest to what she'd wear in everyday life. "If I wear that one," she says, pointing to the magenta headscarf with the tassels, "it's like false advertising." As she looks at herself in the mirror, the black *jilbab* with its fringe of lace framing her face, she sees a version of herself which is just a little bit prettier, a little bit more elegant, than the everyday, but which is still *her*.

"You do look really pretty," Putri says, laying her head on Aisha's shoulder.

Now it's time to assemble the rest of the outfit. Putri parades graphic t-shirts with snarky cartoons on the front, but she knows Aisha won't bite—she's mostly doing it for her own amusement. Aisha has taken out a selection of *Paras* Indonesian fashion magazines and is paging through them for inspiration. Finally, she settles on a flowing white blouse, with top like a man's formal shirt with a collar and a row of buttons, but a skirt bottom that billows out, ending just below the knees. "I'd like him to think I am a business woman, that I'm successful, but the dress shows I am still a woman," Aisha explains.

In the shoes department, as it strikes 4:30 p.m., Aisha falls for a pair of gleaming white pumps with a tiny window at the front so her big toe can be seen, but which otherwise cover her skin. No arguments from Putri: the shoes are that nice. Since the dress and shoes are both white, they decide that color is obviously the theme of the outfit. So that Aisha doesn't look like a blank canvas, they add purple waist-belt and cream colored slacks. Putri likes the first pair of pants Aisha tries on, which show a half-moon of her plump bottom, but Aisha decides to buy a size up. "Better safe than sorry," she says again. That too is a sentiment from an article in *Paras*.

Jilbabs and headscarves are part of a greater Islamic practice known as 50 *hijab*, an Arabic word which means "cover" or "curtain." *Hijab* usually refers to appropriate Islamic dress for women, of which a *jilbab* is just a part. Body contours are allowed to be vaguely discernible, but too-tight clothing is looked on as "cheating" and "and not much different from being naked." *Hijab* can also mean the veil, impossible to penetrate, drawn between man and Allah.

Some Islamic theorists, especially those supporting burkas, suggest that *hijab* was established not only to protect female modesty from men, but to guard women against their own vanity. A black featureless sheet, they argue, makes it hard to be vain about one's body or clothing, allowing a woman to focus on spiritual concerns.

In Islamic countries where burkas are not the norm, *hajib* has often had the opposite effect, making women extremely conscious of their dress. Women are brought up to see their clothes as expressing their religion and identities. Expecting to be judged on their dress, women calibrate their outfits down to the smallest accessory. Because so much attention is focused on women's clothing, fashion becomes especially important to the population. The Middle East plays a key role in supporting the French *haute couture* industry, though most of the designer garments are shown off only in private.

Just as there are glossy fashion magazines in the West, they exist too in Indonesia, albeit without showing an inch of skin besides the face and hands. Walk into any bookstore and you will find magazines pitched to every degree of religiosity. The most liberal magazines are the international stalwarts, *Vogue*, etc., translated into Indonesian, with the same photos as anywhere else, and a few country-specific articles thrown in, but those are difficult to find in Banda Aceh. Magazines targeted at Muslim women, such as *Paras*, are more popular in Aceh and significantly more conservative, showing only hand and facial skin, though occasionally there are suggestive form-hugging outfits and articles like, "Sex: The First Night" and "Asymmetrical *Jilbab* Arrangement." Truly conservative magazines feature burkas. All of them are filled out with recipes, gossipy profiles of Indonesian or Arab pop stars, light reportage, informative articles about Islam (a sample title, "Islamic Info: the Tradition of Kissing the Hand"), and encouragement to remain true to the magazine's interpretation Islam. They also, of course, display sponsored fashion shoots, advertisements, and pages of outfits and beauty products.

In one advertisement titled, "Secret Garden Collection," an Indonesian woman with very white skin poses before the ivy-entangled wall of an English manor, leaning slightly into the vines as if pushed by an invisible force. She wears a duchess's riding jacket with a pattern of roses, a high-waisted Victorian dress which nearly screams "corset beneath!" and a red velvet sunhat with a gift-wrap bow. Mixed in with all this is a *jilbab* and, in a quirk of some Indonesian models, a wedding ring.

55   Many of the fashions displayed in the magazines and most of the outfits seen in Banda Aceh's packed cafes on a Saturday night rely on suggestion. Putri, for example, has been noticing a certain style: a bang carefully combed so that it dangles just under the lip of the *jilbab*, almost like gravity has innocently teased it into that position. What is that lock hinting at?

Aisha and Putri analyze the bang like it is evidence in a murder mystery. When Putri tries to explain her reactions to the hairstyle, she finds herself tripping on her own words. Perhaps what she means by calling it "sexy but not really sexy" is that the hair is not explicitly flirtatious, but rather hints that the woman *has* sexuality—but is that actually seductive? More importantly, that twist of hair suggests the girl disagrees with the authorities, that she's braver, a little westernized. . . .

Aisha points out that maybe the bang signals the girl is "approachable," that you could "ask her on a date." Putri picks up on this, "Some women in Banda Aceh do not date before they get married. Sometimes the guy shows up, asks her father first, talks to her last, and right away, that day, it's agreed. Maybe it's a way to have a choice about guys. Because it's a lot harder to ask someone on a date if they're in a very religious *jilbab*."

In the end, neither Aisha nor Putri can quite pin the styled bang down. They agree it probably has meanings they can't puzzle out. What is the bang trying to say? Maybe only the woman knows. Maybe the woman couldn't quite say herself.

By now, it's 5:15 p.m., and Aisha is supposed to meet Fajar at 7:30 p.m., after the *magrib* evening prayers. As they hustle towards the cashier, Putri stops and pulls a headscarf from a rack: it is crimson with a leopard-skin pattern of black spots. "How about this one?" she giggles.

Aisha can't stop laughing. "Do you want him to think I am a wild animal?"   60
But Putri gets her to try it on and pulls her to a mirror. The face that stares back at Aisha is recognizable as her own, but also different: someone she only vaguely knows, capable of doing deeds she would never be brave (or stupid) enough to dare. It's like meeting a long lost twin, someone she shares a primordial connection with, but who she doesn't know how to talk to.

"It's so amazing. If you're not going to buy it, I am," Putri says.

When Aisha and Putri get home at 6:00 p.m., they take off their *jilbabs*. *Jilbabs* are required in public by sharia law, but not in private or among family members. Even Aisha is a glad to be free of the scarf now that it's appropriate. The cloth had been scratching her cheek and one of the pins kept poking her in the neck.

A bucket shower is Aisha's first order of business. Aisha's mother takes a break from translating the Koran to cook the two a fortifying snack of fried bananas. After washing, Aisha stands in front of a fan to dry her hair enough to put a headscarf over it.

Once Aisha is dressed, it is time for the *jilbab*. She gathers up her hair, bunching it so that she can slip on a *songkong*, an extra tight-fitting hood that goes under a loose headscarf to make sure no hair escapes (not to be confused with *jilbab sonkong*).

Putri sighs in disgust, "Your hair's so pretty, at least let a few pieces out."   65
If Putri could, she wouldn't wear a *jilbab*. There were times in her youth when she didn't. Even though her rebellious phase was before 2001, when sharia law was made official, she still got plenty of verbal harassment and

"advice" from teachers and authority figures, and overheard the rumors tip-toeing through the neighborhood. Eventually, she proved the whispers true by dating a Norwegian NGO worker after the tsunami. Over the years, one might think she'd have grown numb to the criticism, but that's not the case at all: she's just gotten better at hiding her frustration and hurt. She hopes to get a scholarship soon, to America or Europe, somewhere she can abandon her *jilbab* and all the baggage that goes with it.

When travelling in more liberal parts of Indonesia—in westernized parts of Jakarta or in Indonesian provinces where Christians are the majority—Aisha has experimented with not wearing a headscarf. She liked how the wind tangled in her hair. Even better, her hair didn't smell of sweat after taking her veil off. But ultimately she decided to keep wearing a *jilbab*. She has tried to explain to Putri that it's not that she felt naked or threatened without it—it's that she felt like the style wasn't *her*. The *jilbab* is part of her faith, part of how she sees herself, part of her identity.

In the West, many organizations and individuals have attacked headscarves as anachronistic and repressive. There is an assumption that if women had a choice, they would remove them. Aisha knows many women for whom this is true, but she doubts the majority would. All the other provinces in Indonesia lack sharia law, she reasons, and most women in those places still wear headscarves.

Putri does not agree with Aisha. She is sure that if sharia law were lifted, "ninety percent" of the population would fling off their veils. She believes most women, like her, wear the *jilbab* in frustrated acquiescence. "Just look at the teenagers downtown on a Saturday night. Already some of them are getting braver. Sometimes they wear very loose veils, sometimes none at all. I like seeing their hair. It is beautiful."

70   The exact number of women who would choose either side is uncertain. Apocryphal figures about how many Acehnese women wore *jilbabs* before sharia law was introduced vary wildly, usually depending on the speaker's degree of religious devotion. (Though it is perhaps telling that liberals confidently claim ninety percent of people would abandon their *jilbabs*, while conservatives hedge and haw, before asserting that "less than half, maybe forty percent, would remove their veils: many of the young people don't like it.") Both sides claim a silent majority. Both allege a higher moral ground. Liberal activists claim the practice is Neolithic and barbaric. Some male *imams* warn that if a woman does not wear a *jilbab* she will go to hell.

One point, however, most women, liberal and conservative, seem to agree on, is that individuals who abstain from wearing *jilbabs* are not damned.

"How do people even know," Putri asks, "exactly what someone was saying a thousand years ago meant? Maybe Muhammad only meant it for his time. And there are a lot of interpretations of those verses. They can't say I'm going to hell for not wearing it."

"Allah," Aisha agrees, "is very kind. Allah is mostly concerned with people not doing evil, not hurting each other. It is pretty silly saying you'll go to hell for not wearing a *jilbab*."

Most women they know hold a similarly benign view of future punishments. It is usually men who make more drastic claims.

As for accusations that *jilbabs* are repressive and anachronistic, Banda Aceh's women are acutely aware of the image of headscarves in Western eyes. Less than two weeks before Aisha's date with Fajar, students from Banda Aceh's universities took over the main intersection in the city, waving placards that read, "I am beautiful in my *jilbab*." Some of the women wore very conservative dress with their headscarves; others matched their veils with jeans and other Western clothes. They were protesting French laws that ban headscarves in public institutions and burkas outside the home. 75

Putri cheers the French ban on headscarves, her smirk suggesting she sees irony in other Muslim woman being forbidden to wear veils while she is forced to cover up. When asked to describe what it feels like to wear a *jilbab*, her voice roughens with frustration and humiliation. "How can I be myself wearing this? Headscarves stop me from being myself; they stop society from being fair in judging people because no one sees *me* when I don't wear *this*. They only see—," she flails her hand. "It makes it impossible to be equal between men and women. And it stops me from being normal and accepted in the international community. They will always look down on me because I am a Muslim."

Part of France's rational for banning veils is that they erase a woman's identity. But, according to Aisha, while full-body burkas strip women of their identities, *jilbabs* do not always do so. Certainly, a *burka* is very different than the *jilbab* Aisha now wears: as Aisha looks into the mirror, she recognizes herself. The simple black cloth with the fringe of lace—it's her—the same way the aquamarine and black zebra-stripe *jilbab* is, in some way, Putri. Aisha would be concealing something if she didn't wear it.

At 6:45 p.m., Putri paints Aisha's toenails red so that her big toe shines bright as a diamond, emphasized by the oval window in the toe of her white shoe. The single drop of color is glaringly evident against the otherwise white and black outfit.

Aisha dusts her face with whitening powder. Its crisp dryness and sweet smell sooths her nerves. Then she completes her preparations by pinning the folds of her *jilbab* across her chest with an heirloom brooch. Her grandmother, who lived before the implementation of sharia law, once used the same piece of jewelry to fasten her *jilbab* on holidays or when her grandchildren came to visit. That is when the old woman wore a *jilbab*. Sometimes she chose not to.

80   Aisha pulls into the parking lot of Q&L Coffee fashionably late, at 7:40 p.m.

She glances around, wondering if she will see Fajar lounging at a table, smoking, scrutinizing her. Instead, a young couple rushes by, almost elbowing her into the gutter.

Aisha is about to snap at them, but then she notices the girl's headscarf: it is not crimson, but it has a leopard-print pattern. She stares at their retreating backs, noticing how close they walk, a thin inch apart, with such comfortable familiarity that she is sure they must touch when no one else is around. She remembers the girl's face: pouty, a little defiant, certainly in love.

What if Aisha had worn the crimson leopard-print headscarf? She has a vision of herself in that *jilbab*, strutting into the café, a different person, another future waiting for her. Some part of her will always be wondering what it would be like to sport a provocative headscarf, even to let her hair free, just as she knows Putri will always be questioning, in the attic of her heart, if it is her divinely mandated duty to happily wear a *jilbab*.

Aisha shakes the question away. *I am who I am*, she thinks. She takes out a pocket mirror, adjusts the black *jilbab*, and reapplies her lipstick.

85   She is ready to be judged.

(Author's note: A few names, places, and events have been altered to protect individuals who participated in this project.)

Analyze

1. The author seems to have access to the inner thoughts of both women in his essay. How do you imagine he gained access to them? How does that affect your confidence in the authenticity of the reading? Under what conditions do you think it's permissible to "connect the dots" or make interpretations in your writing without revealing or verifying your sources?

2. "She has tried to explain to Putri that it's not that she felt naked or threatened without it—it's that she felt like the style wasn't *her*. The *jilbab* is part of her faith, part of how she sees herself, part of her identity" (paragraph 67). How is wearing a *jilbab* the same as or different from wearing a uniform? Describe a time when you had to wear something (like a uniform) for a professional, religious, or official reason. Did it become part of your identity?

3. Do you consider yourself more like Putri or Aisha when you prepare yourself to go out in the social world? Why?

Explore

1. "Only the luckiest, and fairest, can get away with bright hues; sometimes, Aisha gets jealous just seeing an orange *jilbab* float through a crowd. Her favorite color is orange and it has always seemed unfair that she cannot wear the color because of her muddy complexion." Drawing from Clark's observations of beauty in this selection, write an essay in which you consider standards of beauty in your own cultural and/or religious background. Explain how it determines what you choose (or don't choose) to wear.

2. "The number of styles is almost endless, as are the signals they send, in a society that very much judges a woman on what she wears" Create a visual presentation of the different veils worn by Islamic women that answers the question, "What signals do veils send in Islamic society?" Although this is open to your interpretation, you should provide a research-substantiated rationale for that interpretation. In analyzing these signals, what insight have you gained about wearing veils?

3. Imitating Clark's article, write a third-person narrative about a man or woman choosing what to wear and deciding how to present him- or herself on a date. As Clark did, choose someone from outside your

immediate culture (you may need to do research on customs and gender roles, among other topics). Be sure to include two different characters to represent contrasting views as Clark did with Putri and Aisha.

Leila Ahmed
"Reinventing the Veil"

Leila Ahmed is the Victor S. Thomas Professor of Divinity at the Harvard Divinity School. She is the author of *A Quiet Revolution: The Veil's Resurgence from the Middle East to America* (Yale University Press, 2012), which examines the history of veil-wearing in Egypt and challenges the common assumption that its resurgence signifies a step backward for Muslim women. The following article on this subject was published on May 20, 2011, in the *Financial Times Magazine*, which covers world events, politics, and art from a global perspective. In her research, Ahmed encountered many young Egyptian women who wear the veil not in obedience to patriarchal traditions, but as a way of "raising consciousness about the sexist messages of our society."

Is there such a thing as a courageous—or dangerous—statement to be made by your choice of dress in your community? If you could signal your religious faith or political affiliation to the world through something as visible as a veil, would you? In what contexts?

I grew up in Cairo, Egypt. Through the decades of my childhood and youth—the 1940s, 1950s and 1960s—the veil was a rarity not only at home but in many Arab and Muslim-majority cities. In fact, when Albert Hourani, the Oxford historian, surveyed the Arab world in the mid-1950s, he predicted that the veil would soon be a thing of the past.

Hourani's prophecy, made in an article called *The Vanishing Veil: A Challenge to the Old Order*, would prove spectacularly wrong, but his piece is nevertheless a gem because it so perfectly captures the ethos of that era. Already the veil was becoming less and less common in my own country, and, as Hourani explains, it was fast disappearing in other "advanced Arab countries", such as Syria, Iraq and Jordan as well. An unveiling movement had begun to sweep across the Arab world, gaining momentum with the spread of education.

In those days, we shared all of Hourani's views and assumptions, including the connections he made between unveiling, "advancement" and education (and between veiling and "backwardness"). We believed the veil was merely a cultural habit, of no relevance to Islam or to religious piety. Even deeply devout women did not wear a hijab. Being unveiled simply seemed the modern "advanced" way of being Muslim.

Consequently the veil's steady "return" from the mid-1980s, and its growing adoption, disturbed us. It was very troubling for people like me who had been working for years as feminists on women and Islam. Why would educated women, particularly those living in free western societies where they could dress as they wished, be willing (apparently) to take on this symbol of patriarchy and women's oppression?

The appearance of the hijab in my own neighbourhood of Cambridge,   5 Massachusetts, in the late 1990s was the trigger that launched my own studies into the phenomenon. I well remember the very evening that generated that spark. While I was walking past the common with a friend, a well-known feminist who was visiting from the Arab world, we saw a large crowd with all the women in hijab. At the time, this was still an unusual sight and, frankly, it left us both with distinct misgivings.

While troubling on feminist grounds, the veil's return also disturbed me in other ways. Having settled in the US, I had watched from afar through the 1980s and 1990s as cities back home that I had known as places where scarcely anyone wore hijab were steadily transformed into streets where the vast majority of women now wore it.

This visually dramatic revolution in women's dress changed, to my eyes, the very look and atmosphere of those cities. It had come about as a result of the spread of Islamism in the 1970s, a very political form of Islam that was worlds away from the deeply inward, apolitical form that had been common in Egypt in my day. Fuelled by the Muslim Brotherhood, the spread of Islamism always brought its signature emblem: the hijab.

Those same decades were marked in Egypt by rising levels of violence and intellectual repression. In 1992, Farag Foda, a well-known journalist and critic of Islamism, was gunned down. Nasr Hamid Abu Zayd, a professor at Cairo University, was brought to trial on grounds of apostasy and had to flee the country. Soon after, Naguib Mahfouz, the Egyptian novelist and Nobel Laureate, was stabbed by an Islamist who considered his books blasphemous. Such events seemed a shocking measure of the country's descent into intolerance.

The sight of the hijab on the streets of America brought all this to mind. Was its growing presence a sign that Islamic militancy was on the rise here too? Where were these young women (it was young women in particular who wore it) getting their ideas? And why were they accepting whatever it was they were being told, in this country where it was entirely normal to challenge patriarchal ideas? Could the Muslim Brotherhood have somehow succeeded in gaining a foothold here?

10   My instinctive readings of the Cambridge scene proved correct in some ways. The Brotherhood, as well as other Islamist groups, had indeed established a base in America. While most immigrants were not Islamists, those who were quickly set about founding mosques and other organisations. Many immigrants who grew up as I did, without veils, sent their children to Islamic Sunday schools where they imbibed the Islamist outlook—including the hijab.

The veiled are always the most visible, but today Islamist-influenced people make up no more than 30 to 40 per cent of American Muslims. This is also roughly the percentage of women who veil as opposed to those who do not. This means of course that the majority of Muslim American women do not wear the veil, whether because they are secular or because they see it as an emblem of Islamism rather than Islam.

My research may have confirmed some initial fears, but it also challenged my assumptions. As I studied the process by which women had been persuaded to veil in Egypt in the first place, I came to see how essential women themselves had been in its promotion and the cause of Islamism. Among the most important was Zainab al-Ghazali, the "unsung mother" of the Muslim Brotherhood and a forceful activist who had helped keep the organisation going after the death of its founder.

For these women, adopting hijab could be advantageous. Joining Islamist groups and changing dress sometimes empowered them in relation to their parents; it also expanded job and marriage possibilities. Also, since the veil advertised women's commitment to conservative sexual mores, wearing it paradoxically increased their ability to move freely in public space—allowing them to take jobs in offices shared with men.

My assumptions about the veil's patriarchal meanings began to unravel in the first interviews I conducted. One woman explained that she wore it as a way of raising consciousness about the sexist messages of our society. (This reminded me of the bra-burning days in America when some women refused to shave their legs in a similar protest.) Another wore the hijab for the same reason that one of her Jewish friends wore a yarmulke: this was religiously required dress that made visible the presence of a minority who were entitled, like all citizens, to justice and equality. For many others, wearing hijab was a way of affirming pride and rejecting negative stereotypes (like the Afros that flourished in the 1960s among African-Americans).

Both Islamist and American ideals—including American ideals of   15
gender justice—seamlessly interweave in the lives of many of this younger generation. This has been a truly remarkable decade as regards Muslim women's activism. Perhaps the post-9/11 atmosphere in the west, which led to intense criticism of Islam and its views of women, spurred Muslim Americans into corrective action. Women are reinterpreting key religious texts, including the Koran, and they have now taken on positions of leadership in Muslim American institutions: Ingrid Mattson, for example, was twice elected president of the Islamic Society of North America. Such female leadership is unprecedented in the home countries: even al-Ghazali, vital as she was to the Brotherhood, never formally presided over an organisation which included men.

Many of these women—although not all—wear hijab. Clearly here in the west, where women are free to wear what they want, the veil can have multiple meanings. These are typically a far cry from the old notions which I grew up with, and profoundly different from the veil's ancient patriarchal meanings, which are still in full force in some countries. Here in the west—embedded in the context of democracy, pluralism and a commitment to gender justice—women's hijabs can have meanings that they could not possibly have in countries which do not even subscribe to the idea of equality.

But things are changing here as well. Interestingly, the issue of hijab and whether it is religiously required or not is now coming under scrutiny among women who grew up wearing it. Some are re-reading old texts and concluding that the veil is irrelevant to Islamic piety. They cast it off even as they remain committed Muslims.

It is too soon to tell whether this development, emerging most particularly among intellectual women who once wore hijab, will gather force and become a new unveiling movement for the 21st century: one that repeats, on other continents and in completely new ways, the unveiling movement of the early 20th century. Still, in a time when a number of countries have tried banning the hijab and when typically such rules have backfired, it is worth noting that here in America, where there are no such bans, a new movement may be quietly getting under way, a movement led this time by committed Muslim women who once wore hijab and who, often after much thought and study, have taken the decision to set it aside.

Occasionally now, although less so than in the past, I find myself nostalgic for the Islam of my childhood and youth, an Islam without veils and far removed from politics. An Islam which people seemed to follow not in the prescribed, regimented ways of today but rather according to their own inner sense, and their own particular temperaments, inclinations and the shifting vicissitudes of their lives.

20   I think my occasional yearning for that now bygone world has abated (not that it is entirely gone) for a number of reasons. As I followed, a little like a detective, the extraordinary twists and turns of history that brought about this entirely unpredicted and unlikely "return" of the veil, I found the story itself so absorbing that I seemed to forget my nostalgia. I also lost the vague sense of annoyance, almost of affront, that I'd had over the years at how history had, seemingly so casually, set aside the entirely reasonable hopes and possibilities of that brighter and now vanished era.

In the process I came to see clearly what I had long known abstractly: that living religions are by definition dynamic. Witness the fact that today we have women priests and rabbis—something unheard of just decades ago. As I followed the shifting history of the veil—a history which had reversed directions twice in one century—I realised that I had lived through one of the great sea changes now overtaking Islam. My own assumptions and the very ground they stood on had been fundamentally challenged. It now seems absurd that we once labelled people who veiled "backward" and those who did not "advanced", and that we thought that it was perfectly fine and reasonable to do so. Seeing one's own life from a new perspective can be unsettling, of course—but it is also quite bracing, and even rather exciting.

Analyze

1. What is the difference between Islamism and Islam according to Ahmed?
2. Why does the author say that her research "may have confirmed some initial fears," but that it also challenged her assumptions? What were

her fears? What were her assumptions? How does she feel about the veil by the end of the reading?

3. What other significant clothing item, accessory, or body art has gone through a reinvention similar to the way the author describes the reinvention of the veil?

Explore

1. Choose a particular region or culture and create (either on hard copy or digitally) a visual timeline of how women and men dressed. Be sure to cite your sources for each outfit. Write a brief analysis of how each costume represents gender roles for that period and the influences— cultural, geopolitical, and/or historical—that influenced its change.

2. In paragraph 16 Ahmed notes, "Here in the west—embedded in the context of democracy, pluralism and a commitment to gender justice— women's hijabs can have meanings that they could not possibly have in countries which do not even subscribe to the idea of equality." Do you feel there is "a commitment to gender justice" in your own society? Why or why not? What is your evidence?

3. One country that has banned women wearing veils in public is France. In 1989, three girls of Moroccan descent were expelled from their middle school because of their refusal to remove their hijabs; the furor has yet to settle. Write a research essay about how this national concern turned into a global controversy.

Oliver Broudy
"Body-Building in Afghanistan"

Freelance journalist Oliver Broudy's magazine assignments have taken him around the world, to China, New Zealand, and Afghanistan. "Body-Building in Afghanistan" was published in the June 2007 issue of *Men's Health* magazine, which focuses on such issues as health, nutrition, lifestyle, travel, and sports. Available in 39 international editions, *Men's Health* is the largest men's magazine brand in the world. In this article, Broudy talks about the "muscle revolution" that has taken over Afghanistan. For some Afghani men, body building has become a metaphor for rebuilding a land torn by war and the Taliban, and a way to draw strength from the rubble.

Why do people work out or exercise in your community?

I 've just agreed to deliver a rug to David Beckham. Not just any rug, but one depicting Beckham himself, midstride, plus all his vital statistics: height, weight, birth date, nationality. If I can take the rug to Beckham, the carpet maker reasons, maybe the famous soccer player will agree to provide funding for disabled athletes in Afghanistan. Athletes like himself.

Do I know David Beckham? No. Do I have the slightest idea of how to contact him? No. Then again, consider the following: The man who asked me is ex-mujahideen. He fought the Soviet invasion for 9 years, living like a bee on licks of congealed fruit nectar. The Soviets shot his father when the carpet maker was 14, then his brother 2 years later. In 1989, he took a bullet in the leg. Two of his friends, running beside him, were killed. Three days later, with no anesthesia, a poorly trained doctor amputated the leg with a butcher knife. After the Taliban came into power in 1996, he was thrown into prison for protesting their draconian laws, and was released only after they sold his house and stole his money.

Now this same man is asking me to deliver a rug to a towering celebrity with whom I have no personal connection whatsoever. So, really, how hard could it be?

The rug is the handiwork of Haji Abdul Rahman Mohammadi, the director of a sports association for Afghans disabled by war. I'm talking with him at Kabul Stadium, where the Taliban once sought to solve the crime problem by chopping off the hands of thieves, and the adultery problem by stoning. Today, Afghan workers are squatting in the blood-soaked field, resowing the grass by hand. Outside the stadium, soldiers are honing their parade skills in preparation for Afghan Independence Day on August 19. Independence from whom? The British, in 1919? The Soviets, in 1989? Or the Pakistan-sponsored Taliban, in 2001? When your history is this turbulent, it can be hard to keep track.

5   In Mohammadi's office an assistant serves tea. Someone had referred me to him, thinking he might be able to shed a little light on a question

I had about the recent fitness craze sweeping Afghanistan. Since the fall of the Taliban, 80 new gyms have opened in Kabul alone, up from a total of 15. You see them everywhere, tucked into garage-size storefronts beneath huge pieces of plywood bearing the hulking likeness of Arnold Schwarzenegger, Ronnie Coleman, or some other bodybuilder. The gyms have names like Gold Gym, Super Gym, and Super Gold Top Gym. They stand in the shadow of shattered buildings, beside other shops selling sacks of cement and cases of Coke—the foundations on which all great nations are built.

"The private gyms are suddenly everywhere," Thomas Gouttierre, director of the center for Afghanistan studies at the University of Nebraska at Omaha, had told me before I departed for Kabul. Indeed, during my 2-week stay, it seemed as if a couple of new ones popped up overnight. Other evidence of the get-fit revolution here: Workout gear has replaced burkas on store shelves, protein powder tops every gym-rat's wish list, and the Mr. Afghanistan bodybuilding contest has become the hot ticket.

What, I wanted to know, could possibly explain this trend in a place where 70 percent of the population is chronically malnourished, the average citizen dies before reaching age 45, and the pollution is so thick that even a short ride through downtown Kabul will leave you with a nose full of black snot? How is it that, even as the fanatics are detonating their bodies in the marketplace, in the gyms men of a new generation of Afghans are exercising and building their bodies? For the careful student, there's a lot to learn here about what it means to be strong.

The alarm goes off. It's 8 a.m. Do you really have the juice to hit the gym this morning? As soon as you ask the question, you're in trouble. Now, as you waste time deliberating, sleep takes you by the pinky and pulls you back toward the warm void. The only way to escape is to stop thinking and just move.

Several time zones distant and a few hours earlier, in a dry, dusty place where the per-capita income approximates that of your average gumball machine, another man reaches for his cellphone, to stop the alarm before it starts. You might forgive him for wanting to delay the day. Here's what he has to look forward to: first of all, darkness. It's 4 a.m. when he wakes, and there's no electricity. He locates the lantern by feel, lightly taps the reservoir to check the kerosene level, and slips from the room so as not to wake his two brothers. Feeling his way down the stairs, he heads to the courtyard, where he lights the lantern and washes himself at the well.

10   A more-or-less normal 21-year-old Afghan, Najibullah Mohammed
Shayef (Najib for short) works as a carpenter. Right now he's building a table
for an American rooming house. It should take him about 6 hours. His real
ambition is to be an engineer—building on a larger scale. He was accepted to
study at the local university, but as the sole breadwinner for his family of nine,
he can't afford to go. How, then, to explain Shayef's upbeat attitude, easy
smile, and relaxed manner? And the fact that he wakes before dawn every day
to attend a private English class and work out at the gym, after a breakfast of
bread and tea? Tell me, I say to him. How do you do it? Shayef shrugs. It's
easier in the summer, he admits, when watermelon is in season.

Afghans are a tough, practical people, and not particularly given to
lengthy explanations. (Getting Mohammadi to tell me his story took
hours.) You have to follow them around for a while to understand what
motivates them. Shayef works out at Super Gym, just down the block from
Kabul Stadium. The gym occupies the first floor of what was once a 2- or
perhaps 3-story concrete building. With the current building boom under
way in Kabul, it can sometimes be hard to distinguish the half-built structures from the half-destroyed ones. But when you approach, the bullet-
pocked walls remove all doubt. Rebar blown loose by rocket attacks hangs
from the ceiling, and razor wire swirls along a low wall in front. On an external stairway, red script points the way to a computer class on a floor that
no longer exists. Reduced to its bare bones, the building resembles nothing
so much as a half-demolished parking garage.

Five years ago, Aimal Kabiri beheld this shattered pile and saw promise.
His gym across town had recently been closed by some religious types who
wanted to use the space for an Islamic school. As the owners of the building,
in which Kabiri was merely a squatter, they were within their legal rights.
Kabiri had recently returned from Pakistan, where he had spent the previous
10 years selling ornamental statuary. He had no money, no connections, and
little hope of securing a lease on a new space. Luckily, Kabul has nothing if
not surplus abandoned buildings, so for an enterprising businessman, the
opportunities are endless. With 10 members from his old gym lending a
hand, Kabiri cleared the rubble out of the new location and patched the
holes in the walls. The cleanup took 45 days, and then, with new, modern
weight-lifting machines bought on credit, the gym opened for business.

The building, Kabiri says, used to be occupied by a governmental youth
organization. Conceivably, they could boot him out at any time, but he
doesn't think it likely. And even if they do, he'll just move elsewhere. Today,

the gym has more than 400 members. The membership fee is 400 afghanis a month, or $8. It's not perfect. There's no air-conditioning, and in the summer the mercury regularly blows past 100. In the winter the snow piles up past the razor wire and the temperature drops well below zero. Still, they come, wearing hats and mittens.

Ahmed Khamosh is one of the trainers here. We're sitting in his tiny office, lovingly adorned with posters of Western bodybuilders, grinning Goliaths with biceps as big as horse heads. A dusty shelf holds a row of trophies. The office, like many I visit in Kabul, is jammed with plus-size sofas, an expression of Afghan hospitality and a reflection of how much they like to hang out. Of course, with unemployment at 40 percent here, hanging out for many is a way of life.

"Ambition is dead here," says one of Khamosh's friends. It's easy to be- 15 lieve, given the beating this country has taken in the past 30 years—from the Soviets, then rogue mujahideen, then the Taliban, then the American rescuers, and now the Taliban insurgency. But Khamosh doesn't buy those excuses. He's 22 years old and studying economics at Kabul University. Here's his short list of things to do: 1. Build some factories, so Afghans no longer have to work on the street. 2. Build housing, so Afghans won't have to live in ruins. 3. Build a new university, so Afghans can learn, and better themselves. As we talk, the daylight fades and soon I can no longer see my notebook. I'm scribbling blindly when someone cranks up the generator and the fluorescent lights flicker on, illuminating rows of shiny exercise equipment. Such modern gear is relatively novel here in Kabul, where jacking the handle of a U.N.-supplied water pump remains the most common way to build triceps.

It's in listening to Khamosh that I begin to get a sense of how the fitness trend—something of an oddity, it may seem, in this ravaged land—actually coincides quite sensibly with an underlying natural order. It's an order that begins with rubble. From the rubble they build a gym. In the gym, they build their bodies. And with those bodies, tuned for strength and achievement, they build a nation. When you have nothing, no plumbing, no electricity, no heat, a glass of milk for breakfast if you're lucky, when all you have are your own two arms, your own two legs—and sometimes not even that—that's where you begin.

Khoja Sediqi works out on the north side of town, at the Young Nation Bodybuilding Club (YNBC). "We are tired of war," he says. "We want to be healthy. We want to be famous in the world, not for our fighting, not for war. We want to be famous for our good behavior, our health." The YNBC occupies the basement of a newish apartment building. The neighborhood, constructed post-Taliban, doesn't look like a war zone. It just looks poor. Outside, in the parking lot, an old man shovels dirt into a wheelbarrow. You see men like this everywhere in Kabul. They've been here for thousands of years, shoveling, slaves to the dirt. Inside, men from a younger generation study themselves in mirrors, lifting weights to the beat of Iranian pop. Their workout form leaves something to be desired (you can practically hear the muscle tearing), and their clothing is somewhat unorthodox (many work out in collared shirts and long pants), but unlike gyms in America, where many men tackle their workouts the same way they walk the dog or take out the garbage—joylessly—the atmosphere is energized, hopeful, full of purpose.

Sediqi is built like a pit bull: small but powerfully muscled. The kind of dude you'd want to stuff in a cannon and fire over enemy lines. He caught the fitness bug in Iran, from which he fled in 1997 after the Taliban came to power. Before that, the number of gyms in Kabul could be counted on two hands. They were allowed to remain open, but long pants and long-sleeved shirts were mandatory, even in summer, as were beards. And the Taliban regularly conducted raids to ensure compliance. Anyone found breaking the rules was thrown in prison for 5 days, sometimes longer. Khamosh, the trainer at Super Gym, recalled a time when the Taliban caught him trying to buy a workout shirt at a local store. They beat him senseless with a rubber hose. When his mother objected, they beat her, too, there in the shop.

Sediqi could see what was coming under the Taliban, and wanted no part of it. His flight to Iran is crucial to understanding how Afghanistan works. As one gym owner told me, when trouble comes, the rich split to Europe, and the poor take refuge in places like Iran or Pakistan. When peace is restored, the refugees come streaming back, bringing the foreign culture with them. This explains how communism first came to Afghanistan, by way of the Soviet Union, as well as Wahhabism (one of the more ultraconserva- tive forms of Islam), from Saudi Arabia. And of course bodybuilding, from Pakistan and Iran.

20   That bodybuilding should be the real engine behind the Afghan fitness craze is not surprising. Imagine what it means to be a refugee. You're forced from your home. You can take only so much with you. You hope you can travel with family or friends. You hope you know people who can help you. But maybe you don't. Either way, you're adrift in a foreign place, you speak

the language poorly, and despite your education and experience, you can find only menial work. In the meantime, your country is being overrun by brutes and hooligans, and there's nothing you can do. For all you know, your home has been pillaged, your loved ones slaughtered. You haven't felt this powerless since you were a child.

Then one day you look up and see a billboard of a shirtless dude with biceps like bowling balls. He looks like he could squeeze out Tarzan's last yodel. Strength is always attractive, but never as much as when you're weak. Think of those early Charles Atlas ads that used to run in the back of comic books, showing a bully kicking sand in the face of some skinny kid. Sand is sand, whether it's on a California beach or the arid hills of southern Afghanistan.

And no one likes to be bullied.

But that, and summer melon, is only part of the story for guys like Shayef when the alarm clock goes off at 4 a.m. It takes me a while to understand the rest. The key, it turns out, has been staring me in the face, his sainted image hanging on every wall: the hero of Sediqi and countless other Afghans: Arnold Schwarzenegger. Given the number of signs and billboards on which he appears, you'd be forgiven for thinking he owns half the gyms in Kabul. It makes sense, in a way, this ubiquitous homage. After all, with *Pumping Iron*, the 1977 bodybuilding documentary, Schwarzenegger pretty much single-handedly transformed the image of bodybuilding from an obscure sport followed only by a hardcore group of weirdos to a popular pastime—and the basis of a whole new attitude toward physical health. (Sediqi has seen the movie more than 200 times.) But it goes much deeper than that.

"He has been a symbol here," says Bawar Hotak, the president of the Afghanistan Bodybuilding Federation. "Everyone, when he first starts this exercise, when he first goes to the gym, this is his wish, to become like Arnold." Hotak is as big as Arnold, at 6'3", 247 pounds, with 20-inch biceps. His hands are like Ping-Pong paddles, his fingers too thick for any trigger guard. With his huge, animated face and flaring nostrils, he is one of the more "alive" people I've ever encountered. Talking to him, you have the feeling that at any moment he might just lean across the table and inhale you.

Hotak's passion for Schwarzenegger verges on alarming, so I keep   25
pressing him for exactly what Arnold means to him, as an Afghan. All I hear are answers like, "I am opposite of war, but if a soldier should be the same as he is, it would be so good for defense of his or her country." No doubt there's truth to this, but it still doesn't explain Schwarzenegger's

cultlike status in a country where the only thing showing in the local movie theaters is a view of the mountains, through holes in the wall where the screens used to be.

After talking with Hotak, I pick up a copy of his favorite movie, *Commando*, in hopes of securing some further clue. Notably, the movie is adored not just by Hotak, but also by every other Afghan I talked to. It had been 20 years since I'd seen it last. This time, though, I watch it through the eyes of Hotak.

First you see the boots, crunching through the mountain dust. Then the chain saw, swinging from his right hand. Finally, the legendary biceps. ("His bicep is the most beautiful thing!"—Hotak.) When he comes into full focus, Schwarzenegger is walking out of the forest with a tree trunk on his shoulder, a Paul Bunyan-like figure whose enormous size indicates not just strength but an almost magical exemption from the rules reality imposes on us. Rules like, if a bad guy kidnaps your daughter, you have to do what he says. Or, if a bad guy tears out your truck transmission, you can't chase after him.

The film hasn't aged very well, but who didn't love *Commando* when it was first released? Where before has a hero so concisely embodied the virtues of strength, ethical focus, and self-determination, while still finding time to crack a joke? Expected to roll over and play the victim, Schwarzenegger immediately turns the tables and becomes the predator. Going along with his tormentor's carefully staged game plan never even crosses his mind. And that's what the film is about: not aggression, not winning the game, but controlling it.

For decades Afghans have been the victims in a game far beyond their control as the real players moved their pieces from the Soviet Union, the United Kingdom, even the United States. It should come as no surprise, then, that Afghans love Commando. For them it represents a crucial principle: self-determination. And it's this principle that drives Najib Shayef to the gym every morning. There's an awful lot in life that's beyond his control, from the current Taliban resurgence to his low-paying job, but there is one thing he can control: his own body.

30   Zekria Shafaati, the owner of the YNBC, where Sediqi works out, points out another curious fact about Schwarzenegger. "In most of the Arnold movies I've seen," he says, "I have never seen him making sex with a girl."

It's true. And in a country where most men remain virgins until marriage, the appeal makes sense. Life is hard enough without having to watch your favorite actor get lucky, when you can't even get a peck on the cheek.

Codes of behavior have relaxed since the United States first ousted the Taliban in 2001, but the vibe in Afghanistan today is not exactly spring break. Women in burkas remain a common sight, floating through the streets like ghosts on errands. And women not wearing burkas are sporting chadors, which reveal the eyes but conceal everything else. Meeting ladies is not easy, outside of the Chinese hookers who service the international-aid community, and most Afghans find prostitutes highly distasteful.

There is no bar scene, either, so men work out solely for themselves, to stay fit and ward off unhealthy behavior. In the States, "unhealthy behavior" might mean back-sliding into a cigarette habit. In Afghanistan the stakes are a lot higher: heroin. Afghanistan supplies more than 92 percent of the world's opium. According to the director of Kabul's only drug-treatment program, the city has more than 100,000 addicts, up from 60,000 the previous 2 years. Given the hardship most Afghans face, the balm of a good high is particularly enticing.

Shafaati's gym provides another option. Is it vanity, I ask as we watch big guys flex in the mirror? My translator looks confused. The word "vanity" is new to him. After I explain, he says there is no word for this in Dari. When I finally convey my meaning, Shafaati dismisses my question with a wave. The person we might call vain he calls azkhodrazi—literally, to be in agreement with your body. More broadly, the word describes a person pleased with his own actions. Physical fitness is the basis of good character, Shafaati says, and good character is the basis of success. "We can even call the mirrors teachers," he says, "because they show us where our flaws are."

The gender breakdown at Shafaati's gym is decisive: 400 men, 0 women.   35
We do hear rumors of a women's gym somewhere in Kabul—it's still fairly hush-hush, even 6 years after the fall of the Taliban. We find it one day at the end of a long, meandering drive through the exhaust-clogged streets. The dust in Kabul covers everything. Our driver, Fraydon, was forever (pointlessly, it seemed) wiping down his car. Even the few roads that are paved quickly become dirt roads again. It may be the dust that inspires the fondness for tea in Afghanistan—it's a great cure for a scratchy throat.

The women-only gym occupies a modest one-story structure in east Kabul with a metal roof and peeling pink paint. Heavy curtains cover the windows, one of which is marred by a bullet hole.

An assistant meets us halfway to the door and asks us to wait, which we do, under the blazing Afghan sun. Eventually, the owner, Freshta Farah, comes out to greet us and invite us inside. She has agreed to talk to me, but only because the gym is not officially open at the moment. Farah is 34 years old, with attentive green eyes and luxurious, shoulder-length hair that I'm not supposed to be looking at. She opened this gym 5 months ago, and already it has 350 members. After two trips to the States in 2003 and 2004 to learn how to run a business, she planned to open a driving school and an Internet café, but her friends convinced her that a gym would be more lucrative.

Recently, some of her members quit after the husband of one of her trainers was shot and killed in the street. The trainer was wounded in the attack but survived. I ask Farah for details about the shooting, but she refuses to say more. I strike another sore point when I ask about her sisters. She has 10 of them, but not one is a member of the gym. They all stay at home. She won't say why. All the same, she's going ahead with plans to open up more gyms in the other provinces. At this my translator says something, and Farah laughs lightheartedly. "I told her not to go to the provinces, because she will get killed," my translator says. Then tea is served.

The gym itself resembles a modern office space: one large, gray-carpeted room with exercise bikes and weight machines around the perimeter. The walls are bare—no pictures of Arnold. The women here like to be fit, Farah says, but not for men. The small vein on my translator's temple starts pounding as he struggles to render her meaning: "Just to have dress on and look in a beautiful body, they stand in front of the mirror and see themselves nice and beautiful," he manages finally, concluding with a shrug. "So they enjoy themselves. That is no problem."

40   I ask about her toenails, which are painted purple. There is a difference, she explains, between Islam and tradition. "Islam is a free religion, and some of the people prefer their tradition to Islam." It is tradition, for instance, that mandates the burka—not Islam. Nor does Islam have much to say on the subject of toenails.

Does she look toward a day when men and women can work out together and be free of all these restrictions? Her answer, surprisingly, is no. Her tradition is strong, and just because she wants to be able to exercise doesn't mean she's prepared to cast that tradition aside.

The conversation with the intrepid Farah returns me to my original question about what it means to be strong. Hotak had told me how Afghan bodybuilders used to keep fit by benching tank parts. In the brutally efficient economy that hard times give rise to, scavengers would strip abandoned Soviet hardware and sell whatever they salvaged. The tread sprockets from old Soviet T62s—ideal for weight lifting—would go for a fraction of a dollar. The treads found new life as speed bumps. One day my photographer ran across an old Olympic swimming pool, built by the Soviets in the mid-'80s. It never held water, but the Taliban are said to have used it as an instrument of justice. Homosexuals and political dissidents were shoved from the highest diving board, and those who survived the fall were considered innocent. Today, Afghan youth use the pool as a soccer field.

Strength is resourcefulness, determination, adaptability in the face of the most challenging conditions. Imagine what it's like to be invaded. How would you respond? What if you were hopelessly outnumbered? What if members of your family had been killed? Where is that hard point within you that keeps you straight and strong? That steel shank that runs through your core?

I bring these questions to a man I think may be able to answer them, an ex-mujahideen who now makes his living peddling spare parts, gathering the broken pieces of his country so others can put something together with them. Abdel Khayum waited until he was 16, and then he went to war. His father was killed by the Soviets 2 years prior, in 1981, shot in the foot, the stomach, and the forehead. Khayum was living in Kabul at the time but moved north with his family to Panjshir. When the Soviets came, searching house to house for mujahideen, he and his family hid in the mountains. His grand-parents were too old to hide. His grandfather was knifed to death in his house. Rather than face capture, his grandmother jumped from a cliff into the Panjshir River. The river was running fast. Her body was never found.

Khayum sits across from me in a sparse office near Kabul Stadium. He is broad-shouldered, with a black weight-lifting belt around his waist. He has thick, sturdy legs—one made of flesh, the other of plastic. He is 39 years old, but like many Afghans, he looks 10 years older. He fought the Soviets for 6 years, and after that fought for the fledgling Afghan government against rogue mujahideen. He remembers going to the tailor to pick up a shirt one morning, then hearing the sounds of war approaching. He remembers running toward the fighting, gun drawn, when a jolt from below dropped him into the dirt. He remembers trying to stand up three times before he realized why he couldn't. The answer lay a few yards away, wearing one of the boots he had pulled on that morning. A land mine had taken his leg.

Khayum can't run anymore, so he lifts weights instead, every day. The events of his life do not seem to have altered his resolve. I ask him how this can be, and he tells me a story. It's an old story, from a time before Islam. The country was under attack by foreign invaders, but they were repulsed again and again. When the would-be conquerors returned to their own country, their people asked them, What country is this that has beaten you so thoroughly? The warriors couldn't answer. So the people said, Go and bring us some of the dust of this place, so that we may learn. So the soldiers went, and they brought back the dust. When the people shook the dust loose, it rose in the air and they fought against it, swinging their arms and covering their faces. That's when they understood that just to survive in an inhospitable place like Afghanistan, you have to be a fighter, someone who does not ever give up.

Khayum finishes his story and laughs shyly, tapping his plastic leg. Later, he invites me to his home, 30 minutes away by car, 45 on foot. It was destroyed by war, but he's rebuilt most of it. He leads me to a red-carpeted sitting room, intact by all appearances. A square of sunlight hits the northern wall. Soon, his 5-year-old son comes in carrying a bottle fully half his height. A metal tray holds glasses. The boy pours the tea, washing a little into each cup to rinse out the dust, and then filling each glass to the brim. We sit there in the quiet of the afternoon, cross-legged on the floor.

Khayum's son is very excited about the new Spider-Man movie. Did he know, I ask him, that in New York everyone travels by web? The boy smiles dubiously, reluctant to offend his guest. I ask what he wants to be when he grows up. He doesn't hesitate. Like most sons in Afghanistan, he dreams of being an engineer.

The children here grow up listening to their fathers. They want to build.

Analyze

1. Of the young bodybuilders he profiles, Broudy observes: "When all you have are your own two arms, your own two legs—and sometimes not even that—that's where you begin." What do you think Broudy means by this statement?

2. Who is the "new generation of Afghans exercising and building their bodies" to whom Broudy refers? What does the author discover about them?

3. Broudy defines strength as "resourcefulness, determination, adaptability in the face of the most challenging conditions." How does he arrive

at this definition? Do you think men and women have different kinds of strength? In what ways and under what conditions? How does Broudy's article confirm or challenge your opinion?

Explore

1. Broudy summarizes Khamosh's "short list of things to do" in paragraph 15: "1. Build some factories, so Afghans no longer have to work on the street. 2. Build housing, so Afghans won't have to live in ruins. 3. Build a new university, so Afghans can learn, and better themselves." Write your own comparable "short list of things to do." How does your list compare to Khamosh's?

2. The men Broudy interviews have been visited by extreme violence as have members of their families. How has the legacy of violence affected their identities as men? What might men (and women) from other cultures and nations learn from the Afghani men interviewed in this article?

3. How did Broudy shape his language and choose his words and content to appeal to the readership of *Men's Health*? Did you find his writing stereotypically male? Look at other articles from *Men's Health*, and then consider an international magazine that is geared more toward women. What words, phrases, and topic matters have been chosen to appeal to each gender? What are the exceptions, if any? Have they appealed to you and your peers? As an editor of an international magazine appealing to either men or women, how would you advise your authors to address an audience of one gender or another?

Mark Levine
"Killing Emos, and the Future, in Iraq"

Mark Levine is a professor of Middle Eastern history at the University of California, Irvine, and a distinguished visiting professor at the Center for Middle Eastern Studies at Lund University in Sweden. His research interests focus on the role of music in political struggles, culture jamming, and critical

theory. An author of several books, he is also a journalist and regular contributor to *Al Jazeera* English, part of the Qatar-based Al Jazeera news organization. In the following article, which appeared on the *Al Jazeera* website
on March 20, 2012, Levine examines the 2012 murders of young Iraqis who
shared an interest in "emo" music.

What kinds of circumstances lead to people being ostracized for their
tastes in music, art, or fashion?

With everything else plaguing Iraq today—continued sectarianism,
rampant corruption, irregular electricity, barely functioning healthcare, ten years' worth of depleted uranium shells (courtesy of the US occupation) causing cancer and birth defects—hardcore Shia militants have
decided that the gravest threat to Iraq comes from the small (but growing)
number of fans of the genre of post-punk music known as "emo".

In the past several weeks, an unknown number of young Iraqis have
been murdered—in cold blood—reportedly because of their supposed love
for emo, a genre of hardcore rock that emerged in Washington, D.C., in the
late 1980s and early 1990s and known originally as "emotional hardcore"
or "emocore". Emo is distinguished from other forms of hardcore by its
more "pop" sound and its lyrical focus on emotional, expressive or confes-
sional lyrics.

Critics of the genre consider the music effete, or feminine, as it lacks the
hard and supposedly masculine edge of more traditional punk, hardcore or
heavy metal.

Attacks on young people in the Muslim world because of their taste in
music is neither new nor unique to the region. So-called "extreme" forms of
heavy metal, hip-hop, punk and hardcore music have long been popular,
not merely in the West but globally—precisely because the anger, despair
and intensity of the music reflect the tumult of emotions and uncertain
identities that define adolescence and young adulthood in every culture.

5   The Middle East is a particularly welcoming environment for these
types of music because young people across the region have suffered the
pain and ravages of war, authoritarian and social oppression with particular
ferocity. As a founder of the Moroccan metal scene put it: "We play heavy
metal because our lives *are* heavy metal."

If that's how the kids feel in Morocco, imagine the appeal of metal in a war-torn, occupation-torn and terror-torn country such as Iraq (or its neighbour Iran, which boasts far more developed metal and hip-hop scenes than Iraq). We can see first-hand how relevant the music is in Iraq from one of the most powerful scenes of the documentary "Heavy Metal in Baghdad", which brought the plight of Iraq's small but powerful metal scene to the world's attention. Pointing to the violent cover art of an Iron Maiden CD, "Death on the Road", one of the members of the band Acrassicauda, which was featured in the film, said: "This is what life looks like here." Another member explained: "If I didn't play drums as hard as I can, I would kill somebody."

Until now, it was largely metalheads who faced the most extreme ire of conservatives in the Muslim world. The genre's reputation for "Satanism" and debauchery have long since made it a lightning rod for attacks by Christian conservatives in the West. In recent decades, it has been attracting similar attention from religious and political leaders in the Muslim world. In the 1990s and early 2000s, "Satanic metal" scares saw scores of metalheads arrested, beaten, prosecuted and threatened with execution by their countries' religious and political establishments.

With their focus on violence, war and corruption, hardcore metal and hip-hop were natural channels for young people in the Arab and Muslim world to express their anger at their countries' patriarchal, repressive and sclerotic political and social systems. Whether it was Indonesia in 1998, Tehran in 2009, Tunis in 2010 or Cairo a few weeks later, metalheads, rappers and punks anticipated and could be found at the front lines of most of the major political upheavals of the past decade and a half in the Arab and larger Muslim world.

Indeed, the anger, despair and emotion so effectively channelled by these genres of music are the same anger, despair and emotion that drove Mohamed Bouazizi to set himself on fire, and that drove hundreds of thousands of young Tunisians, Egyptians, Bahrainis, Yemenis, Libyans and others into the streets against such great odds.

Even before the Arab Spring, metal and hip-hop had become increasingly 10 tolerated in countries such as Morocco, Egypt and even Saudi Arabia. On the other hand, earlier this year a group of young punks in Indonesia's Aceh province, which is governed according to a strict interpretation of Sharia, were arrested, had their heads shaved and were sent for "re-education" with the goal of "saving them" and keeping them from "shaming their parents".

But this is nothing compared with the horrific practice of "death by blocking" ("*mawt al-blokkah*")—smashing cinderblocks onto each side of a person's head, which was allegedly used to kill the Iraqi emos.

Why is it that emos are under such fierce attack?

First of all, there is a chance that the number of actual murders based on supposed affiliation to emo music is well below the numbers offered by the media, which vary from well under two dozen to almost 100 victims. Indeed, according to a Human Rights Watch report, several of those killed were heavy metal musicians, while young women were severely beaten merely for "dressing fashionably".

According to one source in the Iraqi police, the actual number is likely well under a dozen, although that number is probably low. Even this number represents a horrible crime. What's worse, it's a crime that was motivated at least in part by the Iraqi Interior Ministry's accusations that the emo community engaged in Satan worship and other "immoral activities". The ministry allegedly created a special police task force to "hunt" them, clearly setting the public tone that legitimised violence by extremist Shia.

15   Indeed, regardless of the actual number of victims, it's doubtful all of them would have classified themselves as emos; that is, as hardcore fans of the genre. The bloody photos of the murdered young men that are circulating around the internet feature the kinds of clothing that young men in the Arab world who are trying to look fashionable have long worn. And their haircuts, while particularly styled, were not far outside the norm for young Arabs.

An Iraqi friend pointed out to me: "I have two brothers in the police, including the police intelligence. They dress like this and one has the same haircuts as the emos. No one has bothered them." And yet, as a report by al-Arabiya makes clear, there is a growing emo subculture in Baghdad. In fact, there are a growing number of stores in Baghdad that openly sell rock 'n' roll merchandise, including, until the wave of killings, emo-related paraphernalia.

The fact that stores are opening across Baghdad that cater to rock 'n' roll tastes is a testament to the real, if slow and unsteady, process of normalisation in Iraq—residents of Baghdad still don't have regular access to electricity, but until last week they could buy the trademark emo skull on a t-shirt. And it is precisely this process of slow normalisation, of seeming "Westernisation" without the direct interference and presence of the US occupation, that is so frightening various elements of Iraqi society with the means and willingness to stigmatise, ostracise and attack anyone who threatens their perception of what a proper Iraqi should look like, and how he or she should behave.

In a conservative society, few behaviours or identities are more threatening to the keepers of public morality than perceived homosexuality. Especially in a culture in which men and women spend so much time segregated by gender, the need to police the boundaries between homosocial and homosexual becomes a central focus of government and social action in order to preserve the social order.

Yet the attacks on suspected homosexuals have much less to do with their sexual orientation than they do with power and control. Indeed, in more than half a dozen years of attacks on suspected gays in Iraq, attackers have raped the gay men they attacked for being gay, a phenomenon that is not at all uncommon and is related to the similar types of sexual violence visited upon prostitutes, who have also been the victims of police death squads in Iraq.

A leading Iraqi gay activist describes the situation today: "The government has declared war on sexual minorities. They are trying to rally the streets of Baghdad. Yesterday and the last six or seven days—we have videos and films of those patrols—with a megaphone, they're saying: 'If anyone who has any information about anyone who is a pervert, an infidel, part of the homosexual network, you have to declare it or you face consequences.' Anyone who harbours anyone who is, according to them, an illegal citizen, will face consequences." 20

To be gay in Iraq today is to be automatically removed from any of the rights of citizenship, and even life. As one Iraqi blogger pointed out, during Baathist rule, similar language was deployed against Communists. In either case, the condemned group became the mechanism for continually testing the fidelity and loyalty of the community as a whole.

The discourse of the government, the various militia and the ultra-conservatives who support them, centres on the supposed "poisoning" of the still-fragile and only partially reanimated Iraqi social body. And so emos and gays are accused of being deviant and abnormal (*shuzzuz*, which also means homosexual), being "weird" and "strange" (*gharaba*), engaging in Satan worship, drug use, and even the sucking of blood and biting off the heads of babies.

The similarities with the Nazi discourse on Jews is too obvious to ignore. And yet, while some fanatical Iraqi Shia, like their Sunni Salafi counterparts, might indeed hate gays with a pathological intensity, the larger dynamic in which such hatred is supported and even promoted is quite different. And before we blame this on some inherent backwardness or violence within Islam, a similar discourse operates in Uganda based on supposedly Christian moral imperatives, and, with only somewhat less intensity in the US Bible Belt.

First of all, as for many conservative Christians, many conservative Muslims consider homosexuality an identity and a chosen behaviour and thus can be changed (unlike one's ethnicity or religion, which is permanent). And so, in several "night letters" that featured the names of suspected gays and emos who were threatened with execution, local militia declared: "We strongly warn you, to all the obscene males and females, if you will not leave this filthy work within four days, the punishment of God will descend upon you at the hand of the mujahideen. . . . If you do not get back to sanity and the right path, you will be killed."

25   There is at least the chance to repent, similar to the extremist Salafi discourse surrounding their attacks on Copts and other Christians, which also often involves calling on them to convert to Islam as the best solution for their situation.

In fact, the whole process can be understood as one of disciplining a community which, with the slow emergence from a decade of war and opening up economically and culturally (especially through the internet) to the outside world, has unprecedented options for shaping identities— and, through them, religious and political beliefs—outside the control of, and potentially opposed to, the interests of the current Shia leadership, whose performance in government has been defined by corruption, a lack of democratic accountability, and a failure to rebuild the country in any meaningful sense.

Indeed, while gays in Iraq are almost completely outside the bounds of society, they are not outside enough for the state itself to engage in the summary murder of suspected homosexuals. But they are outside enough for government officials and some religious figures to use the threat they supposedly pose to mobilise poor and uneducated young militiamen, who have known little but oppression and war, to do their dirty work for them, under the guise of protecting their community from a mortal threat. As several Iraqi commentators have pointed out, deploying these gangs for such activities is one way to keep them occupied, and ensuring their anger and discontent is not directed at more appropriate targets, while using the "defence of society" to gain even more wealth and power. An English-language Iraqi blog post put it most succinctly: "Then we will figure out why this man killed the emo . . . and we can tell the masses that he killed them because it makes money. . . ."

If there is an underappreciated aspect to the sad story of Iraq's emos, it is the complex network of relations and conflicts between Iraq's political and religious elites, the various militia and gangs under their control, and the still fuzzy shape, function and boundaries of the post-occupation Iraqi state. The still-tenuous state has yet to capture a level of hegemony that would allow it to claim a legitimate monopoly of both force and political loyalty. The confusion its lack of authority can produce is revealed by none other than the once-radical and now largely co-opted Muqtada al-Sadr.

In response to the spate of attacks, al-Sadr pronounced on his website that emos were "crazy and fools . . . a plague on Muslim society". Nevertheless, he cautioned that "those responsible should eliminate them through legal means".

But this is, of course, precisely the problem—there is no effective law in Iraq today, in good measure because of the way religious-cum-militia leaders such as al-Sadr shaped the post-occupation political environment. With so much wealth and power up for grabs, and the ethnic and sectarian divide still defining the country's political life, the most useful "state" for most political actors is one whose boundaries with other social, political and economic actors are both porous and able to be reshaped as necessary by the governing elite.

While such a fuzzy state has clear advantages for those at the centre to gain control of as much power and resources as possible, at some point a functioning political system with a more definite shape and lines of power will have to take shape—if the country is to achieve a level of socio-economic development that will satisfy the basic needs and aspirations of its young population. As one of Iraq's most shrewd political operators, al-Sadr clearly knows this, which is why he calls on "responsible" parties— that is, those officially sanctioned by the government—to "eliminate" the threat of emos and homosexuals rather than the kind of militia gangs who helped facilitate his rise to power.

The problem with a more well-defined state for many holders of extreme views is that it offers citizens better protection for their basic human, political and civil rights. Such a state would not only find it harder to "eliminate" people merely for dressing strangely or even being gay, it would also circumscribe the ability of upstarts such as al-Sadr to overstep the power of

30

more traditional leaders such as Grand Ayatollah Sistani, who are not directly part of the emerging political system, and who forcefully condemned the killings as an act of terrorism, and who, along with Ayatollah Mohammed al-Yakoubi, called for dialogue and "advising of the youth".

And so it's not surprising that, soon after al-Sadr's comments became known, one of his assistants clarified them, saying that "in this issue and in all such problems we always use peaceful and educational methods to correct any wrongdoings. We are not connected in any way to those groups allegedly responsible for killing those young people".

Even al-Sadr has to distance himself from unsanctioned violence in order to maintain his position as a legitimate political player in Iraq's emerging post-conflict order.

35   If there is one silver lining in this tragic situation, it is the growing role of human rights discourse as a weapon for society to fight against such extra-legal violence against even its most marginal members. A look at the Arabic-language Iraqi coverage of the emo affair reveals that everyone from Iraqi parliamentarians to religious leaders is using the discourse of human rights as a marker to fight back against the current violence against emos and "non-conformists". Iraq's Parliamentary Commission on Human Rights has become involved in the affair, while one MP, Safia al-Suhail, called on the committees on human rights, security and defence to work together with the interior minister to investigate and stop the killings.

It is hard to underestimate the consequences of this struggle for the future of Iraq. What is clear, however, is that the metalheads, emos, gays and other young Iraqis who are the victims of this horrible violence are unwitting participants in a much larger struggle over the future of their country. By their willingness to put their lives at risk—and in too many cases, lose their life—merely for the right to exercise their freedom of identity and cultural expression, these young people have earned the right to be considered among the martyrs of the democratic revolutionary wave still sweeping across the Arab world.

Update: As this article went to press, I was contacted by a prominent Iraqi blogger who has closely followed the killings of rock fans and gays in his country. He informed me that just in the past two days—which happen to be the ninth anniversary of the US invasion of his country—many more people have been killed, including two girls—just because "they liked pop and punk. The people are terrified by the brutal killing. They mixed attacks on the emo youth and gays, so people have no idea what is the difference, and it [has become] a social attack on any one with long hair or who listens to western music".

The blogger agreed that these attacks were directed by forces in and outside the government who stand the most to lose by any greater opening of Iraq to the outside world, which would lead to greater exposure of their own abuses, corruption and criminality, and which would offer people options for a future aside from their own narrow vision.

Analyze

1. In this article, Levine uses nonsexist language and never specifies one gender when he refers to emos. As you were reading, did you think that emos could be either male or female? Why or why not?
2. How does the author explain and support his claim that "the attacks on suspected homosexuals have much less to do with their sexual orientation than they do with power and control"? Are you convinced? Why or why not?
3. Why do you think that the domain of "emotion" has been associated with being effeminate? Why is that seen as a negative in men? Do you think that this might be changing? If so, in what ways? If not, why?
4. The article refers to "normalization" as a kind of "westernization." How can gender and sexual identities be influenced by globalization?

Explore

1. Do you agree with Levine's claim in paragraph 4 that "the anger, despair and intensity of ["extreme" forms of heavy metal, hip-hop, punk and hardcore] music reflect the tumult of emotions and uncertain identities that define adolescence and young adulthood in every culture"? Do adolescence and young adulthood transcend culture? Write a research paper in which you explore responses to adolescence and young adulthood in other, less familiar regions or cultures. What did you discover?
2. The author mentions intolerance toward gays in fundamentalist communities such as Uganda, the Aceh region in Indonesia, and the Bible Belt in the US South. Choose one of these regions or Iraq itself and explore the political climate that has turned a clampdown on sexual orientation into a global human-rights issue.

3. Write an essay that traces how emo pop, with its roots in 1980s Washington, DC, emerged as a global subculture. What has been the source of its appeal to young men and women? Or consider another powerful music genre, such as hip-hop, in Jackson Allers's "Voice of the Streets: The Birth of a Hip-Hop Movement" (chapter 8).

Chloé Lewis
"The Invisible Migrant Man: Questioning Gender Privileges"

A former intern with Amnesty International USA in San Francisco and a migrant support caseworker at the Coventry Refugee Centre in England, Chloé Lewis is a doctoral candidate in the Department of International Development at the University of Oxford in England, where she researches gender, armed conflict, and forced migration. "The Invisible Migrant Man" is an overview of an interdisciplinary workshop given at the Barn Middlesex University in London. The workshop was intended to "explore areas of migration scholarship, policy and law where the male experience is marginalised or under-researched." The article appeared on May 29, 2012, on *openDemocracy*, an independent nonprofit website dedicated to the idea that "facilitating argument and understanding across geographical boundaries is vital to preventing injustice."

What privileges have you experienced by virtue of your gender?

Migration is often depicted and perceived as a 'quintessentially masculine' activity, 'imbued with masculine attributes, including risk, adventure and courage'. More negative images of male migrants and asylum seekers are also fairly common, portrayed in mainstream media either as 'dangerous and undesirable', 'criminals' and sometimes even as 'rapists'. All in all, the figure of the 'threatening young (migrant) male' is one that is relatively well known within British society and one which tends to lie in contrast, and even in opposition to, the almost universally victimised female migrant.

By focusing on female migrants, in particular on their vulnerabilities, most feminist and gender analyses of migration tend to overlook the diverse experiences of migrant men, for instance as fathers, marriage migrants, immigration detainees, LGBT asylum seekers, and sex workers to name but a few. It is this particular insight that inspired 'The Invisible (Migrant) Man' workshop held at Middlesex University earlier this year, which aimed to highlight the ways in which the needs and perspectives of male migrants are often marginalised—if not outright excluded—from legal and policy discourse surrounding migration and asylum. Presentations at the workshop identified the fact that men's 'affective ties and needs and their vulnerabilities are rarely fore-grounded', while addressing the myriad ways 'immigration systems often operate to marginalise men'. The larger point that was reinforced for me throughout this conference, is the value of stepping outside of understandings of 'gender' that continually equate 'women' with emotionality, vulnerability and passivity; while assumptions of privilege, aggression and oppression are perpetually tied to 'men'. Such approaches sustain unhelpful gender stereotypes which are ultimately detrimental to both male and female migrants—as well as to men and women more generally.

'Love is of a man's life a thing apart/ 'Tis woman's whole existence'. Opening her presentation with this quote from Lord Byron's *Don Juan*, Helena Wray, traced the marginalisation of men's emotional lives and capacities within British immigration law, noting the sustained perception towards male migrants as being exclusively 'economic agents'. According to Wray, the Commonwealth Immigrants Act of 1962 marked a turning point in U.K. immigration policy imposing immigration controls on (non-white) Commonwealth citizens as a means of limiting the influx of Commonwealth migrants and non-European political refugees. This piece of legislation effectively ended circular labour migration from Britain's former colonies. The subsequent rise in family migration as an alternative immigration channel was also hastily regulated by the 1968 Commonwealth Immigration Act which introduced, among other restrictions, the 'Primary Purpose Rule' (abolished in 1997) requiring that men show that the primary reason for marriage was not immigration. Within this context of increased suspicion towards family migration that the perception of the 'bad (male) family migrant' untrustworthy and whose emotional lives should be viewed with cynicism merged.

Wray indicated that 'in family migration, men are regarded as having less invested in affective relationships, as more prone to engage in manipulation or abuse and to act primarily as economic agents', and that 'men who do succeed in the family migration category often have some other characteristic of vulnerability that marks them out as different to the mainstream' usually assessed against a high standard of proportionality, exceptionality and/or the 'insurmountable obstacles' test. The stringency of these standards, however, should not be underestimated as shown in the case of *LH*. (Truly Exceptional—Ekinci applied) Jamaica [2006] UKAIT 00019 UR The case involved a husband and father of two children, one of whom was severely disabled, and who had overstayed his visa. Notwithstanding the extensive evidence presented of the appellant's central role in the care of his severely disabled child, especially significant in light of his wife's depression, the case failed on the grounds that his familial situation was insufficiently 'exceptional'. In this regard, Wray suggests that the father's involvement in the care of family was 'reduced to its practical elements', while 'emotional aspects were entirely disregarded'.

5   In addition to restricting male migrants' ability to make and sustain a credible claim under Article 8, this depiction of the 'bad male migrant' as the norm has also serves to eclipse vulnerabilities faced by migrant men in their respective host communities. One such example that is as stark as it is perhaps controversial is that of a number of Pakistani and Turkish male marriage migrants in Britain and Denmark respectively. Conventionally, much of the attention paid to transnational marriages has focused on (Muslim) brides, honing in on questions of forced marriage and honour killings in particular. Keenly wary of promoting an evaluation of relative suffering between female and male marriage migrants, Katherine Charsley's presentation on her work in progress (co-authored with Anika Liversage) shed light on the parallel hardships faced by a number of Muslim male marriage migrants revealing their weak(er) position in domestic structures of power in relation to both their in-laws as well as their wives.

In her earlier work, Charsley commented on the use of the term *ghardamad* by her Pakistani informants in Bristol and in Pakistan to refer to male marriage migrants. Not unlike the 'the conventional daughter-in-law', the appellation connotes of being 'dependent on and subservient to the in-laws', thus an undesirable position, especially—Charsley suggests—for Pakistani men. A rarer phenomenon as marriage migrants are predominantly women, the process of male migration effectively creates new domestic, and asymmetrical, power relationships. In most cases this is manifested in a constant sense of 'belittling', while in more extreme cases, in domestic abuse. These men are, furthermore, generally unable to give voice to their difficulties either within or outside their communities for fear of undermining 'cultural logics of masculine honour'.

Social, economic, and cultural pressures emanating from migration were identified as the primary source of male migrants' dependence on their in-laws. Additionally, however, the research also points to the potential impact of immigration laws and residency requirements in particular, which further limit their autonomy and restrict possible sources of exit, at least until citizenship is acquired, at which point some are able to file for divorce. Yet, by doing so Pakistani marriage migrants contribute to widespread perceptions of 'bogus' transnational marriages, that is, that South East Asian men ' "trick" local (British) Asian families into allowing them to marry their daughters, only to divorce them immediately after their acquire citizenship'. Moreover, in doing so, Pakistani divorced male marriage migrants interviewed by Charsley recounted some of the challenges they faced in relation to homogenised constructions of Muslim men within legal institutions. One of her informants described feeling like 'an American movies villain'. Overall, by revealing the potentially vulnerable position of Muslim male marriage migrants, these findings destabilise stereotypical portrayals of Muslim husbands and fathers as universally oppressive, but also serve to complicate assumptions of 'bogus' transnational marriages within the British Pakistani population especially.

Another 'group' of (predominantly) male migrants whose vulnerabilities are continually silenced both by their invisibility and negative stereotyping as epitomes of 'bad' migrants, are immigration detainees and failed asylum seekers. Exploring the tensions in representations of immigration detainees and failed asylum seekers, Melanie Griffiths highlighted the 'complex, emotional and gendered' experiences of failed asylum seeking men in Campsfield Immigration Removal Centre in Oxford. In particular, she drew attention to the tensions in their being 'demonised as criminal, deceptive and too dangerous for British society', while simultaneously facing 'emasculation and infantilisation as a result of forced idleness, dependence and a lack of self-determination'. A number of Griffiths' interviewees resisted being labelled as 'criminals' distancing themselves from 'real' criminals, and almost desperately seeking to affirm their identity as, for instance, a 'good father' and 'hard worker'. This point is well captured by the following quote from one interviewee, a Sri Lanka detainee, who stated: 'I'm not being convicted of committing a crime, I'm not a danger to the public, I'm a well-educated person, I can speak several languages including Tamil, Sinhalese, Urdu, Japanese'. In essence, Griffiths' work has uncovered at least two ways in which male refused asylum seekers and those placed in detention face particular vulnerabilities. The first is through their not having a full legal identity; and the second, 'counter-intuitively' she notes, emerges from 'gendered assumptions regarding *privileged patriarchy*, including an expectation that men can cope with destitution, detention and the loss of family'.

The question that was raised during one of the discussion sessions and then thread through much of the research presented was the question of gender privileges. 'Men', taken as a holistic category, are often assumed to be the privileged sex—socially, economically, politically and legally owing to the 'patriarchal dividend'. Writing the foreword for *The Boundaries of International Law*, a seminal publication within feminist international legal scholarship, Elizabeth Evatt observed that 'the law has not always served women well', and that 'for centuries, the legal system, shaped and enforced exclusively by men, denied women the attributed of citizenship and personhood, and subordinated them to the decisions of men'. What is clear from this overview of diverse experiences of male migrants, however, is that 'the law' does not always serve men well either. A paradoxical yet prevalent perception within migration and asylum law especially is that 'women' are often seen as 'privileged' over male migrants and asylum seekers by virtue of their presumed 'vulnerability', a notion which is in fact sometimes strategically drawn upon by legal actors and female asylum seekers themselves.

10   The effectiveness of this strategy is not necessarily sustained empirically given that rates of refusal for male and female asylum seekers were almost equal in 2010 and 2011, averaging at around 72% and 74% respectively. Beyond such pragmatic considerations, the (perceived) privileging of female vulnerability and victimhood bears a certain cost for women as well as men. As I have suggested elsewhere, this trend functions to portray migrants as defenceless victims of their 'culture' (or religion) and elides the various ways through which women express their agency. Equally, however, and less often acknowledged, such gender stereotypes concomitantly serve to eclipse vulnerabilities and hardships faced by men as migrants, husbands, fathers, (refused) asylum seekers, detainees, and quite possibly, as all of these at once.

Analyze

1. How have the research studies cited in this reading challenged "homogenized constructions" about male migrants? How have these challenged or confirmed your own constructs?
2. How have men become victims of male stereotypes? How and under what conditions do you think of men as victims?
3. How does the author demonstrate that "Such approaches sustain unhelpful gender stereotypes which are ultimately detrimental to both male and female migrants—as well as to men and women more generally"?

Explore

1. Consider the experience of someone you know—in your family, community, campus, or classroom—who is an immigrant. In an interview, see if you can find out how his or her gender affected the immigration experience. Be sensitive to how gender overlaps with other identity markers such as age, race, culture, religion, and education. Write up the interview, and as you do, consider how you can provide a portrait of one person's experience, rather than making broad statements about gender and immigration. As you share your portrait with others in your class, what patterns about gender stereotypes and gender inequalities emerge?
2. There are several excellent films with strong narratives that include male immigrants such as *A Better Life*, *El Norte*, *The Edge of Heaven* (*Auf der anderen Seite/Yaşamın Kıyısında*), *The Lost Boys of Sudan*, and *Man Push Cart*. Watch one of them. How does the film you chose confirm and/or refute the claim that male migrants are typically threatening and female migrants are typically victims? How has reading this article provided you with an alternative lens through which to consider male migrants?

Forging Connections

1. How does the language used to describe men and women throughout this chapter shift and change? Look most closely at Larsen's description of women in "The Startling Plight of China's Leftover Ladies," Clark's "Crimson Leopard-Print Headscarves: Wearing the Veil in

Banda Aceh, Indonesia," and Broudy's "Body-Building in Afghanistan." Does their language—the imagery and tone—perpetuate established gender stereotypes? If so, how? How does their language anticipate the reader's gender or attitudes about gender? Why does this matter? Explore these questions in a thoughtfully developed essay.

2. Gender (along with race, eye color, height, and weight) is one of the most obvious identifying markers we use. What legacy of being male and female have we witnessed in this chapter? Write a paper in which you consider how globalization has helped you to have more nuanced perceptions of what it can mean to be male and female. Use this as an opportunity to define and redefine your concept of globalization and gender.

Looking Further

1. Write a research paper in which you explore "the geopolitics of sexual frustration" discussed in Martin Walker's article "The World's New Numbers" (chapter 9). Walker notes that the rate of criminal behavior of unmarried men is "many times higher than that of married men." How has this been affected by gender demographics, particularly in places where baby boys are valued more than baby girls?

2. Write an essay in which you contemplate the meaning of costume and custom in a globalized world, particularly as they may promote, inhibit, or perpetuate gender inequality. In addition to the selections in this chapter on wearing the veil, what can you glean from "Body-Building in Afghanistan" about the way men dress in Afghanistan? What is mandatory and why? Who ensures compliance? Also consider Damon Tabor's "If It's Tuesday, It Must Be the Taliban" (chapter 9), in which the author himself, as a tourist in Afghanistan, dresses like an Afghani.

8   Pop Culture

The joy and delight of pop culture are often derived from its notoriety and rejection by the status quo. In contrast to high-brow, traditional, or so-called legitimate art, popular culture can be associated with immediate gratification, easy entertainment, and mainstream trends that are here today, gone tomorrow. It has been derisively considered commercial, unskilled, do-it-yourself, and unsophisticated. Some might say that because of its easy imitation and youthful appeal, pop culture travels easily on a global level. Some are critical of what it is that travels and in which direction: There's the concern that American culture dominates, other cultures with, for example, Mickey Mouse and McDonald's, as we considered in chapter 1.

As if it were an unruly teenager, there seems to have always been concern that pop culture would corrupt a society's cultural traditions—television and film subverting literature and theater; folk music, jazz, and rock 'n' roll subverting classical or traditional music. And yet therein is its appeal and irony—the pop culture of yesterday seems to have become the tradition of today. What seemed so simple and gratuitous, under critical analysis is serious, complex, and creative. Geography is even more forgiving than time as we see in the selections chosen for this chapter exploring the globalizing function of pop culture in the world and the impact of the world upon pop culture itself.

The selections that follow refer to genres of popular culture that may have originated or come to be defined in the United States—television, graffiti, cinema, and hip-hop—but as you read, consider the role of popular culture in defining and exposing what it can mean to express oneself in a globalized world.

We begin with Roozbeh Shirazi's critique of the reality television program *Shahs of Sunset*. By contrasting its depiction of American-Iranians with his own first-hand experience of growing up Iranian in the United States, Shirazi calls into question the impulse to reduce groups into stereotypes—a fine line that a global perspective can make bold. Should those paragons of rebellion, graffiti artists, become legitimate artists and participate in the commerce of the art world? Or must they work only with a "revolution in the can?" Blake Gopnik makes his own claims while analyzing the form and content of graffiti in the world's revolutionary hotspots. Sarah Lacy reports on Nigeria's blossoming cinema industry—one of the largest industries emerging out of sub-Saharan Africa to date. She also has become the subject of her article as she sits in a makeshift courtroom, waiting to be tried for essentially being in the wrong place at the wrong time. Anyone who thinks that the pop culture commercialism isn't also political will think differently after reading "You Think Hollywood Is Rough? Welcome to the Chaos, Excitement and Danger of Nollywood." In India, where Bollywood has had a more established place in the memories of fervent cinemagoers, Charukesi Ramadurai is inspired to write nostalgically about the demise of large-screen theaters as she reports on the end of an era in the "Fading Lights in Mumbai."

Whether or not your concern is that the United States and the West in general are globalizing the world and eroding indigenous cultures, it's hard not to be moved by the ways in which pop culture permeates youth culture worldwide and gives voice and meaning to those impassioned by its universal message. A publication like *World Hip Hop Market*, which published

Jackson Allers's "Voice of the Streets: The Birth of a Hip-Hop Movement," demonstrates the global passion for and the international language of hip-hop music. The last selection of the chapter, Jeff Chang's "So You Think They Can Break-Dance?" takes us into South Korea's world of b-boy battles, including the government's surprisingly enthusiastic sponsorship. Chang teases out subtle readings of life in South Korea where K-Pop, "Gangnam Style," and other pop phenomena are themselves going global.

Roozbeh Shirazi
"Beyond Mullahs and Persian Party People: The Invisibility of Being Iranian on TV"

After earning his doctorate from Columbia University's Teachers College in international and comparative education, Roozbeh Shirazi became a post-doctoral fellow at the University of Minnesota. His areas of interest include youth citizenship, empowerment, and political participation; globalization, migration, and education. The following selection, excerpted from Shirazi's forthcoming book of the same name, appeared in February 2012 on *Jadaliyya*, an independent e-zine published by the Arab Studies Institute (ASI). *Jadaliyya* provides insight and critical analysis in both English and Arabic about all matters concerning the Arab world. In this piece, Shirazi ponders whether American media will continue to demonize and play up long-standing stereotypes about Iranian culture in light of Bravo's latest reality show, *Shahs of Sunset*.

In what ways should creators of television programs be held accountable for the promotion and perpetuation of false or hurtful stereotypes of cultural, gender, or racial groups?

A t first glance, the impending premiere of Bravo's *Shahs of Sunset* would seem to herald that Iranian Americans have finally achieved melting pot bliss in the cauldron of American multiculturalism. After three decades of villainy, cultural essentialism, and protagonistic invisibility in American media, six youngish southern Californian (SoCal) adults—who party, shop, and date(!)—are poised to catapult Iranians into the American mainstream as ethnic bon vivants.

A short while ago, such an about-face would have seemed like an impossibility. Growing up in the 1980s and 1990s, being Iranian onscreen was limited to grim news stories detailing the religious fanaticism of post-revolutionary Iran, Iranian enmity for all things American, tragically terrible movies, and the exploits of memorable wrestling villain, The Iron Sheik. Real life did not seem to offer much respite from what was being shown on television.

When my parents were graduate students in Michigan during the early 1980s, these tropes were more enduring than even living in the United States. And the unfolding of the Iranian revolution resulted in the overthrow of a vital American autocratic ally in the late Shah, severed diplomatic relations, and an unforgettable hostage crisis—to name but a few of the earlier hits of US-Iran relations. Incessant American news coverage of these events, notably in Ted Koppel's *Nightline*, did its part in introducing a terrified American audience to the now-familiar spectacle of hysterical hijab-clad women and angry bearded men loudly denouncing the United States in the streets. This imagery became an enduring leitmotif in media portrayals of political opinion throughout the Middle East. The hostage crisis—and in a broader stroke, the revolution that caused it—created a lasting swell of American hostility towards Iran and Iranians living in the United States.

My parents were idealistic, energetic student-activists who had taken to working in a popular college eatery to be able to continue their educations and pay their bills. Their visa status was in question, and they were experiencing financial hardship after their government-funded scholarships were abruptly cut amid Iran's revolutionary upheaval. As an avid reader, my dad would bring Persian-language newspapers and pamphlets to work with him to catch up on the news during his shift breaks. One day, he returned to the break area to find that his reading material had been thrown in the trash. Asking around, he soon learned that the restaurant owner had thrown them away. When my dad confronted him, the owner was enraged and exclaimed that he paid my father to work, not to read "that shit." Never mind that my dad was reading on his break time; the owner followed up with a timeless "patriotic" truism, telling my father if he did not like his job, he was free to leave it. Our family's precarious situation did not allow for such luxuries, so my father continued working there—enjoying his reading despite his boss' bigotry until he finished graduate studies several years later.

Around the same time, my mother was trying to balance the compet-   5
ing demands of being a new parent, working, and going to school full-time in a tensely charged atmosphere. At the height of the hostage crisis, her faculty advisor chided her for registering for a high number of semester credits, and wanted her to drop her course load in half. When my mother told him she was trying to graduate sooner due to the uncertainty of her situation, he told her that she should not feel any pressure to finish her studies. After all, was it not "the men who made decisions and provided in Iranian society?"

It is tempting to say that these were isolated incidents of Midwestern provincialism in a bygone era. However, if you speak with enough Iranian Americans, you will hear many similar anecdotes from those who experienced them firsthand, or have seen their loved ones subject to discrimination, undue surveillance, and harassment. Yes, even in California.

It was these experiences, and the ongoing demonization of Iran in the news, that became productive in certain representational strategies of many Iranians living in the United States—brilliantly captured in the 2010 online public service announcement made by Iranican: an Iranian American volunteer-based organization. In the video clip, a young female census worker interviews different Iranians—all played by the comedian Maz Jobrani—who resist to participating in the 2010 US Census as "Iranians." One respondent, a young Iranian male named Kambiz, tells the census officer to put down "white" for him on the form. "Veer vite, just put vite," he says. When asked about how they self-identify racially, all of the Jobrani-characters decide to identify as Italian.

The punch line of the video highlights an unspoken but widely understood practice among many Iranian Americans to deny their ethnicity or categorize themselves in ways that do not call negative attention to themselves. This is facilitated by the construction of racial categories in the United States that encourages the underreporting of Iranians. According to the 2010 American Community Survey (ACS), there are a total of 448,772 Iranians in the United States, a number thought to be much lower than the actual population by several Iranian American civic organizations. Add to this fact that all peoples of North Africa and the Middle East are generally considered to be "white" according to US federal guidelines, and it makes sense why Kambiz and many other Iranian Americans would not think twice about ticking the "white" box on government forms. Still, claiming that being Iranian is being white remains problematic, because of the ways in which the Iranians are typically imagined and represented in very non-white and "un-American" social roles. (The same can be said of Americans of Arab descent.)

While the Census provides the opportunity to pick the least imperfect race box to check once every ten years, Iranian Americans make choices about how to position themselves ethnically every day. Importantly, the "Persian" moniker so popular among some Iranian Americans is often used to highlight either a non-Islamic or a secular Iranian identity, which permits a nationalist respite from the messy connotations of calling the Islamic Republic of Iran "home." Being Persian does not eliminate the difference between being Iranian and being white; it anesthetizes it.

> "Iran has remained entrenched as one of the United States' most indomitable bogeymen."

10   Given the right amount of Orientalist historical cherry picking, "Persianness" is nearly synonymous with being white (being empire-builders rather than imperial subjects). The term "Persian" is ostensibly evocative of exotic culture and grandeur, whereas "Iranian" is usually redolent of less glamorous associations. In this curious "post-racial" age where diversity is celebrated—yet xenophobia is on the rise—being Persian is the seemingly sexy way for the Iranian Americans to be ethnic without sticking out amid growing Islamophobia and anti-immigrant sentiments.

Not sticking out is pretty important, when one considers that Iran has remained entrenched as one of the United States' most indomitable bogeymen for over thirty years running. Iran is routinely denounced by the United States as the most active state sponsor of terrorism and a regional trouble-maker. President Obama and his bevy of Republican challengers are falling over themselves to proclaim that "no option is off the table," when it comes to dealing with the perceived Iranian nuclear threat. Lest we think that a defiant Iran only poses a threat to American national security, critics unfailingly remind us that Iran is considered to be an existential threat to Israel too, and "the mullahs" also regularly commit human rights atrocities against their own restive populace that Western journalists delight in telling us who long for more "Western" lifestyles. Put it all together, and

Bravo's central casting could not have dreamed up a better foil for self-congratulatory American morality.

In light of this political history, a reality TV series starring wealthy Iranians is bound to attract some notoriety. In fact, Ryan Seacrest and the Bravo Network are betting on it. They are not even the first to come up with the idea; Doron Ofir's *Persian Version* never came to pass, but was the first show that proposed to cast glamorous Persian party people with no credit limits and no problems. It is fair to say that Seacrest knows a TV hit when he sees one. The enormously successful entertainment personality has built his considerable cache by hosting *American Idol* and supplying us with an endless diet of *Keeping Up with the Kardashians*. With *Shahs of Sunset*, he now turns his entrepreneurial gaze crosstown to Tehrangeles, to follow the lives of several Los Angeles (LA)-based "Persian-American friends" who "try to balance their social lives and work lives."

Shahs of Sunset has cast a very specific young adult cohort to personify what Bravo TV personality Andy Cohen calls an affluent community. "[It] exists all over the place. . . . If you live in LA, you know that the Persian American community is really strong. . . . It is really family-oriented. And it is really affluent." Cohen also reminds us that these Persian princes and princesses do not just "spend a lot of money." He goes on to tell us that "this is a group of people that does not exist on television anywhere, and that is another reason that I am excited to do the show. It is new and different."

In a sneak preview show, the cast tells their viewers that they do not "work in buildings, they own them." They add that their lives are all about "cash, flash, Cristal, gold, cars, and houses with big columns." They are also well-integrated model immigrants who apparently partied and slept their way through 9/11 and the resurgent xenophobia of the last decade. As one cast member gushes, "Who does not love America? This place is fantastic. It is really the land of milk and honey!"

It is no secret that Seacrest, like Bravo, is in the business of making addictive TV and oodles of money. They are not out to educate audiences, and it is likely that they had no problem casting for the show in "Tehrangeles." The LA area boasts the largest Iranian population in the United States, and very wealthy individuals among them live the many cultural clichés that *Shahs of Sunset* will showcase. But lest we forget, Iranian Americans are not all rich real estate playboys and trust fund divas who bleed red, white, and blue. They come in all stripes. They are rich, poor, liberal, conservative, gay, straight, Muslim, Jewish, Baha'i, and atheist, among other things. As an ethnic community in the United States, while they tend to be very well educated, not all are super-rich. According to 2010 ACS data, the median family income among Iranian Americans is $83,375—higher than the national average to be certain, but hardly in the "one percent" stratosphere that Bravo is selling as typically "Persian."

In other words, *Shahs* is not a show that examines Iranian American issues as they are lived by most Iranian Americans. Its aim is to entertain by marketing lithe bodies and big personalities who have no major problems other than who to date, how to please their parents, and where to spend lots of money. By dispensing with the diverse realities of being Iranian in the United States—notably the multiple ways in which Iranians articulate, enact, and experience race, citizenship, and community—and by instead magnifying a shallow Persian party scene, the *Shahs of Sunset* appears guilty of replacing one cultural stereotype with another.

Building a show around a specific Persian party scene embodies a neo-liberal multiculturalism of sorts, in which members of an ethnic group—even those from countries considered to be "enemies"—can be made socially acceptable through their hyper-consumerism and engagement in familiar reality TV hijinks.

It seems for now that Iranians can be in the American public imagination predominantly as still-scary fanatics or approachable ethnic party people who can shop, hook up, and drive fast cars with the best of them. You all know they have made it in America, however, when they can stand for more than just party people in the public eye.

Analyze

1. What do you know about the Iranian hostage crisis of 1980? This was also portrayed in the 2012 Hollywood film *Argo* directed by Ben Affleck. Do you agree with the author that it "created a lasting swell of American hostility towards Iran and Iranians living in the United States"?

2. What kind of "special authority" does the writer, an Iranian-American born in the US, have in regard to Iranian culture? How does he use it to give his article more credibility? Is it persuasive for you?

3. "Being Persian does not eliminate the difference between being Iranian and being white; it anesthetizes it" (paragraph 9). What does the author mean by this?

Explore

1. "In this curious 'post-racial' age where diversity is celebrated—yet xenophobia is on the rise—being Persian is the seemingly sexy way for the Iranian Americans to be ethnic without sticking out amid growing Islamophobia and anti-immigrant sentiments" (paragraph 10). Why are Iranians considered Persian? How does being Persian distinguish Iranians from people of other Islamic nations?

2. Why might creating stereotypes for television be appealing? Is this something that could be said about most reality TV shows—or about American TV in general? To whom would this be appealing? Who might it offend? Explore the impact of a television show's stereotypes on a particular group—ethnic, racial, gender, sexual preference, or age.

3. Several articles, including this one, have referenced *neoliberalism*: "Building a show around a specific Persian party scene embodies neoliberal multiculturalism of sorts." What do you think of when you hear this term? Explain in your own words what neoliberalism means in this context and how it is used elsewhere. Explore the dynamic use of the term and how it can take on different meanings in different contexts. You may want to consider how it is similar to or different from other terms like "multiculturalism" and "globalization."

Blake Gopnik
"Revolution in a Can"

In 2010, after spending 10 years as the chief art critic for *The Washington Post*, Blake Gopnik moved on to *Newsweek* and *The Daily Beast* to write about art and design. Gopnik earned his doctorate in art history from Oxford University and has written on aesthetic topics ranging from Facebook to gastronomy. "Revolution in a Can" originally appeared in the November 2011 edition of *Foreign Policy*, an influential bi-weekly magazine that covers international politics and global affairs. Gopnik draws comparisons between the "high-art" graffiti of America and other parts of the West, and the political and revolutionary graffiti of other parts of the world, namely South America, Africa, and the Middle East.

What other kinds of self-expression have served as markers of rebellion—regionally, nationally, or globally?

The worst moment in the history of graffiti came during what was also its heyday, in the early 1980s in New York. That was when mainstream culture adopted graffiti as something called "art." A counterculture medium that had, at least for a bare moment, been about communication and empowerment became saddled with the oldest high-culture clichés. Graffiti came to be about "personal style," "aesthetic innovation," and "artistic self-expression"; about looking good and catching the eye; about stylistic influence and the creation of a self-conscious visual tradition. That left it perfectly positioned to be co-opted by consumerist culture. You could say that the grand murals of graffiti art, known to their makers as "pieces"—short for "masterpieces," another hoary cliché—were a kind of stand-in for missing advertising billboards, made by artists from neighborhoods that had been left out of Calvin Klein's underwear ad buy. It was only by chance that those murals had no commodity to sell—until they realized they could sell themselves, as that high-end good called art.

Then, by way of contrast, think about graffiti as it appears to us around the world today, in places where painting on a wall is about speaking truth to power. The Arab Spring was marked by spray-painted taunts to dictators, and Haiti's chaos led to impassioned scrawls. A crackdown against anti-regime graffiti in the town of Daraa was even the inspiration this year for Syria's tank-defying protest movement. In many of these cases, the artfulness of the graffiti takes a distant second place to what someone is actually trying to say. "Free doom—Get out Hamad," reads one spray-painted text from Bahrain. During the rebellion in Libya, "Freedom=Aljazeera" written on a wall makes the value of a free press perfectly clear; on another wall, the simple tracing of an AK-47 is enough to invoke an entire ethos of rebellion. In Guatemala City, stenciled portraits of the "disappeared" of Guatemala's long civil war, with the Spanish words for "Where are they?" written below, stand as eloquent witness to one of the country's most crucial concerns. (The portrait style is loosely derived from the British street artist Banksy.)

In all these cases, graffiti is being used as a true means of communication rather than as purely aesthetic exchange. These 21st-century scrawls leapfrog back to a prehistory of graffiti, when wall writing was mostly about voicing forbidden thoughts in public. And they take us back to the first years of graffiti in New York, when some members of the underclass declared their incontrovertible presence by "tagging" every square inch of the city as they transgressed the normal boundaries set by class and race. As German scholar Diedrich Diederichsen has written, "graffiti was a form of cultural and artistic production that was illegible from the dominant cultural perspective." When some of those same taggers realized that they could also make "pieces" that would count as something called "art," they began quickly buying into the values of the mainstream they'd once confronted.

By now, grand graffiti gestures are as tired as could be, at least in the context of the Western art world. But across the rest of the planet, the static language of the American "piece" has moved on to a second life as the visual lingua franca of genuine political speech. The most elaborate images from Egypt, Libya, and Haiti today look very much like the 1980s paint jobs on New York subway cars and warehouse facades, and yet their point is not to function as art but to work as carriers of content and opinion. In Managua, the swooping letters developed for New York graffiti spell out the initials of the Sandinista party. In the Palestinian West Bank, a big-eyed figure you'd expect to see decorating a wall in Los Angeles wears a keffiyeh and proclaims a longing for a "free Palestine," as the text beside him says, in English.

It's not clear whether the use of English in so much of this wall-painting 5 represents a desire to speak to Western eyes or whether English has simply become the standard idiom for political protest, even of the local variety. (It could be that the two are almost the same.) But it does seem clear that the stylistic clichés of graffiti in the West—the huge loopy letters, the exaggerated shadows dropped behind a word—have become an international language that can be read almost transparently, for the content those clichés transmit. Look at New York-style graffiti letters spelling "Free Libya" on a wall in Benghazi or proclaiming "revolution" in Tahrir Square: Rather than aiming at a new aesthetic effect, they take advantage of an old one that's so well-known it barely registers.

That thing called "art" in the West is essentially an insider's game, thrilling to play but without much purchase on the larger reality outside. We have to look at societies that are truly in crisis to be reminded that images—even images we have sometimes counted as art—can be used for much more than game-playing. In a strange reversal, the closer graffiti comes to being an empty visual commodity in the West, the better it serves the needs of the rest of the world's peoples, who eagerly adopt it to speak about their most pressing concerns. It is as though Coca-Cola, as it spread across the globe, turned out to be a great nutritional drink.

Analyze

1. What is Gopnik's central claim about the role of graffiti? Consider his opening comment, "The worst moment in the history of graffiti came during what was also its heyday, in the early 1980s in New York." Why does he think this was a "worst moment" for graffiti? Do you agree?

2. Write a history of the word *graffiti*. Begin by tracing its etymological roots to the Ancient Greek, modern Italian, and now to its status as a word understood globally. Consider how its meaning has changed over time, and provide visual examples.

3. "Then, by way of contrast, think about graffiti as it appears to us around the world today, in places where painting on a wall is about speaking truth to power." What does the expression "speaking truth to power" mean, and what examples does Gopnik provide that illustrate what he means?

Explore

1. Do you consider it "selling out" if an artist is compensated for his political or social commentary artwork? Can an artist be a political/ social commentator *and* earn a living with her work? Research political art and provide a well-reasoned response, with examples to support your point of view.

2. "In all these cases, graffiti is being used as a true means of communication rather than as purely aesthetic exchange." How might someone argue against what Gopnik claims here? Is a means of expression ever separate from its "aesthetic exchange?"

3. "It's not clear whether the use of English in so much of this wall-painting represents a desire to speak to Western eyes or whether English has simply become the standard idiom for political protest, even of the local variety. (It could be that the two are almost the same.)" What is

the role of English in political protest art? In a research paper, look into the uses of English in recent global political protests and make a case for whether it's intended for "Western eyes," or "has become a standard idiom for political protest," or something altogether different.

Sarah Lacy
"You Think Hollywood Is Rough? Welcome to the Chaos, Excitement and Danger of Nollywood"

Sarah Lacy, an American author and technology journalist, is the founder and editor-in-chief of *PandoDaily*, a technology news site that was launched in January 2012. She has been covering technology news for more than 15 years, most recently as a senior editor for *TechCrunch*, an online publication that was founded in June 2005 and is dedicated to profiling startups, reviewing new Internet products, and breaking tech news. "You Think Hollywood Is Rough? Welcome to the Chaos, Excitement, and Danger of Nollywood" was posted on *TechCrunch* in May 2011.

How does the filmmaking of a region, a culture, or a nation reflect its values and ideals? Is it reasonable to assume that much can be learned about a society from the films it produces?

It was when they pulled out the machetes that I started to worry.

I'd seen men with machetes in Africa before, but they were rusty, practical tools used for clearing away brush by the side of the highway. These were long, shiny and housed in decorative sheaths, pulled out ostensibly so the men could sit down more comfortably, but done with a clear, understated flair. They were more like sultan swords than jungle tools.

The kicking in my six-month pregnant belly had gone eerily silent since we entered the vigilante court at Alaba. I reassured myself that I'd been through things like this before. The time I went to visit Brazilian entrepreneur Marco Gomes' hometown in the crime-ridden slums of central Brazil, comforted only by his reassurance that "No foreigner has ever died in my hometown, because no foreigner has ever been to my hometown." And the time I was driving along the border between Rwanda and the Democratic Republic of Congo and armed Rwandan guards stopped our car, wordlessly got in the backseat and hitched a ride for several miles. And then there was the time we were charged by a baboon.

Looking at those beady baboon eyes rushing towards me, I was instantly convinced I was losing an arm. Now, in this Nigerian "courtroom," my husband was looking at the machetes having the same thought. I was just hoping they didn't realize he'd slipped the camera's memory card in his pocket. I tried to pat my stomach as apologetically as I could. Sorry, son. Welcome to life as my kid.

5   Sometimes I write provocative leads that aren't quite what they seem. Like the time I said I was in a wheelchair getting a blood transfusion in Singapore. As the second graph explained, I was actually at a hospital-themed bar where you sit in wheelchairs and drink out of IV bags. My cocktail was called a "blood transfusion."

But this time, I'm not being hyperbolic or clever. There's no twist coming. My husband, our unborn child and I were actually sitting in a Nigerian vigilante court being tried for—as near as I could tell—taking photos and not respecting authority. The makeshift courthouse looked like a set of a Western. The judge was named "Bones." The police? Well, there was a station not too far from here, but the police ceded Bones authority in Alaba. They didn't want to get involved.

It could have been a scene in a movie. That irony wasn't lost on us, because our accusers, the people speaking for us, and the judge, jury and—well, let's just call them the guys with the machetes—were there to protect the interests of the rough-and-tumble world of the Nigerian filmmaking. They call it Nollywood.

Nollywood sprung up a few decades ago and is the second largest film industry in the world by volume. Producers churn out hundreds of movies a month, most shot on a shoe-string budget of about $15,000 per picture. We visited a set of a film called "The Stripers." It reminded me of the photos in Larry Sultan's book about low-frills porn sets, "The Valley," sans sex and nudity of course.

The film—a romantic comedy where one of Nollywood's hottest actresses turns a gay man straight—was shot in an empty suburban house rented for a few days with a crew of no more than ten. The assistant did the hair and makeup, and the producer did most everything else.

There are few theatrical releases in Nollywood. Most of these movies— which Nigerians consume as rabidly as Brazilians devour their telenovelas— are seen on local TV stations and sold over DVDs. And these producers move fast: Last week we saw a movie on the market called "Dead at Last: Osama Bin Laden, Complete Season One: Life and Death."

Like most industries in emerging markets, Nollywood is developing in a very different time than Hollywood or even Bollywood developed, and that alone means it's developing in a very different way. On the plus side, cheap modern digital production tools have made it all possible. But rampant digital piracy means there's no honeymoon period for producers to build an industry around protected copyrights. They produce content millions of people love, but most of these scrappy street producers are constantly operating on shoe-string budgets, lucky to break even on each film.

Alaba International Market is where the producers all have their storefronts and distribution hubs. We met dozens of them inside a long, dark cave-like hallway where each producer operated out of a cell-sized office, filled with paper records, movie posters pasted over movie posters, and spindles of thousands of DVDs.

Some of these producers are highly-educated entrepreneurs following their passion the same way the best entrepreneurs in Silicon Valley have. We met one man named Ulzee, a Nollywood pioneer who decided to make movies after getting a science degree. His wife, trained as a lawyer, joined him along the seemingly crazy journey. His biggest hit was "Osuofia in London," one of the first Nollywood films to get international attention. He shot it on location in London and it cost about $6,500 to make—a jaw-dropping investment for a Nollywood picture back in 2003. But it grossed more than $650,000.

Much like the 419 scam business, members of Nigeria's 50 million-person unemployed class see the glamorous, seemingly easy money of Nollywood and have flooded into the business. Ulzee doesn't respect many of them, saying they aren't artists. They shoot once and release the same movie with four different covers just to make an extra buck. Of course, given the rampant piracy that's destroyed their margins, you can understand why these producers are constantly trying to milk revenues out of the same film.

Here's what makes the mood at the Alaba market so tense: Before you get to that hallway of producers peddling their movies in their cell-like offices, you walk past the open air markets where the software and DVD pirates have set up shop. Unlike Hollywood where the producers reside in glamourous offices and pirates operate in the shadows and basements of the Internet, in Alaba the content creators and those destroying their hopes of revenues reside in the same place, selling the same product side-by-side. Fire-and-brimstone evangelical preachers set up keyboards and microphones in the middle of the street to save souls, only adding to the chaos. So I could understand why Bones and his council occasionally need some machetes to keep the peace.

After 40 weeks in emerging countries, markets tend to blur together, but Alaba was unlike any place I've seen before. It was rawly and intensely Nigerian. Nigeria isn't a culture based on pleasantries. A local saying painted on the backs of trucks sums it up: "No Paddy for Jungle," or no one has friends in the jungle.

And Lagos is like a jungle. On Victoria Island—the ritzy section of Lagos—incomes are high even for a dual economy, thanks to oil and corruption. The most basic four-star hotels cost upwards of $500 a night, and the rich buy up rooms for a whole year or more, artificially constricting supply. Plots of land cost millions and a middle-of-the-road dinner for two without drinks can run $100 or more. But on the mainland in Lagos, you see the real Nigeria, the one where one-third of the population is unemployed. I talked to people furious by the corruption in the country, and what they felt was an unfair nepotism among the rich that made it almost impossible to climb the societal ladder.

Even the people I met in "easy money" businesses such as scamming and Nollywood toil entrepreneur's hours to build their fortunes, constantly under pressure to outsmart the people out to kill their livelihoods—whether that's law enforcement in the case of scammers or pirates in the case of Nollywood.

The tension is palpable. Stuck in traffic on the freeways, we saw fistfights break out. Unlike some other developing countries where hawkers will smile and flatter Westerners in an attempt to sell them outrageously priced goods, Nigerians don't play that game. They're happy to sell you something if you show the cash. Otherwise, keep moving. They have little use for smiling, nodding and pandering. It's not necessarily that there's more anger, resentment or corruption in Nigeria than the rest of the emerging world; Nigerians just wear it on their sleeves.

Part of me loves that. The warm hospitality many people showed us— 20
in both poor and rich areas of the city—was genuine. You know where you
stand in these places; it's all out in the open. But it makes walking through
these markets intimidating. Look at a hawker and smile on the wrong day,
and you'll get screamed at just for being there. As one 419 scammer told
me, "If I can't even trust a man with the black flesh, why should I ever
trust you?"

Our guide through Nollywood was an entrepreneur named Jason
Njoku. His parents are Nigerian, but he grew up in the United Kingdom.
He became entranced with Nollywood a few years ago and was bored with
London. So he moved here, stunning his family and friends. He started
Iroko Partners to catalog this vast Nollywood inventory and give it a new
global distribution life on the Web. It sounds like a recipe for a city boy to
get fleeced, but so far that hasn't been the case.

Njoku spent weeks trolling the Alaba markets introducing himself to
producers and trying to explain to them how a YouTube channel could be
an answer for revenues, not simply another channel for the pirates to steal
their intellectual property. Once he sold a few of the bigger ones like Ulzee,
word spread and more producers piled in. Just four months in to his business, Njoku has bought the online rights to 500 movies from 100 different
one-man production houses. Last month his YouTube channel had 1.1 million
uniques, 8 million streams, and is on pace to do more than $1 million in
revenues this year from YouTube ads. Those numbers are massive for a
Nigerian-based Web company, particularly in such a short time. Facebook
has one of the largest user-bases here, feeling ubiquitous in the city. And yet
it has less than three million users.

Njoku is playing a long-game. Most of his traffic is from outside
Nigeria, because broadband penetration is still so low there. He's paying
more than he would have to for rights; about $3,000 per film, roughly
what TV stations pay. That immediately returns about one-third of the
production costs, a welcome surprise for a new medium that most of
these producers had never really considered before. He provides a lot of
other value-added services too, like creating an IMDB-equivalent for the
messy Nollywood industry, and watching all movies to strip out things
like the unauthorized use of a Beyoncé song. In the future, he's going
to provide French subtitles so the movies can find new audiences in
surrounding West African nations.

The checks have endeared Njoku to this rag-tag community of producers. One of Njoku's several cell phones rings constantly with producers calling him to check on contracts, release dates and when they're getting their next checks.

25   And that loyalty came in handy about the time a screaming mob broke out in Alaba over the presence of two unknown Americans taking pictures. I'm still not sure if they actually thought we were spying on their business or just wanted to extort us for cash. I'm still not sure whether it was the pirates, the producers or other rabble rousers who were the instigators. The ring leader appeared to be a terrifyingly huge, enraged, bald guy wearing a tight, white muscle shirt that said "SKULL SHIT" in big letters.

We barricaded ourselves in Ulzee's cell-like office until it died down. We didn't have another choice. We were half way down a long, dark hallway of offices, and there was no way out without going through the mob. Ulzee's wife, who'd been lounging on some boxes when we arrived, sprung into action, explaining to the accusers that we were their guests and welcome to do what we wanted.

Eventually, the chaos died down, we promised not to take any more pictures and we tried to leave. But as soon as we left the office, it erupted again and the crowd encircled us. The screaming intensified, echoing through the cave-like hallway. I tried to go back into Ulzee's office, but the doors were being locked behind me by Bones' crew. We were trapped, and the angry faces were circling in tighter, the screaming unintelligible as it echoed from wall-to-wall.

"Trust me, it's better that this plays out here than on the street," Njoku said. "Half of the people yelling are on our side."

News of the uproar reached Bones, the man entrusted to keep the peace between producers, pirates and rare interlopers like ourselves. And that's when we were summoned to his court. A phalanx of producers escorted us through the streets making sure no more harm came to us before we got there. "Don't worry," Njoku whispered. "As long as I have my checkbook, they still need me alive."

30   We sat on one bench. The producers sat on the other. And that's when Bones and the machete-men strolled in. After hearing all the evidence, our insistence that we respected his authority, the producers vouching for us, and of course, some cash changed hands, the machetes stayed sheathed and they let us go.

Njoku didn't break a sweat. Rather than convincing me he was trying to regulate something that couldn't possibly be regulated, the whole episode made me more bullish on his company. It was clear how much the legitimate entrepreneurs in this community valued him, the depth of his relationships after just four months, and his innate understanding for navigating crisis in a terrifying situation.

If a business like this were being built in the West, there'd be few barriers to entry. Someone can always just pay higher license fees. But in a country like Nigeria, these sorts of relationships, this kind of trust in a place where no one trusts anyone are more solid barriers to entry than patents.

The demand is there. The supply is there. Nollywood will emerge out of this chaos as something hugely profitable. There's suspicion, competition and chaos surrounding the market, but that's business in emerging markets. At the end of the day the producers weren't unreasonable. They asked that next time Njoku bring guests, he give them a heads up and they'd provide protection. They're justifiably suspicious because their industry is finally starting to take off, and they sit next to the people trying to erode it every day. And my bet is that when Nollywood does take off, Njoku will be one of the guys to reap the benefits.

Of course, we couldn't leave without pressing our luck and asking to take Bones & Co.'s picture. It's below, and he's on the bottom right.

(Note: Those smiles were nowhere to be seen before the cash changed hands.)

Analyze

1. There are two threads going through Lacy's article: her firsthand experience of Nollywood corruption, and her report on Nollywood. Summarize each of them, and explain how they relate to each other.
2. How is Nollywood part of an emerging market? How is it different from Hollywood or Bollywood according to the author? What further questions do you have about Nollywood?
3. Who is the primary audience for Nollywood films, and how does it view them?

Explore

1. Lacy does not consider the films aesthetically or politically. See if you can watch one of the films she mentions (e.g., *Osuofia in London* or another one with the actor Nkem Owoh). What does this film tell you about Nollywood and the film industry in Nigeria? How does it compare to films you typically watch?
2. Bollywood and Nollywood have been given their titles in reference to Hollywood. Why? What do they have in common with Hollywood and each other? Where in the world might be the next emerging "–ollywood," and why? Research the answers to these questions and write an expository paper in which you explain the local significance of a global industry.
3. Movie stars have had the public in thrall since the beginning of cinema not much more than a hundred years ago. Who are the biggest movie stars that you have never heard of? With others in your class, create a magazine in which you profile movie stars from around the world. Together, decide what aspects of their lives you want to include and describe.

Jackson Allers
"Voice of the Streets: The Birth of a Hip-Hop Movement"

Jackson Allers, a successful producer of hip-hop music, became a full-time journalist in 2002. Since the spring of 2006, Allers has been based in the Middle East, working as an editor, journalist, and documentary filmmaker. He is writing a book about the rise of Arab hip-hop in the Middle East and lecturing on its role in the Arab Spring. In January 2012, he became managing editor of World Hip Hop Market (WHHM), a music and event promotion and merchandizing company specializing in international (non-American) hip-hop music. The following post appeared on the WHHM website on January 20, 2012, just five days before the one-year anniversary of the Egyptian uprisings.

Why do you think hip-hop, with its roots in urban America, has been so readily adopted by Arab youth—particularly in a time of political upheaval?

L ast November, 12 of the region's best-known Arab rappers were set to perform together at a public youth center in the swanky central Cairo district of Zamalek. Organizers billed *Voice of the Streets* as a concert to remind people about "the continued struggle for freedom of expression in the wake of the Arab uprisings." Indeed, it was an Arab hip-hop event without precedent.

Unlikely rap torchbearer, Tunisia's MC El Général whose song *Rayess Labled (Head of State)* was a musical anthem for the uprisings, and MC Swat from Libya, who was featured in numerous international stories about the musical scions of the Libyan rebel movement, were both "prize-winning" elements to the stellar line-up.

But the day before the event was scheduled to take place, event organizer Martin Jakobsen, director of the educational NGO Turntables in the Camps and founding member of the legendary Danish DJ collective Den Sorte Skole (The Black School) told WHHM that neither rapper was going to make it.

"Do you expect any trouble at the event or with the event?" I asked Jakobsen in a late-night interview at an activist hostel on Abd El Khaliq Tharwat street downtown—about one half-klick[1] northwest of Egypt's protest epicentre, Tahrir Square.

5   "We sure as hell hope not," he said, clearly worried about the contingencies. "We got our security clearances. Actually, we had to pay for the security clearances."

He told me that they got through to the "right" people in the military regime.

I'd heard from activists and journalists for months that changes to the regime since the fall of longtime dictator Hosni Mubarak were cosmetic at best. Jakobsen one-upped that. "Everything has stayed the same. You have to bribe your f*#@ng way through the process. The bribes we had to pay off to organize this event were unbelievable," he said.

In the two days leading up to the event, Jordanian organizers Immortal Entertainment—owner and photographer Nasser Kalaji and his partner, filmmaker, editor and street photographer Laith Majali—were out with the MCs shooting footage of them breaking into impromptu guerrilla raps on the streets of Cairo.

The energy with the MCs was manic according to Kalaji. "What we did was hit areas with high concentrations of students. And to see the reaction of kids and students walking by pausing—totally dialled in to what these guys were spitting—that was incredible."

10   It was a bold move. Besides the marketing potential of the stunt, such actions would have landed the MCs (and entourage) in jail pre-Mubarak. "One time we were shooting a video for Arabian Knightz," Kalaji explained referring to Egypt's power rap crew, "And while we were shooting, a national security officer almost arrested us. Luckily, we were able to buy him off with $20."

Mai'a, a blogger in Cairo who runs *guerrilla mama medicine* wrote:

> on wednesday night, happened to be sitting next to a group of guys
> at a bar. when one of them starts beat boxing and another starts
> rhyming in arabic. it was this beautiful unexpected moment. after
> that me and my friends took pictures of them and talked with them
> and found out that they were holding a show called, the voice of the
> street, based on the arab spring, two days later.

Ground Zero

On the day of the event, I headed over to the Gezira Youth Center in Zamalek. It was not the location I had envisioned for the concert itself—more Upper West Side Manhattan than South Bronx—home to a preponderance of European expats.

The concert venue was adjacent to the members-only Gezira Sporting Club, built by the British in 1882, but the youth center itself was community enough, with 3 football pitches and a fair amount of green-space for the general public to enjoy.

I arrived around 2 in the afternoon to interview the artists and record the sound check, having bought some wheat paste for the organizers in a Zamalek art store so heads could bomb Cairo with posters later on.   15

As I walked through the gates of the Gezira Youth Center, the massive stage was being built on one of the soccer pitches, but with three hours until the start of the show, it was far from ready. (Par for the course in Egypt, my homies told me.)

What was worse was the presence of two suited spooks skulking around the youth center grounds asking questions of the organizers as the stage hands continued to build.

"Where are all the MCs?" I asked photographer Majali.

He pointed to a small cafe on the youth center grounds that had little kiddie rides and plastic picnic tables scattered near the center's admin building. "All the guys are there," he told me.

Over the years I had been in contact with or worked with nearly all of   20
the artists assembled for the event, but as *they* must have felt when meeting all of their hip-hop peers for the first time, I was nervous when I walked up to their table to greet them.

Jordanian hip-hop stalwart, Hicham Ibrahim aka DJ Sotusura, that unpretentiously smooth musical/DJ backbone of the Jordanian hip-hop underground and the DJ for the Voice of the Street event, was the first to greet me.

"Yo! Brother Jacks. What's up!?"

After a pound, a handshake and a hug, I looked up to see an Arab hip-hop summit in full effect. They all extended an obligatory hip-hop "What ups?" with their hands raised, and I was fully humbled.

There was Boikutt formerly of Ramallah Underground repping Palestine; two young lions Khotta Ba and Tareq Abu Kwaik aka El Far3i from

Jordan; veterans Edd from the Lebanese live hip-hop group Fareeq al Atrash and Malikah also from Lebanon representing as the lone female MC of the event; and you had your bevy of the best Egyptian talent—Deeb and theArabian Knightz (E-Money, Sphinx, Rush) and MC Amin from a dusty-city called Mansoura 120 km north of Cairo.

25   I made my way around table giving pounds to the MCs from Jordan and from Egypt who, with the exception of Deeb, I hadn't met yet. It didn't take me long to notice that despite the historic occasion, these MCs were serious about their purpose in Cairo. While the stage was frantically getting built, these homies were making the most of the delayed soundcheck.

Sotusura went over set lists with the artists while they figured out where the collabo tracks were going to fit in with the solo sets. He played Instrumentals off his computer and the MCs each took turns spitting their verses around the table, tweaking things until they were tight. Listening in to the various sessions was this rare glimpse at their talent, especially because the laptop speaker volume wasn't very loud. (Shit was so impressive.)

Then the first sounds came from the stage and slowly the MCs made their way across the football pitch. The time was 5:30 in the afternoon or thereabouts—a full 30 minutes after the intended start time and more than 4 hours later than the originally scheduled pre-performance warm-up.

By that time the crowds were beginning to grow outside the Gezira Youth Center gate, and the organizers and local MCs all began getting calls that people were being refused entry at the gate.

Hip-Hop Response

For nearly 3 hours the crowds grew outside the gates of the youth center. Egyptian b-boys and b-girls, college students, activists, ex-pats, and a group of people invited by the organizers who had been injured during the revolution—all clamored to get in.

30   As the impatience grew on both sides of the gates, people that had managed to get into the venue early—mostly young MCs and hip-hop heads— started to mingle with some of the performers.

"What's going on? Are you guys going to perform?" came the question— in Arabic—from a young head with a Philadelphia Phillies straight brim on.

"Yo! Whatever happens . . . even if it has to be on the streets . . . we'll perform for you," Rush from Arabian Knightz yelled back—flashing a peace sign.

What happened next will go down as the essence of hip-hop cultural response to pressure. Impromptu freestyle rap cyphers began forming in little pockets around the soccer pitch as the lights from the stage shined down on the 80 or so people gathered there.

One MC after another started facing off. Locals flexed their lyrical games with veterans that had come to Cairo from around the region to perform—shit was serious. And in those cyphers, all bets were off—the playing field was leveled. One cypher in particular put Boikutt, Khotta Ba, and El Far3i together with a local MC Shamsedein.

El Far3i set down the gauntlet first with a devastating set of punch-lines   35
and half-written flows from his up-coming album. Then Khotta Ba and Shamsedeine jumped in—Khotta Ba's flow more measured and smooth Shamsedein's like an Egyptian version of Supernatural—fast and furious incorporating everything he was seeing around him.

Boikutt came in and kind of slapped all the crowd-goers and the MCs with this ill, developed delivery—clear and concise—about being in Egypt and being from Palestine. He talked about the brotherhood of the revolutionaries on the streets and with the MCs, and then Khotta Ba and Shamsedein got into a rap head-cutting contest to the sheer admiration of each. When it ended the bond between the MCs was like soul epoxy.

Limbo

Then the news came in. Security was not letting the wounded of the revolution into the venue, with Gezira club security accusing the event organizers of using their hip-hop event as a "cover to honor the victims and their families."

The organizers talked to the director of the Gezira Sports Club whose position was that the wounded—many visibly scarred, some on crutches and others wearing eye patches—were "criminals who were at the event to cause trouble."

Kalaji, who had spent time taking photographs of these wounded members of the revolution offered to ask them to leave. "I was close enough with these people that they wouldn't be insulted," Kalaji told WHHM.

40   The Gezira director refused saying that if they were told to leave then the press would accuse the club of refusing the victims entry. Then Kalaji told the director that they would stay with the victims during the performance with the private security hired, but she denied that request as well, saying they might have weapons and could hurt people.

The Interior Ministry of Egypt sent their final decree at around 8pm. Without new permitting, organizers were in danger of being hauled off to jail, and with more than 300 people having been refused entry at the gate, effectively 2 months of planning the biggest Arab hip-hop event to date was suddenly a "non-event!"

Epic Switch

One distinguishing element of hip-hop organizing is its ability to adapt. It's a code of the streets that anything can happen at anytime—forced power outages, police crackdowns, squeamish venue owners—are all aspects of hip-hop event history that have often led to the most memorable performances.

With all of the hype from the controversy at the gate and the energy of the MCs that had come from so many different places to perform for the people, frantic calls went out to resuscitate the Voice of the Streets. Would the MCs take it to the streets? Would the Cairo Jazz Club—friendly to performers in the past—be the next venue?

As the MCs all made their way to the crowd waiting outside, a local arts and culture center Darb 17 18 assumed responsibility for salvaging the event—and the word went out through Facebook, Twitter and mobile telephones.

45   Darb 17 18 was in an industrial part of Old Cairo, and was described in a local zine as "one of the main cultural venues of Cairo despite its not so central location." After a herculean effort to get the sound ready and set up the space for an ad hoc concert, the MCs and organizers wondered how many people would make their way across town to attend.

They did come, in droves, lining the street below the 2nd floor balcony of the space that served as the stage for the night.

MC Amin opened the show with his street anthems *Rap Saleni Abuqueda, Madinat al Khataya (Sin City)* and upcoming new release *The Arabs are the Roots Part 3*, showing why he is widely regarded as the future of Egyptian rap with his direct connections to the Egyptian street—his philosophical Egyptian turns of phrase punctuating condemnations of the government.

Malikah then took the stage and joined Amin on an unnamed collaboration. Malikah continued—lyrical guns blazing—showing the audience that there was at least one female MC living in the Arab world that could hold it down in a sea of testosterone.

What came next was perhaps the most fun collaboration of the evening. Malikah was joined on the stage by Edd and MC Amin for the tentatively titled song *Hip-Hop* that melded into the refrain of the chorus the phrase "Cairo City," which the crowd all chanted back in a rousing call-and-response.

"The energy was crazy out there, but I'm so tired," Malikah told me after 50 her performance. She'd told the story earlier at the youth center that two days prior to the event she was in Columbia for a hip-hop festival in Cali with the revolutionary female Columbian rapper Diana. She'd slept hardly at all and was suffering from a serious case of jet-lag.

"But nothing's gonna stop me on a night like this!" she said, and the fans uniformly praised the press-dubbed "Queen of Arab hip-hop" who after 5 solid years in the game had carved near celebrity status—her raps an homage to her home city Beirut.

After the trio left the stage it was another Beirut-city MC that showed just how good the Lebanese hip-hop scene is. Edd, one of two veteran MCs from Fareeq al Atrash (a word play on the famous Syrian-Egyptian T'arab singer, composer, actor Farid al Atrash) proceeded with three songs from the bands repertoire ending his set with a track from their new album *Baladi*.

Edd's flow, a mixture of hard-hitting political intonations with a laid back but sharp delivery, earned him a sort of rappers fan-base among the MCs themselves, and in a nod to the Egyptian revolution, a track that had burned up the internet airwaves with Arab hip-hop fans, Edd performed the self-produced track *Alamna Marfou3* with Egyptian MC, Mohammed el Deeb aka Deeb, formerly of the Egyptian crew Asfalt. Deeb dropped the track at the height of the revolution at the same time as his EP *Cairofornication*.

"When the people in Egypt heard it, they got the sense that all Arabs were facing the same problems—unemployment, corruption, lack of social and cultural awareness—and were in a constant battle to remember a past before Mubarak" Deeb explained.

55   His song *Masrah Deeb* or "Deebs Stage" was a crowd favorite, not the least because of the production of the song that features a perfectly placed BB King sample. "It's a song reflecting on my daily experiences; my personal relationship with music," Deeb told me, adding, "now people are yearning for songs against oppression with meaning that will also reflect their daily lives."

During one part of the song that night, Deeb intoned, "The microphone is my true friend that appreciates my honesty," and in the hook of the song, what Deeb calls an affaya or punchline, he mentions to the crowd how he is trying to wake people up to the situation in Egypt—a track which he incidentally recorded in the weeks before the January 25 protest date.

After Deeb performed an a cappella version of *Um al Masri*, the Jordanian contingent proved why they were on the bill with more veteran rappers. Khotta Ba and El Far3i cut through a gruff, hard-hitting set of political tracks from their up-coming solo albums that are sure to put Jordan on the map in the Arab hip-hop massive like never before.

In the most polished performance of the night, having just played in the Shatilla Palestinian refugee camp in Beirut a month earlier and having gone through a series of events with his experimental audio-visual group Tashweesh also in Beirut, was Boikutt representing Ramallah in the West Bank.

No doubt the liquid clarity of Boikutt's mic control set the bar for the night as there was no one better than the slight-of-frame Palestinian rhyme-styler at getting his lyrical content through to the audience with a sound system that was pushed to its max the entire night. For many in the audience, it was their first time seeing Boikutt, whose rep as a co-founder of the now defunct Ramallah Underground preceded him.

60   Rounding out the night before the more unknown local MCs capped off the event was the mega-crew and the local crowd favorites—Arabian Knightz. A crew that rolls around 15-deep at its periphery had all three of its core members on stage—Rush, E-Money and Sphinx, recently back from his stint with US Immigration Services in California justifying his life as a rapper in Egypt.

Their songs *Rebel* with Palestinian singer and rapper Shadia Mansour and *Not Your Prisoner* were the most listened to Egyptian hip-hop tracks of the revolution. Preparing for the release of their debut LP *Unknighted State of Arabia,* they performed to a thinned out crowd at around 2 in the am. But, it was a crowd that literally knew all the lyrics to their songs, and who definitely were not going to miss out after the Gezira Youth Center gig was shut down.

The three MCs showed that they were still psyched to be performing despite constant sound struggles with their microphones, and no doubt, they left you wanting another follow-up concert that would better showcase their skills after a night that favored solo performances.

End Game

Finally, when the last speaker was carted out, people continued to mill about well after the performances ended, endorphin's running high, wondering where to go for the after-party. Fans and MCs were lost in conversation in the chill-night air, sweating and amazed, as dozens of empty orange bean bags set out by the organizers hours earlier formed what looked like a huge art installation on a grassy knoll in the middle of the street below the stage.

One conversation with Jordan's El Far3i summed up the evening. Speaking about his own amazement at the show, he recognized that as in any underground rap scene, since hip-hop time began, there were your abstract rappers, your grind-time rappers, your conscious rappers and your street rappers. Certainly, that was what such an historic event was able to convey—that there is an evolution of styles coming through in Arabic detailing the realities of rappers in their various locales.

As the Arab uprisings have shown in the last year, resistance has become a truism for the Arab youth. They have made up the overwhelming majority of the bodies in the crush against state authorities throughout the region. And while the Arab hip-hop heads can be seen as presaging the messaging of these revolutions and their calls to stand up against the machinations of state oppression, until this year, Arab hip-hop was mostly an insular clique whose music had little impact on the larger society.

Now it's fair to say that if ever there was a sense of this elusive idea of an Arabic hip-hop movement that had often seemed more hypothesis than cultural fact, in Cairo on November 4 at the Voice of the Streets event—that hypothesis became tangible.

NOTE

1   A "half-klick" is half a kilometer, or 500 meters.

Analyze

1. How does the author credit the Arab Spring for the birth of an Arab hip-hop movement?
2. How was the *Voice of the Streets* concert organized; what went wrong; and how, in the end, did it go on? What does this communicate to you about hip-hop as a global culture?
3. How does the author position himself in his account of the *Voice of the Streets* concert? Why does he choose to use words like "homies," "spooks," and "wheat paste" without explaining what the terms mean? How would you translate these terms and others for an audience who is not entirely familiar with hip-hop culture?

Explore

1. The author references Tunisia's MC El Général's song *Rayess Labled (Head of State)* as "a musical anthem for the uprisings." Research another key political moment where popular music provided a political voice.
2. Write your own account of a public event that included entertainment. Describe how the event was organized and for what purpose; where it was held; who attended; and the response of the participants.
3. In a 1991 interview, legendary hip-hop DJ Afrika Bambaataa observed of the global impact of hip-hop: "A lot of rap artists are the most vocal people who'll speak whatever is on their mind, from any angle or culture that they want to speak upon. . . . This is music for the young adults and the youth that's speaking upon the government, the community, whites or blacks. Hip-hop can deal with all types of subjects, in addition to peace, unity or 'love you baby—I wanna get down tonight.' It's the fact that the message in rap telling it like it is what's really grabbing hold of young adults throughout the world." Research the spread of hip-hop culture since Bambaataa's 1991 quote. Compare the goals and ideals of its early adherents to those of today's most popular hip-hop artists. Consider the effects of geography, language, culture, and social/political engagements on how global hip-hop artists are "keeping it real."

Charukesi Ramadurai
"Fading Lights in Mumbai"

Charukesi Ramadurai is a freelancer writer, journalist, and photographer from India. She is a regular blogger for *The New York Times* and a columnist for the *South China Morning Post.* The following article, in which she laments the disappearance of Mumbai's traditional single-screen cinema houses in favor of American-style multiplexes, originally appeared on *More Intelligent Life*, a web-based lifestyle and culture publication from the British magazine *The Economist.*

How have you experienced the changes in movie-watching culture over the years? What do you think are the long-term effects of those changes?

These buildings in Mumbai could be ageing courtesans from another time and place. Faded, wrinkled, abused and world-weary, they are the old single-screen cinema houses scattered all over the city. Some still have the spirit to don the war paint in the hopes of luring customers. Others have just given up the struggle.

At four in the afternoon, Royal Talkies near Grant Road in South Mumbai appears desolate. In a hall capable of seating over 600, around 40 heads are visible in the dim light. All eyes are on the screen where an old mother is pleading with her wayward son to mend his ways. The movie is from the 1980s, with stars who have long since retired. The large posters outside the cinema hall announce other obscure films starring macho men from the Hindi hinterlands of North India. "We sell tickets for 20 rupees (roughly 30p / 45 cents)," says the cinema manager. "Anything above that and even this audience will not come. But how can we afford to screen new movies at that cost?"

Tickets at multiplex theatres cost ten times as much, so the crowd here is more forgiving of whatever film is on. Everyone claps and whistles, jeers and cries along with the demands of the story. During the interval (a convention of Indian cinema) the audience steps out to the road, where vendors are ready with cut fruit, chewy omelettes, tepid tea and local sodas called Banta; no concessions are available inside, not even a bottle of drinking water. A cinema employee stands nearby and calls out the name of the film and the ticket prices to passers-by. These ticket callers seem in keeping with the seedy beckoning of the neighbourhood next door, the squalid red-light district of Kamathipura.

The security guards patrolling these cinemas seem inexplicably paranoid. Anyone asking questions or taking photographs is viewed with suspicion, even hostility, though the films themselves are fairly benign. (A few theatres do have discreet 10am shows of what are called "sexy films", but customers in the know tend to quietly troop in on time.)

5   But after their initial wariness, some managers open up. "Why don't you sell these photographs and give us the money to convert this theatre into a multiplex?" jokes one. "That is what people want anyway, that air-conditioned comfort." Another has a different take: "The enemy is not the multiplex theatres. We cater to completely different audiences." He then explains that the real problem is the ready availability of pirated DVDs of new films, which sell for 30 rupees. "The entire family can watch the movie and then return the DVD at half the rate to the seller. How can we compete with anything like that?"

Nestled in the city's noisy bustle, Mumbai's single-screen theatres are exotic anachronisms. Many of them have grand English names—Strand, Metro and, most famously, Opera House—which have long been used to identify the surrounding neighbourhoods. In their heyday, these cinemas were mostly playhouses patronised by upper-class Brits. The now-seedy Alfred was originally the Ripon, one of Mumbai's first playhouses for regional drama.

The road along which many of these theatres sit is still called Pila Haus (a phonetic adaptation), although the entertainment is now limited mainly to old action films. Some owners of once-prosperous theatres in South Mumbai have been investing in restoration and reinvention. The Edward, for instance, has gamely tried to mask its ageing soul with a fresh coat of paint, and has lately been hosting a series of world cinema classics. The Roxy, having been shut for 12 years, now gleams with steel and chrome. Other popular theatres, such as Sterling and Metro, have been converted into multiplexes in recent years with sponsorship from large cinema production houses or theatre chains, such as Reliance Big Cinema and Inox.

But many have not been so lucky. Mumbai may have the largest number of art deco buildings after Miami, but conservation is not on the minds of most Mumbaikars. The few locals who lament the destruction of the city's architectural heritage are not inclined towards activism. And the suburbs up north have readily embraced the spanking new multiple-screen theatres, which show new "multiplex movies" with slick production values, offbeat stories and timely celebrities.

In a city that can be fast and hard, there is very little room for nostalgia. Deepa Gahlot, a film writer and critic, sums up this view with an incident that left her frustrated. She had e-mailed a famous film actor asking for his help in preserving Capitol theatre, known for its superior architecture. His reply was bluntly dismissive: "Everything changes, we can't cling to the past."

Everyone in Mumbai has a single-screen story. My own has to do with   10
late-night shows on Fridays with friends at Sterling in South Mumbai (when it was still Bombay). Specifically, with the taste of the caramel popcorn—then still a novelty—that lingered through the week. And the joy of finding tickets available for that much-anticipated film on the first day of its release, at a time when Internet bookings and simultaneous shows on several screens were unknown. Sometimes this would mean buying "black tickets" (i.e., from touts who sell them at a premium). Built in 1969, Sterling is not as old as some of the other cinema halls in Mumbai, but it was one of the few that screened only English films, and was patronised by a rather young and hip clientele.

This is long before the word "multiplex" became part of the Indian vocabulary. Single-screen cinemas were the only option available. Some were known for their particularly good samosa, others for their dreaded creaky overhead fans, or for a reputation for attracting "rowdy elements." Some were massive sprawls with hundreds of seats while others were smaller and cosier. Every theatre had its own character and charm. Those were the days when I took them for granted.

Analyze

1. Write a description of a nostalgic place from your past where you used to hang out as a child or teenager. Share your description with a group in your class.
2. Why do the theatres that Ramadurai describes have English names? What do those names evoke for you? Why?

3. Why have single-screen cinemas been replaced by multiplexes? Why would people want to preserve old movie theatres? What are the different views expressed in this reading? With whom do you agree?
4. Do you think cities and countries should preserve their old movie theatres in tribute to the past; or do you agree with this quote from the article: "In a city that can be fast and hard, there is very little room for nostalgia"?

Explore

1. Research the "heyday" of cinema in Mumbai (the city formerly known as Bombay). How did it come to be called "Bollywood," and how did it resemble and differ from the heyday of Hollywood? Consider the films that were produced, the movie stars, and the theatres that were built to show them.
2. Cinema has long been recognized as a global art form. Choose an Indian cinema director or film star and discuss his or her influence on popular culture at the time of his or her greatest fame. To what extent did he or she have a global presence or recognition?
3. Ramadurai is wistfully nostalgic about movie theatres in Mumbai. Write a similar piece about something in your popular culture that you're nostalgic about. Set it in the future and make it about something that seems as integral to your current experience as movie houses were to Ramadurai.

Jeff Chang
"So You Think They Can Break-Dance?"

Jeff Chang is an American journalist and hip-hop music and culture critic. He won an American Book Award in 2005 for *Can't Stop, Won't Stop*, his chronicles of the early hip-hop scene in America. His work has appeared in numerous publications, including the *Village Voice*, *Vibe*, *Mother Jones*, *The Nation*, *Spin*, and *Salon*, the award-winning news site that covers breaking news, politics, culture, technology, and entertainment. In "So You Think They Can Break-Dance?" which appeared on *Salon* in June 2008, Chang writes about the ascendance of hip-hop dance culture in South Korea.

What are other examples of pop culture imports that have "gone global" in ways similar to hip-hop dancing? What global influences have you noticed in Anglo-American pop culture?

This summer, the United States is reaching new heights of dance fever as TV shows like Fox's "So You Think You Can Dance" and MTV's "Randy Jackson Presents: America's Top Dance Crew" have returned to the airwaves. MTV's runaway hit is considered especially cutting edge, showcasing hip-hop dance groups from across America. But if MTV really wants the *best* dance crew, it should be looking in South Korea.

"Of the top six or seven crews in the world, I'd say half of them are from Korea," says Christopher "Cros One" Wright, 33, an American dance promoter and b-boy who was recently in Suwon, South Korea, to judge the second annual global invitational hip-hop dance competition, called R16, that was held at the end of May.

The development of South Koreans' hip-hop dancing could be seen a cultural parallel to their sharp global ascendance in electronics and automaking. A decade ago, Koreans were struggling to imitate the Bronx-style b-boy and West Coast funk styles that are the backbone of the genre. Now, a handful of these crews are the safest bets to win any competition anywhere.

Certainly no country takes its hip-hop dance more seriously. The Korean government—through its tourism board and the city of Suwon—invested nearly $2 million in this year's competition. Two of the most successful teams, Gamblers and Rivers, have been designated official ambassadors of Korean culture. Once considered outcasts, the b-boys now seem to embody precisely the kind of dynamic, dexterous and youthful excellence that the government wants to project.

Although hip-hop dance goes back at least 35 years, the top Korean 5
b-boys trace their histories back just 11 years, to 1997, the Year Zero of Korean breaking. By 2001, the first year that a Korean crew entered the Battle of the Year—the world's biggest b-boy contest—they won "best show" honors and a fourth-place trophy. Every year since, a Korean crew

has placed first or second. Says Battle of the Year founder Thomas Hergenrother, "Korea is on a different planet at the moment."

The R16 competition, held at the Olympic Sports Complex, is broadcast live in prime time in South Korea and dozens of other countries. The government expects to gross $35 million from advertising and TV rights this year. And it isn't the only one profiting: Gamblers Crew, formed in 2001, may now be one of the most world's most lucrative hip-hop dance groups. The members regularly tour Asia, have endorsement deals with Fila, Kookmin Bank and Enerzen energy drinks, and will star opposite American teen idol Omarion in the $25 million movie "Hype Nation," the latest in the Hollywood dance-ploitation genre, set to open next year.

While some fans on the message boards for "America's Best Dance Crew" still don't know what a "b-boy" is, the word in South Korea has become synonymous with national pride. B-boy contests around the world attract mostly young males, but the R16 Sports Complex is full of grandparents, high school couples and teenage girls in their school uniforms. When one holds up a sign that reads "I (Heart) Physics!" she isn't referring to her college-prep curriculum, but to the 24-year-old, Bogart-faced, elbow-spinning star of the Rivers crew, Kim "Physicx" Hyo-Geun.

In South Korea, b-boying rules. The question even Americans are asking is, "How did this happen?"

During the 1970s, an array of dances practiced by black and Latino kids sprang up in the inner cities of New York and California. The styles had a dizzying list of names: "uprock" in Brooklyn, "locking" in Los Angeles, "boogaloo" and "popping" in Fresno, and "strutting" in San Francisco and Oakland. When these dances gained notice in the mid-'80s outside of their geographic contexts, the diverse styles were lumped together under the tag "break dancing."

10   The most physically demanding style—the Bronx dance called "breaking" or "b-boying"/"b-girling"—fueled a global fascination. In the mid-'80s, b-boys could be found spinning at the Olympics or at President Reagan's inauguration and promoting consumer products. But after the explosion, the dancers were cast off, the detritus of an exhausted fad.

Still, the dances took root around the world. While South Koreans have often been hostile to American imports, from Hollywood films to Washington beef (massive street protests against the government's lifting of the ban on U.S. beef broke out in Seoul the day before R16), hip-hop dance has been welcomed.

That may be partly because of South Korea's history of cultural repression of youth countercultures. During the 1970s, young Koreans in Seoul were being exposed to "Soul Train" and funk music via the U.S. Armed Forces Korea Network. A club scene arose in Itaewon to service American G.I.s. But as early as the summer of 1971, U.S.-backed dictator Park Chung-hee ordered his police to round up longhaired Korean men and cut their hair.

As the decade wore on, he escalated his "social purification" campaign, detaining artists, intellectuals and church leaders. In the first six months of 1976 alone, police reported checking over 600,000 men on hair length and possession of "obscene" T-shirts. Park's censorship committee blocked hundreds of American songs, from "We Shall Overcome" to "Me and Mrs. Jones."

"Black music was considered illegal because it was not good for the youth. The only music allowed was folk music," said Lee "MC Meta" Jaehyun of the influential Korean rap group Garion, through a translator. "The music scene itself died. Influential music makers left the country." When he and his peers became enthralled with images of b-boys at the 1984 Olympics, they had no outlet for their creativity.

It was not until opposition leader Kim Young-sam became South 15 Korea's first civilian leader in 1992 that youth culture seemed to flower again. At first, dance-friendly pop imports like Bobby Brown and MC Hammer spawned a host of Korean copies. "Up until then, it was all ballads," said Choi "DJ Wrecks" Jae-hwa, a pioneering Korean DJ who now spins for the Rivers crew, through a translator. But, Lee added, "the curiosity began and people became hungry for the real thing."

In just five years, Koreans would have their own thing.

It's a cool evening in front of the Ibis Hotel, an imposing postmodern gray slab that commands the Suwon skyline. Dozens of b-boys from around the world gather in groups in the lobby, bolts of color and noise against the hotel's minimalist white marble.

The Dutch crew, Funky Dope Manouvres, looks as ethnically diverse as Supercrew, the American one (which will fly directly from R16 to tape "America's Top Dance Crew"). Drawing dancers not just from Holland but Scandinavia too, FDM includes second-generation kids whose parents come from Brazil, Indonesia, Poland, Ghana and Suriname. Iranian-Swede Mahan "King Foolish" Noubarzadeh, 21, talks about how b-boying has brought together Muslims and Christians. Then he scans the lobby and sizes up the competition: "The favorites here? Gamblers and Rivers."

The next day is the marquee event, head-to-head elimination battles that are the heart of b-boying. Two crews challenge each other with aggressive, stylized choreographed steps and freestyle solo and ensemble moves. Egos are on the line. Tempers sometimes flare. "America's Best Dance Crew" doesn't dare approach this kind of a format. But the heat of the battle often makes the dancing spectacular.

20   Outside the hotel entrance, a Belgian dancer is challenging Kim "Bang Rock" Hyun-jin, 24, a genial round-faced dancer from Rivers, the defending R16 champs. They don't speak each other's language, but the Belgian is calling out the Korean by pointing to the ground and staring out from a chin-up tilt. Kim won't step in the cipher, the space between the dancers surrounded by a circle of onlookers that forms the battleground. So the Belgian starts with a six-step, then drops to a flurry of footwork and ends with a shoulder roll.

Now Kim has to respond. He humiliates the Belgian by imitating the European's movements, and climaxes with a series of virtuoso body spins. When he comes to a stop, he is leaning upside down at an inverted angle, balanced on a shoulder and a hand. He grins up at his opponent. This encounter is over. The Belgian offers a congratulatory hand.

Later, sucking on an ice cream treat, Kim laughs. "I didn't want to battle. I keep asking, 'Why?'" Of course, he knows the answer. It's the reason Korean crews regularly practice five hours a day, seven days a week. "We know there's always somebody trying to catch up with us," says 27-year-old Gamblers crew spokesman Chung "B-Boy Sick" Hyung-sik through a translator. "We always have to be ahead."

R16 co-organizer Johnjay Chon says that a decade ago, there were just five crews in the whole country. This spring, more than 50 entered the country's qualifying competition for R16. At events or clubs in Seoul, Chon regularly spots unknown b-boys taking out experienced pros. "What happens is they practice on the lowdown until they're up at a level where they can actually come out and shock somebody," he says. "They practice in the shadow."

Cho "C4" Chung-woon of Rivers says through a translator, "We've been praised for our technical skills, but that's because we would practice head spinning all day long. That's what sets us apart."

25   Still, the old "Asian work ethic" explanation is just part of the story. When Koreans first emerged, Americans praised them for their power

moves—the highflying crowd-pleasing spins, freezes and gymnastics moves—but criticized the Seoul b-boys for lacking soul. They were thought to be mechanical, unable to rock with the beat, and lacking in "foundation skills," such as the top-rock and footwork moves that form the historical roots of the dance.

"What the Americans said really influenced them," says Charlie Shin, Chon's business partner and a Korean b-boy advocate. "They went back in the lab. It changed them."

They mastered routines, the choreographed ensemble moves that are essential parts of a showdown. They immersed themselves in the music and the rhythms. They studied the history of b-boying and hip-hop culture. Three members of the Rivers crew—Born, C4 and Red Foot—are now affiliates of Mighty Zulu Kings, a crew whose lineage can be traced back to hip-hop pioneer Afrika Bambaataa's Bronx River Project dances in the early 1970s. Even their crew name, Rivers, was chosen to capture an aspect of the hip-hop aesthetic.

"You know how rivers flow? Rivers flow swiftly, and that's also how we move and how we think," C4 says. "B-boys in other countries do it as a hobby, but to the Korean b-boys, our life is b-boying."

R-16 organizers Shin, 31, and Chon, 32, are what Asian-Americans call one-point-fivers—young people born in Asia but raised bilingual and bicultural in America. Shin's 15th birthday came days after riots erupted in Los Angeles on April 29, 1992, after the Rodney King verdict, a traumatic period that Korean-Americans now simply call Sa-I-Gu or "4-2-9" the way one might refer to "9/11." Parts of Koreatown were still in flames and hundreds of Korean-American businesses had been reduced to ashes. The era had poisoned mainstream perceptions of Asian immigrants. White pundits used them to score rhetorical points against welfare and affirmative action, while black leaders boycotted their shops. But neither Shin nor Chon was close enough to the fires to have been burned by them. You could call them members of the post-Sa-I-Gu generation.

Hip-hop formed a crucial part of their identity, and a source of redemption. "For me, growing up in the States, I had been called all kinds of names," Shin says. When he moved to Seoul eight years ago, supporting Korean b-boys became a cause. Seeing them win respect from others, he says, "kind of dissolved all that racial bullshit I grew up with." The Korean-Americans became exemplars of hip-hop culture at a moment when young South Koreans were trying to define a new national identity.

Chon was born in Japan and raised in Seattle. After forming and competing nationally with the multiracial Circle of Fire crew, he came to Seoul on a summer trip in 1997 to visit family. Armed with videos and DVDs of dozens of contests, Chon began scouring the clubs for b-boys to battle. He met the Expression crew—now a hip-hop dance theater troupe—and gave it a video of a legendary Los Angeles b-boy competition called Radiotron.

"A year later I came back and I later I came back and I just saw there were more b-boys. They were telling me, 'Oh you gotta see this footage,'" Chon says. "I'm watching it and it's the Radiotron that I brought out a year ago. It's been dubbed so many times the screen is shaking."

During the year Chon was gone, teenagers such as the Gamblers' B-Boy Sick had caught religion after watching grainy videos like that one. Lively Internet groups brought hip-hop fans together. Japan's obsession with underground American hip-hop was at its peak, and CDs and videos found their way to South Korea through Tokyo. As South Korea's economy spiraled downward in 1997, a vibrant counterculture was emerging in Seoul.

At the Master Plan club in the Chungjeong neighborhood, rap groups like Garion, Artisan Beats & Keeproots and Drunken Tiger JK explored the rhythms of their native tongue and sometimes disclosed personal traumas or attacked social ills. In Taehongno, an area rich in college campuses, nightclubs, galleries and theaters, b-boys suddenly appeared. The Rivers crew and Expression crew, South Korea's first Battle of the Year winners, were among the b-boys who gathered there.

35   They battled all evening in front of the crowds at the popular Maronie Park, then moved to the clubs in the early morning hours. When dawn broke, they headed to school. Their intensity impressed Chon. "I'm like, 'OK how does this work?'" he says he asked the b-boys. "I just sleep in school" was their invariable reply.

These Korean hip-hop heads were the first generation to grow up after authoritarian rule. Those before them had come of age on the front lines of demonstrations against American-backed dictators. But these youths lived under relative, if yet unstable, democracy and prosperity.

They were also mostly working-class outsiders. "The minute you're born in Korea, depending on what your economic background is, or who your parents are, what network you're in, what neighborhood you're in, what high school you went to, what college you went to, your life is pretty much decided for you," Shin says. "The b-boys, it's not like they're the most highly educated kids, but they're good at what they do, and they put as much effort into practicing as the other kids do into the Korean SATs."

Because South Korea is still a country at war, looming over every young man's life is mandatory military service. For working-class b-boys, it acts as a passage into a bleak future. "If they're not in college, they have to do some kind of menial job," according to Shin. Many say that the prospect of military service is the main factor that has accelerated the Korean breaking scene's development. "You see that hunger and that drive," says Korean-American filmmaker Benson Lee, whose 2007 hit documentary "Planet B-Boy" featured a DMZ scene with members of Gamblers and Rivers as battling soldiers.

They know that the freedom of b-boying can't last. "The service will come up when you're 21, 22. But they can always extend that using some excuse," Chon says. "A lot of the b-boys—now they're like 26, 27, they haven't gone. They have to go soon. They keep putting it off because the culture is kind of peaking now."

He estimates that four out of five b-boys currently competing in South 40 Korea have postponed their service or have illegally evaded their conscription. Chon and Shin say they know many b-boys who have mutilated themselves to dodge the army. Kim "Bang Rock" Hyun-jin of the Rivers crew says through a translator, "Everyone tries to avoid the service." Then he switches to English for emphasis. "It's like going to hell."

On the final day of R16, there are more government officials in suits wandering around backstage, the crowd is thicker and louder, the TV crews are everywhere, and the energy is high.

Through the opening rounds of the crew-on-crew battles, the Gamblers and Rivers dispatch their rivals easily. In the semifinals, the Gamblers face the fluid and elegant Brasil All-Stars, whose moves vibrate with the traditions of capoeira. They win in a pleasingly close contest, three judges to two. But when the Rivers crew faces Russia's Top 9 crew from St. Petersburg in the other semifinal—potentially a classic duel of power versus finesse—tension builds.

On an arena stage, crews must face each other across the floor, as if across a DMZ turned battleground. This staging emphasizes the metaphor of the attack. By the rules, each crew must give the other its space on the floor while it is performing. They alternate their turns. No touching of opponents is allowed.

But minutes into the contest, Physicx begins dancing before Russia's tiny dynamo Flying Buddha has finished his solo. When Buddha moves over to stare down Physicx, who has begun a difficult flare sequence, a Rivers member pushes him away. Physicx backs out of the cipher, comes around to high-five Buddha and motions for him to retake the floor. Instead Top 9 starts a three-man routine. Physicx steps back in to disperse Top 9, then motions again to Flying Buddha. The Russian takes a wide berth, flings off his light blue shirt, does a six-step, then launches into a spectacular one-armed move known as an air chair. Now Top 9 is fired up.

45   B-boy Robin, Russia's assassin in a brown Yankees hat, oversize polo shirt and cargo slacks, circles the floor and then taunts the Koreans by pulling back his eyes. Some in the crowd gasp at Robin's slanted-eye dis. But his subsequent solo, featuring a Tony Hawk-style hand plant and surging rolls broken up with one-armed freezes, is flawless. In what b-boys call a "commando" attack—a routine in which a run is begun by one or more b-boys but finished by another, named for the post-gang-era Bronx dancers who invented it as a tactic to prevent the other crew from immediately responding—C4 dives through two Rivers members and leaps straight at Robin, pulling his own eyes back, then miming a castration of Robin. The crowd roars.

But as the battle continues, Rivers seems exhausted, while Top 9 gains momentum. In their final routine, the Top 9 b-boys do a number of clever duet Lindy Hop-style routines, jumping off each other, flipping each other into spins and forming circles for crewmates to leap through. When Top 9 wins 5-0, some in the crowd boo. But this won't be Rivers' day. It finishes fourth behind the Brasil All-Stars.

In the finals, South Korea's Gamblers crew counters Top 9's routines with elaborate commandos and ample personality. As the clock ticks down, the dancers play "pass the hat." B-boy Pop handstands across the stage and balances on his left hand. Then he arches his body into the heart of the Top 9 line and passes a white baseball cap to a hand-spinning Soul Soy. On the Gamblers' last run, b-boy Sick chases Robin and Top 9 out of the cipher, drops down for some fleet footwork, then quickly contorts himself through a set of wire-doll freezes that wouldn't look out of place on a Cirque du Soleil stage.

When the Gamblers are announced as the champions, Pop flings his shirt into the crowd and strikes a kung-fu matinee idol pose at the edge of the stage. Cameras and cellphones flash. Soul Soy announces to the media that it is donating its R16 winnings to victims of the earthquakes in China and Myanmar. It's an audacious statement. The $15,000 first-place prize is the largest that has ever been offered at any b-boy event in the world.

Later, Sick signs autographs and takes pictures with two stricken schoolgirls. As he waves and disappears into the bus, they clutch their autographed programs and continue blushing and bowing. There are few big-name b-girls now in South Korea, but who knows? Perhaps those girls will form the next generation of champion dance crews. "The world is a big place, man, and there's another hungry competitor stepping up," R-16 judge and legendary Rock Steady crew b-boy Ken Swift says. "It's a cycle, and the cycle is based upon crews like these Korean crews who go out and inspire these new fans. And then five years from now, those new people are going to be saying, 'OK *we're* the shit now.'"

Analyze

1. Why did the South Korean government have such a stark turn-around in its attitude toward youth culture, and especially b-boys?
2. "The Korean-Americans became exemplars of hip-hop culture at a moment when young South Koreans were trying to define a new national identity." How did these "one-point-fivers" influence the South Koreans to define a new national identity? What does one-point-fiver refer to?
3. How do you account for the popularity of competitions such as the "crew on crew battles" described in this article? What about poetry jams or "American Idol"?

Explore

1. Choose a pop culture trend that impassions and/or intrigues you. Focus on one geographical scene and explore and document its emergence as Chang has done with the b-boys in Seoul.
2. Notice Chang's descriptive language of the b-boys as they "battle" against each other. Attend a live performance of a music, dance, or theatre group you love, and write a description so that those who are not familiar with the group can "see" it through your eyes.
3. Can you imagine pop culture competitions becoming globally unified like the Olympics or nationally sponsored like those in South Korea?

Imagine a program for the first biannual Global Pop Culture Competition. Where would it take place? What would the categories be? Who would be eligible to compete? What would the criteria for winning be?

Forging Connections

1. What connections can you make between the functions of hip-hop in North Africa and Korea and those of graffiti as Gopnik describes it in "Revolution in a Can"?

2. Roozbeh Shirazi and Jeff Chang mention immigrants' children in their articles. Shirazi is the son of Iranian immigrants, and Chang discusses "one-point-fivers" (referring to generation 1.5), immigrants who have come to their new countries as children or teenagers. Write an essay that explores what the benefits might be of growing up in two different cultures. Consider how this knowledge might be cultivated into a more globalized perspective. Use Shirazi and Chang or other authors as examples and evidence, as well as your own experiences or those of your friends.

Looking Further

1. There have been a number of readings in this book that have cited war (Afghanistan, Iraq), rebellion (North Africa and Middle East), military service (South Korea), and conflict-torn regions (Sierra Leone). Write a paper that examines how pop culture provides a platform for responding to and promoting awareness of such issues while engaging people. What are the general themes you see across genres of popular culture and across cultural, national, or regional concerns?

2. How has pop culture become globalized? One theme emerging from the chapters in this book has been the ways in which pop culture travels so easily across national, linguistic, and cultural borders, adapting and even reinventing itself within local contexts. In chapter 5, "Communication and Technology," we saw hip-hop culture affecting the Arab Spring through social media, and Latin America *telenovelas* at the center of public resistance in Iran thanks to illegal satellite dishes. In chapter 2, "Identity and Place," and chapter 4, "Languages in Contact," we read about video games (to the chagrin of the selection's

author) infiltrating the Arctic Circle. Write a research paper in which you identify and examine other ways in which pop culture has crossed borders. How has it "traveled," and how have people adapted or reinvented it to fit their local contexts? In what ways has it connected them to the larger world? Based on what you've discovered, how might you describe the process of globalizing pop culture? You may want to include audio and video clips in your paper, as well as images. Or you may want to organize your research using entirely digital platforms.

9 Change & Transformation

There have been many thematic strands threading through this book's readings on globalization. Certainly we can see that place and identity, language and culture, gender matters and money matters, health, happiness, and hunger, conflict and rebellion, land and climate are all changing and transforming personal lives and global perspectives. This last chapter revisits many of these themes, and I ask you to also consider as you read the theme of change and transformation: how we read the unfolding of events; how our actions (or inactions) contribute to change, wanted and otherwise; and how writing itself (whether by the authors represented here or our own) effects change and in so doing transforms lives.

As you take in this next set of readings, see if you can look at them through the lens of globalization you've cultivated—a lens that helps you perceive more deeply and more broadly what is immediately in front of you. That "perceiving" doesn't always come from knowing and having information at hand, but rather from practicing the habits of mind that promote inquiry, curiosity, openness, and the ability to suspend judgment.

We begin by looking at what Martin Walker, a veteran journalist and global business policy expert, calls "The World's New Numbers." He demonstrates how we might understand, use, and interpret global demographics to formulate, address, and resolve some of our current challenges and conundrums: Will the biosphere be able to sustain a growing population? How will decreased fertility and increased longevity affect the culture of family, community, and work? In a world with increased transnational migration, how are immigrants affected by their new cultures, and how in turn does that affect fertility rates? How has a decreased population of women prompted what Walker calls "the geopolitics of sexual frustration"? How can demographic statistics and trends help to track change and enable transformation?

Next, Damon Tabor takes us on an adventure of a lifetime in "If It's Tuesday, It Must Be the Taliban." What risks are we willing to endure in order to "see the world," and why do we set out to see it in the first place? How do the goals of *tourists* differ from those of *travelers*? How can we have traveled somewhere only to find, like Tabor, that "it still felt just out of reach"? Our travels continue with writer Petina Gappah, who returns to her childhood home in "Zimbabwe," retracing as an adult the changes that occurred in her schooling as the country transitioned from colonial Rhodesia to postcolonial Zimbabwe. Have the prospects of an education that can transform the lives of black Zimbabweans actually changed, and why?

Change continues with Paul Salopek in "The Last Famine." Walking with pastoral herdsmen of the Daasanach people in Northern Kenya, he is witness to the contemplation of the end of "a venerable way of life and a 10,000-year-old economy." As we read, we can consider what has pushed the Daasanach to make these choices; what alternatives they might have; and how we might generalize their situation to those of other cultures and indigenous peoples worldwide. In a very different genre of writing, Francis Kuria writes about the same situation in "It's Time for the Turkana to Leave Their Wastelands and Settle Down." Why does Kuria's opinion piece seem so much more urgent than Salopek's?

Our chapter—and book—concludes with a selection written by economists Abhijit Banerjee and Esther Duflo (a recipient of the MacArthur "genius grant"). While the title, "More Than 1 Billion People Are Hungry in the World," sounds dire, the intelligence with which Banerjee and Duflo frame their research and findings is surprising, creative, and casts "hunger" in a very different light. They open our eyes to the surprising complexity of assumptions and responses to hunger, poverty, and aid—on the part of those who are poor and hungry recipients of aid, and on the part of those who seek to alleviate that hunger and its causes.

More than anything, I hope that you read these selections as the emerging writer you've become while responding thoughtfully to the themes of globalization throughout this book. Notice how you've broadened and refined your sense of audience and the diverse readership you can address as a writer. In anticipating your readers' questions and concerns, notice how you're already formulating ways to define and explain your terms. Although you are willing to argue and persuade when appropriate, you might now feel equally comfortable using writing as a way to test, share, and articulate thoughts and interpretations that are as yet tentative and not fully formed. I also hope you realize that just as you can be a reader of many voices, you can also adapt many different voices in your writing—and that all of them can be yours.

Martin Walker
"The World's New Numbers"

Martin Walker, a senior scholar at the Woodrow Wilson Center, is also the senior director of the Global Business Policy Council for A. T. Kearney, a global management consultant firm. He was a journalist with the British newspaper *The Guardian* for 25 years, serving as bureau chief in Moscow and the United States, and is editor-in-chief emeritus of United Press International. "The World's New Numbers" appeared in the spring 2009 edition of *The Wilson Quarterly*, published by the Woodrow Wilson International Center for Scholars. Since 1976, the *Quarterly* has provided a nonpartisan, non-ideological lens on questions related to policy, culture, religion, science, and other fields that bear upon public life.

Why are birthrates such an important statistic for governments as they consider public policies? In what ways do the advantages and disadvantages of high birthrates shift and change when talking about national birthrate scales compared to international or global birthrate scales?

Something dramatic has happened to the world's birthrates. Defying predictions of demographic decline, northern Europeans have started having more babies. Britain and France are now projecting steady population growth through the middle of the century. In North America, the trends are similar. In 2050, according to United Nations projections, it is possible that nearly as many babies will be born in the United States as in China. Indeed, the population of the world's current demographic colossus will be shrinking. And China is but one particularly sharp example of a widespread fall in birthrates that is occurring across most of the developing world, including much of Asia, Latin America, and the Middle East. The one glaring exception to this trend is sub-Saharan Africa, which by the end of this century may be home to one-third of the human race.

"Despite their many uncertainties, demographic projections have become an essential tool."

The human habit is simply to project current trends into the future. Demographic realities are seldom kind to the predictions that result. The decision to have a child depends on innumerable personal considerations and larger, unaccountable societal factors that are in constant flux. Yet even knowing this, demographers themselves are often flummoxed. Projections of birthrates and population totals are often embarrassingly at odds with eventual reality.

In 1998, the UN's "best guess" for 2050 was that there would be 8.9 billion humans on the planet. Two years later, the figure was revised to 9.3 billion—in effect, adding two Brazils to the world. The number subsequently fell and rose again. Modest changes in birthrates can have bigger consequences over a couple of generations: The recent rise in U.S. and European birthrates is among the developments factored into the UN's latest "middle" projection that world population in 2050 will be just over 9.1 billion.

In a society in which an average woman bears 2.1 children in her lifetime—what's called "replacement-level" fertility—the population remains stable. When demographers make tiny adjustments to estimates of future fertility rates, population projections can fluctuate wildly. Plausible scenarios for the next 40 years show world population shrinking to eight billion or growing to 10.5 billion. A recent UN projection rather daringly assumes a decline of the global fertility rate to 2.02 by 2050, and eventually to 1.85, with total world population starting to decrease by the end of this century.

Despite their many uncertainties, demographic projections have 5
become an essential tool. Governments, international agencies, and private
corporations depend on them in planning strategy and making long-term
investments. They seek to estimate such things as the number of pensioners, the cost of health care, and the size of the labor force many years into
the future. But the detailed statistical work of demographers tends to seep
out to the general public in crude form, and sensationalist headlines soon
become common wisdom.

Because of this bastardization of knowledge, three deeply misleading
assumptions about demographic trends have become lodged in the
public mind. The first is that mass migration into Europe, legal and illegal, combined with an eroding native population base, is transforming
the ethnic, cultural, and religious identity of the continent. The second
assumption, which is related to the first, is that Europe's native population
is in steady and serious decline from a falling birthrate, and that the aging
population will place intolerable demands on governments to maintain
public pension and health systems. The third is that population growth in
the developing world will continue at a high rate. Allowing for the uncertainty of all population projections, the most recent data indicate that all of
these assumptions are highly questionable and that they are not a reliable
basis for serious policy decisions.

In 2007, *The Times* of London reported that in the previous year
Muhammad had edged out Thomas as the second most popular name
for newborn boys in Britain, trailing only Jack. This development had
been masked in the official statistics because the name's many variants—
such as Mohammed, Mahmoud, and Muhamed—had all been counted
separately. *The Times* compiled all the variants and established that
5,991 Muhammads of one spelling or another were born in 2006,
trailing 6,928 Jacks, but ahead of 5,921 Thomases, 5,808 Joshuas, and
5,208 Olivers. *The Times* went on to predict that Muhammad would
soon take the top spot.

On the face of it, this seemed to bear out the thesis—something of a rallying cry among anti-immigration activists—that high birthrates among
immigrant Muslims presage a fundamental shift in British demography.
Similar developments in other European countries, where birthrates among
native-born women have long fallen below replacement level, have pro-
voked considerable anxiety about the future of Europe's traditionally
Christian culture. Princeton professor emeritus Bernard Lewis, a leading

authority on Islamic history, suggested in 2004 that the combination of low European birthrates and increasing Muslim immigration means that by this century's end, Europe will be "part of the Arabic west, of the Maghreb." If non-Muslims then flee Europe, as Middle East specialist Daniel Pipes predicted in *The New York Sun*, "grand cathedrals will appear as vestiges of a prior civilization—at least until a Saudi-style regime transforms them into mosques or a Taliban-like regime blows them up."

The reality, however, looks rather different from such dire scenarios. Upon closer inspection, it turns out that while Muhammad topped Thomas in 2006, it was something of a Pyrrhic victory: Fewer than two percent of Britain's male babies bore the prophet's name. One fact that gets lost among distractions such as the *Times* story is that the birthrates of Muslim women in Europe—and around the world—have been falling significantly for some time. Data on birthrates among different religious groups in Europe are scarce, but they point in a clear direction. Between 1990 and 2005, for example, the fertility rate in the Netherlands for Moroccan-born women fell from 4.9 to 2.9, and for Turkish-born women from 3.2 to 1.9. In 1970, Turkish-born women in Germany had on average two children more than German-born women. By 1996, the difference had fallen to one child, and it has now dropped to half that number.

10   These sharp reductions in fertility among Muslim immigrants reflect important cultural shifts, which include universal female education, rising living standards, the inculcation of local mores, and widespread availability of contraception. Broadly speaking, birthrates among immigrants tend to rise or fall to the local statistical norm within two generations.

The decline of Muslim birthrates is a global phenomenon. Most analysts have focused on the remarkably high proportion of people under age 25 in the Arab countries, which has inspired some crude forecasts about what this implies for the future. Yet recent UN data suggest that Arab birthrates are falling fast, and that the number of births among women under the age of 20 is dropping even more sharply. Only two Arab countries still have high fertility rates: Yemen and the Palestinian territories.

In some Muslim countries—Tunisia, the United Arab Emirates, Bahrain, Kuwait, and Lebanon—fertility rates have already fallen to near-European levels. Algeria and Morocco, each with a fertility rate of 2.4, are both dropping fast toward such levels. Turkey is experiencing a similar trend.

Revisions made in the 2008 version of the UN's *World Population Prospects Report* make it clear that this decline is not simply a Middle Eastern phenomenon. The report suggests that in Indonesia, the country with the world's largest Muslim population, the fertility rate for the years 2010–15 will drop to 2.02, a shade below replacement level. The same UN assessment sees declines in Bangladesh (to 2.2) and Malaysia (2.35) in the same period. By 2050, even Pakistan is expected to reach a replacement-level fertility rate.

Iran is experiencing what may be one of the most dramatic demographic shifts in human history. Thirty years ago, after the shah had been driven into exile and the Islamic Republic was being established, the fertility rate was 6.5. By the turn of the century, it had dropped to 2.2. Today, at 1.7, it has collapsed to European levels. The implications are profound for the politics and power games of the Middle East and the Persian Gulf, putting into doubt Iran's dreams of being the regional superpower and altering the tense dynamics between the Sunni and Shiite wings of Islam. Equally important are the implications for the economic future of Iran, which by midcentury may have consumed all of its oil and will confront the challenge of organizing a society with few people of working age and many pensioners.

The falling fertility rates in large segments of the Islamic world have   15 been matched by another significant shift: Across northern and western Europe, women have suddenly started having more babies. Germany's minister for the family, Ursula von der Leyen, announced in February that the country had recorded its second straight year of increased births. Sweden's fertility rate jumped eight percent in 2004 and stayed put. Both Britain and France now project that their populations will rise from the current 60 million each to more than 75 million by midcentury. Germany, despite its recent uptick in births, still seems likely to drop to 70 million or less by 2050 and lose its status as Europe's most populous country.

In Britain, the number of births rose in 2007 for the sixth year in a row. Britain's fertility rate has increased from 1.6 to 1.9 in just six years, with a striking contribution from women in their thirties and forties—just the kind of hard-to-predict behavioral change that drives demographers wild. The fertility rate is at its highest level since 1980. The National Health Service has started an emergency recruitment drive to hire more midwives, tempting early retirees from the profession back to work with a bonus of up to $6,000. In Scotland, where births have been increasing by five percent a year, Glasgow's *Herald* has reported "a mini baby boom."

Immigrant mothers account for part of the fertility increase throughout Europe, but only part. And, significantly, many of the immigrants are arrivals from elsewhere in Europe, especially the eastern European countries admitted to the European Union in recent years. Children born to eastern European immigrants accounted for a third of Scotland's "mini baby boom," for example.

In 2007, France's national statistical authority announced that the country had overtaken Ireland to boast the highest birthrate in Europe. In France, the fertility rate has risen from 1.7 in 1993 to 2.1 in 2007, its highest level since before 1980, despite a steady fall in birthrates among women not born in France. France's National Institute of Demographic Studies reports that the immigrant population is responsible for only five percent of the rise in the birthrate.

A similar upturn is under way in the United States, where the fertility rate has climbed to its highest level since 1971, reaching 2.1 in 2006, according to the National Center for Health Statistics. New projections by the Pew Research Center suggest that if current trends continue, the population of the United States will rise from today's total of some 300 million to 438 million in 2050. Eighty-two percent of that increase will be produced by new immigrants and their U.S.-born descendants.

20   By contrast, the downward population trends for southern and eastern Europe show little sign of reversal. Ukraine, for example, now has a population of 46 million; if maintained, its low fertility rate will whittle its population down by nearly 50 percent by mid-century. The Czech Republic, Italy, and Poland face declines almost as drastic.

In Russia, the effects of declining fertility are amplified by a phenomenon so extreme that it has given rise to an ominous new term—hypermortality. As a result of the rampant spread of maladies such as HIV/AIDS and alcoholism and the deterioration of the Russian health care system, says a 2008 report by the UN Development Program, "mortality in Russia is 3–5 times higher for men and twice as high for women" than in other countries at a comparable stage of development. The report—which echoes earlier findings by demographers such as the Woodrow Wilson Center's Murray Feshbach—predicts that within little more than a decade the working-age population will be shrinking by up to one million people annually. Russia is suffering a demographic decline on a scale that is normally associated with the effects of a major war.

It is important to consider what this means for the future of the Russian economy. Identified by Goldman Sachs as one of the BRIC quartet (along with Brazil, India, and China) of key emerging markets, Russia has been the object of great hopes and considerable investments. But a very large question mark must be placed on the economic prospects of a country whose young male work force looks set to decrease by half.

The Russian future highlights in exaggerated fashion another challenge facing the European countries. Even absent Russia's dire conditions, the social and political implications of an aging population are plain and alarming. At a 2004 conference in Paris, Heikki Oksanen of the European Commission's Directorate-General for Economic and Financial Affairs noted that the European social model of generous welfare states is facing a crisis because the number of retirees is rising while the number of working-age people is declining. "People are aware that there is a problem, but they do not know how serious it is and [what] drastic reforms are necessary," he said.

Oksanen went on to describe the dire implications for European tax systems. A pay-as-you-go pension scheme would take "only" 27 percent of wages if Europeans had replacement-level fertility, retired at age 60, and lived to 78. But if fertility decreased to 1.7 while longevity increased gradually to 83—close to where Europe is now—the tax would rise to 45 percent of the wage bill. Because of its low birthrate, Germany's problem is particularly acute. It currently has about four people of working age for every three dependents. Under one scenario for 2050, those four working-age Germans would be required to support five dependents.

But these sorts of projections don't capture the full picture. There are at least three mitigating factors to be considered, which suggest that the German welfare state and others in Europe might not have to be dismantled wholesale. 25

The first is that the traditional retirement age of 60 in Italy, France, and Germany is very early indeed, especially considering that life expectancy is approaching 80 and that modern diets and medicine allow many elderly people to continue working well into their seventies. An increase of the retirement age to 65, which is being slowly introduced in France and Germany, would sharply reduce the number of nonworkers who depend on the employed for support, as would more employment for people below the age of 20. A retirement age of 70 in Germany would virtually end the problem, at least until life expectancy rose as high as 90 years.

Second, the work force participation rate in Germany (and much of continental Europe) is relatively low. Not only do Germans retire on the early side, but the generous social welfare system allows others to withdraw from work earlier in life. An increase in employment would boost the revenues flowing into the social security system. For example, only 67 percent of women in Germany were in the work force in 2005, compared with 76 percent in Denmark and 78 percent in Switzerland. (The average rate for the 15 "core" EU states is 64 percent; for the United States, 70 percent.)

David Coleman, a demographer at Oxford University, has suggested that the EU's work force could be increased by nearly a third if both sexes were to match Denmark's participation rates. The EU itself has set a target participation rate of 70 percent for both sexes. Reaching this goal would significantly alleviate the fiscal challenge of maintaining Europe's welfare system, which has been aptly described as "more of a labor-market challenge than a demographic crisis."

The third mitigating factor is that the total dependency ratios of the 21st century are going to look remarkably similar to those of the 1960s. In the United States, the most onerous year for dependency was 1965, when there were 95 dependents for every 100 adults between the ages of 20 and 64. That occurred because "dependents" includes people both younger and older than working age. By 2002, there were only 49 dependents for every 100 working-age Americans. By 2025 there are projected to be 80, still well below the peak of 1965. The difference is that while most dependents in the 1960s were young, with their working and saving and contributing lives ahead of them, most of the dependents of 2009 are older, with more dependency still to come. But the point is clear: There is nothing outlandish about having almost as many dependents as working adults.

30   Population growth on a scale comparable to that which frightened pundits and demographers a generation ago still exists in 30 of the world's least developed countries. Each has a fertility rate of more than five. With a few exceptions—notably, Afghanistan and the Palestinian territories—those countries are located in sub-Saharan Africa. Depending on the future course of birthrates, sub-Saharan Africa's current 800 million people are likely to become 1.7 billion by 2050 and three billion by the end of the century.

One striking implication of this growth is that there will be a great religious revolution, as Africa becomes the home of monotheism. By midcentury, sub-Saharan Africa is likely to be the demographic center of Islam, home to as many Muslims as Asia and to far more than inhabit the Middle East. The non-Arab Muslim countries of Africa—Niger, Mali, Burkina Faso, and Senegal—constitute the one region of the Islamic world where birthrates remain high. In several of these countries, the average woman will have upward of five children in her lifetime.

Christianity will also feel the effects of Africa's growth. By 2025, there will be as many Christians in sub-Saharan Africa—some 640 million—as in South America. By 2050, it is almost certain that most of the world's Christians will live in Africa. As Kenyan scholar John Mbiti writes, "The centers of the church's universality [are] no longer in Geneva, Rome, Athens, Paris, London, New York, but Kinshasa, Buenos Aires, Addis Ababa, and Manila."

But awareness of Africa's religious revolution is usually overshadowed by the fearful possibilities raised by the continent's rapid population growth. By 2050, the national populations are expected to more than double in the Democratic Republic of the Congo and Uganda, reaching 147 million and 91 million, respectively. Smaller countries—such as Liberia, Niger, Mali, Chad, and Burundi—are expected to experience growth of 100 to 200 percent. These are the countries with the weakest state institutions, the least infrastructure, the feeblest economies, and thus the poorest health and education systems. They also face daunting problems of environmental degradation—and the lesson from Darfur and the Rwanda genocide is that disaster can follow when population growth strains local environments so badly that people cannot feed themselves.

The various demographic changes I have described arrived with remarkable speed. At the turn of this century, the conventional wisdom among demographers was that the population of Europe was in precipitous decline, the Islamic world was in the grip of a population explosion, and Africa's population faced devastation by HIV/AIDS. Only a handful of scholars questioned the idea that the Chinese would outnumber all other groups for decades or even centuries to come. In fact, however, the latest UN projections suggest that China's population, now 1.3 billion, will increase slowly through 2030 but may then be reduced to half that number by the end of the century.

Because there are so many assumptions embedded in it, this forecast of 35 the Chinese future could well be wrong. There is one area, however, in which demography relies on hard census data rather than assumptions about the future, and that is in mapping the youth cohort. All of the teenagers who will be alive in 2020 have already been born. So a strong indication of the eventual end of China's dominance of world population statistics is apparent in the fact that there are now 372 million Indians under the age of 15, but only 270 million Chinese. This gap will grow. India seems very likely to become the world's most populous country by 2030 or thereabouts, but only if nothing changes—China maintains its one-child policy and India does not launch the kind of crash program of birth control that Prime Minister Indira Gandhi so controversially attempted in the 1970s.

There is another development that could affect future Indian and Chinese birthrates: the use of sonograms to ascertain the sex of a fetus. Wider availability of this technology has permitted an increase in gender-specific abortions. The official Chinese figures suggest that 118 boys are now being born in China for every 100 girls. As a result, millions of Chinese males may never find a mate with whom to raise a conventional family. The Chinese call such lonely males "bare branches." The social and political implications of having such a large population of unattached men are unclear, but they are not likely to be happy.

Gender imbalances are not limited to China. They are apparent in South Korea, Taiwan, Pakistan, Bangladesh, and increasingly in India, particularly among the Sikhs. Valerie Hudson of Brigham Young University and Andrea den Boer of Britain's University of Kent at Canterbury calculate that there are 90 million "missing" women in Asia, 40 million each in China and India, six million in Pakistan, and three million in Bangladesh.

In a recent paper Hudson and den Boer asked, "Will it matter to India and China that by the year 2020, 12 to 15 percent of their young adult males will not be able to 'settle down' because the girls that would have grown up to be their wives were disposed of by their societies instead?" They answered, "The rate of criminal behavior of unmarried men is many times higher than that of married men; marriage is a reliable predictor of a downturn in reckless, antisocial, illegal, and violent behavior by young adult males." Resulting cross-border "bridal raids," rising crime rates, and widespread prostitution may come to define what could be called the geopolitics of sexual frustration.

The state's response to crime and social unrest could prove to be a defining factor for China's political future. The U.S. Central Intelligence Agency asked Hudson to discuss her dramatic suggestion that "in 2020 it may seem to China that it would be worth it to have a very bloody battle in which a lot of their young men could die in some glorious cause." Other specialists are not as alarmed. Military observers point out that China is moving from a conscript army to a leaner, more professional force. And other scholars contend that China's population is now aging so fast that the growing numbers of elderly people may well balance the surge of frustrated young males to produce a calmer and more peaceful nation.

China is also a key site of another striking demographic change: the   40
rapid growth of the global middle class, perhaps the fastest-growing discrete
segment of the world's population. While the planet's population is
expected to grow by about one billion people by 2020, the global middle
class will swell by as many as 1.8 billion, with a third of this number residing
in China. The global economic recession will retard but not halt the expansion of the middle class—nobody expected growth without interruption.

The lower the birthrate, the greater the likelihood that a given society is
developing—investing in education, accumulating disposable income and
savings, and starting to consume at levels comparable to those of the middle
classes in developed societies. Absent a shock factor such as war or famine,
a society with a falling birthrate tends to be aspirational: Its members seek
decent housing, education for their children, provision for health care and
retirement and vacations, running water and flush toilets, electricity and
appliances such as refrigerators and televisions and computers. As societies
clamber up the prosperity chain, they also climb the mobility ladder, seeking
bicycles, motor scooters, and eventually cars; they also climb the protein
ladder, seeking better, more varied foods and more meat.

This pattern is apparent in China, India, and the Middle East. China's
new middle class, defined as those in households with incomes above about
$10,000 a year, is now estimated to number between 100 million and 150
million people. Some put the figure in India as high as 200 million. But it
is apparent from the urban landscape across the developing world—whether
in Mumbai or Shanghai, São Paulo or Moscow, Dubai or Istanbul—that a
growing proportion of consumers seek to emulate a Western-international
lifestyle, which includes an air-conditioned house with a car in the garage, a
private garden, satellite TV, and Internet access, along with the chance to
raise a limited number of children, all of whom will have the opportunity to
go to college. Whether the biosphere can adapt to such increases in consumption remains a critical question.

Perhaps the most striking fact about the demographic transformation
now unfolding is that it is going to make the world look a lot more like
Europe. The world is aging in an unprecedented way. A milepost in this
process came in 1998, when for the first time the number of people in the
developed world over the age of 60 outnumbered those below the age of 15.
By 2047, the world as a whole will reach the same point.

The world's median age is 28 today, and it is expected to reach 38 by the
middle of the century. In the United States, the median age at that point

will be a youngish 41, while it will be over 50 in Japan and 47 in Europe. The United States will be the only Western country to have been in the top 10 largest countries in terms of population size in both 1950 and 2050. Russia, Japan, Germany, Britain, and Italy were all demographic titans in the middle of the 20th century. Today, only Russia and Japan still (barely) make the top 10. They will not stay there long. The world has changed. There is more and faster change to come.

Analyze

1. How does the author account for the "mini baby boom" in Europe? He notes that immigrant mothers account for part of it. What are the other explanations for it?

2. What cultural shifts does the author see reflected in the "sharp reduction in fertility among Muslim immigrants" in Europe?

3. Walker writes that "[d]espite their many uncertainties, demographic projections have become an essential tool." For whom have demographic projections become "an essential tool"? Why?

4. Walker warns that key assumptions underlying population predictions are "highly questionable and that they are not a reliable basis for serious policy decisions." What are those assumptions, and how does Walker try to persuade us that these are unfounded?

5. What impact does religion have upon birthrates in sub-Saharan Africa compared to other parts of the world? What are the specific concerns of the continent's rapid population growth?

6. How has the world's median age shifted over the past 50 years, and what are Walker's predictions for the next 50 years? What are the implications, and how are they relevant to your own life?

Explore

1. Demographers study, describe, and interpret features and characteristics of human populations. In turn, these "numbers" are used to make predictions and shape policies. What populations has Walker looked at in this reading, and how has he interpreted the "world's numbers"? Write a summary of this article that communicates your understanding of these numbers and their significance.

2. The author makes many striking assertions. He notes that "Iran is experiencing what may be one of the most dramatic demographic shifts in human history," that "Russia is suffering a demographic decline on a scale that is normally associated with the effects of a major war," and that sub-Saharan Africa could double its population in 50 years. In what ways are the changing demographics transforming the world? How does this global perspective transform your own understanding of your role as a global citizen?

3. "It is apparent," Walker writes, "from the urban landscape across the developing world [...] that a growing proportion of consumers seek to emulate a Western-international lifestyle, which includes an air-conditioned house with a car in the garage, a private garden, satellite TV, and Internet access, along with the chance to raise a limited number of children, all of whom will have the opportunity to go to college. Whether the biosphere can adapt to such increases in consumption remains a critical question." Explore the issue of the compatibility of a rising global middle class with environmental sustainability in a research paper.

Damon Tabor
"If It's Tuesday, It Must Be the Taliban"

Damon Tabor is a freelance journalist based in New York City. He holds a graduate degree in journalism from Columbia University and has traveled widely in Asia, South America, and Europe. His work, which covers subjects ranging from surviving kidnapping in a failed state to search-and-rescue robotics, has appeared in *The New York Times*, *Wired*, *Backpacker*, *National Geographic Adventure*, and *Outside* magazine. *Outside*, in which "If It's Tuesday, It Must Be the Taliban" appeared in December 2010, covers sports, environmentalism, travel, and other issues of interest to readers who pursue active and adventurous lives.

Is it responsible, or even ethical, to be a "tourist" in a conflict-ridden country? Who should be responsible for the safety of such travelers?

The Taliban charged us only $1 to get through the first roadblock. At the second, we paid two.

It was highway robbery, but that seemed unimportant. We were traveling in an unarmored Toyota minibus with bald tires and a faded red allah sticker on the back window. The men at the roadblocks had guns, so we gladly would've paid more.

But by the time we reached the next roadblock, the mood on the bus had soured. Everyone was edgy about the possibility of getting kidnapped. We were worn out from several days of hard travel on roads that were little more than cratered, ditch-ridden goat tracks. We were tired of lamb kabob.

At the third roadblock, a pink nylon rope was strung between two wooden posts. We stopped, and a sneering man in his forties with deeply lined brown skin slowly walked up to the vehicle. A younger man with a Kalashnikov sat under a tree by the road while a group of turbaned men stood a short distance away, one holding an automatic rifle and another a cell phone. The man spoke to our driver in Dari, and the driver, young and normally brash, replied quietly. The man turned and looked at us. His eyes were bright and cold and he made our driver nervous. Then he stepped back, untied the pink rope, and let it drop to the ground.

5   We continued up the road and entered a dusty, ramshackle village called Chisht-e Sharif. A U.S. military helicopter buzzed overhead. Pickup trucks loaded with Afghan National Army soldiers—wearing black masks and carrying weapons—sped down the road, heading in the direction we'd come from.

"You couldn't come to Afghanistan without seeing some Taliban, right?" asked our guide, a seventy-something Englishman named Geoff Hann. He had a ruddy complexion and thick eyebrows, and with a beard and skullcap he could pass for an Afghan. Hann had been leading tours through the country intermittently for more than 30 years, but now even he looked shaken.

I was on "vacation," part of a small tour group whose members had paid Hann, the owner of a UK-based company called Hinterland Travel, $3,700 for the pleasure of traveling in a war zone. His job was to make sure that the people who'd signed up stayed alive while moving through one of the most hazardous countries on earth. Hann operates in safer places, too, but he has a reputation as a specialist who can shepherd adventurous tourists through countries like Iraq and Afghanistan—places that other guides won't touch, no matter how much cash you slap down.

It was August 2010, and it would have been hard to think of a less desirable getaway spot than this Texas-size Central Asian nation. U.S. and NATO forces were engaged in a major offensive to crush a Taliban insurgency entrenched in Afghanistan's south and east but also blooming in the once peaceful north and west. The month before had been the most deadly for American troops since the Taliban's ouster in 2001 by the U.S. military and its Afghan allies, after several years of brutal fundamentalist rule. Suicide bombings were frequent, armed bandits stalked the country's roads, and kidnapping was now a commercial enterprise. The central government—shakily presided over from Kabul by U.S.-backed president Hamid Karzai—exerted little control outside major cities, and safety anywhere was tenuous at best. The U.S. State Department warned its citizens against traveling to Afghanistan, while the *Lonely Planet* guide to the country strenuously undersold its attractions. "Hundreds of what are now called 'illegally armed groups' operate freely," it read. "Kidnapping remains a threat. . . . Criminal groups have been known to sell hostages to the highest bidder, usually the insurgents." Increasingly, NGO workers, journalists, and a trickle of tourists—the only foreigners in the country aside from the military—were confined to cities and usually traveled in armored SUVs with armed guards.

The sundry security threats mocked the best-laid travel plans, so Hann's itineraries were strings of guesswork that he referred to as "theories." Ours had initially called for flying into Peshawar, Pakistan, then driving over the Khyber Pass to Jalalabad, Afghanistan, but NATO forces were using the Khyber to move resupply convoys, which made it irresistible to insurgents and impassable for us. Thus, prior to our group's arrival, Hann had notified all his clients that they would fly from Dubai into Kabul instead. The plan after that was to hire minibuses to carry us several hundred miles across central Afghanistan from Kabul to Herat, a city near the Iranian border, then dogleg up to Mazar-e Sharif, in the north, and finally return to Kabul, all without armor or armed security.

The journey would avoid the country's most deadly regions—the south-   10
ern provinces of Kandahar and Helmand—but no part of Afghanistan was truly safe. In Kabul, there were kidnappers and suicide bombs. On the road, there were bandits, Taliban, jihadis, land mines, and improvised explosive devices (IEDs). In the northwest, there was the worst road in Afghanistan and a notoriously lawless town, Bala Murghab, teeming with insurgents. In the northeast, once considered generally secure, the Taliban

had recently overrun a government checkpoint north of Kabul and beheaded six policemen. Even livestock was dangerous; in December 2009, the Taliban attacked British troops using a "donkey bomb."

Hann sells his Afghanistan tours as a chance to see the country's rugged outback while sleeping on dirty teahouse floors and tackling the country's roads in minibuses that buck like mechanical bulls. It's also an opportunity to gamble your life on his instincts and experience in order to be a tourist in a place that barely has any. There are no backpackers or bus-tour day-trippers in Afghanistan, and proximity to danger is the real essence of a Hann trip. His tour is a chance to court your own demise—a short walk on the Hindu Kush's dark side. If you were lucky, you would feel more alive at the end. If you weren't? It was best not to think about that.

For Hann, the road to this career started in 1970, when he drove a Volkswagen camper from Britain to Bombay, chasing after an errant wife living on an ashram—an impromptu cannonball run with an intact marriage as the prize. The wife came back—though Hann later left her and courted a woman he met on one of his tours—and the trip gave him a glimpse of a more exciting way of life. A native of Surrey who dropped out of school at 17, Hann had served in the Royal Air Force in the mid-1950s and then worked for several uneventful years as an electroplater at his father's company.

The wife-fetching mission aroused an appetite for untamed travel, and the timing was right. In the sixties and early seventies, Afghanistan, then a constitutional monarchy, was getting besieged by repurposed double-deckers and flagrantly painted VW Kombis ferrying unkempt Westerners from London to India and Nepal—the so-called Hippie Trail. In 1971, Hann started Hann Overland and guided "a handful of weirdos" in a 12-seat Land Rover from London to Bombay. Along the way, the group dodged bandits, got robbed in Turkey, and drove through the wilds of Afghanistan. "By the end of the trip," he told me, "we were all a bit rattled, but it was exciting."

Hann's company, which was primarily running Iraq tours, went under after the first Gulf war grounded flights to Baghdad. He launched Hinterland after the war ended in 1991, focusing mostly on Afghanistan and Iraq. But Hann has also led trips through a marquee list of danger zones, including Kashmir, Burma, and Pakistan. He's been jailed in India, interrogated by various security services, and smacked in the head with a rifle butt. He carries a commando knife and keeps a pistol stashed with a Pakistani rug dealer he calls "Mr. Ralph." During a now-legendary trip through Iraq following the 2003 U.S. invasion, Hann's group watched as a mob beat a man to death in Mosul; later, they were only a block away when a car bomb detonated outside the Turkish embassy in Baghdad. In 2007, Hann stumbled into a gun battle between two warring clans in Afghanistan, then negotiated an on-the-fly ceasefire and led his group, Moses-like, through the parted factions. Remarkably, none of his clients has been kidnapped or killed over the past 40 years, but Hann believes they'd better sign up with eyes wide open.

"People come on a trip like this of their own free will," he says. "If something happens to them, I'm very sorry—I do my best to make sure it doesn't. But if it does, then that's what happened. Anyone who says they didn't know is an idiot. It's on television every day." Though fiery and occasionally volatile, Hann is generally cautious, but he can become distracted, and he allows his clients to wander freely and alone in cities—something most Western companies and NGOs working in war zones would consider insanely risky. Obviously, Hann's tours attract adventurous travelers, but they're not adrenaline freaks or war junkies. Most are past middle age, unmarried, fairly mild-mannered, and childless. They carry passports sporting ink from countries like Syria, Pakistan, and Sudan—places that Westerners usually prefer to see as flickering images on a screen. Some are ticking off items on a bucket list, but many seem driven by a desire to see all the world's splendors and have simply been everywhere else. Afghanistan, to them, is the next logical frontier. The fact that it's dangerous is part of the appeal.

Not surprisingly, Hann has a few critics. One veteran Western traveler with extensive experience in Afghanistan—who asked not to be named—told me that what Hann does is irresponsible.

"There are a couple of companies in Kabul that I would trust to take people in Afghanistan," he said. "They are local, have established security procedures, work as fixers for journos, businesses, and NGOs, and they're completely plugged in. Hinterland is not. . . . Just because Hann has gotten away with it so far doesn't make these tours safe."

Hann knows he takes risks, of course, but he argues that the security situation is more nuanced than government travel bulletins and jumpy journalists would have you believe. He thinks it's possible to move through Afghanistan with the right combination of information and prudence, hopping to islands of safety like rocks in a river. On every trip, he's attempting to disprove the world's conventional wisdom about where humans should and shouldn't go.

"I'm trying to do the impossible, which is to give people the freedom to move about in restricted areas," he says with conviction. "It's not easy. At the end of the day, they get the rough with the smooth."

"We've already been here too long," Hann had declared two days after we flew into Kabul and checked into the Spinzar Hotel, which had lazy guards with gleaming new Kalashnikovs at a checkpoint out front. He had rules about being a tourist, which made being a tourist difficult: You didn't stay anywhere long and you told no one where you were going. You avoided military trucks and UN vehicles, which was hard because they were everywhere.

20   On the morning of our third day, we packed into a white minibus to head north to Bamiyan, the site of some famous Buddhist ruins. There were reports of Taliban activity on the road ahead, but no one in the group seemed anxious. Sue Hynard, an executive assistant from London in her late fifties, had once been on a tour in Pakistan's Swat Valley when fighting broke out between the military and insurgents, and her attitude was pretty typical of the group.

"Tourists go on package tours to places like Torremolinos," she said, referring to the overdeveloped British-resort kennel in southern Spain. "We're travelers."

The others apparently felt the same way. Peter Haug, a 58-year-old professor of supply-chain management from Bellingham, Washington, had gotten lost in Bhutan's wilderness and been rescued by army troops. Cameron Rose, a tall, pale retired math teacher at England's Eton school, had made a midnight run with a sugar smuggler going from Lebanon into Syria. Kent Rausner, a 44-year-old Danish hotelier living in Thailand, had had a knife pulled on him in Dakar. The oldest person in our group was a tiny, 75-year-old Indian woman named Bithi Das, who walked with a cane and exuded Yoda-like tranquility. She was going to Libya and Uzbekistan after this, and seemed to have a philosophical take about risk.

"I will die," she told me at one point. "We all will die. It's OK."

Spumes of dust were blowing into the air as we inched through Kabul's apocalyptic streets, and military convoys stopped traffic for blocks. Sue, Bithi, and Valerie Godsalve, a dyspeptic pathologist who'd flown in late from Saskatoon, Canada, were wearing veils. Peter, Cameron, Kent, and I wore shalwar kameez, the long tunic and baggy pants that U.S. soldiers call "man jammies." Afghans still stared when they saw us; they weren't used to seeing kuffar, or "nonbelievers," in unarmored minibuses.

An hour north of the city, the sky turned the color of pressed tin and   25
rain began falling in thick drops that turned the road to mud. Abbas pulled
up behind a long line of cars stopped in front of a torrent of water surging
down from the mountains and across the road. It looked impassable, but an
enterprising local had driven an orange backhoe into the washout and was
using the bucket to carve out an improvised road—and charged 100 afghanis, or about $2, to let cars across.

We arrived so late that the only place to sleep was the police barracks. In the
morning, I followed the group across a dry, dusty field to see the now destroyed
Bamiyan Buddhas. These were once a premier attraction, but in 2001 the
Taliban used anti-aircraft guns and dynamite to reduce both statues—carved
into a tall sandstone cliff as early as the third century and standing 120 and
175 feet tall—into a fenced-off pile of dusty rubble. The cliff was honeycombed
with grottoes inhabited 1,500 years ago by hermetic Buddhist monks, though
many were now littered with bone shards and animal feces. I walked up a
twisting staircase cut into the sandstone cliff and, at the top, looked out at
nothing. To visit Bamiyan's Buddhas was to contemplate a void—appropriate,
since the taller statue had represented *sunyata*, or emptiness.

A day later, we set out west across the spine of the Hindu Kush toward
Band-e Amir, a glittering string of topaz-colored lakes set high amid cliff-
studded mountains. Backhoes and yellow bulldozers were scraping the
road, part of a USAID project attempting to smooth Afghanistan's ex-
panses for exports other than opium. It was early afternoon when we
reached the first lake, where cars filled a dirt parking lot. In 2009, the
Afghan government had declared this area the country's first national park.
Hotels and restaurants were planned. Locals were dissuaded from using
hand grenades to fish. During the dedication, Karl Eikenberry, a former
Army lieutenant general and the U.S. ambassador to Afghanistan, had
ridden a swan paddleboat—one of the site's main attractions—around one
of the lakes, grinning like a schoolboy.

Now, women in burkas watched from shore while their husbands paddled around. Families ate picnics on blankets and boys jumped into the
cold water in their underwear. Peter, Sue, and I climbed into a red boat with
flaking paint, quickly trailed by a small swan-boat flotilla of curious
Afghans. Two boys in a yellow boat approached first, one smiling widely
and showing teeth like a tumbledown fencerow.

Another boat approached, filled with three men in their thirties wearing
light-colored tunics. From a distance, they'd been pointing and laughing at

the infidels in the swan boat. "Excuse me, where are you from?" shouted one, giggling with his friends. Another pulled out a digital camera and began taking pictures of us.

30   "America and England," Peter said, smiling. I'd nicknamed him Operation American Caress, because he waved at every scowling Afghan on the road, though often as not they just stared. "What is your job?" Abdullah, the older boy, asked.

"We are tourists," I said. He looked surprised.

"In Band-e Amir, security is very good," one of the men said proudly.

"Is there anything like this in America?" Abdullah asked.

"America is Los Angeles and California and Mexico and Chicago!" one of the older men yelled giddily.

35   "You are very friendly and kind men!" one of the older men yelled, and then they paddled away, laughing like children.

We drove all the next day, crossed the 11,000-foot Shahtu Pass, and then stopped for the night at a teahouse with an ill-tempered donkey in the back. Cameron unrolled an air mattress as large as an airplane's evacuation slide. Valerie surreptitiously tortured her hair into a helmet of pink rollers. Bithi snored in the corner, a surprisingly baritone rumble. Later, Hann, who had been outside talking on a sat phone, walked into the room. "There's been a really bad killing," he said, announcing that the Taliban had shot and killed ten members of a medical team, including six Americans, near the northeast border with Tajikistan.

It was possible sometimes to forget that the sawtooth mountains and apple orchards flashing past the minibus windows were in Afghanistan at all, but the perils now seemed very real again. No one slept well.

We woke up at dawn and drove west, now somewhere in the middle of the country. Soviet personnel carriers, stripped to their frames, rusted in the scraggly grass; yellow-eyed herding dogs loped after the minibus. We stopped for lunch in a teahouse with posters of grim-faced legislative candidates tacked to the wall, and Hann asked the owner, a delicate-featured man named Jarwald, about the road ahead.

"In Bala Murghab, is the Taliban there or is it just *badmash*?" he asked, using a word for bandits.

40   "They aren't here in this province," Jarwald said. "The other provinces—the Taliban are there. Around Chaghcharan, the security is very good. After that, it may be some problems for you."

"Are they your sons?" Bithi asked, indicating a group of Afghan men sitting impassively against a wall, listening to our conversation.

"No, they are my friends," Jarwald said, chuckling. "He is older than me." Jarwald was one of the Hazara Shia, a group ill-treated by the fundamentalist Pashtun Taliban, who consider them heretical Muslims. President Karzai, also a Pashtun, seemed to ignore them. Jarwald said he would support Karzai going forward if, and only if, he paved the road.

"You can't build a road unless there's security and unless there's money," Hann said.

"Sometimes one before the other."

Jarwald conferred with his friends for a moment. "They want to fight   45 after that because the government haven't any attention for us," he said. "They want to enjoy the Taliban." By which he meant join them.

"What's your duty here?" Jarwald asked Hann.

"I bring tourists to Afghanistan," he said.

The Afghan men said something to Jarwald and they all laughed. "They are saying we can arrest you, so the government make our roads," Jarwald said.

We laughed nervously. The bill arrived and Hann bickered with the waiter about it, which seemed imprudent. Men like Jarwald were Hann's main source of information about security conditions. Though Hann's Web site claims otherwise, he had performed no real intelligence gathering—checking Afghan news sites or e-mailing local sources—before arriving in-country. Instead, he chatted with waiters and taxi drivers once he was on the ground, forging ahead or retreating depending on what they told him. But since most Afghans don't speak English and Hann speaks almost no Dari or Pashto, this process often involved a questionably effective game of charades.

We drove along a winding dirt road until late in the day, then pulled   50 into Chaghcharan, a dusty traders' settlement on a wind-swept plateau. Hann disliked the town intensely and said it was filled with hustlers. At dusk, after languishing in a cramped room for several hours, I asked Bithi if she wanted to take a walk. She hadn't moved much since Kabul and wasn't eating or drinking enough. We went down a narrow alley and onto a wide, half-paved road. Mud-brick buildings lined the street, and the town's small shops were mostly shuttered. A group of young men stood on the street corner, staring as we walked past. I didn't like the way they watched us, but Bithi seemed unafraid.

"I took a trip to Kashmir," she said, holding my arm as we shuffled along. "A pilgrimage Indians take to a mountain called Amarnath. This is where Shiva shared the secret of creation with his wife, Parvati, but two white doves overheard and so now they are reborn again and again."

She kept talking as we passed several men working on the road. It had grown dark; wind whipped grit through the air. I suggested we go back to the teahouse. We crossed the street and walked by a dark-skinned man with a red turban and bloodshot eyes. I said "Salaam," but he only glared. Up ahead, the young men were still at the corner. Three dirty boys with stained tunics followed behind us, one clutching a plastic pistol. Bithi was quiet for a moment, and I asked if she was afraid of dying. She had had heart surgery six months before, knee surgery before that, and took 20 pills every day. Her body had become a kind of cage, and she was ready to be done with it.

"If God told me I would die tomorrow, I would be happy," she said.

The next afternoon we passed through the Taliban roadblocks. The last one rattled Hann and the driver and everybody else. Valerie soon began emitting breathy yelps whenever we went over bumps. Cameron had grown thin-skinned. Earlier in the day, at the Minaret of Jam, a 213-foot tower covered in elaborate script next to the Hari River, he had unloaded on the driver for swiping an empty plastic water bottle. "You can't just take people's things!" he screamed. "This belongs to me!" It was a low point in Westerner-Afghan relations, and it seemed like a bad omen.

55   A few hours later, we were drinking greasy green tea in a town several miles past the Taliban roadblocks, and the group was mutinous. Hann wanted to stay on the road another night, but the group wanted instead to press on to Herat, a major city close to the border with Iran. It was a long day's drive, but there were beds, non-lamb meals, and, presumably, fewer Taliban. Hann got in the minibus, muttering darkly.

The hills soon flattened out, and we drove into the sun-blasted western half of Afghanistan. Nomads' black domed tents lined the road. A current of air like an opened oven door—Afghans call it the Wind of 120 Days— buffeted the minibus. Cameron, Sue, and Peter had struck up a lively, semi-geriatric conversation about ailments, but I suggested that our first Taliban encounter warranted further comment.

"I've not particularly enjoyed the road or the roadblocks," Sue said. "The rest of it's been lovely. I think if my parents were alive, I probably wouldn't have come."

"I've never taken into account anything to do with dependents, because it's never been an issue," Cameron added. "Even when Mother was alive. I leave my will on the study table, but I do that when I go to the Antarctic. I really need to get it done professionally now."

We reached Herat at dusk. It was a cosmopolitan city with roadside shops selling red velvet dresses and knockoff cell phones. In the morning, we walked through the Musalla Complex, a 15th-century compound of minarets, mosques, and madrassas that had been devastated over time by British dynamite, Soviet artillery, and earthquakes. A remaining minaret was held upright by steel block and tackle airlifted from Kabul and installed by a UNESCO crew that included the same Italian who'd stabilized the Leaning Tower of Pisa a few years ago. Hann, who had a weakness for Afghan carpets, added another to the already extensive collection he'd amassed since Kabul. We visited Gazar Gah, a Sufi shrine where men prayed on red rugs beneath a green ilex tree. Males passed on one side of the tree, females on the other. The Afghans snickered at Peter for walking the wrong way. We were infidels in a Muslim holy place and I stuffed 100 afghanis into a donation box.

Later, Hann arrived at dinner preoccupied. The plan had been to drive north the next day from Herat to Mazar-e Sharif via a town called Maimana. Maimana was considered safe, but south of it was Bala Murghab, riddled with insurgents and bandits. Last year, the military had turned Hann's group back. The local police had also made Lonely Planet writer Paul Clammer sleep in their compound after the Taliban attacked an NGO office in town the day before he arrived.

"They were very kind, made us tea and gave us beds outside," Clammer had told me. "At midnight, we were awoken by the sound of much automatic gunfire, and the sky lit up with tracers."

Now, Hann said at the table, we had to decide if we wanted to drive through this. He'd been trying to hire a driver all afternoon, but he'd been rebuffed everywhere. "I said they had no testicles," he said. "I personally think it's safe enough to go, but they were telling me it's too dangerous. Bala Murghab is nasty. It's full of crooks, bandits, smugglers, and Taliban. I'm disappointed."

Hann laid out two options. He had a driver willing to take us to a town south of Bala Murghab, but once there we'd have to hire another driver to get to Maimana. We might get lucky. We might also get killed. The iffiest

60

stretch of road was about 40 miles long, an island of danger—what Afghans sometimes called a yagistan, or lawless place—in an already choppy sea. We could probably make it, but the decision to go would be a deeply existential one. Or, Hann said, we could catch a short flight to Kabul and then another to Mazar-e Sharif—lifted above Afghanistan's perils by a credit card.

"I quite like the sound of that," Sue said. "Everybody seems to be saying it's not a good idea."

65   "It's silly to say at my age, but I say go with the flow of the country you're experiencing," Cameron said. He looked as relaxed and happy as I'd seen him on the trip. "Fine by me," Peter said, turning his attention back to a pretty Spanish woman who'd joined us for dinner.

"I would sneak up there and do it," Hann said, "but if the locals say the risk is too great, then it's really irresponsible for us to go. There's risks, and there's risks."

We took the flight. In Mazar-e Sharif, which felt like the frontier town that it was, we quickly located a seedy expat café serving green $4 cans of Tuborg beer, likely trucked in illegally from Uzbekistan. A large TV blared CNN. A worn-looking blonde, a Western man with a shaved head, and a Maori security contractor with an oily perm and tattooed forearms were drinking at another table. They blew plumes of smoke and talked about an aid project. Our group had been reduced by two: Kent had flown back to Thailand from Kabul to run his two hotels. Valerie's camera was stolen in Herat and she'd flown back to Saskatoon without a word to anyone.

Hann hired two taxis the next morning and we drove to Haji Piyada, a stucco mosque that is the oldest in Afghanistan and now sits covered by what looks like an enormous protective carport. The building's caretaker, a bent-legged man with a long scar across his jaw, squatted in the dirt. Two Afghan policemen sat under a rough-looking shack by a stream. A field of marijuana plants grew nearby. We walked quietly through the mosque, and I asked Bithi what she thought of the journey.

"There is rise and fall of terrorists all the time," she said. "It's a kind of adventure to see one of the Taliban."

70   "What would you say if you met one?" I asked.

"As-*Salamu Alaykum*," she said, smiling a little wickedly. It's an Islamic greeting that means "Peace be upon you."

One of the policemen approached Bithi and spoke to her in Hindi. He was young-looking and wore a jaunty white scarf with his green uniform.

"He says the Taliban's attitude is to kill no matter who it is," she translated. "They want to have the pride that they have killed someone. They are
very near, 10 to 15 kilometers." As we were leaving, she handed the propri-
etor 100 afghanis, which Hann protested was too much.

The next morning, Hann hired a rickety minibus to take us west to
Andkhoy, a town near the border with Turkmenistan. Our driver was an
Uzbek named Abdullah, and he drank black tea and smoked cheap cigarettes during the holy month, which made me trust him. Hann had never
been to Andkhoy before, but he'd heard they had good carpets. From there
we would drive to a village called Daulatabad, then return to Mazar-e
Sharif through the Dasht-e Leili desert. This was the last, and potentially
worst, leg of the trip. A one-eyed taxi driver had warned Hann that
Daulatabad was teeming with Taliban.

On the outskirts of Mazar, a graveyard of T-62 Russian tanks and   75
Katyusha rocket launchers sat by the road. Goats lounged in the shade of
a gas pipeline. Off to the right, a road led to Qala-e Jangi, a sprawling 19th-
century military fortress and the site of a seven-day prison uprising led by
the Taliban in November 2001. Earlier, Peter and I had taken a side trip
there, tried unsuccessfully to bribe the guard to let us in, and were then
passed off to Jeff and Stan, two cops from Texas who were helping train
Afghan police at a nearby military base. "Maaannn," Stan had said, looking concerned when I told him we were tourists.

"Y'all be careful. It's like the fucking Wild West out there," Jeff said,
scribbling our names on the back of a business card in case something
happened.

At midday, we drove into Daulatabad, a small village with tree-lined
streets crowded with donkey carts and kaleidoscopically painted, three-
wheeled rickshaws. Abdullah parked on a side street. The plan was to
quickly explore the town, then return to the bus. I followed Hann, Sue,
Peter, and Cameron into a market of crowded stalls selling tools, shoes, and
scraps of cloth. A young boy led a camel caravan through the street.
Another boy laughed at my shalwar kameez and called me *farangi*, or
"foreigner." I trailed Hann down an alley and into a courtyard filled with
wood. Afghan men, squatting in the dirt, turned and stared.

"I think we better go back," Hann said, after walking quickly through
the courtyard. Back at the minibus, a crowd had gathered around the
vehicle and Abdullah was discussing our route through the desert with
several men. "Too dangerous, not safe, Taliban," one of them said.

Hann had climbed into the passenger seat and turned around to look at us. "Who's up for going through the desert?" he asked. "He says that it's not a problem for him but could be a problem for us."

80   "I think it's up to the driver," Sue said.

"We go back to Andkhoy then," Peter said.

"I was trying to find rare carpets just to have a look, but nobody seems to know where they are," Hann muttered. He looked unhappy to be retreating again.

Tactically, our vacation had begun to feel similar to a military raid—rush in and rush out—and it was both exhilarating and unsatisfying. You were trying to be a tourist in a place that didn't allow for it. You could strike up a conversation with a shopkeeper, but he might be a Taliban informant. You could wander down some beckoning side street, but you might not be seen again. It was the central paradox of a Hann trip: we were in Afghanistan, but the country still felt just out of reach.

On my last day in Afghanistan, I ate runny eggs and stale naan with weak tea for breakfast at Kabul's Spinzar Hotel. Hann and I were setting out for Ghazni, a notoriously dangerous town on a notoriously dangerous road between Kabul and Kandahar. In July 2007, the Taliban had kidnapped 23 South Korean volunteers on this road, two of whom were later executed. The month before we arrived, two U.S. Navy sailors had been found dead after a mysterious, unsanctioned drive in the area.

85   Hann's itinerary had called for an optional half-day trip to Ghazni at the tour's end, but he canceled it because the security risk was too high. I wanted to see more of the country—and perhaps indulge some darker urge, too—and he had agreed to take me, provided I absolved him of responsibility. It was a potential suicide run with no point, but we found a taxi driver willing to do it for 4,000 afghanis, or about $90. If we were killed, sensible people would say we'd gotten what we deserved. When I asked Hann to assess the danger level, he said, "Fairly high."

We wove through Kabul's backstreets and alleys and passed two dogs fucking, which I took as a good sign. Then we drove by a humble-jumble of rocks in the middle of the road, a grave, which I took as a bad sign. I sat low in the taxi's backseat, wearing a shalwar kameez and a checkered scarf over my head. Hann sat up front, wearing a white skullcap, black vest, and several weeks' worth of beard. At the edge of the city, we were flagged off the road at a police checkpoint.

"We're tourists," I told the officer, showing him Hann's camera, which was small and pink and looked like a teenage girl's.

"You should not be on this road. It is too dangerous," the officer said. He said something to the driver, and I thought he would make us turn back, but we were let through.

We picked up the Kabul-Kandahar highway, a long, straight two-lane road that ran southwest through flat, sandy plains and low foothills. I could feel the city's protective grip, thin as it was, slipping away. A man in a black vest and turban stood under a billboard watching the traffic. A military helicopter flew overhead. The driver looked nervous and began driving too slow. He pointed behind us and said, "Kabul, Kabul." Hann ignored him and stabbed his finger in the direction ahead and said, "Ghazni, Ghazni." Then the driver pulled over to the side of the road and stopped.

"This is not good, mate," Hann said, looking around anxiously.   90

The driver popped the hood, got out, and fiddled with the engine. The sun was almost directly overhead now, the car sweltering. A minute ticked by, and another. Cars raced by. An Afghan police compound stood off the road several hundred yards ahead. I wondered if they would mistake us for insurgents and start shooting. I was furious at the driver for stopping here, for risking our lives.

He got back in the taxi and turned the key, but the engine quit. He turned it again, we lurched forward, and the engine quit again. He said something unintelligible except for the word "Taliban." He was faking engine trouble, I suspected. We were making him a target and he wanted to be rid of us.

"Bullshit," Hann yelled. "He's a fucking prick. He's not getting paid, either. We're only 50 K from Ghazni. He shouldn't have taken us if that's how he felt."

It was reckless to sit on the road, and I suggested we go back. Hann relented. The taxi's engine caught after a few tries and we swung around in the road and retreated toward Kabul. Then the driver abruptly slowed again. I looked up and saw a cloud of white smoke next to the road a few hundred yards ahead—what looked like an IED or land-mine explosion, though there'd been no sound. The cars around us slowed to a crawl and we drove down the highway in a loose, hesitant convoy. Our driver chewed on the collar of his shalwar kameez.

Near the smoke, a dead goat lay in the road with its insides strewn across   95
the asphalt. A minute later, three SUVs, filled with turbaned men carrying

Kalashnikovs and an RPG, suddenly turned around ahead of us and went speeding past. A small unit of Afghan police was standing in the road ahead with AK-47's at the ready. They had a pickup-mounted .50-caliber machine gun pointed in our direction. Their faces looked anxious, and they seemed prepared to fight. We were slipping toward something chaotic and lethal. I did not want to die in an Afghan taxi on this road. We were no longer tourists.

We sped through the roadblock and, after a few miles, the driver seemed to relax. The car's engine improved, and soon we approached the crumbling perimeter mud wall and shack-covered hills that marked the city's edges. White kites made of plastic bags flew in the air. A red archway over the road read WELCOME.

Hann was quiet and looked out the window. At a roundabout, a seemingly endless military convoy of American Humvees and heavily armored MRAPs rumbled past, the battered minibuses and sedans snarled around it in a tightening knot. My head hurt and my stomach burned. I wanted to get off the road, to board a wobbly 707 and leave Afghanistan behind. We got out of the taxi near the Spinzar, and Hann paid the driver 1,000 Afghanis. The driver protested, waving the bills indignantly in the air, and I thought Hann was going to punch him. I slipped him a few hundred more, but it still didn't seem like nearly enough.

Analyze

1. Why did the author call the article "If It's Tuesday, It Must Be the Taliban"?

2. How does Bithi's attitude toward death and her travel plans explain why someone might go to a dangerous place like Afghanistan?

3. Sue Hynard distinguishes travelers from tourists in the article. What is your own interpretation of the difference between a tourist and a traveler?

4. What is the significance of visiting specific places that might be considered hallowed grounds—ruins, former battlefields, and in this reading, the Bamiyan Buddhas? Is this something that interests you? Why or why not?

5. Create a play with others in your class that dramatizes the action in this article. What do you learn about the characters as you bring them to life that you might not have noticed simply by reading? What more did you want to know about them?

6. Tabor writes that Geoff Hann's tour "is a chance to court your own demise—a short walk on the Hindu Kush's dark side. If you were lucky, you would feel more alive at the end." What do you think is the appeal of traveling in a war zone?

7. What kind of ethics do you feel are necessary to write about different places? Do you feel that Tabor's piece sensationalizes Afghanistan, or does it provide insight into it as a troubled place? Is it an impartial picture of others' perceptions of Afghanistan? What was the purpose of this article, do you think, based on its content?

Explore

1. How does Tabor deal with quotidian life in Afghanistan, and what does this communicate to you about his attitudes, the publication he writes for, and his intended audience? How might the article be different if he were writing for another kind of publication? As a writer, how would you deal with describing the deaths of people in Afghanistan? Research three other publications' articles about contemporary Afghanistan, and write an essay in which you consider how the purpose and audience influence what a writer chooses to convey.

2. Of the people who go on the Hinterland tour, Tabor writes, "Some are ticking off items on a bucket list, but many seem driven by a desire to see all the world's splendors and have simply been everywhere else." Who are these people? Write a profile of one of them. Make it a first-person narrative and put as many details down as you can: their age, profession, etc. Tell their version of the adventure in Afghanistan and other places you imagine they have traveled to. Consider consulting a tourist guide, such as *Lonely Planet*, to a remote place to get ideas.

3. Tabor writes, "It was the central paradox of a Hann trip: we were in Afghanistan, but the country still felt just out of reach." Why did the country feel just out of reach? Did you see opportunities in the article when Tabor and the others on the trip could have felt in reach of the country? What are the best ways to get to know a place? How does being a tourist keep you at a distance by default? What is the alternative? Write an essay in which you thoughtfully consider these questions using your own experiences or those you have read about in this book and others.

Petina Gappah
"Zimbabwe"

Lawyer and writer Petina Gappah earned law degrees from the University of Zimbabwe, the University of Cambridge, and the University of Graz. She was born in Zimbabwe and returned there to live in 2010. Her collection of short stories, *An Elegy for Easterly* (Faber & Faber, 2009), won the Guardian First Book Award in 2009. The following selection was published in January 2012 as part of *Guernica*'s Writers Bloc project—a collection of essays about education systems around the world. *Guernica* is a bimonthly global online magazine of ideas, art, poetry, and fiction. Its contributors hail from dozens of countries and write in nearly as many languages.

> If you were to go back to your primary or secondary school and speak at the graduation ceremony, as Gappah does in this article, what words of advice would you have for the children?

If Zimbabwe were human, the country would need more years of therapy than its 30 years of independence. According to *Foreign Policy*, in 2010, Zimbabwe was fourth on the "Failed State Index." In 2006, it was declared to be the unhappiest place on earth—ahead of Zimbabwe on the "Happiness Index" were countries like the Democratic Republic of Congo, Sudan, and North Korea. In 2008, it had inflation rates not seen since the Weimar Republic: prices of goods changed as customers walked to the tills. By any measure, Zimbabweans should just have given up, switched off what little lights remained burning, and hightailed it to the nearest border.

Zimbabwe's collapse is jarring because it has been so fast. Particularly, in education, where it once led all of Africa, Zimbabwe has had a dizzying fall. The papers are full of stories of teachers at government schools threatening to strike, of pupils being sent home for not paying school fees, of overcrowded classrooms and poorly maintained schools.

At the beginning of 2011, I planned to write about the state of education in coalition Zimbabwe.

In September 2008, Zimbabwe woke to a new chapter in its history. For the first time since independence, Zanu PF, the party of the rooster emblem, was no longer cock of the walk. Mugabe's party entered into a power-sharing arrangement with the MDC, the opposition party that has sworn to reverse the economic decline. Ministerial portfolios were divvied up between the three parties to the coalition. The Ministry of Education, or, to give it its full name, The Ministry of Education, Sport, Art, and Culture, went to the smaller of the two MDC parties, and is headed by David Coltart, a lawyer and senator from Bulawayo. Senator Coltart is known as one of the most accessible of the ministers. His door was open when I walked in to tell him about my project, and to ask for his permission to visit government schools.

My initial plan had been to go to all of Zimbabwe's ten provinces, and 5 visit two primary schools and two secondary schools in each province. I soon came to realize that bureaucracy had not quite caught up with the reality of the new coalition government. The head of the first government school I visited would not see me because I did not have the authority of the provincial head.

"But the Minister signed my letter," I protested and produced the letter signed by Senator Coltart.

Not good enough, clearly.

"That letter was not signed by the provincial director," I was told.

I went to Chester House in Harare to see the Provincial Director, a small man in an over-furnished office who put a stamp on it, signed it, and wrote, "APPROVED" above his signature, effectively approving his boss's approval. After that, I had to see the District Officer, a smiling woman with a complicated hairstyle who put down her tea and biscuits to stamp the minister's letter, appending her own approval to the other two approvals. A friend who works closely with the Ministry of Education shrugs when I tell him this anecdote. He explains that the Senator's Permanent Secretary—said to be a staunch Zanu PF supporter—is apparently involved in a war of attrition with his MDC minister, almost, my source says, as though he does not want the minister to succeed.

I decide to limit my visits to the schools to which I have a personal con- 10 nection: a writer visiting her old schools to write about them, I reason, is an entirely different thing to an unknown person walking into strange schools, even with ministerial and provincial level approval.

Besides, I am lucky to have gone to five schools in Zimbabwe, six if I include the University of Zimbabwe.

"Why so many?" my photographer, Rudo Nyangulu asks.

I explain to her that I am of the generation that started school in Rhodesia, continued in Zimbabwe-Rhodesia and finished in Zimbabwe. Those were the days of social mobility, of dismantled racial barriers. I did the first year of my primary education at Chembira Government Primary School, did Grade 2 at Kundai Government Primary School, and then did Grades 4 to 7 at Alfred Beit Primary School before completing my secondary education at St. Dominic's Secondary School and St. Ignatius' College. It is to these old schools that Rudo and I turn in the company of our driver, Innocent.

My first school was Chembira School, the first government primary school to be built in Glen Norah, a black township established in the early 1970s. There were more children than there were school places, which meant that about 80 pupils shared a classroom, with a group of children coming to school in the mornings and another in the afternoons. Until the classroom cleared, my classmates and I sat under a tree with our teacher. "Hot seating" only ended when a new school opened the following year.

15   Behind the administration block is the tap from where we drank water in our cupped hands. "A DAY IN SCHOOL IS A GAIN ON ETERNITY" says a notice on the board inside the reception. Below this is a large poster outlining the school's plans for the next five years, the most ambitious being to build a new block of classrooms. When I tell the deputy headmistress that I am an old pupil, she welcomes me with a hug of delight, especially when I mention where I have been since 1978. This being Zimbabwe, it turns out that she knows one of my aunts—they did their teacher training together in the 70s.

Hot seating is back again as there are simply too many children for the available classrooms—1, 315 in all. Glen Norah is in the catchment area of the Hopley Farm informal settlement, she explains, which means that they have many children from very poor families. The BEAM programme is important for them, the deputy head says, and shows me a group of parents assisting in sorting through applications in the staff room.

By the BEAM programme, she means the "Basic Education Assistance Module," a donor-funded scheme that aims to ensure that children from poor families stay in school: it is aimed at what its multilateral donors call OVCs—orphans and other vulnerable children. They have their fees and levies paid for them and are supplied with uniforms and stationery.

"But what about children not covered under the BEAM? Would you expel children whose parents cannot pay fees?" I ask.

There have been several stand-offs between schools and the Ministry, with the latter insisting that schools cannot expel children for not paying fees, while schools point out that without fees, they are unable to run. In addition to the government-set school fees of about 20 dollars for a term of three months, there is the "development levy," which varies from small amounts at the poorer schools to hundreds, and even thousands, of dollars at the better-off schools. The levy is charged directly by each School Development Association—the SDAs are made up of parents and teachers. Faced with a perpetually broke government, the SDAs have been the drivers of school development. In fact, the plan to build a new classroom block at Chembira is an SDA project.

"We do not expel children," the deputy headmistress says. "You find that many such children have just one parent, and so, even if they are not orphans exactly, they will be covered somehow."

She tells me that the SDA levies at Chembira have enabled them to pay for two extra teachers, and for their Traditional Dance coach. The school has won the country's leading Traditional Dance competition for school children. In 2010, Chembira came top in the whole country, she tells me proudly.

"We are doing really well. We have an excellent coach," she beams, "Someone who really believes in his job."

Does the same commitment extend to the classroom, I ask. Are their teachers as committed to excellence as the dance coach?

"There are challenges," she admits. "There are simply not enough teachers for all the children."

As we walk around the school, I meet the two oldest teachers; they must have been there when I was, I prod them eagerly for memories of my old teacher, but 1978 is too far in the past. Our tour of the school coincides with break-time. The children, eager for any diversion, follow us around. Rudo's camera is like a magnet; they jostle to have their pictures taken. As the deputy headmistress tries to keep the children at a distance, I ask her about the pressures facing the schools. She tells me what I will hear at the two other primary schools I will visit: that the Grade Zero classes are adding pressure to already pressured schools.

In 2005, the government introduced an Early Development class, ECD, informally called Grade Zero. It was intended to address the reality that not all parents could afford to send their children to crèches, which were all privately run and tended to be expensive.

The idea was that all children should, before the formal start of primary school, be equipped with the social skills they need to start school.

A wonderful initiative in theory, but, as with many things in Zimbabwe, the devil was in the implementation. The government did not build more classrooms to accommodate Grade Zero children, who need toys, picture books and specialized learning aids. In the first few years, there were no teachers who were properly qualified in early childhood development. Many government schools were already struggling with too many children, falling infrastructure and indifferent and unmotivated teachers, if they were not absent. Grade Zero has thus added more children to schools without accompanying improvements in infrastructure.

I remark to the deputy head that Chembira has the same number of toilets it had 30 years ago.

30   "That's when they are working," she says, ominously.

We visit the Grade Zero classroom. It is the room that was once the library, and still has LIBRARY written on the door. Efforts have gone into making it cheerful. The floor has been carefully swept. Children learn to distinguish shapes from old boxes of different sizes. The walls are decorated with collages made of pictures from newspapers and magazines. It is woefully inadequate, and, at the same time, heroic in a way that is heartbreaking.

"When the new classroom block is built," the headmistress says, "then this can be a library again.

"But we have no books," she adds as an afterthought. "You see why we need help?"

To understand what has gone wrong at schools like Chembira requires an understanding of what Zimbabwe used to do well. What Zimbabwe did particularly well in the first twenty years of its life was to correct the racial injustice that had denied quality universal education to the majority of the country's black children: throughout the history of the colony, state education was bottlenecked to ensure that fewer and fewer blacks had access to education as they progressed up to tertiary education.

35   Government schools for whites, and to a lesser extent, those for Coloreds and Indians, had the best resources, while the "Africans only" schools, the Group B schools like Chembira, suffered from overcrowding, inadequately trained teachers and no resources. It is no wonder that at independence, the government, and its first leader, Mugabe, a teacher, considered it the chief

priority, even ahead of land reform, to respond to the thirst for education. But in the last ten short years of Zimbabwe's political and economic crisis, these hard won gains have been all but lost.

My next school is a short drive from Chembira. I walked down this same dusty road on a day in January 1979, when the school opened to new pupils. This was during the short-lived Zimbabwe-Rhodesia regime, led by Bishop Muzorewa. Our hot-seating class was told to get up and walk with our teacher to our new school, where we found ourselves among the first pupils at Glen Norah Number 6 Government Primary School.

The school is now called Kundai. It is smaller than I remember it. It is also impressively neat. There are new trees all around the school. They were not there when I last visited the school two years ago. They are labeled with Latin names written out in a neat hand. The headmaster, Mr. Ingidzai Kamudyarwa, is a keen botanist.

His enthusiasm flourishes everywhere.

"Some of the children are now very interested in trees and plants," he tells us.

The children here look smarter than at Chembira, perhaps it is the uniform that makes the difference, an attractive blue and white checked fabric that does not seem to reflect the harshness of the sun as does the darker green of Chembira. The children are all in class as we walk around the school, they spring up with one motion when we enter the classrooms. As at Chembira, there are far too many children at the school—a total of 1,300 in all.

I last visited Kundai in 2008, when Zimbabwe was at its very worst. My cousin, Eddison Murwira, who taught there, had asked me to talk to his Grade 7 class, to fire them with ambition. He told me then that teachers' salaries were barely sufficient to cover their transport.

"And you still come to work?" I marvelled.

"*Vana vevanhu,*" he said. "You look at them and think well, if you don't teach them, who will? You get frustrated and angry; you vow not to come to work. Then you look at these children, such innocent souls, and you think, how is it their fault?"

Kundai is the only school in Glen Norah that offers education specifically tailored to children with special needs. There are two special classes at the school: one for hearing-impaired children, and another for mentally-challenged

40

children, a class of children whom the headmaster calls "slow-learners." The teacher in this class explains that they need rugs because the children like to play on the cold floor. They also need toys and books. In the obsession over the shortage of textbooks, she says, the requirements of the special needs children often get less priority. The class has a small collection of makeshift and homemade toys—bricks, bottle tops and dried seeds. They have needles and thread, a doll and a few charts.

45   "The doll causes a lot of problems because it is the only one," the teacher laughs.

The bricks make me smile—for Zimbabwean children with no toys, discarded bricks can, with the appropriate sounds, become anything from a racing car to a haulage truck.

From the special classes, Mr. Kamudyarwa takes us around the playground he designed for the Grade Zeros. Rudo and I run exclaiming from one section to another: there is a mini stadium for story telling, there is a little patch where the little ones have planted beans, there is a mini garage with stop signs and a petrol pump.

"That," says Mr. Kamudyarwa, pointing to the animals painted on a wall, "is the game park."

Outside the playground, under a tree, a hot-seating class listens as their teacher reads to them. As we leave, I look again at the small, neat-pin school. Rudo and I talk all the way back and we find ourselves reaching again and again for that old cliché, about the difference that one person can make.

50   From the township of Glen Norah to the suburb of Mabelreign is a distance of a few kilometers. It is a twenty-minute drive if there is no traffic. It took my parents 15 years to traverse that distance, their journey impeded by Rhodesia's segregationist policies. In the year of Zimbabwe's independence, we moved from the township to the suburb. The former Group A schools were forced to open up to children from all backgrounds and I began my education at Alfred Beit School. I was one of its first black pupils.

The school was named for the mining magnate whose statue sits outside Imperial College in London and outside Zimbabwe's National Archives, and whose sizeable fortune launched the education charity the Beit Trust. In the reception, Rudo and I sit facing a large tapestry of painted seeds glued on canvas to form the school crest and motto, in French: *Fait bien, fait tout.* At the bottom is a legend that says, "In memory of Grade 7 M 1984."

My shock is almost palpable. That is the year that I left school. Our class made this collage, in art class, our teacher Mr. Makwarimba directing us. Twenty-eight years later, it is still intact.

Below the collage is a sign that says THERE ARE NO SCHOOL PLACES AVAILABLE. Opposite, under the portrait of Alfred Beit, is a poster: YOU CAN SURVIVE HIV. There is a shining plaque: Alfred Beit School received the Secretary's Bell for the best results in 1994. Below this is yet another notice: THERE ARE NO SCHOOL PLACES AVAILABLE.

As the deputy headmistress walks us around Alfred Beit, I am unable to shake my sense of dislocation. This cannot be the school of my childhood. Over there was the music room where Miss Roberts taught us the recorder. Behind the Grade 7 classroom were the tennis courts. In this classroom, we learned TS Eliot's *Macavity* for the Allied Arts Competition. In that one, Mr. Wallace made us put our heads down on the better to let the waves, the parrot calls and the pirate cries wash over us as we listened to an audiotape of *Treasure Island*. That distant field, where the grass is now taller than a Grade 4 child, was the scene of our second team's hockey triumph over the unbeatable Northpark. Everywhere, voices from the past: "I sprang to the stirrup and Joris and he. I galloped, Dirk galloped, we galloped all three. Do you remember an inn, Miranda, do you remember an inn?"

I feel as though I am in a Bizarro Alfred Beit, a dystopic nightmare of 55 neglect. The bicycle shed is overgrown with weeds. The swimming pool, scene of my brother Ratiel's spectacular rescue by Michelle Sawyer, is a dirty greenish-blue hole in the ground.

"When I was at Alfred Beit," I tell the headmaster, Mr. Zvareva, "the average used to be 26 children to a class."

"Those were the days," he says. "Now it is about 48 to 50 children per class."

The school has 1,422 children in total, with the largest group being the five Grade 1 classes.

There are no new classrooms.

I am puzzled to know how the school has managed to fit 1,422 children 60 in a school that had a maximum of maybe 400 children, until Mr. Zvareva explains that they have had to convert all the arts and music rooms and library into ordinary classrooms. I ask about drama, the pride of our school when I was there, and the Allied Arts Competition.

"That is now long gone," says the deputy headmistress.

We pass a group of Grade Zeros who look like they are playing dress up with their older siblings' clothes.

The most absent thing at Alfred Beit School are books. There is not a single book in sight that could be read for pleasure. When I was here, there were books in every classroom. There was a school library, and even better, at the shops was the Queen Victoria Memorial Library. It is now called the Harare City Library. Recalling the eagerness with which I once walked up these steps, my mouth watering at the thought of another new book, I go to the library. There are just 12 subscribers at the library now, the librarian there tells me.

Of these, only three are children.

As we leave the school, there is a tightness in my chest. In the distance, the sports fields are covered in long grass. For a mad minute, I think it is maze. In the faint breeze, a sign flutters on the gate: THERE ARE NO SCHOOL PLACES AVAILABLE.

Chishawasha is a short drive from central Harare. It would be shorter still if the dust road from the turn off at Enterprise Road were tarred. The surrounding Shawasha Hills have become a fashionable new development, dotted with new houses built with new money. The valley itself remains resolutely rural: Innocent stops the car to let two small boys herd their cows across the road.

Chishawasha is Catholic Central, with four schools, a clinic, the regional seminary and a cathedral all built on land that Rhodesia's founder, Cecil John Rhodes, gave to the Jesuits in 1890s. It is prime land. The school overlooks the old Valley of the Millionaires—after the Federation of the two Rhodesias and Nyasaland collapsed, its last Governor-General, Simon Ramsay, Lord Dalhousie, set up a farm here.

We drive to St Dominic's Secondary school. Everything seems to be exactly the same. The redbrick classrooms. The convent with its Dominican sisters. The school hall where mass was held and where we sat exams. The statue of the Virgin in the grotto. There is Sister Elizabeth, with her gentle face and German accent, and there, Mr. Madubeko, the headmaster and my old science teacher.

A highly selective girls' school, St Dominic's was every parent's dream. It offered a first class education in an austere but nurturing Catholic environment, far from the temptations of town. Daughters of the wealthy mixed with girls from poor rural families, their common bond academic excellence.

"Is the school still committed to educating girls from all backgrounds?" 70 I ask my former teachers.

"We really want to educate poor children but we can't educate anyone without money, no?" says Sister Elizabeth.

Mr. Madubeko confirms this but clarifies that even though only those able to pay fees come to the school, they aim to keep the fees low. The fees are currently less than 400 dollars a term. Sister Elizabeth explains that in years when they got donations from overseas, they could pay for girls who may have lost their parents and were unable to continue.

The more I look, the more I see changes. The library has moved to a room twice its former size. There is a new A-Level block, built in 2001, which offers accommodation for 40 girls. St Dominic's has received an impressive number of Secretary's Bells; at a hundred percent, the school consistently has the highest pass rate for A-Levels in the country.

"We do not take girls with less than 5 As at O-Level if they were here," Sister Elizabeth says. "And if they come from outside the school, they have to have 8 As."

Mr. Madubeko bemoans the current pass-rate of 90 percent at O-Level, 75 the lowest it has been in ten years.

"When I was at St Dominic's," I remark, feeling smug, "The pass-rate was 100 percent."

Mr. Madubeko sighs and says that they are often under pressure to take girls who are not up to standard. One of the girls tells me later that one of Zimbabwe's top army generals had a daughter here. An army truck drove up every Saturday to bring her food, even though this was against the school rules. Mr. Madubeko is circumspect about the kind of pressures he is under, saying only that these pressures prevent a perfect pass rate.

The same faces I crept past those many years ago, trying very hard not to attract any attention, are still here, among them Sister Elizabeth, Sister Veronica, the deputy headmaster and his wife, who teaches science, Mai Farai, the Librarian, and Mr. Madubeko himself who has been here since 1975.

For the Dominican nuns, it is clear: the convent, and so the school, is their home. "But the others, why do the other teachers stay so long?" I ask.

80   Mr. Mutangara, deputy head since 1987, laughs and says, "There is nowhere else to go."

Mr. Madubeko explains it has been a stable home and a wonderful
environment for his children who all grew up in the valley. It also
helps, he says, that the staff receives a better salary than the ministry
salary—it is topped up by money from fees. He becomes wistful as he
wonders whether his staying so long has been good or bad for the
school.

We move around the school taking photographs. The girls are hard at
work. A class in social geography is exploring the concept of equality under
socialism. In the food and nutrition class, the girls are learning to make a
curry. In this same room, my classmates and I were taught to make food
meant for cold English winters, shepherd's pie and toad-in-the-hole, York-
shire pudding and apple crumble. At the end of the corridor is a literature
room. There are five girls there now, with books before them, discussing
Measure for Measure.

As we leave, I take a look at the school's vision statement on the notice
board. One of the aims of the school, according to this, is "preparation for
life in all its dimensions, its profound meaning and transformation beyond
death to eternal life." There is no way of measuring whether the school
achieves this. What it achieves without question are stellar results: twenty-
three years after I left, St Dominic's is still one of the top schools in the
country.

From St Dominic's, I went to St Ignatius College as one of the 40 girls at
Zimbabwe's finest Jesuit school for boys. Our mission was partly to help the
boys move with ease between the all-boys environment of Form 1 to 4 to
the co-educational A-Levels. With us, they got used to girls before being
unleashed on an unsuspecting world. But we were there mainly because
Mary Ward, a forward-thinking English nun who founded the Institute of
the Blessed Virgin Mary, now called the Congregation of Jesus, dreamed of
setting up girls' schools on the Jesuit model. The Mary Ward girls, as we
were called, shared classes with the boys.

85   We received a first class education.

Since its establishment on 1962, St Ignatius has educated generations of
brilliant boys from poor and modest backgrounds: better-off families in

search of a Jesuit education tend to send their sons to St. Ignatius' posher brother school in town, St George's College.

When I visit St Ignatius with Rudo and Innocent, it is like stepping into the achingly familiar. I was very happy here. The school is built on a hill, with the Chishawasha valley on one side and a view of the Valley of the Millionaires from Mary Ward House. Rich red earth is everywhere, at one with the red bricks of the well-maintained buildings. Father Roland von Nidda, the rector, is expansive in his welcome. He takes us from classroom to classroom.

My visit inspires him to invite me to the Prize-Giving Day as a guest of honor.

It is here that I see my old school at its very best.

I speak to the boys and girls about what the school meant to me, about 90 the Jesuits priests and Mary Ward sisters who taught me, about the fierce ambition they burned in me to not only do exceptionally well but also, in the words of St Ignatius of Loyola, to find a way to set the world on fire. I tell them about my little rebellions, abandoning Catholicism for Buddhism, only to find myself as lonely as my headmaster Father Berridge had predicted: I would probably be the only Buddhist in Zimbabwe, he had said.

"I also want to be a Buddhist," whispers a small Form 2 boy to me later, as I give out his prize.

Father Von Nidda emphasizes in his speech that the school aims for a holistic education.

Over tea, he tells me that he wants to send into the world compassionate young men and women with critical minds.

"And they are so bright," he says. "My goodness they are bright. I do worry though that some of them take religion too seriously."

The prizes follow. The sun hits my eyes as I give out certificate after cer- 95 tificate, for best A-Level results, for the top ten in each class. There are school colors in volleyball, swimming, netball, rugby, soccer, basketball and chess. It is inspiring to see both the fierce competition and the pleasure in the pursuit of excellence. There is humor and camaraderie in the competitiveness. Peels of ululation ring out as exultant parents dance little jigs to celebrate their children. The teachers are just as competitive. They receive prizes for every record they break.

As I hand out their certificates and congratulate the A-level students who did exceptionally well in both the Cambridge and Zimbabwe school examinations, I ask where they are headed, and what they will read.

"I will do medicine in South Africa," says one.

"I am off to York University in Canada," says another.

They want to study medicine and accountancy, law and engineering, architecture and actuarial science.

100   "If I can't go anywhere else," the former head girl, Nancy Kachingwe, tells me, "Then it will have to be the University of Zimbabwe."

Zimbabwe's Prime Minister, Morgan Tsvangirai, likes to say that the real scope of the tragedy of Mugabe's most recent years in power is that he has destroyed not only what he inherited at independence, but also what he built himself. My journey around my childhood confirms that, far from being an enabler and builder, the government has actually been an inhibitor and destroyer. The successful schools are those where government interference is felt the least, private schools that, untainted by government control, have managed to thrive.

Even in the government schools, all is not quite lost. Individuals have managed to make a difference, even against the odds; ordinary people like the headmaster and teachers at Kundai; the engaged parents in the SDA at Chembira. Even Alfred Beit, which fell the furthest of my previous schools, has barely hung on because parents have agreed to pay more fees than government demands.

It is hard to shake the sense I got that money has replaced race in Zimbabwe. In Rhodesia, race determined whether a child was guaranteed a good education. In post-crisis Zimbabwe, it is now class that is the determinant. It is the ability of the parents to pay that determines whether their children get a good education. A Zimbabwean PhD student has written a thesis that argues that this generation of children will be less literate then their parents, a terrifying possibility that brings with it the specter of social upheavals to come.

In one respect, the Zimbabwe of my education is the same Zimbabwe today. It is a country filled with children who manage to find happiness in difficult circumstances, who make toys out of bricks, who study in the light of candles, and who are filled with imaginations and ambitions that are bigger than the collapse of their failed state.

Analyze

1. Gappah explains that she was "of the generation that started school in Rhodesia, continued in Zimbabwe-Rhodesia and finished in Zimbabwe." What lessons of colonial rule and postcolonial transformation are related in this reading?

2. Gappah claims that the Rhodesian government expressly did not want the black population to be educated. Why not? How did that change when Rhodesia became Zimbabwe? How is it different now?

3. How does your own education compare to Gappah's? Do you feel that children whose parents can afford private schools are receiving a better education? Explain.

4. Gappah describes the fierce ambition her teachers burned into her and the children at her former school: "to not only do exceptionally well but also, in the words of St Ignatius of Loyola, to find a way to set the world on fire." Have your teachers burned into you any "fierce ambition"? What did Gappah's teachers mean when they encouraged her to "set the world on fire"?

Explore

1. What impression do you have of Gappah's high school's curriculum? What do you think is important to include in a curriculum? Write a description of your own primary, middle, and/or secondary school— what did it look like, and what did you learn? What was considered important? Why? Looking back on it now, do you think there was a "political" aspect to it that you were not aware of at the time? If you went back today, how might it have changed? Would it have changed for the better?

2. Gappah writes, "A Zimbabwean PhD student has written a thesis that argues that this generation of children will be less literate then their parents, a terrifying possibility that brings with it the specter of social upheavals to come." Why is this a terrifying possibility? What social upheavals would result from a less literate society in Zimbabwe? What has challenged Zimbabwe's educational system? Research a country in sub-Saharan Africa that has a positive model for an equitable education system. What were its greatest challenges and, and how were they solved?

Paul Salopek
"The Last Famine"

In 1998, foreign correspondent Paul Salopek won the Pulitzer Prize in Explanatory Reporting for two articles profiling the Human Genome Diversity Project. In 2001, he won another Pulitzer, this time in International Reporting, for his work on the political conflicts and disease epidemics ravaging Africa. He is at work on *The Mule Diaries*, a book about wandering. "The Last Famine" appeared on March 2, 2012, in *Foreign Policy*, one of the leading publications on international politics and global affairs. Readers of *Foreign Policy* will find expert analyses about such pressing global challenges as famine and starvation. Salopek chronicles the journey he took with his wife and the pastoral nomads of northern Kenya across the starving regions of the Horn of Africa, offering an intimate look at the complicated issue of famine.

What factors do you think make a journalist's reporting especially authoritative? Should a journalist always maintain an objective distance, or are there times when a journalist can only tell the "truth" through direct personal experience?

Early in February, without much fanfare, the United Nations officially declared the famine over in the Horn of Africa. This is welcome news. Last summer, when the worst drought in 60 years was wasting the region, 13 million people faced starvation. The misery was most acute in Somalia, where al-Shabab, the fanatical Islamist militia with links to al Qaeda, had blocked aid groups from working in the areas under its control. In the end, an estimated 35,000 Somalis—along with some Kenyans and Ethiopians— are thought to have died; most were children under five. The handling of the calamity nonetheless has been rated an overall success. Context helps in measuring such victories. Twenty years ago, a quarter of a million Somalis perished during a similar wartime drought. And before that, in the Sahelian emergencies of the mid-1980s, a million emaciated bodies were spooned prematurely into sandy graves.

Last August, I took a long walk with Daasanach nomads in northern Kenya, well inside the disaster zone, to see what it was like to move, as most famine victims do, on foot, through a landscape of chronic hunger. It was a way to look at hunger beyond the carefully framed shots of television cameras, and an occasion to ask: When will Africa's vast hunger pangs finally end?

I made no pretense of suffering myself. I was joined by my wife, Linda, a seasoned hiker, and neither of us stinted on our personal food supply: We carried rucksacks heavy with energy bars and bottled water. Our host was a rope-thin goatherd named Inas Lonyaman, a smiling, bald-headed elder at 35, who answered to Mister Inas. He wore sandals cut from old tires and a kind of faded sarong, and he brought along his usual herding kit—a throwing stick and a tiny wooden stool on which to sit. His sterner colleague, Haskar Lotur, shouldered a rusty AK-47 rifle slung on a rawhide cord as defense against the Gabra, a competing and similarly armed group of herders. A young entomology student, Luke Lomeiku, also of Daasanach ancestry, joined us as interpreter. Lomeiku had equipped himself with a shiny-red plastic thermos that held perhaps two cups of water, and a butterfly net. Every few hours, he crept up to shriveled acacias and swept them for insects. But our trek promised lean prospects for science. Mister Inas's pastures—located in the immense, arid core of the Turkana Basin—were overgrazed to the appearance of a gravel parking lot. Temperatures in the netted shade of the thorn trees hovered, at noon, around 100 degrees Fahrenheit. In two days of plodding across 25 miles of cauterized terrain, Lomeiku captured a single bee.

Mister Inas seemed grateful for the company. Pushing 80 goats through the coming desert was melancholy work. For three years, precipitation had fallen erratically, if at all, in his isolated corner of the world, a Kenyan outback located 500 miles northwest of the famine's epicenter in Somalia. It was not the focus of the massive international relief effort, in which the U.S. government played a leading role, having donated by then some $459 million in humanitarian assistance. But the epidemic of hunger here was just as old and stunting. While an army of foreign journalists and relief workers converged on refugee camps on the distant Somali border, Daasanach children were starving in the more typical nomad way—more or less permanently and beyond the restless glare of the TV lights. Half of the Turkana Basin's population of 500,000 livestock herders and subsistence farmers was on food aid. Indeed, some people had been collecting rations for 30 years. Even so, Mister Inas, a veteran of many starveling years, ranked the current dry spell the toughest he had ever experienced. Droughts used to be spaced further apart, he said. Nowadays, they came brutally hard and fast, and his goats were dying of thirst. He'd lost half his herd already. His seven children he parceled out among various relatives to avert starvation. When I asked how long he was prepared to endure such catastrophes, he shrugged.

5   "We have no education," he said, knocking his bony forehead with a fist. "If the Daasanach go to school, then all these troubles will end. But we are stupid." He talked at length about abandoning the nomad life altogether.

But I'd heard such declarations before. They weren't credible. For the Daasanach, owning animals means everything—status, wealth, life. And like many disempowered minorities, they frequently said what they thought outsiders wished to hear. Trudging behind him for hours, I became convinced that the surer measure of Mister Inas's future lay at the opposite end of his anatomy.

Horny with calluses, flat as slabs of jerked meat, his feet swung from his high, girlish hips like the weights on a metronome: smoothly, tirelessly—I am tempted to say, eternally—as though the surface of the savanna consisted not of burning dust, but greased ball bearings. His sandals rode the earth like skates. It was a gait of superhuman efficiency: transcontinental, very old, designed for chasing clouds, for swallowing endless miles of geography in the pursuit of the country of rain. Once Africa stops producing such supremely educated feet, I thought—only *then* will the stereotypical images of her dying babies, the bloat-bellied infants of nomads, disappear from the world's TV screens. The Mister Inases will have become extinct. Or, they will have finally pulled on socks and shoes. And from that point on, the mass hungers we hear about will be protagonized by victims whose soft soles are shod in wingtips, work boots, high-heeled pumps, tennis shoes. They will be urban. Which is to say, they will belong to us.

The Turkana Basin is a freakishly beautiful place. A gargantuan wilderness of hot wind and thorn stubble, it covers all of northwestern Kenya and spills into neighboring Uganda, Ethiopia, and South Sudan. Black volcanoes knuckle up from its pale-ocher horizons. Lake Turkana—the largest alkaline lake in the world, 150 miles long—pools improbably in its arid heart. The lake is sometimes referred to, romantically, as the Jade Sea; from the air, its brackish waters appear a bad shade of green, like tarnished brass. Turkana, Pokot, Gabra, Daasanach, and other cattle nomads eke out a marginal existence around its shores. The basin's dry sediments, which form part of the Great Rift Valley, hold a dazzling array of hominid remains. Because of this, the Turkana badlands are considered one of the cradles of our species.

Richard and Meave Leakey, the scions of the eminent Kenyan fossil-hunting family, have been probing deep history here for 45 years. Their oldest discovery, a pre-human skull, about 4 million years old, was found on a 1994 expedition led by Meave. An earlier dig headed by Richard uncovered a fabulous, nearly intact skeleton of *Homo ergaster*, dating back 1.6 million years, dubbed the Turkana Boy. Both Leakeys told me the modern landscape had changed nearly beyond recognition since their excavations began in the 1960s. The influx of food aid and better medical services had more than tripled the human population and stripped the region of most of its wild meat, wiping out the local buffalo, giraffe, and zebra. Domestic livestock—exploding and then crashing with successive droughts—had scalped the savannas' fragile grasses. While driving one day near his headquarters, the Turkana Basin Institute, Richard pointed at a dusty cargo truck, its bed piled high with illegally cut wood. "Charcoal for the Somali refugee camps," he said with a puckish smile. "The U.N. pays for it."

Leakey is not only a celebrity thinker. He is also an incorrigible provocateur and a man of big and restless ambitions. Bored with the squabbles of academic research ("I could never go back to measuring one tooth against another"), he abandoned the summit of paleoanthropology in the late 1980s to assume the directorship of Kenya's enfeebled wildlife service, where he became a hero to conservationists by ordering elephant poachers shot on sight. A few years later, he helped organize Kenya's first serious opposition party, and those activities invited years of police harassment. (A 1993 plane crash, which Leakey blames on sabotage, resulted in the loss of both his legs below the knee; he now gets around—driving Land Rovers, piloting planes—on artificial feet.) At one point, I asked him about heavy bandages on his head and hands at a recent lecture at New York's Museum of Natural History. He had been suffering from skin cancers, he explained, that metastasized from old police-baton injuries. Leakey tends to view humankind through a very long lens, and pessimistically.

When we met, Leakey warned me that the killer drought throttling the Horn of Africa was another opening act for full-bore global warming. Northern Africa was a canary in the mine shaft. Even worse famines awaited. On the planetary stage, Leakey framed the problem bluntly as a matter of feeding 6 billion excess people. (He put the world's carrying capacity at 1 billion humans and suggested our species would fall back to that level this century, probably via a pandemic.) Droughts and famines have been integral to the human story, he went on. We have 200,000 years of experience with climate change, yet today, he complained, "We can't think even 50 years ahead." He said he was glad he was old—he was 67—because he had seen the best of life. He did offer one palliative for our future of deepening starvation: synthetic foods. Leakey's oratory was so hypnotic that I neglected to ask what exactly he meant—food grown by bacteria? In labs? I asked whether there was any hope for people like the Daasanach.

"Pastoral nomadism is nearly gone," he said. "We're seeing the last kicks and wiggles of a dying way of life. The people are getting progressively poorer, and you can't afford to feed them and their goats forever."

One anthropological study pegs the number of African pastoralists, classic drought victims, at 20 million. When agro-pastoralists—herders who also scratch out a bit of farming—are included, the total grows to 280 million, about a quarter of the entire African population. Surely they must be accommodated. "There are large aquifers here," Leakey said. "You could set up a Palm Springs-type area—casinos, hotels. There's no end to opportunities for tourism. Turkana could be the Nevada of Africa."

Meave Leakey was sitting beside her husband, on a shaded rock veranda, as he visualized golf carts in Kenya's most desolate hinterland. "Casinos," she muttered. She grimaced out over lion-colored plains that were largely bereft of lions now. "Imagine."

15　　At dawn, Mister Inas gulped a cup of gruel made with maize flour donated by USAID, the American development agency. It was impossible to tell whether this food was new aid, sent to combat the famine, or just more of the billions of dollars in international relief that has become a semipermanent fixture in Africa's ragged margins. Even Mister Inas didn't know. He'd been collecting rations in a nearby town for so long—in exchange for manual labor on public works or as a reward for having his children immunized—that it all blurred together. Either way, the gruel, beaten cold in a fire-blackened pot by his wife, Eyomo, would be his only meal until nightfall. He set off on the walk from his kraal, or brushy goat corral, having consumed perhaps 500 calories.

Mister Inas used a repertoire of vocalizations to keep his goats on track. This consisted of a peculiar medley of clucks, chirrups, and whistles. Shouts of "Hah!" put the herd on alert against jackals. "Woup! Woup! Woup!" summoned the animals to water. Or so he told me. I honestly couldn't discern any significant change in the herd's behavior. The goats—they had mottled pelts and square pupils that appraised you unnervingly from inside chromium yellow eyes—seemed to graze at will, moving audibly through the scrub across a broad front, like a rustling breeze. With no grass left to gnaw, they stood on their hind hooves, cropping the undersides of thorn bushes as level as topiary.

I wondered how the nomads perceived this scene.

The British anthropologist Colin M. Turnbull, in his classic study of Mbuti Pygmy life in the rain forests of Congo, described taking one of his informants, a man named Kenge, out into the open savanna for the first time. The forest-dweller, adapted to a field of vision cramped by billions of leaves, spotted black dots on a distant plain. "He asked me what kind of insects they were, and I told him they were buffalo, twice as big as the forest buffalo known to him," Turnbull wrote. "He laughed loudly and told me not to tell such stupid stories." When Turnbull drove up to the animals, the astonished Pygmy asked "why they had been so small, and whether they *really* had been small and had suddenly grown larger, or whether it had been some kind of trickery."

I began to suspect that Mister Inas's own depth perception was shaped by the gargantuan space of the Turkana Basin. He paid scant attention to the termite mounds and dry gulches that corrugated our route and seemed riveted instead by the horizons. He scanned them incessantly, swinging his head slowly back and forth like a Doppler radar. He said he was looking for rain. Quite possibly he was searching for the tippy-tops of clouds peeking above the curvature of the Earth, 60 miles away. I discerned nothing of the sort, though later in the afternoon a high, muzzy overcast developed.

In the past, herders had tended to outcompete farmers in many of Africa's desert borders. Mobility was the key. If your pastures dried up, you drove your animals toward the slightest hint of precipitation, knowing grass would eventually sprout there. But this strategy worked only when old boundaries were observed. What appeared to me a featureless wasteland was parsed, in the eyes of a Daasanach, by a dense web of regulation and ownership, something akin to urban zoning: The savannas were crisscrossed by invisible migration routes, seasonal pasturage rights, proprietary water holes. In a place as destitute as the Turkana Basin, food aid hadn't just swollen human populations, but undermined those antique rules. It had also encouraged the nomads, ruinously, to maintain more animals than the fragile pastures could sustain; living on donations, they saw little need to eat or sell off their herds in times of drought. And so, the rangelands eventually wore away, becoming sterile as concrete.

"This country is too crowded," Haskar Lotur, the gunman, snorted. He flicked his skinny wrist dramatically at the ringing emptiness. "Nobody stays in their place anymore."

The sun was devastatingly hot, and Linda and I sucked down bottled water. Seeing our thirst, Mister Inas and Lotur politely declined offers of drinks. They accepted granola bars, but judging from their exchanged deadpan glances, must have found them disappointing. Mister Inas then showed us a few wild plants the Daasanach resorted to during famines: the berries of the kadite bush and a gnarled tree that produced a currant-like fruit called *miede*. People were forgetting their use. "Today, we eat food aid instead," he said.

At that time, the U.N. World Food Program was helping feed 265,000 people in the Turkana region. The nomads, once canny at eking out a livelihood on the gauntest of Kenyan landscapes, had been settling into ramshackle outposts, essentially rural slums, where each household received a monthly allotment of 10 kilograms of maize. They were losing what relief workers termed "famine-coping mechanisms"—their ancestral survival skills. Cutting off assistance cold was unthinkable; countless people would die. So after having helped fund these supplemental feeding programs for decades, the U.S. government, through its African Development Foundation, decided last year to put its foot down. It earmarked $10 million for a pilot program in the Turkana area that might be called aid methadone— still more aid, but this time in the form of fishponds and irrigated market gardens, all intended to pry people off the old aid.

The Bible is rife with divinely ordained famines. No surprise there. Who were the Israelites, after all, if not rain-obsessed pastoralists and dry-land farmers? "Gladness and joy have been taken away from the fruitful land of Moab; I have made the wine cease from the wine presses; no one treads them with shouts of joy; the shouting is not the shout of joy." (Jeremiah 48:33)

Sharman Apt Russell, in her survey of our primordial craving,   25
Hunger: An Unnatural History, quotes a 4,000-year-old inscription on
the tomb of an Egyptian noble: "All of Upper Egypt was dying of hunger
to such a degree that everyone had come to eating his children." Two-
thirds of Italy, she reminds us, starved to death during the black plagues
of the 14th century. Five-hundred years later, a microscopic potato
fungus scythed down a million Irishmen (and women and children) and
sent at least a million more into famished exodus. And proving once
again that we humans are perhaps the worst crop of pestilence of all, she
cites the 2 million to 3 million Ukrainians methodically starved to
death by Stalin's forced collectivization. A grim coda: The deadliest
famine recorded—ever—was man-made and happened within living
memory: The Great Leap Forward, Mao's rush to industrialize the countryside, killed tens of millions of Chinese between 1958 and 1962.
"Hunger," Russell writes, "is as big as history."

Reaching back much deeper in time, some scientists argue that, by repeatedly winnowing our species' ranks, droughts and famines made us
fully human.

For example, a so-called "thermal hypothesis" of evolution, supported
by evidence of sweltering temperatures in the prehistoric Turkana Basin,
posits that repeated, hot, waterless interludes encouraged our apelike ancestors to finally rise up off their knuckles; bipedalism minimized the body's
exposure to intense solar radiation. Sweat glands replaced fur. Standing up,
we caught a breeze.

Closer to the present, sediment cores drilled at Lake Malawi in southern
Africa suggest that an awesome "mega-drought" struck just as our species
was gaining a tentative foothold on the continent, nearly killing off *Homo
sapiens* altogether. This epic dry spell began 135,000 years ago and lasted
for 50 millennia. The sands of the Sahara and Kalahari deserts merged,
smothering the woodlands and savannas where we evolved. The drought
unleashed what very nearly became our last famine. Geneticists calculate a
population of survivors no larger than 10,000. (Researchers at Stanford
University narrow that bottleneck even more; they contend that only 2,000
anatomically modern humans escaped extinction, and they are the fore-
bears of every single person alive today.) The stragglers migrated to the
African coasts, where for millennia they scavenged "famine food" at low
tide: mussels, snails, clams. The switch from red meat to seafood proved
fateful. It elevated our intake of omega-3 fatty acids—brain food: a new

diet that may have inadvertently accelerated the development of verbal skills. Such "water's-edge" theories of human evolution have gained credence in recent years with the discovery of enormous shell middens at coastal shelters in South Africa and Eritrea. The sites date to the time of the super-drought.

"Place a species under stress, and you can't tell what will happen," Meave Leakey told me. "It could go extinct, or a new mutation will arise, in this case, maybe something that led to advanced language."

30   What seems clear from the fossil record is that the great Pleistocene famine nudged us out of the African nursery. For the first time, we began marching beyond the continent in earnest, eventually to conquer the world. Empty bellies transformed us into the wandering ape.

We walked, squinting for hours through hot panes of light. Mister Inas steered his goats toward Lake Turkana. It was the animals' second day without water and time to quench their thirst. I knew we were nearing the lake because livestock began to multiply on the threadbare savanna. The air grew thick with dust and was filled with the clanking of neck bells and the calling of other nomads. I asked Mister Inas how he kept track of his animals in all the traffic, and he stared at me with genuine incredulity. "I know my goats," he said.

The lake was another desert—an oxidized mirror shining up dully at the overcast. Its gray surface was swept by a sultry wind that didn't cool the skin. Muddy waves gummed the beach, and the grass on the shore was nibbled down to a vegetative five o'clock shadow. There was a famous drought story here.

Back in the early 1970s, in an effort to break the cycles of starvation in the Turkana region, Kenyan officials had delegated the Norwegian development agency Norad the task of retraining local herders to fish. The lake swarmed with tilapia and Nile perch. The idea was to wean the people off their boom-and-bust livestock economy, swap animal for fish protein, and make the nomads productive, sedentary citizens. The Scandinavians built a modern freezer plant near the lake. They taught people how to cast nets. And they distributed 20 large, modern fiberglass skiffs. The project was a colossal failure. As it turned out, freezing the catches cost more than the fish were worth. And, astoundingly, the foreigners hadn't bothered to ask whether the milk- and meat-addicted nomads even liked fish. (They didn't.) A decade after donors had sunk millions into the scheme, the Turkana pastoralists were as poor and hungry as ever. Many gave up and returned to the bush. A few of the more enterprising families found a novel use for their upturned fishing vessels as crude shelters.

Lake Turkana's beached fishing fleet became an icon of asinine philanthropy in Africa.

That said, the earnest Norwegians had been onto something. They were   35 simply premature; it took more decades of lethal droughts for the idea to catch on. Today, big cooler trucks loaded with fresh fish rattle between Lake Turkana and markets in Nairobi, a two-day drive away. Fishing keeps several thousand ex-herders marginally employed, though admittedly, with the price of their catches inflated 16-fold between the lakeshore and the supermarkets, urban middlemen are the real beneficiaries. And critics may get the last laugh. Lake Turkana's fish stocks are already collapsing.

Mister Inas watered his goats near two Daasanach men drying their fishing nets on the shore. They were the only human beings visible for hundreds of yards along the beach. Mister Inas pointedly ignored them. Bent at their work, they returned the snub. Men who don't possess hoofed animals are despised as worthless in Daasanach culture.

A few steps away, a 6-foot crocodile lay rotting in the surf. Its skull was pierced by two neat bullet holes. A few weeks before, a child had been dragged into the lake by a croc. Several herders had seen it happen. "There was nothing they could do," Mister Inas said. "They just ran to tell the family that their boy was swallowed by a crocodile." Later, one of the boy's relatives walked to the lake with a Kalashnikov and shot the first crocodile he saw.

Mister Inas invited me to join him for a bath. He grinned when I declined, but he wasn't swaggering. The proximity of so much water, even brackish water, was a luxury not to be passed up. He hitched up his wrap, revealing a pair of blue soccer shorts, and, with a look of intense bliss, waded into the murky shallows on the pin legs of a heron.

Lodwar, the frontier outpost that serves as the capital of the Turkana District, is located across Lake Turkana, about 120 miles southwest of Mister Inas's barren pastures. Roads are scarce in northern Kenya. So the simplest way of getting there was by plane. A Cessna flown by Leakey's bush pilot deposited us at the town's airstrip. Two huge jet engines, relics of a previous crash, lay bleaching atop boulders next to the runway like a negative monument to air safety. The airport terminal consisted of an open-sided hut. Signs of humanitarian engagement were everywhere.

40   White Toyota Land Cruisers with long whip antennas and logos of various relief agencies stamped on their doors crowded a dirt parking lot. There were large numbers of listless young men on the unpaved streets, and the streets themselves were littered with thousands of squashed plastic water bottles—refuse from donated rations. At the airport, a forlorn souvenir booth featured a Japanese flag and the sign, "Japan-Kenya Livelihood & Peace Building Committee." It sold beaded belts, wooden carvings, and a single copy of a book on anthropology written by an Irish Catholic missionary. The lonesome clerk was startled that I wanted to buy the book.

Later, while escaping the sun in what was possibly the slowest cybercafe in the world—downloading a single email took 17 minutes and a notice on the wall warned, perversely, "No Idlers Please"—I read a document that someone had been composing at my rented computer: "Incident Reporting Sheet for the Kenya Field Monitors."

It was a memo from an intergovernmental security commission that summarized a recent spike in fighting between nomads in the Turkana region. In one skirmish "Toposa bandits" had maneuvered 25 stolen donkeys belonging to a Mr. Namocho toward the Sudanese border. Armed Turkana "warriors" gave chase, cutting off the rustlers and igniting a firefight with "negative impact on human lives." Another raid at a settlement called Kibish involved a herd of pigs. Two thieves were shot dead "as intensive cross-fire exploded in the air."

The bloodiest episode by far was the coldblooded murder, nine days before, of eight ethnic Turkana women in the Todonyang area near the border with Ethiopia. The aggressors were Merille from Ethiopia—kin to the Daasanach. Snapshots accompanying the report, all the more wrenching for their amateur quality, featured crude graves and babies with horribly bruised faces. Their dead mothers had dropped them trying to escape the gunfire. The extreme brutality of such attacks baffled me until a Turkana businessman who ran a development organization in Lodwar explained their logic. "Nothing demoralizes the enemy more than killing their women," he said. "Women are targeted because it is a war of ethnic survival. And between the Merille and Turkana, access to shrinking pasturelands equals survival." Roughly a hundred nomads annually, from various ethnic groups, have died in battles in the Turkana region in recent years.

Outsiders tend to see their pet causes played out in African famines. Everyone brings something to hunger's table.

Anti-globalization groups condemn stock market speculators for jacking 45 up the costs of the world's food staples (thus pricing the poor out of their next meal). Washington worries about famine's role in political instability, particularly if relief is diverted to terrorist groups. (Secretary of State Hillary Clinton was obliged last summer to rescind the threat of legal sanctions against aid groups working in parts of Somalia controlled by the Islamist al-Shabab guerrillas; millions of civilians might have died otherwise.) Nowadays, the latest meta-concern to be piggybacked onto the backs of the starving is global warming. Some reporters, agreeing with Richard Leakey, have labeled the bloody clashes in the Turkana Basin one of the world's first "climate-change conflicts." Like most other imposed narratives, though, this one is blinkered.

"At this stage, I don't think there is any hard evidence to show conclusively that droughts are getting worse in the region, compared with the past," Philip Thornton, a leading climate scientist at the International Livestock Research Institute in Nairobi, wrote me in an email. "To call this a 'climate change war' may well be simply wrong."

Nobody disputes that the Horn of Africa is reeling through a period of harrowing droughts. Water levels in Lake Turkana have sunk 50 feet over the past 40 years. And Mister Inas and other herders insisted that the recent dry seasons have broken all records for longevity. But the point Thornton and other climate scientists make is that events in one lifetime aren't a reliable enough gauge of what droughts loom ahead. Long-term rainfall statistics collected in the region—going back to British colonial times—are ambiguous, sometimes oscillating just as radically as today. And according to the most recent report issued by the Intergovernmental Panel on Climate Change, the international agency spearheading the study of the man-made pollutants that cause global warming, East Africa is expected to get wetter, not dryer, in coming decades. "Even if East Africa does become wetter, this does not imply that the climate will be more conducive for agricultural production," Thornton cautioned. Increases in temperature are likely to lead to decreased crop yields.

In Lodwar, the people closest to the violence naturally had their own interpretations.

"I would put climate change second or third," said Epem Esekon, a senior administrator at Lodwar's hospital. "The redrawing of land boundaries under Kenya's new constitution comes first, then maybe climate, then maybe guns." Local violence has erupted in Kenya over political boundaries overhauled in 2010. In addition, Esekon said, pastoral groups had clashed and stolen each others' livestock using spears. Now an abundance of cheap assault rifles from wars both defunct and active in South Sudan and Uganda had upped the ante of such raids.

50   Esekon's hospital had already discharged the survivors of the assault on Todonyang. But other victims of such carnage were lying about. One Turkana man, shot through the back by competing Pokots, curled glassy-eyed with pain in bed No. 20. The bullet's exit would was two inches above his navel. He had limped four days to seek medical help.

"There is a lot of grass in the area where they are killing us," Peter Akure Lothike, the chief of the area where the skirmish took place, told me. He spoke affably, even as he toted a Belgian FAL assault rifle through the stifling ward. "The Pokots increase their cattle raids about now, to pay for their children's school fees."

And I thought again of Mister Inas's antediluvian feet. The Pokots, it seemed, were walking out of their last famines as nomadic herders. They were headed for the shoe stores.

Russell, in her book on hunger, uncovers the world record for fasting.

"Mr. A.B.," a patient at the University Department of Medicine in Dundee, Scotland, was a morbidly obese young man who weighed 456 pounds. In June 1965, under medical supervision, he stopped eating. In fact, he didn't eat, according to the *Postgraduate Medical Journal*, for more than a year—a boggling 382 days. Occasionally he was plied with vitamins. He drank water. He lost more than 250 pounds. "He must, at times, have felt like a god," Russell writes. "He lived like a tree, a rowan or oak, on air and sunshine. He lived more like a spirit than matter. Did he try and walk through walls? Did he think of himself as a ghost?" Whatever else Mr. A.B. may have felt, a gutting loneliness surely must have haunted him. Our bodies are like beads, rings of flesh wrapped about a hollow tube. What strings us all together is bread—bread and stories.

The longest I have survived without food is eight days. I remember the 55 experience well. It occurred while I was on hunger strike in prison, five years ago, after being detained while reporting on the Darfur war in Sudan. What lingers is a strange placidity, an unexpected and feverish clarity. By the third or fourth day without eating, I could feel myself weakening, but almost in compensation the surfaces of the everyday world appeared to take on a luminous polish; calls to prayer broadcast from a nearby mosque, the orange sunsets seen through window bars, the glossy red bodies of ants rummaging about my cell: Everything seemed freighted with deeper meanings. I began to understand how prolonged periods of hunger underpin bouts of mysticism—why the eyes of the starved, sunk brightly in their skulls, burn like a clairvoyant's. Scientists tell us it's actually the effect of ketones being released into the bloodstream by the liver's metabolization of stored fatty acids. This is the same mood-altering byproduct that accumulates with lengthy exercise—the biochemical buzz of "runner's high." Of course, I never approached the phases of malnutrition suffered by famine victims: agonizing intestinal cramps, bleeding gums, painfully inflamed joints, and finally, a coma-like stupor. I didn't get anywhere near that.

When we staggered back from our trek through the hunger zone to his kraal at dusk, Mister Inas ordered a kid goat slaughtered. I would reimburse him $25 for it later. But the simple gesture remained an act of surpassing generosity; goats were his family's sole bank account. That capital was ominously depleted. Mister Inas hadn't tasted meat for three months.

We crouched around a sparking fire, under dust-bleared stars, roasting gobbets of goat on upright sticks. The offal, bundled in the butchered animal's abdominal sack, went to the women "because they need soft things to eat"; Linda scored the intestine. It became apparent, as we cracked open the bones for marrow, why generations of Western anthropologists fell in love with nomads. Even in the middle of a drought, Mister Inas's encampment of brush huts, which would be abandoned in a few days, buzzed like a playground. It burbled with gossip and laughter. Naked children horsed about in a moonlit wadi until midnight. Even grim Haskar Lotur softened, pressing his Kalashnikov on me for the night, ostensibly as a defense against starving hyenas. He advised me to be sure of my target; people wandered the dark, too, to relieve themselves. The rifle was adorned about the muzzle with a hairy goatskin fetish. It belonged in a gallery of contemporary art.

The United Nations expects hunger to return again this year to the Horn of Africa. The next dry season begins in May. From that month on, it simply becomes a waiting game.

Aid workers employ a highly mathematical definition for the word "famine": It means that at least 20 percent of families in a region face extreme food shortages and acute malnutrition affects more than 30 percent of the population; there must be two starvation-related deaths per 10,000 people every day. Richard Leakey says these numbers toll, like a distant bell, for all of us. For a certain Dr. Francis Kuria of the Inter-Religious Council of Kenya, who published a well-reasoned column in the *Daily Nation* of Nairobi that quoted both the Roman poet Virgil and his country's bleak ranking on the Human Development Index, they ring the end, at last, for a venerable way of life and a 10,000-year-old economy. Of the nomads he wrote: "It's time for the Turkana to leave their wastelands and settle down." The optimists are few. Mostly, they are the desert wanderers themselves.

60   The last we saw of Mister Inas, he stood on the savanna, waving under shrouded skies. Two days later, rain poured down on the bone-colored dust of the Turkana Basin. The newspapers reported the drought broken. As many as eight people were killed in flash floods.

Analyze

1. As Salopek walks with the Daasanach nomads, what does he discover about moving "through a landscape of chronic hunger"?
2. Leakey "put the world's carrying capacity at 1 billion humans and suggested our species would fall back to that level this century, probably via a pandemic." How does Leakey's assessment jibe with Walker's "The World's New Numbers"? What in Leakey's demeanor (as described by Salopek) establishes (or undermines) his credibility?
3. How has humanitarian aid contributed to the savannas in the Turkana Basin "becoming sterile as concrete"? How does this resonate with the readings on aid and social entrepreneurship in chapter 6?
4. "Anti-globalization groups condemn stock market speculators for jacking up the costs of the world's food staples (thus pricing the poor out of their next meal)." How is globalization perceived in this sentence in paragraph 45?

Explore

1. Does the author believe Mr. Inas's assertion that the Daasanach need to go to school and possibly give up herding? If this happens, what will be lost? What will be gained? Answer these questions in an essay by researching herding cultures in the 21st century. How have they contributed to the economy, culture, and environmental stability of specific regions? Are they still valuable and/or sustainable in the 21st century? Why or why not?

2. "He wore sandals cut from old tires and a kind of faded sarong, and he brought along his usual herding kit—a throwing stick and a tiny wooden stool on which to sit." Draw pictures and/or find photos online that illustrate the various characters you came across in this reading. What have you learned about the choices people make in their clothing and adornments? How have other cultures, modern technology, and contemporary exigencies encroached upon more traditional costumes?

3. Meave Leakey wonders whether casinos like those in Nevada will replace the Daasanach. What is your response when you read that entire ways of traditional life may be ending—in this case, pastoral nomads? What if agrarians (i.e., farmers) were also to become extinct? What other way of life is moving toward extinction? Imagine in a fictional account that takes place some time in the not-so-distant future what would happen to a land and its people (and what the impact on a global scale would be) if a traditional way of life were to end.

Francis Kuria
"It's Time for the Turkana to Leave Their Wastelands and Settle Down"

Francis Kuria is the executive director of the Inter-Religious Council of Kenya, a coalition of all-faith communities working together to deepen interfaith dialogue in Kenya. This opinion piece appeared in the Kenyan newspaper *The Daily Nation*, Kenya's leading newspaper and one of the largest in Africa, in August 2011.

According to Kuria, a people's welfare is not typically what motivates a government to move a population group from one area to another. In what other parts of the world has forced removal of a people—under the guise of it being for their own welfare—taken place?

And what so potent cause took you to Rome?
Freedom, which, though belated, cast at length
No hope of freedom, and no thought to save.
Though many a victim from my folds went forth,
Never laden with hands returned home
There instant answer gave he to my suit
Feed, as before, your kine, boys, rear your bulls
So in old age, you happy man, your fields
Will still be yours, ample for your need!
Though with bare stones o'erspread, the pastures all.
—Virgil

In 35 BC in Rome, Virgil, the much-celebrated poet, asked the rhetorical question why a country man would hearken to the city of Rome.

The answer was, to obtain freedom from want and war, and to eat.

After all, he reasoned, when the country man is old, the pastures, strewn with bare stones, will still be his.

5   Was the celebrated sage writing about our Turkana? Isn't it time the Turkana abandoned nomadic pastoralism and moved to urban areas to seek other means of survival?

The images of the effects of drought in the region, which is perennial, requires a rethink of the current policy, if a policy exists.

The situation is likely to get worse as the cumulative effect of climate change and the spread of the Sahara Desert southwards continue.

The stance of most policy-makers is to wring their hands, make feeble gestures towards Ethiopia, and promise more relief food.

But what really is the vision for the region in the next 50 years. Shall we be still distributing relief food to emaciated women and children in the region?

10   Neighbouring Sudan has shown that it is possible to turn a wasteland into a highly productive region given the right investment.

Relying entirely on the waters of River Nile, the Sudanese have shown, with the Kenana Sugar Factory, what is possible.

They were replicating what the Egyptians have done for eons.

Can we not do the same with River Turkwel and the mighty Lake Turkana?

The waters of this lake are adequate to turn the riparian area into viable irrigated lands where the Turkana can be concentrated.

Such an undertaking would require the translocation of a significant   15
part of the population.

Massive translocation of people is not a new phenomenon. It has happened throughout the ages in response to life-threatening natural disasters, and in more recent times, due to man-made disasters.

The total population of Turkana County, according to the 2009 Population Census, is 855,399.

That is roughly equivalent to the population of Embakasi in Nairobi.

Just trying to reach the people with social services over an area of 69,000 square kilometres—roughly the size of Rwanda and Burundi combined—is a logistical nightmare.

In the past, the government has moved people to pave the way for big   20
projects like dams. Recently, we saw people being moved to make way for mining in Kwale.

When such populations are moved, it is not their welfare that is the driving force. But rather it is the whims of some bureaucrats and commercial interests of others far away from the local population.

It should thus be more attractive to move people to new settlements for their own good.

In a few years, there shall be created a new Tatu City for Sh24 billion and the new Malili ICT City for Sh800 billion.

From a human development standpoint, those two projects will have zero effect on our Human Development Index.

With just a fraction of this money, we could build three or four major   25
irrigation projects and settlement schemes for all the Turkana within a 10-km radius of the lake.

Such projects may be worthier than the preoccupation with economic growth that does not yield jobs nor reduce poverty.

It will be much easier to build schools, hospitals and other social amenities within such concentrated settlements than in the vast region, and eliminate widespread human suffering and grinding poverty within a generation.

Such irrigation schemes will permanently deal with hunger for the Turkana. Education, healthcare, water, sanitation, skills, security, employment and sustainable development can thereafter be delivered rapidly and cost-effectively.

Of course, there may be many counter-arguments to such a policy, including the danger of creating white elephants, and also destroying the culture and traditions of the Turkana.

30   People could argue about crime, drugs, violence and many other vices, or about the need to respect the socio-economic lifestyles of indigenous people.

But it is not possible to argue like that with the death-stare of a starving grandmother in your face.

Analyze

1. What do you make of Kuria's invocation of an ancient Roman poet to address the fate of the Turkana? What does this tell you about the kind of audience he is trying to appeal to?
2. "With just a fraction of this money, we could build three or four major irrigation projects and settlement schemes for all the Turkana within a 10-km radius of the lake. Such projects may be worthier than the pre-occupation with economic growth that does not yield jobs nor reduce poverty." How might Salopek respond to this?
3. How does Kuria back up this statement: "It will be much easier to build schools, hospitals and other social amenities within such concentrated settlements than in the vast region, and eliminate widespread human suffering and grinding poverty within a generation."

Explore

1. Research how advocates of the Turkana might respond to Kuria's opinion. In order to do this, you may need to know more about Kuria. Why is his opinion significant? What are the interests of the Turkana? As always, carefully evaluate the reliability of your sources.
2. "Of course, there may be many counter-arguments to such a policy, including the danger of creating white elephants, and also destroying the culture and traditions of the Turkana." Explain what kinds of counterarguments there may be. What does Kuria mean by the

expression "white elephants"? What would the white elephants be in this case? Can you think of other solutions to complex problems that have become white elephants?

3. How might the plight of the Turkana people be relevant to your own life? There are a number of contemporary films that address geopolitical issues in East Africa including the environment and arms (*Darwin's Nightmare*), literacy (*The First Grader*), displacement camps (*War Dance*), and genocide (*The Devil Came on Horseback*). Watch one of these films, and explore and clarify for yourself the issues it raises. How do you view your personal engagement with regional issues far from your own life?

Abhijit Banerjee and Esther Duflo
"More than 1 Billion People Are Hungry in the World"

In 2003, Abhijit Banerjee and Esther Duflo co-founded the Abdul Latif Jameel Poverty Action Lab (J-PAL)—a research center in the economics department at the Massachusetts Institute of Technology (MIT). It has since grown into a global network of researchers focused on developing strategies for fighting poverty. Banerjee, an Indian economist and the Ford Foundation International Professor of Economics at MIT, is the author of three books including *Poor Economics* (Public Affairs, 2012), which he co-wrote with Duflo. Duflo is a French economist, Professor of Poverty Alleviation and Development Economics at MIT, and a MacArthur Foundation Fellow (also known as the "genius grant"). She serves on the board of the Bureau for Research and Economic Analysis of Development (BREAD) and is director of the Center for Economic and Policy Research's development economics program. The following article appeared in the May/June 2011 issue of *Foreign Policy*—one of the leading publications on international politics and global affairs.

How do you define what it means to live in poverty?

For many in the West, poverty is almost synonymous with hunger. Indeed, the announcement by the United Nations Food and Agriculture Organization in 2009 that more than 1 billion people are suffering from hunger grabbed headlines in a way that any number of World Bank estimates of how many poor people live on less than a dollar a day never did.

But is it really true? Are there really more than a billion people going to bed hungry each night? Our research on this question has taken us to rural villages and teeming urban slums around the world, collecting data and speaking with poor people about what they eat and what else they buy, from Morocco to Kenya, Indonesia to India. We've also tapped into a wealth of insights from our academic colleagues. What we've found is that the story of hunger, and of poverty more broadly, is far more complex than any one statistic or grand theory; it is a world where those without enough to eat may save up to buy a TV instead, where more money doesn't necessarily translate into more food, and where making rice cheaper can sometimes even lead people to buy less rice.

But unfortunately, this is not always the world as the experts view it. All too many of them still promote sweeping, ideological solutions to problems that defy one-size-fits-all answers, arguing over foreign aid, for example, while the facts on the ground bear little resemblance to the fierce policy battles they wage.

Jeffrey Sachs, an advisor to the United Nations and director of Columbia University's Earth Institute, is one such expert. In books and countless speeches and television appearances, he has argued that poor countries are poor because they are hot, infertile, malaria-infested, and often landlocked; these factors, however, make it hard for them to be productive without an initial large investment to help them deal with such endemic problems. But they cannot pay for the investments precisely because they are poor—they are in what economists call a "poverty trap." Until something is done about these problems, neither free markets nor democracy will do very much for them.

5   But then there are others, equally vocal, who believe that all of Sachs's answers are wrong. William Easterly, who battles Sachs from New York University at the other end of Manhattan, has become one of the most influential aid critics in his books, *The Elusive Quest for Growth* and *The White Man's Burden*. Dambisa Moyo, an economist who worked at Goldman Sachs and the World Bank, has joined her voice to Easterly's with her recent book, *Dead Aid*. Both argue that aid does more bad than good.

It prevents people from searching for their own solutions, while corrupting and undermining local institutions and creating a self-perpetuating lobby of aid agencies. The best bet for poor countries, they argue, is to rely on one simple idea: When markets are free and the incentives are right, people can find ways to solve their problems. They do not need handouts from foreigners or their own governments. In this sense, the aid pessimists are actually quite optimistic about the way the world works. According to Easterly, there is no such thing as a poverty trap.

This debate cannot be solved in the abstract. To find out whether there are in fact poverty traps, and, if so, where they are and how to help the poor get out of them, we need to better understand the concrete problems they face. Some aid programs help more than others, but which ones? Finding out required us to step out of the office and look more carefully at the world. In 2003, we founded what became the Abdul Latif Jameel Poverty Action Lab, or J-PAL. A key part of our mission is to research by using randomized control trials—similar to experiments used in medicine to test the effectiveness of a drug—to understand what works and what doesn't in the real-world fight against poverty. In practical terms, that meant we'd have to start understanding how the poor really live their lives.

Take, for example, Pak Solhin, who lives in a small village in West Java, Indonesia. He once explained to us exactly how a poverty trap worked. His parents used to have a bit of land, but they also had 13 children and had to build so many houses for each of them and their families that there was no land left for cultivation. Pak Solhin had been working as a casual agricultural worker, which paid up to 10,000 rupiah per day (about $2) for work in the fields. A recent hike in fertilizer and fuel prices, however, had forced farmers to economize. The local farmers decided not to cut wages, Pak Solhin told us, but to stop hiring workers instead. As a result, in the two months before we met him in 2008, he had not found a single day of agricultural labor. He was too weak for the most physical work, too inexperienced for more skilled labor, and, at 40, too old to be an apprentice. No one would hire him.

Pak Solhin, his wife, and their three children took drastic steps to survive. His wife left for Jakarta, some 80 miles away, where she found a job as a maid. But she did not earn enough to feed the children. The oldest son, a good student, dropped out of school at 12 and started as an apprentice on a construction site. The two younger children were sent to live with their grandparents. Pak Solhin himself survived on the roughly 9 pounds of subsidized rice he got every week from the government and on fish he caught at a nearby lake. His brother fed him once in a while. In the week before we last spoke with him, he had eaten two meals a day for four days, and just one for the other three.

Pak Solhin appeared to be out of options, and he clearly attributed his problem to a lack of food. As he saw it, farmers weren't interested in hiring him because they feared they couldn't pay him enough to avoid starvation; and if he was starving, he would be useless in the field. What he described was the classic nutrition-based poverty trap, as it is known in the academic world. The idea is simple: The human body needs a certain number of calories just to survive. So when someone is very poor, all the food he or she can afford is barely enough to allow for going through the motions of living and earning the meager income used to buy that food. But as people get richer, they can buy more food and that extra food goes into building strength, allowing people to produce much more than they need to eat merely to stay alive. This creates a link between income today and income tomorrow: The very poor earn less than they need to be able to do significant work, but those who have enough to eat can work even more. There's the poverty trap: The poor get poorer, and the rich get richer and eat even better, and get stronger and even richer, and the gap keeps increasing.

10   But though Pak Solhin's explanation of how someone might get trapped in starvation was perfectly logical, there was something vaguely troubling about his narrative. We met him not in war-infested Sudan or in a flooded area of Bangladesh, but in a village in prosperous Java, where, even after the increase in food prices in 2007 and 2008, there was clearly plenty of food available and a basic meal did not cost much. He was still eating enough to survive; why wouldn't someone be willing to offer him the extra bit of nutrition that would make him productive in return for a full day's work? More generally, although a hunger-based poverty trap is certainly a logical possibility, is it really relevant for most poor people today? What's the best way, if any, for the world to help?

The international community has certainly bought into the idea that poverty traps exist—and that they are the reason that millions are starving. The first U.N. Millennium Development Goal, for instance, is to "eradicate extreme poverty and hunger." In many countries, the definition of poverty itself has been connected to food; the thresholds for determining that someone was poor were originally calculated as the budget necessary to buy a certain number of calories, plus some other indispensable purchases, such as housing. A "poor" person has essentially been classified as someone without enough to eat.

So it is no surprise that government efforts to help the poor are largely based on the idea that the poor desperately need food and that quantity is what matters. Food subsidies are ubiquitous in the Middle East: Egypt spent $3.8 billion on food subsidies in the 2008 fiscal year, some 2 percent of its GDP. Indonesia distributes subsidized rice. Many states in India have a similar program. In the state of Orissa, for example, the poor are entitled to 55 pounds of rice a month at about 1 rupee per pound, less than 20 percent of the market price. Currently, the Indian Parliament is debating a Right to Food Act, which would allow people to sue the government if they are starving. Delivering such food aid is a logistical nightmare. In India it is estimated that more than half of the wheat and one-third of the rice gets "lost" along the way. To support direct food aid in this circumstance, one would have to be quite convinced that what the poor need more than anything is more grain.

But what if the poor are not, in general, eating too little food? What if, instead, they are eating the wrong kinds of food, depriving them of nutrients needed to be successful, healthy adults? What if the poor aren't starving, but choosing to spend their money on other priorities? Development experts and policymakers would have to completely reimagine the way they think about hunger. And governments and aid agencies would need to stop pouring money into failed programs and focus instead on finding new ways to truly improve the lives of the world's poorest.

Consider India, one of the great puzzles in this age of food crises. The standard media story about the country, at least when it comes to food, is about the rapid rise of obesity and diabetes as the urban upper-middle class gets richer. Yet the real story of nutrition in India over the last quarter-century, as Princeton professor Angus Deaton and Jean Drèze, a professor at Allahabad University and a special advisor to the Indian government, have shown, is not that Indians are becoming fatter: It is that they are in fact eating less and less. Despite the country's rapid economic growth, per capita calorie consumption in India has declined; moreover, the consumption of all other nutrients except fat also appears to have gone down among all groups, even the poorest. Today, more than three-quarters of the population live in households whose per capita calorie consumption is less than 2,100 calories in urban areas and 2,400 in rural areas—numbers that are often cited as "minimum requirements" in India for those engaged in manual labor. Richer people still eat more than poorer people. But at all levels of income, the share of the budget devoted to food has declined and people consume fewer calories.

15   What is going on? The change is not driven by declining incomes; by all accounts, Indians are making more money than ever before. Nor is it because of rising food prices—between the early 1980s and 2005, food prices declined relative to the prices of other things, both in rural and urban India. Although food prices have increased again since 2005, Indians began eating less precisely when the price of food was going down.

So the poor, even those whom the FAO[1] would classify as hungry on the basis of what they eat, do not seem to want to eat much more even when they can. Indeed, they seem to be eating less. What could explain this? Well, to start, let's assume that the poor know what they are doing. After all, they are the ones who eat and work. If they could be tremendously more productive and earn much more by eating more, then they probably would. So could it be that eating more doesn't actually make us particularly more productive, and as a result, there is no nutrition-based poverty trap?

One reason the poverty trap might not exist is that most people have enough to eat. We live in a world today that is theoretically capable of feeding every person on the planet. In 1996, the FAO estimated that world food production was enough to provide at least 2,700 calories per person per day. Starvation still exists, but only as a result of the way food gets shared among us. There is no absolute scarcity. Using price data from the Philippines, we calculated the cost of the cheapest diet sufficient to give 2,400 calories. It would cost only about 21 cents a day, very affordable even for the very poor (the worldwide poverty line is set at roughly a dollar per day). The catch is, it would involve eating only bananas and eggs, something no one would like to do day in, day out. But so long as people are prepared to eat bananas and eggs when they need to, we should find very few people stuck in poverty because they do not get enough to eat. Indian surveys bear this out: The percentage of people who say they do not have enough food has dropped dramatically over time, from 17 percent in 1983 to 2 percent in 2004. So, perhaps people eat less because they are less hungry. And perhaps they are really less hungry, despite eating fewer calories. It could be that because of improvements in water and sanitation, they are leaking fewer calories in bouts of diarrhea and other ailments. Or maybe they are less hungry because of the decline of heavy physical work. With the availability of drinking water in villages, women do not need to carry heavy loads for long distances; improvements in transportation have reduced the need to travel on foot; in even the poorest villages, flour is now milled using a motorized mill, instead of women grinding it by hand. Using the average calorie requirements calculated by the Indian Council of Medical Research, Deaton and Drèze note that the decline in calorie consumption over the last quarter-century could be entirely explained by a modest decrease in the number of people engaged in heavy physical work.

Beyond India, one hidden assumption in our description of the poverty trap is that the poor eat as much as they can. If there is any chance that by eating a bit more the poor could start doing meaningful work and get out of the poverty trap zone, then they should eat as much as possible. Yet most people living on less than a dollar a day do not seem to act as if they are starving. If they were, surely they would put every available penny into buying more calories. But they do not. In an 18-country data set we assembled on the lives of the poor, food represents 36 to 79 percent of consumption among the rural extremely poor, and 53 to 74 percent among their urban counterparts.

It is not because they spend all the rest on other necessities. In Udaipur, 20 India, for example, we find that the typical poor household could spend up to 30 percent more on food, if it completely cut expenditures on alcohol, tobacco, and festivals. The poor seem to have many choices, and they don't choose to spend as much as they can on food. Equally remarkable is that even the money that people do spend on food is not spent to maximize the intake of calories or micronutrients. Studies have shown that when very poor people get a chance to spend a little bit more on food, they don't put everything into getting more calories. Instead, they buy better-tasting, more expensive calories.

In one study conducted in two regions of China, researchers offered randomly selected poor households a large subsidy on the price of the basic staple (wheat noodles in one region, rice in the other). We usually expect that when the price of something goes down, people buy more of it. The opposite happened. Households that received subsidies for rice or wheat consumed less of those two foods and ate more shrimp and meat, even though their staples now cost less. Overall, the caloric intake of those who received the subsidy did not increase (and may even have decreased), despite the fact that their purchasing power had increased. Nor did the nutritional content improve in any other sense. The likely reason is that because the rice and wheat noodles were cheap but not particularly tasty, feeling richer might actually have made them consume less of those staples. This reasoning suggests that at least among these very poor urban households, getting more calories was not a priority: Getting better-tasting ones was.

All told, many poor people might eat fewer calories than we—or the FAO—think is appropriate. But this does not seem to be because they have no other choice; rather, they are not hungry enough to seize every opportunity to eat more. So perhaps there aren't a billion "hungry" people in the world after all.

None of this is to say that the logic of the hunger-based poverty trap is flawed. The idea that better nutrition would propel someone on the path to prosperity was almost surely very important at some point in history, and it may still be today. Nobel Prize-winning economic historian Robert Fogel calculated that in Europe during the Middle Ages and the Renaissance, food production did not provide enough calories to sustain a full working population. This could explain why there were large numbers of beggars— they were literally incapable of any work. The pressure of just getting enough food to survive seems to have driven some people to take rather extreme steps. There was an epidemic of witch killing in Europe during the Little Ice Age (from the mid-1500s to 1800), when crop failures were common and fish was less abundant. Even today, Tanzania experiences a rash of such killings whenever there is a drought—a convenient way to get rid of an unproductive mouth to feed at times when resources are very tight. Families, it seems, suddenly discover that an older woman living with them (usually a grandmother) is a witch, after which she gets chased away or killed by others in the village.

But the world we live in today is for the most part too rich for the occasional lack of food to be a big part of the story of the persistence of poverty on a large scale. This is of course different during natural or man-made disasters, or in famines that kill and weaken millions. As Nobel laureate Amartya Sen has shown, most recent famines have been caused not because food wasn't available but because of bad governance—institutional failures that led to poor distribution of the available food, or even hoarding and storage in the face of starvation elsewhere. As Sen put it, "No substantial famine has ever occurred in any independent and democratic country with a relatively free press."

25   Should we let it rest there, then? Can we assume that the poor, though they may be eating little, do eat as much as they need to?

That also does not seem plausible. While Indians may prefer to buy things other than food as they get richer, they and their children are certainly not well nourished by any objective standard. Anemia is rampant; body-mass indices are some of the lowest in the world; almost half of children under 5 are much too short for their age, and one-fifth are so skinny that they are considered to be "wasted."

And this is not without consequences. There is a lot of evidence that children suffering from malnutrition generally grow into less successful adults. In Kenya, children who were given deworming pills in school for two years went to school longer and earned, as young adults, 20 percent more than children in comparable schools who received deworming for just one year. Worms contribute to anemia and general malnutrition, essentially because they compete with the child for nutrients. And the negative impact of undernutrition starts before birth. In Tanzania, to cite just one example, children born to mothers who received sufficient amounts of iodine during pregnancy completed between one-third and one-half of a year more schooling than their siblings who were in utero when their mothers weren't being treated. It is a substantial increase, given that most of these children will complete only four or five years of schooling in total. In fact, the study concludes that if every mother took iodine capsules, there would be a 7.5 percent increase in the total educational attainment of children in Central and Southern Africa. This, in turn, could measurably affect lifetime productivity.

Better nutrition matters for adults, too. In another study, in Indonesia, researchers tested the effects of boosting people's intake of iron, a key nutrient that prevents anemia. They found that iron supplements made men able to work harder and significantly boosted income. A year's supply of iron-fortified fish sauce cost the equivalent of $6, and for a self-employed male, the yearly gain in earnings was nearly $40—an excellent investment.

If the gains are so obvious, why don't the poor eat better? Eating well doesn't have to be prohibitively expensive. Most mothers could surely afford iodized salt, which is now standard in many parts of the world, or one dose of iodine every two years (at 51 cents per dose). Poor households could easily get a lot more calories and other nutrients by spending less on expensive grains (like rice and wheat), sugar, and processed foods, and more on leafy vegetables and coarse grains. But in Kenya, when the NGO that was running the deworming program asked parents in some schools to pay a few cents for deworming their children, almost all refused, thus depriving their children of hundreds of dollars of extra earnings over their lifetime.

30   Why? And why did anemic Indonesian workers not buy iron-fortified fish sauce on their own? One answer is that they don't believe it will matter— their employers may not realize that they are more productive now. (In fact, in Indonesia, earnings improved only for the self-employed workers.) But this does not explain why all pregnant women in India aren't using only iodine-fortified salt, which is now available in every village. Another possibility is that people may not realize the value of feeding themselves and their children better—not everyone has the right information, even in the United States. Moreover, people tend to be suspicious of outsiders who tell them that they should change their diet. When rice prices went up sharply in 1966 and 1967, the chief minister of West Bengal suggested that eating less rice and more vegetables would be both good for people's health and easier on their budgets. This set off a flurry of outrage, and the chief minister was greeted by protesters bearing garlands of vegetables wherever he went.

It is simply not very easy to learn about the value of many of these nutrients based on personal experience. Iodine might make your children smarter, but the difference is not huge, and in most cases you will not find out either way for many years. Iron, even if it makes people stronger, does not suddenly turn you into a superhero. The $40 extra a year the self-employed man earned may not even have been apparent to him, given the many ups and downs of his weekly income.

So it shouldn't surprise us that the poor choose their foods not mainly for their cheap prices and nutritional value, but for how good they taste. George Orwell, in his masterful description of the life of poor British workers in *The Road to Wigan Pier*, observes:

> The basis of their diet, therefore, is white bread and margarine, corned beef, sugared tea and potatoes—an appalling diet. Would it not be better if they spent more money on wholesome things like oranges and wholemeal bread or if they even, like the writer of the letter to the *New Statesman*, saved on fuel and ate their carrots raw? Yes, it would, but the point is that no ordinary human being is ever going to do such a thing. The ordinary human being would sooner starve than live on brown bread and raw carrots. And the peculiar evil is this, that the less money you have, the less inclined you feel to spend it on

wholesome food. A millionaire may enjoy breakfasting off orange juice and Ryvita biscuits; an unemployed man doesn't. . . . When you are unemployed . . . you don't *want* to eat dull wholesome food. You want something a little bit "tasty." There is always some cheaply pleasant thing to tempt you.

The poor often resist the wonderful plans we think up for them because they do not share our faith that those plans work, or work as well as we claim. We shouldn't forget, too, that other things may be more important in their lives than food. Poor people in the developing world spend large amounts on weddings, dowries, and christenings. Part of the reason is probably that they don't want to lose face, when the social custom is to spend a lot on those occasions. In South Africa, poor families often spend so lavishly on funerals that they skimp on food for months afterward.

And don't underestimate the power of factors like boredom. Life can be quite dull in a village. There is no movie theater, no concert hall. And not a lot of work, either. In rural Morocco, Oucha Mbarbk and his two neighbors told us they had worked about 70 days in agriculture and about 30 days in construction that year. Otherwise, they took care of their cattle and waited for jobs to materialize. All three men lived in small houses without water or sanitation. They struggled to find enough money to give their children a good education. But they each had a television, a parabolic antenna, a DVD player, and a cell phone.

This is something that Orwell captured as well, when he described how 35 poor families survived the Depression:

> Instead of raging against their destiny they have made things tolerable by reducing their standards.

> But they don't necessarily lower their standards by cutting out luxuries and concentrating on necessities; more often it is the other way around— the more natural way, if you come to think of it. Hence the fact that in a decade of unparalleled depression, the consumption of all cheap luxuries has increased.

These "indulgences" are not the impulsive purchases of people who are not thinking hard about what they are doing. Oucha Mbarbk did not buy his TV on credit—he saved up over many months to scrape enough money together, just as the mother in India starts saving for her young daughter's wedding by buying a small piece of jewelry here and a stainless-steel bucket there.

We often see the world of the poor as a land of missed opportunities and wonder why they don't invest in what would really make their lives better. But the poor may well be more skeptical about supposed opportunities and the possibility of any radical change in their lives. They often behave as if they think that any change that is significant enough to be worth sacrificing for will simply take too long. This could explain why they focus on the here and now, on living their lives as pleasantly as possible and celebrating when occasion demands it.

We asked Oucha Mbarbk what he would do if he had more money. He said he would buy more food. Then we asked him what he would do if he had even more money. He said he would buy better-tasting food. We were starting to feel very bad for him and his family, when we noticed the TV and other high-tech gadgets. Why had he bought all these things if he felt the family did not have enough to eat? He laughed, and said, "Oh, but television is more important than food!"

NOTE

1 Food and Agricultural Organization of the United Nations.

Analyze

1. What was the key research question that the authors set out to answer? How was this different from previous questions about famine? What were their findings, and how were they surprising?

2. How do economists define the "poverty trap"? Summarize the different points of view of Jeffrey Sachs, "an advisor to the United Nations and director of Columbia University's Earth Institute," and his ideological opponent, the vociferous aid critic William Easterly.

3. "We were starting to feel very bad for him and his family, when we noticed the TV and other high-tech gadgets. Why had he bought all these things if he felt the family did not have enough to eat? He laughed, and said, 'Oh, but television is more important than food!'" Why do you think the authors chose this to be the last line of their article? What impression do you think they intended to leave on their readers? Consider their overall purpose in writing. Was this ending effective? Explain.

Explore

1. In an age of globalization, one can say that it is of utmost importance "to be able to distinguish the facts on the ground from the policy battles being raged." Why?

2. "The poor often resist the wonderful plans we think up for them because they do not share our faith that those plans work, or work as well as we claim. We shouldn't forget, too, that other things may be more important in their lives than food." What are important things that people should spend their money on? What about you? What is "tasty" for you? Why?

3. Amartya Sen, the Nobel Laureate economist says, "No substantial famine has ever occurred in any independent and democratic country with a relatively free press." This supports the authors' claim that famines are less the result of lack of available food and more what? Explain how, according to the authors, most recent famines could have been avoided.

4. The authors were surprised to find that "among these very poor urban households, getting more calories was not a priority: Getting better-tasting ones was." What does this help you understand about the nature of hunger? Write about the time when you were most hungry. What did you crave the most? Many children in the West are told to eat everything on their plates because "people in Africa are starving." What do you think the intention behind that statement is? How has this article affected your understanding of hunger, famine, and poverty?

5. The authors note that the first UN Millennium Development Goals is to "erad is to "eradicate extreme poverty and hunger." What are the other U.N. Millennium Development Goals, and how are they being addressed? How has greater knowledge helped to refine these goals? Choose one goal, and research what actions have been taken and what the results were. What surprises and debates were generated?

Forging Connections

1. "It was impossible to tell whether this food was new aid, sent to combat the famine, or just more of the billions of dollars in international relief that has become a semipermanent fixture in Africa's ragged margins" (Salopek, "The Last Famine"). How does knowing what we read about

in chapter 6, "Earning and Spending," complicate your notion of aid in northern Kenya? What about Banerjee and Duflo's argument in "More than 1 Billion People Are Hungry in the World"?

2. In "Zimbabwe," Gappah writes, "It is hard to shake the sense I got that money has replaced race in Zimbabwe. In Rhodesia, race determined whether a child was guaranteed a good education. In post-crisis Zimbabwe, it is now class that is the determinant." The theme of education comes up often throughout the readings in these chapters. In what ways can locally educated populations address current global challenges? What would a good education need to consist of? Use the observations and interpretations of the authors in this chapter's readings, as well as your own written responses and group work, to provide a framework for your vision of an education that would be suited for and benefit a globalized world.

Looking Further

1. What do you make of Damon Tabor's portrait of Geoff Hann in "If It's Tuesday, It Must Be the Taliban"? How does Hann compare to Kwame Anthony Appiah's portrait of Richard Burton in "The Shattered Mirror" (chapter 1)? Does Hann's way of life fit Appiah's definition of "cosmopolitanism"? Why or why not? Find other examples of "cosmopolitans" you've "met" in this book—either the writers themselves or the people they describe—who transcend their national identities for more globalized viewpoints.

2. Paul Salopek writes, "Lake Turkana's beached fishing fleet became an icon of asinine philanthropy in Africa." What are examples of asinine philanthropy in other parts of the world? He also writes, "It earmarked $10 million for a pilot program in the Turkana area that might be called aid methadone—still more aid, but this time in the form of fishponds and irrigated market gardens, all intended to pry people off the old aid." There have been several discussions of humanitarian aid in this book—its efficacy, who gives it, who gets it, and what some better alternatives might be. How would you apply the global perspective you've gained from the readings in this book? What might be a more authentic and complex way of understanding the meanings of aid and the various roles that we can take as members of a global community?

3. With a long glance back at human evolution, Meave Leakey tells Paul Salopek in "The Last Famine": "Place a species under stress, and you can't tell what will happen. . . . It could go extinct, or a new mutation will arise, in this case, maybe something that led to advanced language." Salopek muses that, perhaps, "empty bellies transformed us into the wandering ape." What does this say about our challenges as humans today and the potential benefits of adversity? Can this help us reframe how we look at and address the many challenges we face as a global community? Is it possible to actively transform our current adversities into beneficial traits? Choose one theme that has emerged for you in your responses to the readings in this book, and develop a framework through which we might understand it from a globalized perspective.

Researching and Writing about Globalization

Barbara Rockenbach and Aaron Ritzenberg[1]

Research-based writing lies at the heart of the mission of higher education: to discover, transform, and share ideas. As a college student, it is through writing and research that you will become an active participant in an intellectual community. Doing research in college involves not only searching for information but also digesting, analyzing, and synthesizing what you find in order to create new knowledge. Your most successful efforts as a college writer will report on the latest and most important ideas in a field, as well as make new arguments and offer fresh insights.

It may seem daunting to be asked to contribute new ideas to a field in which you are a novice. After all, creating new knowledge seems to be the realm of experts. In this guide, we offer strategies that demystify the research and writing process, breaking down some of the fundamental steps that scholars take when they do research and make arguments. You'll see that contributing to scholarship involves strategies that can be learned and practiced.

Throughout this guide, we imagine doing research and writing as engaging in a scholarly conversation. When you read academic writing, you'll see that scholars reference the studies that came before them and allude to the studies that will grow out of their research. When you think of research as

---

1   Barbara Rockenbach, Director of Humanities & History Libraries, Columbia University; Aaron Ritzenberg, Associate Director of First-Year Writing, Columbia University.

engaging in a conversation, you quickly realize that scholarship always has a social aspect. Even if you like to find books in the darkest corners of the library, even if you like to draft your essays in deep solitude, you will always be awake to the voices that helped you form your ideas and to the audience who will receive your ideas. As if in a conversation at a party, scholars mingle: They listen to others and share their most recent ideas, learning and teaching at the same time. Strong scholars, like good conversationalists, will listen and speak with an open mind, letting their own thoughts evolve as they encounter new ideas.

You may be wondering, "What does it mean to have an open mind when I'm doing research? After all, aren't I supposed to find evidence that supports my thesis?" We'll be returning to this question soon, but the quick answer is: To have an open mind when you're doing research means that you'll be involved in the research process well before you have a thesis. We realize this may be a big change from the way you think about research. The fact is, though, that scholars do research well before they know any of the arguments they'll be making in their papers. Indeed, scholars do research even before they know what specific topic they'll be addressing and what questions they'll be asking.

When scholars do research, they may not know exactly what they are hunting for, but they have techniques that help them define projects, identify strong interlocutors, and ask important questions. This guide will help you move through the various kinds of research that you'll need at the different stages of your project. If writing a paper involves orchestrating a conversation within a scholarly community, there are a number of important questions you'll need to answer: How do I choose what to write about? How do I find a scholarly community? How do I orchestrate a conversation that involves this community? Whose voices should be most prominent? How do I enter the conversation? How do I use evidence to make a persuasive claim? How do I make sure that my claim is not just interesting but important?

GETTING STARTED

You have been asked to write a research paper. This may be your first research paper at the college level. Where do you start? The important thing when embarking on any kind of writing project that involves research is to find something that you are interested in learning more about. Writing and research are easier if you care about your topic. Your instructor may have given you a topic, but you can make that topic your own by finding something that appeals to you within the scope of the assignment.

Academic writing begins from a place of deep inquiry. When you are sincerely interested in a problem, research can be a pleasure, because it will satisfy your own intellectual curiosity. More important, the intellectual problems that seem most difficult—the questions that appear to resist obvious answers—are the very problems that will often yield the most surprising and rewarding results.

Presearching to Generate Ideas

When faced with a research project, your first instinct might be to go to Google or Wikipedia, or even to a social media site. This is not a bad instinct. In fact, Google, Wikipedia, and social media can be great places to start. Using Google, Wikipedia, and social media to help you discover a topic is what we call "presearch"—it is what you do to warm up before the more rigorous work of academic research. Academic research and writing will require you to go beyond these sites to find resources that will make the work of researching and writing both easier and more appropriate to an academic context.

Google Let's start with Google. You use Google because you know you are going to find a simple search interface and that your search will produce many results (screen capture 1). These results may not be completely relevant to your topic, but Google helps in the discovery phase of your work. For instance, you are asked to write about globalization and language.

This Google search will produce articles from many diverse sources—magazines, government sites, and corporate reports among them. It's not a bad start. Use these results to begin to hone in on a topic you are interested in pursuing. A quick look through these results may yield a more focused topic, such as how globalization is affecting language and culture around the world. A particular source mentions this impact in the context of Japan, while others examine how the spread of English as a dominant language is a result of globalization.

Wikipedia

A Wikipedia search on globalization and language will lead you to several articles that address both concepts. The great thing about Wikipedia is that it is an easy way to gain access to a wealth of information about thousands of topics. However, it is crucial to realize that Wikipedia itself is not an

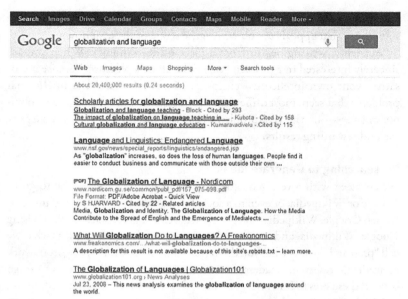

Screen capture 1 Results of a Google search for "globalization and language."

authoritative source in a scholarly context. Even though you may see Wikipedia cited in mainstream newspapers and popular magazines, academic researchers do not consider Wikipedia a reliable source and do not consult or cite it in their own research. Wikipedia itself says that "Wikipedia is not considered a credible source. . . . This is especially true considering that anyone can edit the information given at any time." For research papers in college, you should use Wikipedia only to find basic information about your topic and to point you toward scholarly sources. Wikipedia may be a great starting point for presearch, but it is not an adequate ending point for research. Use the References section at the bottom of the Wikipedia article (screen capture 2) to find other, more substantive and authoritative resources about your topic.

Using Social Media

Social media such as Facebook and Twitter can be useful in the presearch phase of your project, but you must start thinking about these tools in new ways. You may have a Facebook or Twitter account and use it to keep in touch with friends, family, and colleagues. These social networks are

References

1. ^ a b Al-Rodhan, Nayef R.F. and Gérard Stoudmann. (2006, 19 June). "Definitions of Globalization: A Comprehensive Overview and a Proposed Definition." 📄
2. ^ a b Albrow, Martin and Elizabeth King (eds.) (1990). *Globalization, Knowledge and Society* London: Sage. ISBN 978-0803983243 p. 8. "...all those processes by which the peoples of the world are incorporated into a single world society."
3. ^ Carpenter, John B., 1999, "Puritan Missions as Globalization," *Fides et Historia*, 31:2, p. 103.
4. ^ Stever, H. Guyford (1972). "Science, Systems, and Society." *Journal of Cybernetics*, 2(3):1-3. doi:10.1080/01969727208542909 ⊘
5. ^ a b Frank, Andre Gunder. (1998). *ReOrient: Global economy in the Asian age.* Berkeley: University of California Press. ISBN 978-0520214743
6. ^ "*Globalization and Global History* (p.127)" 📄. Retrieved 3 July 2012.
7. ^ Ritzer, George (2011). *Globalization: The Essentials*. NY: John Wiley & Sons.
8. ^ Google Books Ngram Viewer: Globalization ⊘

Screen capture 2 List of references from a Wikipedia search on globalization. Use these links to further your research.

valuable, and you may already use them to gather information to help you make decisions in your personal life and your workplace. Although social media is not generally useful to your academic research, both Facebook and Twitter have powerful search functions that can lead you to resources and help you refine your ideas.

After you log in to Facebook, use the "Search for people, places, and things" bar at the top of the page to begin. When you type search terms into this bar, Facebook will first search your own social network. To extend beyond your own network, try adding the word "research" after your search terms. For instance, a search on Facebook for "globalization research" will lead you to a Facebook page for the Centre for Research on Globalization. The posts on the page link to current news stories on globalization, links to other similar research centers, and topics of interest in the field of globalization research. You can use these search results as a way to see part of the conversation about a particular topic. This is not necessarily the scholarly conversation we referred to at the start of this guide, but it is a social conversation that can still be useful in helping you determine what you want to focus on in the research process.

Twitter is an information network where users can post short messages (or "tweets"). Although many people use Twitter simply to update their friends ("I'm going to the mall" or "Can't believe it's snowing!"), more and more individuals and organizations use Twitter to comment on noteworthy events or link to interesting articles. You can use Twitter as a presearch tool because it aggregates links to sites, people in a field of research, and noteworthy sources. Communities, sometimes even scholarly communities, form around topics on Twitter. Users group posts together by using hashtags—words or phrases that follow the "#" sign. Users can respond to other users by using the @ sign followed by a user's Twitter name. When searching for specific individuals or organizations on Twitter, you search using their handle (such as @ barackobama or @ whitehouse). You will retrieve tweets that were created either by the person or organization, or tweets that mention the person or organization. When searching for a topic to find discussions, you search using the hashtag symbol, #. For instance, a search on # globalization will take you to tweets and threaded discussions on the topic of globalization.

There are two ways to search Twitter. You can use the search book in the upper right-hand corner and enter either a @ or # search as described above. Once you retrieve results, you can search again by clicking on any of the words that are hyperlinked within your results, such as #antiglobalization.

If you consider a hashtag (the # sign) as an entry point into a community, you will begin to discover a conversation around topics. For instance, a search on Twitter for #globalization leads you to YaleGlobal Online (@YaleGlobal), a community that explores globalization and the growing interconnectedness in economics, security, trade, politics, and the environment. News agencies such as Reuters are also active on Twitter, so an article from a Reuters publication can be retrieved in a search. Evaluating information and sources found in social media is similar to evaluating any information you encounter during the research process. And, as with Wikipedia and Google searches, this is just a starting point to help you get a sense of the spectrum of topics. This is no substitute for using library resources. Do not cite Facebook, Twitter, or Wikipedia in a research paper; use them to find more credible, authoritative sources. We'll talk about evaluating sources in the sections that follow.

Create a Concept Map

Once you have settled on a topic that you find exciting and interesting, the next step is to generate search terms, or keywords, for effective searching. Keywords are the crucial terms or phrases that signal the content of any given source. Keywords are the building blocks of your search for information. We have already seen a few basic keywords like "globalization" and "language." One way to generate keywords is to tell a friend or classmate what you are interested in. What words are you using to describe your research project? You may not have a fully formed idea or claim, but you have a vague sense of your interest. A concept map exercise can help you generate more keywords and, in many cases, narrow your topic to make it more manageable.

A concept map is a way to visualize the relationship between concepts or ideas. You can create a concept map on paper, or there are many free programs online that can help you do this (see, for instance, http://vue.tufts.edu/, http://www.wisemapping.com, or http://freeplane.sourceforge.net). There are many concept mapping applications available for mobile devices; the concept map here was created using the app SimpleMind (screen capture 3).

Here is how you use a concept map. First, begin with a term like globalization. Put that term in the first box. Then think of synonyms or related words to describe globalization such as "global economy," "global culture," "neoliberalism," "worldwide business," "world economy," and "global outsourcing." This brainstorming process will help you develop keywords for searching. Notice that keywords can also be short phrases.

After some practice, you'll discover that some phrases make for excellent keywords and others make for less effective search tools. The best keywords are precise enough to narrow your topic so that all of your results are relevant, but are not so specific that you might miss helpful results. Concept maps created using apps such as SimpleMind allow you to use templates, embed hyperlinks, and attach notes, among other useful functions.

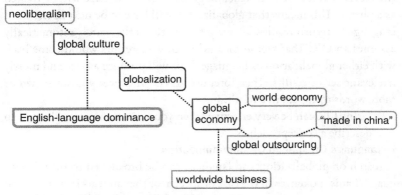

Screen capture 3   A concept map.

Keyword Search

One of the hardest parts of writing is coming up with something to write about. Too often, we make the mistake of waiting until we have a fully formed idea before we start writing. The process of writing can actually help you discover what your idea is and, most important, what is interesting about it.

Keyword searches are most effective at the beginning stages of your research. They generally produce the highest number of results and can help you determine how much has been written on your topic. You want to use keyword searches to help you achieve a manageable number of results, but *what* is manageable? This is a key question when beginning research. Our keyword search in Google on globalization and language produced over 18 million results. The same search in JSTOR.org produced over 28,000 results. These are not manageable results sets. Let's see how we can narrow our search.

Keyword searches, in library resources or on Google, are most effective if you employ a few search strategies that will focus your results.

1. Use AND when you are combining multiple keywords. We have used this search construction previously:

   globalization AND language

The AND ensures that all your results will contain both the terms globalization and language. Many search engines and databases will assume an AND search, meaning that if you type

   globalization language

the search will automatically look for both terms. However, in some cases the AND will not be assumed, and globalization language will be treated as a phrase. This means that globalization will have to be next to the word language to return results. Worse yet, sometimes the search automatically assumes an OR. That would mean that all your results would come back with either globalization or language. This will produce a large and mostly irrelevant set of results. Therefore, use AND whenever you want two or more words to appear in a result.

2. Using OR can be very effective when you want to use several terms to describe a concept such as

   language OR speech OR communication

A search on globalization and language can be broadened to include language that is spoken, as in the case of speech, or that appears in written and spoken form, such as communication. The following search casts a broader net because results will come back with globalization and either language, speech, or communication:

globalization AND (language OR speech OR communication)

Not all of these words will appear in each record. Note also that the parentheses set off the OR search indicating that globalization must appear in each record and then language, speech, or communication needs to appear along with globalization.

3. Use quotation marks when looking for a phrase. For instance, if you are looking for information on language and globalization in multinational corporations, you can ensure that the search results will include all of these concepts and increase the relevance by using the following search construction:

globalization AND language AND "multinational corporations"

This phrasing will return results that contain both the word globalization and the phrase "multinational corporations."

4. Use NOT to exclude terms that will make your search less relevant. You may find that a term keeps appearing in your search that is not useful. Try this:

globalization NOT politics

If you are interested in the linguistic side of this debate, getting a lot of results that discuss the politics of globalization may be distracting. By excluding the keyword politics, you will retrieve far fewer sources, and hopefully more relevant results.

Researchable Question

In a college research paper, it is important that you make an argument, not just offer a report. In high school, you may have found some success by merely listing or cataloging the data and information you found; you might have offered a series of findings to show your teacher that you investigated your topic. In college, however, your readers will not be interested in data or information merely for its own sake; your readers will want to know what you make of these data and why they should care.

In order to satisfy the requirements of a college paper, you'll need to distinguish between a topic and a research question. You will likely begin with a topic, but it is only when you move from a topic to a question that your research will begin to feel motivated and purposeful. A topic refers only to the general subject area that you'll be investigating. A researchable question, on the other hand, points toward a specific problem in the subject area that you'll be attempting to answer by making a claim about the evidence you examine.

"Globalization and language" is a topic, but not a researchable question. It is important that you ask yourself, "What aspect of the topic is most interesting to me?" It is even more important that you ask, "What aspect of the topic is most important to illuminate for my audience?" Ideally, your presearch phase will have yielded questions about globalization and language that you'd like to investigate.

A strong researchable question will not lead to an easy answer, but rather will lead you into a scholarly conversation in which there are many competing claims. For instance, the question, "What are the official languages of the United Nations?" is not a strong research question, because there is only one correct answer, and thus there is no scholarly debate surrounding the topic. It is an interesting question (the answer is Arabic, Chinese, English, French, Russian, and Spanish), but it will not lead you into a scholarly conversation.

When you are interested in finding a scholarly debate, try using the words "why" and "how" rather than "what." Instead of leading to a definitive answer, the words "why" and "how" will often lead to complex, nuanced answers for which you'll need to marshal evidence in order to be convincing. "Why did Arabic become an official language of the UN in 1973?" is a question that has a number of complex and competing answers that might draw from a number of different disciplines (political science, history, economics, linguistics, and geography, among others). If you can imagine scholars having an interesting debate about your researchable question, it is likely that you've picked a good one.

Once you have come up with an interesting researchable question, your first task as a researcher is to figure out how scholars are discussing your question. Many novice writers think that the first thing they should do when beginning a research project is to articulate an argument, and then find sources that confirm it. This is not how experienced scholars work. Instead, strong writers know that they cannot possibly come up with a strong central argument until they have done sufficient research. So, instead of looking for sources that confirm a preliminary claim you might want to make, look for the scholarly conversation.

Looking at the scholarly conversation is a strong way to figure out if you've found a research question that is suitable in scope for the kind of paper you're writing. Put another way, reading the scholarly conversation can tell you if your research question is too broad or too narrow. Most novice writers begin with research questions that are overly broad. If your question is so broad that there are thousands of books and articles participating in the scholarly conversation, it's a good idea for you to focus your question so that you are asking something more specific. If, on the other hand, you are asking a research question that is so obscure that you cannot find a corresponding scholarly conversation, you will want to broaden the scope of your project by asking a slightly less specific question.

Keep in mind the metaphor of a conversation. If you walk into a room and people are talking about globalization and language, it would be out of place for you to begin immediately by making a huge, vague claim like "New technology affects the way that people speak to each other around the world." It would be equally out of place for you to begin immediately by making an overly specific claim like "Social media usage in Doha is a strong indicator of Facebook's growing strength in Qatar." Rather, you would gauge the scope of the conversation and figure out what seems like a reasonable contribution.

Your contribution to the conversation, at this point, will likely be a focused research question. This is the question you take with you to the library. In the next section, we'll discuss how best to make use of the library. Later, we'll explore how to turn your research question into an argument for your essay.

Your Campus Library

You have probably used libraries all your life, checking out books from your local public library and studying in your high school library. The difference between your previous library experiences and your college library experience is one of scale. Your college library has more stuff. It may be real stuff like books, journals, and videos, or it may be virtual stuff like online articles, e-books, and streaming video. Your library pays a lot of money every year to buy or license content for you to use for your research. By extension, your tuition dollars are buying a lot of really good research material. Resorting to only Google and Wikipedia means that you are not getting all you can out of your college experience.

Your college library has not only a much larger collection; it has a more up-to-date and relevant collection than your high school or community public library. Academic librarians spend considerable time acquiring research materials based on classes being taught at your institution. You may not know it, but librarians carefully monitor what courses are being taught each year and are constantly trying to find research materials appropriate to those courses and your professors' research interests. In many cases, you will find that the librarians know about your assignment and may already have ideas about the types of sources that will make you most successful.

Get to Know Your Librarians!

The most important thing to know during the research process is that there are people to help you. Although you may not yet be in the habit of going to the library, there are still many ways in which librarians and library staff can be helpful. Most libraries now have an email or chat service set up so you can ask questions without even setting foot in the building. No question is too basic or too specific. It's a librarian's job to help you find answers, and all questions are welcome. The librarian can even help you discover the right question to ask given the task you are trying to complete.

Help can also come in the form of consultations. Librarians will often make appointments to meet one-on-one with you to offer in-depth help on a research paper or project. Chances are you will find a link on your library website for scheduling a consultation.

Among the many questions fielded by reference librarians, three stand out as the most often asked. We suggest that students ask these questions when they begin their research. You can go to the library and ask in person, or you can ask vie email or online chat.

1. How do I find a book relevant to my topic? The answer to this question will vary from place to place, but the thing to remember is that finding a book can be either a physical process or a virtual process. Your library will have books on shelves somewhere, and the complexity of how those shelves are organized and accessed depends on factors of size, the number of libraries, and the system of organization your library uses. You will find books by using your library's online catalogue (screen capture 4) and carefully noting the call number and location of a book.

Your library is also increasingly likely to offer electronic books or e-books. These books are discoverable in your library's online catalogue as well. When looking for the location of a book, you will frequently see a link for e-book versions. You will not find an e-book in every search, but when you do, the advantage is that e-book content is searchable, making your job of finding relevant material in the book easier.

If you find one book on your topic, use it as a jumping-off point for finding more books or articles on that topic. Most books will have

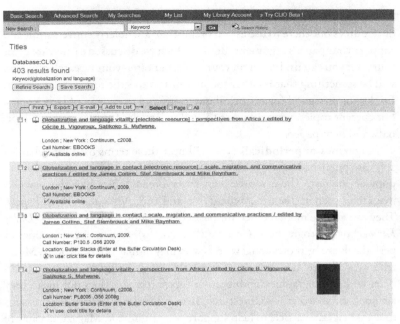

Screen capture 4 Library catalog search for "globalization and language."

bibliographies either at the end of each chapter or at the end of the book in which the author has compiled all the sources used. Consult these bibliographies to find other materials on your topic that will help support your claim.

Another efficient way to find more sources once you've identified a particularly authoritative and credible book is to go back to the book's listing in your library's online catalogue. Once you find the book, look carefully at the record for links to subjects. By clicking on a subject link, you can find other items in your library on the same subject. For instance, a search on

globalization AND language
will lead you to items with subjects such as

language and culture

English language—21st century

Language and languages—study and teaching.

2. What sources can I use as evidence in my paper? There are many types of resources out there to use as you orchestrate a scholarly conversation and support your paper's argument. Books, which we discussed earlier, are great sources if you can find them on your topic, but often your research question will be something that is either too new or too specific for a book to cover. Books are very good for historical questions and overviews of large topics. For current topics, you will want to explore articles from magazines, journals, and newspapers.

Magazines or periodicals (you will hear these terms used interchangeably) are published on a weekly or monthly schedule and contain articles of popular interest. These sources can cover broad topics like the news in magazines such as *The Economist, Time,* and *U.S. News and World Report.* They can also be more focused for particular groups, such as farmers (*Dairy Farmer*) or photographers (*Creative Photography*). Articles in magazines or periodicals are by professional writers who may or may not be experts. Magazines typically are not considered scholarly and generally do not contain articles with bibliographies, endnotes, or footnotes. This does not mean they are not good sources for your research. In fact, there may be very good reasons to use a magazine article to help support your argument. Magazines capture the point of view of a particular group on a subject, like how farmers feel about increased globalization of food production. This point of view may offer support for your claim or an opposing viewpoint to counter. Additionally, magazines can also highlight aspects of a topic at a particular point in time. Comparing a *Time* article from 1989 on Japan and globalization to an article on the same topic in 2009 allows you to draw conclusions about the changing relationship between the US and Japan over that 20-year period.

Journals are intended for a scholarly audience of researchers, specialists, or students of a particular field. Journals such as *Globalization and Health, Modern Language Journal,* and *Anthropological Linguistics* are all examples of scholarly journals focused on a particular field or research topic. You may hear the term "peer-reviewed" or "referred" in reference to scholarly journals. This means that the articles contained in a journal have been reviewed by a group of scholars in the same field before the article is published in the journal. This ensures that the research has been vetted by a group of peers before it is published. Articles from scholarly journals can help provide some authority to your argument. By citing the experts in a field, you are bolstering your argument and entering into the scholarly conversation we talked about at the beginning of this guide.

Newspaper articles are found in newspapers that are generally published daily. There is a broad range of content in newspapers, from articles written by staff reporters, to editorials written by scholars, experts, and general readers, to reviews and commentary written by experts. Newspapers are published more frequently and locally than magazines or journals, making them excellent sources for very recent topics and events, as well as those with regional significance. Newspaper articles can provide you with a point of view from a particular part of the country or world (How do Texans feel about globalization compared to New Yorkers), or a strong opinion on a topic from an expert (an economist writing an editorial on the effects of globalization on the Chinese economy).

A good argument uses evidence from a variety of sources. Do not assume you have done a good job if your paper cites only newspaper articles. You need a broad range of sources to fill out your argument. Your instructor will provide you with guidelines about the number of sources you need, but it will be up to you to find a variety of sources. Finding two to three sources in each of the categories above will help you begin to build a strong argument.

3. Where should I look for articles on my topic? The best way to locate journal, magazine, or newspaper articles is to use a database. A database is an online resource that organizes research material of a particular type or content area. For example, *PsycINFO* is a psychology database where you would look for journal articles (as well as other kinds of sources) in the discipline of psychology. Your library licenses or subscribes to databases on your behalf. Finding the right database for your topic will depend upon what is available at your college or university because every institution has a different set of resources. Many libraries will provide subject or research guides that can help you determine what database would be best for your topic. Look for a section on the library's website on databases, and then look for a search box in that section. For instance, if you type "language" in a database search box, you may find that your library licenses a database called *MLA* (Modern Language Association) *International Bibliography*. A search for "history" in the database search box may yield *American History and Life* or *Historical Abstracts*. In most instances, your best bet is to ask a librarian which database or databases are most relevant to your research.

When using the databases that your library provides for you, you will know that you are starting to sufficiently narrow or broaden your topic when you begin to retrieve 30 to 50 sources during a search. This kind of narrow result field will rarely occur in Google, which is one of the reasons why using library databases is preferable to Google when doing academic research. Databases will help you determine when you have begun to ask a manageable question.

When you have gotten down to 30–50 sources in your result list, begin to look through those results to see what aspects of your topic are being written about. Are there lots of articles on globalization, language, and China? If so, that might be a topic worth investigating since there is a lot of information for you to read. This is when you begin to discover where your voice might add to the ongoing conversation on the topic.

Using Evidence

The quality of evidence and how you deploy it are ultimately what will make your claims persuasive. You may think of evidence as the thing that will help prove your claim. But if you look at any scholarly book or article, you'll see that evidence can be used in a number of different ways. Evidence can be used to provide readers with crucial background information. It can be used to tell readers what scholars have commonly thought about a topic (but which you may disagree with). It can offer a theory that you use as a lens. It can offer a methodology or an approach that you would like to use. And finally, of course, evidence can be used to back up the claim that you'll be making in your paper.

Novice researchers begin with a thesis and try to find all the evidence that will prove that their claim is valid or true. What if you come across evidence that doesn't help with the validity of your claim? A novice researcher might decide not to take this contradictory evidence into account. Indeed, when you come across contradictory evidence, you might be tempted to pretend that you never saw it! But rather than sweeping imperfect evidence under the rug, you should figure out how to use this evidence to enhance your own ideas.

The best scholarly conversations take into account a wide array of evidence, carefully considering all sides of a topic. As you probably know, often the most fruitful and productive conversations occur not just when you are talking to people who already agree with you, but when you are fully engaging with people who might disagree with you.

Coming across unexpected, surprising, and contradictory evidence, then, is a good thing! It forces you to make a complex, nuanced argument and ultimately allows you to write a more persuasive paper.

Other Forms of Evidence

We've talked about finding evidence in books, magazines, journals, and newspapers. Here are a few other kinds of evidence you may want to use.

Interviews Interviews can be a powerful form of evidence, especially if the person you are interviewing is an expert in the field that you're investigating. Interviewing can be intimidating, but it might help to know that many people (even experts) will feel flattered when you ask them for an interview. Most scholars are deeply interested in spreading knowledge, so you should feel comfortable asking a scholar for his or her ideas. Even if the scholar doesn't know the specific answer to your question, he or she may be able to point you in the right direction.

Remember, of course, to be as courteous as possible when you are planning to interview someone. This means sending a polite email that fully introduces yourself and your project before you begin asking questions. Email interviews may be convenient, but an in-person interview is best, as it allows you and the interviewee to engage in a conversation that may take surprising and helpful turns.

It's a good idea to write down a number of questions before the interview. Make sure not to get just facts (which you can likely get somewhere else). Ask the interviewee to speculate about your topic. Remember that "why" and "how" questions often yield more interesting answers than "what" questions.

If you do conduct an in-person interview, act professionally. Be on time, dress respectfully, and show sincere interest and gratitude. Bring something to record the interview. Many reporters still use a pad and pen, since these feel unobtrusive and are very portable. Write down the interviewee's name, the date, and the location of the interview, and have your list of questions ready. Don't be afraid, of course, to veer from your questions. The best questions might be the follow-up questions that couldn't have occurred to you before the conversation began. You're likely to get the interviewee to talk freely and openly if you show real intellectual curiosity. If you're not a fast writer, it's certainly OK to ask the interviewee to pause for a moment while you take notes. Some people like to record their interviews. Just make sure that you ask permission if you choose to do this. It's always nice to send a brief thank you note or email after the interview. This would be a good time to ask any brief follow-up questions.

Images Because we live in a visual age, we tend to take images for granted. We see them in magazines, on TV, and on the Internet. We don't often think about them as critically as we think about words on a page. Yet, a critical look at an image can uncover helpful evidence for a claim. For example, if you are writing about the impact of globalization on language, you could introduce an image of a sign, such as the one pictured below (figure 1).

This is an image of a Coca-Cola boxcar in Haikou, Hainan, China. Though we may not be able to read the language, it is recognizable as an advertisement for Coca-Cola. This image enables you to discuss how visual elements (the distinctive Coca-Cola stripe, the vertical lettering on the can, etc.) can be read like a language—a language that is increasingly global. You could also use this image as evidence for a claim that the language of branding is becoming an international or global language. Images can add depth and variety to your argument, and they are generally easy to find on the Internet. Use Google Image search or Flickr.com to find images using the same keywords you used to find books and articles. Ask your instructor for guidance on how to properly cite and acknowledge the source of any images you wish to use. If you want to present your research outside of a

Figure 1 A Coca-Cola boxcar in Haikou, Hainan, China.

classroom project (for example, publish it on a blog or share it at a community event), ask a research librarian for guidance on avoiding any potential copyright violations.

Multimedia Like images, multimedia such as video, audio, and animation are increasingly easy to find on the Internet and can strengthen your claim. For instance, if you are working on globalization and language, you could find audio or video news clips illustrating the effects of globalization on local languages. There are several audio and video search engines available such as Vimeo (vimeo.com) or Blinkx (blinkx.com), and a search engine featuring audio and video from the BBC, Reuters, and the Associated Press, among others. As with images, ask your instructor for guidance on how to properly cite and acknowledge the source of any multimedia you wish to use. If you want to present your research outside of a classroom project (for example, publish it on a blog or share it at a community event), ask a research librarian for guidance on avoiding any potential copyright violations.

Evaluating Sources

A common problem in research isn't a lack of sources, but an overload of information that is more accessible than ever. How many times have you done an online search and asked yourself: "How do I know what is good information?" Librarians can help. Evaluating online sources is more challenging than traditional sources, because it is harder to make distinctions between good and bad online information than with print sources. It is easy to tell that *Time* magazine is not as scholarly as an academic journal, but everything online may look the same. There are markers of credibility and authoritativeness when it comes to online information, and you can start to recognize them. We provide a few tips here, but be sure to ask a librarian or your professor for more guidance whenever you're uncertain about the reliability of a source.

Domain The "domain" of a site is the last part of its URL. The domain indicates what type of website it is. Noting the web address can tell you a lot. An ".edu" site indicates that an educational organization created that content. This is no guarantee that the information is accurate, but it does suggest less bias than a ".com" site, which will be commercial in nature and have a motive to sell you something, including ideas.

Date Most websites include a date somewhere on the page. This date may indicate a copyright date, the date something was posted, or the date the site was last updated. These dates tell you when the content on the site was last changed or reviewed. Older sites might be outdated or contain information that is no longer relevant.

Author or editor Does the online content indicate an author or editor? As with print materials, authority comes from the creator or the content. It is now easier than ever to investigate an author's credentials. A general Google search may lead you to a Wikipedia entry on the author, a LinkedIn page, or even an online résumé. If an author is affiliated with an educational institution, try visiting the institution's website for more information.

Managing Sources

Now that you've found sources, you need to think about how you are going to keep track of the sources and prepare the bibliography that will accompany your paper. Managing your sources is called "bibliographic citation management," and you will sometimes see references to bibliographic citation management on your library's website. Don't let this complicated phrase deter you; managing your citations from the start of your research will make your life much easier during the research process and especially the night before your paper is due when you are compiling your bibliography.

EndNote and RefWorks Chances are your college library provides software, such as *EndNote* or *RefWorks*, to help you manage citations. These are two commercially available citation management software packages that are not freely available to you unless your library has paid for a license. *EndNote* and *RefWorks* enable you to organize your sources in personal libraries. These libraries help you manage your sources and create bibliographies. Both *EndNote* and *RefWorks* also enable you to insert endnotes and footnotes directly into a Microsoft Word document.

Zotero If your library does not provide *EndNote* or *RefWorks*, a freely available software called *Zotero* (Zotero.org) will help you manage your sources. *Zotero* helps you collect, organize, cite, and share your sources, and it lives right in your web browser where you do your research. As you are searching Google, your library catalogue, or library database, *Zotero* enables you to add a book, article, or website to a personal library with one click. As you add items to your library, *Zotero* collects both the information you need for you bibliography and any full-text content. This means that the content of journal articles and e-books will be available to you right from your *Zotero* library.

To create a bibliography, simply select the items from your *Zotero* library you want to include, right click and select "Create Bibliography from Selected Items . . . ," and choose the citation style your instructor has asked you to use for the paper. To get started, go to Zotero.org and download *Zotero* to the browser of your choice.

Taking Notes It is crucial that you take good, careful notes while you are doing your research. Not only is careful note-taking necessary to avoid plagiarism, it can help you think through your project while you are doing research.

While many researchers used to take notes on index cards, most people now use computers. If you're using your computer, open a new document for each source that you're considering using. The first step in taking notes is to make sure that you gather all the information you might need in your bibliography or works cited. If you're taking notes from a book, for instance, you'll need the author, the title, the place of publication, the press, and the year. Be sure to check the style guide assigned by your instructor to make sure you're gathering all the necessary information.

After you've recorded the bibliographic information, add one or two keywords that can help you sort this source. Next, write a one- or two-sentence summary of the source. Finally, have a section on your document that is reserved for specific places in the text that you might want to work with. When you write down a quote, remember to be extra careful to capture the quote exactly as it is written and enclose it in quotation marks. Do not use abbreviations or change the punctuation. Remember, too, to write down the exact page numbers from the source you are quoting. Being careful with small details at the beginning of your project can save you a lot of time in the long run.

Writing about Globalization

In your writing, as in your conversations, you should always be thinking about your audience. Although your most obvious audience is the instructor, most college professors will want you to write a paper that will be interesting and illuminating for other beginning scholars in the field. Many students are uncertain about how "smart" they can presume their audience to be. A good rule of thumb is to write for your instructor but also for other students in your class and other students in classes similar to yours. You can assume a reasonably informed audience that is curious but also skeptical.

Of course, it is crucial that you keep your instructor in mind. After all, your instructor will be giving you feedback and evaluating your paper. The best way to keep your instructor in mind while you are writing is to periodically reread the assignment while you are writing. Are you answering the assignment's prompt? Are you adhering to the assignment's guidelines? Are you fulfilling the assignment's purpose? If your answer to any of these questions is uncertain, it's a good idea to ask the instructor.

From Research Question to Thesis Statement

Many students like to begin the writing process by writing an introduction. Novice writers often use an early draft of their introductions to guide the shape of their papers. Experienced scholars, however, continually return to their introduction, reshaping and revising it as their thoughts evolve. After all, since writing is thinking, it is impossible to anticipate the full thoughts of your paper before you have written it. Many writers, in fact, only realize the actual argument they are making after they have written a draft or two of the paper. Make sure not to let your introduction trap or narrow your thinking. Think of your introduction as a guide that will help your readers down the path of discovery—a path you can only fully know after you have written your paper.

A strong introduction will welcome readers to the scholarly conversation. You'll introduce your central interlocutors and pose the question or problem that you are interested in resolving. Most introductions contain a thesis statement, which is a sentence or two that clearly states the main argument. Some introductions, you'll notice, do not contain the argument, but merely contain the promise of a resolution to an intellectual problem.

Is Your Thesis an Argument?

So far, we've discussed a number of steps for you to take when you begin to write a research paper. We started by strategizing about ways to use presearch to find a topic and ask a researchable question, then we looked at ways to find a scholarly conversation by using your library's resources. Now we'll discuss a crucial step in the writing process: coming up with a thesis.

Your thesis is the central claim of your paper—the main point that you'd like to argue. You may make a number of claims throughout the paper; when you make a claim, you are offering a small argument, usually about a piece of evidence that you've found. Your thesis is your governing claim, the central argument of the whole paper. Sometimes it is difficult to know if you have written a proper thesis. Ask yourself, "Can a reasonable person disagree with my thesis statement?" If the answer is no, then it is likely that you have written an observation rather than an argument. For instance, the statement "There are six official languages of the UN" is not a thesis, because this is a true fact. A reasonable person cannot disagree with this fact, so it is not an argument. The statement "Arabic became an official language of the UN for economic reasons" is a thesis, because it is a debatable point. A reasonable person might disagree (by arguing, for instance, that "Arabic became an official language of the UN for political reasons"). Remember to keep returning to your thesis statement while you are writing. Not only will you be able to make sure that your writing remains on a clear path, but you'll also be able to keep refining your thesis so that it becomes clearer and more precise.

Make sure, too, that your thesis is a point of persuasion rather than one of belief or taste. "Chinese food tastes delicious" is certainly an argument you could make to your friend, but it is not an adequate thesis for an academic paper, because there is no evidence that you could provide that might persuade a reader who doesn't already agree with you.

Organization

In order for your paper to feel organized, readers should know where they are headed and have a reasonable idea of how they are going to get there. An introduction will offer a strong sense of organization if it

- introduces your central intellectual problem and explains why it is important;
- suggests who will be involved in the scholarly conversation;
- indicates what kind of evidence you'll be investigating; and
- offers a precise central argument.

Some readers describe well-organized papers as having a sense of flow. When readers praise a sense of flow, they mean that the argument moves easily from one sentence to the next and from one paragraph to the next.

This allows your reader to follow your thoughts easily. When you begin writing a sentence, try using an idea, keyword, or phrase from the end of the previous sentence. The next sentence, then, will appear to have emerged smoothly from the previous sentence. This tip is especially important when you move between paragraphs. The beginning of a paragraph should feel like it has a clear relationship to the end of the previous paragraph.

Keep in mind, too, a sense of wholeness. A strong paragraph has a sense of flow and a sense of wholeness; you should allow your reader to trace your thoughts smoothly and ensure that the reader understands how all your thoughts are connected to the large, central idea. Ask yourself as your write each paragraph: What does this paragraph have to do with the central intellectual problem that I am investigating. If the relationship isn't clear to you, then it won't be clear to the readers either.

Novice writers often use the form of a five-paragraph essay. In this form, each paragraph offers an example that proves the validity of the central claim. The five-paragraph essay may have worked in high school because it meets the minimum requirement for making an argument with evidence. You will quickly notice, though, that experienced writers do not use the five-paragraph essay. Indeed, your college instructors will expect you to move beyond the five-paragraph essay. This is because a five-paragraph essay relies on static examples rather than fully engaging new evidence. A strong essay will grow in complexity and nuance as the writer brings in new evidence. Rather than thinking of an essay as something that offers many examples to back up the same static idea, think of it as the evolution of an idea that grows ever more complex and rich as the writer engages with scholars who view the idea from various angles.

Integrating Your Research

As we have seen, doing research involves finding an intellectual community by looking for scholars who are thinking through similar problems and may be in conversation with one another. When you write your paper, you will not merely be reporting what you found; you will be orchestrating the conversation that your research has uncovered. To orchestrate a conversation involves asking a few key questions: Whose voices should be most prominent? What is the relationship between one scholar's ideas and another scholar's ideas? How do these ideas contribute to the argument that your own paper is making? Is it important that your readers hear the exact words of the conversation, or can you give them the main ideas and important points of the conversation in your own words? Your answers to these questions will determine how you go about integrating your research into your paper.

Using evidence is a way of gaining authority. Even though you may not have known much about your topic before you started researching, the way you use evidence in your paper will allow you to establish a voice that is authoritative and trustworthy. You have three basic choices to decide how best you'd like to present the information from a source: summarize, paraphrase, or quote. Let's discuss each one briefly.

Summary You should summarize a source when the source provides helpful background information for your research. Summaries do not make strong evidence, but they can be helpful if you need to chart the intellectual terrain of your project. Summaries can be an efficient way of capturing the main ideas of a source. Remember to be fully sympathetic to the writer's point of view when you are summarizing. Put yourself in the scholar's shoes. If you later disagree with the scholar's methods or conclusions, your disagreement will be convincing because your reader will know that you have given the scholar a fair hearing. A summary that is clearly biased is not only inaccurate and ethically suspect; it makes your writing less convincing because readers will be suspicious of your lack of rigor.

Let's say you come across the following quote that you'd like to summarize. Here's an excerpt from *The Language Wars: A History of Proper English*, by Henry Hitchings:

> No language has spread as widely as English, and it continues to spread. Internationally the desire to learn it is insatiable. In the twenty-first century the world is becoming more urban and more middle class, and the adoption of English is a symptom of this, for increasingly English serves as the lingua franca of business and popular culture. It is dominant or at least very prominent in other areas such as shipping, diplomacy, computing, medicine and education. (300)

Consider this summary:

> In *The Language Wars*, Hitchings says that everyone wants to learn English because it is the best language in the world (300). I agree that English is the best.

If you compare this summary to what Hitchings actually wrote, you will see that it is a biased and distorted version of the actual quote. Hitchings did not make a universal claim about whether English is better or worse than other languages. Rather, he made a claim about why English is becoming so widespread in an increasingly connected world.

Now let's look at another summary, taken from the sample paper at the end of this research guide:

> According to Hitchings, English has become the go-to choice for global communications and has spread quickly as the language of commerce and ideas (300).

This is a much stronger summary than the previous example. The writer shortens Hitchings's original language, but she is fair to the writer's original meaning and intent.

Paraphrase Paraphrasing involves putting a source's ideas into your own words. It's a good idea to paraphrase if you think you can state the idea more clearly or more directly than the original source does. Remember that if you paraphrase, you need to put the entire idea into your own words. It is not enough for you to change one or two words. Indeed, if you only change a few words, you may put yourself at risk of plagiarizing.

Let's look at how we might paraphrase the Hitchings quote that we've been discussing. Consider this paraphrase:

> Internationally the desire to learn English is insatiable. In today's society, the world is becoming wealthier and more urban, and the use of English is a symptom of this (Hitchings 300).

You will notice that the writer simply replaced some of Hitchings's original language with synonyms. Even with the parenthetical citation, this is unacceptable paraphrasing. Indeed, this is a form of plagiarism, because the writer suggests that the language is his or her own, when it is in fact an only slightly modified version of Hitchings's own phrasing.

Let's see how we might paraphrase Hitchings in an academically honest way:

> Because English is used so frequently in global communications, many people around the world want to learn English as they become members of the middle class (Hitchings 300).

Here the writer has taken Hitchings's message but has used his or her own language to describe what Hitchings originally wrote. The writer offers Hitchings's ideas with fresh syntax and new vocabulary and gives Hitchings credit for the idea in a parenthetical citation.

Quotation The best way to show that you are in conversation with scholars is to quote them. Quoting involves capturing the exact wording and punctuation of a passage. Quotations make for powerful evidence, especially in humanities papers. If you come across evidence that you think will be helpful in your project, you should quote it. You may be tempted to quote only those passages that seem to agree with your main claim. But remember to write down the quotes of scholars who may not seem to agree with you. These are precisely the thoughts that will help you build a powerful scholarly conversation. Working with fresh ideas that you may not agree with can help you revise your claim to make it even more persuasive, because it will force you to take into account potential counterarguments. When your readers see that you are grappling with an intellectual problem from all sides, and that you are giving all interlocutors a fair voice, they are more likely to be persuaded by your arguments.

To make sure that you are properly integrating your sources into your paper, remember the acronym ICE, which stands for Introduce, Cite, and Explain. Let's imagine that you've found an idea that you'd like to incorporate into your paper. We'll use a quote from David Harvey's *A Brief History of Neoliberalism* as an example. On page 7, you find the following quote that you'd like to use: "The assumption that individual freedoms are guaranteed by freedom of the market and of trade is a cardinal feature of neoliberal thinking, and it has long dominated the US stance towards the rest of the world."

1. The first thing you need to do is **introduce** the quote ("introduce" gives us the "I" in ICE). To introduce a quote, provide a context so that your readers know where it is coming from, and you must integrate the quote into your own sentence. Here are some examples of how you might do this:

   In his book *A Brief History of Neoliberalism*, David Harvey writes . . .
   One expert on the relationship between economics and politics claims . . .
   Professor of Anthropology David Harvey explains that . . .
   In a recent book by Harvey, he contends . . .

Notice that each of these introduces the quote in such a way that readers are likely to recognize it as an authoritative source.

2. The next step is to **cite** the quote (the C in ICE). Here is where you indicate the origin of the quotation so that your readers can easily look up the original source. Citing is a two-step process that varies slightly depending on the citation style that you're using. We'll offer an example using MLA style. The first step involves indicating the author and page number in the body of your essay. Here is an example of a parenthetical citation that gives the author and page number after the quote and before the period that ends the sentence:

> One expert on the relationship between economics and politics claims that neoliberal thinking has "long dominated the US stance towards the rest of the world" (Harvey 7).

Note that if it is already clear to readers which author you're quoting, you need only give the page number:

> In *A Brief History of Neoliberalism*, David Harvey contends that neoliberal thinking has "long dominated the US stance towards the rest of the world" (7).

The second step of citing the quote is providing proper information in the works cited section or bibliography of your paper. This list should include the complete bibliographical information of all the sources you have cited. An essay that includes the quote by David Harvey should also include the following entry in the Works Cited section:

> Harvey, David. *A Brief History of Neoliberalism*. New York: Oxford UP, 2005. Print.

3. Finally, the most crucial part of integrating a quote is **explaining** it. The E in ICE is often overlooked, but a strong explanation is the most important step for involving yourself in the scholarly conversation. Here is where you explain how you interpret the source you are citing, what aspect of the quote is most important for your readers to understand, and how the source pertains to your own project. For example:

> David Harvey writes, "The assumption that individual freedoms are guaranteed by freedom of the market and of trade is a cardinal feature of neoliberal thinking, and it has long dominated the US stance towards the rest of the world" (7). As Harvey explains, neoliberalism suggests that free markets do not limit personal freedom but actually lead to free individuals.

Or:

> David Harvey writes, "The assumption that individual freedoms are guaranteed by freedom of the market and of trade is a cardinal feature of neoliberal thinking, and it has long dominated the US stance towards the rest of the world" (7). For Harvey, before we understand the role of the United States in global politics, we must first understand the philosophy that binds personal freedom with market freedom.

Novice writers are sometimes tempted to end a paragraph with a quote that they feel is especially compelling or clear. But remember that you should never leave a quote to speak for itself (even if you love it). After all, as the orchestrator of this scholarly conversation, you need to make sure that readers are getting exactly what you'd like them to take from each quote. Notice, in the above examples, that the first explanation suggests that the writer quoting Harvey is centrally concerned with neoliberal philosophy, while the second explanation suggests that the writer is centrally concerned with US politics. The explanation, in other words, is the crucial link between your source and the main idea of your paper.

Avoiding Plagiarism

Scholarly conversations are what drive knowledge in the world. Scholars using each other's ideas in open, honest ways form the bedrock of our intellectual communities and ensure that our contributions to the world of thought are important. It is crucial, then, that all writers do their part in maintaining the integrity and trustworthiness of scholarly conversation. It is crucial that you never claim someone else's ideas as your own, and that you are always extra careful to give the proper credit to someone else's writing. This is what we call responsible scholarship.

The best way to avoid plagiarism is to plan ahead and keep careful track of notes as you read your sources. Remember the advice on *Zotero* and taking notes: Find the way that works best for you to keep track of which ideas are your own and which ideas come directly from the sources you are reading. Most acts of plagiarism are accidental. It is easy when you are drafting a paper to lose track of where a quote or idea came from; plan ahead, and this won't happen. Here are a few tips for making sure that confusion doesn't happen to you.

1. Know what needs to be cited. You do not need to cite what is considered common knowledge, such as facts (the day Lincoln was born), concepts (the earth orbits the sun), or events (the day Martin Luther King was shot). You do need to cite the ideas and words of others from the sources you are using in your paper.
2. Be conservative. If you are not sure if you should cite something, either ask your instructor or a librarian, or cite it. It is better to cite something you don't have to than omit something you should cite.
3. Direct quotations from your sources need to be cited, as well as any paraphrases of the ideas or words of your sources.
4. Finally, extensive citation not only helps you avoid plagiarism, it also boosts your credibility and enables your reader to trace your scholarship.

Citation Styles

It is crucial that you adhere to the standards of a single citation style when you write your paper. The most common styles are MLA (Modern Language Association, generally used in the humanities), APA (American Psychological Association, generally used in the social sciences), and Chicago (*Chicago Manual of Style*). If you're not sure which style you should use, you should ask your instructor. Each style has its own guidelines regarding the format of the paper. Although proper formatting within a given style may seem arbitrary, there are important reasons behind the guidelines for each style. For instance, while MLA citations tend to emphasize author's names, APA citations tend to emphasize the date of publications. This distinction make sense, given that MLA standards are usually followed by departments in the humanities and APA standards are usually followed by departments in the social sciences. While papers in the humanities value original thinking about arguments and texts that are canonical and often old, papers in the social sciences tend to value arguments that take into account the most current thought and latest research.

There are a number of helpful guidebooks that will tell you all the rules you need to know in order to follow the standards for various citation styles. If your instructor hasn't pointed you to a specific guidebook, try the following online resources:

Purdue Online Writing Lab: owl.english.purdue.edu/

Internet Public Library: www.ipl.org/div/farq/netciteFARQ.html

Modern Language Association (for MLA style): www.mla.org/style

American Psychological Association (for APA style): www.apastyle.org/

The Chicago Manual of Style Online: www.chicagomanualofstyle.org/tools_citationguide.html

SAMPLE STUDENT RESEARCH PAPER

Mich   1

Sarah Mich
Professor Ritzenberg
English 101
15 March 2013

Earth Goes Flat, English Goes Round

In cities across the United States, students practice Spanish, Chinese, and French in order to communicate with people around the world and to gain exposure to different cultures. The reverse current is even stronger: globally, people clamor to learn English. This latter trend is fueled by recent developments in globalization, and what journalist Thomas Friedman calls "the flattening of the world," in which commerce has expanded from the hands of select countries to also including developing nations, companies, and, increasingly, individuals and small groups. English has become the go-to choice for these communications and has spread quickly as the language of commerce and ideas (Hitchings 300). But the resulting desire of millions to learn English, and become versed in Western culture, is a complicated prospect. Many see the trend as destructive, threatening languages and eroding cultures for the sake of multinational consumerism (Leonard). When done well, however, the teaching of English as a Foreign Language (EFL) need not be destructive. Focusing the discussion on *how*— not whether—English is taught ensures that students around the world are offered the same benefits that American students receive in their language classes: global communication skills that do not undermine their own language or culture.

In order to help protect other languages, EFL instruction should treat English as a complementary language, not a replacement. Teachers of Chinese students note that their students believe English is better than their native tongue (Traves), and a recent trend shows that interregional families in India opt to speak English with their children instead of the regional languages they share (Sharma). But under-valuing language in this manner could have significant negative impacts on human communication. Lera Boroditsky, a linguist at Stanford, has shown that language shapes the way humans think and behave, and that the loss of language could limit human access to certain concepts and behaviors (118). A recent study by Boroditsky illustrates these findings by having participants arrange a set of cards according to a temporal progression. The scientists then study the direction in which the participants oriented the cards. English speakers arranged the cards left to right, while Hebrew-speakers mostly arranged right to left, in the direction of Hebrew writing. A third case was conducted with the Kuuk Thaayorre, an aboriginal community in Australia that describes directions such as "left" and right" using cardinal coordinates. The researchers found that the Kuuk arranged their cards from east to west, independent of the direction in which they were seated, using "spatial orientation to construct their representations of time" (123). Language thus allows us to create and articulate unique concepts that are linked with diverse cultures. EFL instruction can work to support this diversity. Classes could include information about research connecting language and thought, asking learners of a language to reflect on the ideas that they are able to express in a native tongue that do not carry over to English. Students could even be asked to complete exercises that incorporate some of their native language into English. The resulting phenomenon—in which speakers craft a "version" of English to reflect their own language, culture, and needs—has been documented in certain areas of the world and should be encouraged (Hitchings 308). The more students are asked to value the contributions of their own language and culture during EFL instruction, the more incentivized they will be to maintain multiple languages and the rich concepts and cultures associated with each.

Like their native tongues, the past experiences and desired outcomes of English language learners vary widely across the globe, and effective language instruction should respond to this diversity. In many ways, instruction already addresses local needs. The English training of Afghan youth in India offers a different model for local empowerment. As Afghanistan became the first epicenter for the military campaign against terrorist organizations in the wake of September 11th, English took root as a near-essential skill for Afghans wishing to advance in business or government (Polanki). Starting in 2011, the government began sponsoring a program to meet this need, sending seventy students to India for a rigorous 20-month training certificate in English. Students speak eagerly about the program, sharing their aptitude in English, recognizing the advantages it will give them, and promising to give back: "God-willing, when we return, we will teach the new generation English" (Polanki). The Afghan government supports these efforts by giving out scholarships to students training as English teachers abroad. The program thus uses language to aid something larger than individual development, by creating a means for sustaining and scaling future language instruction and empowering its participants based on local need. Such programs thus avoid the trap described by journalist Julia Traves: "where once English facilitated the staffing of colonial offices, now it helps fill the cubicles of multinational

Mich   5

corporations." By promoting instructional programs that respond to particular social contexts, and creating sustainable
opportunities for local communities to grow, EFL instruction
ensures that it does more good than harm.

It is not enough, however, for EFL instruction to honor
native languages and local needs; it must also expose students to content about globalization, such that informed EFL
learners will be able to make more active choices about the
way they learn and use English. Many of these changes would
be simple to implement. EFL students could be taught that
by the end of the century, linguists predict fifty percent of
world languages will no longer be spoken—including the
native tongues of many EFL students—thus helping students
think about the implications of learning English and make
informed choices about their role in globalization (Leonard).
Language instruction would also benefit from a discussion of
why English serves as the language of choice for globalization. David Hill, who teaches English in Istanbul, writes that
"English is global for highly dubious reasons: colonial, military and economic hegemony, first of the British, now of the
US" (qtd. in Traves). He then goes on to argue, "If we are not
to be imperialists then we must help our students to express
themselves, not our agenda" (qtd. in Traves). Indeed, self-
expression should be a key part of EFL education, and for
that project it is essential that students learn about the
larger system in which their language instruction operates.
As English classrooms frequently serve as an EFL learner's
first structured education on international issues, they are

an important environment for discussions on globalization. Thus, individuals become informed members of global processes, using English to serve needs other than Western ones, and gaining the opportunity to develop autonomous thoughts about globalization.

Some may argue that such a teaching approach to EFL instruction—one that emphasizes the value of native languages, fits the needs of its learning population, and discusses issues of globalization—is too prescriptive. True, this approach condones a certain set of values. But all teaching occurs around a value set, and this particular approach highlights the needs and contributions of the learners, not those who pushed English in the first place. The focus is thus on helping empower individuals around the world to take an active role in global and local processes. Is this approach feasible, though? It is, though it won't be easy. The industry for EFL is huge: a $7.8-billion one, with western instructors pulling in sizeable salaries (Traves). Textbook companies in the UK and US often teach western values such as consumerism and materialism (Traves). But though the industry is a behemoth, new approaches are emerging that could pressure EFL institutions and instructors into thinking critically about their teaching practices. At Glendon College in Ontario, for example, the Certificate in the Discipline of Teaching English as an International Language pays "close attention to issues of cultural sensitivity and autonomy when training teachers" (Traves). An English teacher halfway around the world offered a similar sentiment on an internet discussion board: "I feel the need of reminding our students and young colleagues that the purpose of learning English is not for us to 'speak and act' like an English person . . . but to 'speak English' as an educated Indonesian" (Traves). Teachers thus play a key role in this transformation. By having more teachers—and the institutions and companies that train them—take an intentional and sensitive approach, EFL instruction could become a tool of widespread empowerment, not subjugation.

English, however, is here to stay—and growing. The way we teach English matters now and will have impacts both tomorrow and years down the road. If instruction is done blindly—with the same uncritical eye that led to years of colonialism on the part of England and the United States—we risk losing the talent and engagement of many around the world in solving global problems. This would be a loss to the world: we all own these problems and their solutions. But if English as a Foreign Language instruction is made intentional—used to complement other languages, engage the needs of its learners, and deliver content about globalization—we may have a shot at increasing communication and empowerment in a globalizing world.

Mich   8

Works Cited

Boroditsky, Lera. "How Does Our Language Shape the Way We Think?" *What's Next? Dispatches on the Future of Science: Original Essays from a New Generation of Scientists.* Ed. Max Brockman. New York: Vintage, 2009. 116–129. Print.

Friedman, Thomas. "It's a Flat World, After All." *New York Times Magazine.* New York Times, 3 Apr. 2005. Web. 25 Jan. 2013.

Hitchings, Henry. *The Language Wars: A History of Proper English.* New York: Farrar, 2011. Print.

Leonard, Stephen Pax. "Death by Monoculture." *University of Cambridge Research.* University of Cambridge, 2 Sep. 2011. Web. 25 Jan. 2013.

Nadeem, Shehzad. "Accent Neutralisation and a Crisis of Identity in India's Call Centres." *The Guardian.* The Guardian, 9 Feb. 2011. Web. 25 Jan. 2013.

Polanki, Pallavi. "Operation Mind Your Language." *Open.* Open Mag., 29 May 2010. Web. 25 Jan. 2013.

Sharma, Reshma Krishnamurthy. "The New Language Landscape." *The Hindu Life & Style.* The Hindu, 12 Feb. 2012. Web. 25 Jan. 2013.

Traves, Julie. "The Church of Please and Thank You." *This Magazine.* This Magazine, March–April 2005. Web. 25 Jan. 2013.

credits

index

"The Accidental Bricoleurs"
(Horning), 184, 229–40

Afridi, Humera, "A Gentle
Madness," 30, 48–53

Ahmed, Leila, "Reinventing the
Veil," 282, 304–9

Akam, Simon, "The Long and
Winding Road," 244, 264–69

Ali, Tanveer, "The Subway
Falafel Sandwich and the
Americanization of Ethnic
Food," 2, 24–27

Allers, Jackson, "Voice of the
Streets: The Birth of a Hip-Hop
Movement," 339, 357–66

"All the Disappearing Islands"
(Whitty), 62–76

Angelos, James, "Passing the Test,"
134, 149–64

Appiah, Kwame Anthony, "The
Shattered Mirror," 2, 10–20

Banerjee, Abhijit, "More Than
1 Billion People Are Hungry in
the World," 384–85, 447–60

"Beyond Mullahs and Persian
Party People: The Invisibility of

Being Iranian on TV" (Shirazi),
339–45

Bhuyan, Avantika, "The Enchanted
Bylanes," 244, 260–64

"Birth" (Fadiman), 78–88

"Body-Building in Afghanistan"
(Broudy), 282, 309–21

Boroditsky, Lera, 133–34
"How Does Our Language
Shape the Way We Think,"
135–45

Broudy, Oliver, "Body-Building in
Afghanistan," 282, 309–21

Bures, Frank, "Can You Hear Us
Now," 184, 192–97

"Can You Hear Us Now" (Bures),
184, 192–97

Chang, Jeff, "So You Think They
Can Break-Dance," 339,
370–80

"The Church of Please and Thank
You" (Traves), 134, 172–80

Clark, Doug, "Crimson Leopard-
Print Headscarves: Wearing the
Veil in Banda Aceh, Indonesia,"
282, 289–304

Cole, Teju, "The White Savior Industrial Complex," 184, 210–18
"Crimson Leopard-Print Headscarves: Wearing the Veil in Banda Aceh, Indonesia" (Clark), 282, 289–304

"Death by Monoculture" (Leonard), 134, 145–49
DeLong-Bas, Natana J., "The New Social Media and the Arab Spring," 184, 197–210
"Do Some Cultures Have Their Own Ways of Going Mad?" (Nasser), 88–94
Duflo, Esther, "More Than 1 Billion People Are Hungry in the World," 384–85, 447–60
Dwoskin, Elizabeth, "Why Americans Won't Do Dirty Jobs," 115–24

The Economist, 151–52, 153, 243, 286
    "The New Grand Tour," 244–52
"The Enchanted Bylanes" (Bhuyan), 244, 260–64

Fadiman, Anne, "Birth," 78–88
"Fading Lights in Mumbai" (Ramadurai), 338, 367–70

Gappah, Petina, "Zimbabwe," 384, 414–27
"A Gentle Madness" (Afridi), 30, 48–53
Gleiser, Marcelo, "Globalization: Two Visions of the Future of Humanity," 2, 7–10

"Globalization: Two Visions of the Future of Humanity" (Gleiser), 2, 7–10
Goldberg, Stefany Anne, "You Can Take It with You," 124–31
Gopnik, Blake, 338
    "Revolution in a Can," 345–49
Guest, Andrew, "Pursuing the Science of Happiness," 94–103

"Haiti Doesn't Need Your Old T-Shirt" (Kenny), 244, 252–55
Hill, Julian, "In Search of Black Identity in Uganda," 30, 53–62
Horning, Ron, "The Accidental Bricoleurs," 184, 229–40
"How Does Our Language Shape the Way We Think" (Boroditsky), 135–45
"How Oliberté, the Anti-TOMS, Makes Shoes and Jobs in Africa" (Watkins), 244, 256–60

"If It's Tuesday, It Must Be the Taliban" (Tabor), 384, 397–413
"In Search of Black Identity in Uganda" (Hill), 30, 53–62
"The Invisible Migrant Man: Questioning Gender Privileges" (Lewis), 330–35
"In Zarafshan" (Olsen), 2–7
"It's Time for the Turkana to Leave Their Wastelands and Settle Down" (Kuria), 384, 443–47
Iyer, Pico, "Lonely Places," 30, 31–37

Kenny, Charles, "Haiti Doesn't Need Your Old T-Shirt," 244, 252–55
"Killing Emos, and the Future, in Iraq" (Levine), 282, 322–30

Kuria, Francis, 442
  "It's Time for the Turkana to
    Leave Their Wastelands
    and Settle Down," 384,
    443–47

Lacy, Sarah, 338
  "You Think Hollywood Is
    Rough? Welcome to the
    Chaos, Excitement and
    Danger of Nollywood,"
    349–56
Larsen, Christina, "The Startling
  Plight of China's Leftover
  Ladies," 281–89
"The Last Famine" (Salopek), 384
"The Last Inuit of Quebec" (Nobel),
  30, 38–48
Leonard, Stephen Pax, "Death by
  Monoculture," 134, 145–49
Levine, Mark, "Killing Emos, and
  the Future, in Iraq," 282,
  322–30
Lewis, Chloé, "The Invisible
  Migrant Man: Questioning
  Gender Privileges," 330–35
"Lonely Places" (Iyer), 30, 31–37
"The Long and Winding Road"
  (Akam), 244, 264–69
"The Luxury Frontier" (Orth),
  269–80

Manseau, Peter, "Plasticize Me,"
  104–15
"A Mickey Mouse Approach to
  Globalization" (Wasserstrom),
  2, 20–24
"More Than 1 Billion People
  Are Hungry in the World"
  (Banerjee and Duflo), 384–85,
  447–60

Nasser, Latif, "Do Some Cultures
  Have Their Own Ways of Going
  Mad?," 88–94
"The New Grand Tour" (The
  Economist), 243–44
"The New Language Landscape"
  (Sharma), 134, 164–67
"The New Social Media and the
  Arab Spring" (DeLong-Bas),
  184, 197–210
Nobel, Justin, "The Last Inuit of
  Quebec," 30, 38–48

Olsen, Tyler, "In Zarafshan," 2–7
"Operation Mind Your Language"
  (Polanki), 134, 167–72
Orth, Maureen, "The Luxury
  Frontier," 269–80

Pakravan, Rudabeh, 184
  "Territory Jam," 219–28
"Passing the Test" (Angelos), 134,
  149–64
"Plasticize Me" (Manseau), 104–15
Polanki, Pallavi, "Operation Mind
  Your Language," 134, 167–72
"Pursuing the Science of Happiness"
  (Guest), 94–103

Ramadurai, Charukesi, "Fading
  Lights in Mumbai," 338, 367–70
"Reinventing the Veil" (Ahmed),
  282, 304–9
"Revolution in a Can" (Gopnik),
  345–49

Salopek, Paul, "The Last Famine,"
  384, 428–43
Sharma, Reshma Krishnamurthy,
  "The New Language Landscape,"
  134, 164–67

"The Shattered Mirror" (Appiah),
2, 10–20
Shirazi, Roozbeh, "Beyond Mullahs
and Persian Party People: The
Invisibility of Being Iranian on
TV," 339–45
"A Small World After All"
(Zuckerman), 183–84, 185–91
"So You Think They Can Break-
Dance" (Chang), 339, 370–80
"The Startling Plight of China's
Leftover Ladies" (Larsen),
281–89
"The Subway Falafel Sandwich and
the Americanization of Ethnic
Food" (Ali), 2, 24–27

Tabor, Damon, "If It's Tuesday,
It Must Be the Taliban," 384,
397–413
"Territory Jam," (Pakravan),
219–28
Traves, Julie, "The Church of Please
and Thank You," 134, 172–80

"Voice of the Streets: The Birth of
a Hip-Hop Movement" (Allers),
339, 357–66

Walker, Martin, "The World's
New Numbers," 384, 385–96
Wasserstrom, Jeffery N., "A
Mickey Mouse Approach to
Globalization," 2, 20–24
Watkins, Tate, "How Oliberté, the
Anti-TOMS, Makes Shoes and
Jobs in Africa" (Tate), 244, 256–60
"The White Savior Industrial
Complex" (Cole), 184, 210–18
Whitty, Julia, "All the Disappearing
Islands," 62–76
"Why Americans Won't Do Dirty
Jobs" (Dwoskin), 115–24
"The World's New Numbers"
(Walker), 384, 385–96

"You Can Take It with You"
(Goldberg), 124–31
"You Think Hollywood Is Rough?
Welcome to the Chaos,
Excitement and Danger of
Nollywood" (Lacy), 338, 349–56

"Zimbabwe" (Gappah), 384,
414–27
Zuckerman, Ethan, "A Small World
After All," 183–84, 185–91

Printed in the USA/Agawam, MA
January 17, 2018

667788.029